DOCUMENTS
ON
AMERICAN FOREIGN RELATIONS
1943–1944

WORLD PEACE FOUNDATION

40 Mt. Vernon Street, Boston, Massachusetts

Founded in 1910

THE World Peace Foundation is a non-profit organization which was founded in 1910 by Edwin Ginn, the educational publisher, for the purpose of promoting peace, justice and good-will among nations. For many years the Foundation has sought to increase public understanding of international problems by an objective presentation of the facts of international relations. This purpose is accomplished principally through its publications and by the maintenance of a Reference Service which furnishes on request information on current international problems. Recently increased attention has been focused on American foreign relations by study groups organized for the consideration of actual problems of policy.

DOCUMENTS
ON
AMERICAN FOREIGN
RELATIONS

VOL. VI
JULY 1943—JUNE 1944

EDITED BY

LELAND M. GOODRICH

Director, World Peace Foundation

AND

MARIE J. CARROLL

Chief, Reference Service

Copyright, 1945, by
World Peace Foundation

PREFACE

This is the sixth in a series of volumes published by the World Peace Foundation for the purpose of contributing to a better popular understanding of American foreign relations. In this series an attempt has been made to present in accessible and convenient form all important available documentary material bearing on the conduct of American foreign relations. Obviously, no such collection published so nearly contemporaneously can be expected to be complete. Because of the special need of preserving the secret and confidential character of certain documents in time of war, the collection is less complete than would be possible in time of peace.

While the previous year had seen the United Nations turn from the defensive to the offensive, the year under review saw this offensive action assume such proportions and meet with such notable success that there could no longer be any reasonable doubt with regard to the outcome. Furthermore, the invasion of Italy followed by the surrender of King Victor Emmanuel's Government, the German reverses in Eastern Europe and the success of American island-hopping tactics in the Pacific produced a general conviction that the end of the War was much nearer than had originally been thought. It was natural that under these circumstances more thought should have been given to the problems which would follow the actual fighting. So it is not surprising that in this volume there is much more evidence of concern with postwar problems than in earlier volumes. Documents concerned with such matters as international security, currency stabilization, loans for developmental purposes, the production of food and the raising of nutritional standards occupy in this volume, as compared with earlier volumes, a relatively more important place than documents having to do with the effective prosecution of the war.

This growing shift of emphasis has seemed to justify a rather radical change in the general pattern of the volume. While chapters dealing with the prosecution of the war, relations with the enemy powers and United Nations cooperation in the conduct of the war have been retained, it has seemed advisable to set up new chapter headings for documents bearing upon post-war problems. These have been introduced following the chapter on *The United Nations* on the principle that they show the development of policies and programs for the realization of which the United Nations have joined their forces in a common war effort, and

v

more particularly, of course, the policies and acts of the United States Government in respect to these particular matters. Thus, following Chapter 7, *The United Nations,* come chapters on *Relief and Rehabilitation, International Peace and Security, Trade and Finance, Transportation and Communications, Agriculture and Use of Natural Resources, Labor and Social Questions,* and *Cultural Relations.* Policies and activities relating to these matters which have been general in their application and effects, i.e. not intended to be peculiar to particular regions or to relations with particular countries, are covered in these chapters. In general, the final three chapters are reserved for what is peculiar to our relations with particular regions or countries. With the emphasis upon the development of general policies and programs, the amount of space devoted to American relations within particular regions and with particular countries thus comes to be proportionally reduced.

It is the hope of the editors, and of the Trustees of the Foundation, in presenting this volume to the public, that it will be of assistance, as we are led to believe that its predecessors have been, in contributing to a better understanding of American foreign relations. This seems particularly desirable at the present time when we are faced not only with the need of the most effective cooperation with the other United Nations in the winning of the war but also with the necessity of deciding how best to deal with urgent and complicated problems of our post-war relationships. It has come to be a truism that we should not win the war only to lose the peace, but it is perhaps not so generally realized that the problems of our post-war relationships with foreign countries will be infinitely more difficult and more demanding of understanding and wisdom than the problems that we now face in winning the war.

In preparing this collection of documents, we are of course greatly indebted to the staff of the World Peace Foundation for its loyal cooperation and assistance. More particularly, we wish to express appreciation of the assistance rendered by Mrs. Ralph de Miranda, formerly of the staff, for her work in the preparation of the index.

LELAND M. GOODRICH
MARIE J. CARROLL

February 16, 1945

CONTENTS

CONTENTS

CONTENTS

CONTENTS

CONTENTS

CONTENTS

CONTENTS

CONTENTS

CHAPTER I

PRINCIPLES AND POLICY:
GENERAL STATEMENTS

(1) *Address by the President (Roosevelt) before the Canadian Parliament at Ottawa, August 25, 1943* [1]

[Excerpt]

YOUR EXCELLENCY, MEMBERS OF THE PARLIAMENT, MY GOOD FRIENDS AND NEIGHBORS OF THE DOMINION OF CANADA:

It was exactly five years ago last Wednesday that I came to Canada to receive the high honor of a degree at Queen's University. On that occasion — one year before the invasion of Poland, three years before Pearl Harbor — I said:

> We in the Americas are no longer a far-away continent, to which the eddies of controversies beyond the seas could bring no interest or no harm. Instead, we in the Americas have become a consideration to every propaganda office and to every general staff beyond the seas. The vast amount of our resources, the vigor of our commerce, and the strength of our men have made us vital factors in world peace whether we choose it or not.[2]

We did not choose this war, and that "we" includes each and every one of the United Nations.

War was violently forced upon us by criminal aggressors, who measure their standards of morality by the extent of the death and the destruction that they can inflict upon their neighbors.

.   .   .   .

We have been forced to call out the sheriff's posse to break up the gang in order that gangsterism may be eliminated in the community of nations.

We are making sure — absolutely, irrevocably sure — that this time the lesson is driven home to them once and for all. We are going to be rid of outlaws this time.

Every one of the United Nations believes that only a real and lasting peace can justify the sacrifices we are making, and our unanimity gives us confidence in seeking that goal.

It is no secret that at Quebec there was much talk of the post-war world. That discussion was doubtless duplicated simultaneously in dozens of nations and hundreds of cities and among millions of people.

[1] Department of State, *Bulletin*, IX, p. 122.
[2] *Documents on American Foreign Relations, I, 1938–39*, p. 23 (hereinafter series cited as *Documents*, etc.).

1

There is a longing in the air. It is not a longing to go back to what they call "the good old days." I have distinct reservations as to how good "the good old days" were. I would rather believe that we can achieve new and better days.

Absolute victory in this war will give greater opportunities to the world because the winning of the war in itself is proving that concerted action can accomplish things. Surely we can make strides toward a greater freedom from want than the world has yet enjoyed. Surely by unanimous action in driving out the outlaws and keeping them under heel forever we can attain a freedom from fear of violence.

I am everlastingly angry only at those who assert vociferously that the Four Freedoms and the Atlantic Charter are nonsense because they are unattainable. If they had lived a century and a half ago they would have sneered and said that the Declaration of Independence was utter piffle. If they had lived nearly a thousand years ago they would have laughed uproariously at the ideals of Magna Carta. And if they had lived several thousand years ago they would have derided Moses when he came from the mountain with the Ten Commandments.

We concede that these great teachings are not perfectly lived up to today, and we concede that the good old world cannot arrive at Utopia overnight. But I would rather be a builder than a wrecker, hoping always that the structure of life is growing, not dying.

May the destroyers who still persist in our midst decrease. They, like some of our enemies, have a long road to travel before they accept the ethics of humanity.

Some day — in the distant future perhaps, but some day with certainty — all of them will remember with the Master: "Thou shalt love thy neighbor as thyself."

Ma visite à la ville historique de Québec rappelle vivement à mon esprit que le Canada est une nation fondée sur l'union de deux grandes races. L'harmonie de leur association dans l'égalité peut servir d'exemple à l'humanité toute entière — un exemple partout dans le monde.

(2) *Our Foreign Policy in the Framework of Our National Interests. Radio Address by the Secretary of State (Hull), September 12, 1943* [1]

I

In July of last year, in an address over these networks, I outlined, as definitely as was possible at that time, the chief problems and conditions confronting us in the field of foreign relations and sought to indicate some

[1] Broadcast over the network of the National Broadcasting Company. Department of State, *Bulletin*, IX, p. 173.

of the policies necessary for meeting these problems. I pointed out that in the present conflict each of the United Nations is fighting for the preservation of its freedom, its homes, its very existence; and that only through united effort to defeat our enemies can freedom or the opportunity for freedom be preserved — for all countries and all peoples. I spoke of the need to chart for the future a course based on enduring spiritual values which would bring our nation and all nations greater hope for enduring peace and greater measure of human welfare. To this end, I urged intensive study, hard thinking, broad vision, and leadership by all those, within each nation, who provide spiritual, moral, and intellectual guidance.

At that time, the military picture was still dark. The United Nations were still fighting a desperate war of defense against better prepared foes. We had suffered a succession of grim defeats.

Since then, the military picture has greatly changed.

We are now winning heartening victories — in the air, at sea, and on land. Our counterblows are steadily increasing in power and effectiveness. They are stepping-stones to our final triumph over the forces of conquest and savagery.

Attainment of complete victory, although now certain, is still a formidable task. Our lesser enemies are fast losing heart and strength. Italy has already surrendered. But our principal enemies, Germany and Japan, though shaken, still possess great resources and enormous strength. They still control vast portions of Europe and of Asia. To defeat them completely, the United Nations need to make, on the battlefront and at home, efforts even greater than those thus far made.

In making these more intensified efforts, it is more important than ever for all concerned to have a clear understanding of what is at stake, now and in the future.

During recent months, public discussion and debate on a high plane have revealed the profound concern of our people with the issues of the country's foreign relations. These issues need to be seen in their full perspective. Unless our people so see them, and unless our people are willing to translate their understanding of them into action, the well-being of the nation — and even its very life — may be gravely menaced.

The foreign policy of any country must be expressive of that country's fundamental national interests. No country can keep faith with itself unless that is so.

In determining our foreign policy we must first see clearly what our true national interests are. We must also bear in mind that other countries with which we deal in the conduct of foreign relations have their national interests, which, of course, determine their policies.

Obviously there are, even between friendly nations, differences as regards their respective aims and purposes and as regards the means of attaining them. But there are also immense areas of common interest. By cooperating within those areas, the nations not only can advance more effectively the aims and purposes which they have in common, but can also find increased opportunity to reconcile, by peaceful means and to mutual advantage, such differences as may exist among them.

II

At the present time, the paramount aim of our foreign policy, and the paramount aim of the foreign policy of each of the other United Nations, is to defeat our enemies as quickly as possible. Here we have a vast area of common interest and a broad basis of cooperative action in the service of that interest.

Every weapon of our military and economic activity and every instrumentality of our diplomacy have been and are directed toward the strengthening of the combined war effort. All these necessarily go together.

The land, air, and sea forces of the United States are fighting with surpassing skill and heroism in the Mediterranean, over the Nazi-held fortress of Europe, in the far reaches of the Pacific and of Asia. In each of the theaters of war they are operating shoulder to shoulder in a spirit of superb comradeship with the gallant forces of one or more of our Allies.

The resolute will and devoted effort of our people have brought about the greatest miracle of production and delivery in all history. Our war supplies are flowing outward in a constant and ever-increasing stream, not alone to those areas in which our own forces are engaged, but to every point on the globe at which the armed forces of the United Nations are fighting.

We are in continuous consultation with our Allies on various phases of military, economic, and political activity — as required by the exigencies of a constantly changing situation.

Our cooperation with our Allies has long since reached the state where contingents of the forces of various Allies are serving side by side under unified command. We have developed this type of cooperation with invincible Britain; with intrepid and resolute Canada, Australia, New Zealand, and South Africa; with valiant and determined China; and with the forces of other Allies. It is being rapidly extended as the military operations progress.

To the Soviet Union, whose heroic armies and civilian population have earned everlasting renown through their magnificent feats of courage and sacrifice, we have been glad to render all possible aid. It is our desire and our settled policy that collaboration and cooperation between our two countries shall steadily increase during and following the war.

With the reemerging military power of France we have been and are developing a heartening degree of coordinated effort. We look forward to the day when reborn France will again take her rightful place in the family of free nations.

With governments which the Axis powers have driven from their invaded and brutally oppressed but unconquerable countries we have the most friendly relations. These relations reflect our profound and active sympathy for the suffering of their peoples and our determination that the victory of the United Nations shall restore their nations to freedom.

With all but one of the nations of the Western Hemisphere we have today the closest ties of solidarity and association — the fruit of 10 years of unremitting labor on the part of all of these nations to build in this hemisphere a fraternity of Good Neighbors. Each of our American associates is making a magnificent contribution to the war effort. Here we have, in peace and in war, a highly successful example of cooperation between sovereign nations.

The victories of the United Nations have been the direct result, not of separate and uncoordinated military, economic, and diplomatic action, but of close coordination of all three types of action, both within each of the nations and among all of them. It is well to recall some outstanding examples.

Our protracted diplomatic effort to achieve a fair and peaceful solution of difficulties in the Far East afforded our military authorities and those of other countries now in the ranks of the United Nations many months of precious time for strengthening defenses against the combined Axis threats in the Atlantic and in the Pacific, in case Japan should reject a peaceful settlement as she eventually did.

The drawing-together of the American Republics to assure their common defense made it possible to establish a line of communications through the Caribbean, Brazil, and the South Atlantic. That line proved to be of invaluable importance alike in transporting equipment to the British forces at El Alamein; in supplying our own expedition to North Africa; and, at a desperate hour, in putting our warplanes into the air over the Pacific islands and in China.

Diplomatic foresight and patient and vigorous activity by the agencies of our foreign policy played an indispensable part in preparing the way by which the huge strategic North African area was brought without heavy losses into the sphere of the United Nations and the French fleet was kept out of German hands. Had Vichy felt it feasible to ignore our diplomatic pressure directed toward preventing the surrender of the North and West African areas to the Nazis and the delivery of the French fleet to Hitler as Laval had planned, or had Spain entered the war on the side of the Axis as Hitler had hoped, control of the Mediterranean would have early fallen into the hands of our enemies. Instead, the Allied forces converged, with a skill and precision unequaled in military annals, upon this gateway through which we are now invading the European Continent.

The Mediterranean operations weakened the German air force available on the Soviet front just as the Russian resistance, by holding the German armies on the eastern battle line, prevented Hitler from parrying our thrust toward his southern flank. Meanwhile, our constant military pressure against Japan had its inevitable effect in deterring Japan from aggression against the Soviet Union.

Our diplomatic agreements with fearless Danish officials on free soil and with the Government of Iceland made it possible to guard the great North Atlantic passage as a precious route for our supplies and troops and as defense against attack from the north.

The perseverance of China, the first victim of the movement of aggression, in resistance to Japan has been aided in no small measure by the faith of her leaders in us, based on their knowledge of our history and policy and on their observation, as time went on, of our efforts to achieve a fair and peaceful settlement in the Far East, our economic support, and more recently, our military assistance. China's resistance has held enmeshed on her front substantial Japanese forces which might otherwise have been loosed against us and other of the United Nations in the Pacific; and China is playing an important part in the United Nations' program for the winning of the war and achievement of a stable peace.

The agencies of our foreign policy are at all times at work as instruments of national defense. Since the attack upon us, they have been intensively at work in assisting our armed forces to achieve the victories which are now fast increasing in numbers and significance.

III

Beyond final victory, our fundamental national interests are — as they always have been — the assuring of our national security and the fostering of the economic and social well-being of our people. To maintain these interests, our foreign policy must necessarily deal with current conditions and must plan for the future in the light of the concepts and beliefs which we, as a nation, accept for ourselves as the guiding lines of our international behavior.

Throughout our national history, our basic policy in dealing with foreign nations has rested upon certain beliefs which are widely and deeply rooted in the minds of our people. Outstanding among these are:

1. All peoples who, with "a decent respect to the opinions of mankind," have qualified themselves to assume and to discharge the responsibilities of liberty are entitled to its enjoyment.

2. Each sovereign nation, large or small, is in law and under law the equal of every other nation.

3. All nations, large and small, which respect the rights of others, are entitled to freedom from outside interference in their internal affairs.

4. Willingness to settle international disputes by peaceful means, acceptance of international law, and observance of its principles are the bases of order among nations and of mankind's continuing search for enduring peace.

5. Nondiscrimination in economic opportunity and treatment is essential to the maintenance and promotion of sound international relations.

6. Cooperation between nations in the spirit of good neighbors, founded on the principles of liberty, equality, justice, morality, and law, is the most effective method of safeguarding and promoting the political, the economic, the social, and the cultural well-being of our nation and of all nations.

These beliefs are among the most important tenets of our national faith. They are capable of universal application as rules of national and international conduct. In their application by other nations and in willingness and preparedness on the part of all peacefully inclined nations to join together to make them effective lies the greatest hope of security, happiness, and progress of this country and for all countries.

Vigorous participation in efforts to establish a system of international relations based on these rules of conduct, and thus to create conditions in which war may be effectively banished, is and must be a fundamental feature of our foreign policy — second only to our present over-riding preoccupation with the winning of complete military victory. Here, too, our nation and other peacefully inclined nations have a vast and crucial area of common interest.

In the Atlantic Charter and in the Declaration by United Nations, the nations now associated in this war for self-preservation have clearly expressed their recognition of the existence of this area of common interest. Our task and that of our associates is to utilize this common interest to create an effective system of international cooperation for the maintenance of peace.

As I read our history and the temper of our people today, our nation intends to do its part, jointly with the other peace-seeking nations, in helping the war-torn world to heal its wounds. I am sure also that our nation and each of the nations associated today in the greatest cooperative enterprise in history — the winning of this war — intends to do its part, after the victory of the United Nations, in meeting the immense needs of the post-war period. Those needs will embrace the task of taking practical steps to create conditions in which there will be security for every nation; in which each nation will have enhanced opportunities to develop and progress in ways of its own choosing; in which there will be, . for each nation, improved facilities to attain, by its own effort and in cooperation with others, an increasing measure of political stability and of economic, social, and cultural welfare.

If our nation and like-minded nations fail in this task, the way will be open for a new rise of international anarchy, for new and even more destructive wars, for an unprecedented material and spiritual impoverishment of mankind. Many times in the course of history nations have drifted into catastrophe through failure, until too late, to recognize the dangers which confronted them and to take the measures necessary to ward off those dangers. Post-war cooperation to maintain the peace is for each peace-seeking nation scarcely less essential for its self-preservation than is the present cooperative effort to win the war.

IV

If there is anything on which all right-thinking people are agreed, it is the proposition that the monstrous specter of a world war shall not again show its head. The people of this and other lands voice this demand insistently. There is danger in complacency and wishful thinking. The nations that stand for peace and security must now make up their minds and act together — or there will be neither peace nor security.

It is abundantly clear that a system of organized international cooperation for the maintenance of peace must be based upon the willingness of the cooperating nations to use force, if necessary, to keep the peace. There must be certainty that adequate and appropriate means are available and will be used for this purpose. Readiness to use force, if necessary, for the maintenance of peace is indispensable if effective substitutes for war are to be found.

Differences between nations which lead toward armed conflict may be those of a non-legal character, commonly referred to as political, and those capable of being resolved by applying rules of law, commonly referred to as justiciable. Another cause of armed conflict is aggression by nations whose only motive is conquest and self-aggrandizement. We must, therefore, provide for differences of a political character, for those of a legal nature, and for cases where there is plain and unadulterated aggression.

Political differences which present a threat to the peace of the world should be submitted to agencies which would use the remedies of discussion, negotiation, conciliation, and good offices.

Disputes of a legal character which present a threat to the peace of the world should be adjudicated by an international court of justice whose decisions would be based upon application of principles of law.

But to assure peace there must also be means for restraining aggressors and nations that seek to resort to force for the accomplishment of purposes of their own. The peacefully inclined nations must, in the interest of general peace and security, be willing to accept responsibility for this task in accordance with their respective capacities.

The success of an organized system of international cooperation with the maintenance of peace as its paramount objective depends, to an important degree, upon what happens within as well as among nations. We know that political controversies and economic strife among nations are fruitful causes of hostility and conflict. But we also know that economic stagnation and distress, cultural backwardness, and social unrest within nations, wherever they exist, may undermine all efforts for stable peace.

The primary responsibility for dealing with these conditions rests on each and every nation concerned. But each nation will be greatly helped in this task by the establishment of sound trade and other economic relations with other nations, based on a comprehensive system of mutually beneficial international cooperation, not alone in these respects, but also in furthering educational advancement and in promoting observance of basic human rights.

There rests upon the independent nations a responsibility in relation to dependent peoples who aspire to liberty. It should be the duty of nations having political ties with such peoples, of mandatories, of trustees, or of other agencies, as the case may be, to help the aspiring peoples to develop materially and educationally, to prepare themselves for the duties and responsibilities of self-government, and to attain liberty. An excellent example of what can be achieved is afforded in the record of our relationship with the Philippines.

Organized international cooperation can be successful only to the extent to which the nations of the world are willing to accept certain fundamental propositions.

First, each nation should maintain a stable government. Each nation should be free to decide for itself the forms and details of its governmental organization — so long as it conducts its affairs in such a way as not to menace the peace and security of other nations.

Second, each nation should conduct its economic affairs in such a way as to promote the most effective utilization of its human and material resources and the greatest practicable measure of economic welfare and social security for all of its citizens. Each nation should be free to decide for itself the forms of its internal economic and social organization — but it should conduct its affairs in such a way as to respect the rights of others and to play its necessary part in a system of sound international economic relations.

Third, each nation should be willing to submit differences arising between it and other nations to processes of peaceful settlement and should be prepared to carry out other obligations that may devolve upon it in an effective system of organized peace.

All of this calls for the creation of a system of international relations based on rules of morality, law, and justice as distinguished from the anarchy of unbridled and discordant nationalisms, economic and political. The outstanding characteristic of such a system is liberty under law for nations as well as individuals. Its method is peaceful cooperation.

The form and functions of the international agencies of the future, the extent to which the existing court of international justice may or may not need to be remodeled, the scope and character of the means for making international action effective in the maintenance of peace, the nature of international economic institutions and arrangements that may be desirable and feasible — all these are among the problems which are receiving attention and which will need to be determined by agreement among governments, subject, of course, to approval by their respective peoples. They are being studied intensively by this Government and by other governments. They are gradually being made subjects of consultation between and among governments. They are being studied and discussed by the people of this country and the peoples of other countries. In the final analysis, it is the will of the peoples of the world that decides the all-embracing issues of peace and of human welfare.

V

The outbreak of war made it clear that problems of crucial importance in the field of foreign relations would confront this country as well as other countries upon the termination of hostilities. It became the obvious duty of the Department of State to give special attention to the study of conditions and developments relating to such problems. As the war spread over the earth, the scope of these studies was extended and work upon them was steadily increased, so far as was compatible with the fullest possible prosecution of the war.

By direction of the President and with his active interest in the work, the Department of State undertook, through special groups organized for the purpose, to examine the various matters affecting the conclusion of the war, the making of the peace, and preparation for dealing with post-war problems. In doing this work, we have had collaboration of representatives of other interested agencies of the Government and of many national leaders, without regard to their political affiliation, and the assistance of a specially constituted and highly qualified research staff. We have been aided greatly by public discussion of the problems involved on the part of responsible private individuals and groups and by the numerous suggestions and expressions of opinion which we have received from all parts of the country. In proceeding with this work we envisage the fullest cooperation between the executive and the legislative branches of the Government.

We have now reached a stage at which it becomes possible to discuss in greater detail some of the basic problems outlined in this address and in my previous statements. I hope to be able to undertake this from time to time in the early future.

The supreme importance of these problems should lift them far above the realm of partisan considerations or party politics. It is gratifying that both in the Congress and elsewhere great numbers of thoughtful men have so approached them. A heavy responsibility rests upon all of us to consider these all-important post-war problems and to contribute to their solution in a wholly non-partisan spirit.

(3) *Address by the Secretary of State (Hull) Delivered before a Joint Meeting of Both Houses of Congress on the Work of the Moscow Conference, November 18, 1943* [1]

For text of the Declarations, emanating from the Moscow Conference, see p. 229–31. For account of work of Conference in relation to other Allied Conferences, see p. 226.

MR. PRESIDENT, MR. SPEAKER:

I appreciate deeply the high compliment of being invited to meet with you today. But I appreciate even more the fact that by your invitation you have emphasized your profound interest in the principles and policies for which the Moscow Conference stood and in the progress made by the participating governments in carrying them forward.

In the minds of all of us here present and of the millions of Americans all over the country and at battle-stations across the seas, there is and there can be at this moment but one consuming thought — to defeat the enemy as speedily as possible. We have reached a stage in the war in which the United Nations are on the offensive in every part of the world. Our enemies are suffering defeat after defeat. The time will come when their desperate movement to destroy the world will be utterly crushed. But there are in store for us still enormous hardships and vast sacrifices. The attainment of victory will be hastened only in proportion as all of us, in this country and in all the United Nations, continue to exert all possible effort to press home our advantage without the slightest relaxation or deviation.

The glorious successes which have already attended our arms and the confidence which we all feel today in assured, though still immensely difficult, victory would have been impossible if this country, and Great Britain, and the Soviet Union, and China, and the other victims of aggression had not each risen as a unit in defense of its liberty and independence. They would have been equally impossible if all these nations had not come together in a brotherhood of self-preservation.

[1] *Ibid.*, p. 341.

While we are thus engaged in the task of winning the war, all of us are acutely conscious of the fact that the fruits of our victory can easily be lost unless there is among us whole-hearted acceptance of those basic principles and policies which will render impossible a repetition of our present tragedy, and unless there is promptly created machinery of action necessary to carry out these principles and policies. The Moscow Conference is believed to have been an important step in the direction both of shortening the war and of making provision for the future.

The convocation of the Conference was the result of a profound conviction on the part of President Roosevelt, Prime Minister Churchill, and Marshal Stalin that, at this stage of the war, frank and friendly exchanges of views between responsible representatives of their three Governments on problems of post-war, as well as war, collaboration were a matter of great urgency. Up to that time, such exchanges of views had taken place on several occasions between our Government and that of Great Britain. But the exigencies of war had been obstacles to the participation of the Soviet Government in such exchanges to the same extent. With the acceleration of the tempo of war against Germany, the necessity became daily more and more apparent for more far-reaching discussions and decisions by the three Governments than had occurred theretofore.

I went to Moscow, by direction of President Roosevelt, to discuss with the representatives of Great Britain and the Soviet Union some basic problems of international relations in the light of principles to which our country, under the President's leadership, has come to give widespread adherence. It has never been my fortune to attend an international conference at which there was greater determination on the part of all the participants to move forward in a spirit of mutual understanding and confidence.

The Conference met against the background of a rapidly changing military situation. From the east and from the south, the Nazi armies were being steadily hammered back into narrower and narrower confines. From the west, the Allied air forces were relentlessly and systematically destroying the nerve centers of German industrial and military power.

Formidable as the war task still is, it has been increasingly clear that the time is nearing when more and more of the territory held by the enemy will be wrested from his grasp, and when Germany and its remaining satellites will have to go the way of Fascist Italy. In these circumstances, new problems arise which require concerted action by the Allies, to hasten the end of the war, to plan for its immediate aftermath, and to lay the foundation for the post-war world. Our discussions in Moscow were concerned with many of these problems. Important agreements were reached, but there were no secret agreements, and none was suggested.

Of the military discussions which took place it can be stated that they were in the direction of facilitating closer cooperation between the three countries in the prosecution of the war against the common enemy. I am glad to say that there is now in Moscow a highly competent United States Military Mission, headed by Maj. Gen. John R. Deane.

The attention of the Conference was centered upon the task of making sure that the nations upon whose armed forces and civilian efforts rests the main responsibility for defeating the enemy will, along with other peacefully minded nations, continue to perform their full part in solving the numerous and vexatious problems of the future. From the outset, the dominant thought at the Conference was that, after the attainment of victory, cooperation among peace-loving nations in support of certain paramount mutual interests will be almost as compelling in importance and necessity as it is today in support of the war effort.

At the end of the war, each of the United Nations and each of the nations associated with them will have the same common interest in national security, in world order under law, in peace, in the full promotion of the political, economic, and social welfare of their respective peoples — in the principles and spirit of the Atlantic Charter and the Declaration by United Nations. The future of these indispensable common interests depends absolutely upon international cooperation. Hence, each nation's own primary interest requires it to cooperate with the others.

These considerations led the Moscow Conference to adopt the four-nation declaration [1] with which you are all familiar. I should like to comment briefly on its main provisions.

In that document, it was jointly declared by the United States, Great Britain, the Soviet Union, and China "That their united action, pledged for the prosecution of the war against their respective enemies, will be continued for the organization and maintenance of peace and security."

To this end, the four Governments declared that they "recognize the necessity of establishing at the earliest practicable date a general international organization, based on the principle of the sovereign equality of all peace-loving states, and open to membership by all such states, large and small." I should like to lay particular stress on this provision of the declaration. The principle of sovereign equality of all peace-loving states, irrespective of size and strength, as partners in a future system of general security will be the foundation stone upon which the future international organization will be constructed.

The adoption of this principle was particularly welcome to us. Nowhere has the conception of sovereign equality been applied more widely in recent years than in the American family of nations, whose contribution to the common effort in wartime will now be followed by representation in building the institutions of peace.

[1] See this volume, p. 229.

The four Governments further agreed that, pending the inauguration in this manner of a permanent system of general security, "they will consult with one another and as occasion requires with other members of the United Nations with a view to joint action on behalf of the community of nations" whenever such action may be necessary for the purpose of maintaining international peace and security.

Finally, as an important self-denying ordinance, they declared "That after the termination of hostilities they will not employ their military forces within the territories of other states except for the purposes envisaged in this declaration and after joint consultation."

Through this declaration, the Soviet Union, Great Britain, the United States, and China have laid the foundation for cooperative effort in the post-war world toward enabling all peace-loving nations, large and small, to live in peace and security, to preserve the liberties and rights of civilized existence, and to enjoy expanded opportunities and facilities for economic, social, and spiritual progress. No other important nations anywhere have more in common in the present war or in the peace that is to follow victory over the Axis powers. No one, no two of them can be most effective without the others, in war or in peace.

Each of them had, in the past, relied in varying degrees upon policies of detachment and aloofness. In Moscow, their four Governments pledged themselves to carry forward to its fullest development a broad and progressive program of international cooperation. This action was of world-wide importance.

As the provisions of the four-nation declaration are carried into effect, there will no longer be need for spheres of influence, for alliances, for balance of power, or any other of the special arrangements through which, in the unhappy past, the nations strove to safeguard their security or to promote their interests.

The Conference faced many political problems growing out of the military activities in Europe. It was foreseen that problems of common interest to our three Governments will continue to arise as our joint military efforts hasten the defeat of the enemy. It is impracticable for several governments to come to complete and rapid understanding on such matters through the ordinary channels of diplomatic communication. The Conference accordingly decided to set up a European Advisory Commission with its seat in London. This Commission will not of itself have executive powers. Its sole function will be to advise the Governments of the United States, Great Britain, and the Soviet Union. It is to deal with non-military problems relating to enemy territories and with such other problems as may be referred to it by the participating governments. It will provide a useful instrument for continuing study and formulation of recommendations concerning questions connected with the termination of hostilities.

For the purpose of dealing with problems arising from the execution of the terms of surrender of Italy and with related matters growing out of the developing situation in that country, the Conference established an Advisory Council for Italy. This Council will consist of representatives of the Governments of the United States, Great Britain, and the Soviet Union, of the French Committee of National Liberation, and of the Governments of Yugoslavia and Greece, as early as practicable. The members of the Council will advise the Allied Commander-in-Chief and will make recommendations to the respective governments and to the French Committee concerning non-military problems relating to Italy.

It was clearly understood that the setting up of these two agencies was not intended to supersede the usual diplomatic channels of communication between the three Governments. On the contrary, arrangements were made for expeditious and effective handling of questions of concern to the three Governments through tripartite diplomatic conversations in any one of the three capitals.

In a declaration on Italy, the Conference set forth a number of principles on the basis of which democratic restoration of that country's internal political structure should take place. These principles — including freedom of religion, of speech, of the press, and of assembly, and the right of the people ultimately to choose their own form of government — are among the most basic human rights in civilized society.

In a declaration on Austria, the forcible annexation of that unhappy country was pronounced null and void. It was further declared that Austria is to be given an opportunity to become reestablished as a free and independent state, although the Austrians were put on notice that in final analysis the treatment to be accorded them will depend upon the contribution which they will make toward the defeat of Germany and the liberation of their country.

The Conference also served as an occasion for a solemn public declaration by the heads of the three Governments with regard to the perpetrators of the bestial and abominable crimes committed by the Nazi leaders against the harassed and persecuted inhabitants of occupied territories — against people of all races and religions, among whom Hitler has reserved for the Jews his most brutal wrath. Due punishment will be administered for all these crimes.

Finally, the Conference gave preliminary attention to a number of other specific problems relating to the eventual transition from war to peace. A fruitful exchange of views took place on such questions as the treatment of Germany and its satellites, the various phases of economic relations, the promotion of social welfare, and the assurance of general security and peace.

These were among the outstanding developments at the Moscow Conference. The intensive discussion, lasting two weeks, did not and was not intended to bring about the solution of all the problems that are before us. Much less could we anticipate the problems that are bound to arise from day to day and from year to year. There were other problems, such, for example, as questions relating to boundaries, which must, by their very nature, be left in abeyance until the termination of hostilities. This is in accordance with the position maintained for some time by our Government.

Of supreme importance is the fact that at the Conference the whole spirit of international cooperation, now and after the war, was revitalized and given practical expression. The Conference thus launched a forward movement which, I am firmly convinced, will steadily extend in scope and effectiveness. Within the framework of that movement, in the atmosphere of mutual understanding and confidence which made possible its beginning in Moscow, many of the problems which are difficult today will as time goes on undoubtedly become more possible of satisfactory solution through frank and friendly discussion.

I am happy on this occasion to pay personal tribute to those with whom it was my privilege to confer in Moscow. Mr. Molotov arranged for the business of the Conference in a most efficient manner. Both as chairman and participant he manifested throughout the highest order of ability and a profound grasp of international affairs. Mr. Eden, with his exceptional wisdom and experience, exhibited the finest qualities of statesmanship. I found in Marshal Stalin a remarkable personality, one of the great statesmen and leaders of this age.

I was deeply impressed by the people of Russia and by the epic quality of their patriotic fervor. A people who will fight against ruthless aggression, in utter contempt of death, as the men and women of the Soviet Union are fighting, merit the admiration and good-will of the peoples of all countries.

We of today shall be judged in the future by the manner in which we meet the unprecedented responsibilities that rest upon us — not alone in winning the war but also in making certain that the opportunities for future peace and security shall not be lost. As an American, I am proud of the breadth and height of vision and statesmanship which have moved you, ladies and gentlemen, in each House of the Congress, to adopt, by overwhelming non-partisan majorities, resolutions in favor of our country's participation with other sovereign nations in an effective system of international cooperation for the maintenance of peace and security.

Only by carrying forward such a program with common determination and united national support can we expect, in the long range of the future, to avoid becoming victims of destructive forces of international anarchy which in the absence of organized international relations will rule the world. By the procedure of cooperation with other nations likewise intent upon security we can and will remain masters of our own fate.

(4) *Radio Address by the President* (*Roosevelt*), *December 24, 1943* [1]

[Excerpt]

This address was given following the President's return from the Cairo Conference with Prime Minister Churchill and Generalissimo Chiang Kai-shek, and the Tehran Conference with Prime Minister Churchill and Marshal Stalin. For descriptions of these two Conferences, see p. 232-8.

. . . .

Britain, Russia, China, and the United States and their Allies represent more than three quarters of the total population of the earth. As long as these four nations with great military power stick together in determination to keep the peace there will be no possibility of an aggressor nation arising to start another world war.

But those four powers must be united with and cooperate with all the freedom-loving peoples of Europe and Asia and Africa and the Americas. The rights of every nation, large or small, must be respected and guarded as jealously as are the rights of every individual within our own republic.

The doctrine that the strong shall dominate the weak is the doctrine of our enemies — and we reject it.

But, at the same time, we are agreed that if force is necessary to keep international peace, international force will be applied — for as long as it may be necessary.

It has been our steady policy — and it is certainly a common-sense policy — that the right of each nation to freedom must be measured by the willingness of that nation to fight for freedom. And today we salute our unseen allies in occupied countries — the underground resistance groups and the armies of liberation. They will provide potent forces against our enemies, when the day of invasion comes.

Through the development of science the world has become so much smaller that we have had to discard the geographical yardsticks of the past. For instance, through our early history the Atlantic and Pacific Oceans were believed to be walls of safety for the United States. Time and distance made it physically possible for us and for the other American Republics to obtain and maintain our independence against infinitely stronger powers. Until recently very few people, even military experts, thought that the day could ever come when we might have to defend our Pacific coast against Japanese threats of invasion.

At the outbreak of the first World War relatively few people thought that our ships and shipping would be menaced by German submarines on the high seas or that the German militarists would ever attempt to dominate any nation outside of central Europe.

After the Armistice in 1918, we thought and hoped that the militaristic philosophy of Germany had been crushed; and being full of the milk of human kindness we spent the next 15 years disarming, while the Germans

[1] Broadcast from Hyde Park, New York, *ibid.*, X, p. 3.

whined so pathetically that the other nations permitted them — and even helped them — to rearm.

For too many years we lived on pious hopes that aggressor and warlike nations would learn and understand and carry out the doctrine of purely voluntary peace.

The well-intentioned but ill-fated experiments of former years did not work. It is my hope that we will not try them again. No — that is too weak — it is my intention to do all that I humanly can as President and Commander-in-Chief to see to it that these tragic mistakes shall not be made again.

There have always been cheerful idiots in this country who believed that there would be no more war for us, if everybody in America would only return into their homes and lock their front doors behind them. Assuming that their motives were of the highest, events have shown how unwilling they were to face the facts.

The overwhelming majority of all the people in the world want peace. Most of them are fighting for the attainment of peace — not just a truce, not just an armistice — but peace that is as strongly enforced and as durable as mortal man can make it. If we are willing to fight for peace now, is it not good logic that we should use force if necessary, in the future, to keep the peace?

I believe, and I think I can say, that the other three great nations who are fighting so magnificently to gain peace are in complete agreement that we must be prepared to keep the peace by force. If the people of Germany and Japan are made to realize thoroughly that the world is not going to let them break out again, it is possible, and, I hope, probable, that they will abandon the philosophy of aggression — the belief that they can gain the whole world even at the risk of losing their own souls.

. . . .

(5) *Statement of the President (Roosevelt), January 1, 1944* [1]

Many of us in the United States are observing this first day of the New Year as a day of prayer and reflection and are considering the deeper issues which affect us as part of the family of nations at a crucial moment in history. It is fitting on this day that we direct our thoughts to the concept of the United Nations which came into being on another and infinitely bleaker New Year's Day two years ago.

It was but three weeks after Pearl Harbor that the Declaration by United Nations was promulgated at Washington. Twenty-six nations subscribed immediately, eight more have adhered subsequently, all pledging themselves to stand together in the struggle against common enemies.

[1] From the Office of the Secretary to the President.

Two years ago the United Nations were on the defensive in every part of the world. Today we are on the offensive. The walls are closing in remorselessly on our enemies. Our armed forces are gathering for new and greater assaults which will bring about the downfall of the Axis aggressors.

The United Nations are giving attention also to the different kind of struggle which must follow the military phase, the struggle against disease, malnutrition, unemployment, and many other forms of economic and social distress.

To make all of us secure against future aggression and to open the way for enhanced well-being of nations and individuals everywhere, we must maintain in the peace to come the mutually beneficial cooperation we have achieved in war. On the threshold of the New Year, as we look toward the tremendous tasks ahead, let us pledge ourselves that this cooperation shall continue both for winning the final victory on the battlefield and for establishing an international organization of all peace-loving nations to maintain peace and security in generations to come.

(6) *Annual Message of the President (Roosevelt) to the Congress, January 11, 1944* [1]

[Excerpts]

TO THE CONGRESS OF THE UNITED STATES:

This Nation in the past two years has become an active partner in the world's greatest war against human slavery.

We have joined with like-minded people in order to defend ourselves in a world that has been gravely threatened with gangster rule.

But I do not think that any of us Americans can be content with mere survival. Sacrifices that we and our Allies are making impose upon us all a sacred obligation to see to it that out of this war we and our children will gain something better than mere survival.

We are united in determination that this war shall not be followed by another interim which leads to new disaster — that we shall not repeat the tragic errors of ostrich isolationism — that we shall not repeat the excesses of the wild twenties when this Nation went for a joy-ride on a roller coaster which ended in a tragic crash.

When Mr. Hull went to Moscow in October, and when I went to Cairo and Tehran in November, we knew that we were in agreement with our Allies in our common determination to fight and win this war. But there were many vital questions concerning the future peace, and they were discussed in an atmosphere of complete candor and harmony.

In the last war such discussions, such meetings, did not even begin

[1] From the Office of the Secretary to the President; H. Doc. 377, 78th Cong.; Department of State, *Bulletin*, X, p. 76.

until the shooting had stopped and the delegates began to assemble at the peace table. There had been no previous opportunities for man-to-man discussions which lead to meetings of minds. The result was a peace which was not a peace.

That was a mistake which we are not repeating in this war.

And right here I want to address a word or two to some suspicious souls who are fearful that Mr. Hull or I have made "commitments" for the future which might pledge this Nation to secret treaties, or to enacting the role of Santa Claus.

To such suspicious souls — using a polite terminology — I wish to say that Mr. Churchill, and Marshal Stalin, and Generalissimo Chiang Kai-shek are all thoroughly conversant with the provisions of our Constitution. And so is Mr. Hull. And so am I.

Of course we made some commitments. We most certainly committed ourselves to very large and very specific military plans which require the use of all allied forces to bring about the defeat of our enemies at the earliest possible time.

But there were no secret treaties or political or financial commitments.

The one supreme objective for the future, which we discussed for each nation individually, and for all the United Nations, can be summed up in one word: Security.

And that means not only physical security which provides safety from attacks by aggressors. It means also economic security, social security, moral security — in a family of nations.

In the plain down-to-earth talks that I had with the Generalissimo and Marshal Stalin and Prime Minister Churchill, it was abundantly clear that they are all most deeply interested in the resumption of peaceful progress by their own peoples — progress toward a better life. All our Allies want freedom to develop their lands and resources, to build up industry, to increase education and individual opportunity, and to raise standards of living.

All our Allies have learned by bitter experience that real development will not be possible if they are to be diverted from their purpose by repeated wars — or even threats of war.

China and Russia are truly united with Britain and America in recognition of this essential fact:

The best interests of each nation, large and small, demand that all freedom-loving nations shall join together in a just and durable system of peace. In the present world situation, evidenced by the actions of Germany, Italy and Japan, unquestioned military control over disturbers of the peace is as necessary among nations as it is among citizens in a community. And an equally basic essential to peace is a decent standard of living for all individual men and women and children in all nations. Freedom from fear is eternally linked with freedom from want.

There are people who burrow through our Nation like unseeing moles, and attempt to spread the suspicion that if other nations are encouraged to raise their standards of living, our own American standard of living must of necessity be depressed.

The fact is the very contrary. It has been shown time and again that if the standard of living of any country goes up, so does its purchasing power — and that such a rise encourages a better standard of living in neighboring countries with whom it trades. That is just plain common sense — and it is the kind of plain common sense that provided the basis for our discussions at Moscow, Cairo and Tehran.

．　．　．　．　．　．　．

The foreign policy that we have been following — the policy that guided us at Moscow, Cairo and Tehran — is based on the common sense principle which was best expressed by Benjamin Franklin on July 4, 1776: "We must all hang together, or assuredly we shall all hang separately."

I have often said that there are no two fronts for America in this war. There is only one front. There is one line of unity which extends from the hearts of the people at home to the men of our attacking forces in our farthest outposts. When we speak of our total effort, we speak of the factory and the field and the mine as well as of the battleground — we speak of the soldier and the civilian, the citizen and his Government.

Each and every one of us has a solemn obligation under God to serve this Nation in its most critical hour — to keep this Nation great — to make this Nation greater in a better world.

(7) *Bases of the Foreign Policy of the United States. Memorandum Given to the Press by the Secretary of State (Hull), March 21, 1944* [1]

On March 21, 1944, Secretary of State Cordell Hull informed press and radio correspondents that after returning from his recent trip to Florida he had noted a growing interest in the foreign policy of the United States and an increasing number of requests for information about various points in our foreign policy. He said that he was glad of this increased interest. The Secretary said that, in addition to many statements and declarations by the President, he had himself made a number of basic statements on foreign policy during the past two years. He thought it would be a convenience and help to the public generally if there could be compiled a brief memorandum of a number of them.

OUR FUNDAMENTAL NATIONAL INTERESTS

In determining our foreign policy we must first see clearly what our true national interests are.

At the present time, the paramount aim of our foreign policy is to defeat our enemies as quickly as possible.

[1] Department of State, *Bulletin*, X, p. 275.

Beyond final victory, our fundamental national interests are the assuring of our national security and the fostering of the economic and social well-being of our people.

INTERNATIONAL COOPERATION

Cooperation between nations in the spirit of good neighbors, founded on the principles of liberty, equality, justice, morality, and law, is the most effective method of safeguarding and promoting the political, the economic, the social, and the cultural well-being of our nation and of all nations.

INTERNATIONAL ORGANIZATION BACKED BY FORCE

Some international agency must be created which can — by force, if necessary — keep the peace among nations in the future.

A system of organized international cooperation for the maintenance of peace must be based upon the willingness of the cooperating nations to use force, if necessary, to keep the peace. There must be certainty that adequate and appropriate means are available and will be used for this purpose.

POLITICAL DIFFERENCES

Political differences which present a threat to the peace of the world should be submitted to agencies which would use the remedies of discussion, negotiation, conciliation, and good offices.

INTERNATIONAL COURT OF JUSTICE

Disputes of a legal character which present a threat to the peace of the world should be adjudicated by an international court of justice whose decisions would be based upon application of principles of law.

REDUCTION OF ARMS

International cooperative action must include eventual adjustment of national armaments in such a manner that the rule of law cannot be successfully challenged and that the burden of armaments may be reduced to a minimum.

MOSCOW FOUR-NATION DECLARATION

Through this declaration the Soviet Union, Great Britain, the United States, and China have laid the foundation for cooperative effort in the post-war world toward enabling all peace-loving nations, large and small, to live in peace and security, to preserve the liberties and rights of civilized existence, and to enjoy expanded opportunities and facilities for economic, social, and spiritual progress.

SPHERES OF INFLUENCE AND ALLIANCES

As the provisions of the four-nation declaration are carried into effect, there will no longer be need for spheres of influence, for alliances, for balance of power, or any other of the special arrangements through which, in the unhappy past, the nations strove to safeguard their security or to promote their interests.

SURVEILLANCE OVER AGGRESSOR NATIONS

In the process of reestablishing international order, the United Nations must exercise surveillance over aggressor nations until such time as the latter demonstrate their willingness and ability to live at peace with other nations. How long such surveillance will need to continue must depend upon the rapidity with which the peoples of Germany, Japan, Italy, and their satellites give convincing proof that they have repudiated and abandoned the monstrous philosophy of superior race and conquest by force and have embraced loyally the basic principles of peaceful processes.

INTERNATIONAL TRADE BARRIERS

Excessive trade barriers of the many different kinds must be reduced, and practices which impose injuries on others and divert trade from its natural economic course must be avoided.

INTERNATIONAL FINANCE

Equally plain is the need for making national currencies once more freely exchangeable for each other at stable rates of exchange; for a system of financial relations so devised that materials can be produced and ways may be found of moving them where there are markets created by human need; for machinery through which capital may — for the development of the world's resources and for the stabilization of economic activity — move on equitable terms from financially stronger to financially weaker countries.

ATLANTIC CHARTER: RECIPROCAL OBLIGATIONS

The pledge of the Atlantic Charter is of a system which will give every nation, large or small, a greater assurance of stable peace, greater opportunity for the realization of its aspirations to freedom, and greater facilities for material advancement. But that pledge implies an obligation for each nation to demonstrate its capacity for stable and progressive government, to fulfil scrupulously its established duties to other nations, to settle its international differences and disputes by none but peaceful methods, and to make its full contribution to the maintenance of enduring peace.

SOVEREIGN EQUALITY OF NATIONS

Each sovereign nation, large or small, is in law and under law the equal of every other nation.

The principle of sovereign equality of all peace-loving states, irrespective of size and strength, as partners in a future system of general security, will be the foundation-stone upon which the future international organization will be constructed.

FORM OF GOVERNMENT

Each nation should be free to decide for itself the forms and details of its governmental organization — so long as it conducts its affairs in such a way as not to menace the peace and security of other nations.

NON-INTERVENTION

All nations, large and small, which respect the rights of others are entitled to freedom from outside interference in their internal affairs.

LIBERTY

There is no surer way for men and for nations to show themselves worthy of liberty than to fight for its preservation, in any way that is open to them, against those who would destroy it for all. Never did a plainer duty to fight against its foes devolve upon all peoples who prize liberty and all who aspire to it.

All peoples who, with "a decent respect to the opinions of mankind," have qualified themselves to assume and to discharge the responsibilities of liberty are entitled to its enjoyment.

DEPENDENT PEOPLES

There rests upon the independent nations a responsibility in relation to dependent peoples who aspire to liberty. It should be the duty of nations having political ties with such peoples, of mandatories, of trustees, or of other agencies, as the case may be, to help the aspiring peoples to develop materially and educationally, to prepare themselves for the duties and responsibilities of self-government, and to attain liberty. An excellent example of what can be achieved is afforded in the record of our relationship with the Philippines.

(8) *Foreign Policy of the United States of America. Radio Address by the Secretary of State (Hull), April 9, 1944* [1]

I want to talk with you this evening about the foreign policy of the United States. This is not, as some writers assume, a mysterious game carried on by diplomats with other diplomats in foreign offices all over the world. It is for us the task of focusing and giving effect in the world outside our borders to the will of 135 million people through the constitutional processes which govern our democracy. For this reason our foreign policy must be simple and direct and founded upon the interests and purposes of the American people. It has continuity of basic objectives because it is rooted in the traditions and aspirations of our people. It must, of course, be applied in the light of experience and the lessons of the past.

In talking about foreign policy it is well to remember, as Justice Holmes said, that a page of history is worth a volume of logic. There are three outstanding lessons in our recent history to which I particularly wish to draw your attention. In the first place, since the outbreak of the present war in Europe, we and those nations who are now our allies have moved from relative weakness to strength. In the second place, during that same period we in this country have moved from a deep-seated tendency toward separate action to the knowledge and conviction that only through unity of action can there be achieved in this world the results which are essential for the continuance of free peoples. And, thirdly, we have moved from a careless tolerance of evil institutions to the conviction that free governments and Nazi and Fascist governments cannot exist together in this world because the very nature of the latter requires them to be aggressors and the very nature of free governments too often lays them open to treacherous and well-laid plans of attack.

An understanding of these points will help to clarify the policy which this Government has been and is following.

In 1940, with the fall of France, the peoples of the free world awoke with horror to find themselves on the very brink of defeat. Only Britain in the west and China in the east stood between them and disaster, and the space on which they stood was narrow and precarious. At that moment the free nations were militarily weak, and their enemies and potential enemies were strong and well prepared. Even before that this country had begun its preparations for self-defense. Soon thereafter we started upon the long hard road of mobilizing our great natural resources, our vast productive potentialities, and our reserves of manpower to defend ourselves and to strengthen those who were resisting the aggressors.

[1] Broadcast over the network of the Columbia Broadcasting System, *ibid.*, p. 335.

This was a major decision of foreign policy. Since that decision was made we have moved far from the former position. We and our Allies are attaining a strength which can leave no doubt as to the outcome. That outcome is far from achieved. There are desperate periods still before us, but we have built the strength which we sought and we need only to maintain the will to use it.

This decision which we have made and carried out was not a decision to make a mere sporadic effort. An episode is not a policy. The American people are determined to press forward with our Allies to the defeat of our enemies and the destruction of the Nazi and Fascist systems which plunged us into the war. And they are also determined to go on, after the victory, with our Allies and all other nations which desire peace and freedom to establish and maintain in full strength the institutions without which peace and freedom cannot be an enduring reality. We cannot move in and out of international cooperation and in and out of participation in the responsibilities of a member of the family of nations. The political, material, and spiritual strength of the free and democratic nations not only is greatly dependent upon the strength which our full participation brings to the common effort but, as we now know, is a vital factor in our own strength. As it is with the keystone of an arch, neither the keystone nor the arch can stand alone.

This growth of our strength entails consequences in our foreign policy. Let us look first at our relations with the neutral nations.

In the two years following Pearl Harbor, while we were mustering our strength and helping to restore that of our Allies, our relations with these neutral nations and their attitude toward our enemies were conditioned by the position in which we found ourselves. We have constantly sought to keep before them what they, of course, know — that upon our victory hangs their very existence and freedom as independent nations. We have sought in every way to reduce the aid which their trade with the enemy gives him and to increase the strength which we might draw from them. But our power was limited. They and we have continually been forced to accept compromises which we certainly would not have chosen.

That period, I believe, is rapidly drawing to a close. It is clear to all that our strength and that of our Allies now makes only one outcome of this war possible. That strength now makes it clear that we are not asking these neutral nations to expose themselves to certain destruction when we ask them not to prolong the war, with its consequences of suffering and death, by sending aid to the enemy.

We can no longer acquiesce in these nations' drawing upon the resources of the allied world when they at the same time contribute to the death of troops whose sacrifice contributes to their salvation as well as ours. We have scrupulously respected the sovereignty of these nations;

and we have not coerced, nor shall we coerce, any nation to join us in the fight. We have said to these countries that it is no longer necessary for them to purchase protection against aggression by furnishing aid to our enemy — whether it be by permitting official German agents to carry on their activities of espionage against the Allies within neutral borders, or by sending to Germany the essential ingredients of the steel which kills our soldiers, or by permitting highly skilled workers and factories to supply products which can no longer issue from the smoking ruins of German factories. We ask them only, but with insistence, to cease aiding our enemy.

The allied strength has now grown to the point where we are on the verge of great events. Of military events I cannot speak. It is enough that they are in the hands of men who have the complete trust of the American people. We await their development with absolute confidence. But I can and should discuss with you what may happen close upon the heels of military action.

As I look at the map of Europe, certain things seem clear to me. As the Nazis go down to defeat they will inevitably leave behind them in Germany and the satellite states of southeastern Europe a legacy of confusion. It is essential that we and our Allies establish the controls necessary to bring order out of this chaos as rapidly as possible and do everything possible to prevent its spread to the German-occupied countries of eastern and western Europe while they are in the throes of reestablishing government and repairing the most brutal ravages of the war. If confusion should spread throughout Europe it is difficult to overemphasize the seriousness of the disaster that may follow. Therefore, for us, for the world, and for the countries concerned, a stable Europe should be an immediate objective of allied policy.

Stability and order do not and cannot mean reaction. Order there must be to avoid chaos. But it must be achieved in a manner which will give full scope to men and women who look forward, men and women who will end Fascism and all its works and create the institutions of a free and democratic way of life.

We look with hope and with deep faith to a period of great democratic accomplishment in Europe. Liberation from the German yoke will give the peoples of Europe a new and magnificent opportunity to fulfill their democratic aspirations, both in building democratic political institutions of their own choice and in achieving the social and economic democracy on which political democracy must rest. It is important to our national interest to encourage the establishment in Europe of strong and progressive popular governments, dedicated like our own to improving the social welfare of the people as a whole — governments which will join the common effort of nations in creating the conditions of lasting peace and in promoting the expansion of production, employment, and the exchange and consumption of goods, which are the material foundations of the liberty and welfare of all peoples.

It is hard to imagine a stable Europe if there is instability in its component parts, of which France is one of the most important. What, then, is our policy toward France? Our first concern is to defeat the enemy, drive him from French territory and the territory of all the adjacent countries which he has overrun. To do this the supreme military commander must have unfettered authority. But we have no purpose or wish to govern France or to administer any affairs save those which are necessary for military operations against the enemy. It is of the utmost importance that civil authority in France should be exercised by Frenchmen, should be swiftly established, and should operate in accordance with advanced planning as fully as military operations will permit. It is essential that the material foundations of the life of the French people be at once restored or resumed. Only in this way can stability be achieved.

It has always been our thought in planning for this end that we should look to Frenchmen to undertake civil administration and assist them in that task without compromising in any way the right of the French people to choose the ultimate form and personnel of the government which they may wish to establish. That must be left to the free and untrammeled choice of the French people.

The President and I are clear, therefore, as to the need, from the outset, of French civil administration — and democratic French administration — in France. We are disposed to see the French Committee of National Liberation exercise leadership to establish law and order under the supervision of the Allied Commander-in-Chief. The Committee has given public assurance that it does not propose to perpetuate its authority. On the contrary, it has given assurance that it wishes at the earliest possible date to have the French people exercise their own sovereign will in accordance with French constitutional processes. The Committee is, of course, not the government of France, and we cannot recognize it as such. In accordance with this understanding of mutual purposes the Committee will have every opportunity to undertake civil administration and our cooperation and help in every practicable way in making it successful. It has been a symbol of the spirit of France and of French resistance. We have fully cooperated with it in all the military phases of the war effort, including the furnishing of arms and equipment to the French armed forces. Our central and abiding purpose is to aid the French people, our oldest friends, in providing a democratic, competent, and French administration of liberated French territory.

In Italy our interests are likewise in assisting in the development at the earliest moment of a free and democratic Italian government. As I said some moments ago, we have learned that there cannot be any compromise with Fascism — whether in Italy or in any other country. It must always be the enemy, and it must be our determined policy to do all in our power to end it. Here again, within these limits, it is not our purpose or policy to impose the ultimate form or personnel of government. Here again we wish to give every opportunity for a free expression of a free Italy. We had hoped that before this enough of Italy would have been freed so that we might have had at least a preliminary expression of that will. Events have not progressed according to our hopes.

The present situation, then, is this: In October 1943 the President, Mr. Churchill, and Marshal Stalin accepted the active cooperation of the Italian Government and its armed forces as a cobelligerent in the war against Germany under the supervision of an Allied Control Commission.[1] The declaration regarding Italy made at Moscow by the British, Soviet, and American Governments confirmed the policy initiated by the British and American Governments that the Italian Government shall be made more democratic by the introduction of representatives of those sections of the Italian people who have always opposed Fascism; that all institutions and organizations created by the Fascist regime shall be suppressed; that all Fascists or pro-Fascist elements shall be removed from the administration and from the institutions and organizations of a public character; and that democratic organs of local governments shall be created. Finally, it recites that nothing in the declaration should operate against the right of the Italian people "ultimately to choose their own form of government."[2]

This policy has been and is being carried out. Only that part which calls for the introduction into the central government of more democratic elements has not yet been put into effect. This does not signify any change in the clear and announced policy. Thus far it has been thought by those chiefly responsible for the military situation that it would be prejudiced by an imposed reconstruction of the government, and a reconstruction by agreement has not yet been possible. But there is already promise of success in the activities of the political parties which are currently holding conferences with a view to drawing up a program for the political reconstruction of their country along democratic lines. The Permanent Executive Junta is seeking a solution which will provide for the cooperation of the liberal political groups within the government. Thus, after 21 years, we see a rebirth of political consciousness and activity in Italy, which points the way to the ultimate free expression of the Italian people in the choice of their government.

What I have said related to some of the most immediate of our problems and the effect of our policy toward them as we and our Allies have moved from a position of weakness to one of strength. There remain the more far-reaching relations between us and our Allies in dealing with our

---

[1] See this volume, p. 160.   [2] *Ibid.*, p. 230.

enemies and in providing for future peace, freedom from aggression, and opportunity for expanding material well-being. Here I would only mislead you if I spoke of definitive solutions. These require the slow, hard process, essential to enduring and accepted solutions among free peoples, of full discussion with our Allies and among our own people. But such discussion is now in progress. After two years of intensive study, the basis upon which our policy must be founded is soundly established; the direction is clear; and the general methods of accomplishment are emerging.

This basis of policy and these methods rest upon the second of the lessons which I said at the outset of my remarks was found in the pages of our recent history. It is that action upon these matters cannot be separate but must be agreed and united action. This is fundamental. It must underlie the entire range of our policy. The free nations have been brought to the very brink of destruction by allowing themselves to be separated and divided. If any lesson has ever been hammered home with blood and suffering, that one has been. And the lesson is not yet ended.

However difficult the road may be, there is no hope of turning victory into enduring peace unless the real interests of this country, the British Commonwealth, the Soviet Union, and China are harmonized and unless they agree and act together. This is the solid framework upon which all future policy and international organization must be built. It offers the fullest opportunity for the development of institutions in which all free nations may participate democratically, through which a reign of law and morality may arise, and through which the material interests of all may be advanced. But without an enduring understanding between these four nations upon their fundamental purposes, interests, and obligations to one another, all organizations to preserve peace are creations on paper and the path is wide open again for the rise of a new aggressor.

This essential understanding and unity of action among the four nations is not in substitution or derogation of unity among the United Nations. But it is basic to all organized international action because upon its reality depends the possibility of enduring peace and free institutions rather than new coalitions and a new pre-war period. Nor do I suggest that any conclusions of these four nations can or should be without the participation of the other United Nations. I am stating what I believe the common sense of my fellow countrymen and all men will recognize — that for these powers to become divided in their aims and fail to recognize and harmonize their basic interests can produce only disaster and that no machinery, as such, can produce this essential harmony and unity.

The road to agreement is a difficult one, as any man knows who has ever tried to get two other men, or a city council, or a trade gathering, or a legislative body, to agree upon anything. Agreement can be achieved only by trying to understand the other fellow's point of view and by going as far as possible to meet it.

Although the road to unity of purpose and action is long and difficult we have taken long strides upon our way. The Atlantic Charter was proclaimed by the President and the Prime Minister of Great Britain in August 1941. Then, by the Declaration of the United Nations of January 1, 1942, these nations adopted the principles of the Atlantic Charter, agreed to devote all their resources to the winning of the war, and pledged themselves not to conclude a separate armistice or peace with their common enemies.

After that came the declaration signed at Moscow on October 30, 1943.[1] Here the four nations who are carrying and must carry the chief burden of defeating their enemies renewed their determination by joint action to achieve this end. But they went farther than this and pledged cooperation with one another to establish at the earliest practicable date, with other peace-loving states, an effective international organization to maintain peace and security, which in principle met with overwhelming non-partisan approval by the Congress in the Connally and Fulbright resolutions.[2]

Further steps along the road of united allied action were taken at the the conference at Cairo,[3] where the President and Mr. Churchill met with Generalissimo Chiang Kai-shek, and at the conference at Tehran,[4] where they met with Marshal Stalin. At Tehran the three Allies fighting in Europe reached complete agreement on military plans for winning the war and made plain their determination to achieve harmonious action in the period of peace. That concert among the Allies rests on broad foundations of common interests and common aspirations, and it will endure. The Tehran declaration made it clear also that in the tasks of peace we shall welcome the cooperation and active participation of all nations, large and small, which wish to enter into the world family of democratic nations.

The Cairo declaration as to the Pacific assured the liquidation of Japan's occupations and thefts of territory to deprive her of the power to attack her neighbors again, to restore Chinese territories to China, and freedom to the people of Korea.

No one knows better than we and our Allies who have signed these documents that they did not and do not settle all questions or provide a formula for the settlement of all questions or lay down a detailed blueprint for the future. Any man of experience knows that an attempt to do this would have been as futile as it would have been foolish.

There has been discussion recently of the Atlantic Charter and of its application to various situations. The Charter is an expression of funda-

[1] *Ibid.*, p. 229.   [2] *Ibid.*, p. 315–16.   [3] *Ibid.*, p. 232.   [4] *Ibid.*, p. 234.

mental objectives toward which we and our Allies are directing our
policies. It states that the nations accepting it are not fighting for the
sake of aggrandizement, territorial or otherwise. It lays down the common principles upon which rest the hope of liberty, economic opportunity,
peace, and security through international cooperation. It is not a code of
law from which detailed answers to every question can be distilled by
painstaking analysis of its words and phrases. It points the direction in
which solutions are to be sought; it does not give solutions. It charts the
course upon which we are embarked and shall continue. That course
includes the prevention of aggression and the establishment of world
security. The Charter certainly does not prevent any steps, including
those relating to enemy states, necessary to achieve these objectives.
What is fundamental are the objectives of the Charter and the determination to achieve them.

It is hardly to be supposed that all the more than 30 boundary questions in Europe can be settled while the fighting is still in progress. This
does not mean that certain questions may not and should not in the
meantime be settled by friendly conference and agreement. We are at all
times ready to further an understanding and settlement of questions
which may arise between our Allies, as is exemplified by our offer to be of
such service to Poland and the Soviet Union. Our offer is still open. Our
policy upon these matters, as upon all others, is the fundamental necessity
for agreed action and the prevention of disunity among us.

So it is with the basic conviction that we must have agreed action
and unity of action that we have gone to work upon the form and substance of an international organization to maintain peace and prevent
aggression and upon the economic and other cooperative arrangements
which are necessary in order that we maintain our position as a working
partner with other free nations. All of these matters are in different
stages of development.

It is obvious, of course, that no matter how brilliant and desirable any
course may seem it is wholly impracticable and impossible unless it is a
course which finds basic acceptance, not only by our Allies but by the
people of this country and by the legislative branch of this Government,
which, under our Constitution, shares with the Executive power and
responsibility for final action.

A proposal is worse than useless if it is not acceptable to those nations
who must share with us the responsibility for its execution. It is dangerous for us and misleading to them if in the final outcome it does not have
the necessary support in this country. It is, therefore, necessary both
abroad and at home not to proceed by presenting elaborate proposals,
which only produce divergence of opinion upon details, many of which
may be immaterial. The only practicable course is to begin by obtaining
agreement, first, upon broad principles, setting forth direction and

general policy. We must then go on to explore alternative methods and finally settle upon a proposal which embodies the principal elements of agreement and leaves to future experience and discussion those matters of comparative detail which at present remain in the realm of speculation.

It is a difficult procedure and a slow procedure, as the time which has been required to work out the arrangements for such a universally accepted objective as international relief makes evident. It is a procedure in which misunderstanding, the premature hardening of positions, and uninformed criticism frequently cause months of delay and endless confusion, sometimes utter frustration. It is a procedure in which the people, who are sovereign, must not only educate their servants but must be willing to be educated by them.

In this way we are proceeding with the matter of an international organization to maintain peace and prevent aggression. Such an organization must be based upon firm and binding obligations that the member nations will not use force against each other and against any other nation except in accordance with the arrangements made. It must provide for the maintenance of adequate forces to preserve peace and it must provide the institutions and procedures for calling this force into action to preserve peace. But it must provide more than this. It must provide for an international court for the development and application of law to the settlement of international controversies which fall within the realm of law, for the development of machinery for adjusting controversies to which the field of law has not yet been extended, and for other institutions for the development of new rules to keep abreast of a changing world with new problems and new interests.

We are at a stage where much of the work of formulating plans for the organization to maintain peace has been accomplished. It is right and necessary that we should have the advice and help of an increasing number of members of the Congress. Accordingly, I have requested the Chairman of the Senate Committee on Foreign Relations to designate a representative, bipartisan group for this purpose. Following these and similar discussions with members of the House of Representatives, we shall be in a position to go forward again with other nations and, upon learning their views, be able to submit to the democratic processes of discussion a more concrete proposal.

With the same determination to achieve agreement and unity we talked with our Allies at Tehran regarding the treatment of Nazi Germany and with our Allies at Cairo regarding the treatment which should be accorded Japan. In the formulation of our policy toward our enemies we are moved both by the two lessons from our history of which I have spoken and by the third. This is that there can be no compromise with Fascism and Nazism. It must go everywhere. Its leaders, its institutions, the power which supports it must go. They can expect no negotiated peace, no compromise, no opportunity to return. Upon that this people and this Government are determined and our Allies are equally determined. We have found no difference of opinion among our Allies that the organization and purposes of the Nazi state and its Japanese counterpart, and the military system in all of its ramifications upon which they rest, are, and by their very nature must be, directed toward conquest. There was no disagreement that even after the defeat of the enemy there will be no security unless and until our victory is used to destroy these systems to their very foundation. The action which must be taken to achieve these ends must be, as I have said, agreed action. We are working with our Allies now upon these courses.

The conference at Moscow, as you will recall, established the European Advisory Commission, which is now at work in London upon the treatment of Germany. Out of these discussions will come back to the governments for their consideration proposals for concrete action.

Along with arrangements by which nations may be secure and free must go arrangements by which men and women who compose those nations may live and have the opportunity through their efforts to improve their material condition. As I said earlier, we will fail indeed if we win a victory only to let the free peoples of this world, through any absence of action on our part, sink into weakness and despair.

The heart of the matter lies in action which will stimulate and expand production in industry and agriculture and free international commerce from excessive and unreasonable restrictions. These are the essential prerequisites to maintaining and improving the standard of living in our own and in all countries. Production cannot go forward without arrangements to provide investment capital. Trade cannot be conducted without stable currencies in which payments can be promised and made. Trade cannot develop unless excessive barriers in the form of tariffs, preferences, quotas, exchange controls, monopolies, and subsidies, and others are reduced or eliminated. It needs also agreed arrangements under which communication systems between nations and transport by air and sea can develop. And much of all this will miss its mark of satisfying human needs unless we take agreed action for the improvement of labor standards and standards of health and nutrition.

I shall not on this occasion be able to explain the work which has been done — and it is extensive — in these fields. In many of them proposals are far advanced toward the stage of discussion with members of the Congress prior to formulation for public discussion.

I hope, however, that I have been able in some measure to bring before you the immensity of the task which lies before us all, the nature of the difficulties which are involved, and the conviction and purpose with which we are attacking them. Our foreign policy is comprehensive, is stable, and is known of all men. As the President has said, neither he nor I have made or will make any secret agreement or commitment, political or financial. The officials of the Government have not been unmindful of the responsibility resting upon them, nor have they spared either energy or such abilities as they possess in discharging that responsibility.

May I close with a word as to the responsibility which rests upon us. The United Nations will determine by action or lack of action whether this world will be visited by another war within the next 20 or 25 years, or whether policies of organized peace shall guide the course of the world. We are moving closer and closer to the hour of decision. Only the fullest measure of wisdom, unity, and alertness can enable us to meet that unprecedented responsibility.

All of these questions of foreign policy which, as I said earlier, is the matter of focusing and expressing your will in the world outside our borders, are difficult and often involve matters of controversy. Under our constitutional system the will of the American people in this field is not effective unless it is united will. If we are divided we are ineffective. We are in a year of a national election in which it is easy to arouse controversy on almost any subject, whether or not the subject is an issue in the campaign. You, therefore, as well as we who are in public office, bear a great responsibility. It is the responsibility of avoiding needless controversy in the formulation of your judgments. It is the responsibility for sober and considered thought and expression. It is the responsibility for patience both with our Allies and with those who must speak for you with them. Once before in our lifetime we fell into disunity and became ineffective in world affairs by reason of it. Should this happen again it will be a tragedy to you and to your children and to the world for generations.

(9) Sovereign Equality for All Nations. Statement by the Secretary of State (Hull), June 1, 1944 [1]

At his press and radio news conference on June 1 the Secretary of State made this statement in answer to the question whether there was anything he could say that might be of reassurance to the small nations. The correspondent who asked the question pointed out that some of the small nations seemed to think that they would not be properly represented in the proposed international organization.

That is a matter in which the small nations and the large nations as well should be at all times especially interested. It is a mutual affair. The future welfare of each nation depends upon the welfare of all. In view of that common interest and that self-interest in every mutual sense, I doubt whether there would be many nations, large or small, which would have any other purpose than to cooperate in all legitimate and practicable international relationships that would be mutually advan-

[1] Department of State, *Bulletin*, X, p. 509.

tageous and mutually profitable. As far as this Government is concerned, whenever I have said anything on this subject, it has always emphasized the all-inclusive nature of the world situation and our disposition and purpose to see that all nations, especially the small nations, are kept on a position of equality with all others and that, in every practicable way, there will be cooperation.

Now, it is not possible at this stage for this Government or any government to give anybody a blueprint as to all of the details of how these relationships between all of the different nations will be gradually developed and perfected. There is no occasion to be especially concerned about the attitude of this Government in view of the declarations that the President, and I, and others have made. The truth is that even those declarations are not necessarily called for in the light of our entire history and our traditions. We have for 150 years preached liberty to all the nations of the earth, to all the peoples of the earth, and we have practiced it. We have encouraged all nations to aspire to liberty, and to enjoy it. Our attitude toward the Philippines is a striking example. Nobody had to put us on the witness stand to know what we were doing for them.

Even back in our earlier days we preached the same spirit of liberty with which we, ourselves, were inspired in acquiring our own liberty, to all the nations — especially those that were in chains of despotism, as the South American countries were for centuries under Spanish rule. Nobody asked us to do it. That was our philosophy. That was our spirit, both at home and toward all peoples who might aspire to liberty. As soon as our American neighbors threw off the Spanish yoke we proceeded to recognize them, right and left. We had the same spirit toward Greece and other countries desiring liberty as we demonstrated in the Philippines. That has been our consistent record, a record of championship of liberty for everybody, encouraging them at all times and in all places. I see no reason why this country, this great free people who through generations have dedicated themselves to this wonderful human cause and preserved it — I see no reason why they should be catechized every morning before breakfast as to their loyalty to liberty, or their consistent desire of liberty for everybody and freedom for aspiring peoples everywhere.

I have spoken of this often in speeches and at other times before, during, and after my trip to Europe. Here is an example from my address to the Congress: "The principle of sovereign equality of all peace-loving states, irrespective of size and strength, as partners in a future system of general security will be the foundation stone upon which the future international organization will be constructed." That is our objective. I think I have indicated sufficiently to you the policy of this nation and this Government representing it.[1]

[1] For President's statement of June 15, 1944, see this volume, p. 325.

CHAPTER II

CONDUCT OF FOREIGN RELATIONS

1. THE MAKING OF INTERNATIONAL AGREEMENTS

A. Procedure in Making United Nations Relief and Rehabilitation Administration Agreement [1]

After more than a year of negotiations carried on between the Governments of the United States, the United Kingdom, the Soviet Union and China, a preliminary draft of an agreement setting up the United Nations Relief and Rehabilitation Administration was finally agreed upon as the basis for further discussions. The text of the Draft Agreement was published on June 11, 1943.[2] This Draft Agreement contained in its preamble a broad statement of purposes; provided in Article I for the establishment of a United Nations Relief and Rehabilitation Administration, the powers, purposes and functions of which were defined in broad terms; provided in Articles II, III and IV for the organization of the Administration; and in Articles V and VI obligated member governments to contribute to the financial support of the relief and rehabilitation program and its administration. Article V, par. 1, read in part as follows:

"Each member government pledges its full support to the Administration, within the limits of its available resources and subject to the requirements of its constitutional procedure, through contributions of funds, materials, equipment, supplies and services, for use in its own, adjacent or other areas in need, in order to accomplish the purposes of Article I, paragraph 2 (a)."

Article VI (Administrative Expenses), after describing how administrative *expenses* were to be allocated, concluded as follows:

"Each member government pledges itself, subject to the requirements of its constitutional procedure, to contribute to the Administration promptly its share of the administrative expenses so determined."

Article VIII provided that provisions of the Agreement might be amended "by unanimous vote of the Central Committee and two-thirds vote of the Council." The Agreement was to enter into force with respect to each Signatory on the date of signature, "unless otherwise specified by such signatory." There was no provision for withdrawal.

In reply to a letter from Senator Arthur H. Vandenberg of Michigan, Secretary of State Hull said: [3]

"It has been decided, after consultation with the majority and minority leaders of both houses of Congress, that United States participation in the establishment of the United Nations administration should be through an executive agreement."

On July 6, Senator Vandenberg introduced Senate Resolution 170,[4] which was referred to the Senate Committee on Foreign Relations. This resolution instructed the Committee to investigate the agreement and report whether in its

[1] For information on Agreement for United Nations Relief and Rehabilitation Administration and functions of organization, see this volume, p. 248.

[2] Department of State, *Bulletin*, VIII, p. 523.

[3] *Congressional Record*, vol. 89, p. 7512 (daily edition, July 8, 1943).

[4] *Ibid.*, p. 7312 (daily edition, July 6, 1943).

judgment it constituted a treaty requiring Senate approval. On July 8, Senator Vandenberg made a statement before the Senate in which he explained the purpose he had in view in introducing the resolution and the developments that had thus far occurred.[1]

As the result of conversations between members of the Department of State, and members of the Senate Committee on Foreign Relations, and the House Committee on Foreign Affairs, and more particularly between State Department representatives and members of a subcommittee of the Senate Committee, agreement was reached on a revised draft which would eliminate binding financial commitments and would make it clear that such commitments would only be assumed by regular constitutional procedures. Furthermore, a procedure was agreed upon under which the agreement would come before Congress for approval in the form of a resolution authorizing the President to spend such moneys as Congress might appropriate, to be followed by the introduction and adoption of appropriation bills in the regular way. The story is told in some detail in Mr. Sayre's statement, given below. The exhibits given below throw light on the nature and significance of the procedure followed in accomplishing American acceptance of an agreement for the establishment of an important post-war international organization.

(1) *Statements of Senators Vandenberg* (*Michigan*) *and Green* (*Rhode Island*) *to the Senate, July 8, 1943* [2]

MR. VANDENBERG. Mr. President, I wish to make a brief statement regarding a vital and basic matter pending before the Senate Foreign Relations Committee. It will take me only a few moments.

On July 6, I submitted Senate Resolution 170, which was referred to the Senate Foreign Relations Committee, and which states the following in a single sentence:

Resolved, That the Committee on Foreign Relations is instructed to investigate the draft agreement for a United Nations Relief and Rehabilitation Administration published by the State Department on June 11, 1943, and to report to the Senate whether in its judgment this draft agreement partakes of the nature of a treaty, and should be submitted to the Senate for ratification.

Mr. President, when the Foreign Relations Committee met on yesterday morning there was an immediate unanimous agreement, without regard to political parties, that the subject matter of this resolution must be promptly explored, not presently in respect to the merits of the arrangements which are contemplated for United Nations relief and rehabilitation, but in respect to the procedure involved in the creation of this tremendous instrumentality.

Mr. President, as a result of the action of the Foreign Relations Committee a subcommittee was immediately appointed to confer with the State Department upon this subject, with the distinguished Senator from Texas, who is chairman of the full committee, as chairman of the subcommittee. The interest was so general and so intense that a conference

[1] *Ibid.,* p. 7511 (daily edition, July 8, 1943).
[2] *Ibid.,* p. 7511, 7513.

was immediately arranged for yesterday afternoon at 2:30, when the subcommittee met with the distinguished Secretary of State, Mr. Hull, and the able Assistant Secretary of State, Mr. Acheson, who freely and fully provided us with all available information.

As a result of the conference the entire subject matter of the resolution — involving, as it does, the whole question of constitutional authority in respect to war settlements and post-war plans — is under mutual consideration by the Department and the Senate committee. But I do not want the Senate to separate for the recess without making the subject matter clear in the RECORD so that there may be no mistake about the point at issue, and so that the importance of the point in the life of the Nation may not be overlooked.

Mr. President, I repeat that this discussion does not involve the merits of the draft agreement for United Nations relief and rehabilitation administration. That can be weighed later on its merits.

Obviously there is need for some such action; that is conceded. Obviously advanced planning is the only course of prudence; that is conceded. I commend the State Department for proceeding with concrete studies in this direction. This draft agreement, as a matter of fact, may be the appropriate nucleus for ultimate action. The only question here raised, Mr. President, is the question of procedure and jurisdiction, yet nothing could be more important as we prepare to face these transcendental questions involved in the liquidation of the war.

To what extent is it safe, to what extent is it wise, to what extent is it constitutional for executive authority to proceed independent of Congress with respect to the great decisions now impending, in respect to the determination of the problems growing out of this war? That is at the base of this inquiry.

Mr. President, I do not raise the question in a spirit of controversy; I raise it in a spirit of constructive exploration. That was the attitude of the subcommittee of the Foreign Relations Committee yesterday — a searching for a formula which will invite ultimate unity for sound purposes. If I err at any point in my statement I hope I may be corrected by the distinguished Senator from Rhode Island (Mr. Green), who is a member of the subcommittee with me and who is familiar with the subject matter which I discuss.

It seems to me, Mr. President, that now is the time, on the threshold of many such international settlements and determinations, to find out precisely what pattern of things to come we shall follow. The best objectives may be defeated by the wrong approach; the finest aims may be dissipated by failure to pursue them appropriately. We know that from our own history. Bluntly, Mr. President, this episode poses the question as to the extent to which the Congress is to be a constitutional partner in the plans and the decisions which shall liquidate this war; to what extent, on the other hand, the President and his executive administration shall settle these war and post-war problems to suit their own discretion and their own purposes.

I repeat that I do not want to discuss the merits of this particular plan, I want to refer only to the procedure, and I refer to the contents of this draft agreement only to indicate the almost illimitable extent of the moral commitments which can live within the four corners of this draft agreement, as we view it. [At this point Senator Vandenberg asked that the text of the Draft Agreement be inserted in the RECORD.[1] Text is omitted here.]

For the purpose of this brief comment, I merely point to the fact that the draft agreement contemplates the treatment of almost the total subject, not only of relief, but also of rehabilitation, not only in the war world, not only in respect to those areas which may fall to our responsibility as a result of our serial victories in the war, but also, quoting the language it covers:

The period following the cessation of hostilities.

It sets up for this purpose a complete international machine which is partially reminiscent of the League of Nations itself in respect to its creation of a general body representing all the signatory powers and then a superbody representing only the four major powers, namely, China, Russia, Britain, and the United States, and binding the latter to operate by unanimous consent.

Mr. President, I leave the document to speak for itself, but in Article V it finally reads as follows:

Each member government pledges its full support to the administration, within the limits of its available resources and subject to the requirements of its constitutional procedure, through contributions of funds, materials, equipment, supplies, and service for use in its own, adjacent, or other areas in need, in order to accomplish the purposes of Article I.

And those purposes are the all-out purposes to which I have previously referred.

Mr. President, it seems to me that this is a moral commitment, if nothing more, of all the available resources of the United States to whatever plan may evolve from the administrative agency, world-wide in its scope and in the dedication which is created by this document. I think it is a moral commitment from which we could never recede when ultimate appropriations are sought from a Congress which was never consulted in respect to the commitments. I do not believe that is the democratic, the constitutional way.

[1] *Ibid.,* p. 7512; also printed in Department of State, *Bulletin,* VIII, p. 523.

Mr. President, I said I wanted to discuss only the question of procedure because that is the thing involved in the present episode. I wrote to the distinguished Secretary of State on June 22 and asked him whether it was contemplated that this draft agreement would be submitted to the Senate for ratification. I read one sentence from the Secretary's letter of July 6 in reply:

It has been decided, after consultation with the majority and minority leaders of both Houses of Congress, that United States' participation in the establishment of this United Nations administration should be through an executive agreement.

That is the point at issue, Mr. President. The point at issue is whether a commitment of this incalculable magnitude in respect not only to policy but to resources is merely an executive agreement which can totally bypass the Congress of the United States except at that "long last" moment when finally an appropriation is to be sought from Congress to implement the pledges and promises which have been made in the name of the total resources of the United States, by the President and his executive associates.

Under the draft agreement and under the Secretary's letter there is no point at which this plan, I repeat, of illimitable consequences, reaches the Congress for any consultation or action except at "long last" when everything has been done, the machinery created, the commitments made, our share of the cost assessed to us, and we are finally given the unavoidable privilege in Congress of finally making the appropriation. We pay the bills — that is, the people do — but we have nothing to say about what the bills shall be. I respectfully submit that government by executive decree could not aspire to much greater totalitarian authority.

Mr. President, I submit that if any agreements or commitments in international relationships could ever rise to the dignity and importance of a treaty as contemplated by the Constitution of the United States, here is Exhibit A. I totally disagree with the conception that commitments of this nature can be made without ratification by the Senate of the United States.

In presenting the matter now I am hoping — and I know the distinguished and unanimous Senators who were sitting in yesterday's conference are of the same mind — that we may find common ground between Congress, the State Department, and the office of the President upon which we can proceed with least possible friction in the development of the answers to the utterly terrific problems which one after another will confront us in the liquidation of the war.

I do not believe that we can hope to arrive at that concert of interest and action if the State Department and the President are to proceed in the fashion indicated in this initial exhibit.

Therefore, Mr. President, I wanted the RECORD to show precisely what had happened, I wanted the RECORD to carry the text of this draft agreement. It is the preliminary text, it is subject to change by consultation with other nations. The final text will probably not be available for 60 days at the earliest.

The State Department representatives, including the very distinguished Secretary of State, Mr. Hull, than whom no finer public servant has appeared in the public life of this Nation in my time, listened to us respectfully yesterday, and have agreed to consider the whole matter anew. By the whole matter I mean not only the text of this draft, but also the general subject of the better constitutional relationships which must be established in the pursuit of the settlement of our war problems, if the virtue of the settlements is not to be lost in the quarrel over the method of making the settlements.

It is for the reasons I have given, Mr. President, that I have made this statement, not in a spirit of controversy, but in a spirit of hope that this very frank disclosure, this very frank discussion of what I believe is a substantial error in the attitude of the State Department and the President in this initial venture, may lead to those contacts between us which may find a better and a happier way in which to solve the remaining problems which will pile in upon us as we liquidate the war and justify our conclusive victory.

MR. GREEN. The distinguished Senator from Michigan (Mr. Vandenberg), in his remarks about what happened yesterday at a meeting of the Committee on Foreign Relations and, after the meeting, of the subcommittee appointed by the committee to confer with the Secretary of State, asked that I note what he said, and that I draw his attention to any unintentional misstatement he might make. I am glad to say that I listened attentively, and he has given a correct statement of what occurred at the two meetings.

(2) House Joint Resolution to Enable the United States to Participate in the Work of the United Nations Relief and Rehabilitation Organization, Approved March 28, 1944 [1]

[For text of Resolution, see p. 293.]

This resolution (H. J. Res. 192) was significant not only as defining the conditions under which the United States joined the United Nations Relief and Rehabilitation Administration,[2] but also as an important step in the procedure which was evolved for accomplishing American acceptance of the Agreement without the requirement of approval by two-thirds vote of the Senate.

The statement of Mr. Sayre, given below, gives the pre-legislative history of this resolution.

[1] Public Law 267, 78th Cong.
[2] See this volume, p. 248.

The United Nations Relief and Rehabilitation Agreement was signed, in its revised form, at the White House on November 9, 1943.[1] On November 15, the President sent a message to Congress recommending to the Congress "the enactment of a bill authorizing the appropriation of funds as Congress may from time to time determine to permit the participation of the United States in the work of UNRRA."[2] On the same day, Mr. Sol Bloom, Chairman of the House Committee on Foreign Affairs, introduced H. J. Res. 192 "to enable the United States to participate in the work of the United Nations relief and rehabilitation organization,"[3] which was referred to the House Committee on Foreign Affairs. Hearings were held by the Committee on December 7–10, 15–17, 1943 and January 11, 1944.[4] On January 17, 1944 the Committee reported the resolution favorably with certain amendments.[5] The resolution was adopted by the House, with amendments adopted in the Committee of the Whole, on January 25 by the vote of 338 to 54.[6] On January 26 the resolution was referred to the Senate Committee on Foreign Relations, which held brief hearings on February 9 and 10,[7] and then reported the resolution favorably with an amendment.[8] In the Senate, the resolution was discussed at considerable length,[9] and on February 17, it was adopted, in amended form, by a vote of 47 to 14, 35 members not voting.[10] The House asked for a conference on February 23 and on March 3 the Senate agreed. The Conference Report was submitted on March 15.[11] The Report was considered and finally adopted by the Senate on March 21 by a vote of 47 to 9, 40 members not voting.[12] It was discussed and adopted by the House on March 22 by a vote of 285 to 58, 85 members not voting.[13] The resolution was approved by the President on March 28, 1944.

(a) Statement of Mr. Francis B. Sayre, Special Assistant to the Secretary of State, before the House Committee on Foreign Affairs, December 15, 1943 [14]

The question has been asked as to who is responsible for the form of language of the joint resolution (H. J. Res. 192) now under consideration. It will be remembered that after more than a year of negotiations carried on between the United States, the United Kingdom, the Soviet Union, and China, a preliminary draft of an agreement setting up the United Nations Relief and Rehabilitation Administration was finally agreed

[1] For text, see this volume, p. 251.

[2] *Congressional Record*, vol. 89, p. 9593, 9637 (daily edition, November 15, 1943).

[3] *Ibid.*, p. 9665.

[4] *Hearings before the Committee on Foreign Affairs, House of Representatives, on H. J. Res. 192*, 78th Cong., 1st and 2nd sess. (Washington, Govt. Printing Office, 1944).

[5] House Report No. 994, 78th Cong., 2nd sess.

[6] *Congressional Record*, vol. 90, p. 683–700 (daily edition, January 25, 1944).

[7] *Hearings before the Committee on Foreign Relations, United States Senate, on H. J. Res. 192*, 78th Cong., 2nd sess. (Washington, Govt. Printing Office, 1944).

[8] Senate Report No. 688, 78th Cong., 2nd sess.

[9] *Congressional Record*, vol. 90, p. 1735, 1737–64, 1808–25, 1826–40 (daily edition, February 16 and 17, 1944).

[10] *Ibid.*, p. 1840.

[11] House Report No. 1260, 78th Cong., 2nd sess.

[12] *Congressional Record*, vol. 90, p. 2845–53 (daily edition, March 21, 1944).

[13] *Ibid.*, p. 2969–76.

[14] *Hearings before the Committee on Foreign Affairs, House of Representatives, on H. J. Res. 192*, 78th Cong., 1st and 2nd sess., p. 158.

upon as the basis for further discussions. In July 1943, this preliminary draft was informally shown to and discussed with the members of the Senate Committee on Foreign Relations and the House Committee on Foreign Affairs. Various changes in the draft of the agreement were suggested as a result of these discussions and these changes were incorporated in the final form of the agreement.

During the course of the discussions in the Senate Committee on Foreign Relations, Senator Vandenberg raised the question of whether the United Nations Relief and Rehabilitation Administration agreement should not be considered as a treaty and therefore submitted for ratification by two-thirds of the Senate. The Senate Committee on Foreign Relations thereupon appointed a subcommittee to consider and discuss this question, consisting of Senator Connally, Senator Green, Senator Thomas of Utah, Senator Vandenberg, and Senator LaFollette. In the ensuing discussions which took place between the members of this subcommittee and Assistant Secretary Acheson and myself, representing the State Department, it was made clear that the draft agreement was not intended to impose binding obligations on the part of the United States but to set up the machinery for an international organization to administer relief and rehabilitation providing that contributions of funds should be made by each member government "within the limits of its available resources and subject to the requirements of its constitutional procedure."

After considerable discussion, the subcommittee reached the conclusion that in view of certain modifications which Senator Vandenberg and others had suggested in the text of the agreement and which were incorporated in the final text, the best method of procedure would be along the following lines: That an effort be made to secure the agreement of the other 43 United Nations and associated governments to the changes proposed by Senator Vandenberg and by others in the Senate Committee on Foreign Relations and the House Committee on Foreign Affairs and that if this could be done the President should sign the agreement and the Administration should be organized in accordance with the agreement. Following this a joint resolution should be introduced in Congress authorizing the President to expend such moneys as Congress might from time to time appropriate for participation by the United States in the United Nations Relief and Rehabilitation Administration. Such a joint resolution presumably would be discussed and considered both in the House Committee on Foreign Affairs and in the Senate Committee on Foreign Relations and would also be debated on the floors of the House and the Senate. This would give to Congress full opportunity to consider the extent to which the United States should participate in the work of the United Nations Relief and Rehabilitation Administration.

Following the passage of the joint resolution, appropriation bills would then be introduced and would be considered first by the Appropriation Committees of the House and the Senate and then on the floor by the House and the Senate. In this way everyone concerned would have full opportunity to consider the whole program. I understand that the sub-committee of the Foreign Relations Committee concluded that if the changes which had been proposed were made in the text and above pro-gram were followed, the introduction of a joint resolution would be an appropriate constitutional procedure.

Mr. Acheson and I were in constant touch with your committee and the Senate Foreign Relations Committee and with other congressional leaders.

In accordance with this program, the changes proposed in the text of the United Nations Relief and Rehabilitation Administration agreement were then put before the other 43 nations and their agreement was se-cured to them. We also set about drafting a joint resolution to be intro-duced in Congress in accordance with the program.

Senator Vandenberg insisted that the joint resolution should carry within it the full text of the United Nations Relief and Rehabilitation Administration agreement as signed by the President. To this Mr. Acheson and I both agreed.

Following these conversations we set to work drafting such a joint resolution as proposed. Our aim was to make it as simple and as short as possible, simply authorizing the appropriation from time to time to the President of such sums as the Congress might determine to be appropriate for participation by the United States in the work of the United Nations Relief and Rehabilitation Administration and reciting the text of the agreement as desired by Senator Vandenberg.

In working out this draft, I consulted all those who I felt would have an interest in the question. The draft was worked out in consultation with Mr. Hackworth, the legal adviser of the State Department, and with Mr. McDougal, general counsel of the Office of Foreign Relief and Rehabilitation Operations. It was also taken up informally with repre-sentatives of the Bureau of the Budget. The draft, as proposed, was submitted to Senator Green who, in turn, sent it in a letter to Senator Vandenberg who wrote back approving the form of the resolution.

The resolution was also submitted to Mr. Sol Bloom, the chairman of your committee, and was discussed and examined carefully by Mr. Morgan, assistant legislative counsel of Congress. The text was laid before your Committee on Foreign Affairs in executive session on Sep-tember 23, 1943 and before the Senate Committee on Foreign Relations on September 22, 1943 and before members of the House Committee on Appropriations. Further discussions were held with the Senate Foreign Relations Committee on November 5, 1943 and with the House Foreign Affairs Committee in November 1943.

So far as I know all of those consulted in both the House and the Senate and elsewhere were in full agreement on the text of the joint resolution which is now before you. We sought in the bill to avoid contentious issues and to make it as short and general as possible. I believe that no one has raised any serious objection to the language of the bill.

(b) Statements of Assistant Secretary of State Acheson before the Senate Committee on Foreign Relations, February 9, 1944 [1]

[Excerpts]

.   .   .   .

The draft agreement was subject to many criticisms. Many of those were made by the subcommittee of this committee. The ones that you gentlemen did not think of, some of the foreign countries did; so as a result of all of the discussion we went all over that draft very carefully with the subcommittee of this committee, and there it was substantially rewritten in two major respects: one, as Senator Vandenberg has said, in the preamble; and in the section which I have just read, which is Article I, paragraph 2, the scope of the activities was very much more specifically stated and more restrictedly stated. Everything which might look like reconstruction or long-term rebuilding was taken out.

Furthermore, in Articles V and VI there was a complete rewriting of those articles to make it clear that there was no commitment and could be no commitment to participate in this work without the authorization of the constitutional bodies in each country which had the authority to do that. So that the document as rewritten merely set up machinery to accomplish the purposes of relief and such rehabilitation as was incident to relief. What was to be done with that machinery was entirely within the power of the constitutional bodies of the member countries.

.   .   .   .

Now, that is the agreement, and as I say, that agreement was worked out after thorough discussion with the subcommittee of this committee, which led it to believe that all commitments on the part of this country are in the hands of Congress, that no one had undertaken to commit the United States to any act, and that therefore the issue as to whether this was a treaty had been removed from discussion.

Senator VANDENBERG. Mr. Acheson, at that point I would like to have the record show the language in Article V,[2] because I think it is very important. The only actual obligation which we accept in a financial sense is set out in Article V, is it not?

_____

[1] Hearings before the Committee on Foreign Relations, United States Senate on H. J. Res. 192, 78th Cong., 2nd sess. Washington, Govt. Printing Office, 1944.

[2] See this volume, p. 255.

Mr. ACHESON. Article V and Article VI, which have to do with the administrative expenses; yes, sir.

Senator VANDENBERG. And, in each instance, quoting from the text —

The amount and character of the contributions of each member government under this provision will be determined from time to time by its appropriate constitutional bodies.

In other words, we are accepting no fiscal obligation under this agreement except as the obligation is specifically accepted by acts of appropriation by the Congress, is that correct?

Mr. ACHESON. That is correct, Senator Vandenberg.

. . . .

Senator VANDENBERG. Before you get away from the financial problem, Mr. Secretary, I want to refer to the question of administrative expenses. I assume the same rule applies to the payment of administrative expenses.

Mr. ACHESON. The administrative expenses, which are dealt with under Article VI of the agreement, are also dealt with in the financial plan, and they have been distributed differently. That distribution has been made on a basis by which the United States would pay much less than the relative amount of its total contribution to the total assets of UNRRA. A budget has been approved for the first year in the amount of $10,000,000. That is the total administrative expense of the organization. That was allocated on the basis of a different formula, which leaves the American contribution at $4,000,000, provided the Congress of course wishes to do it; so that, whereas on the basis of the total American contribution to the total contributions to the operations of UNRRA, and the administrative contributions would be somewhere in the neighborhood of $6\frac{1}{2}$; it is now, under this other plan, 4.

The purpose of that was that it was thought necessary, and the other countries were willing to agree, that every country should bear some part, and a substantial part, of the administrative expenses, and that therefore a percentage contribution was desirable and necessary.

Senator VANDENBERG. If Congress became critical at any time of the administrative set-up and thought it was extravagant or improvident, I assume that under the terms of Article VI, since each member government undertakes to make its contribution only "subject to the requirements of its constitutional procedure," the administrative problem would also be entirely within congressional control insofar as our share of sustaining it is concerned.

Mr. ACHESON. That is correct. Congress would have complete power at any time to stop its contributions or to lay down the conditions as to their uses.

Senator VANDENBERG. I constantly emphasize that point, Mr. Chairman, because it was one upon which our subcommittee put major emphasis in indicating the change in the character of the document.

.   .   .   .

Senator VANDENBERG. Are we making any contribution to UNRRA and its administrative budget during this formulative period?

Mr. ACHESON. We are not, Senator, and that is one reason why I hope it will be possible to act with some expedition. We have taken the attitude, which I think is the correct one, that this matter has been laid before the Congress; now, therefore, while it may be within the legal power to turn over some funds to UNRRA for administrative expenses, that should not be done until the Congress has expressed itself on the whole matter. Whether or not there is power to use the Presidents' emergency fund I do not know.

At any rate, it is not proposed to use it until the Congress had acted upon this resolution. If the Congress acts upon the resolution then appropriation requests will be made, and it may be at that time that someone will consult with the Appropriation Committees and ask whether they would be willing to have an advance payment made so that we can go in on the administrative expenses. Already, other countries which are members of UNRRA have contributed a million dollars or more to the administrative expenses, and if Congress approved of this we would like to be in a position as soon as possible of taking our part in carrying the administrative expenses of the Administration.

Senator VANDENBERG. That is the statement I wanted you to make, because I think it is the final demonstration of the integrity of the whole cooperative effort between the Congress and the State Department in connection with this whole undertaking.

(c) Statement of Senator Vandenberg (Michigan) to the Senate, February 16, 1944 [1]

In the course of Senate debate, Senator Taft of Ohio had argued that under Article VIII of the UNRRA Agreement an amendment might be made imposing further obligations upon the United States by the action of the President alone.

Mr. VANDENBERG. Mr. President, I totally dissent from the construction which the able Senator from Ohio places upon what we are doing here in respect to this agreement. When the agreement was originally proposed last June it was intended to be exclusively an executive agreement. It was at that point that the Senate Foreign Relations Committee intervened, as the result of the resolution which I submitted; and as a further result we had our subsequent conferences with the State De-

[1] Congressional Record, vol. 90, p. 1746–50 (daily edition, February 16, 1944).

partment and produced what we both understand is to be not merely an executive agreement, but an agreement approved by Congress.

Mr. President, I believe that the agreement embodied in the joint resolution is subject to the same kind of reservations, if Congress desires to attach them, as would be the case if this were a treaty pending for our consideration. I think the Congress can attach any reservations it wishes to attach to this agreement, because the theory upon which the agreement now comes to Congress is that it has ceased to be an executive agreement alone, which in our opinion would have been a gross violation of the proprieties as well as of the law. It has been submitted to Congress for congressional approval and not merely for congressional information. If the Senator from Ohio wishes any reservations to the agreement, so far as I am concerned he is just as free to offer reservations to this agreement as he would be to offer reservations to a treaty if we were considering it as a treaty.

As to the meaning of the language to which reference has been made, in view of that history of the situation, I submit that when the agreement says that amendments shall take effect for each member government only on acceptances by it, in the face of the clear record, and in the face of the equally clear understanding which exists between the State Department and at least the Senate Foreign Relations Committee, "it" means the same legislative process by which the agreement is approved in the first instance. That is my interpretation of the word "it." If there is any doubt about it, I refer further to the letter which Assistant Secretary of State Sayre wrote to the able Senator from Rhode Island [1] in response to a question which I submitted to him as to what is meant by the escape clause, and whether the President or the Congress could invoke the escape clause. I do not believe that in the face of the record there can be any doubt on earth as to what "it" means in this instance.

(i) Letter of Mr. Francis B. Sayre, Special Assistant to the Secretary of State, to Senator Theodore Francis Green (Rhode Island), August 28, 1943 [2]

[Excerpt]

With respect to Senator Vandenberg's question, I presume that he refers to the concluding article of the UNRRA draft the first sentence of which reads as follows:

"Any member government may give notice of withdrawal from the Administration at any time after the expiration of six months from the entry into force of the Agreement for that government."

Since the UNRRA agreement is a multilateral undertaking by many governments, the general form of the agreement must be such as to be readily applicable to various types of constitutions and governmental frameworks. The foregoing provision is in a form well established in general international usage.

[1] See this volume, p. 49.   [2] Text of letter received from Senator Green.

The answer to Senator Vandenberg's question of who decides whether or not the United States Government is to exercise the right of withdrawal depends, of course, upon our own Constitution. Since under our Constitution the President is charged with the responsibility for communicating with foreign governments, it would be for the President to give the formal notice of withdrawal should such a course of action become desirable.

As a practical matter, however, it seems clear that either the Congress or the President would have the power to cause the withdrawal of the United States from active participation in the UNRRA. Certainly the President would have it within his power to do so. It is equally obvious that if Congress indicated its desire by concurrent resolution or otherwise to have this Government withdraw, since Congress possesses the power to make all appropriations and since the United States could not continue to participate in the relief program without the support of Congress, the United States could not continue to participate in the work of the United Nations Relief and Rehabilitation Administration.

B. Lend-Lease Agreements

(1) Statements of Senators Vandenberg (Michigan) and Connally (Texas) before the Senate on Authority of President to Enter into Commitments on Post-War Foreign Policy under Provisions of Section 3(b) of Lend-Lease Act, May 8, 1944 [1]

The Senate Committee on Foreign Relations in its report on H. R. 4254 [2] emphatically reaffirmed the principles regarding the authority of the President to enter into commitments on post-war policies which it had stated in its report of the previous year.[3] It added: "If there is any necessity for Congress to formally declare its adherence to these principles in order to insure their recognition, the Committee believes that the proviso [4] added by section 2 of the House bill adequately takes care of the situation."

In the debate on the Senate floor, Senators Vandenberg and Connally expressed views which, apparently, were shared generally by members of that body, as well as by members of the House.

Mr. VANDENBERG. Mr. President, because of certain testimony before the Foreign Relations Committee, I wish to refer to one phase of the pending bill. I have in mind the proviso on page 2 of the bill, reading as follows:

Provided, however, That nothing in this paragraph shall be construed to authorize the President in any final settlement to assume or incur any obligations on the part of the United States with respect to post-war economic policy, post-war military policy, or any post-war policy involving international relations except in accordance with established constitutional procedure.

Mr. President, at the time the subject of lend-lease was before the Senate 1 year ago the Foreign Relations Committee definitely and specifically challenged certain things which were being done in the master

[1] *Congressional Record*, vol. 90, p. 4181–2 (daily edition, May 8, 1944).
[2] Senate Report No. 848, 78th Cong., 2d sess., p. 2.
[3] Senate Report No. 99, 78th Cong., 1st sess.; *Documents, V, 1942–43*, p. 129.
[4] Substantially as finally adopted.

agreements which were made between the United States and its lend-lease debtors. The committee found that in Article VII of those master agreements there was an exchange of commitments which promised and pledged that in the ultimate settlement of lend-lease accounts provision should be made "to the elimination of all forms of discriminatory treatment in international commerce, and to the reduction of tariffs and other trade barriers," and so forth.

Mr. President, the Foreign Relations Committee came to the unanimous conclusion 1 year ago — and there was no partisan difference of opinion on the subject as the committee was a unit on it — that by no stretch of the imagination is the executive branch of the Government entitled to commit the Government upon its own exclusive responsibility "to the elimination of all forms of discriminatory treatment in international commerce, and to the reduction of tariffs and other trade barriers."

Regardless of what the aspect of the barriers may be, and without respect to the validity of that objective, it is perfectly clear that the sole initial power to deal with any such subjects does not rest in the Executive, but rests exclusively, under the Constitution, in the Congress of the United States.

Therefore, the Foreign Relations Committee in its report 1 year ago said:

The committee believes that there is no authority in the Lend-Lease Act to warrant any general post-war commitments or post-war policies in agreements made under the terms of the Lend-Lease Act.

Mr. President, when the administrators of lend-lease came before the Foreign Relations Committee this year I was curious to find out how much attention had been paid to the clear mandate of the Senate Foreign Relations Committee which subsequently had the endorsement of the Senate at least to the extent that it never confronted any dissent. I read from a few questions and answers:

Senator VANDENBERG. Are you still writing the same master agreements, in the same language, which the Senate Foreign Relations Committee criticized a year ago so appropriately?
Mr. Cox. —
Speaking for the Lend-Lease Administration —
I would say "Yes." I do not think there have been any substantial number of master agreements since that time, if any. We can check that, however.
Senator VANDENBERG. But, if any?
Mr. Cox. They would be in the same language.

In spite of the fact that the Congress itself had deliberately and specifically notified the executive authorities, the lend-lease authorities, and the negotiating authorities of this country that they could have no authority under the Constitution to include any such pledges as they have written into Article VII of the master agreements under the Lend-Lease Act.

I continue reading from the testimony:

Senator VANDENBERG. Obviously, the Wadsworth proviso is aimed at the same thing the Foreign Relations Committee was talking about in its last report?

Mr. Cox. I think so, although it is limited to the post-war economic, military, or international policy that is tied in with any settlements that are made.

Senator VANDENBERG. But you would have to pay more attention to this than you do to the committee's report of a year ago?

Mr. Cox. I would think so.

In other words, Mr. President, the effort of the Senate Foreign Relations Committee and of the Senate itself to be rather polite in their disagreement with the executive authorities was a total failure. The constitutional opinion of the committee and the Senate apparently carried no weight at the other end of Pennsylvania Avenue. Therefore, it became necessary to write into the bill the proviso to which I have referred.

In emphasizing the matter, I voice the hope that the authority of Congress as expressed in a statute may succeed in being more effective than the constitutional opinion of the Senate as expressed in a committee report; and I express the belief that the proviso which is now in the pending extension act not only prohibits the President from writing into his lend-lease agreements any obligation which primarily rests within the constitutional jurisdiction, but that it also is intended to confine lend-lease absolutely to the military operation of this war, that it does not extend it 1 minute or $1 into the post-war period.

.   .   .   .

Mr. CONNALLY. Mr. President, with relation to what has been said by the Senator from Michigan [Mr. VANDENBERG] I desire to observe that, while the bill as reported to the Senate adopts the provision carried in the House bill, indicating that no commitments are to be made by the Executive other than the express ones authorized by the law, yet I do not think that under the Constitution the President can make any commitments with relation to the post-war era that in any way affect the constitutional powers of the two Houses of Congress. The President might agree, whether in lend-lease or in any other way, that we would reduce our tariff or change our tariff, but that in no sense under our Constitution would be a commitment of the Government; the Congress would have to act in any event. So I do not regard it as absolutely imperative that the amendment be carried in order to effectuate that purpose although it is a good expression of our policy and our attitude, and I favored the inclusion of the amendment in the pending bill.

Mr. VANDENBERG. Mr. President, will the Senator yield?

Mr. CONNALLY. I yield.

Mr. VANDENBERG. I completely agree with the able Senator's analysis factually. Of course, the President cannot exceed his constitutional authority and ultimately "get away with it." But I am suggesting that any pretense or suggestion that he might be able to do so in respect to suggestions made to others of the United Nations may invite an ultimate disillusionment which would not make for post-war amity and that it is far better — and I know the Senator is in agreement with me regarding the basic facts — that the situation should be totally clear and not muddled.

Mr. CONNALLY. As I stated a moment ago to the Senator from Michigan, I favored the inclusion of the House amendment and still adhere to that position, although I wanted to make it clear that by what we have done heretofore we had in nowise compromised the constitutional power of the Houses of Congress, whatever the President may have done or promised to do in any of these master agreements.

Mr. President, one general statement and then I shall yield back the floor to the Senator from Illinois. Of course, the lend-lease policy and all agreements under it contemplate the aid of the war; they contemplate military action. As one who originally voted for the lend-lease, I do not think that we ever intended lend-lease to serve any purpose except to aid in the military operations in carrying on the war.

C. Cooperation in Formulating Plans for a General International Organization

By being a party to the Moscow Declaration of October 30, 1943, the Administration recognized "the necessity of establishing at the earliest practicable date a general international organization . . . for the maintenance of international peace and security." By the Connally Resolution, adopted November 5, 1943, the Senate gave its support to this principle, earlier affirmed in somewhat more general terms by the House of Representatives in the Fulbright Resolution, adopted September 21.[1]

In his radio address of April 9, 1944,[2] Secretary Hull, in discussing the question of post-war agreements, said:

"It is obvious, of course, that no matter how brilliant and desirable any course may seem it is wholly impracticable and impossible unless it is a course which finds basic acceptance, not only by our Allies but by the people of this country and by the Legislative branch of this government, which, under our Constitution, shares with the Executive power and responsibility for final action."

Further on he stated:

"We are at a stage where much of the work of formulating plans for the organization to maintain peace has been accomplished. It is right and necessary that we should have the advice and help of an increasing number of members of the Congress. Accordingly, I have requested the Chairman of the Senate Committee on Foreign Relations to designate a representative

[1] See this volume, p. 315.   [2] *Ibid.*, p. 25.

bipartisan group for this purpose. Following them and similar discussions with members of the House of Representatives, we shall be in the position to go forward again with other nations and, upon learning their views, be able to submit to the democratic processes of discussion a more concrete proposal."

At his press conference on April 12, Speaker Rayburn of the House of Representatives stated that he had been assured by Secretary Hull, in the course of a telephone conversation, that members of the House would be consulted as well as members of the Senate. While the Secretary made it clear that he would ask the Senate group first, he added that House conferees would also be asked to join him for discussion.[1]

In a statement to the press, released for publication, April 23,[2] Senator Connally, Chairman of the Senate Foreign Relations Committee stated that Secretary of State Hull had invited him "to designate a group from the Committee to meet with the Secretary of State in an initial meeting to discuss further plans and steps relating to conferences and cooperation between the Executive Department and the Senate regarding the whole question of a post-war program, with special reference to the formation and structure of an organization to preserve the peace of the world." Continuing, he said: "After consultation with members of the Committee, I designated the following: Senators Connally, George, Barkley, Gillette, Democrats; Senator LaFollette, Progressive; Senators Vandenberg, White and Austin, Republicans. The members of this group were selected from the Subcommittee which considered and reported the so-called Connally Peace Resolution, which was adopted by the Senate in the fall of 1943. It was felt that their studies over a period of several months in connection with that resolution would be very helpful in their prospective duties.

"The invitation of the Secretary of State related only to a preliminary informal discussion between the State Department and the Committee representatives which is intended to serve the purpose of developing each other's slant of mind with respect to various phases of future international questions and to a suitable program of conference and discussion as developments may arise. Such initial meeting is to be exploratory and consultative in character."

On May 21, the Senate Liaison Committee was reported to have reached a preliminary accord with Secretary Hull on the broad principles of the post-war international peace organization. There apparently was no attempt at this stage to reach agreement in detail.[3] On May 29, Secretary Hull announced the successful conclusion of these conversations.

(1) Preliminary Discussions on Establishment of International Peace and Security Organization. Statement of the Secretary of State (Hull), May 29, 1944 [4]

The first phase of the informal conversations with the eight Senators has been concluded. We had frank and fruitful discussions on the general principles, questions, and plans relating to the establishment of an international peace and security organization in accordance with the principles contained in the Moscow four-nation declaration, the Connally resolution, and other similar declarations made in this country. I am definitely encouraged and am ready to proceed, with the approval of the President, with informal discussions on this subject with Great Britain, Russia, and China, and then with governments of other United Nations.

[1] From the Office of the Chairman of the Senate Committee on Foreign Relations; see also *New York Times*, April 23, 1944.   [2] *Ibid.*
[3] *Ibid.*, May 22, 1944.   [4] Department of State, *Bulletin*, X, p. 510.

Meanwhile, I shall have further discussions with these and other leaders of both parties in the two Houses of Congress, and with others. The door of nonpartisanship will continue to be wide open here at the Department of State, especially when any phase of the planning for a post-war security organization is under consideration.

2. DEPARTMENT OF STATE

A. Organization

(1) *Resignation of Sumner Welles and Appointment of Edward R. Stettinius, Jr., as Under Secretary of State, White House Press Release, September 25, 1943* [1]

The President has announced the resignation of Sumner Welles as Under Secretary of State and the appointment of his successor, Edward R. Stettinius, Jr., now Lend-Lease Administrator.

In announcing Mr. Welles' resignation, the President stated that he had accepted it with deep and sincere regret. He said that Mr. Welles had advised him of his desire to be relieved of his heavy governmental duties in view of his wife's health, and he could understand and sympathize with that desire.

The President commended Mr. Welles' long service in the Department and said: "Mr. Welles has served the Department of State and this Government with unfailing devotion for many years."

Commenting on the Stettinius appointment, the President said that his broad experience with our Allies both before and after Pearl Harbor as Lend-Lease Administrator, and his long experience as an executive in business, splendidly equipped him for his new post.

(2) *Reorganization of the Department. Departmental Order 1218, January 15, 1944, with Subsequent Amendments* [2] *to June 30, 1944* [3]

[Excerpts]

The new organization of the Department is described in detail in the following Departmental order as revised up to June 30, 1944. It was designed to free the Assistant Secretaries and principal officers of the Department from administrative duties in order that they might devote the greater part of their time to matters of important foreign policy. Clearer lines of responsibility and authority are established inside the Department which simplify its structure and eliminate overlapping jurisdictions and diffusion of responsibility by means of a logical grouping of functions and divisions in twelve major "line" offices. The work of the higher officers of the Department is coordinated more closely through the creation of two principal committees — a Policy Committee and a Committee on Post War Programs.

[1] *Ibid.*, IX, p. 208.

[2] The amending orders are enclosed in brackets.

[3] Department of State, *Bulletin*, X, p. 45. Detailed information on the personnel in the various divisions will be found in the *Register of the Department of State*, 1944.

The Policy Committee assists the Secretary of State in the consideration of major questions of foreign policy, and the Committee on Post War Programs assists him in the formulation of post-war foreign policies and the execution of such policies by means of appropriate international arrangements.

The Secretary of State also established an Advisory Council on Post War Foreign Policy and designated Mr. Norman H. Davis,[1] Mr. Myron C. Taylor, and Dr. Isaiah Bowman as Vice Chairmen of this new Council, which is under his Chairmanship with the Under Secretary as his deputy.

The new organization assigns specific fields of activity to each of the Assistant Secretaries and to the Legal Adviser. Coordination among the Assistant Secretaries is provided by the Policy Committee.

The twelve major "line" offices are new organizational units in the Department. Within each major office are more diversified divisional units than existed previously. This results in broadening the base of the Department's organizational structure permitting the more flexible and efficient adjustment of the Department's functions to rapidly changing conditions. Further, the setting-up of the new "line" offices enables the Department to bring in additional outstanding personnel at a high level.

Five of these offices — those dealing with the major geographic areas (Europe, Far East, Near East and Africa, and American Republics) and with special political affairs report directly to the Secretary and Under Secretary. The four geographic offices are charged with the coordination of all aspects of our relations with the countries in their respective jurisdictions and not exclusively with political relations as has been the tendency during the past few years. The Special Political Affairs Office is concerned with political matters of world-wide scope and importance such as international security and organization.

Designations of personnel, and of routing symbols are omitted from the text when feasible.

PURPOSE OF ORDER

The purpose of this Order is to facilitate the conduct of the foreign relations of the United States, in war and in peace, by making adjustments in the organization of the Department of State.

PREVIOUS ORDERS REVOKED

All previous Departmental Orders and other administrative instructions concerning —

1. the organization of the Department of State;
2. the definition and assignment of functions and responsibilities among the various divisions and offices of the Department; and
3. the designation of ranking officers of the Department

are hereby revoked and superseded.

NEW ORGANIZATION OF THE DEPARTMENT

A chart showing the new organization of the Department of State is attached.[2]

The definition and assignment of functions and responsibilities among the various Offices and Divisions of the Department, and the designation

[1] Deceased July 2, 1944.   [2] Not reproduced here.

of its ranking officers, shall henceforth be as set forth below, subject to modification or amendment by Departmental Order.

As hereinafter provided, all matters concerning the organization of the Department, the definition and assignment of functions and responsibilities among its several Offices and Divisions, and the designation of its ranking officers below the Assistant Secretary level, shall be dealt with by the Office of Departmental Administration. Problems which may arise in connection with the new organization of the Department shall be referred to the Director of this Office.

OFFICE OF THE SECRETARY OF STATE

The following are hereby designated Special Assistants to the Secretary of State with functions and responsibilities as indicated:

1. Mr. Leo Pasvolsky. Mr. Pasvolsky, in addition to such other functions and responsibilities as may be assigned to him from time to time by the Secretary, shall serve as hereinafter provided as Executive Director of the Committee on Post War Programs.
2. Mr. Joseph C. Grew.[1] Mr. Grew shall perform such duties as may be assigned to him from time to time by the Secretary.
3. Mr. George T. Summerlin. In addition to such other responsibilities as may be assigned to him from time to time by the Secretary, Mr. Summerlin shall serve as Chief of Protocol.
4. Mr. Michael J. McDermott. Mr. McDermott shall serve as the Secretary's principal assistant in matters concerning the Department's relations with the press.

|*Special Assistant to the Secretary — Press Relations.*[2]

The Special Assistant to the Secretary, Mr. McDermott, as the Secretary's principal assistant in matters concerning the Department's relations with the press, shall have responsibility for: (a) liaison between the Department and the domestic and foreign press, including the conduct of the press conferences of the Secretary, the Under Secretary, and other officials of the Department; (b) liaison between the Department and other agencies of the Government, particularly the Office of War Information, the Office of Censorship, the Coordinator of Inter-American Affairs, and the public relations bureaus of the War and Navy Departments, in connection with the current operations of such agencies relating to the dissemination abroad of information regarding the war effort,

[1] By Departmental Order 1266, May 1, 1944, effective same date, Mr. Grew was designated as Director of Office of Far Eastern Affairs, Department of State, *Bulletin*, X, p. 420.

[2] Departmental Order 1229, February 22, 1944, effective February 21, *ibid.*, p. 209.

where such information is of an immediate news character; (c) clearance, in consultation with the appropriate officers of the Department, of speeches submitted to the Department by the Office of War Information and the Coordinator of Inter-American Affairs, and submission of speeches by the Department to the Office of War Information for clearance as may be required; (d) coordination of the Department's relations with agencies concerned in psychological warfare and related activities, including representation of the Department on the Board of Overseas Planning for Psychological Warfare of the Office of War Information; and (e) preparation and distribution within the Department and to the Foreign Service of clippings, daily press summaries and bulletins bearing upon foreign relations. . . .

The Division of Current Information is hereby abolished.

To assist Mr. McDermott in carrying out his responsibilities (a) in connection with the current operations of other agencies relating to the dissemination abroad of information of an immediate news character regarding the war effort and (b) for the coordination of relations with agencies concerned in psychological warfare, a Special Assistant shall be designated in each of the four geographical Offices. This Special Assistant may be the same as, and in any case will work in association with, the chief information liaison officer prescribed in section III of this Order.

The Special Assistant to the Secretary, Mr. McDermott, shall be a member of the Department of State Policy Committee and of the Committee on Post War Programs.

5. Mr. Thomas K. Finletter.[1] Mr. Finletter shall perform such duties as may be assigned to him from time to time by the Secretary.

6. Mr. Joseph C. Green. Mr. Green shall perform such duties as may be assigned to him from time to time by the Secretary.

[Mr. Robert Woods Bliss,[2] Mr. Stanley K. Hornbeck [3] and Mr. George A. Gordon [4] were appointed subsequent to January 15, 1944.]

The following additional designations are made in the Office of the Secretary:

1. Mr. Cecil W. Gray is hereby designated an Executive Assistant to the Secretary of State with responsibility for the administration of the Secretary's immediate office.

2. Mrs. Blanche R. Halla is hereby designated an Executive Assistant to the Secretary of State with responsibility for the review and co-

---

[1] Resigned from the Department, effective March 9, 1944, Department of State, ibid., p. 211.

[2] By Departmental Order 1222, February 11, 1944, effective February 10, ibid., p. 184.

[3] By Departmental Order 1265, May 1, 1944, effective same date, ibid., p. 420. Mr. Joseph C. Grew replaced Mr. Hornbeck as Director of the Office of Far Eastern Affairs.

[4] By Departmental Order 1262, April 27, 1944, effective May 1, ibid., p. 400.

ordination of all correspondence prepared for signature by the Secretary and Under Secretary.

3. Mr. George W. Renchard and Mr. James E. Brown are hereby designated Assistants to the Secretary of State.

4. Mr. Carlton Savage is hereby designated a General Consultant to the Secretary of State.

5. Mr. Orme Wilson is hereby designated Liaison Officer [1] with responsibility for assisting the Secretary and the Under Secretary in their liaison with the War and Navy Departments and such other duties as may be assigned to him.

[Mr. Frederick W. Nichol has been appointed as Special Adviser on Administration. He will assist the Department in implementing the reorganization plan announced on January 15, 1944.[2]] . . .

OFFICE OF THE UNDER SECRETARY OF STATE

1. The Under Secretary of State, Mr. Edward R. Stettinius, Jr., shall serve as the Secretary's deputy in all matters of concern or interest to the Department. . . .

ASSISTANT SECRETARIES AND LEGAL ADVISER

1. The Assistant Secretary, Mr. Adolf A. Berle, Jr., shall have general responsibility in matters of Controls and in matters of Transportation and Communications. . . .

2. The Assistant Secretary, Mr. Breckinridge Long, shall have general responsibility for all matters concerning the Department's relations with the Congress, with the exception of matters relating to appropriations and the administration of the Department and the Foreign Service. . . .

3. The Assistant Secretary, Mr. Dean Acheson, shall have general responsibility in the field of Economic Affairs.[3] . . .

4. The Assistant Secretary, Mr. G. Howland Shaw, shall have general responsibility for the administration of the Department and the Foreign Service and for matters of Public Information both at home and abroad. . . .

5. The Legal Adviser, Mr. Green H. Hackworth, shall have equal rank in all respects with the Assistant Secretaries and he shall have general responsibility for all matters of a legal character concerning the Department, including matters of a legal character formerly dealt with by the Treaty Division, which is hereby abolished. . . .

[1] By Departmental Order 1277, June 7, 1944, the functions of this office were transferred to the Office of Foreign Activity Correlation and the Liaison Office was abolished, *ibid.*, p. 543.

[2] *Ibid.*, p. 227.

[3] Designated as Chairman of Executive Committee on Foreign Policy by Departmental Designation 29, issued June 30, 1944, effective same date, *ibid.*, XI, p. 54.

POLICY COMMITTEE

1. There is hereby created the Department of State Policy Committee which shall assist the Secretary in the consideration of major questions of foreign policy.

This Committee shall meet every Monday, Wednesday and Friday at 9:30 A.M. in the Secretary's Conference Room.

The Committee on Political Planning is hereby abolished.

2. The Secretary shall be Chairman and the Under Secretary shall be Vice Chairman of the Policy Committee.

The Assistant Secretaries, the Legal Adviser, and the Special Assistant to the Secretary, Mr. Pasvolsky, shall be members of the Committee; and the Directors of Offices, as hereinafter provided for, shall be *ex officio* members of the Committee. [Mr. Charles W. Yost was designated as Executive Secretary on February 22, 1944.] [1]

3. Responsibility for the preparation of agenda, the keeping of minutes and the performance of such other duties as may be assigned by the Chairman or Vice Chairman of the Policy Committee shall be vested in an Executive Secretary who shall be assisted by such staff as may be determined. . . .

COMMITTEE ON POST WAR PROGRAMS

1. There is hereby created the Department of State Committee on Post War Programs which shall assist the Secretary in the formulation of post-war foreign policies and the execution of such policies by means of appropriate international arrangements.

2. The Secretary shall be Chairman, the Under Secretary shall be Vice Chairman, and the Special Assistant to the Secretary, Mr. Pasvolsky, shall be Executive Director of the Committee on Post War Programs. The Vice Chairmen of the Advisory Council on Post War Foreign Policy. the Assistant Secretaries, and the Legal Adviser, shall be members of the Committee; and the Directors of Offices, as hereinafter provided for, shall be *ex officio* members of the Committee.

3. The Executive Director of the Committee on Post War Programs shall have full authority under the Secretary to organize the Committee's work and to call upon the various Offices and Divisions of the Department for such assistance as may be required in carrying out the Committee's responsibilities. . . .

[Mr. C. Easton Rothwell was designated as Executive Secretary on Political Affairs and John H. Fuqua as Executive Secretary on Economic Affairs on March 18, 1944.] [2]

[1] Departmental Order 1231, February 23, 1944, effective February 22, *ibid.*, X, p. 212.
[2] Departmental Order 1242, March 20, 1944, effective March 18, *ibid.*, p. 293.

[INFORMATIONAL LIAISON REPRESENTATIVES AND THEIR DUTIES [1]

A chief informational liaison officer shall be designated in each Office of the Department by the Director thereof, subject to the approval of the Director of the Office of Departmental Administration. He shall be provided with the assistance needed to effectuate this Order.

Informational Servicing of Missions

For the purpose of strengthening the flow of information to each of the missions, including confidential information about developments of crucial interest in other parts of the world, there is hereby established the Information Service Committee, which shall be composed of a representative from Mr. McDermott's office and the chief informational liaison officers from each of the following Offices: American Republic Affairs, European Affairs, Far Eastern Affairs, Near Eastern and African Affairs, Public Information, and Foreign Service Administration. The Director of the Office of Foreign Service Administration shall act as chairman of the Committee.

The representatives of the geographical Offices shall ordinarily give full time to the task of obtaining and collating information drawn from Divisions of their Offices, and from other Offices in the Department, which may usefully be made known to the heads of missions throughout the world as well as to appropriate officers in the Department. These representatives, subject to the direction of the Directors of their Offices, shall advise on the selection of information for transmission to the particular missions with which the Office is concerned.

It shall be the duty of the Information Service Committee (acting where necessary with the informational liaison officers in all the Offices of the Department) to aid in supplying the missions and the Department with pertinent information. Especially (taking account of the material which already is being prepared and transmitted regularly) the Committee shall supplement this material by systematic, highly selective, confidential summaries of developments involving all parts of the world which should be known to the heads of missions.

The Secretary and the Under Secretary will designate an officer in their Offices to communicate to the Committee over-all information not available through other channels which is essential to the objective of supplying the heads of missions with information.

The Chairman of the Committee shall take care that the summaries are prepared and distributed to the missions on a weekly schedule. The summaries shall also be supplied to the Secretary, the Under Secretary, the members of the Policy Committee, and the Chiefs of Divisions in the four geographical Offices. In addition to the special and confidential

[1] Departmental Order 1229, February 22, 1944, effective February 21, *ibid.*, p. 210.

service just described, it shall be the general duty of the Committee to survey the entire flow of information from the Department to the missions, in whatever form, and to initiate action for improving this service.

Liaison with the Special Assistant, Mr. McDermott

It shall be the duty of the informational liaison officers to keep the Special Assistant to the Secretary, Mr. McDermott, and officers designated by him, currently informed as to all developments within their Offices.

Liaison with the Office of Public Information

It shall be the duty of the informational liaison officers, individually or as a group, upon request, to advise and assist the Director of the Office of Public Information on matters within the scope of that Office.]

OFFICE OF CONTROLS

There is hereby created an Office of Controls which shall have responsibility, under the general direction of the Assistant Secretary, Mr. Berle, for initiating and coordinating policy and action in all matters pertaining to the control activities of the Department of State. . . .

The Office of Controls shall be composed of the following divisions, with functions and responsibilities as indicated.

1. Passport Division.

The Passport Division shall have responsibility for initiating and co-ordinating policy and action in all matters pertaining to: (a) the administration of laws and regulations relating to the control of American citizens and nationals entering and leaving territory under the jurisdiction of the United States; (b) limitation of travel of American citizens in foreign countries; (c) determination of eligibility to receive passports or to be registered as citizens or nationals of the United States in American consulates of persons who claim to be American citizens, citizens of Puerto Rico, citizens of the Virgin Islands, citizens of the Commonwealth of the Philippines, or inhabitants of the Canal Zone, Guam, or American Samoa, owing permanent allegiance to the United States; (d) prevention and detection of fraud in passport matters and the preparation of cases involving fraud for prosecution in the courts; (e) issuance of passports, issuance of instructions to American diplomatic and consular officers concerning matters relating to nationality, passports, registrations, and the protection of American nationals in foreign countries, the release of persons inducted into foreign military service, the refund of taxes imposed for failure to perform military service, the preparation of reports of births of American citizens abroad and reports of marriages; (f) administration of passport work performed by the executive officers of American Samoa, Guam, Hawaii, Puerto Rico, the Virgin Islands, and by the United States High Commissioner to the Philippine Islands; (g) supervision of the passport agencies in New York, San Francisco, and Miami; and (h) direction of clerks of courts in the United States with regard to passport matters. . . .

2. *Visa Division.*

The Visa Division shall have responsibility for the initiation and coordination of policy and action in all matters pertaining to: (a) alien visa control; (b) the assembling and examination of all information necessary to determine the admissibility of aliens into the United States in the interest of public safety; (c) the issuance of exit and reentry permits; (d) recommendations to American Foreign Service officers for their final consideration concerning individual visa applicants; (e) the control of immigration quotas; (f) the issuance of licenses within the purview of paragraph XXV of the Executive Order of October 12, 1917 relating to the Trading with the Enemy Act and title VII thereof, approved June 15, 1917; and (g) collaboration with interested offices and divisions of the Department, as well as with other agencies of the Government, concerning the control of subversive activities and the transportation of enemy aliens. . . .

3. *Special War Problems Division.*[1]

The Special War Problems Division shall be charged with the initiation and coordination of policy and action in all matters pertaining to: (a) the whereabouts and welfare of, and transmission of funds to, Americans abroad; (b) the evacuation and repatriation of Americans from foreign countries; (c) financial assistance to Americans in territories where the interests of the United States are represented by Switzerland; (d) liaison with the American Red Cross and the President's War Relief Control Board for the coordination of foreign relief operations of private agencies with the foreign policy of this Government; (e) representation by this Government of the interests of foreign governments in the United States; (f) representation by a third power of United States interests in enemy countries; (g) supervision of the representation in the United States by third powers of the interests of other governments with which the United States has severed diplomatic relations or is at war; (h) the exchange of official and non-official American and Axis Powers personnel; (i) civilian internees and prisoners of war, and the accompanying of representatives of the protecting powers and the International Red Cross on prisoner-of-war and civilian-enemy-alien camp inspections.

[1] For a detailed description of this Division see "Special War Problems Division" by Graham H. Stuart, *ibid.*, XI, p. 6.

4. *Division of Foreign Activity Correlation.*[1]

The Division of Foreign Activity Correlation shall have responsibility for the initiation and coordination of policy and action in all matters pertaining to such foreign activities and operations as may be directed.

．　．　．　．　．　．

OFFICE OF TRANSPORTATION AND COMMUNICATIONS

There is hereby created an Office of Transportation and Communications which shall have responsibility, under the general direction of the Assistant Secretary, Mr. Berle, for initiating and coordinating policy and action in all matters concerning the international aspects of transportation and communications.

．　．　．　．　．　．

The Division of International Communications is hereby abolished.

The Office of Transportation and Communications shall be composed of the following divisions, with functions and responsibilities as indicated.

1. *Aviation Division.*[2]

[The Aviation Division shall have responsibility for initiating, developing and coordinating policy and action in all matters pertaining to:

(*a*) International aviation, including the development and operation of airlines and air transportation, the acquisition of landing rights abroad, and matters relating to airports and airways.

(*b*) Discussions with foreign countries on matters relating to civil aviation and the drafting of agreements on this subject.

(*c*) Assembling basic material and otherwise preparing for international aviation conferences.

(*d*) Representation of the Department on the International Technical Committee of Aerial Legal Experts (CITEJA), the United States National Commission of the Permanent American Aeronautical Commission (CAPA) and other international bodies dealing with aeronautical affairs.

(*e*) Matters of policy relating to international air mail.

(*f*) Presentation to the Munitions Assignments Committee (Air) or other appropriate allocation authorities of foreign requests for aircraft and collaboration with other offices and divisions of the Department and of other Departments and agencies of the Government concerned in the export of aircraft.

---

[1] Transfer of functions of the Secretary's Liaison Office to this division, Departmental Order 1277, June 7, 1944, *ibid.*, X, p. 543.

[2] Amendment introduced by Departmental Order 1246, March 28, 1944, effective March 27, *ibid.*, p. 302; for original text, see *ibid.*, p. 49.

(*g*) Training of foreign aircraft and ground personnel in the United States and abroad, including collaboration and coordination with the Civil Aeronautics Board, the Civil Aeronautics Administration and other Departments and agencies of the Government and with foreign agencies engaged in like activities.

(*h*) Obtaining military and civil flight permits for United States aircraft proceeding abroad and for foreign aircraft visiting the United States and its possessions on request of diplomatic missions accredited to the United States.

(*i*) Screening of non-military requests for travel priorities for civilian personnel and the presentation of these requests to military authorities.

(*j*) Representation on interdepartmental committees considering problems involving aviation.

(*k*) Miscellaneous matters involving aviation in general including liaison with the Department of Commerce, Civil Aeronautics, Civil Aeronautics Administration, the War, Navy, and Post Office Departments, Defense Supplies Corporation and other Departments and agencies of the Government.

In carrying out these functions and responsibilities, the Aviation Division shall work in close cooperation with all other interested divisions of the Department.] . . .

2. *Shipping Division.*

The Shipping Division shall have responsibility for the initiation and coordination of policy and action in all matters pertaining to (*a*) international shipping, excepting functions relating to shipping requirements and allocations vested in the wartime economic divisions, and including the development of shipping policy; and (*b*) liaison with the War Shipping Administration, Maritime Commission, Navy Department, Office of Censorship, and such other departments and agencies as may be concerned. . . .

3. *Telecommunications Division.*

The Telecommunications Division shall have responsibility for the initiation and coordination of policy and action in matters pertaining to (*a*) international aspects of [mail and telephone] [1] radio, telegraph, and cable communications, including the development of telecommunications policy [motion pictures, (other than responsibilities assigned to the Office of Public Information) and liaison with the Post Office Department]; [1] and (*b*) liaison with the Federal Communications Commission, War and Navy Departments, Office of Censorship, and such other departments and agencies as may be concerned. . . .

[1] Additional responsibilities, enumerated in brackets, issued in Departmental Order 1224, February 14, 1944, effective February 11, *ibid.*, p. 195.

OFFICE OF WARTIME ECONOMIC AFFAIRS

There is hereby created an Office of Wartime Economic Affairs which, in collaboration with the Office of Economic Affairs hereinafter provided for, shall have responsibility, under the general direction of the Assistant Secretary, Mr. Acheson, for the initiation and coordination of policy and action, so far as the Department of State is concerned, in all matters pertaining to the wartime economic relations of the United States with other governments.

The Office of Wartime Economic Affairs and its component Divisions shall be the focal points of contact and liaison, within the scope of their functions, with the Foreign Economic Administration,[1] War Production Board, War Shipping Administration, Treasury, War and Navy Departments, United Nations Relief and Rehabilitation Administration, and such other agencies as may be concerned. For this purpose, there shall be full and free exchange of information and views between the Office of Wartime Economic Affairs and its component Divisions, and the appropriate political and economic offices and divisions of the Department.

The Office of Wartime Economic Affairs shall be composed of the following divisions, with functions and responsibilities as indicated.

1. *Supply and Resources Division.*

The Supply and Resources Division shall have responsibility, so far as the Department of State is concerned, for the initiation and coordination of policy and action in all matters pertaining to: (*a*) the procurement and development abroad of all materials needed for the prosecution of the war or the relief of enemy, enemy-held or reoccupied territory (excepting European Neutrals and their possessions, and French North and West Africa and projects in Latin America); (*b*) Lend-Lease matters (excepting French and British possessions), reciprocal aid arrangements, as they relate to the procurement and development of materials abroad, and White Paper matters; (*c*) War Shipping matters; (*d*) the administration of Section 12 of the Neutrality Act of November 4, 1939 governing the movement of arms, ammunition and implements of war, the Helium Act of September 1, 1937 and the Tin Plate Scrap Act of February 15, 1936; (*e*) representation, within the scope of its responsibilities, of the Department before the Combined Boards and their operating, advisory and other committees (excepting only in cases of a special nature in which the Department's point of contact is through membership on special area committees); before the Foreign Economic Administration, War Production Board, War Shipping Administration, War Food Administration, and other departments and agencies concerned, in connection with

[1] For Executive Order establishing the Foreign Economic Administration, see this volume, p. 98.

requirement programs and requests for allocations for commodities and shipping submitted by other divisions of the Department; and (f) liaison within the scope of the Divisions' responsibilities, with such other departments and agencies as may be concerned. . . .

2. *Liberated Areas Division.*

The Liberated Areas Division shall have responsibility so far as the Department of State is concerned for the initiation and coordination of policy and action in all wartime economic matters pertaining to areas now occupied by the enemy and to Southern Italy and Sicily, including: (a) preparation of requirement programs for the liberated areas, and, as required by the Director of the Office, programs for purchases from those areas, and the importation of supplies and materials into the United States; (b) [1] fiscal matters, including banking matters; and financial and property controls, including the application of Executive Order No. 8389, as amended, to property located in the United States of governments of those areas and their nationals, and questions relating to the Alien Property Custodian and to the property control measures of other United Nations; (c) in collaboration with the Division of Financial and Monetary Affairs hereinafter provided for, reconstruction and rehabilitation of industrial and agricultural structures including supply and economic development; (d) liaison, within the scope of the Division's responsibilities, with the Foreign Economic Administration, Civil Affairs Division of the War Department, the United Nations Relief and Rehabilitation Administration, and such departments and agencies as may be concerned. . . .

3. *American Republics Requirements Division.*

The American Republics Requirements Division shall have responsibility so far as the Department of State is concerned for the initiation and coordination of policy and action in all wartime economic matters pertaining to the other American republics and British and Dutch colonies and possessions in the Caribbean area including: (a) the preparation of requirement programs for, and the functioning of control of exports to, that area; (b) assistance in regard to procurement programs, shipping schedules and other economic operations relating to the other American republics; (c) representation of the Department before the Foreign Economic Administration and other agencies in connection with applications for projects for the other American republics recommended by the Division of Financial and Monetary Affairs; and (d) liaison, within the scope of its responsibilities, with such other departments and agencies as may be concerned. . . .

[1] Functions listed under (b) transferred to Office of Economic Affairs, Division of Financial and Monetary Affairs, by Departmental Order 1252, April 1, 1944, effective March 30, Department of State, *Bulletin*, X, p. 328, see this volume, p. 70.

4. *Eastern Hemisphere Division.*

The Eastern Hemisphere Division shall have responsibility so far as the Department of State is concerned for the initiation and coordination of policy and action in all wartime economic matters pertaining to countries of the Eastern Hemisphere, except those presently occupied by the enemy, and Southern Italy and Sicily; and, in the Western Hemisphere, to all French possessions, Iceland, Greenland, Canada, and British Colonies and Possessions, except in the Caribbean area and in South America, including (a) economic blockade of enemy and enemy-occupied territories; (b) formulation of requirement programs and of purchase programs constituting the counterpart of requirement programs; (c) Lend-Lease matters arising in connection with French and British possessions; (d) representation of the Department, within the scope of the Division's responsibilities, before the United States Commercial Company and special area committees organized with representatives of the French, Belgian, British Dominion, and other governments, where the problems arise from a diverse group of articles and materials rather than one or a few commodities; and (e) liaison, within the scope of its responsibilities, with such departments and agencies as may be concerned. . . .

5. *Division of World Trade Intelligence.*[1]

The Division of World Trade Intelligence shall have so far as the Department of State is concerned responsibility for the initiation and coordination of policy and action in all matters pertaining to (a) the administration of the Proclaimed List of Certain Blocked Nationals and related lists; (b) the administration of Executive Order No. 8389, as amended, issued under Sec. 5 (b) of the Trading with the Enemy Act and relating to the regulation of transactions in foreign exchange and foreign-owned property (excepting with respect to Liberated Areas), and the application of the recommendations of the Inter-American Conference on Systems of Economic and Financial Control, excepting matters relating to the replacement or reorganization of Axis firms; (c) the collection, evaluation and organization of biographical data; (d) liaison, within the scope of its responsibilities, with the Treasury Department, Foreign Economic Administration, Office of the Coordinator of Inter-American Affairs, and such other departments and agencies as may be concerned.

OFFICE OF ECONOMIC AFFAIRS

There is hereby created an Office of Economic Affairs which, in collaboration with the Office of Wartime Economic Affairs, shall have

[1] For Departmental Order 1252, April 1, 1944 for redefinition of relations between this Division and the Division of Financial and Monetary Affairs, see this volume, p. 70.

responsibility, under the general direction of the Assistant Secretary, Mr. Acheson, for the initiation and coordination of policy and action in all matters pertaining to international economic affairs, other than those of a wartime character.

The Office of the Adviser on International Economic Affairs, the Office of the Petroleum Adviser, and the Division of Economic Studies are hereby abolished and their functions and responsibilities shall henceforth be carried on in the Office of Economic Affairs.

The Office of Economic Affairs shall be composed of the following divisions, with functions and responsibilities as indicated.

1. *Division of Commercial Policy.*

The Division of Commercial Policy shall have responsibility for the initiation and coordination of policy and action in all matters pertaining to: (a) the protection and promotion of American commercial and agricultural interests in foreign countries under the terms of Reorganization Plan No. II as authorized by the Reorganization Act of April 3, 1939; (b) the formulation, negotiation, and administration of commercial treaties, of reciprocal trade agreements under the Act of June 12, 1934, and of such other commercial agreements as may be assigned to it by the Director of the Office of Economic Affairs; (c) the tariff, general trade, and international commercial policy of the United States; and (d) liaison, within the scope of its responsibilities, with the Department of the Treasury, the Department of Commerce, the Department of Agriculture, the United States Tariff Commission, and such other departments or agencies as may be concerned.

2. *Division of Financial and Monetary Affairs.*

The Division of Financial and Monetary Affairs shall have responsibility for the initiation and coordination of policy and action in all matters pertaining to (a) general international financial and monetary policy; (b) public and private foreign investment; (c) industrialization and development programs, including matters relating to the reorganization of Axis firms and requirements for long-range development projects; (d) international financial agreements and arrangements; (e) certification, under Section 25 (b) of the Federal Reserve Act, of the authority of designated persons to dispose of various foreign properties deposited in this country; (f) liaison, within the scope of its responsibilities, with the Treasury Department, Export-Import Bank, Departments of Commerce, Justice, and Agriculture, Foreign Economic Administration, Alien Property Custodian, Office of the Coordinator of Inter-American Affairs, and such other departments or agencies as may be concerned.

The Financial Division is hereby abolished and its functions and responsibilities transferred to the Division of Financial and Monetary Affairs.

[1][In order to concentrate in one Division responsibility for financial matters, responsibility for these matters in the above areas is hereby transferred from the Liberated Areas Division to the Divisions of Financial and Monetary Affairs. The relationships between the Division of Financial and Monetary Affairs and the Liberated Areas Division and the Division of World Trade Intelligence are hereby redefined.

Transfer of Functions From the Liberated Areas Division

Departmental Order 1218 is hereby amended by the transfer of functions listed in section (b) of the Liberated Areas Division to the Division of Financial and Monetary Affairs: "(b) fiscal matters, including banking matters; and financial and property controls, including the application of Executive Order no. 8389, as amended, to property located in the United States of governments of those areas and their nationals, and questions relating to the Alien Property Custodian and to the property control measures of other United Nations."

Relations With the Liberated Areas Division

In carrying out its responsibilities, the Division of Financial and Monetary Affairs shall work in close collaboration with the Liberated Areas Division. The Liberated Areas Division continues to be responsible for the initiation and coordination of policy and action in all wartime economic matters pertaining to enemy, enemy-occupied and liberated areas, except those matters covered in (b) above. The area representatives in this Division will be the focal point of contact regarding all matters in the area.

Relations With the Division of World Trade Intelligence

The Division of World Trade Intelligence shall have primary responsibility for the initiation and formulation of policy and for action with respect to the application and administration of foreign funds control (Executive Order 8389, as amended) except with respect to the governments or nationals of enemy, enemy-occupied, or liberated areas. In carrying out its responsibilities, the Division of World Trade Intelligence shall consult with the Division of Financial and Monetary Affairs in the formulation of policy on foreign funds control matters, such as the extension of controls to additional countries, the lifting or relaxing of controls, modifications of control through general licenses or rulings, and arrangements for the utilization of the funds of governments or their official banks.

The Division of Financial and Monetary Affairs shall have primary responsibility for the initiation and formulation of policy and for action

[1] From Departmental Order 1252, April 1, 1944, effective March 30, *ibid.*, X, p. 328.

in matters relating to the application of foreign funds control measures to property of governments or nationals of enemy, enemy-occupied or liberated areas. The Division of Financial and Monetary Affairs shall keep the Division of World Trade Intelligence informed of policy developments with regard to these matters. As policies become established, the Division of World Trade Intelligence shall assume the handling of individual cases within the framework of these policies.

The Division of Financial and Monetary Affairs shall also have primary responsibility for policy and action in cases involving the control of imported securities under General Ruling 5, pursuant to Executive Order 8389, as amended, and in matters pertaining to the servicing of dollar bonds. Subject to the foregoing exceptions, the Division of World Trade Intelligence shall handle all individual freezing cases and license applications.]

3. *Commodities Division.*

The Commodities Division shall have responsibility for the initiation and coordination of policy and action in all matters pertaining to: (a) the production and control and the distribution in international commerce of major commodities such as rubber, tin and the heavy metals,[1] coffee, sugar, wheat and cotton; (b) international commodity arrangements; (c) international fisheries, including fisheries surveys for the purpose of providing food fish for the American armed forces and for our Allies; and (d) within the scope of its responsibilities, liaison with intergovernmental agencies concerned with international commodity problems, with the Department of Agriculture, and such other departments and agencies as may be concerned. . . .

[*Industry Branch* [2]

The policies of the United States Government on cartels and related international industrial arrangements are inseparable aspects of United States commercial policy, and accordingly are of direct concern to the Department of State. During the coming periods of peace settlement, post-war adjustment, industrial rehabilitation, and revival of international trade, cartel problems will be a major concern in international affairs.

In order that responsibility for the Department's policy and action on all matters regarding international industrial arrangements may be clearly fixed and properly coordinated, there is hereby established an Industry Branch in the Commodities Division of the Office of Economic

---

[1] The text is given with deletions provided for in Departmental Order 1245, March 27, 1944, effective March 24, *ibid.*, p. 302.

[2] Departmental Order 1254, April 10, 1944, effective April 17, *ibid.*, p. 365.

Affairs. Departmental Order 1218 of January 15, 1944, is accordingly amended.

The Industry Branch shall be responsible for initiation, formulation, and coordination of policy and action on all cartel and related international industrial arrangements. This will include such activities as:

(a) Assembling and analyzing basic data and information, and preparing background and policy studies on international cartels, intercorporate relations of United States and foreign firms, patent and other market regulating agreements, trademarks and trade names, intergovernmental industrial agreements, and related matters.

(b) Development of policies and programs for controlling cartels, combines, restrictive patent agreements, and other restrictive international business arrangements.

(c) Determination and promotion of standards for intergovernmental industrial agreements and of the forms of international organization required to implement such standards and general programs.

(d) Development of data, recommendations, and policies, in collaboration with other Divisions of the Department and other interested Federal agencies, such as the Department of Justice, Department of Commerce, Office of Strategic Services, and the Foreign Economic Administration, for use in international discussions and negotiations regarding international cartel matters.

(e) Formulation of policy on matters of international industrial arrangements involved in the treatment of industry in enemy and ex-enemy countries during the period of military occupation.

(f) Review of policy documents pertaining to foreign industrial arrangements submitted to the Department by other Federal agencies and interdepartmental committees.

(g) Provision of a central source of current information for other Offices of the Department on cartels and related aspects of international industrial arrangements, including agreements allocating quotas or areas, price-fixing arrangements, and patent and trade-mark agreements.

(h) Provision of secretariat (agenda, supporting documents, and minutes), and participation in the work of interdivisional or interdepartmental committees concerned with problems of international industrial organization.

(i) Review of legislative proposals and discussions relating to foreign contracts, patents, trademarks, cartels, etc.

(j) Policy advice to Divisions of the Department and other Federal agencies with regard to current supply arrangements involving industrial combines, cartels, and similar problems.

In carrying out these responsibilities, the Industry Branch of the Commodities Division shall work in close collaboration with other

Divisions of the Department whose work bears upon cartel questions, particularly the Division of Financial and Monetary Affairs, the Division of Commercial Policy and other Divisions of the Office of Economic Affairs, the Liberated Areas Division and other Divisions of the Office of Wartime Economic Affairs, and the Divisions of the Office of Special Political Affairs.

The Industry Branch shall act as the Department's liaison with the Department of Justice on any matters affecting international cartels and industrial arrangements.]

4. *Division of Labor Relations.*[1]

The Division of Labor Relations shall have responsibility for initiating and coordinating policy and action in matters pertaining to (*a*) the effects on the foreign relations of the United States of policies and practices in foreign countries concerning wage and hour standards, working conditions and similar matters of interest and concern to labor in the United States and abroad; (*b*) the interest of labor in the United States in matters of broad international policy; (*c*) international arrangements for the promotion of full employment, health, economic and social welfare in general; and (*d*) within the scope of its responsibilities, liaison with the Department of Labor and other departments and agencies concerned, and with international agencies. . . .

[*Petroleum Division.*[2]

There is hereby established in the Office of Economic Affairs a Petroleum Division which shall have responsibility for the initiation, development and coordination of policy and action in all matters pertaining to petroleum and petroleum products and, within that scope, responsibility for liaison with intergovernmental agencies concerned with international problems in this field and with the Petroleum Administration for War, the Foreign Economic Administration and other departments and agencies which are or may hereafter be concerned with petroleum and petroleum products. Since the Department's policy with regard to petroleum and with regard to other commodities must be consistent, it is important that this Division collaborate closely with the Commodities Division. Other divisions concerned should also be consulted as occasion may arise.] . . .

[1] The Department announced on May 29, 1944 that Mr. Robert J. Watt, International Representative of the American Federation of Labor, Mr. J. Raymond Walsh, Director of Research and Education of the Congress of Industrial Organizations, and Professor Sumner Slichter, of Harvard University, had been appointed as advisers to the Division of Labor Relations, *ibid.*, p. 513.

[2] Departmental Order 1245, March 27, 1944, effective March 24, *ibid.*, p. 302.

Office of American Republic Affairs

There is hereby created an Office of American Republic Affairs which shall have responsibility, under the general direction of the Secretary and Under Secretary, for the initiation and, in particular, the coordination of policy and action in regard to all aspects of relations with Argentina, Bolivia, Brazil, Chile, Colombia, Costa Rica, Cuba, Dominican Republic, Ecuador, El Salvador, Guatemala, Haiti, Honduras, Mexico, Nicaragua, Panama, Paraguay, Peru, Uruguay, and Venezuela. In addition, the Office of American Republic Affairs shall have responsibility for supervising so far as the Department of State is concerned the program of the Interdepartmental Committee for Cooperation With the Other American Republics.

All other offices and divisions in the Department shall assure full participation by the Office of American Republic Affairs and its component divisions, as hereinafter provided for, in the formulation and execution of policy affecting relations with the countries under the jurisdiction of this Office. . . .

The Office of American Republic Affairs shall be composed of the following divisions, which shall have primary responsibility for the functions of the Office in regard to relations with the countries indicated in each case.

1. *Division of Mexican Affairs.* Mexico.

.   .   .   .

2. *Division of Caribbean and Central American Affairs.* Costa Rica, Cuba, Dominican Republic, El Salvador, Guatemala, Haiti, Honduras, Nicaragua, and Panama, and, in collaboration with the appropriate divisions in the Office of European Affairs, relations with European possessions in the area, the Guianas and British Honduras.

The Caribbean Office is hereby abolished and its functions and responsibilities, including liaison with the American Section of the Anglo-American Caribbean Commission, are hereby transferred to the Division of Caribbean and Central American Affairs.

[2. *Relationships of the United States Section of the Anglo-American Caribbean Commission to the Department.*[1] In fiscal and administrative matters, the United States Section of the Anglo-American Caribbean Commission shall be under the jurisdiction of the Assistant Secretary in charge of the administration of the Department of State. Matters of policy affecting relations with possessions of European countries in the Caribbean area dealt with by the United States Section of the

[1] By Departmental Order 1274, May 23, 1944, effective same date, *ibid.*, p. 502.

Commission shall be cleared through the appropriate Divisions of the Office of European Affairs. Those policy matters affecting relations with American Republics in the Caribbean area shall be cleared through the Division of Caribbean and Central American Affairs of the Office of American Republic Affairs. When necessary, the United States Section of the Commission and the geographic Offices shall consult with other interested Offices or Divisions of the Department. The United States Section of the Commission shall keep the Office of European Affairs and the Office of American Republic Affairs currently informed of matters which it is handling within their respective fields; those Offices, and other Divisions and Offices of the Department, particularly the Division of Communications and Records, shall keep the United States Section of the Commission currently informed of matters in Which the United States Section is interested.

The United States Section shall be represented on the interdivisional Working Committee on Problems of Dependent Territories of the Division of International Security and Organization.] . . .

3. *Division of Brazilian Affairs.* Brazil. . . .

4. *Division of Bolivarian Affairs.* Colombia, Ecuador, and Venezuela. . . .

5. *Division of River Plate Affairs.* Argentina, Paraguay, and Uruguay. . . .

6. *Division of West Coast Affairs.* Bolivia, Chile, and Peru. . . .

[*Division of American Republics Analysis and Liaison* [1]

1. *Establishment of the division.* There is hereby established a Division of American Republics Analysis and Liaison in the Office of American Republic Affairs. The Division of American Republics Analysis and Liaison shall be responsible for: (*a*) analysis of data and preparation of special studies and reports on developments within and among the Latin-American countries; (*b*) liaison with other offices of the Department and with other agencies of the Government on matters of general policy in the inter-American field which are outside the scope of the geographic divisions of the Office; and (*c*) formulation of policy to be adopted by the Office of American Republic Affairs concerning inter-American organizations, conferences, and conventions.

2. *Organization of the division.* The Division of American Republics Analysis and Liaison shall consist of three sections: Analysis Section; Liaison Section; and Inter-American Section.

3. *Analysis Section.* (*a*) The Analysis Section is responsible for the collection and analysis of data from all sources, including regular Departmental despatches and memoranda, reports of other Federal agen-

[1] Departmental Order 1271, May 3, 1944, effective same date, *ibid.*, p. 443.

cies, and published documents bearing on the work of the Office of American Republic Affairs; the conduct of special studies on current conditions, trends and policy questions of interest to the divisions of the Office of American Republic Affairs; the assembling and digesting of research materials on background and policy developments of interest to officers of the Office, the missions, and selected officers of the Department; cooperation with other divisions of the Department on research relating to the other American Republics, particularly the divisions of the Office of Special Political Affairs and the Office of Economic Affairs; cooperation with the research staff of other Government agencies engaged in research on Latin-American problems; contact, when appropriate, with the Division of Research and Publication; and maintenance of a reference service on data concerning the other American Republics for all officers of American Republic Affairs, other officers of the Department and other Federal agencies who may have occasion to call on this service.

(b) This section shall serve as the research staff to the Director and Deputy Director of the Office on problems with which they are dealing, and to the Chiefs of the divisions on special problems. In rendering this assistance, the section shall take the initiative in selecting topics warranting analysis and shall develop recommendations bearing on policy, as well as answering requests for information and research. The section will work with the planning staff of the Office of Foreign Service Administration on the development of standards for the improvement of reporting from the missions and for the evaluation of Foreign Service reports.

4. *Liaison Section.* (a) The Liaison Section is responsible for maintaining liaison on policy matters of the Office of American Republic Affairs, outside the scope of the geographic divisions, with other offices of the Department concerned with general inter-American activities, and for advising the Coordinator of Inter-American Affairs and other agencies of the Government carrying on programs in the other American Republics on the relation of their programs to the policy of the Office of American Republic Affairs.

(b) The Liaison Section will assist the Chief Informational Liaison Officer in carrying on the work of the Information Service Committee; in advising with the Special Assistant, Mr. McDermott, on press matters; and in consulting with the Office of Public Information on its public information activities and its cultural relations programs.

5. *Inter-American Section.* The Inter-American Section will formulate and recommend policy and action to be adopted by the Office of American Republic Affairs on Departmental problems of an inter-American character as distinguished from problems falling within the scope of the geographic divisions. The section will also, working closely with the Division of International Conferences and the Division of International Security

and Organization, handle for the Office of American Republic Affairs policy matters relating to American participation in inter-American organizations, meetings, treaties, and conventions.

6. *Assistance from other divisions of the Office.* In performing its work the division will call upon the geographic divisions of the Office of American Republic Affairs for assistance in keeping currently apprised of developments in and policy toward the several countries.

7. *Transfer of personnel to the division.* Personnel presently performing any of the functions cited in this order are hereby transferred to the Division of American Republics Analysis and Liaison.] . . .

OFFICE OF EUROPEAN AFFAIRS

There is hereby created an Office of European Affairs which shall have responsibility, under the general direction of the Secretary and the Under Secretary, for the initiation and the coordination of policy and action in regard to all aspects of relations with the following countries: Albania, Australia, Austria, Belgium, Bulgaria, Canada, Czechoslovakia, Denmark, Estonia, Finland, France, Free City of Danzig, Germany, Great Britain (including British territories and possessions except India and those in Africa), Hungary, Iceland, Ireland, Italy, Latvia, Lithuania, Luxemburg, Netherlands, New Zealand, Norway, Poland, Portugal, Rumania, Spain, Sweden, Switzerland, Union of South Africa, Union of Soviet Socialist Republics, Yugoslavia, and European possessions in the Far East (in conjunction with the Office of Far Eastern Affairs).

All other offices and divisions in the Department shall assure full participation by the Office of European Affairs and its component divisions as hereinafter provided for in the formulation and execution of policy affecting relations with the countries under the jurisdiction of this Office. . . .

The Office of European Affairs shall be composed of the following divisions which shall have primary responsibility for carrying out the functions of the Office in regard to relations with the countries indicated in each case.

1. *Division of British Commonwealth Affairs.* British Commonwealth of Nations and possessions, except India and possessions in Africa. . . .

2. *Division of Eastern European Affairs.* Union of Soviet Socialist Republics, Poland, and other areas of Eastern Europe. . . .

3. *Division of Central European Affairs.* Germany, Austria, Czechoslovakia. . . .

4. *Division of Southern European Affairs.* Albania, Bulgaria, Hungary, Italy, Rumania, San Marino, Yugoslavia. The Division shall also have responsibility for matters relating to the Vatican. . . .

5. *Division of Northern European Affairs.* Denmark, Finland, Iceland, Netherlands, Norway, Sweden, and possessions of these countries. . . .

6. *Division of Western European Affairs.* Andorra, Belgium, France, Liechtenstein, Luxemburg, Monaco, Portugal, Spain, Switzerland, and possessions of those countries. . . .

OFFICE OF SPECIAL POLITICAL AFFAIRS

There is hereby created an Office of Special Political Affairs which shall have responsibility, under the general direction of the Secretary and Under Secretary, for the initiation and coordination of policy and action in special matters of international political relations.

The Division of Political Studies is hereby abolished and its functions and responsibilities transferred to the Office of Special Political Affairs.

All other offices and divisions in the Department shall assure full participation by the Office of Special Political Affairs and its component divisions as hereinafter provided for in the formulation and execution of policy affecting the responsibilities of this Office. . . .

The Office of Special Political Affairs shall be composed of the following divisions, with functions and responsibilities as indicated.

1. *Division of International Security and Organization.*

The Division of International Security and Organization shall have responsibility for the initiation and coordination of policy and action in matters pertaining to: (*a*) general and regional international peace and security arrangements and other arrangements for organized international cooperation; (*b*) liaison with international organizations and agencies concerned with such matters; and (*c*) liaison within the scope of its responsibilities with the War and Navy Departments and such other departments and agencies of the Government as may be concerned. . . .

2. *Division of Territorial Studies.*

The Division of Territorial Studies shall have responsibility for: (*a*) analyzing and appraising developments and conditions in foreign countries arising out of the war and relating to post-war settlements of interest to the United States; (*b*) maintaining liaison in this field with other departments and agencies of the Government; and (*c*) formulating policy recommendations in regard to these matters in collaboration with other divisions in the Department. . . .

OFFICE OF FAR EASTERN AFFAIRS

There is hereby created an Office of Far Eastern Affairs which shall have responsibility, under the general direction of the Secretary and the Under Secretary, for the initiation and, in particular, the coordination of policy and action in regard to all aspects of relations with the following countries: China, Japan, and Thailand, and (in conjunction with the Office of European Affairs, and other interested offices and divisions) the possessions and territories of Occidental countries in the Far East and in the Pacific area. The Office also shall have charge of such matters as concern the Department in relation to American-controlled islands in the Pacific and, in particular, of such matters as concern the Department in relation to the Philippine Islands.

All other offices and divisions in the Department shall assure full participation of the Office of Far Eastern Affairs and its component divisions, as hereinafter provided for, in the formulation and execution of policy affecting relations with the countries under the jurisdiction of this Office. . . .

The Office of Far Eastern Affairs shall be composed of the following divisions which shall have primary responsibility for carrying out the functions of the Office in regard to relations with the countries indicated in each case.

1. *Division of Chinese Affairs.* China and adjacent territories. . . .

2. *Division of Japanese Affairs.* Japanese Empire, Japanese Mandates, and, in cooperation with the Division of Eastern European Affairs, matters relating to the Soviet Far East. . . .

3. *Division of Southwest Pacific Affairs.* Thailand, and, in cooperation with other interested offices and divisions, Indo-China, Malaya, British North Borneo, Netherlands East Indies, Portuguese Timor and British and French Island Possessions in the Pacific. . . .

4. *Division of Philippine Affairs.* Philippine Islands and other American-controlled islands of the Pacific.

The Office of Philippine Affairs is hereby abolished and its functions and responsibilities are hereby transferred to the Division of Philippine Affairs. . . .

OFFICE OF [NEAR] EASTERN AND AFRICAN AFFAIRS [1]

There is hereby created an Office of [Near] Eastern and African Affairs which shall have responsibility, under the general direction of the Secretary and the Under Secretary, for the initiation and, in particular, the coordination of policy and action in regard to all aspects of relations with the following countries: Afghanistan, Burma, Ceylon, Greece, India, Iran, Iraq, Lebanon, Palestine and Trans-Jordan, Saudi Arabia and other countries of the Arabian Peninsula, Syria, Turkey, Egypt, Ethiopia, Liberia and all colonies, protectorates, and mandated territories in Africa, excluding Algeria.

[1] Title changed to Office of Near Eastern and African Affairs and symbol to NEA by Departmental Order 1226 of February 17, 1944, effective February 15, *ibid.*, p. 194.

All other offices and divisions in the Department shall assure full participation by the Office of [Near] Eastern and African Affairs and its component divisions as hereinafter provided for in the formulation and execution of policy affecting relations with the countries under the jurisdiction of this Office. . . .

The Office of [Near] Eastern and African Affairs shall be composed of the following divisions which shall have primary responsibility for carrying out the functions of the Office in regard to relations with the countries indicated in each case.

1. *Division of Near Eastern Affairs.* Egypt, Greece, Iraq, Lebanon, Palestine and Trans-Jordan, Saudi Arabia and other countries of the Arabian Peninsula, Syria and Turkey. . . .

2. *Division of Middle Eastern Affairs.* Afghanistan, Burma, Ceylon, India and Iran. . . .

3. *Division of African Affairs.* Ethiopia, Liberia and all other territories in Africa. . . .

OFFICE OF DEPARTMENTAL ADMINISTRATION

There is hereby created the Office of Departmental Administration which shall have responsibility, under the general direction of the Assistant Secretary, Mr. Shaw, for all matters of administration and organization of the Department of State, including (a) budget development and control and fiscal management; (b) administrative and procedural planning; (c) personnel administration; (d) communications and records; (e) geographic and cartographic research; (f) protocol; (g) administrative aspects of international conferences and the fulfillment of international obligations; and (h) liaison with the Civil Service Commission, Bureau of the Budget, General Accounting Office, and such other agencies as may be concerned. . . .

The Office of Departmental Administration shall be composed of the following divisions, with functions and responsibilities as indicated.

1. *Division of Budget and Finance.*

The Division of Budget and Finance shall have responsibility in the following matters: (a) supervision of the budgetary and fiscal affairs of the Department, including the Foreign Service (subject to legal requirements), including the acquisition and distribution of funds, auditing, accounting, fiscal management, purchasing, and related activities; (b) formulation of budgetary and fiscal policies and controls in cooperation with staff and program offices and divisions; (c) liaison with Congressional Appropriations Committees, Bureau of the Budget, General Accounting Office, Treasury Department, Government Printing Office, and other departments and agencies on budgetary, fiscal or procurement matters.

The Office of Fiscal and Budget Affairs and the Division of Accounts are hereby abolished and their functions and responsibilities transferred to the Division of Budget and Finance. . . .

2. *Division of Administrative Management.*

The Division of Administrative Management shall have responsibility for all matters pertaining to: (*a*) general administration and organization; (*b*) effective administrative coordination between offices and divisions within the Department; (*c*) inter-office and inter-divisional definitions of responsibility; (*d*) the drafting and issuance of Departmental Orders and Administrative Instructions; (*e*) effective administrative relationships between the Department and other departments and agencies and inter-governmental agencies; and (*f*) such other duties as may be assigned by the Director of the Office and Departmental Administration. . . .

The Office of the Chief Clerk and Administrative Assistant is hereby abolished and, except as may hereafter be determined, its functions and responsibilities transferred to the Division of Administrative Management.

3. *Division of Departmental Personnel.*

The Division of Departmental Personnel shall have responsibility in the following matters: (*a*) assisting the Director of the Office of Departmental Administration in the formulation and effectuation of policies and practices which assure sound personnel management throughout the Department and proper utilization and training of employees of the Department; and (*b*) administration of the Civil Service rules and regulations and the execution of the provisions of the Classification, Retirement, and Employees' Compensation Acts, involving recruitment, classification, personnel relations, efficiency ratings, Selective Service, and related personnel functions; and liaison with the Civil Service Commission and such other departments and agencies as may be concerned. . . .

[*Personnel Utilization Section* [1]

There is hereby established within the Division of Departmental Personnel a Personnel Utilization Section which will have the responsibility for the development of a personnel utilization program in the Department. In this section will be centralized the responsibility for the continuous surveys in the personnel utilization program requiring careful planning, scheduling, and follow-through. These surveys are to be con-

[1] Departmental Order 1236, March 10, 1944, effective March 9, *ibid.*, p. 240.

ducted at the operating levels and will be designed to ascertain employee and supervisory attitudes, to promote maximum use of skills and abilities, and to analyze and evaluate personnel and administrative practices currently employed in the divisions. As a result of these surveys confidential reports with recommendations will be submitted to the Division Chiefs. Analyses of these reports will give direction to the attainment of better supervisory and employee effort, productivity and morale.

Recommendations as a result of the personnel utilization program shall be worked out between the Chief of Departmental Personnel and the Divisions concerned. Matters involving recommended major changes as a result of the surveys shall be dealt with by the Director of the Office of Departmental Administration.]

4. *Division of Communications and Records.*

The Division of Communications and Records shall have responsibility in the following matters: (*a*) dispatch and receipt of all telegraphic correspondence of the Department; encoding and decoding of messages exchanged in the conduct of foreign relations; (*b*) review of all outgoing correspondence; coordination of the correspondence for consideration and initialing before signing, and submission to the appropriate officers for signature; and furnishing of information concerning diplomatic precedence, accepted styles of correspondence, and related matters;[1] (*c*) classification, recording, distribution, and preservation of correspondence, and the conduct of research therein; (*d*) commenting upon, censoring and grading of reports and other information received from the Foreign Service on commercial, agricultural and economic matters, and the distribution of such information to the Departments of Commerce and Agriculture and to such other departments and agencies as may appropriately receive it; and (*e*) liaison, within the scope of its responsibilities, between the Department and, in particular, the Departments of Commerce and Agriculture, and such other departments and agencies as may be concerned.

The Office of Coordination and Review[1] is hereby abolished and its functions and responsibilities transferred to the Division of Communications and Records. . . .

[*Division of Coordination and Review.*

[1] There is hereby established a Division of Coordination and Review in the Office of Departmental Administration. . . .

Responsibility for the initiation and coordination of policy and action in matters pertaining to: (*a*) the review of all outgoing correspondence;

[1] Established as Division of Coordination and Review in the Office of Departmental Administration by Departmental Order 1221, February 10, 1944, effective February 8, *ibid.*, p. 184.

(b) the coordination of correspondence for consideration and initialing before signing, and submission to appropriate officers for signature; and (c) the furnishing of information concerning diplomatic precedents, accepted styles of correspondence, and related matters, is hereby transferred from the Division of Communications and Records (as set forth under 4(b), page 35, of Departmental Order No. 1218 of January 15, 1944) to the Division of Coordination and Review.] . . .

5. *Division of Geography and Cartography.*

The Division of Geography and Cartography shall have responsibility in the following matters: (a) the assembling, analysis, interpretation and presentation in the form of maps, charts, or reports, of data of a geographic, geodetic or cartographic nature on land and water areas throughout the world in connection with current and post-war considerations and negotiations concerning international or inter-regional relations involving questions of political, economic, historic or commercial geography; and the furnishing of related geographic information or advice; (b) determination or revision of population statistics in connection with the fixing of immigration quotas for specific areas or countries, when occasion arises; (c) maintenance of the Department's collection of maps, atlases and gazetteers; and (d) liaison with the United States Geological Survey, Coast and Geodetic Survey, Hydrographic Office, and other departments and agencies in matters of geography, geodesy and cartography.

The Office of the Geographer is hereby abolished and its functions and responsibilities transferred to the Division of Geography and Cartography. . . .

6. *Division of Protocol.*

The Protocol Division shall have responsibility in the following matters: (a) arranging for presentation to the President of ambassadors and ministers accredited to this Government; (b) correspondence concerning their acceptability to this Government and correspondence concerning the acceptability to foreign governments of like officers of the United States; (c) questions regarding rights and immunities in the United States of representatives of foreign governments; (d) arrangements for all ceremonials of a national or international character in the United States or participated in by the United States abroad; (e) arrangements for and protection of distinguished foreign visitors; (f) questions concerning customs and other courtesies abroad; (g) making arrangements for the casual or ceremonial visits of foreign naval vessels and of foreign military organizations to the United States and visits of the same character of United States naval vessels and military organizations abroad; (h) arrangements for the entry of troops of Allied Nations and their baggage, arriving at United States ports en route to training centers in this hemisphere and en route to foreign duty; (*i*) arrangements for release, as international courtesy, of certain war materials, ammunitions, models, et cetera, used in fulfilling contracts for Allied Nations; (*j*) matters with respect to visits of aliens to industrial factories and plants where war contracts are being executed; (*k*) questions affecting the Diplomatic Corps under the commodities rationing program; (*l*) matters of ceremonial in connection with the White House and the Department of State; (*m*) preparation of the Diplomatic List; (*n*) maintenance of a record of all officers and employees of foreign governments in the United States and its possessions; (*o*) questions of exemption of such foreign government officials from military training and service; (*p*) preparation of exequaturs, certificates of recognition, and notes granting provisional recognition to foreign consular officers in the United States, and correspondence relating thereto; (*q*) preparation of the List of Foreign Consular Offices in the United States; (*r*) questions concerning the medals and decorations conferred by foreign governments upon officers of the United States; and (*s*) preparation of communications from the President to the heads of foreign states. . . .

[The functions and responsibilities of the Protocol Division [1] shall henceforth be exercised under the direction of the Special Assistant to the Secretary and Chief of Protocol, Mr. George T. Summerlin.

These functions and responsibilities shall be subject to the fiscal control of the Assistant Secretary, Mr. Shaw, who shall also be consulted fully by Mr. Summerlin and his staff concerning other administrative aspects of protocol matters.

Mr. Stanley Woodward will continue as Chief of the Division of Protocol which shall report to the Secretary through the Special Assistant, Mr. Summerlin.] . . .

7. *Division of International Conferences.*

The Division of International Conferences shall have responsibility in the following matters: (*a*) planning and executing arrangements for participation by this Government in international organizations, conferences, congresses, expositions and conventions at home and abroad, including the organization of delegations to international conferences and collaboration in the preparation of instructions to such delegates; (*b*) fulfillment of the international obligations of the United States with respect to membership and expenditures for international treaty commissions, committees, bureaus, and other official organizations; (*c*) collaboration in carrying out agreements, resolutions and recommendations of official international meetings; (*d*) supervision of appropriations for

[1] Departmental Order 1243, March 21, 1944, effective March 20, *ibid.*, p. 292.

conference activities; and (e) liaison, within the scope of its functions and responsibilities, with permanent international organizations. . . .

BOARD OF FOREIGN SERVICE PERSONNEL, BOARD OF EXAMINERS FOR THE FOREIGN SERVICE, AND FOREIGN SERVICE OFFICERS TRAINING SCHOOL BOARD

The duties of the Board of Foreign Service Personnel, under Executive Order 5642 of June 8, 1931, are: to submit to the Secretary of State for approval, lists of Foreign Service officers prepared in accordance with law by the Division of Foreign Service Personnel in which they are graded in accordance with their relative efficiency in value to the Service; to recommend promotions in the Foreign Service and to furnish the Secretary of State with lists of Foreign Service officers who have demonstrated special capacity for promotion to the grade of minister; to submit to the Secretary of State, for approval and transmission to the President, the names of those officers and employees of the Department of State who are recommended for appointment by transfer to the position of Foreign Service officer; to submit to the Secretary of State the names of those Foreign Service officers who are recommended for designation as counselors of embassies or legations; to recommend the assignment of Foreign Service officers to posts and the transfer of such officers from one branch of the Service to the other; to consider controversies and delinquencies among the Service personnel and to recommend appropriate disciplinary action where required; to determine, after considering recommendations of the Division of Foreign Service Personnel, when the efficiency rating of an officer is unsatisfactory, in order that the Secretary of State may take appropriate action.

The duties of the Board of Examiners for the Foreign Service, under Executive Order 5642 of June 8, 1931, are to conduct the examinations of candidates for appointment to the Foreign Service.

The duties of the Foreign Service Officers Training School Board are to exercise direction over the Foreign Service Officers Training School.

The Assistant Secretary, Mr. Shaw, shall continue to serve as a Member and Chairman, and Assistant Secretaries, Mr. Berle and Mr. Acheson, shall continue to serve as Members, of these Boards.

OFFICE OF THE FOREIGN SERVICE [1]

There is hereby created an Office of Foreign Service Administration which shall have responsibility, under the general direction of the Assistant Secretary, Mr. Shaw, for all aspects of the administration of the Foreign Service of the United States. . . .

[1] Title changed from Office of Foreign Service Administration by Departmental Order 1273, May 6, 1944, *ibid.*, p. 488.

[*Planning Staff* [1]

In order to strengthen the Office of Foreign Service Administration to carry out effectively its responsibility under Departmental Order 1218, there is hereby created special staff [2] in the Office of Foreign Service Administration for the purpose of rendering staff assistance on programming and planning with a view toward continual adjustment and improvement in the over-all administration of the Foreign Service. This staff shall assist the Director, under the immediate direction of a Deputy Director for planning, in carrying out the following responsibilities of the Office of Foreign Service Administration:

(*a*) Reviewing and evaluating projects, programs, and surveys originating in the Department or in other departments and agencies and to be undertaken by the Foreign Service;

(*b*) Making recommendations as to the number and character of Foreign Service personnel required for the execution of such projects, programs, and surveys;

(*c*) Making recommendations for the maintenance of the efficiency of Foreign Service personnel responsible for implementing the programs originated by other departments and agencies;

(*d*) Making recommendations, after consultation with other Offices and Divisions of the Department, particularly the Office of Economic Affairs and the Office of Wartime Economic Affairs, for improving the services rendered by the Foreign Service to American agricultural, commercial, shipping, industrial, and other interests;

(*e*) Maintaining working liaison with the Office of Departmental Administration to assure effective coordination of Foreign Service and Departmental administrative policies and practices;

(*f*) Arranging, in collaboration with other Offices and Divisions of the Department, particularly the Office of Public Information, and with other departments and agencies, trade and other conferences and itineraries of returning Foreign Service and auxiliary Foreign Service officers; and

(*g*) Developing standards for the improvement of reporting from the missions and for the evaluation of Foreign Service reports. . . .]

The Office of Foreign Service Administration shall be composed of the following divisions, with functions and responsibilities as indicated.

1. *Division of Foreign Service Personnel.*

The Division of Foreign Service Personnel shall have responsibility in the following matters: (*a*) recruitment, appointment, and training of

[1] Departmental Order 1234, March 6, 1944, effective March 1, *ibid.*, p. 241.
[2] For a description of the Joint Survey Group, as organized by the Planning Staff, see article by Alan N. Steyne, *ibid.*, p. 589.

the classified, auxiliary, and clerical personnel of the Foreign Service of the United States; (b) maintenance of the required efficiency standards of the Service and custody of the confidential records of all personnel; (c) recommendation to the Board of Foreign Service Personnel of administrative action regarding assignments, transfers, promotions, demotions, disciplinary action, and separations from the Service, based upon conclusions drawn from an evaluation of efficiency reports, inspection reports, and official authentic information from chiefs of diplomatic missions and consular establishments, from competent officers of the Department, and from other informed sources; (d) preparation, under the supervision of the Chairman of the Board of Foreign Service Personnel, of biannual rating lists in which all Foreign Service officers are graded in accordance with their relative efficiency and value to the Service, and from which list recommendations for promotions are made in the order of ascertained merit within classes; (e) consultation with chiefs of missions, principal consular officers, and the heads of divisions and offices of the Department in regard to the proper functioning of field offices; (f) reception of officers and clerks of the Foreign Service on home leave of absence and discussion with them of their work and problems; (g) information with respect to entrance into the Foreign Service; (h) records of the Board of Examiners for the Foreign Service and matters connected with the holding of examinations. . . .

2. *Division of Foreign Service Administration.*

The Division of Foreign Service Administration shall have general responsibility for all matters concerning the administration of the Foreign Service of the United States except such matters as are or may be assigned to other divisions in the Office of Foreign Service Administration or to the Division of Budget and Finance in the Office of Departmental Administration. Specifically, the Division of Foreign Service Administration shall have responsibility in the following matters: (a) the drafting of regulations and the coordinating of instructions in regard thereto; (b) the preparation and justification of budget estimates for the Foreign Service; (c) the control of expenditures from the various appropriations for the Foreign Service; (d) analysis of cost of living at the various posts in connection with equitable distribution of allowances and clerical salaries; (e) the granting of leaves of absence; (f) the administration of the law governing the payment of annuities to retired Foreign Service officers and their widows; (g) the establishment, operation, or closing of diplomatic and consular offices; (h) the administration and maintenance of government property abroad, including supervision of contracts; (i) the furnishing of equipment and supplies with maintenance of inventories; (j) the operation of the diplomatic pouch service and the supervision of diplomatic couriers; (k) supervision of the despatch agencies and of matters relating to the designation of military, naval, and other attachés abroad; (*l*) recommendation of legislation affecting the Foreign Service and keeping the Foreign Service informed concerning new statutes; (*m*) maintenance and revision of the Foreign Service regulations; (*n*) handling of emergency wartime problems such as the evacuation of staffs and dependents from dangerous areas; (*o*) Selective Service; (*p*) general administrative assistance to missions sent abroad by other departments and agencies; (*q*) claims made by Foreign Service personnel for personal losses caused by the war; (*r*) the documentation of merchandise; (*s*) matters relating to the estates of American citizens dying abroad; (*t*) notarial services performed by consular officers; (*u*) reports of death of American citizens; (*v*) extradition cases handled in collaboration with the Office of the Legal Adviser; (*w*) services for the Veterans' Administration; (*x*) certain matters relating to diplomatic and consular rights and privileges.

The Foreign Service Buildings Office and the Office of Foreign Service Furnishings are hereby abolished,[1] and their functions and responsibilities are hereby vested in the Division of Foreign Service Administration, as follows: (*a*) the housing and furnishing of diplomatic and consular establishments abroad; (*b*) the protection and maintenance of properties owned or to be acquired by the United States for such purpose; and (*c*) programs of expenditures for the acquisition, construction, alteration, or furnishing of such properties. . . .

[2. *Creation of the Division of Foreign Buildings Operations.*[1] There is hereby established a Division of Foreign Buildings Operations in the Office of the Foreign Service to perform the functions of housing and furnishing diplomatic and consular establishments abroad as required by the Foreign Service Buildings Act of Congress, approved May 7, 1926.

3. *Organization and Functions of the Division of Foreign Buildings Operations.* Within the Division of Foreign Buildings Operations are three Sections, functioning under the direction of the Chief and Assistant Chief of the Division: Buildings Projects Section, Property Management Section, and Furniture and Furnishings Section.

4. *Building Projects Section.* The Building Projects Section is responsible for the analysis, approval and development of projects for the purchase of properties and construction of buildings for the housing of the diplomatic, consular and other agencies of the United States Government abroad. This includes such activities as:

(*a*) The maintenance of complete information and records concerning property purchases, initial construction, and major improvements of properties.

---

[1] Division of Foreign Buildings Operations established by Departmental Order 1273, May 6, 1944, effective same date, *ibid.*, p. 488.

(*b*) Analysis and determination of the needs for acquiring new sites and constructing or altering buildings for these purposes.

(*c*) Providing of architectural and engineering designs, plans and specifications for the housing of the Foreign Service of the United States.

(*d*) Analysis and determination upon projects submitted by the missions and other Government agencies for the purchase of property and buildings, for new construction or for major alterations and repairs work.

(*e*) Supervision and inspection of the construction, alterations, repairs and maintenance operations on Foreign Service buildings and properties.

5. *Property Management Section.* The Property Management Section is responsible for the supervision of the physical maintenance and use of Foreign Service real properties. This shall include such activities as:

(*a*) Maintenance of information and records regarding Government-owned diplomatic and consular establishments abroad.

(*b*) Formulation and execution of plans for the physical maintenance, and routine alteration and repair of such properties.

(*c*) Analysis and approval of requests for alterations and repairs on Foreign Service properties.

(*d*) Advice to the missions on property matters.

(*e*) Conduct of field inspections and surveys of Foreign Service properties.

6. *Furniture and Furnishings Section.* The Furniture and Furnishings Section is responsible for the initial purchase and replacement of articles of residential furniture and furnishings. This includes such activities as:

(*a*) Collection and maintenance of complete records and inventories on all Government-owned residential furniture, furnishings, and related articles of equipment in buildings owned or leased by the Department of State.

(*b*) Preparation of programs for the furnishing of buildings constructed, purchased or leased for Foreign Service residences abroad, and the maintenance of existing furnishings.

(*c*) Preparation of designs, layouts, specifications, contracts, and orders for such articles of furniture and furnishings.

(*d*) Analysis and approval of proposals from the field for purchase or maintenance of furniture and furnishings.

(*e*) Conduct of factory, warehouse, showroom, or field inspections necessary to carry out its responsibilities.

7. *Responsibilities of the Chief of Division.* (*a*) The Chief of the Division of Foreign Service Buildings is responsible for general supervision and direction of the work of the Division and the Sections. He shall act as Executive Secretary of the Foreign Service Buildings Commission, established by Act of Congress May 7, 1926, on which are represented the Secretary of State, the Secretary of the Treasury, the Secretary of

Commerce, the Chairman and the ranking minority member of the Committee on Foreign Relations of the Senate, and the Chairman and the ranking minority member of the Committee on Foreign Affairs of the House of Representatives. The Chief of the Division is responsible for the preparation and submission to the Commission of reports on the status and projects of the Foreign Service Buildings program, and of reports for the Congress of the United States, and for carrying out the directions of the Foreign Service Buildings Commission.

(b) The Chief of the Division is responsible for the preparation of budgetary programs for initial construction work, property acquisitions, alterations, repairs, maintenance, residential furnishings, and supervision of construction, and is responsible for the expenditure of funds appropriated for such purposes.

(c) The Chief of the Division shall work in close collaboration with the Division of Foreign Service Administration, and shall render to that Division, when required, technical services, including:

(1) Inspection and recommendation of properties for lease; recommendations on lessor-lessee obligations, rental rates and terms and layout requirements.

(2) Inspection of existing leased properties; reports and recommendations on contract party obligations and programs of improvement of existing facilities.

(d) The Chief, in carrying out the responsibilities of the Division, will also work closely with the Division of Foreign Service Personnel, the Division of Budget and Finance, the Legal Adviser, and the geographical Offices.

8. *Departmental Order Amended.* Departmental Order 1218 of January 15, 1944, page 42, is hereby amended, and the functions, personnel and records concerned with this work are hereby transferred to the Division of Foreign Buildings Operations. . . .]

OFFICE OF PUBLIC INFORMATION

For the purpose of assuring full understanding of the foreign policy and relations of the United States, within this country and in other countries, there is hereby created an Office of Public Information which shall have responsibility, under the general direction of the Assistant Secretary, Mr. Shaw, for the public information program and policy of the Department of State. The Office of Public Information shall be responsible for development and coordination of policy and execution of programs in all matters pertaining to: (a) the Department's relations with private groups and organizations interested in the formulation of foreign policy; (b) the collection and analysis of materials relating to public attitudes on current foreign policy questions; (c) relations with the domestic and foreign press, radio, and newsreels; (d) research on international affairs and publication of official documents; (e) the cultural exchange program of the United States Government with foreign countries, coordination of international cultural and educational programs of Federal agencies, and facilitating relationships between United States private, professional, scientific, and educational organizations and similar groups in other countries; and (f) liaison within the field of responsibilities with the Office of War Information, the Office of the Coordinator of Inter-American Affairs, and such other Government departments and agencies as may be concerned.

[*Postwar Information Policies* [1]

The Office of Public Information shall be responsible for coordinating the Department's interests in, and for participating with other Departments and agencies of the Government in the formulation of policies relative to post-war overseas informational activities.]

The Division of Cultural Relations is hereby abolished and its functions and responsibilities transferred to the Office of Public Information.

．　　．　　．　　．　　．　　．　　．

The Office of Public Information shall be composed of the following divisions, with functions and responsibilities as indicated:

1. *Division of Current Information.*

[Abolished by Departmental Order 1229, February 24, 1944; see Special Assistant to the Secretary — Press Relations, p. 57.]

[*Division of Public Liaison* [1]

There is hereby established in the Office of Public Information a Division of Public Liaison, which shall be responsible for:

(a) The Department's relations with private groups and organizations interested in the formulation of foreign policy;

(b) The collection and analysis of materials relating to public attitudes on foreign policy questions;

(c) Assistance to the officers of the Department in the public interpretation of foreign policy; and

(d) Handling of correspondence expressing public views on foreign policy (transfer of functions from the Division of Research and Publication). . . .]

2. *Division of Research and Publication.*

The Division of Research and Publication shall have responsibility in matters pertaining to: (a) conduct of historical research studies in inter-

[1] Departmental Order 1229, February 22, 1944, effective February 21, *ibid.*, p. 210.

national relations, including studies of the Department's wartime policies and operations; (b) preparation for the Secretary of State, the Under Secretary and other officers of the Department of historical information pertaining to current problems; (c) compilation of the *United States Statutes at Large, Foreign Relations of the United States, Treaties and Other International Acts of the United States of America, The Territorial Papers of the United States, The Department of State Bulletin,* special volumes on foreign policy, and other publications; (d) collection, compilation and maintenance of information pertaining to treaties and other international agreements, the performance of research and the furnishing of information and advice, other than of a legal character, with respect to the provisions of such existing or proposed instruments; procedural matters, including the preparation of full powers, ratifications, proclamations and protocols, and matters related to the signing, ratification, proclamation and registration of treaties and other international agreements (except with respect to proclamations of trade agreements, which shall be handled in the Division of Commercial Policy); and custody of the originals of treaties and other international agreements; (e) maintenance of the Department's Library; (f) editing of publications of the Department; codification of regulatory documents; maintenance of the Department's mailing lists; custody and control of the distribution of the Department's publications and processed material; and procurement for and allocation to various Government agencies of foreign publications received through American Foreign Service officers; and release of unpublished documents to private individuals; (g) handling of "public comment" correspondence in collaboration with other interested divisions; [1] (h) administration of the Printing and Binding Appropriation for the Department; and (i) liaison for the Department with The National Archives and the Government Printing Office, and representation of the Department on the National Historical Publications Commission and on the National Archives Council.

The Office of the Editor of the Treaties is hereby abolished and its functions and responsibilities transferred to the Division of Research and Publication. . . .

Treaty Section.[2]

[To meet the need for a repository of treaty information and a corps of technical experts on treaty matters a Treaty Section has been established in the Division of Research and Publication. Under Departmental Order 1218 of January 15, 1944 the Division of Research and Publication and the Legal Adviser's office are assigned certain responsibilities in

---

[1] The responsibility for handling this correspondence has been transferred to the Division of Public Liaison by Departmental Order 1229, February 22, 1944, *ibid.*

[2] *Ibid.,* p. 399.

carrying out the functions of the former Treaty Division. Those assigned the Division of Research and Publication are as follows: ". . . collection, compilation and maintenance of information pertaining to treaties and other international agreements, the performance of research and the furnishing of information and advice, other than of a legal character, with respect to the provisions of such existing or proposed instruments; procedural matters, including the preparation of full powers, ratifications, proclamations and protocols, and matters related to the signing, ratification, proclamation and registration of treaties and other international agreements (except with respect to proclamations of trade agreements, which shall be handled in the Division of Commercial Policy); and custody of the originals of treaties and other international agreements. . . ."

. . . .

It is intended that the Treaty Section shall become as useful as possible to officers of the Department who are concerned with the negotiation and drafting of treaties and other international agreements, particularly with reference to background information, substance, style, and procedure. Through the maintenance of authoritative up-to-date records on the status of existing treaties and other international agreements between the United States and other countries, as well as between foreign countries, through the publication of current treaty information in the Department of State *Bulletin*, and through making readily available in printed form true copies of treaties and other international agreements in the Treaty Series and Executive Agreement Series, there will be a continuance and expansion of services which the new Section may render in an informational capacity to the Department, other Government agencies, members of Congress, and the public in general.

The organization of the Treaty Section is planned not only with a view to meeting current requirements for authoritative information and expert assistance on treaty matters but also to meeting the demands that will be made of the Section in connection with the making of post-war settlements.]

3. *Motion Picture and Radio Division.*[1]

[The Motion Picture and Radio Division, Office of Public Information, shall act as liaison between the Department and other agencies in connection with the current operations of such agencies relating to overseas motion picture and radio programs, and dissemination abroad of printed features and other informational material which is not of an immediate news character.

The functions and responsibilities of the Informational Unit of the former Division of Current Information/Liaison are hereby transferred to the Motion Picture and Radio Division.

[1] Departmental Order 1229, February 22, 1944, effective February 21, *ibid.*, p. 209.

The functions and responsibilities on the matters mentioned above, which were formerly exercised by the Latin American Unit of the former Division of Current Information/Liaison, are hereby transferred to the Motion Picture and Radio Division.

The responsibility for liaison with the Coordinator of Inter-American Affairs concerning the operations of the Coordination Committees and the transmittal of communications between the Coordinator's Office and the Committees, previously exercised by the former Division of American Republics, is transferred to the Motion Picture and Radio Division. . . .]

4. *Science, Education and Art Division.*

The Science, Education and Art Division shall have responsibility in matters pertaining to international cooperation in the fields of science, education and art including (*a*) exchanges of materials in these fields, including books, periodicals, and other printed materials in the various fields of learning and art; (*b*) development of American libraries and schools in foreign countries; (*c*) administration of cultural institutes; (*d*) administration of programs for aiding special research and teaching projects in American colleges and universities abroad; (*e*) cooperation with American private agencies and associations participating in international cultural activities; and (*f*) liaison with the Office of Education, the Coordinator of Inter-American Affairs, and such other departments and agencies as may be concerned.

5. *Central Translating Division.*

The Central Translating Division shall have responsibility for all the translating and interpreting work of the Department of State, including (*a*) translation from English of certain publications of the Government for distribution to the other American Republics, and, in cooperation with other divisions and offices of the Department and the Interdepartmental Committee on Cooperation With the American Republics, the formulation and administration of programs for the distribution of such translations; (*b*) translation from English of addresses, as required, such translations to serve as the accepted official translated version of those public utterances; (*c*) review of material published in Spanish and Portuguese by other Government departments and agencies, and review of Spanish, Portuguese and French script for motion pictures and radio programs to be distributed through official channels in the other American Republics; (*d*) translation of communications addressed to the President by heads of foreign states and other material referred by the White House, and of diplomatic notes and miscellaneous material; and (*e*) the critical examination of foreign texts of draft treaties to which the United States is to be a party, with a view to the closest adjustment thereof to the English text.

The Central Translating Office and the Translating Bureau are hereby abolished and their functions transferred to the Central Translating Division. . . .

B. Records

(1) *Records of the Department of State. Statement of the Department, September 25, 1943* [1]

[Excerpt]

Since the establishment of The National Archives in Washington by the act of Congress approved June 19, 1934, the Department of State has been gradually transferring its non-current records to that agency in pursuance of a policy designed to assure the preservation of the records and to make them available for examination by historians, scholars in the field of international relations, and other interested persons. The bulk of the departmental records, as distinguished from diplomatic and consular post records, for the period 1789–1910 has already been transferred to the custody of The National Archives. The shipping to Washington of the records of embassies, legations, and consulates, which commenced in 1930, was accelerated by the inauguration in 1938 of a program looking to the ultimate transfer to The National Archives of all diplomatic and consular post records for the period prior to August 15, 1912.

The year 1910 (1912 for post records) was selected as a convenient dividing point for the transfer of records to The National Archives because at that time the Department's system of filing was reorganized on the principle of the Dewey decimal library-classification system. Before 1906 the departmental records were, generally speaking, bound in strict chronological order according to country (as Despatches, Great Britain), post (as Consular Despatches, Montevideo), source (as Notes from the Mexican Legation), or subject matter (as Credences). From 1906 to 1910 the records were filed according to subject matter only. In transferring records to The National Archives, the Department has not, however, made the years 1910 and 1912 a rigid line of demarcation. A few groups of departmental records as well as some post records covering more recent years have been sent to The National Archives as permanent accessions, *e.g.*, the signed original treaties of the United States for the period 1778–1932 and the records of the Legation at Tirana, Albania, for the period 1903–39.

The departmental and post records for the period 1789–1910 may be examined freely at The National Archives, with a few exceptions, subject to regulations prescribed by that agency. The records of the Department for the period 1910 to December 31, 1920 which are filed in the Department of State, as well as those departmental and post records for the same period which are in the custody of The National Archives, may be examined upon authorization by the Chief of the Division of Research and Publication of the Department. Because of the wartime demands upon the personnel of the Department as well as the constant use which is being made of the current files, it is not practicable at present to make the records of the Department of State for the period after December 31, 1920 available for examination by persons other than officers of the Government.

[1] *Ibid.*, IX, p. 209.

C. Appropriations

(1) Comparative Statement of State Department Appropriations for 1944 and 1945 [1]

TITLE OF APPROPRIATION	APPROPRIATIONS FOR 1945	APPROPRIATIONS FOR 1944	(+) INCREASE (−) DECREASE FOR 1945
Department Proper . . .	$11,268,000.00	$ 8,001,600.00	$+3,266,400.00
Foreign Service (exclusive of the Emergency Fund) . .	27,104,500.00	25,666,600.00	+1,437,900.00
Emergency Fund	1,500,000.00	12,000,000.00	−10,500,000.00
Foreign Service Buildings .	220,000.00	144,000.00	+ 76,000.00
International Obligations .	3,596,000.00	2,868,808.00	+ 727,192.00
Cooperation with the American Republics	3,450,000.00	4,500,000.00	− 1,050,000.00
Claims Approved		8,666.19	− 8,666.19
TOTALS	$47,138,500.00	$53,189,674.19	$−6,051,174.19

D. Diplomatic Representation

(1) Changes in Foreign Service Posts, July 1, 1943–August 15, 1944 [2]

OFFICES CLOSED

Post	Rank [3]	Date
Bahia Blanca, Argentina	VC	June 30, 1944
Bone, Algeria	VC	January 11, 1944
Brighton, Trinidad	CA	May 13, 1944
Cayenne, French Guiana	C	July 10, 1944
Ciudad Bolivar, Venezuela	VC	April 26, 1944
Corumba, Brazil	VC	March 31, 1944
Helsinki, Finland	L	June 30, 1944
Kweilin, China	C	June 25, 1944
(Reopened prior to August 12, 1944)		
Manta, Ecuador	VC	April 29, 1944
Matanzas, Cuba	C	July 31, 1943
Melbourne	CG	June, 1944
Office maintained in connection with representation to the Government of the Netherlands East Indies. The regular Melbourne Consulate remains open.		
Nueva Gerona, Cuba	C	July 8, 1944
Osorno, Chile	VC	March 31, 1944
St. Lucia, British West Indies	C	November 20, 1943
St. Pierre — Miquelon	C	December 15, 1943
São Vicente, Cape Verde Islands	VC	December 12, 1943

[1] Compiled by the Department of State as of June 30, 1944, subject to change in accordance with subsequent acts of Congress.   [2] Compiled by the Department of State
[3] Key to symbols used:

C — Consulate	CG — Consulate General	M — Mission
CA — Consulate Agency	E — Embassy	MD — Diplomatic Mission
	L — Legation	VC — Vice Consulate

OFFICES ESTABLISHED

Post	Rank	Date
Adana, Turkey	VC	July 17, 1944
Addis Ababa, Ethiopia	L	August 31, 1943
Almirante, Panama	CA	September 15, 1943
Angra do Heroismo, Azores	MD	February 15, 1944
Athens and Belgrade		December 2, 1943
(E) Separate office established at Cairo with representation to the Governments of Greece and Yugoslavia.		
Gibraltar	C	July 25, 1944
Grenada, British West Indies	C	April 6, 1944
Halsingborg, Sweden	CA	April 24, 1944
Hull, England	C	April 24, 1944
Kweilin, China	C	Reopened prior to
(Reported closed June 25, 1944 and subsequently reopened).		August 12, 1944
Melilla, Spanish North Africa	C	August 16, 1943
Mendoza, Argentina	VC	July 14, 1943
Naples, Italy	CG	February 19, 1944
Palermo, Italy	C	November 21, 1943
Puerto Armuelles, Panama	CA	September 15, 1943
San Sebastian, Spain	C	April 5, 1944
Southampton, England	C	April 30, 1944
Tela, Honduras	CA	July 1, 1943

CHANGE IN RANK

Post	Old Rank	New Rank	Date
Algiers, Algeria	CG	M	November 11, 1943
Caracas, Venezuela	C`	CG	July 1, 1944
Curaçao, West Indies	C	CG	August 15, 1944
Dakar, French West Africa	M	CG	July 1, 1944
Fortaleza, Brazil	VC	C	July 1, 1943
Leopoldville, Belgian Congo	C	CG	July 1, 1944
Lisbon, Portugal	L	E	June 20, 1944
Ottawa, Canada	L	E	November 19, 1943
Rosario, Argentina	VC	C	September 1, 1943

Combination of Offices

Chungking, China   E

A consular section was established and the Mission combined on May 1, 1944.

3. AGENCIES OTHER THAN THE DEPARTMENT OF STATE

From the beginning of the tremendous proliferation of Federal administrative mechanisms which has occurred since the summer of 1940, the problem of overall coordination of selected activities performed by independent agencies has been particularly difficult in the field of foreign economic relations. In June 1943, the following agencies, among others, were engaged in foreign economic activities related to the prosecution of the war or the handling of situations resulting directly therefrom: the State, Treasury, Commerce, War and Navy Departments, the Office of Lend-Lease Administration, the Office of Foreign Relief and Rehabilitation Operations, the Board of Economic Warfare, the War Shipping Board, the War Production Board, the Reconstruction Finance Corporation and a number of specially constituted corporations, such as the Rubber Development Corporation and the Petroleum Reserves Corporation.

The need of more effective coordination of civilian agencies operating in liberated areas was immediately apparent as Allied military forces pressed forward with the progressive occupation and liberation of areas hitherto under Axis control, first in North Africa, and then in Sicily and Italy. In his letter of June 3, 1943, to Secretary Hull, the President stressed the importance of proper coordination and set forth the general principles which should be applied.[1] The President specifically recognized the Secretary of State as having the responsibility for seeing that this coordination was achieved. By Departmental Order 1166, dated June 24, 1943, an Office of Foreign Economic Coordination was established in the Department.[2]

This, however, left unresolved difficulties arising from conflicts between agencies concerned more broadly with the foreign economic relations of the United States. The conflict between the Secretary of Commerce and the Vice-President, in his capacity as Chairman of the Board of Economic Warfare, which assumed the form of "acrimonious public debate"[3] brought the whole matter to a head and led to the establishment in the Office for Emergency Management, by Executive Order 9361, of the Office of Economic Warfare to which were transferred the functions and duties of the Board of Economic Warfare, and those of the United States Commercial Company, the Rubber Development Corporation, the Petroleum Reserves Corporation and the Export-Import Bank of Washington together with the functions and duties of the Reconstruction Finance Corporation and those of the Secretary of Commerce with respect to them.

This order, however, like the State Department's Departmental Order of June 24, 1943, dealt with only a part of the larger problem. It still remained necessary to coordinate more fully the activities of the new Office of Economic Warfare, the State Department's Office of Foreign Economic Coordination, the Office of Lend-Lease Administration, and the Office of Foreign Relief and Rehabilitation Operations. Executive Order 9380 was the answer. It concentrated in the newly-erected Foreign Economic Administration responsibility for the conduct of foreign economic operations hitherto performed by agencies referred to above while leaving the definition of policy to the Department of State.

(1) *Executive Order 9380 Establishing the Foreign Economic Administration, September 25, 1943* [4]

By virtue of the authority vested in me by the Constitution and the statutes of the United States, as President of the United States and Commander-in-Chief of the Army and Navy, and in order to unify and consolidate governmental activities relating to foreign economic affairs, it is hereby ordered as follows:

1. There is established in the Office for Emergency Management of the Executive Office of the President the Foreign Economic Administra-

---

[1] *Documents, V, 1942–43*, p. 675.   [2] *Ibid.*, p. 681.
[3] Letter from the President to the Honorable Henry A. Wallace and the Honorable Jesse H. Jones, July 15, 1943, *New York Times*, July 16, 1943.
[4] 8 *Fed. Reg.*, p. 13081; Department of State, *Bulletin*, IX, p. 205.

tion (hereinafter referred to as the Administration), at the head of which shall be an Administrator.

2. The Office of Lend-Lease Administration, the Office of Foreign Relief and Rehabilitation Operations, the Office of Economic Warfare (together with the corporations, agencies, and functions transferred thereto by Executive Order No. 9361 of July 15, 1943), the Office of Foreign Economic Coordination (except such functions and personnel thereof as the Director of the Budget shall determine are not concerned with foreign economic operations) and their respective functions, powers, and duties are transferred to and consolidated in the Administration.

3. The Administrator may establish such offices, bureaus, or divisions in the Administration as may be necessary to carry out the provisions of this order, and may assign to them such of the functions and duties of the offices, agencies and corporations consolidated by this order as he may deem desirable in the interest of efficient administration.

4. The powers and functions of the Administration shall be exercised in conformity with the foreign policy of the United States as defined by the Secretary of State. As soon as military operations permit, the Administration shall assume responsibility for and control of all activities of the United States Government in liberated areas with respect to supplying the requirements of and procuring materials in such areas.

5. All the personnel, property, records, funds (including all unexpended balances of appropriations, allocations, or other funds now available), contracts, assets, liabilities, and capital stock (including shares of stock) of the offices, agencies and corporations consolidated by paragraph 2 of this order are transferred to the Administration for use in connection with the exercise and performance of its functions, powers, and duties. In the case of capital stock (including shares of stock), the transfer shall be to such agency, corporation, office, officer or person as the Administrator shall designate. The Administrator is authorized to employ such personnel as may be necessary in the performance of the functions of the Administration and in order to carry out the purposes of this order.

6. No part of any funds appropriated or made available under Public Law 139, approved July 12, 1943, shall hereafter be used directly or indirectly by the Administrator for the procurement of services, supplies, or equipment outside the United States except for the purpose of executing general economic programs or policies formally approved by a majority of the War Mobilization Committee in writing filed with the Secretary of State prior to any such expenditure.

7. All prior Executive Orders in so far as they are in conflict herewith are amended accordingly. This order shall take effect upon the taking of office by the Administrator, except that the agencies and offices consolidated by paragraph 2 hereof shall continue to exercise their respective functions pending any contrary determination by the Administrator.

(2) *Executive Committee on Economic Foreign Policy. Statement of the Department of State, June 3, 1944* [1]

Creation and Authority. — The Executive Committee on Economic Foreign Policy was created by letter of April 5, 1944 from the President to the Secretary of State and by similar letters to the heads of the other interested Departments and agencies listed below.

Purpose. — It is the function of the Committee to examine problems and developments affecting the economic foreign policy of the United States and to formulate recommendations in regard thereto for the consideration of the Secretary of State and, in appropriate cases, of the President. Major interdepartmental committees concerned with general economic affairs including those established in the Department of State are, in accordance with the letter from the President, expected to be appropriately geared into this Committee.

Organization. — The Committee consists of representatives of the Departments of State, the Treasury, Agriculture, Commerce, and Labor, the United States Tariff Commission, and the Foreign Economic Administration. Representatives of other departments and agencies are invited to participate in this Committee or its subcommittees when matters of special interest to them are under consideration. The chairman of the Committee is an officer of the Department of State designated by the Secretary of State.[2]

Activities. — The Committee meets weekly, or more often if necessary. The Committee studies and advises on questions of economic foreign policy. It considers also problems of various Departments and agencies of the Government dealing with domestic matters which have an important bearing on such policy.

Members

Department of State	Dean Acheson, chairman
Department of State	Harry C. Hawkins, vice chairman
Department of the Treasury	Harry D. White
Department of Agriculture	Leslie A. Wheeler
Department of Commerce	Amos E. Taylor
Department of Labor	A. F. Hinrichs
United States Tariff Commission	Oscar B. Ryder
Foreign Economic Administration	Lauchlin Currie

4. INTERNATIONAL CONFERENCES IN WHICH THE UNITED STATES GOVERNMENT PARTICIPATED, JULY 1, 1943–JUNE 30, 1944 [3]

Conference of Ministers and Directors of Public Education, Panamá, Panama. — September 27–October 4, 1943

Inter-American Demographic Congress, Mexico, D. F., Mexico. — October 12–21, 1943

[1] *Ibid.*, X, p. 511.

[2] By Departmental Designation 29, issued June 30, 1944, effective same date, Mr. Dean Acheson was designated chairman, Mr. Harry C. Hawkins, vice chairman and Mr. Robert M. Carr as Executive Secretary, *ibid.*, XI, p. 54.

[3] Compiled by Department of State, Division of International Conferences; for the conferences at Moscow, Cairo and Tehran, see this volume, p. 226–38.

First Session of the Council of the United Nations Relief and Rehabilitation Administration, Atlantic City, New Jersey. — November 10–December 1, 1943

Ninety-first Session of the Governing Body of the International Labor Office, London, England. — December 16–20, 1943

Fourth American Congress of Teachers, Santiago, Chile. — December 26–31, 1943

International Whaling Conference, London, England. — January 4, 13, 19, 31, 1944

Conference of the Ministers of Education of the Allied Governments, London, England. — Convened April 5, 1944

Twenty-sixth Session of the International Labor Conference, Philadelphia, Pennsylvania. — April 20–May 12, 1944

Ninety-second Session of the Governing Body of the International Labor Office, Philadelphia, Pennsylvania. — (Meeting concurrently with the Twenty-sixth Session of the International Labor Conference)

Fifth Pan American Conference of National Directors of Health, Washington, D. C. — April 24–29, 1944

First Pan American Congress on Criminology, Santiago, Chile. — May 29–June 3, 1944

CHAPTER III

DEFENSE AND PROSECUTION OF THE WAR

1. REQUIREMENTS AND COSTS OF TOTAL WAR

(1) *Message of the President (Roosevelt) to the Congress of the United States, September 17, 1943* [1]

[Excerpt]

TO THE CONGRESS OF THE UNITED STATES:

. . . .

The Congress has reconvened at a time when we are in the midst of the Third War Loan Drive seeking to raise a sum unparalleled in history — fifteen billion dollars. This is a dramatic example of the scale on which this war still has to be fought, and presents some idea of how difficult and costly the responsible leaders of this government believe the war will be.

Nothing we can do will be more costly in lives than to adopt the attitude that the war has been won — or nearly won. That would mean a let-down in the great tempo of production which we have reached, and would mean that our men who are now fighting all over the world will not have that overwhelming superiority of power which has dealt so much death and destruction to the enemy and at the same time has saved so many American lives.

That is why I have always maintained that there is no such separate entity as the "home front." Every day lost in turning out an airplane or a ship at home will have its direct effect upon the men now battling up the leg of Italy or in the jungles of the Southwest Pacific or in the clouds over China.

There have been complaints from some sources about the way this production and other domestic activities have been carried on. Some of these complaints of course are justified. On the other hand some of them come from selfish people who merely do not like to give up some of their pleasures, or a part of their butter or meat or milk.

[1] From the Office of the Secretary to the President; *Congressional Record*, vol. 89, p. 7667 (daily edition, September 17, 1943).

Fair-minded citizens, however, will realize that although mistakes have been made, the job that has been done in converting peacetime America to a wartime basis has been a great job and a successful one, of which all our people have good reason to be proud.

It would be nothing short of a miracle if this unprecedented job of transforming a peace-loving, unprepared industrial America into a fighting and production machine had been accomplished without some mistakes being made and some people being given cause for complaint.

The Congress is well aware of the magnitude of the undertaking, and of the many gigantic problems involved. For the Congress has been actively involved in helping to work out the solutions to these un-precedented problems.

A few facts will show how vast an enterprise this war has been — and how we are constantly increasing the tempo of our production.

The total amount spent on the war from May 1940 to date is $128,-123,000,000. The bill is now running at the rate of $250,000,000 per day.

Up to September 1, 1943, among the more important items produced and delivered since the armament program started in May 1940 are the following:

Airplanes	123,000
Airplane engines	349,000
Tanks	53,000
Artillery weapons	93,000
Small arms (rifles, carbines, machine guns, etc.)	9,500,000
Small arms ammunition	25,942,000,000 rounds
Trucks	1,233,000

In most instances more than half of the above total delivered to date was produced during the first eight months of 1943:

Airplanes	52,000
Tanks	23,000
Artillery weapons	40,600
Small arms (rifles, carbines, machine guns, etc.)	4,638,000
Small arms ammunition	13,339,000,000 rounds

The number of fighting ships and auxiliaries of all kinds completed since May 1940 is 2,380 and 13,000 landing vessels.

In the two and a half years between January 1, 1941 and July 1, 1943, the power plants built for installation in Navy vessels had a horsepower equal to all the horsepower of all hydroelectric plants in the United States in January 1941.

The completions of Navy ships during the last six months were equal to completions in the entire year of 1942.

We have cut down the time required to build submarines by almost 50 per cent.

The anti-aircraft and double purpose guns produced by the Navy since the defense program started in May 1940, if fired all together, would throw 4,600 tons of projectiles per minute against the enemy.

The output of under-water ordnance (torpedoes, mines and depth charges) during the first half of 1943 was equal to the total production of 1942.

During the month of August 1943, we produced almost as many torpedoes as during all of World War I.

Anyone who has had to build a single factory, tool it up, get the necessary help, set up an assembly line, produce and ship the product, will have some idea of what that amount of production has meant.

We have had to raise and equip armed forces approaching ten million men. Simultaneously, in spite of this drain on our manpower, we have had to find millions more men and millions of women to operate our war factories, arsenals, shipyards, essential civilian industries — and the farms and mines of America.

There have been the problems of increasing greatly the output of our natural resources — not only for our own Army and Navy and for our civilians at home, but also for our Allies and our own forces all over the world.

Since the outbreak of war in Europe, we have increased our output of petroleum by 66 per cent. We have stepped up our bituminous coal production by 40 per cent; chemicals by 300 per cent; iron ore by 125 per cent; hydroelectric power by 79 per cent; and steel by 106 per cent.

There were the problems of raising and distributing more food than ever before in our history — for our armed services, for our own people, and to help feed our Allies.

There was the formidable problem of establishing a rationing system of the necessities of life which would be fair to all of our people.

There was the difficulty of keeping prices from skyrocketing and fighting off the serious spectre of inflation.

There was the problem of transporting millions of men and hundreds of millions of tons of weapons and supplies all over our own country and also to all corners of the world. This necessitated the largest railroad and shipping operations in all history.

There were the problems involved in our vast purchases in foreign countries; in our control of foreign funds, located in this country; in our custody of alien property; in our occupation of liberated areas. There were new problems of communications, of censorship, of war information.

There was the problem of maintaining proper management-labor relations; of fair treatment and just compensation to our millions of war workers; of avoiding strikes; of preventing the exploitation of workers or natural resources by those who would seek to become war profiteers and war millionaires.

There were the problems of civilian defense, of lend-lease, of sub-contracting war contracts to smaller businesses, of building up stock piles of strategic material whose normal sources have been seized by the enemy — such as rubber and tin.

There was the problem of providing housing for millions of new war workers all over the country.

And touching all of these, there was the great problem of raising the money to pay for all of them.

.   .   .   .

FRANKLIN D. ROOSEVELT

(2) *Statement of the Director of the Bureau of the Budget, August 2, 1944* [1]

[Excerpts]

THE WAR PROGRAM

THE PROGRAM FOR THE FISCAL YEAR 1945

For the last four critical years and the one ahead the Congress has appropriated and authorized a defense and war program of 393 billion dollars. Of this amount, 294 billion dollars, or about three-fourths, had been translated into war contracts and other obligations and commitments by June 30, the end of the fiscal year 1944.

Actual cash expenditures June 30, 1944, amounted to 200 billion dollars for pay and subsistence of the armed forces, for building and equipping hundreds of war plants and shipyards, for acquisition of 200,000 planes, for construction of hundreds of warships and thousands of transports and other water craft, and for the manufacture of the many other weapons needed in total and global war. The appropriations, obligations, and expenditures for the war program are summarized in Table 1, for general and special accounts and Government corporations.

For the fiscal year 1945 the Congress has made available for war obligations in general and special accounts 94.3 billion dollars. Some contract authorizations included in this amount are intended for obligation in subsequent years.

.   .   .   .

New war appropriations of 54.2 billion dollars enacted for the fiscal year 1945 by the Congress are about two billion dollars less than the

[1] From the Bureau of the Budget.

President had recommended. Most of this difference is explained by the fact that the Congress granted a contract authorization in connection with the Navy aviation program instead of a recommended appropriation. In some cases changes in strategic plans adopted after transmission of the Presidential recommendations permitted reductions. Whether all appropriations and authorizations made available by the Congress will be actually needed for obligation during this fiscal year depends, of course, on the development of the war.

ESTIMATED EXPENDITURES FOR THE FISCAL YEAR 1945

During the fiscal year that ended June 30, 1944, actual cash expenditures for war, including net outlays of Government corporations, were 89.7 billion dollars, or 2.5 per cent below the 92-billion-dollar estimate in the President's budget message of January, 1944. For the fiscal year 1945 cash expenditures were estimated last January at 90 billion dollars, and the total of that estimate is not changed at the present time. Adjustments within the total have been made, however, by increasing slightly the War Department figure, reducing the estimated net war outlays of Government corporations, and adding an estimated expenditure for the United Nations Relief and Rehabilitation Administration.

War expenditure estimates of previous years have been based on the assumption that practically all available resources were to be used for meeting war needs, giving second call to civilian requirements. This year's estimates are influenced by the hope that the liberation of Europe may be accomplished before the end of the fiscal year 1945, while the Japanese phase of the war is assumed to continue all through the fiscal year and beyond.

The end of hostilities in Europe should enable us to cut back many war contracts, but cash payments will decline only with a considerable time lag. Particularly, expenditures for pay and subsistence, including mustering-out pay, will remain at a high level all through the fiscal year.

War expenditures in recent months have been running at an annual rate of about 93 billion dollars; thus a 90-billion-dollar estimate for the whole fiscal year implies a decline in war expenditures during the later part of the fiscal year. These estimates are, of course, of a highly tentative character and depend entirely on the assumptions made with respect to the course of the war.

If victory in Europe should be delayed, the production of munitions will be stepped up to whatever may be needed. If German resistance should collapse earlier than assumed, expenditures for the current fiscal year may be somewhat below the 90-billion-dollar estimate.

.   .   .   .

(3) *Comparative Statement of Receipts and Expenditures for the Fiscal Years 1945, 1944 and 1943* [1]

(In millions)

CLASSIFICATION	1945		1944 ACTUAL	1943 ACTUAL
	REVISED ESTIMATES JULY 1944	BUDGET ESTIMATES JAN. 1944		
GENERAL AND SPECIAL ACCOUNTS				
RECEIPTS:				
Direct taxes on individuals . . .	$18,935	$18,113	$20,290	$6,952
Direct taxes on corporations* . . .	16,588	15,404	15,194	9,916
Excise taxes	5,637	4,251	4,462	3,777
Employment taxes . . -. . .	2,081	3,182	1,751	1,508
Customs	362	438	431	324
Miscellaneous receipts	3,643	2,037	3,280	907
Total receipts*	$47,246	$43,425	$45,408	$23,384
Deduct:				
Net appropriations for Federal old-age and survivors insurance trust fund	1,583	2,656	1,259	1,103
Net receipts*	$45,663	$40,769	$44,149	$22,281
EXPENDITURES:				
War activities†				
War Department	$47,900	$47,600	$49,249	$42,294
Navy Department	28,500	28,500	26,537	20,888
U. S. Maritime Commission . .	4,700	4,700	3,812	2,777
War Shipping Administration . .	1,900	1,893	1,922	1,117
Other	5,900	5,507	5,518	5,033
Total war activities	$88,900	$88,200	$87,038	$72,109
Interest on the public debt . . .	$3,750	$3,750	$2,609	$1,808
Other activities:				
Legislative establishment . . .	29	30	29	27
The Judiciary	13	14	13	12
Executive Office of the President	3	3	2	2
Civil departments and agencies‡ .	1,441	1,473	1,338	1,335
Post Office Department (General Fund)	—	—	§ − 22	9
District of Columbia (Federal contribution)	6	6	6	6

* Includes the following estimated amounts for excess-profits taxes refundable in the post-war period: 1945 revised estimates, $810 million; 1945 Budget estimates, $624 million; 1944, $682 million; 1943, $220 million.

† Expenditures from Lend-Lease (Defense Aid) appropriations are included under the various agencies.

‡ Includes general public works program.

§ A minus item due to return $29 million of excess advances in prior years to meet anticipated deficiencies.

[1] From the Bureau of the Budget.

| CLASSIFICATION | 1945 | | 1944 ACTUAL | 1943 ACTUAL |
	REVISED ESTIMATES JULY 1944	BUDGET ESTIMATES JAN. 1944		
EXPENDITURES — *Continued*:				
Veterans' pensions and benefits .	$1,252	$1,252	$724	$600
Aids to agriculture	499	468	765	1,037
Aids to youth	——	——		18
Social-security program	481	485	511	498
Work relief	17	2	23	317
Refunds	¶1,507	¶1,799	¶267	79
Retirement funds	506	472	440	322
Total other activities . . .	$5,754	$6,004	$4,096	$4,262
Total expenditures, general and special accounts, excluding statutory public debt retirement	$98.404	$97,954	$93,743	$78,179
Statutory public debt retirement . .	——	——	——	3
Total expenditures	$98,404	$97,954	$93,743	$78,182
Excess of expenditures, general and special accounts . .	$52,741	$57,185	$49,594	$55,901
GOVERNMENT CORPORATIONS AND CREDIT AGENCIES				
NET EXPENDITURES (from checking accounts):				
War activities	$1,100	$1,800	$2,682	$2,976
Redemption of obligations in the market	1,450	1,346	2,873	694
Other activities	ª475	15	ª1,152	ª1,476
Net expenditures	$2,075	$3,161	$4,403	$2,194
TRUST ACCOUNTS				
RECEIPTS:				
Transfers from general and special accounts	$1,021	$987	$556	$435
Net appropriation from general account receipts	1,583	2,656	1,260	1,103
Other receipts	3,012	3,104	3,237	2,388
Total receipts	$5,616	$6,747	$5,053	$3,926
EXPENDITURES:				
Investments in U. S. obligations . .	$4,634	$5,778	$4,129	$3,016
Other expenditures	949	922	572	577
Total expenditures	$5,583	$6,700	$4,701	$3,593
Excess of receipts over expenditures	$33	$47	$352	$333

¶ Includes transfers to public debt accounts for excess-profits tax refund bonds issued.

ª Excess of receipts over expenditures.

CLASSIFICATION	1945		1944 ACTUAL	1943 ACTUAL
	REVISED ESTIMATES JULY 1944	BUDGET ESTIMATES JAN. 1944		
THE PUBLIC DEBT				
Public debt at beginning of year . .	$201,003	$197,600	$136,696	$72,422
Net increase in public debt during year:				
General and special accounts, excess of expenditures over receipts . .	$52,741	$57,185	$49,594	$55,901
Government corporations and agencies, net expenditures.	2,075	3,161	4,403	2,194
Trust accounts, excess of receipts over expenditures	− 33	− 47	− 352	− 333
Statutory public debt retirement .	——	——	——	− 3
Change in Treasury balance . . .	− 4,500	101	10,662	6,515
Net increase in public debt .	$50,283	$60,400	$64,307	$64,274
Public debt at end of year	$251,286	$258,000	$201,003	$136,696

2. ADMINISTRATIVE POWERS AND ORGANIZATION

[See *Documents, IV, 1941–42*, p. 126; *V, 1942–43*, p. 81.]

Generally speaking, the machinery of war administration had become stabilized by the beginning of the period under review. In the domestic field the only important change occurred in connection with the administration of the Selective Service and Training Act. By Executive Order of December 5, 1942, the administration of the Selective Service Act was made subject to the supervision and direction of the Chairman of the War Manpower Commission.[1] The Act of December 5, 1943, amending the Selective Service and Training Act, authorized the President to delegate to "the Director of Selective Service only" any authority vested in him under the Act.[2]

The important changes that were made in the period under review were in the field of foreign relations. In particular, there was a substantial and thorough overhauling of the administrative organization of the Department of State under the terms of the Department's Administrative Order of January 15, 1944.[3] Also, there were important changes made in the administrative machinery for handling our foreign economic relations, particularly in connection with the prosecution of the war and dealing with problems arising immediately from the war. For a brief account of these changes with texts of relevant documents, see p. 66–73, 137–42.

[1] Executive Order 9279, 7 *Fed. Reg.*, p. 10177; *Documents, V, 1942–43*, p. 92.
[2] Public Law 197, 78th Cong., sec. 3; see this volume, p. 113.
[3] See this volume, p. 55.

3. MILITARY AND NAVAL POLICIES AND ESTABLISHMENTS

A. Financial Statistics

(1) *Appropriations and Contract Authorizations by Appropriation Acts for the Navy Department and War Department, Military Activities for the Fiscal Years 1943, 1944 and 1945, as of July 31, 1944* [1]

NAVY DEPARTMENT

APPROPRIATING ACTS AND DATE APPROVED	BUREAU OF AERONAUTICS	OTHER	TOTAL
Fiscal Year 1943			
Public Law 441, Feb. 27, 1942:			
Appropriations:			
Annual	$1,436,418,585	$12,608,921,389	$14,045,339,974
Permanent — (revised) . .	——	260,958	260,958
Contract authorizations . . .	——	500,000,000	500,000,000
Transferred to Coast Guard, pursuant to Executive Order 9083, Feb. 28, 1942 from:			
U. S. Maritime Commission:			
State Marine Schools . .	——	+ 360,417	+ 360,417
Department of Commerce:			
Bureau of Marine Inspection and Navigation . .	——	+ 3,030,980	+ 3,030,980
Treasury Department:			
Bureau of Customs . . .	——	+ 52,400	+ 52,400
Transferred from Coast Guard, pursuant to Executive Order 9198, July 11, 1942, to:			
Executive Office of the President:			
War Shipping Administration	——	− 48,360,417	− 48,360,417
Public Law 626, June 23, 1942:			
Appropriations	——	209,440,000	209,440,000
Public Law 700, August 6, 1942:			
Contract authorizations . . .	——	974,634,000	974,634,000
Public Law 763, October 26, 1942:			
Appropriations	3,822,000,000	1,766,568,308	5,588,568,308
Public Law 11, March 18, 1943:			
Appropriations	——	793,668	793,668
Public Law 20, March 31, 1943:			
Appropriations	——	3,836,176,119	3,836,176,119
Contract authorizations . . .	——	449,740,400	449,740,400
Public Law 92, June 26, 1943:			
Appropriations	——	172,439,000	172,439,000
Public Law 140, July 12, 1943:			
Appropriations	——	751,140	751,140
Total Fiscal Year 1943:			
Appropriations	$5,258,418,585	$18,550,433,962	$23,808,852,547
Contract authorizations .	——	$1,924,374,400	$1,924,374,400

[1] Copy received from Executive Office of the President, Bureau of the Budget. This statement does not include the indefinite contract authorizations for the construction of the expanded Navy. According to estimates of the Navy Department, appropriations will be required for this purpose after the fiscal year 1945, amounting to about 88.6 billion.

NAVY DEPARTMENT — *Continued*

APPROPRIATING ACTS AND DATE APPROVED	BUREAU OF AERONAUTICS	OTHER	TOTAL
Fiscal Year 1944			
Public Law 92, June 26, 1943:			
Appropriations:			
Annual	$4,583,725,000	$22,851,062,198	$27,434,787,198
Permanent — (revised) . .	——	304,640	304,640
Contract authorizations . . .	2,000,000,000	——	2,000,000,000
Public Law 216, Dec. 23, 1943:			
Appropriations	——	2,708,816	2,708,816
Public Law 224, January 28, 1944:			
Contract authorizations . . .	——	281,060,000	281,060,000
Public Law 279, April 1, 1944:			
Appropriations	——	3,284,708	3,284,708
Contract authorizations . . .	——	120,000,000	120,000,000
Public Law 347, June 22, 1944:			
Appropriations	——	1,081,000,000	1,081,000,000
Public Law 375, June 28, 1944:			
Appropriations	——	5,330,579	5,330,579
Contract authorizations . . .	——	55,000,000	55,000,000
Total Fiscal Year 1944:			
Appropriations	$4,583,725,000	$23,943,690,941	$28,527,415,941
Contract authorizations .	$2,000,000,000	$456,060,000	$2,456,060,000
Fiscal Year 1945			
Public Law 347, June 22, 1944:			
Appropriations:			
Annual	$4,601,128,300	$21,887,670,001	$26,488,798,301
Permanent	——	322,000	322,000
Contract authorizations . . .	3,600,000,000	1,474,931,400	5,074,931,400
Total Fiscal Year 1945:			
Appropriations	$4,601,128,300	$21,887,992,001	$26,489,120,301
Contract authorizations .	$3,600,000,000	$1,474,931,400	$5,074,931,400

WAR DEPARTMENT — MILITARY ACTIVITIES

APPROPRIATING ACTS AND DATE APPROVED	AIR CORPS	OTHER	TOTAL
Fiscal Year 1943			
Public Law 649, July 2, 1942:			
Appropriations	$11,317,416,790	$31,502,586,277	$42,820,003,067
Public Law 678, July 25, 1942:			
Appropriations	——	3,298	3,298
Public Law 11, March 18, 1943:			
Appropriations	——	679,836	679,836
Public Law 140, July 12, 1943:			
Appropriations	——	272,715	272,715
Total Fiscal Year 1943:			
Appropriations	$11,317,416,790	$31,503,542,126	$42,820,958,916

WAR DEPARTMENT — MILITARY ACTIVITIES — *Continued*

APPROPRIATING ACTS AND DATE APPROVED	AIR CORPS	OTHER	TOTAL
Fiscal Year 1944			
Public Law 108, July 1, 1943:			
Appropriations	$23,655,481,000	$35,379,358,673	$59,034,839,673
Public Law 216, Dec. 23, 1943:			
Appropriations	——	130,362	130,362
Public Law 279, April 1, 1944:			
Appropriations	——	427,407	427,407
Public Law 375, June 28, 1944:			
Appropriations	——	1,145,541	1,145,541
Total Fiscal Year 1944:			
Appropriations	$23,655,481,000	$35,381,061,983	$59,036,542,983
Fiscal Year 1945			
Public Law 374, June 28, 1944:			
Appropriations	$1,610,717,000	$13,824,097,795	$15,434,814,795

B. Mobilization of Manpower

Due to the heavy demands of modern war waged simultaneously on many fronts the manpower situation became increasingly critical at certain points during the period under review.

The nature of modern warfare is such that the demand for younger men became particularly insistent. With the exhaustion of the available men in this age group who were not deferred for occupational or other reasons, the pressure to induct fathers, who had hitherto been deferred on grounds of dependency, became increasingly great. When Congress reconvened on September 14, 1943, members were faced with a probable large-scale drafting of fathers under orders of the War Manpower Commission as part of a "work or fight" program. To head off this development S. 763 [1] was introduced which provided for the blanket mandatory exemption from training and service in the land or naval forces of every registrant under the Selective Training and Service Act of 1940, as amended, who was married prior to December 8, 1941, had a bona fide family relationship with his family since that date, and had a child or children under 18 years of age. Both the Secretary of War and the Secretary of the Navy wrote letters to Chairman Reynolds of the Senate Committee on Military Affairs opposing the measure.[2] The bill was adopted by the Senate in revised form and was sent to the House where it was completely rewritten by the House Committee on Military Affairs and reported favorably in its revised form.[3] Following final House action, it was sent to Conference where differences between the Senate and House versions were ironed out.[4] In the finally agreed-on form, the bill was accepted by both House and Senate and approved by the President, December 5, 1943.[5]

[1] Senate 763, 78th Cong., *Exempting Certain Married Men Who Have Children from Liability Under the Selective Service and Training Act of 1940, as Amended.*

[2] Senate Report No. 384, 78th Cong., 1st sess.

[3] House Report No. 787, 78th Cong., 1st sess.

[4] Conference Report No. 780 to Accompany S. 763, 78th Cong., 1st sess.

[5] Public Law 197, 78th Cong., 1st sess. *An Act Amending the Selective Training and Service Act of 1940, as Amended, and for Other Purposes.*

The important provisions of the Act were as follows:

1. Fathers, married before December 8, 1941 and maintaining a bona fide family relationship since then, "will be inducted after the induction of other registrants not deferred, exempted, relieved from liability, or postponed from induction under this Act or the rules and regulations prescribed thereunder who are available for induction and are acceptable to the land and naval forces," this to be done "on a Nation-wide basis within the Nation and a State-wide basis within each State."

2. Except for needed medical, professional and specialist categories, no persons are to be called for induction because of their occupations or by occupation groups, thus eliminating the possibility of establishing work or fight categories.

3. Provision is made for check-ups on continued indispensability of occupationally deferred registrants who have moved beyond jurisdiction of their local boards.

4. Provision is made for a commission of physicians, with civilian representation, to assist in determination of whether physical, mental and moral qualifications for induction into the armed services can be lowered.

5. Provision is made for full information on occupational deferments, rejections, exemptions, etc. among registrants employed by the Federal Government.

6. The President is authorized to delegate his authority only to the Director of Civil Service.

The Act of December 5, 1943, did little to assist in meeting critical manpower requirements. In his message to Congress of January 11, 1944, the President, on the joint recommendation of the War Department, the Navy Department and the Maritime Commission, recommended the enactment of a National Service Law.[1] The reason back of the President's proposal apparently was not any over-all manpower shortage but rather difficulties that had been experienced in getting persons into the right places and in keeping workers steadily on the job, as evidenced by the high rate of labor turnover in war industries.

There seemed to be, however, a general feeling in the country that the time for such drastic action was past, and for this and other reasons Congress showed little inclination to take action on the President's proposal.

The need of the armed services for younger men led to the adoption by the Selective Service Administration of important changes in basic policies regarding the classification of registrants by age groups. In a statement of policy and accompanying memorandum sent to local boards on May 11, 1944,[2] an over-all picture of the manpower situation as regards the armed forces and specific directives as regards classification were given. It was stated that "the number of men required to bring the armed forces to their required strength is relatively small." On April 5 the Army reported that it had reached its authorized strength of 7,700,000. The Navy was reported to have reached a strength of 3,105,000 on the same date, with 300,000 more required before September 1, 1944. In view of this situation, the Memorandum stated that "the number of men who will be required by the armed forces as replacements will, to a large extent, depend upon the fortunes of war: The policy of the selective service system, therefore, cannot be rigid but must be subject to adjustment as the needs of the armed forces change."

It was indicated that the greatest immediate need was for "physically fit men in the younger age groups, capable of the highest degree of efficiency under combat conditions." Under these conditions, it was indicated that registrants between the ages of 18 and 25 faced the prospect of service in the armed forces "unless they meet the specific conditions for deferment which have been established by the Director of Selective Service." The prospect for registrants in the 26–29 age group "who are found to be 'necessary and regularly engaged in'"

[1] See this volume, p. 114.
[2] From the Office of Selective Service Administration.

activities in war production or in support of the national health, safety or interest" was stated to be that "they will remain in civilian life for the time being, subject to adjustment as the needs of the armed forces change." For those in the 30–37 age group, the prospect was declared to be that "they will remain in civilian life for an indefinite period, subject to adjustment as the needs of the armed forces change."

(1) *Message of the President (Roosevelt) Transmitting a Recommendation for the Passage of a National Service Law and Other Acts, January 11, 1944* [1]

[Excerpt]

To the Congress of the United States:

. . . .

Returning from my journeyings,[2] I must confess to a sense of let-down when I found many evidences of faulty perspectives here in Washington. The faulty perspective consists in overemphasizing lesser problems and thereby underemphasizing the first and greatest problem.

The overwhelming majority of our people have met the demands of this war with magnificent courage and understanding. They have accepted inconveniences; they have accepted hardships; they have accepted tragic sacrifices. And they are ready and eager to make whatever further contributions are needed to win the war as quickly as possible — if only they are given the chance to know what is required of them.

However, while the majority goes on about its great work without complaint, a noisy minority maintains an uproar of demands for special favors for special groups. There are pests who swarm through the lobbies of the Congress and the cocktail bars of Washington, representing these special groups as opposed to the basic interests of the Nation as a whole. They have come to look upon the war primarily as a chance to make profits for themselves at the expense of their neighbors — profits in money or in terms of political or social preferment.

Such selfish agitation can be highly dangerous in wartime. It creates confusion. It damages morale. It hampers our national effort. It muddies the waters and therefore prolongs the war.

If we analyze American history impartially, we cannot escape the fact that in our past we have not always forgotten individual and selfish and partisan interests in time of war — we have not always been united in purpose and direction. We cannot overlook the serious dissensions and the lack of unity in our War of the Revolution, in our War of 1812, or in our War Between the States, when the survival of the Union itself was at stake.

---

[1] House Document No. 377, 78th Cong., 2d sess.
[2] The President had just returned from the Cairo and Tehran Conferences.

In the First World War we came closer to national unity than in any previous war. But that war lasted only a year and a half, and increasing signs of disunity began to appear during the final months of the conflict.

In this war, we have been compelled to learn how interdependent upon each other are all groups and sections of the population of America.

Increased food costs, for example, will bring new demands for wage increases from all war workers, which will in turn raise all prices of all things, including those things which the farmers themselves have to buy. Increased wages or prices will each in turn produce the same results. They all have a particularly disastrous result on all fixed income groups.

And I hope you will remember that all of us in this Government represent the fixed-income group just as much as we represent business owners, workers, and farmers. This group of fixed-income people includes teachers, clergy, policemen, firemen, widows and minors on fixed incomes, wives and dependents of our soldiers and sailors, and old-age pensioners. They and their families add up to one-quarter of our 130,-000,000 people. They have few or no high-pressure representatives at the Capitol. In a period of gross inflation they would be the worst sufferers.

If ever there was a time to subordinate individual or group selfishness to the national good, that time is now. Disunity at home — bickerings, self-seeking partisanship, stoppages of work, inflation, business as usual, politics as usual, luxury as usual — these are the influences which can undermine the morale of the brave men ready to die at the front for us here.

Those who are doing most of the complaining are not deliberately striving to sabotage the national war effort. They are laboring under the delusion that the time is past when we must make prodigious sacrifices — that the war is already won and we can begin to slacken off. But the dangerous folly of that point of view can be measured by the distance that separates our troops from their ultimate objectives in Berlin and Tokyo — and by the sum of all the perils that lie along the way.

Overconfidence and complacency are among our deadliest enemies. Last spring — after notable victories at Stalingrad and in Tunisia and against the U-boats on the high seas — overconfidence became so pronounced that war production fell off. In 2 months, June and July, 1943, more than a thousand airplanes that could have been made and should have been made were not made. Those who failed to make them were not on strike. They were merely saying, "The war's in the bag — so let's relax."

That attitude on the part of anyone — government or management or labor — can lengthen this war. It can kill American boys.

Let us remember the lessons of 1918. In the summer of that year the tide turned in favor of the Allies. But this Government did not relax. In fact, our national effort was stepped up. In August 1918, the draft age limits were broadened from 21 to 31 to 18 to 45. The President called for "force to the utmost," and his call was heeded. And in November, only 3 months later, Germany surrendered.

That is the way to fight and win a war — all out — and not with half-an-eye on the battle fronts abroad and the other eye-and-a-half on personal, selfish, or political interests here at home.

Therefore, in order to concentrate all our energies and resources on winning the war, and to maintain a fair and stable economy at home, I recommend that the Congress adopt:

(1) A realistic tax law — which will tax all unreasonable profits, both individual and corporate, and reduce the ultimate cost of the war to our sons and daughters. The tax bill now under consideration by the Congress does not begin to meet this test.

(2) A continuation of the law for the renegotiation of war contracts — which will prevent exorbitant profits and assure fair prices to the Government. For 2 long years I have pleaded with the Congress to take undue profits out of war.

(3) A cost of food law — which will enable the Government (a) to place a reasonable floor under the prices the farmer may expect for his production; and (b) to place a ceiling on the prices a consumer will have to pay for the food he buys. This should apply to necessities only; and will require public funds to carry out. It will cost in appropriations about 1 per cent of the present annual cost of the war.

(4) Early reenactment of the stabilization statute of October 1942. This expires June 30, 1944, and if it is not extended well in advance, the country might just as well expect price chaos by summer.

We cannot have stabilization by wishful thinking. We must take positive action to maintain the integrity of the American dollar.

(5) A national service law — which, for the duration of the war, will prevent strikes, and, with certain appropriate exceptions, will make available for war production or for any other essential services every able-bodied adult in this Nation.

These five measures together form a just and equitable whole. I would not recommend a national service law unless the other laws were passed to keep down the cost of living, to share equitably the burdens of taxation, to hold the stabilization line, and to prevent undue profits.

The Federal Government already has the basic power to draft capital and property of all kinds for war purposes on a basis of just compensation.

As you know, I have for 3 years hesitated to recommend a national service act. Today, however, I am convinced of its necessity. Although I believe that we and our allies can win the war without such a measure, I am certain that nothing less than total mobilization of all our resources of manpower and capital will guarantee an earlier victory, and reduce the toll of suffering and sorrow and blood.

I have received a joint recommendation for this law from the heads of the War Department, the Navy Department, and the Maritime Commission. These are the men who bear responsibility for the procurement of the necessary arms and equipment, and for the successful prosecution of the war in the field. They say:

When the very life of the Nation is in peril the responsibility for service is common to all men and women. In such a time there can be no discrimination between the men and women who are assigned by the Government to its defense at the battle front and the men and women assigned to producing the vital materials essential to successful military operations. A prompt enactment of a national service law would be merely an expression of the universality of this responsibility.

I believe the country will agree that those statements are the solemn truth.

National service is the most democratic way to wage a war. Like selective service for the armed forces, it rests on the obligation of each citizen to serve his nation to his utmost where he is best qualified.

It does not mean reduction in wages. It does not mean loss of retirement and seniority rights and benefits. It does not mean that any substantial numbers of war workers will be disturbed in their present jobs. Let these facts be wholly clear.

Experience in other democratic nations at war — Britain, Canada, Australia, and New Zealand — has shown that the very existence of national service makes unnecessary the widespread use of compulsory power. National service has proven to be a unifying moral force — based on an equal and comprehensive legal obligation of all people in a nation at war.

There are millions of American men and women who are not in this war at all. It is not because they do not want to be in it. But they want to know where they can best do their share. National service provides that direction. It will be a means by which every man and woman can find that inner satisfaction which comes from making the fullest possible contribution to victory.

I know that all civilian war workers will be glad to be able to say many years hence to their grandchildren: "Yes, I, too, was in service in the great war. I was on duty in an airplane factory, and I helped make hundreds of fighting planes. The Government told me that in doing that I was performing my most useful work in the service of my country."

It is argued that we have passed the stage in the war where national service is necessary. But our soldiers and sailors know that this is not true. We are going forward on a long, rough road — and, in all journeys, the last miles are the hardest. And it is for that final effort — for the total defeat of our enemies — that we must mobilize our total resources.

The national war program calls for the employment of more people in 1944 than in 1943.

It is my conviction that the American people will welcome this win-the-war measure which is based on the eternally just principle of "fair for one, fair for all."

It will give our people at home the assurance that they are standing four-square behind our soldiers and sailors. And it will give our enemies demoralizing assurance that we mean business — that we, 130,000,000 Americans, are on the march to Rome, Berlin, and Tokyo.

I hope that the Congress will recognize that, although this is a political year, national service is an issue which transcends politics. Great power must be used for great purposes.

As to the machinery for this measure, the Congress itself should determine its nature — but it should be wholly nonpartisan in its make-up.

· · · · · · · ·

4. LEND–LEASE

[See *Documents, III, 1940–41*, p. 711; *IV, 1941–42*, p. 169; *V, 1942–43*, p. 105.]

A. Extension of Lend-Lease Act

The Lend-Lease Act, officially designated "An Act to Promote the Defense of the United States," [1] conferred powers upon the President which were to terminate on June 30, 1943, or at an earlier date if so determined by concurrent resolution of both Houses of Congress. The authority was extended for a period of one year when H. R. 1501, adopted by both House and Senate, was signed by the President on March 11, 1943.[2]

H. R. 4254 (A Bill to Extend for One Year the Provisions of an Act to Promote the Defense of the United States, Approved March 11, 1941, as Amended) was introduced by Mr. Bloom, February 23, 1944,[3] and referred to the Committee on Foreign Affairs. The Committee held hearings, March 1 to 9, in the course of which the Foreign Economic Administrator (Mr. Crowley), the Under Secretary of State (Mr. Stettinius), the Secretary of War (Mr. Stimson), the Secretary of the Navy (Mr. Knox), the War Shipping Administrator (Admiral Land), and Assistant Secretary of State (Mr. Acheson) submitted statements and answered questions.[4] On March 30, the Committee reported the bill favorably with an amendment to subsection (b) of section 3 of the original Act relating to the authority of the President to make agreements regarding the terms of Lend-Lease assistance.[5] On April 19, 1944, after brief debate, the House adopted the bill, as reported by the Committee on Foreign Affairs, with a clarifying amendment adopted by the Committee of the Whole House, by a vote of 334 to 21.[6] Two amendments which were offered in Committee of the Whole House with a view to requiring Congressional approval of the terms and conditions of

---

[1] Public Law 11, 77th Cong.; *Documents, III, 1940–41*, p. 712.
[2] Public Law 9, 78th Cong.
[3] *Congressional Record*, vol. 90, p. 2028 (daily edition, February 23, 1944).
[4] *Hearings before the Committee on Foreign Affairs, House of Representatives, on H. R. 4254 [Extension of Lend-Lease Act]*, 78th Cong., 2d sess.
[5] House Report No. 1316, 78th Cong., 2d sess.
[6] *Congressional Record*, vol. 90, p. 3643 (daily edition, April 19, 1944).

Lend-Lease settlements were defeated by votes of 114 to 134 and 94 to 114 respectively.[1]

In the Senate the bill was referred to the Committee on Foreign Relations which held a hearing on April 26, which was devoted almost exclusively to receiving a statement by the Foreign Economic Administrator (Mr. Crowley) and accompanying exhibits. The Senate Committee also had the record of the House Committee hearings before it. On May 2, the Committee reported favorably the House bill, as amended by the House.[2] The bill was finally adopted on May 8, with a clarifying amendment offered by Senator Vandenberg, by a vote of 63 to 1.[3] It was approved by the President, May 17, 1944.

(1) *An Act to Extend for One Year the Provisions of an Act to Promote the Defense of the United States, Approved March 11, 1941, as Amended, Approved May 17, 1944* [4]

Be it enacted by the Senate and House of Representatives of the United States of America in Congress assembled, That subsection (c) of section 3 of an Act to promote the defense of the United States, approved March 11, 1941, as amended, is amended by striking out "June 30, 1944" wherever it appears therein and inserting in lieu thereof "June 30, 1945"; by striking out "July 1, 1947" and inserting in lieu thereof "July 1, 1948"; and by striking out "July 1, 1944" and inserting in lieu thereof "July 1, 1945"; and subsection (b) of section 6 of such Act is amended by striking out "June 30, 1947" and inserting in lieu thereof "June 30, 1948."

SEC. 2. Subsection (b) of section 3 is amended by striking out the period after the word "satisfactory" and inserting the following: "*: Provided, however,* That nothing in this paragraph shall be construed to authorize the President to assume or incur any obligations on the part of the United States with respect to post-war economic policy, post-war military policy or any post-war policy involving international relations except in accordance with established constitutional procedure."

(2) *Report from the Senate Committee on Foreign Relations, Submitted to Accompany H. R. 4254 (Extension of Lend-Lease), May 2, 1944* [5]

[Excerpt]

·   ·   ·   ·   ·   ·

NECESSITY FOR CONTINUING LEND-LEASE

The United Nations are now prepared for the decisive battles of this war. Their men and their weapons are deployed for the great offensives

[1] *Ibid.*, p. 3631–42.
[2] Senate Report No. 848, 78th Cong., 2d sess.
[3] *Congressional Record*, vol. 90, p. 4191 (daily edition, May 8, 1944).
[4] Public Law 304, 78th Cong.
[5] Senate Report No. 848, 78th Cong., 2d sess.

to come both in Europe and in the Far East. The plans for these offensives are based upon two great principles — the freest interchange of fighting manpower made possible by unity of command and the most efficient use of resources made possible by lend-lease and reverse lend-lease. Only if we continue to combine our resources through lend-lease and reverse lend-lease can each of the United Nations strike the enemy with the maximum force. We cannot slacken for one moment our efforts of mutual aid at this crucial stage of the war.

There has been no controversy with respect to the necessity for passing this bill. The House Foreign Affairs Committee conducted extensive hearings, continuing over a period of weeks, and made a full and complete record concerning lend-lease operations. This record was fully considered by this committee. In addition, the committee heard testimony from Leo T. Crowley, Foreign Economic Administrator, and Oscar Cox, general counsel of the Foreign Economic Administration.

The committee was greatly assisted in its consideration of the bill by various factual statements, charts, and other data presented to the members of the committee. Most of this information that was not included in the record of the hearings before the House Foreign Affairs Committee has been included in the record of the hearings before this committee. The 14 detailed reports on lend-lease operations which have been submitted to the Congress pursuant to section 5 (b) of the Lend-Lease Act have also been of great assistance in appraising the part played by lend-lease in the conduct of the war.

The facts brought out before your committee at its hearings indicate the vital necessity for continuing the Lend-Lease Act as an essential part of our mechanism for waging war.

MUTUAL WAR AID — REVERSE LEND-LEASE

In view of the comprehensive nature of the reports on lend-lease and reverse lend-lease operations contained in the printed record of the hearings before your committee, in the printed record of the hearings before the House Foreign Affairs Committee, and in the report of the House Foreign Affairs Committee, it is not necessary to include in this report a detailed review of these activities. Your committee would like, however, to comment on several salient features of lend-lease operations.

The mutual war-aid programs of the United Nations [1] are providing the weapons needed for victory on every front and on the production line behind those fronts. Through combined organizations our weapons, our war-production supplies, our food, and our merchant ships are allocated and sent to the various theaters of war in accordance with strategic decisions of the military commanders. The responsibility for

[1] For further information, see this volume, p. 122 and 218.

those over-all decisions rests with the Combined Chiefs of Staff. Whether the aid is provided by the United States under lend-lease or by other United Nations under mutual aid, the guiding principle always followed is, Will the supplies, services, or information furnished hasten the day of victory?

American, British, and Canadian war supplies are moving in ever-increasing quantities to the Soviet Union. By March 1, 1944, we had sent under lend-lease 8,800 planes, 5,200 tanks, and huge quantities of other war materials. American, British, and Canadian war supplies are moving to China in quantities which are increasing at a rate as fast as can be expected under the hampering conditions of air transportation. With the aid of these lend-lease shipments, the Red Army has destroyed important elements of the Nazi war machine and tens of thousands of German planes, tanks and guns, and the Chinese Army has made an impressive showing against the Japanese.

American and British weapons are being used in Africa to reequip French, Polish, Yugoslav, and Greek troops so that they can play their full part in the liberation of their homelands. Already several divisions of these troops have participated in the campaigns in Tunisia, Sicily, Sardinia, Corsica, and Italy, thus reducing the numbers of American and British soldiers that had to be sent to these fronts. And from French north and west Africa we are receiving as reverse lend-lease food for our forces in the Mediterranean area.

Under lend-lease we have sent munitions and war supplies to Britain, India, Australia, and New Zealand. These members of the British Commonwealth in their turn are furnishing our armed forces, as reverse lend-lease without payment by us, ever-increasing quantities of supplies and services. The monthly rate of reverse lend-lease aid from Australia and New Zealand, for example, now approximates the monthly rate of lend-lease shipments to those areas.

COMMERCIAL TRADE

The committee made inquiries to determine to what extent lend-lease operations may have affected the commercial trade of the United States. The committee found that despite the loss of important markets in Axis countries and countries now occupied by the Axis, the drastic limitation of shipping, and the curtailment of civilian production, cash purchase exports from the United States in 1942 and 1943 (excluding all lend-lease shipments) maintained the average of such exports for the years 1930 through 1939. This record contrasts sharply with that of our larger allies who have suffered serious, and in some cases alarming, declines in their foreign trade as the war has progressed.

These declines have resulted in part from the normal consequences of war and in part from the fact that the receipt of lend-lease supplies has operated to restrict the field in which those countries can participate in foreign trade. Thus, in the master lend-lease agreements each of our allies has agreed that it will not retransfer — and hence will not reexport — any article it has received under lend-lease without the approval of the President. In addition, the United Kingdom Government in a White Paper issued September 10, 1941, declared that it would apply substantially similar restrictions to the export of short supply articles, no matter from what source derived, if similar goods are obtained from the United States either for cash or under lend-lease. The effect of this declaration has been to avoid any possibility that British industry could through lend-lease derive a commercial advantage at the expense of United States industry.

CONCLUSION

We and our allies are now ready for the supreme tests of this war. We have come a long way since those dark days of 1940 and 1941 when the Axis aggressors were winning all the victories. Those were the days of weakness and disaster as the peace-loving nations were overrun one by one.

Now as United Nations we have found the strength that comes from unity. We have combined our manpower and our material resources. Every sector of every front manned by our allies with the aid of lend-lease weapons and every battle won with the aid of lend-lease weapons is a sector we will not have to man and a battle we will not have to win. The fight is our fight — and theirs. United, the freedom-loving peoples of the world are certain of final victory and the opportunity to establish a just and durable peace.

B. Amount, Form and Allocation of Lend-Lease Aid

In the period July 1, 1943 to June 30, 1944 the President, acting under the provisions of the Lend-Lease Act of March 11, 1941, section 5 (*b*) (Public Law 11, 77th Cong.), has transmitted the following reports to Congress:[1] Eleventh Report to Congress on Lend-Lease Operations, for the Period Ended July 31, 1943, transmitted to Congress August 25, 1943 (House Doc. 263, 78th Cong., 1st sess.); Twelfth Report to Congress on Lend-Lease Operations, transmitted to Congress November 11, 1943 (H. Doc. 353, 78th Cong., 1st sess.); Thirteenth Report to Congress on Lend-Lease Operations, for the Period Ended November 30, 1943, transmitted to Congress January 6, 1944 (H. Doc. 375, 78th Cong., 2d sess.); Report to Congress on Lend-Lease Operations, from the Passage of the Act, March 11, 1941, to December 31, 1943, transmitted by Mr. Crowley, Administrator, Foreign Economic Administration, March 11, 1944 (H. Doc. 497, 78th Cong., 2d sess.); and the Fifteenth Report to Congress on Lend-Lease Operations, for the Period Ending March 31, 1944, transmitted to Congress May 22, 1944 (H. Doc. 616, 78th Cong., 2d sess.).

[1] For list of earlier reports, see *Documents, V, 1942–43*, p. 130.

(1) *Total Lend-Lease Appropriations and Transfer Authorizations, as of June 30, 1944* [1]

I. LEND-LEASE APPROPRIATIONS TO THE PRESIDENT

First Lend-Lease Appropriation	$7,000,000,000
Second Lend-Lease Appropriation	5,985,000,000
Third Lend-Lease Appropriation	5,425,000,000
Fourth Lend-Lease Appropriation	6,273,629,000
Fifth Lend-Lease Appropriation	3,538,869,000
TOTAL	$28,222,498,000

II. TRANSFERS AUTHORIZED FROM OTHER APPROPRIATIONS

Direct appropriations have been made to the War and Navy Departments and to the Maritime Commission for the procurement of items which are in the main common to the uses of our own armed forces and those of our allies. These items when produced can be used, in other words, by our own armed forces or those of our allies in the manner in which they can be most effective in defeating our common enemies. It is not until they are ready for distribution that they are allocated by the military experts in accordance with the strategic needs. The appropriation Acts in question authorize transfers to our allies up to stated amounts under the Lend-Lease Act. That does not mean that transfers up to the stated amounts have to or will necessarily be made. All that it means is that there is sufficient flexibility for the military experts to assign the supplies where they will do the most good in winning the war.

War Department:

Third Supplemental, 1942	$2,000,000,000
Fourth Supplemental, 1942	4,000,000,000
Fifth Supplemental, 1942	11,250,000,000
Sixth Supplemental, 1942	2,220,000,000
Military Appropriation Act, 1943.	12,700,000,000
Navy Department — Second Supplemental, 1943 . .	3,000,000,000
Departments other than War — Third Supplemental, 1942	800,000,000
TOTAL	$35,970,000,000

Note: In addition to the foregoing, Congress has with certain limitations authorized the leasing of ships of the Navy and merchant ships constructed with funds appropriated to the Maritime Commission without any numerical limitation as to the dollar value or the number of such ships which may be so leased. (See, for example, Public Law 1, 78th Congress, approved February 19, 1943, and Public Law 11, 78th Congress, approved March 18, 1943.)

[1] *Sixteenth Report to Congress on Lend-Lease Operations for the Period Ended June 30, 1944*, p. 49.

(2) *Amount of Lend-Lease Aid, March 11, 1941, through June 30, 1944*

(a) *Lend-Lease Exports to All Countries* [1]

[Thousands of Dollars]

COUNTRY	MAR. 1941– JUN. 1942	JUL. 1942– JUN. 1943	JUL. 1943– JUN. 1944	TOTAL
United Kingdom	1,404,241	3,058,785	4,858,523	9,321,549
U. S. S. R.	511,115	1,931,077	3,489,752	5,931,944
Africa, Middle East & Mediterranean Area . .	288,344	1,139,590	1,642,895	3,070,829
China and India	174,151	430,582	797,693	1,402,426
Australia and New Zealand	101,563	428,624	481,698	1,011,885
Latin America	9,277	74,695	87,998	171,970
Other Countries	86,296	250,476	287,495	624,267
Total	2,574,987	7,313,829	11,646,054	21,534,870

(b) *Goods Consigned to U. S. Commanding Generals, in the Field, for Subsequent Transfer under Lend-Lease to Foreign Governments as of June 30, 1944* [2]

[Thousands of Dollars]

CATEGORY	FRENCH FORCES IN NORTH AND WEST AFRICA	CHINA	OTHER COUNTRIES	TOTAL
Ordnance and Ammunition .	74,329	140,946	8,534	223,809
Aircraft and Parts	56,209	———	101	56,310
Tanks and Other Vehicles .	196,534	63,482	3,318	263,334
Miscellaneous Supplies . .	93,297	22,574	18,917	134,788
Total	420,369	227,002	30,870	678,241

[1] *Ibid.*, p. 56.
[2] *Ibid.*, p. 54.

(c) *Total Lend-Lease Aid, March 1941 through June 30, 1944* [1]

CATEGORY	AMOUNT	% OF TOTAL
Goods Transferred:		
Munitions	$15,162,329,000	53.6
Industrial Materials and Products	6,026,086,000	21.3
Agricultural Products	3,630,585,000	12.9
Total Transfers	24,819,000,000	87.8
Services Rendered:		
Servicing and Repair of Ships, etc.	522,853,000	1.9
Rental of Ships, Ferrying of Aircraft, etc. .	2,210,752,000	7.8
Production Facilities in U. S.	621,700,000	2.2
Miscellaneous Expenses	96,046,000	0.3
Total Services	3,451,351,000	12.2
Total Lend-Lease Aid	28,270,351,000	100.0
Consignments to Commanding Generals * . .	678,241,000	———

* Goods consigned to United States commanding generals for subsequent transfer in the field to lend-lease countries. The value of such goods transferred is not included in the lend-lease aid total of $28,270,351,000.

C. Benefits Received

Section 3 (b) of the Lend-Lease Act provided as follows:

"The terms and conditions upon which any such foreign government receives any aid authorized under subsection (a) shall be those which the President deems satisfactory, and the benefit to the United States may be payment or repayment in kind or property, or any other direct or indirect benefit which the President deems satisfactory."

When the bill extending the Act was under consideration by Congress in 1943, a great deal of attention was given to the nature of the benefits received by the United States. The House Committee on Foreign Affairs and the Senate Committee on Foreign Relations in their reports on the bill devoted considerable space to the benefits to be taken into account in the final settlements.[2] Both Committees recognized that the chief benefit derived from Lend-Lease aid is the earliest possible winning of the war by putting American materials, services and ideas at the disposal of those engaged in fighting the common enemy.

It was apparent, however, from the discussions in committee and on the floor of the House and Senate that members of Congress were interested in more tangible benefits than the winning of the war or the making of a just and lasting peace. A great deal of attention, for example, was given to what the United States was getting through reverse lend-lease. Attention was called to

[1] *Ibid.*, p. 11.

[2] House Report No. 188, 78th Cong., 1st sess.; Senate Report No. 99, 78th Cong., 1st sess.; *Documents, V, 1942-43*, p. 123, 127.

the benefit which the United States would receive from the return of such defense articles as the President might deem of use to the United States. The idea was clearly present, however, in the minds of some that as part of the final settlement the recipients of lend-lease assistance might be asked to pay in money or in other things of value to the United States, such as bases, for assistance which they had received in excess of benefits received by the United States. There thus emerged the possibility of a recurrence of the war debt issue which had plagued international relations after the last war.

In the original letter transmitting the President's "Eleventh Report on Lend-Lease Operations to Congress," the following words appeared:

"The Congress in passing and extending the Lend-Lease Act made it plain that the United States wants no war debts to jeopardize the coming peace. Victory and a secure peace are the only coin in which we can be repaid." [1]

Possibly because of popular and Congressional reaction to this part of his letter, the President later repudiated it, explaining that the letter was printed inadvertently without his approval and that a new copy of the letter was being sent to Congress with these two sentences deleted. [2] There was truth, the President was reported as saying, in the words but it was a condensation of the truth which might lead to misunderstanding. It was perfectly true in a narrow, technical sense that we wanted no debt, but it was the President's thought and that of most of the other countries that they would repay so far as they possibly could. [3]

When the question of the extension of the Lend-Lease Act came up again in 1944, members of Congress showed themselves concerned with the benefits which the United States would receive, and especially with the question as to whether the United States was being asked to make a disproportionate contribution to the war effort. In this connection, further information on the amount of reverse lend-lease aid received from recipients of lend-lease assistance was sought. There was also curiosity expressed as to the use to which lend-lease funds had been put. In an attempt to kill numerous rumors that had been circulating regarding the alleged misuse of lend-lease funds, Mr. Crowley, the Foreign Economic Administrator, had prepared and submitted to the House Committee on Foreign Affairs on March 8, 1944, a statement dealing with some of these "fictions." [4]

Largely as the result of reports brought back by five Senators who visited the world battle fronts in the summer of 1943, the Senate Appropriations Committee voted on November 10, 1943 to join with the Truman Committee in an investigation of lend-lease operations throughout the world, as well as other government expenditures abroad. The Deficiencies Subcommittee, headed by Senator McKellar, was designated to act for the Committee. [5] A preliminary report of the Committee Investigators to the Subcommittee on Deficiencies was made on May 1, 1944 and presented by Senator McKellar on May 4. [6] In this report considerable attention was given to reverse lend-lease, and to the difficulties connected with an accurate accounting of the amount of such assistance received.

---

[1] *Eleventh Report to Congress on Lend-Lease Operations for the Period Ended July 31, 1943*, p. 6.

[2] Department of State, *Bulletin*, IX, p. 168.

[3] *New York Times*, September 8, 1943.

[4] *Hearings before the Committee on Foreign Affairs, House of Representatives, on H. R. 4254* [*Extension of Lend-Lease*], 78th Cong., 2d sess., p. 141, 230.

[5] *New York Times*, November 11, 1943.

[6] Senate Doc. No. 19, 78th Cong., 2d sess.

(1) *Comparative War Expenditures. Report to Congress on Lend-Lease Operations from the Passage of the Act, March 11, 1941, to December 31, 1943, Submitted by the Foreign Economic Administrator (Crowley), March 11, 1944* [1]

The world-wide pattern of lend-lease and reverse lend-lease is an essential part of the war effort of the United Nations. In effect, a pool of resources has been created into which contributions are placed and from which withdrawals are made as the demands of the many fighting fronts dictate. Each of our major fighting partners is contributing fully from its resources to the defeat of the Axis powers, though the contributions of each differ with the circumstances of war and the resources that are available.

The war contribution of some of our allies has of necessity taken the form of direct use of their own production and of those munitions and supplies which have been made available to them by their less hard-pressed allies. Russia and China, fighting to throw back the invader from their own territories, have found a magnificently effective use for all of the guns and tanks and planes that they could produce or that their allies could send to them. The United Kingdom, which has been heavily bombed and is now the base for the combined British-American air offensive on Germany and for the coming invasion, has nevertheless been able to turn over substantial quantities of supplies to the forces of the United States, the Soviet Union, and other United Nations. The United States, which is located far from the fighting zones and has by far the greatest industrial capacity, is able to make available to its allies much larger quantities of munitions and other war supplies, while still retaining far the greater part for its own armed forces.

The costs of mutual aid — of lend-lease and reverse lend-lease — are only a small part of the war expenditures even of those nations which have contributed most heavily to their allies in the form of supplies. For example, 14 per cent of the war expenditures of the United States have been for lend-lease. These expenditures have not been less effective in promoting the defense of the United States and bringing nearer the ultimate defeat of the enemy than has the 86 per cent of our war production which has been used by our own armed forces. The decision as to whether one of the United Nations is to use directly the whole of its own production or is to send a part of it to its allies is made by the military authorities in the light of the over-all military strategy of the war and without regard to purely financial considerations. The production of the United States, the United Kingdom, and Canada is allocated among the United Nations by the Combined Boards on which

[1] House Doc. No. 497, 78th Cong., 2d sess., p. 13.

are represented the military and economic high commands of the three powers.

The over-all costs of the war cannot be measured in dollars. The men who fell in Stalingrad and Salerno, in Tunisia and at Changsha; the immeasurable havoc which the war has created with human lives and happiness; the destruction of homes and cities — these are claims of war that can never be evaluated in monetary terms.

To the extent that the cost of war can be measured in financial terms, probably the best measurement is the proportion of its national production which each of the United Nations is devoting to the war. As long as each country spends roughly the same proportion of its gross national production for the defeat of the Axis powers, the financial burden is distributed equally among the United Nations in accordance with their ability to pay. Those with the most to give, give the most, but they do not contribute more in proportion to their capacity than those that draw upon more limited resources.

Trends of war expenditures of several nations as percentages of their gross national production are shown in Chart 5.[1] These ratios were computed in the Foreign Economic Administration on the basis of the best statistical information available. Obviously the accuracy and reliability of such measurements vary between the different countries. In view of the nature of the basic data, the ratios shown in the chart should be regarded as approximations of trends and relationships rather than as exact statistical measurements. The chart gives a correct picture of the general situation, however.

Our principal allies have been carrying on the war against the Axis longer than we have. Before Pearl Harbor, the United Kingdom, Canada, Australia, and New Zealand were devoting from about one-fourth to one-half of their gross national production to the defeat of the enemy. In 1941 the United States spent only one-tenth of its income for the war. Today the nations of the British Commonwealth are contributing approximately 50 per cent of their gross national production to the war. The United States is just now reaching the point where one-half of our gross national production is devoted to war purposes, including transfers under lend-lease. Thus, at the present time, the financial claims of

---

[1] The Chart here referred to is not reproduced. It was prepared, and in part based on estimates, by the Foreign Economic Administration. The following table represents a rough approximation to the results which the graphs of the Chart show:

War Expenditures as Per Cent of Gross National Production

	1940	1941	1942	1943
United States	3	11	32	48
United Kingdom	46	49	53	54
Canada	12	16	41	49
Australia	20	32	50	52

war against the United States and our principal allies are approximately equal.

When the money costs of the war fall according to the rule of equality of financial sacrifice, no nation grows wealthy from the war effort of its allies and each nation fulfills its responsibility to contribute to the fullest extent to the defeat of the enemy. The claims of war against each are comparatively the same in terms of production and finance.

(2) *Reporting and Valuing Reverse Lend-Lease. Preliminary Report of Committee Investigators to the Committee on Appropriations, United States Senate, on Lend-Lease Aid and Government Expenditures Abroad, May 1, 1944* [1]

[Excerpt]

The problem of reporting and valuing reverse lend-lease aid constitutes one of the most difficult and complex problems with which the United States Government is faced in its program of mutual aid with foreign governments.

. . . .

The reporting of reciprocal aid has been difficult. Originally, the Army and Navy required its overseas commanders to report the aid received in detail as well as the "value" thereof, determined either on the basis of values furnished by foreign governments or, alternatively, estimates by United States military or naval personnel. As the volume of reciprocal aid increased, this reporting requirement became a very heavy burden. In the case of the United Kingdom, particularly, the British Government stated that it could not individually price "issue vouchers" covering goods provided to our forces, inasmuch as its accounting system was not established on such a basis that individual prices could readily be determined, and the manpower which would be required to determine such individual prices could not be spared from more important tasks contributing directly to the prosecution of the war.

Faced with the lack of any indication of costs from the British Government in the great majority of items being obtained, our forces concluded that a separate pricing or estimating of value by them would call for a large staff of price analysts whose services could not be spared from the war effort. Moreover, it was felt that even a large force of price analysts would face grave difficulties in arriving at fair estimates of value, due to the dissimilarity of foreign and United States items, the great variety of items involved, etc.

Accordingly, in October 1942, the instructions to our forces overseas with respect to the reporting and valuation of reciprocal aid were revised to permit the recording of aid in terms of a description of items received,

[1] Senate Doc. No. 190, 78th Cong., 2d sess., p. 6.

in order to permit subsequent evaluation in Washington when that became necessary. Any values furnished by foreign governments, however, were to continue to be reported to Washington. Many reports of this nature have been received and are on file in the Foreign Economic Administration, but up to the present time no action has been taken to evaluate them, as it is felt that any evaluation at the present time would be purely arbitrary and subject to receipt of further information from foreign governments which may not be available until after the war.

As public interest in reverse lend-lease increased during subsequent months, and because of the desire of the Congress and interested Government agencies to obtain, if possible, some monetary measurement of the volume and scope of reciprocal aid, it became apparent that some attempt would have to be made to arrive at a reasonable compromise. Therefore, in June and August 1943, the Army and Navy issued instructions to their overseas commanders requiring that reciprocal aid be reported in the following manner:

1. Values would be requested from responsible foreign government representatives, the values so received representing unilateral estimates by the foreign governments to which the United States Government does not necessarily agree;

2. Any values received from foreign government representatives would not be disputed, but would be reviewed by United States military and naval personnel; and if they were not in agreement with the valuations furnished by foreign governments, they were to submit their own estimate of value for the information of the United States Government; and

3. In the absence of any values furnished by foreign governments, United States military and naval personnel were to arrive at their own estimate of value based upon local cost, market value, or any other reasonable basis.

Simultaneously, negotiations were entered into with the British Government with a view to inducing it to alter its policy on the reporting of reverse lend-lease aid which it has supplied. As a result of these negotiations, the British issued on November 11, 1943, a White Paper [1] indicating an estimate (stated to be incomplete) of their out-of-pocket expenditures up to June 30, 1943, in furnishing reciprocal aid to the United States forces. The British Government agreed further that it would thereafter provide quarterly statements of its expenditures for reciprocal aid rendered to United States forces in the United Kingdom. These statements were to reflect approximately 50 major categories and more than 300 subcategories of goods and services. This statement was

[1] *A Report on Mutual Aid. Text of a White Paper Presented by the Chancellor of the Exchequer to Parliament*, November 11, 1943. N. Y., British Information Services, 1943.

not to be based in each case on individual prices, which it was stated were not available, but was to be prepared from the figures currently available under the British accounting system and was to represent the best estimates possible by the British Government of the reciprocal aid extended by them to United States forces.

It has been agreed that the reports described will be accepted as unilateral estimates of the British Government, and that the American Government will not be deemed either to agree to them or to be committed by them. While it has been agreed that itemized pricing of individual items may represent an unwarranted expenditure of manpower at this time, the United States Government has reserved the right to request that the British Government supply itemized prices at a later date when the required expenditure of manpower would not interfere with the war effort.

Except for shipping services, the British Government's statements apply only to supplies furnished and services rendered within the United Kingdom. In addition, the United Kingdom is extending aid to American forces from its colonies in various parts of the world. Full and complete records of the value of the aid transferred in these areas may never be available, particularly for transfers which have occurred during combat. Insofar as the records are available, reports containing monetary expenditures are now being prepared by the British Government. In the meantime, reports are being made by United States forces in those areas.

The Governments of Australia and New Zealand are also periodically making available statements of the cost to them of providing reverse lend-lease assistance. The problems of reporting encountered in these areas are not so great as in the United Kingdom. For example, in New Zealand all United States supply functions have been centralized in a joint purchasing board on which the Army, Navy, and Marine Corps are represented. When goods or services are obtained, the armed forces certify their receipt and pass the vouchers back to the appropriate New Zealand Government department for payment, and such records then provide a statement of expenditures made. In the case of works projects constructed for us by the New Zealand Government, however, there are the difficulties encountered in assessing post-war values and in allocating expenditures for works jointly constructed by American and foreign forces.

In all other areas records of reverse lend-lease received are obtained from the armed forces. Until July 1943, these reports usually were confined to physical descriptions in quantities of goods and services received, to provide a basis for subsequent valuation if such should be necessary. Since July 1943, however, our forces have been endeavoring to obtain estimates of expenditures for all aid received. While these estimates will be of considerable assistance in the future determination of lend-lease benefits, they do not represent a statement by the foreign government of its costs, and provide only a unilateral estimate by United States military or naval personnel operating under difficult conditions.

The need for uniformity in the reporting and valuation of reciprocal aid has been recognized by the armed forces. Because of the complexities of the problem, particularly in combat areas, it has not yet been possible to arrive at a system which is entirely uniform or acceptable. Efforts are constantly being made, however, to improve both the system used and the reports submitted.

A comment by the Navy Department on reciprocal aid would be of interest to the committee:

The Navy Department reports to the Foreign Economic Administration (formerly the Lend-Lease Administration) monthly all reverse lend-lease or reciprocal aid which has been reported. Reports of such reciprocal aid to the Navy Department are admittedly deficient for various reasons. Vigorous steps have been and are being taken to correct this deficiency and these steps are showing results. Some of the reasons why such reports have not been adequate are as follows: Much of the reciprocal aid has been received on the active fighting fronts where the commanding officers have neither the time nor the facilities to maintain the necessary records and to render the corresponding reports. Reciprocal aid has never been distinctly defined and conceptions of what constitutes reciprocal aid and what constitutes joint military operations vary considerably. Some reciprocal aid is difficult if not impossible to evaluate in terms of dollars. The United Kingdom has been very reluctant to place a price on any reciprocal aid, although the aid has been offered freely. In cases where no value or cost is assigned by the foreign government, but quantities and the nature of services have been reported, it is impossible for the Navy Department to assign any significant valuation. Not only do questions of exchange arise, but it is impossible for our officers to estimate the real cost to the foreign government. Furthermore, even if the approximate cost to the foreign government were known, the question arises as to whether that is the real value, or whether it should be the corresponding value of a similar article or service in this country, or if supplied from this country. Because of these difficulties the instructions have been changed several times.

At present the instructions require our officers to demand a price figure from the foreign government and to submit that figure, together with his own comment, if any. If no price can be obtained from the foreign government our officers are instructed to submit their own best estimate, together with information as to upon what the estimate was based and the rate of exchange used. Obviously, none of these methods of evaluation is entirely satisfactory, but the method by which the foreign government states the cost to it of the aid rendered appears to be the most desirable and is comparable to our own method of evaluating direct lend-lease. Reports on this basis are now being regularly received from Australia and New Zealand and the British Admiralty is being urged to adopt a similar policy.

There is much to be done to develop adequate information on reverse lend-lease. The final story, however, will not be possible until after the cessation of hostilities.

(3) *Reverse Lend-Lease Aid Received by the United States to June 30,*
    1944. Message from the President of the United States
    (Roosevelt) Transmitting the Seventeenth Report to Congress on
    Lend-Lease Operations, November 24, 1944 [1]

To the Congress of the United States of America:

I

I am submitting herewith my Seventeenth Report to Congress on
Lend-Lease Operations.

In fifteen of these reports I have reported on lend-lease aid extended
by the United States. One year ago, the Twelfth Lend-Lease Report
to Congress set forth the reverse lend-lease aid received by the United
States from the British Commonwealth of Nations under the Lend-
Lease Act. That report covered the period up to June 30, 1943.

I now report on reverse lend-lease aid received by the United States
from the British Commonwealth of Nations up to June 30, 1944.

One year ago the governments of the British Commonwealth reported
their expenditures for reverse lend-lease aid to the United States, on
the basis of estimates carefully prepared from their records, as totalling
$1,175,000,000. They now report that by June 30, 1944 — one year
later — these expenditures had risen to $3,348,000,000 — almost three
times the previous total.

The first six months of 1944 showed a significant increase in reverse
lend-lease aid from the British Commonwealth. These were the months
when the final preparations were being made in the United Kingdom
for the liberation of Western Europe and for the offensives aimed at
Germany.

In these six months, United States forces in the British Isles received
the equivalent of almost 3,851,000 ships' tons of supplies from the United
Kingdom under reverse lend-lease exclusive of construction materials
and gasoline, compared with 2,950,000 tons in the entire preceding 18
months. In monetary value, the supplies and services we received in
these six months were greater than for the entire preceding year.

By "D" Day, United States armed forces had reached the United
Kingdom in vast numbers. From the day our first soldiers arrived in
1942, one-third of all the supplies and equipment currently required by
United States troops in the British Isles has been provided under reverse
lend-lease. The percentages of total United States Army requirements
in the European theater provided by the United Kingdom have ranged
as high as 63 percent in the case of quartermaster supplies and 58 percent
for engineers' supplies.

[1] *Seventeenth Report to Congress on Lend-Lease Operations*, House Doc. No. 764,
78th Cong., 2d sess.

Reverse lend-lease has played an essential part in the stupendous job of preparing for and supplying the great allied offensives in Europe.

It would have required a thousand ships to send across the Atlantic what we received for our men through reverse lend-lease from the United Kingdom.

We were able to use these thousand ships instead for carrying supplies and equipment that had to come from the United States.

Without the reverse lend-lease aid that we received from the United Kingdom, we would surely have been forced to delay the invasion of France for many months. Now that this campaign has been success-fully launched and is on the road to ultimate success, it is possible to include in this report facts about specific and vitally important reverse lend-lease projects that could not previously be safely disclosed in a public report.

For the war against Japan, United States forces have also received increased quantities of supplies and services in the past six months as reverse lend-lease from Australia and New Zealand, and in India. These were the months in which the forces under General MacArthur were completing the New Guinea campaign and were preparing to launch the campaign for the liberation of the Philippines.

Our forces in the Pacific have already received 1,850,000,000 pounds of food alone from Australia and New Zealand, including more than 400,000,000 pounds of beef and other meats.

Another important reverse lend-lease program in this theater has been the production for our forces of landing craft, small ships and boats, for the campaign we are waging in the Pacific. Tremendous numbers of these boats are needed for landing and supply operations on hundreds of islands scattered across thousands of miles of water. More than 9,500 of these craft had been produced and delivered by Australia alone in time for the Philippines campaign and over 12,000 more are on the way. In addition, Australia and New Zealand have turned over to our forces many hundreds of coastal steamers, barges, tugs, lighters, yachts, and launches.

In India the increased rate of reverse lend-lease aid we have received in the first six months of 1944 has kept pace with the rising tempo of air, land and sea operations in the Burma-India and China theaters. A significant proportion of the supplies we have received in India has consisted of aviation gasoline and other petroleum products drawn from British oil resources in the Middle East and refined at the British refinery at Abadan. This gasoline, provided to us as reverse lend-lease, without payment by us, is helping to power our B-29 Super-Fortresses in their raids from both China and India on the Japanese homeland and on such enemy-occupied strong points as Singapore. It is also being used by the fighter and bomber planes of the 10th and 14th United States Army Air Forces.

II

I take the occasion of this Report again to point out that the reverse lend-lease aid rendered by nations of the British Commonwealth to the United States is only a part of the aid which we have received from the British in fighting this war. The United States has benefited greatly from reverse lend-lease aid, as the facts set forth in this Report indicate. But we have benefited far more, and in a far larger sense, from the total fighting effort of our allies.

As I have stated in previous Lend-Lease Reports and as the Congress has expressed itself in Reports by its appropriate committees at the time of the virtually unanimous renewals of the Lend-Lease Act in 1943 and 1944, lend-lease and reverse lend-lease are not two sides of a financial transaction. We are not loaning money under lend-lease. We are not receiving payments on account under reverse lend-lease. The lend-lease system is, instead, a system of combined war supply, whose sole purpose is to make the most effective use against the enemy of the combined resources of the United Nations, regardless of the origin of the supplies or which of us uses them against the enemy.

Neither the monetary totals of the lend-lease aid we supply, nor the totals of the reverse lend-lease aid we receive are measures of the aid we have given or received in this war. That could be measured only in terms of the total contributions toward winning victory of each of the United Nations. There are no statistical or monetary measurements for the value of courage, skill and sacrifice in the face of death and destruction wrought by our common enemies.

We in the United States can be justly proud of our contributions in men and materials and of the courage and skill and sacrifice of the men and women in our armed forces and of all those others who have devoted themselves selflessly to the war effort at home. We can also be rightly proud of and grateful for the contributions in men and materials of our allies and the courage and skill and sacrifice of their soldiers, airmen, seamen and peoples.

In this war the United Nations have all drawn strength from each other — our allies from us and we from them. We can now begin to see the full significance of the overwhelming power that this steadily closer partnership has created. We already know how much it did to save us all from disaster. We know that it has brought and will bring final victory months closer than would otherwise have been possible.

Lend-lease and reverse lend-lease are a system of combined war supply. They should end with the war. But the United Nations partnership must go on and must grow stronger. For the tasks of building a workable peace that will endure, we shall need all the strength that a permanent and stronger United Nations can provide in winning security from aggression, in building the economic foundations for a more prosperous world, and in developing wider opportunities for civilized advancement for the American people and for all the other peace-loving peoples of the world.

FRANKLIN D. ROOSEVELT

(a) Reverse Lend-Lease Aid Furnished to United States by British Commonwealth of Nations

	JANUARY–JUNE 1944	CUMULATIVE TO JUNE 30, 1944
United Kingdom	$873,422,000	$2,437,062,000
Australia, New Zealand, and India . . .	350,062,000	911,065,000
Total	$1,223,484,000	$3,348,127,000

(Conversion to dollars at official rates of exchange.)

(b) Reverse Lend-Lease Aid from the United Kingdom

	JANUARY–JUNE 1944	CUMULATIVE TO JUNE 30, 1944
Goods and services transferred in the United Kingdom	$456,527,000	$1,028,787,000
Shipping services	82,010,000	356,050,000
Capital construction in United Kingdom and overseas	148,348,000	704,488,000
Goods and services transferred outside the United Kingdom [1]	186,537,000	347,737,000
Total	$873,422,000	$2,437,062,000

(Conversion from pound sterling at $4.03.)

(c) Reverse Lend-Lease Aid from Australia

	JANUARY–JUNE 1944	CUMULATIVE TO JUNE 30, 1944
Construction	$30,189,000	$123,179,000
Foodstuffs and clothing	23,654,000	118,775,000
Air Force supplies and equipment	4,661,000	40,096,000
Other military supplies and equipment . .	61,633,000	113,233,000
Shipping services and shipbuilding . . .	20,789,000	44,069,000
Transportation and other services	43,980,000	107,918,000
Total	$184,906,000	$547,270,000

(Conversion from Australian pound at $3.23.)

[1] Includes the value of raw materials and foodstuffs and military supplies shipped to or transferred in the United States. Includes transfers in overseas theaters of war to March 31, 1944 only.

(d) Reverse Lend-Lease Aid from New Zealand

	JANUARY–JUNE 1944	CUMULATIVE TO JUNE 30, 1944
Construction	$6,000	$28,570,000
Foodstuffs and clothing	23,011,000	52,511,000
Air Force supplies and equipment	(1)	(1)
Other military supplies and equipment . .	8,526,000	21,893,000
Shipping services and shipbuilding . . .	1,346,000	7,846,000
Transportation and other services	6,404,000	20,359,000
Total	$39,293,000	$131,179,000

(Conversion from New Zealand pound at $3.25.)

(e) Reverse Lend-Lease Aid in India [2]

	JANUARY–JUNE 1944	CUMULATIVE TO JUNE 30, 1944
Construction	$34,202,000	$78,076,000
Foodstuffs and clothing	11,463,000	21,552,000
Air Force and other military supplies and equipment	68,746,000	109,563,000
Shipping services	1,543,000	3,643,000
Transportation and other services	9,909,000	19,782,000
Total [3]	$125,863,000	$232,616,000

5. ECONOMIC WARFARE

A. Organization and Principles

The controversy and acrimonious public debate between Vice President Henry A. Wallace, in his capacity as Chairman of the Board of Economic Warfare, and Secretary of Commerce Jesse H. Jones, in his capacity as head of the Reconstruction Finance Corporation and its numerous subsidiaries, concerning the administration of foreign economic affairs made it necessary for the President "in the public interest," [4] to make certain changes in the administration of measures of economic warfare. These changes were accomplished by Executive Order 9361, establishing the Office of Economic Warfare in the Office for Emergency Management in which were vested powers formerly exercised by a number of separate agencies. Mr. Leo T. Crowley, who had been serving as Alien Property Custodian, was appointed to head this new office.

By Executive Order 9380, September 25, 1943 (see p. 98), the Office of Economic Warfare, and its functions, powers, and duties, were transferred to and consolidated in the Foreign Economic Administration.

[1] Not available separately; included with other military supplies and equipment.

[2] Provided both by the United Kingdom and the Government of India. Based on estimates by the United States Army.

[3] Does not include raw materials and foodstuffs shipped to the United States.

[4] Letter of the President (Roosevelt) to Wallace and Jones, published in the *New York Times*, July 16, 1943.

(1) *Executive Order No. 9361 Supplementing the Executive Order Establishing the Office of War Mobilization and Providing for the Unifying of Foreign Economic Affairs, July 15, 1943* [1]

By virtue of the authority vested in me by the Constitution and the Statutes of the United States, particularly by the First War Powers Act, 1941, as President of the United States and as Commander-in-Chief of the Army and Navy, and in order to provide for the more effective unification of the agencies concerned with foreign economic affairs, it is hereby ordered as follows:

1. The Board of Economic Warfare, existing pursuant to paragraph 2 of Executive Order No. 8839, July 30, 1941, as amended by Executive Order No. 8982, December 17, 1941, is terminated. There is established in the Office for Emergency Management an Office of Economic Warfare, at the head of which shall be a Director, appointed by the President, who shall exercise the functions, powers and duties of the Board of Economic Warfare. The Director shall receive such salary, travel, subsistence or other allowances as the President may determine.

There are transferred to the Office of Economic Warfare for use in connection with the exercise and performance of its functions, powers and duties so much of the unexpended balances, appropriations, allocations and other funds now available for, as well as all the personnel, property and records heretofore used in the administration of the functions, powers and duties of the Board of Economic Warfare.

No part of any funds appropriated or made available under Public 139, approved July 12, 1943, shall be used, directly or indirectly, after August 15, 1943, by the Office of Economic Warfare for the procurement of services, supplies, or equipment outside the United States except for the purpose of executing general economic programs or policies formally approved in writing by a majority of the War Mobilization Committee and such writing has been filed with the Secretary of State prior to any such expenditure.

2. The United States Commercial Company, the Rubber Development Corporation, the Petroleum Reserves Corporation and the Export-Import Bank of Washington and their functions, powers and duties, together with the functions, powers and duties of the Reconstruction Finance Corporation and of the Secretary of Commerce with respect to them are transferred to the Office of Economic Warfare. All personnel, property, records, funds (including all unexpended balances of appropriations, allocations or other funds now available), contracts, assets, liabilities and capital stock of these corporations, together with so much of the personnel, records and property of the Reconstruction Finance Corporation used in the administration of these corporations as the Director of the

---

[1] 8 *Fed. Reg.*, p. 9861.

Bureau of the Budget shall determine, are transferred with these corporations to the Office of Economic Warfare for use in connection with the exercise and performance of its functions, powers and duties. The Director of the Office of Economic Warfare may reconstitute the Boards of Directors of these corporations and take such other action as he deems necessary in respect of them to carry out the purposes of this Order.

3. (a) Until such time as the Congress shall provide other means of financing, the Secretary of Commerce and the Reconstruction Finance Corporation are authorized and directed to supply necessary funds to the corporations transferred to the Office of Economic Warfare by this Order through loans, using for this purpose all the borrowing powers and unobligated funds of the Reconstruction Finance Corporation. Such funds shall be supplied at such times and in such amounts and in such manner and upon such terms and conditions as the Director of War Mobilization, on the request of the Director of the Office of Economic Warfare, may from time to time determine. The disbursement of the funds so supplied shall be under the exclusive direction of the Director of the Office of Economic Warfare, except as otherwise provided by this Order.

(b) The functions, powers and duties and outstanding contracts and obligations relating to activities and transactions in or pertaining to foreign countries, now vested in, or in the name of, any corporation created and organized under Section 5 (d) of the Reconstruction Finance Corporation Act, or of any other corporation organized by the Reconstruction Finance Corporation, shall, unless the Director of War Mobilization otherwise determines, be transferred to the corporation or corporations designated by the Director of the Office of Economic Warfare, and the charter and by-laws of the corporations affected by such transfers, so far as necessary, shall be amended accordingly. Following such transfers, no corporations created and organized by the Reconstruction Finance Corporation, other than those transferred to the Office of Economic Warfare by this Order, shall exercise any of its powers and functions in regard to any activity or transaction in or pertaining to any foreign country except as ordered by the Director of War Mobilization. The Secretary of Commerce, the Reconstruction Finance Corporation, and any corporation organized by it, shall execute and deliver all instruments which may be deemed necessary by the Director of War Mobilization to carry out the provisions of this Order.

4. The functions of the Office of War Mobilization shall include the authority to arrange for the unification and coordination of the activities of the Federal Government relating to foreign supply, foreign procurement and other foreign economic affairs in conformity with the foreign policy of the United States as defined by the Secretary of State. In providing for such unification the Office of War Mobilization may utilize

the facilities of other departments and agencies, including the machinery for the coordination of foreign economic affairs established in the Department of State.

5. All prior Executive orders and directives in so far as they are in conflict herewith are amended accordingly.

(a) Order No. 1 of the Director (Crowley), Office of Economic Warfare, July 16, 1943 [1]

By virtue of the authority vested in me by Executive Order No. 9361 of July 15, 1943, it is hereby ordered as follows:

Pending my further order, all licenses, orders, rules and regulations, procedures, instructions and delegations of authority, of whatever character, heretofore issued, prescribed or executed by, on behalf of, or with respect to, the Board of Economic Warfare, the corporations referred to in paragraph 2 of said Order, and, with respect to their activities and transactions in or pertaining to foreign countries, the corporations referred to in paragraph 3 (b) of said Order, are hereby ratified, confirmed and continued in effect, and any action taken thereunder shall be deemed to be in conformity with said Order, even though performed in the name of the Board of Economic Warfare.

(2) General Economic Programs and Policies. Resolution Approved by the War Mobilization Committee, July 29, 1943 [2]

WHEREAS, under the provisions of Executive Order No. 9361 of July 15, 1943, it is provided —

No part of any funds appropriated or made available under Public 139, approved July 12, 1943 shall be used, directly or indirectly, after August 15, 1943, by the Office of Economic Warfare for the procurement of services, supplies, or equipment outside the United States except for the purpose of executing general economic programs or policies formally approved in writing by a majority of the War Mobilization Committee and such writing has been filed with the Secretary of State prior to any such expenditure.

Now, THEREFORE, BE IT RESOLVED:

That, pursuant to the above-quoted provision, the activities carried on by or on behalf of the Office of Economic Warfare shall be restricted to the executing of the following general economic programs and policies which are hereby approved by the undersigned, who constitute a majority or more of the War Mobilization Committee:

Exports

To control the commercial exportation from the United States and its Territories, dependencies and possessions, of articles, materials, supplies

[1] *Ibid.*
[2] From the Office of Economic Defense, *Comprehensive Export Schedule*, No. 14 (issued by the Foreign Economic Administration, June 5, 1944), p. 3.

and technical data so as to: (1) prevent the exportation of any articles, materials, supplies or technical data to such destinations, in such amounts or to such consignees as might aid directly or indirectly the enemy; (2) prevent the exportation, except for the purposes set forth in items (4) to (8) herein, of articles, materials or supplies required within the United States, its Territories, dependencies or possessions, for the war production effort and the civilian economy; (3) prevent the exportation of technical data except where necessary to assist in the development of industrial and mechanical techniques employed in furtherance of the war program of the United Nations and where adequate assurance is provided that such data will not be made available to unfriendly interests or where the nature of the data is such that indiscriminate disclosure will not impair the national defense or well being of the country; (4) supply materials needed to maintain and expand the production and procurement abroad of strategic and critical materials required for the war effort and civilian economies of the United Nations; (5) supply materials to allied countries of the kinds and in the amounts necessary to maintain their war and domestic economies; (6) supply materials to friendly countries of the kinds and in the amounts necessary to maintain their domestic economies; (7) insure, within the limitations of shipping availabilities, the priority of movement of goods most essential to the economies of such allied or other friendly countries; (8) control the shipment of goods to European and other neutrals with a view to obtaining from them concessions helpful to the war program of the United Nations and detrimental to the war effort of the enemy countries; and, incident to the foregoing, (9) locate stranded critical and strategic materials, including materials the exportation of which has been denied, and direct such materials in active channels where they will further the war program, either through the medium of voluntary resale or requisitioning and, where requisitioning is necessary, determine the fair and just compensation to be paid the owner; and, in the administration of said programs and policies, so administer its controls, consistent with the war exigencies, as to maintain and strengthen private trade channels and protect the trade position of the United States.

Imports

To provide for the procurement and production of materials and commodities in foreign countries so as to: (1) effectuate with maximum speed the execution of directives of the Chairman of the War Production Board and War Food Administrator as to quantities, specifications, delivery time schedules, and priorities of materials and commodities required to be imported for the war production effort and the civilian economy; (2) obtain, through preclusive purchase, materials and commodities, whether or not included in said directives of the War Production Board or the War Food Administrator, which may be vital to the enemy, either for military or civilian needs; (3) at the request of, or in cooperation with, as the case may be, the Department of State, the Lend-Lease Administration, the Army, the Navy or other affected agencies, arrange for the purchase or receipt of commodities for stockpile, stabilization or other approved purposes, and, pursuant to the priority determinations of the War Production Board and in collaboration with the War Shipping Administration, supervise the transportation of said commodities; and in the administration of said programs and policies, so far as consistent with the war exigencies, maintain and strengthen private trade channels, and protect the trade position of the United States.

Economic Warfare Analysis

To recommend or direct appropriate economic warfare measures, within the limits of prescribed authority, and, for these purposes, to collect, analyze and evaluate economic intelligence in order to: (1) maintain and tighten the blockade of the European continent; (2) injure the enemy and aid the United Nations by means of trade controls designed to secure maximum supplies and to restrict the flow of materials to the enemy; (3) work with other interested agencies in the elimination from Latin America of Axis or other economic interests inimical to the United States; (4) work with other interested agencies in the handling of economic problems in reoccupied or liberated areas; (5) perform technical services and operations necessary to the work of the Office of Economic Warfare abroad, in the fields of industrial engineering, petroleum, air transport, economic intelligence, cartography; and (6) assist the armed services in (a) estimating enemy economic war capabilities; (b) analyzing bombing objectives in terms of industrial importance and susceptibility to damage; (c) assessing economic damage caused by bombing of specific targets and relating such damage to the total enemy productive capacity; and (d) meeting the problems of overseas supply.

RESOLVED, FURTHER, that this resolution be executed in triplicate; one copy to be filed with the Secretary of State, one with the Comptroller General, and one retained as part of the permanent records of this Committee.

JAMES F. BYRNES	ROBERT P. PATTERSON
Office of War Mobilization	*Acting Secretary of War*
FRED M. VINSON	FRANK KNOX
Office of Economic Stabilization	*Secretary of the Navy*
MARVIN JONES	D. M. NELSON
Food Administrator	*Chairman, War Production Board*

B. Trading With the Enemy

[See *Documents, IV, 1941–42*, p. 760; *V, 1942–43*, p. 132.]

(1) *Regulations Relating to Trade or Communication with or by an Enemy National. General Ruling No. 11, March 18, 1943,*[1] *as Amended September 3, 1943* [2]

This ruling was made under Executive Order 8389,[3] as amended, Executive Order 9193,[4] and Sections 3 (*a*) and 5 (*b*) of the Trading With the Enemy Act, as amended by the First War Powers Act, 1941.[5]

Under the regulations a special license is required lawfully to engage in any business or commercial communication or intercourse with an enemy national or to effect any act or transaction involving such communication or intercourse. Unlicensed trade or communication with an enemy national is unlawful under Sections 3 (*a*) and 5 (*b*) of the Trading With the Enemy Act, as amended.

The term "enemy national" includes any person within any enemy country or enemy occupied territory and any person whose name appears on The Proclaimed List of Certain Blocked Nationals. The regulations also include within the category of enemy nationals any other person to the extent that he is acting without a license for or on behalf of an enemy national who is within an enemy country or whose name appears on The Proclaimed List. Treasury officials emphasized that subjects of enemy and enemy occupied countries who are not within enemy territory are not by reason of their citizenship alone enemy nationals within the meaning of the regulations. It was also pointed out that the occupying forces of the United Nations and civilians accompanying them who are within enemy territory in the course of their duties are not enemy nationals.

The regulations strike at any act or transaction of a financial, business, trade or commercial character which involves any trade or communication with an enemy national. In substance, the regulations are directed at all transactions included within the definition of the term "to trade" contained in Section 2 of the Trading With the Enemy Act, as amended.

Treasury officials called attention to the fact that the regulations prohibit certain transactions which are not prohibited by the freezing order. In this connection, Treasury officials stated that a transaction on behalf of an enemy national who is within an enemy country or whose name appears on The Proclaimed List which is prohibited by the freezing order may lawfully be effected if licensed under the freezing order, unless it also involves communication with any enemy national. On the other hand, a transaction which is within the purview only of the regulations or involves communication with any enemy national, may lawfully be effected only pursuant to a license which specifically refers to General Ruling No. 11.

Treasury officials noted that compliance with the regulations did not dispense with the necessity of complying with relevant censorship regulations.

------

(1) *Trade and Communication With an Enemy National Prohibited.* Unless authorized by a license expressly referring to this general ruling, no person shall, directly or indirectly, enter into, carry on, complete, perform, effect, or otherwise engage in, any trade or communication with an enemy national, or any act or

[1] See *Documents, IV, 1941–42*, p. 767.
[2] From the Treasury Department.
[3] 6 *Fed. Reg.*, p. 2897, 3715, 6348, 6785.
[4] 7 *ibid.*, p. 5205.
[5] See *Documents, IV, 1941–42*, p. 763.

transaction which involves, directly or indirectly, any trade or communication with an enemy national.

(2) *Acts and Transactions by an Enemy National Prohibited.* Unless authorized by a license expressly referring to this general ruling, no enemy national who is within the United States shall, directly or indirectly, enter into, carry on, complete, perform, effect, or otherwise engage in, any financial, business, trade, or other commercial act or transaction.

(3) *Certain Transactions Licensed Under Section 3 (a).* Every act or transaction prohibited by Section 3 (a) of the Trading With the Enemy Act, as amended, is hereby licensed thereunder unless such act or transaction is prohibited by paragraph (1) or paragraph (2) hereof or otherwise prohibited pursuant to Section 5 (b) of that Act and not licensed by the Secretary of the Treasury. Attention is directed to the fact that the General License under Section 3 (a) of the Act, issued by the President on December 13, 1941, does not license any act or transaction not authorized hereunder.

(4) *Definitions.* As used in this general ruling and in any other rulings, licenses, instructions, etc.:

(a) The term "enemy national" shall mean the following:

(i) The Government of any country against which the United States has declared war (Germany, Italy, Japan, Bulgaria, Hungary, and Rumania) and any agent, instrumentality, or representative of the foregoing Governments, or other person acting therefor, wherever situated (including the accredited representatives of other governments to the extent, and only to the extent, that they are actually representing the interests of the Governments of Germany, Italy, and Japan and Bulgaria, Hungary, and Rumania);

(ii) The government of any other blocked country having its seat within enemy territory, and any agent, instrumentality, or representative thereof, or other person acting therefor, actually situated within enemy territory;

(iii) Any individual within enemy territory, except any individual who is with the armed forces of any of the United Nations in the course of his service with such forces or who is accompanying such armed forces in the course of his employment by any of the Governments of the United Nations or organizations acting on their behalf;

(iv) Any partnership, association, corporation or other organization to the extent that it is actually situated within enemy territory;

(v) Any person whose name appears on The Proclaimed List of Certain Blocked Nationals, and any person to the extent that he is acting, directly or indirectly, for the benefit or on behalf of any such person; *provided* that no person so acting shall be deemed to be an enemy national if he is acting pursuant to license issued under the Order or expressly referring to this general ruling; and

(vi) Any person to the extent that he is acting, directly or indirectly, for the benefit or on behalf of an enemy national (other than a member of the armed forces of the United States captured by the enemy) if such enemy national is within any country against which the United States has declared war; *provided* that no person so acting shall be deemed to be an enemy national if he is acting pursuant to license issued under the Order or expressly referring to this general ruling.

(b) The term "enemy territory" shall mean the following:

   (i) The territory of Germany, Italy, Japan, Bulgaria, Hungary, and Rumania; and

   (ii) The territory controlled or occupied by the military, naval, or police forces or other authority of Germany, Italy, or Japan.
   The territory so controlled or occupied shall be deemed to be the territory of Albania; Austria; that portion of Belgium within continental Europe; Bulgaria; that portion of Burma occupied by Japan; that portion of China occupied by Japan; Czechoslovakia; Danzig; that portion of Denmark within continental Europe; Estonia; that portion of France within continental Europe, including Monaco and Corsica; French Indo-China; Greece; Hong Kong; Hungary; Latvia; Lithuania; Luxemburg; British Malaya; that portion of the Netherlands within continental Europe; that portion of the Netherlands East Indies occupied by Japan; Norway; that portion of the Philippine Islands occupied by Japan; Poland; Rumania; San Marino; Thailand; that portion of the Union of Soviet Socialist Republics occupied by Germany; Yugoslavia; and any other territory controlled or occupied by Germany, Italy or Japan.

(c) The term "The Proclaimed List of Certain Blocked Nationals" shall mean The Proclaimed List of Certain Blocked Nationals, as amended and supplemented, promulgated pursuant to the President's Proclamation of July 17, 1941.

(d) The term "trade or communication with an enemy national" shall mean any form of business or commercial communication or intercourse with an enemy national after March 18, 1942, including, without limitation, the sending, taking, obtaining, conveying, bringing, transporting, importing, exporting, or transmitting, or the attempt to send, take, obtain, convey, bring, transport, import, export, or transmit,

   (i) Any letter, writing, paper, telegram, cablegram, wireless message, telephone message, or other communication, whether oral or written, of a financial, commercial, or business character; or

   (ii) Any property of any nature whatsoever, including any goods, wares, merchandise, securities, currency, stamps, coin, bullion, money, checks, drafts, proxies, powers of attorney, evidences of ownership, evidences of indebtedness, evidences of property, or contracts;

directly or indirectly to or from an enemy national after March 18, 1942; *provided, however,* that with respect to any government or person becoming an enemy national after March 18, 1942, the date upon which such government or person became an enemy national shall be substituted for the date March 18, 1942.

RANDOLPH PAUL
Acting Secretary of the Treasury

C. Export Control

[See *Documents, II, 1939–40,* p. 786; *III, 1940–41,* p. 473; *IV, 1941–42,* p. 718; and *V, 1942–43,* p. 137.]

During the period under review no important changes were made in the system of export control. The decentralization plan of export control, announced on

March 3, 1943,[1] was applied and further developed to meet the special requirements of our trade with the American Republics, and a system of "program
licenses," announced on March 10, 1943,[2] was applied and developed to cover
exports of goods to given destinations (all British Empire or other allied countries) "shipped through private trade and Lend-Lease channels to such destination for specific end-uses." For further and detailed information on the system
of export control as it developed in the light of experience, see *Comprehensive
Export Schedule*, Number 14, issued June 5, 1944, by the Foreign Economic
Administration, Bureau of Supplies, Requirements and Supply Branch, Washington, D. C.

In connection with Latin American trade, the Foreign Economic Administration announced on March 15 [3] that it was lessening some of the controls
over the shipment of several groups of manufactured goods to Latin American
Republics in an attempt "to bring exporter and importer in closer contact
with each other." It was explained that this was in line with the Administration's policy of clearing the way for the expeditious handling of articles at present
in limited supply "when and if" they are in greater supply. The modification
specifically introduced was that exporters would no longer be required to show
an "import recommendation."

D. Foreign Funds Control

[See *Documents, III, 1940–41*, p. 533; *IV, 1941–42*, p. 740; *V, 1942–43*, p. 149.]

(1) *Regulations Relating to Securities Accounts of Banks or Other Financial Institutions Located in Block Countries. General Ruling No. 17, October 20, 1943* [4]

This Ruling was issued under Executive Order 8389,[5] as Amended, Executive
Order 9193,[6] and Sections 3 (*a*) and 5 (*b*) of the *Trading With the Enemy Act*,
as amended by the *First War Powers Act, 1941*.[7]

The new regulations constituted a further measure to prevent Axis nationals
and Axis sympathizers from cloaking their securities holdings and financial
transactions in the United States.

Securities accounts maintained in the United States in the name of foreign
financial institutions were known to contain securities beneficially owned by
clients or customers of such institutions. However, such securities were in no
way differentiated from securities owned by the foreign financial institution
itself. If securities held in an account of a foreign financial institution were
sold, the proceeds reverted to its general blocked account. However, this might
mean that the foreign financial institution would credit the proceeds in its home
office to the account of the beneficial owner of the securities. Such owner might
well be an Axis national who would thus receive the benefits of free foreign
exchange. Furthermore, such Axis national might have acquired his "ownership," either literally or figuratively, at the point of a gun.

For some time the Treasury had been scrutinizing this situation and its various ramifications. Controls had been imposed in specific cases, and this ruling
formalized such controls in a general manner.

Under General Ruling No. 17 there may not be any sales or purchases of
securities or receipt of income on securities held in the account of a foreign finan-

---

[1] *Documents, V, 1942–43*, p. 138.
[2] *Ibid.*, p. 145.
[3] *Current Export Bulletin*, No. 152.
[4] From the Office of Foreign Funds Control, Treasury Department.
[5] 6 *Fed. Reg.*, p. 2897, 3715, 6348, 6785.
[6] 7 *ibid.*, p. 5205.
[7] See *Documents, IV, 1941–42*, p. 763.

cial institution within a blocked country unless the banking institution in the United States which holds the securities has complete information as to the past and present beneficial ownership of the securities. As an alternative to the obtaining of such information, the banking institution in the United States may conduct such securities transactions on the basis of a certification obtained from the foreign financial institution. The terms of the certification are specifically spelled out in the new regulations. Among other things, they require such foreign institutions to commit themselves to submit, upon request, full evidence of beneficial ownership of the securities.

In order to avoid creating additional burdens for domestic coupon and dividend paying agents and to minimize possible losses where neither such information nor certification is available, the regulations also permit sales of securities and the receipt of dividends and interest thereon, provided the proceeds are deposited into a specially restricted account called a General Ruling No. 6 account.

The new regulations exempt from their operation every transaction effected under the general licenses extended to Portugal, Spain, Sweden and Switzerland or their central banks. However, it is to be noted that such general licenses contain restrictive provisions similar to those incorporated into the new regulations. Thus, in using their general licenses, these neutral countries commit themselves not to engage in any transaction involving Axis nationals or Axis interests.

----

(1) *Scope of Ruling.* This ruling is applicable to (*i*) every sale of securities held in any account maintained in the name of any bank or other financial institution which is located in a blocked country and which is not licensed as a generally licensed national, (*ii*) every purchase of securities where the cost thereof is to be debited to any account maintained in the name of any such bank or financial institution, and (*iii*) the receipt of dividends or interest or other income on securities held in any account maintained in the name of any such bank or financial institution, except —

    (*a*) Transactions effected under General Licenses Nos. 49, 50, 52, or 70; or

    (*b*) Sales of securities or the receipt of dividends, interest or other income on securities effected under any other general license or under any specific license, provided that the proceeds thereof are deposited in a General Ruling No. 6 account in the name of such bank or other financial institution; or

    (*c*) Transactions effected pursuant to certification as provided in Section (3) hereof.

(2) *Purchase and sales of securities and the receipt of dividends, interest or other income on securities not authorized in the absence of certain information.* No purchase or sale of securities or the receipt of dividends, interest or other income on securities to which this ruling is applicable may be effected under any specific or general license which does not expressly refer to this General Ruling unless the person with whom the account is maintained is in possession of the following information:

    (*a*) In the case of any proposed sale of securities or the receipt of dividends, interest or other income on securities —

        (*i*) The name, address and nationality of each person having an interest in the securities on the date when such securities were received into the account or on April 8, 1940, whichever is later; and (*ii*) The name, address and nationality of each person having an interest in the securities on the date when the transaction is effected; and

(*iii*) If the information submitted with respect to (*i*) and (*ii*) disclose, that there has been any change in any interest in such securitiess the name, address and nationality of each transferee of any such interest, the date of each such transfer, and the license under the Order, if any, pursuant to which it is claimed that each such transfer was effected; or

(*b*) In the case of any proposed purchase of securities —

(*i*) The name, address and nationality of each person who will have an interest in such securities as a result of such transaction.

(3) *Certification.* Notwithstanding Section (2) hereof, this ruling shall not be applicable to any purchase or sale of securities or the receipt of dividends, interest or other income on securities if the bank or other financial institution in whose name the account is maintained has certified to the person with whom such account is maintained:

(*a*) In the case of any proposed sale of securities or the receipt of dividends, interest or other income on securities —

(*i*) That no person who is a national of any blocked country other than the country in which such bank or other financial institution is located, and that no person whose name appears on The Proclaimed List of Certain Blocked Nationals has an interest in the securities, and that no such person has had an interest in such securities since April 8, 1940, or the date when such securities were received into the account, whichever is later; and

(*ii*) That such bank or other financial institution will upon request at any time promptly submit to the diplomatic or consular representatives of the Government of the United States, duly accredited to the country in which it is located, satisfactory evidence of, and, in any event, will submit to the Treasury Department, Washington, D. C., in duplicate, not later than one year after the termination of the present war, a verified statement disclosing (A) the name, address and nationality of each person having an interest in the securities on the date when such securities were received into the account or on April 8, 1940, whichever is later; (B) the name, address and nationality of each person having an interest in the securities on the date when the transaction was effected; and (C) if the information submitted with respect to (A) and (B) discloses that there has been any change in any interest in such securities, the name, address and nationality of each transferee of any such interest, the date of each such transfer, and the license under the Order, if any, pursuant to which it is claimed that each such transfer was effected; or

(*b*) In the case of any proposed purchase of securities —

(*i*) That no person who is a national of any blocked country other than the country in which such bank or other financial institution is located, and that no person whose name appears on The Proclaimed List of Certain Blocked Nationals will have an interest in such securities as a result of such transaction; and

(*ii*) That such bank or other financial institution will upon request at any time promptly submit to the diplomatic or consular representatives of the Government of the United States duly accredited to the country in which it is located, satisfactory evidence of, and, in any event, will submit to the Treasury Department, in Washington, D. C., in duplicate, not later than one year after the termination of the present war, a verified statement disclosing (A) the name, address and nationality of each person who acquired an interest in the securities at the time of their purchase; (B) the name, address and nationality of each person having an interest in the securities as of any date or dates (hereafter prescribed) subsequent to the deposit of such securities in, and prior to their withdrawal from the account; and (C) if the information submitted with respect to (A) and (B) discloses that there has been any change in any interest in such securities, the name, address and nationality of each transferee of any such interest, the date of each such transfer, and the license under the Order, if any, pursuant to which it is claimed that each such transfer was effected.

(4) *Recording and reporting of information and the effectuation of transactions under Section (2) hereof.* (a) When any sale of securities or the receipt of any dividends, interest or other income to which this ruling is applicable has been effected, the proceeds may be credited to any account authorized by license, provided that, if such account is not maintained in the name or names of the beneficial owner or owners of the securities, a memorandum record is kept of the amount so credited and of the name, address and nationality of each such beneficial owner. In the case of the receipt of dividends, interest or other income on securities, a memorandum record shall also be kept with respect to such securities in the manner prescribed in Section (4) (b) hereof.

(b) When any purchase of securities to which this ruling is applicable has been effected, the securities may be deposited in any account authorized by license, provided that if such account is not maintained in the name or names of the beneficial owner or owners of the securities, a memorandum record is kept of the securities so deposited and of the name, address and nationality of each such beneficial owner.

(c) Any information specified in Section (2) (a) hereof required to be reported on Form TFR-300 by the person holding the securities, but which has not heretofore been so reported, shall be reported on Form TFR-300, as provided in Section 130.4 of the Regulations and Public Circular No. 4, not later than thirty days after a sale of the securities or the receipt of dividends, interest or other income thereon effected under Section (2) hereof. All information specified in Section (2) of this ruling with respect to securities in an account maintained in the name of a bank or other financial institution which is located in a blocked country, and which is not licensed as a generally licensed national, not otherwise required to be reported on Form TFR-300, shall be reported by the person with whom such account is maintained on Form TFR-300, Series L, in the manner provided in Public Circular No. 4 C, as of the date of the receipt of such securities in such account. Every such report on Form TFR-300, Series L, shall be filed within thirty days after a purchase or sale of the securities or the receipt of dividends, interest or other income thereon effected under Section (2) hereof, whichever occurs first, and shall state that it is made in accordance with General Ruling No. 17.

(5) *Effectuation and recording of certified transactions.* When any purchase or sale of securities or the receipt of any dividends, interest or other income thereon to which this ruling would otherwise be applicable has been effected pursuant to the certification specified in Section (3) hereof, the proceeds of the

securities sold, or the dividends, interest or other income received may be credited to, or the securities purchased may be deposited in, any account authorized by license, provided, however, that a memorandum record is kept of the transaction and that it was effected pursuant to certification under Section (3) of this ruling. Each such memorandum record shall bear the name of the bank or other financial institution making the certification, and the number of such certification.

(6) *Form of certification and continuing effect of certain certifications.* (a) No form is prescribed for the certification specified in Section (3) hereof, but the certifications of each bank or other financial institution shall be numbered consecutively and every statement submitted to the Treasury Department in accordance with Sections (3) (*a*) (*ii*) and (3) (*b*) (*ii*) hereof shall refer to the number of the certification pursuant to which the transaction was effected. The certification specified in Section (3) hereof may be made by a cable or wireless message which clearly identifies the transaction, and states, in code or otherwise, that the sender makes the certification specified in Section (3) of General Ruling No. 17.

(*b*) A certification made under Section (3) (*a*) hereof with respect to the receipt of dividends, interest or other income on securities will, unless the bank or other financial institution making the certification expressly stipulates otherwise, be deemed to be a continuing certification applicable to the further receipt of dividends, interest or other income on the same securities, and the phrase "the date when the transaction was effected" in clause (B) of Section (3) (*a*) (*ii*) hereof shall be deemed, in the case of such certification, to mean the date of each receipt of dividends, interest or other income on such securities effected under such certification.

(7) *Proceeds of sales and income from securities to be deposited in General Ruling No. 6 accounts.* All proceeds of sales of securities and all dividends, interest or other income received on securities held in any account maintained in the name of any bank or other financial institution which is located in a blocked country, and not licensed as a generally licensed national, shall be deposited in a General Ruling No. 6 account in the name of such bank or other financial institution, unless —

    (*a*) The person with whom the account is maintained is in possession of the information specified in Section (2) (*a*) hereof with respect to such securities; or

    (*b*) The bank or other financial institution in whose name the account is maintained has made the certification specified in Section (3) (*a*) hereof with respect to such securities; or

    (*c*) The sale of such securities or the receipt of such dividends, interest, or other income was effected under General Licenses Nos. 49, 50, 52, or 70.

(8) *Savings Provision.* None of the provisions of this General Ruling shall be applicable (*a*) to purchases or sales of securities effected within thirty calendar days after the date hereof pursuant to orders to buy or to sell specific securities, provided, however, that such orders are outstanding on the date hereof; or (*b*) to the receipt of dividends, interest or other income on securities within thirty calendar days after the date hereof.

(9) *Dollar accounts maintained with a bank or other financial institution which is a national of a blocked country.* The Secretary of the Treasury may, in his discretion, as a condition to the exercise of the privileges of a license issued, or the issuance of a license, under the Order, or otherwise, require a verified statement from any bank or other financial institution which is a national of a blocked country and maintains a dollar or securities account with a person within the

United States, disclosing the names, nationalities and such other information as may be prescribed, concerning any or all persons who have maintained dollar accounts with such bank or other financial institution since the effective date of the Order with respect to such persons.

(10) *Definitions.* For the purposes of this General Ruling:

(a) The term "bank or other financial institution" shall include every person engaged in the business of (*i*) banking, (*ii*) insurance, (*iii*) buying, selling or otherwise dealing in securities, or (*iv*) managing, operating, conducting or otherwise holding securities or securities accounts for others;

(b) The term "dividends, interest or other income on securities" shall include payments of principal and payments on account of the retirement or redemption of securities; and

(c) The term "nationality" shall mean the names of all countries of which a person is a national within the meaning of the Order.

RANDOLPH PAUL
Acting Secretary of the Treasury

E. Proclaimed List of Certain Blocked Nationals

[See *Documents, IV, 1941–42*, p. 752; *V, 1942–43*, p. 152.]

For a detailed account of the manner in which the Proclaimed List of Certain Blocked Nationals is used, see address entitled "Some Economic Weapons in Total Warfare" by Francis H. Russell, Chief of Division of World Trade Intelligence, Department of State, at the annual meeting of the American Drug Manufacturers Association, Hot Springs, Virginia, May 4, 1944. The text of this address is given in Department of State, *Bulletin*, X, p. 405.

(1) *Revisions of the Proclaimed List of Certain Blocked Nationals, as of June 30, 1944* [1]

REVISION	SUPPLEMENT	DATE	Federal Register	
		1943	*Vol.*	*Page*
V	3	Jul. 2	8	9181
	4	Jul. 30	"	10707
	5	Aug. 27	"	11894
	6	Sept. 24	"	13092
VI		Oct. 7	"	13883
	1	Oct. 22	"	14426
	2	Nov. 19	"	15816
	3	Dec. 17	"	16962
		1944		
	4	Jan. 14	9	652
	5	Feb. 11	"	1693
	6	Mar. 10	"	2772
VII		Mar. 23	"	3285
	1	Apr. 7	"	3833
	2	May 5	"	4858
	3	June 2	"	6056
	4	June 30	"	7369

[1] Continuation of list in *ibid., V, 1942–43*, p. 153.

F. Treatment of Enemy Property

[See *Documents, IV, 1941–42*, p. 830; *V, 1942–43*, p. 156.]

No significant changes were made in the period under review either in the policy or the administrative organization and procedures for dealing with enemy property. The first annual report of the Office of Alien Property Custodian, covering the period beginning March 11, 1942, and ending June 30, 1943, was submitted by the President to the Congress on February 14, 1944.[1] In his letter of transmittal, Mr. Crowley reviewed the work of the Office and the policies which had been in practice pursued. For greater detail on the points covered, see the text of the report and appendices.

(1) *Letter from the Alien Property Custodian (Crowley) to the President (Roosevelt), Transmitting the Annual Report of the Alien Property Custodian for the Period March 11, 1942 to June 30, 1943* [2]

[Excerpt]

The amount of enemy-owned property in the United States at the beginning of the present war was less than it was at the time of our entry into the First World War, even though Japan and Italy were not our enemies in the First World War. In the years intervening between 1920 and 1939, the countries with which we are now at war were in no economic position to export substantial amounts of capital. In fact, the net movement of capital was the other way. The rigid controls which these countries imposed on exchange transactions during most of these years tended to keep their capital at home, while large-scale military preparations absorbed a substantial proportion of their investments abroad.

Nevertheless, the amount of enemy-owned property in the United States was still rather substantial at the time of our entry into this war. Moreover, regardless of the total value of enemy-owned property, much of it was of strategic importance in American industry. Wartime control over enemy-owned property serves the double purpose of eliminating any benefit to the enemy from these assets and of making available productive enterprises and strategic materials to promote our own war effort. In addition, wartime control is essential to prevent property from becoming derelict.

In contrast with the method of handling enemy property that was followed during the last war, a distinction has been drawn this time between two broad classes of property. Cash and investment securities not involving control over specific productive assets have been placed within the jurisdiction of the Treasury Department. Other types of property, particularly productive assets, which must not only be kept from the enemy but which also must be positively controlled if they are to continue as parts of our economic system, have been placed under jurisdiction of the Office of Alien Property Custodian.

[1] House Doc. No. 417, 78th Cong., 2d sess.   [2] *Ibid.*, p. 1.

Property with which the Office deals falls into five main groups:

1. Business enterprises.
2. Patents, trade-marks, and copyrights.
3. Real and personal property.
4. Ships.
5. Property in process of judicial administration.

Three basic forms of control are employed by the Alien Property Custodian in dealing with properties under his jurisdiction. The first involves an outright transfer of title to the property from the foreign owner to the Custodian. Each such transfer is accomplished through what is known as a "vesting" order issued by the Custodian. The second, used in cases where it is not thought desirable to take title or as an interim protective device while true beneficial ownership of properties is being investigated, involves the issuance by the Custodian of a "supervisory" order which has the effect of giving him control of the use and operation of the property without transfer of title. A procedure has been established for receiving and evaluating interim claims of non-enemy persons who are affected by either type of order. The third form of control is exercised through general orders and related regulations, which require persons having interests in certain classes of property to perform certain acts or to refrain from their performance.

During the period covered by this report 1,792 vesting orders were issued. Under these orders, and related supervisory orders, the Office of Alien Property Custodian assumed control of property whose total estimated value is $356,000,000, in which the vested enemy interest is roughly estimated at $125,000,000. In addition, there have been vested 41,000 patents and patent applications, as well as a large number of valuable copyrights and trade-marks, for which values cannot be assigned. Supervisory control without transfer of title was assumed during the period over property valued at about $20,000,000, under supervisory orders.

In terms of ownership, the manufacturing enterprises, patents, and miscellaneous properties were predominantly German, the trading companies, banks, and insurance companies mostly Japanese. Italian properties, except for ships, are of minor significance and little or no property of consequence has been discovered belonging to nationals of Rumania, Hungary, or Bulgaria.

It remains for Congress to determine the ultimate disposition of enemy property subjected to the control of this Office. In the meantime, the functions of the Custodian are twofold — to search out and seize enemy property and property interests, and to administer these and supervised properties in such a way that the American economy and the American war effort will derive the maximum benefits of control.

Some 200 of the enterprises taken over by the Office of Alien Property Custodian, principally trading companies, banks, and insurance companies, are being liquidated. These, it was determined, have no particular contribution to make as going concerns, and can best serve the national interest if their productive assets and the labor they employ are made available to other producers. These liquidations are being carried out under direction of salaried employees of the Office of Alien Property Custodian.

The immediate problem in dealing with the remaining business enterprises which are being continued as going concerns is to make sure that each has a loyal, highly competent management that will make a full contribution to the war effort. In many of these enterprises the Office has retained existing management. In these cases the management was judged to be able and loyal, and production results so far indicate that all productive resources are being fully utilized. The Office has uniformly refrained from interfering with existing arrangements of these companies for legal, engineering, or auditing services. It will continue to be our policy to avoid interference of any sort with managements of controlled companies so long as production results are satisfactory.

Where it has been found necessary to replace management, the task of securing competent and skilled personnel under wartime conditions has been difficult. In today's highly competitive manpower market, men are reluctant to leave secure positions for new places unless they can be assured security of tenure and adequate income. In many cases the Office uses its own salaried employees in vested companies as members of boards of directors and in supervisory capacities.

As a point of national policy it will probably become advisable to dispose ultimately of most or all of the vested properties that are maintained as going concerns. A desirable sales policy must foster continued existence of these enterprises as strong and economically independent producing entities.

The Office of Alien Property Custodian has fixed upon a policy of public sales of properties to the highest bidders, reserving the right to weigh, in addition to monetary considerations, the competence of the bidders to maintain the property as a valuable producing concern, their willingness to maintain it as a freely competing institution, and operate it with due regard for the national interest of the United States.

Wherever feasible a wide distribution of the stock of formerly enemy-owned companies will be encouraged. In some of the more important enterprises the method of voting trusts will be used so as to prevent transfer of the shares to enemy nationals for a specified period of time.

During the past year this Office has vested some 36,000 patents and 5,000 patent applications formerly owned by nationals of Axis and Axis-controlled countries. The inventions and processes covered by these patents and applications relate to every field of industrial activity but are most heavily concentrated in the fields of chemistry, electrical equipment, plastics, and pharmaceuticals. Many of them relate to the production of ordnance and aircraft.

The technical subject matter of both vested patents and patent applications is being made widely known to American industry and to all war agencies. Patents taken from the enemy nationals which are not already under exclusive license to Americans are being licensed by this Office on a nonexclusive, royalty-free basis. The patents taken from nationals of enemy-occupied countries which are not already under license to Americans are to be licensed on a royalty-free basis for the duration of the war with a provision for reasonable royalty payments thereafter. All royalty payments due under vested patents are being collected by this Office.

Many of the vested patents are already under license to American industry and of these some are tied up with agreements restricting price, production, use, sale, and market area. The interests of foreign nationals in contracts relating to United States patents, including the licensed vested patents, are being vested, and wherever possible the contracts will be modified to remove the restrictive provisions.

The copyright interests of foreign nationals in approximately 72,000 works have already been vested by this Office. Royalty due on these is being collected. The publication of works not now available is being fostered. Microfilm reproduction of approximately 500 enemy scientific books and periodicals has been authorized and licenses have been granted to reprint over 250 volumes of German scientific works.

Under terms of Executive Order No. 9325,[1] signed by the President April 7, 1943, necessary administrative costs of the Office of Alien Property Custodian, as approved by the Bureau of the Budget, are chargeable to the properties held by the Office.

G. Capture and Disposition of Prizes

[See *Documents, V, 1942–43*, p. 165.]

(1) *An Act to Amend the Act Approved August 18, 1942, Entitled " An Act to Facilitate the Disposition of Prizes Captured by the United States during the Present War, and for Other Purposes," Approved July 1, 1944* [2]

Prior to August 18, 1942, all prizes, regardless where captured, were required to be returned to the United States for adjudication. The Act of August 18, 1942 [3] exempted from this requirement vessels which, during the present war, were captured "on the high seas" and taken into the territorial waters of a cobelligerent, or were taken or appropriated for the use of the United States "on the high seas or in such territorial waters." It established a procedure whereby district courts of the United States might adjudicate prizes located

8 *Fed. Reg.*, p. 4682.   [2] Public Law 407, 78th Cong.   [3] *Documents, V, 1942–43*, p. 165.

outside their territorial jurisdiction. Section 1 of the Act of July 1, 1944 broadens the coverage of the 1942 Act to permit adjudication, outside the territorial waters of the United States, of captures occurring other than on the high seas, *i.e.*, in harbors, bays, ports and inland waters, and of prizes taken or appropriated for the use of the United States in any waters whatsoever.

The Act originated as H. R. 4348. The bill was recommended by the Navy Department, the War Shipping Administration and the Department of Justice. For reports of the House and Senate Committees on the Judiciary, see House Report No. 1359, 78th Cong., 2d sess., and Senate Report No. 920, 78th Cong., 2d sess.

Be it enacted by the Senate and House of Representatives of the United States of America in Congress assembled, That section 1 of the Act entitled "An Act to facilitate the disposition of prizes captured by the United States during the present war, and for other purposes," approved August 18, 1942 (56 Stat. 746, 50 App. U. S. C. 821 ff.), is amended to read as follows: "That the district courts shall have original jurisdiction of all prizes captured during war if said capture was made by authority of the United States or was adopted and ratified by the President of the United States and the prize was brought into the territorial waters of a cobelligerent or was taken or appropriated for the use of the United States, including jurisdiction of all proceedings for the condemnation of such property taken as prize."

SEC. 2. That section 4 of such Act is amended by striking out the period at the end of said section and by inserting in lieu thereof a colon and by adding immediately thereafter the following: "*Provided,* That notwithstanding any other provision of law, if the seized property is taken or appropriated for the use of the United States whether before or after it comes into the custody of the prize court, the prize court is hereby authorized to proceed to adjudication on the basis of an inventory and survey and an appropriate undertaking by the United States to respond for the value of such property without the necessity for either an appraisement or the deposit of the value of the prize with the Treasurer of the United States or any other public depository."

SEC. 3. That the title of such Act is amended by striking out the words "the present" therein so that the title, as amended, shall read "An Act to facilitate the disposition of prizes captured by the United States during war, and for other purposes."

By Proclamation No. 2594 [1] dated September 27, 1943 the President extended to the Government of Canada "privileges with respect to prizes captured under authority of the said Government and brought into the territorial waters of the United States or taken or appropriated in the territorial waters of the United States for the use of the said Government," Canada having already consented to like treatment for prizes of the United States.

By Proclamation No. 2601 [2] dated November 28, 1943 the President extended like privileges to the Government of India on the same condition.

[1] 8 *Fed. Reg.*, p. 13217.   [2] *Ibid.*, p. 16351.

6. PUBLIC INFORMATION AND PROPAGANDA

[See *Documents, IV, 1941–42*, p. 185; *V, 1942–43*, p. 167.]

Broader responsibility for the clearance of war news to the newspapers and radio was assumed by the Office of Censorship under revised codes of wartime practices for the press and radio issued on December 10, 1943, to become effective immediately.[1] Whereas the original codes urged withholding of information except where it was made available for publication "by appropriate authority," the new documents added "or is specifically cleared by the Office of Censorship."

(1) *Statements of the Secretary of State (Hull) on Alleged Suppression of Political News, March 27 and 28, 1944* [2]

In an address delivered on March 24, Governor Dewey of New York said: "When we find the State Department requesting the British censor to suppress political news sent to American papers by American correspondents abroad, it begins to amount to a deliberate and dangerous policy of suppression of the news at home."

Secretary Hull was asked on March 27 whether he would comment on this statement. In the *New York Times* of March 28, there appeared a cable from the London office in which certain queries were raised regarding the phraseology of Mr. Hull's statement. The statement of March 28 was by way of comment on that.

(a) Statement of March 27

Governor Dewey is 100 percent wrong in the accuracy of his statement. All my life I have not only talked about a free press, I have fought for it. When these rumors of political censorship in England started in November 1942 I wrote Byron Price and cabled Ambassador Winant to tell Mr. Eden my conviction that "fundamentally the long-range interests of international friendship are best served by permitting the people of any country to know what people in friendly countries are thinking and saying about them, however unpleasant some of those opinions may be." Both Mr. Price and Mr. Eden expressed full agreement.

These rumors cropped up again while I was in Florida last month, and Mr. Stettinius made unequivocally clear that that is still our policy. His statement was published widely at the time.

I am glad to see a press dispatch from London yesterday stating that the British Government fully understands, and shares, our opposition to political censorship and our conviction that plain speaking is more healthful than suppression.

---

[1] Press Release of Office of Censorship, December 10, 1943. For texts, see *Code of Wartime Practices for the American Press* (Edition of December 1, 1943); *Code of Wartime Practices for American Broadcasters* (Edition of December 1, 1943).

[2] Department of State, *Bulletin*, X, p. 300.

(b) Statement of March 28

The statement I gave you yesterday is entirely accurate. We have never requested the British for any kind of censorship whatsoever except on grounds of military security or for the safety of high officials while traveling. There seems to be a confusion between the censorship of news in the possession of the press and the avoidance of premature disclosures to the press of confidential information. The disclosure of confidential information is a matter between the governments conducting negotiations, et cetera, and upon which there is usually consultation before publication. We ourselves never think of publishing something in that connection without first conferring with the other government and having an agreement. That is a matter for decisions of the governments and not a matter of censorship.

Where there has occurred in the past premature disclosure to the press by unauthorized officials, usually anonymous, on either the part of this Government or the British Government, each Government has customarily called the attention of the other Government to the infringement of agreement between the two Governments. Any such action is in no way related to the question of censorship upon which our position is unequivocal and clear.

Any claim that the State Department has requested the British censor to suppress political news is therefore entirely wrong.

CHAPTER IV

THE AXIS POWERS

1. AMERICAN POLICY TOWARD ENEMY STATES AFTER CONCLUSION OF HOSTILITIES

[See *Documents, V, 1942–43*, p. 169.]

A. General Statements

(1) Letter of the President (Roosevelt) to Congress Transmitting the Eleventh Report on Lend-Lease Operations, August 25, 1943 [1]

[Excerpt]

. . . .

The subjugated peoples of Nazi Europe are now aware that the European fortress is not impregnable. The great offensives of the Soviet Army on the Eastern Front, the continued heroic struggle of the Chinese, and the British offensives in other areas, aided by lend-lease munitions and supplies, are having their repercussions both on and behind the battle lines. Our might and that of our allies is being felt in the Axis satellite nations of the Balkans and Middle Europe, and in Nazi Germany as well. From Hamburg on the North Sea to Ploesti in Rumania, the people know from first-hand experience with what crushing force the United Nations can strike.

Except for the responsible fascist leaders, the people of the Axis need not fear unconditional surrender to the United Nations. I have said that we shall bring food for the starving and medicine for the sick in the areas liberated by the United Nations. We have done so, under lend-lease, in North Africa. We are doing so in Sicily. We shall continue to do so in other areas, as they are liberated, to prevent economic breakdown and to aid the liberated peoples to produce and to help themselves. We shall provide these necessary civilian supplies in support of our military operations and as a matter of simple humanity. The people of Axis-controlled areas may be assured that when they agree to unconditional surrender they will not be trading Axis despotism for ruin under the United Nations. The goal of the United Nations is to permit liberated peoples to create a free political life of their own choosing and to attain economic security. These are two of the great objectives of the Atlantic Charter.

. . . .

[1] Department of State, *Bulletin*, IX, p. 124, 125; *Eleventh Report on Lend-Lease Operations for the Period Ending July 31, 1943*.

B. Italy

1. SURRENDER OF THE ITALIAN GOVERNMENT

The invasion and occupation of Italian territory provided the first test case of United Nations' policy in the treatment of defeated enemy countries and of actual administration of such countries. For the first time, the personnel of the Allied Military Government had an opportunity to put its plans and machinery into operation in enemy territory.

The invasion of Sicily commenced on the night of July 9, 1943, after months of preliminary preparation, on the east and south coasts of the island. The initial assault was carried out from North Africa by British, American, and Canadian troops, with some Polish, Czech, Yugoslav, Greek and French units. The invasion came at a time when Soviet forces were engaging the Germans in heavy and crucial fighting in Eastern Europe. It was spearheaded by the British Eighth Army, under General Sir Bernard L. Montgomery, and the American Seventh Army, under Lieutenant General George S. Patton. The former landed on Sicily's east coast, struck toward Catania and the ultimate objective of Messina. The latter landed on the south coast, moved west, towards Agrigento and then north with the aim of seizing the heart of the Axis communication system. Everywhere, Italian resistance was somewhat less than determined. Palermo surrendered on July 22 and on August 17 the Third Division of the American Seventh Army entered Messina and the conquest of Sicily was completed in 38 days.

The Algiers radio broadcast a proclamation on July 10, 1943 of General Dwight Eisenhower from Allied Headquarters to the Sicilian people stating that the Fascist party, together with all its connected associations, such as the Fascist Militia, would be dissolved in all Italian territory occupied by the Allies. The spreading of Fascist propaganda, under any form, would be prohibited, and no political activity of any kind would be tolerated during the period of military government. Appropriate measures would be immediately taken for the abrogation of all laws discriminating on the basis of race, color or religion.

On the same day, Hitler and Mussolini met at Verona and decided on military measures to be taken on the Mediterranean and eastern fronts, which they regarded as closely interdependent. On July 24 Mussolini made a statement on the political and military situation at a meeting of the Fascist Grand Council and a resolution presented by Dino Grandi, the President, was passed by 19 votes to 7, inviting Mussolini to ask the King to assume command of the armed forces. Early on July 25, after an all-night session, the Council deposed Mussolini. His resignation as Prime Minister and Secretary of State was accepted by the King on the same day. King Victor Emmanuel III, who had issued a proclamation announcing that he had assumed leadership of the armed forces, named Marshal Pietro Badoglio as the new Prime Minister, and asked him to form a government. Mussolini was taken from the Palazzo Venezia and was imprisoned on the Gran Sasso. The new Council of Ministers decided upon the formal dissolution of the Fascist party on July 27. The unlimited powers of the Grand Council under the law of December 1928 were repealed, the special tribunal for the defense of the State was suppressed and all affairs for which it was responsible were transferred to the military tribunals of the Army Corps for the duration of the war. Marshal Badoglio put the country under martial law and assumed direct control of all armed forces, police, civil guards and the Fascist Militia. He also dissolved all political parties for the duration of the war. The closure of the Senate and Legislature was proposed and the Chamber of Fasces and Corporations was dissolved. A new Chamber of Deputies would be elected within four months after the end of the war and a new Legislature would be set up.

On July 29 a message from General Eisenhower was broadcast to the Italian people commending them and the House of Savoy on ridding themselves of Mussolini, and pointing out that the only remaining obstacle to peace was the

German aggressor, still on Italian soil. He said the Italians could have peace under honorable conditions, which had already been offered by the British and United States Governments. Rome radio stated on July 30 that proposals for unconditional surrender meant the utilization of Italian territory to continue the war against Germany and that this excluded the possibility of a real peace for Italy. A further warning to the Italian people was broadcast from Allied Headquarters in Algiers on August 2 threatening invasion by air and land forces and announcing that the Allies had waited 8 days for the Badoglio Government to accept the terms of surrender.

A proclamation announcing that he had asked General Eisenhower for an armistice and that it had been granted was issued by Marshal Badoglio on September 8. The armistice was actually signed on September 3, upon the fall of Sicily, but the announcement was withheld until September 8, when Allied landings were made on the Calabrian Coast near Naples and at Salerno by the American Fifth Army. The full terms of the armistice have not been made public, but the military terms were published on September 13 and were as follows: [1]

1. Immediate cessation of all hostile activity by the Italian armed forces.

2. Italy will use its best endeavors to deny to Germans facilities that might be used against the United Nations.

3. All prisoners or internees of the United Nations to be immediately turned over to Allied Commissioner-in-Control and none of these may now, or at any time, be evacuated to Germany.

4. Immediate transfer of Italian fleet and Italian aircraft to such points as may be designated by Allied C.-in-C. with details of disarmament prescribed by him.

5. Italian merchant shipping may be requisitioned by the Allied C.-in-C. to meet the needs of the military and naval program.

6. Immediate surrender of Corsica and all Italian territory, both of islands and mainland, to the Allies for such use as operational bases and other purposes as the Allies may see fit.

7. Immediate guarantee of free use by the Allies of all airfields and naval ports in Italian territory, regardless of the rate of evacuation of Italian territory by German forces. These ports and fields to be protected by Italian armed forces until this function is taken over by the Allies.

8. The immediate withdrawal to Italy of Italian armed forces from all participation in the current war from whatever area wherein they may now be engaged.

9. Guarantee by the Italian Government that if necessary it will employ all available armed forces to ensure prompt and exact compliance with all provisions of this armistice.

10. The C.-in-C. of the Allied Forces reserves to himself the right to take any measures which in his opinion may be necessary for the protection and interests of the Allied Forces for the prosecution of the war, and the Italian Government binds itself to take such administrative or other actions as the C.-in-C. may require, and, in particular, the C.-in-C. will establish Allied Military Government over such parts of Italian territory as he may deem necessary in the military interests of the Allied Nations.

11. The C.-in-C. of the Allied Forces will have full right to impose the measures of disarmament, demobilization and demilitarization.

12. Other conditions of political, economic and financial nature, with which Italy will be bound to comply, will be transmitted at a later date.

13. The conditions of the present armistice will not be made public without the previous approval of the Allied C.-in-C. The English version will be considered the official text.

The clauses providing for the turning over of Allied prisoners and internees, the transfer of merchant shipping and aircraft, the surrender of Corsica, the guaranteed use of airfields, ports, etc. had, however, been rendered inapplicable in those parts of Italy where German armed forces had taken control. General

[1] *Bulletin of International News*, XX (1943), p. 825.

Eisenhower emphasized, nevertheless, the importance of the single fact of possession of the Italian fleet, the main portion of which was later massed at Malta.

However, the expulsion of German forces from the rest of Italy remained a colossal task. News of the armistice was the signal for intense German activity and Northern and Central Italy were occupied by German forces. On September 12 Field Marshal Kesselring proclaimed all Italian territory under his jurisdiction to be a war zone under German martial law. Rome, however, was to be recognized as an open city, in accordance with the announcement of the Italian Government of August 14, declaring "formally and publicly without further delay that Rome is an open city, and that all necessary measures in conformity with international law are being taken." [1] The King and Marshal Badoglio departed for southern Italy a few days before the armistice.

From the German radio on September 12 came the announcement of the escape of Mussolini to Germany with the aid of German paratroopers. From his refuge, Mussolini directed the reestablishment of the Fascist Party in Northern Italy and addressed the Fascists in a proclamation announcing that he had resumed supreme direction of Fascism in Italy, and that henceforth the "true party," to be termed the Republican Fascist Party, would be reorganized and reconstituted with the purposes of aiding German forces, aiding the people, seeking out and punishing the party traitors and resuming governmental posts.

(1) *Proclamation of the Commander-in-Chief of the Allied Forces (Eisenhower) to the People of Sicily, Posted Following the Landing of Allied Troops in Sicily, July 10, 1943* [2]

To THE PEOPLE OF SICILY:

As Commander-in-Chief of the Allied forces I transmit this message on behalf of the Governments of the United States and Great Britain.

Allied forces are occupying Italian territory. They are doing so not as enemies of the Italian people but as an inevitable part of their war to destroy the German overlordship of Europe.

Their aim is to deliver the people of Italy from a Fascist regime which led them into the war, and when that has been accomplished to restore Italy as a free nation.

Allied forces have no intention of changing or undermining the traditional laws and customs of the Italian people. They will take necessary steps, however, to eliminate the Fascist system in whatever territory they occupy.

Accordingly, the Fascist organization will be dissolved and its appendages, such as the Fascist Militia and the so-called Youth Organization, will be abolished. Fascist doctrines and propaganda in any form will be prohibited. No political activity whatsoever shall be countenanced during the period of military government.

In furtherance of the policies of the Allied Governments, proper steps will forthwith be taken to stop the operation of all laws which discriminate on the basis of race, color or creed. Freedom of religious worship

[1] *Bulletin of International News*, XX (1943), p. 755.
[2] *New York Times*, July 21, 1943.

will be upheld, and to the extent that military interests are not prejudiced freedom of speech and of the press will be instituted.

Measures will be taken for the prompt release of political prisoners. The Special Tribunal for the Defense of the State will be abolished.

The Military Governor of the occupied territory will take action by proclamation or otherwise to carry into effect the foregoing measures as military conditions may permit.

These evidence the principles to which the Allies are attached and for the reestablishment of which they will relentlessly fight. They are the principles to which the Axis leaders under German domination are opposed. You will be the beneficiaries of their defeat.

It is therefore to your interests as men whose fathers fought for freedom not to resist the Allied arms, but to facilitate their mission — the lifting of the Nazi yoke by quick and total victory.

(2) *Message of the President* (*Roosevelt*) *and the Prime Minister of the United Kingdom* (*Churchill*) *to the People of Italy, July 16, 1943* [1]

At this moment the combined armed forces of the United States and Great Britain under the command of General Eisenhower and his Deputy General Alexander are carrying the war deep into the territory of your country. This is the direct consequence of the shameful leadership to which you have been subjected by Mussolini and his Fascist regime.

Mussolini carried you into this war as the satellite of a brutal destroyer of peoples and liberties. Mussolini plunged you into a war which he thought Hitler had already won. In spite of Italy's great vulnerability to attack by air and sea, your Fascist leaders sent your sons, your ships, your air forces, to distant battlefields to aid Germany in her attempt to conquer England, Russia, and the world. This association with the designs of Nazi-controlled Germany was unworthy of Italy's ancient traditions of freedom and culture — traditions to which the peoples of America and Great Britain owe so much.

Your soldiers have fought not in the interests of Italy but for Nazi Germany. They have fought courageously, but they have been betrayed and abandoned by the Germans on the Russian front and on every battlefield in Africa from El Alamein to Cape Bon. Today Germany's hopes for world conquest have been blasted on all fronts. The skies over Italy are dominated by the vast air armadas of the United States and Great Britain. Italy's seacoasts are threatened by the greatest accumulation of British and Allied sea power ever concentrated in the Mediterranean.

The forces now opposed to you are pledged to destroy the power of Nazi Germany — power which has ruthlessly been used to inflict slavery,

[1] Department of State, *Bulletin*, IX, p. 27.

destruction, and death on all those who refuse to recognize the Germans as the master race. The sole hope for Italy's survival lies in honorable capitulation to the overwhelming power of the military forces of the United Nations. If you continue to tolerate the Fascist regime which serves the evil power of the Nazis, you must suffer the consequences of your own choice. We take no satisfaction in invading Italian soil and bringing the tragic devastation of war home to the Italian people. But we are determined to destroy the false leaders and their doctrines which have brought Italy to her present position.

Every moment that you resist the combined forces of the United Nations — every drop of blood that you sacrifice — can serve only one purpose: to give the Fascist and Nazi leaders a little more time to escape from the inevitable consequences of their own crimes. All your interests and all your traditions have been betrayed by Nazi Germany and your own false and corrupt leaders; it is only by disavowing both that a reconstituted Italy can hope to occupy a respected place in the family of European Nations.

The time has now come for you, the Italian people, to consult your own self-respect and your own interests and your own desire for a restoration of national dignity, security, and peace. The time has come for you to decide whether Italians shall die for Mussolini and Hitler — or live for Italy, and for civilization.

(3) *Address by the President* (*Roosevelt*), *July 28, 1943* [1]

[Excerpts]

Over a year and a half ago I said to the Congress: "The militarists in Berlin, Rome, and Tokyo started this war, but the massed, angered forces of common humanity will finish it."

That prophecy is in the process of being fulfilled. The massed, angered forces of common humanity are on the march. They are going forward — on the Russian front, in the vast Pacific area, and into Europe — converging upon their ultimate objectives, Berlin and Tokyo.

The first crack in the Axis has come. The criminal, corrupt Fascist regime in Italy is going to pieces.

The pirate philosophy of the Fascists and Nazis cannot stand adversity. The military superiority of the United Nations — on sea and land, and in the air — has been applied in the right place and at the right time.

Hitler refused to send sufficient help to save Mussolini. In fact, Hitler's troops in Sicily stole the Italians' motor equipment, leaving Italian soldiers so stranded that they had no choice but to surrender. Once again the Germans betrayed their Italian allies, as they had done

---

[1] Broadcast from the White House; Department of State, *Bulletin*, IX, p. 57.

time and time again on the Russian front and in the long retreat from Egypt, through Libya and Tripoli, to the final surrender in Tunisia.

Mussolini came to the reluctant conclusion that the "jig was up"; he could see the shadow of the long arm of justice.

But he and his Fascist gang will be brought to book and punished for their crimes against humanity. No criminal will be allowed to escape by the expedient of "resignation."

Our terms to Italy are still the same as our terms to Germany and Japan — "unconditional surrender."

We will have no truck with Fascism in any way, shape, or manner. We will permit no vestige of Fascism to remain.

Eventually Italy will reconstitute herself. It will be the people of Italy who will do that, choosing their own government in accordance with the basic democratic principles of liberty and equality. In the meantime, the United Nations will not follow the pattern set by Mussolini and Hitler and the Japanese for the treatment of occupied countries — the pattern of pillage and starvation.

We are already helping the Italian people in Sicily. With their cordial cooperation we are establishing and maintaining security and order, we are dissolving the organizations which have kept them under Fascist tyranny, we are providing them with the necessities of life until the time comes when they can fully provide for themselves.

Indeed, the people in Sicily today are rejoicing in the fact that, for the first time in years, they are permitted to enjoy the fruits of their own labors — they can eat what they themselves grow instead of having it stolen from them by the Fascists and the Nazis.

In every country conquered by the Nazis, the Fascists, or the Japanese militarists, the people have been reduced to the status of slaves or chattels.

It is our determination to restore these conquered peoples to the dignity of human beings, masters of their own fate, entitled to freedom of speech, freedom of religion, freedom from want, freedom from fear.

We have started to make good on that promise.

I am sorry if I step on the toes of those Americans who, playing party politics at home, call that kind of foreign policy "crazy altruism" and "starry-eyed dreaming."

Meanwhile the war in Sicily and Italy goes on. It must go on, and will go on, until the Italian people realize the futility of continuing to fight in a lost cause — a cause to which the people of Italy never gave their whole-hearted approval and support.

.   .   .   .

The same kind of careful planning that gained victory in North Africa and Sicily is required if we are to make victory an enduring reality and do our share in building the kind of peaceful world which will justify the sacrifices made in this war.

The United Nations are substantially agreed on the general objectives for the post-war world. They are also agreed that this is not the time to engage in an international discussion of *all* the terms of peace and *all* the details of the future. We must not relax our pressure on the enemy by taking time out to define every boundary and settle every political controversy in every part of the world. The all-important thing now is to get on with the war — and to win it.

While concentrating on military victory we are not neglecting the planning of the things to come, the freedoms which we know will make for more decency and greater justice throughout the world.

.   .   .   .

(4) *Statement of the Commander-in-Chief of the Allied Forces (Eisenhower) to the Italian People, July 29, 1943* [1]

We commend the Italian people and the House of Savoy for ridding themselves of Mussolini, the man who involved them in the war as a tool of Hitler and brought them to the verge of disaster.

The greatest obstacle which divided the Italian people from the United Nations has been removed by the Italians themselves. The only remaining obstacle on the road to peace is the German aggressor, who is still on Italian soil.

You want peace. You can have peace immediately and peace under honorable conditions which our Governments have already offered you.

We are coming to you as liberators. Your part is to cease immediately any assistance to German military forces in your country. If you do this we will rid you of the Germans and deliver you from the horrors of war.

As you have already seen in Sicily, our occupation will be mild and beneficent.

Your men will return to their normal life and to their productive avocations and, provided all British and Allied prisoners now in your hands are restored safely to us and not taken away to Germany, the hundreds of thousands of Italian prisoners captured by us in Tunisia and Sicily will return to the countless Italian homes who long for them.

Ancient traditions and liberties of your country will be restored.

(5) *Joint Statement by the Treasury Department and the War Department on the Introduction of Allied Military Currency and Postage Stamps, Sicily, August 2, 1943* [2]

Allied expeditionary forces, seeking to establish orderly relationships with the people of liberated Sicily, are introducing into its occupied areas

[1] *New York Times*, July 30, 1943.   [2] From the Treasury Department.

an "Allied Military Currency," speaking a "Lira" language that will be understood by every Sicilian trader and consumer.

It may now be revealed that a distinctive currency, determined upon by British and American officials, was made in the Treasury's Bureau of Engraving and Printing. It was rushed to the scene of action by huge transport planes and is being used as the medium of exchange in that part of Italy that we now hold.

A part of its legend reads "Issued in Italy."

At the same time, it was revealed, a comparable series of postage stamps will be introduced into the areas under military administration.

This is the first truly Allied venture into the field of military monetary expedients and an undertaking without precedent so far as the United States is concerned. The distinctive lira currency will be used in the payment of troops of all the Allied nations on Italian soil, and in payment by the procurement services for local supplies.

Government officials said the undertaking is designed to give the occupied areas a currency in denominations and terms which they know.

It provides an adequate circulating medium in sections where there may be a shortage of local currency because of confiscation or destruction by retreating enemy forces, or from other causes.

It avoids complication of the monetary system which use of foreign currencies might cause.

Previously, the United States forces in North Africa had used a regular "back home" currency with a distinctive seal, while the British had used a "military pound." Now, authorities of the Allied Nations have worked out this cooperative use of a single medium of exchange.

The preparation of this military currency and postage in advance of the invasion of Italy is itself an amazing chapter in the story of the gigantic and minutely-detailed planning that preceded the expedition, a story that must, for the most part, remain untold until after the war. From the standpoint of the physical undertaking alone, there is no precedent for such a job. Presses of the Bureau of Engraving and Printing worked 24 hours a day, not even pausing for meal periods, for weeks, to have the stocks of notes and stamps ready for the final, revealing overprinting when the invasion actually began.

The planning of the job goes back some four months, when high officials of the Treasury, the War and Navy Departments, the Department of State, and officials of the British Government laid the groundwork in a series of extraordinary conferences held in utmost secrecy.

No inkling of the project ever was put in writing, no word of it spoken over a telephone, and no discussions of it carried outside the conference rooms.

Designs for the notes and stamps had to be completed under similar conditions of secrecy, and stocks of distinctive paper and huge amounts of inks of various colors accumulated. In none of this preliminary work was the country for which the notes were intended ever identified.

On the basic designs under consideration, where now the words "Issued in Italy" appear, the words "United States" were placed fictitiously, and where the "lira" designation is printed were such unrevealing terms as "dollars" or "shillings."

Basic printing of the notes began early in June, with the name of the country and the currency designation still omitted. Huge stocks of the partially finished notes were accumulated against the day when the "go" signal should be given.

The invasion news was flashed to the world on the night of July 9. Key employees of the Bureau of Engraving and Printing stood by their telephones throughout Sunday, and continued at their posts until the printing order was released by Army authorities actually on Tuesday, July 13. Huge presses immediately began to roll, overprinting the partially-completed notes with the identifying legends.

By Saturday, July 17, enough had been completed to load a huge transport plane, but transportation was not available until Monday, July 19, when two planes carrying seven tons of the distinctive money took off. Other shipments have followed, both of currency and stamps.

The currency introduced into Sicily is in eight denominations from one to 1,000 lira. The smaller denominations are half the size of United States currency, and the larger denominations the same size. It is made by a lithograph process, since the time element and the size of the undertaking did not permit steel engraving.

Except for the "lira" designation, all the legend on the bills is in English. "The "Four Freedoms," Freedom of Speech, Freedom of Religion, Freedom from Want, and Freedom from Fear, appear prominently on the reverse sides of all the notes. Ornate designs in pantograph, of a neutral nature, are used in the series, so that it might be adapted to the needs of troops in further assaults upon Hitler's European fortress merely by overprinting the proper currency designations and name of country on the basic stock.

Smaller notes, of one, two, five and ten lira bear a wheat field scene in brown on the face, with the denomination in the center. Blue, lavender, green and black borders also identify the respective denominations. The words "Allied Military Currency" appear on the upper margin of the face and in an ornate oval on the reverse side. The face also carries the legends, "Series 1943," "Issued in Italy," and a serial number. The Four Freedoms appear in the four corners of the note on the reverse side.

For notes of 50, 100, 500, and 1,000 lira, borders and ornate design of the front are in blue, lavender, green and black, respectively, with the background on all four notes a pale blue. The denomination appears in each of the four corners on the face, and in an ornate shield in the center. The words "Issued in Italy" appear in ovals at each end, and the words "Allied Military Currency" at the bottom of the note. The face also carries the designation "Series 1943," and serial numbers.

The reverse side of these larger notes is a subdued brown, with "Allied Military Currency" appearing in a center shield, and the Four Freedoms in ovals at either side.

The Allied Military Postage stamps are in denominations of 15, 25, 30, 50, and 60 centesimi, and in 1, 2, 5, and 10 lira. They are all of the same design, distinguished by colors of the usual United States postage series. They bear a pantograph background, with white lettering, and the denomination in the center of the stamp, are perforated, and on a gummed paper. Both the stamp design and the overprint are put on in one operation on a two-color press.

(6) *Announcements of the Surrender of the Italian Government*

(a) *Proclamation by the Commander-in-Chief of the Allied Forces (Eisenhower), September 8, 1943* [1]

This is Gen. Dwight D. Eisenhower, Commander-in-Chief of the Allied Forces.

The Italian Government has surrendered its armed forces unconditionally. As Allied Commander-in-Chief, I have granted a military armistice, the terms of which have been approved by the Governments of the United Kingdom, the United States and the Union of Soviet Socialist Republics. Thus I am acting in the interest of the United Nations.

The Italian Government has bound itself to abide by these terms without reservation. The armistice was signed by my representative and the representative of Marshal Badoglio and it becomes effective this instant.

Hostilities between the armed forces of the United Nations and those of Italy terminate at once. All Italians who now act to help eject the German aggressor from Italian soil will have the assistance and the support of the United Nations.

(b) *Proclamation by the Premier of the Italian Government (Badoglio), September 8, 1943* [2]

[Translation]

The Italian Government, recognizing the impossibility of continuing the unequal struggle against the overwhelming power of the enemy, with the object of avoiding further and more grievous harm to the nation, has requested an armistice from General Eisenhower, Commander-in-Chief of the Anglo-American Allied Forces. This request has been

---

[1] *New York Times*, September 9, 1943.   [2] *Ibid.*

granted. The Italian forces will therefore cease all acts of hostility against the Anglo-American forces wherever they may be met. They will, however, oppose attack from any quarter.

(7) *Message of the President (Roosevelt) and the Prime Minister of the United Kingdom (Churchill) to Marshal Badoglio and the People of Italy, September 10, 1943* [1]

It has fallen to you in the hour of your country's agony to take the first decisive steps to win peace and freedom for the Italian people and to win back for Italy an honorable place in the civilization of Europe.

You have already freed your country from Fascist servitude. There remains the even more important task of cleansing the Italian soil from the German invaders. Hitler, through his accomplice Mussolini, has brought Italy to the verge of ruin. He has driven the Italians into disastrous campaigns in the sands of Egypt and the snows of Russia. The Germans have always deserted the Italian troops on the battlefield, sacrificing them contemptuously in order to cover their own retreats. Now Hitler threatens to subject you all to the cruelties he is perpetrating in so many lands.

Now is the time for every Italian to strike his blow. The liberating armies of the Western World are coming to your rescue. We have very strong forces and are entering at many points. The German terror in Italy will not last long. They will be extirpated from your land and you, by helping in this great surge of liberation, will place yourselves once more among the true and long-proved friends of your country from whom you have been so wrongfully estranged.

Take every chance you can. Strike hard and strike home. Have faith in your future. All will come well. March forward with your American and British friends in the great world movement towards Freedom, Justice and Peace.

(8) *Message of the President (Roosevelt) to the Congress of the United States, September 17, 1943* [2]

[Excerpt]

To the Congress of the United States:

On the tenth of July a carefully prepared expedition landed in Sicily. In spite of heavy German opposition it cleared this large and heavily fortified island in thirty-eight days.

British, Canadian and American losses in killed, wounded and missing in the Sicilian campaign were 31,158, of which the American forces lost

[1] Department of State, *Bulletin*, IX, p. 159.

[2] From the Office of the Secretary to the President; *Congressional Record*, vol. 89, p. 7667 (daily edition, September 17, 1943).

7445. The casualties among the Italians and Germans were approximately 165,000, including 132,000 prisoners.

The unmistakably sincere welcome given to the Allied troops by the Italian people has proved conclusively that even in a country which had lived for a generation under a complete dictatorship — with all of its propaganda, censorship, and suppression of free speech and discussion — the love of liberty was unconquerable.

It has also proved conclusively that this war was not waged by the people of Italy on their own choice. All of Mussolini's propaganda machine could not make them love Hitler or hate us. The less said about the feelings toward Mussolini, the better.

I believe that equal jubilation and enthusiasm will be shown by the people of the other nations now under the German heel when Nazi Gauleiters and native Quislings are removed through force or flight.

How different was this invading army of the Allies from the German forces that had come into Sicily, ostensibly to "protect it." Food, clothing, cattle, medicines and household goods had been systematically stolen from the people of Sicily, and sent North to the "master race" in Germany. Sicily, like other parts of Italy and like the other satellite and conquered nations, had been bled white by the Nazi and Fascist governments. Growers of crops were permitted to retain only a small fraction of their own produce for themselves and their families.

With the Allied armies, however, went a carefully planned organization, trained and equipped to give physical care to the local population — food, clothing, medicine. This new organization is also now in the process of restoring to the people of Sicily freedoms which, for many years, had been denied to them. I am confident that, within a year, Sicily will be once more self-supporting — and, in addition to that, once more self-respecting.

From Sicily the advance of the Allied armies has continued to the mainland. On the third day of September they landed on the toe of the Italian peninsula. These were the first Allied troops to invade the continent of Europe in order to liberate the conquered and oppressed countries. History will always remember this day as the beginning of the answer to the prayer of the millions of liberty-loving human beings not only in these conquered lands but all over the world.

On July 25th — two weeks after our first landings in Sicily political events in Italy startled the world. Mussolini, the incubus of Italy for a generation, the man who is more responsible for all of the sorrows of Italy than anyone, except possibly Hitler himself, was forced out of office and stripped of his power as a result of his own dismal failures, his wanton brutalities, and the overwhelming demand of the Italian people. This was the first break in Axis leadership — to be followed, we are determined, by other and similar encouraging downfalls.

But there is one thing I want to make perfectly clear: When Hitler and the Nazis go out, the Prussian military clique must go with them. The war-breeding gangs of militarists must be rooted out of Germany — and out of Japan — if we are to have any real assurance of future peace.

Early last month, the relentless application of overwhelming Allied power — particularly air and sea power — convinced the leaders of Italy that it could not continue an active part in the war. Conversations were begun by them with us. These conversations were carried on with the utmost secrecy. Therefore, much as I wished to do so, I could not communicate the facts of the case to the Congress, or the press, or to those who repeatedly expressed dismay or indignation at our apparent course in Italy. These negotiations turned out to be a complete surprise to nearly everyone, not only to the Axis but to the Italian people themselves.

I am sure that the Congress realizes that there are many situations in this war — and there will be many more to come — in which it is impossible for me to make any announcement or even to give any indication of the policy which we are following. And I ask the American people as well as the Congress to bear with me and with our Chiefs of Staff. It is difficult to remain silent when unjustified attack and criticism come from those who are not in a position to have all the facts.

But the people and the Congress can be sure that the policy which we follow is an expression of the basic democratic traditions and ideals of this Republic. We shall not be able to claim that we have gained total victory in this war if any vestige of Fascism in any of its malignant forms is permitted to survive anywhere in the world.

The Armistice with Italy was signed on September third in Sicily, but it could not be put into effect until September eighth, when we were ready to make landings in force in the Naples area. We had planned these landings some time before and were determined to go through with them, armistice or no armistice.

Italian leaders appealed to their Army and Navy to end hostilities against us. Italian soldiers, though disorganized and ill-supplied, have been fighting the Germans in many regions. In conformity with the terms of unconditional surrender, the Italian fleet has come over to our side; and it can be a powerful weapon in striking at the Nazi enemies of the Italian people.

.   .   .   .

2. RELATIONS WITH THE BADOGLIO GOVERNMENT

On October 1 Marshal Badoglio announced from Bari the formation of a new government under the King with a small preliminary Cabinet. Marshal Badoglio sent a note to General Eisenhower on October 13 informing him that the King had declared war on Germany and General Eisenhower was asked to communicate this information to the other United Nations Governments. On the same day the Marshal broadcast a proclamation to the Italian people announcing the declaration of war and stating "there will not be peace in Italy so long as a single German remains on our soil." The King issued a proclamation on October 18 calling upon the Army to unite with the Anglo-American forces.

It was announced on October 29 that Marshal Badoglio had signed the full armistice terms on September 29, which contained 40 clauses setting forth all the conditions of a political, economic and financial nature.

General Eisenhower announced on November 10 the formation of the "Allied Control Commission for Italy," which had assumed the duty of carrying out the terms of the armistice and of aligning Italian economy in support of the fight against Germany.

Three bodies will operate in Italy under Allied control until the restoration of the liberated areas to the jurisdiction of the Italian Government: The Allied Military Government (A.M.G.); the Allied Control Commission (A.C.C.), which replaced the military mission under General Mason MacFarlane, who had been appointed to the Badoglio Government at the time of the armistice; and the Advisory Council for Italy (see p. 238).

On November 12 the Committee of National Liberation, an association of all political parties formed in Naples, issued a statement demanding immediate formation of a political government and the abdication of King Victor Emmanuel. Mass meetings in other cities called for the abolition of the Monarchy. The Naples Committee telegraphed to President Roosevelt, Marshal Stalin and Prime Minister Churchill on December 19 protesting against the prohibition by the Allied military authorities of a congress of democratic parties. The ban was withdrawn on December 21 by A.M.G., provided the meeting was held farther from the front than Naples and that no more than 90 people attended.

A congress of Provincial Commissioners of Liberation opened at Bari on January 28 and passed a resolution demanding abdication of the King and calling for the summoning of a constituent assembly at the end of hostilities and the immediate formation of a permanent executive committee composed of all parties in the congress.

The Italian Government announced on March 13 that diplomatic relations had been established with the Soviet Union and that this move had resulted from Italian initiative. The Badoglio Government severed relations with Finland on March 14. The National Council of the Italian Communist Party issued a call on April 1 for the formation of a united democratic, Liberal, anti-Fascist front. At a meeting on April 6 of the Democratic *Junta* it was reported by Signor Croce that negotiations with the King had led to an offer of withdrawal when Rome was freed. The previous day Humbert, Prince of Piedmont, told the press that he was prepared to act as Regent for his father, thereby clearing the way for a coalition government of all the chief parties. On April 12 the King announced in a broadcast his decision to withdraw from public affairs when the Allies entered Rome and to appoint the Prince of Piedmont as Lieutenant of the Realm. A meeting of the *Junta* attended by all six parties agreed on this appointment in lieu of abdication, and on April 17 Marshal Badoglio presented the resignation of the Cabinet to the King. A new Cabinet on a broader foundation was announced on April 21, which included Palmiro Togliatti (better known as Ercole Ercoli or Mario Ercoli), leader of the Communist Party, as Minister without portfolio. The Cabinet issued a declaration of policy on the 27th pronouncing its chief task to be the conduct of the war and proposing to create a small consultative body to take the place of Parliament "in agreement with the committees of liberation."

On May 24 the Government issued a declaration on foreign policy with the following heads: (1) They repudiated the entire foreign policy of the Fascists, (2) the war would be prosecuted until the final defeat of Hitlerism, (3) they condemned the invasion of France, Greece, Yugoslavia and Albania and desired Albania to regain her independence as soon as possible, (4) they intended to adopt a policy of friendly cooperation so that destruction done by the war might be repaired and the injuries wrought by the Fascists determined and (5) they would contribute to the creation of a new international law in accordance with the Atlantic Charter.

(1) *Address by Assistant Secretary of State Berle before the Italian-American Labor Council, New York City, October 12, 1943* [1]

[Excerpt]

. . . .

The relations between the United States and such an Italian government — as, indeed, with all countries — were clearly outlined only a month ago by Secretary Hull: "Cooperation between nations in the spirit of good neighbors, founded on the principles of liberty, equality, justice, morality, and law, is the most effective method of safeguarding and promoting the political, the economic, the social, and the cultural well-being of our nation and of all nations."

Toward this goal we have already traveled a long, difficult, bloody road. We shall have tragic and anxious hours before it is achieved. But faith shall not waver, and courage shall not fail.

Nearly a year ago we met together after the armies of the United Nations, under American command, had entered the Mediterranean and liberated North Africa. This Government clearly stated, first, that the United Nations proposed to restore to liberated Italy her essential nationhood; but, second, that rebirth of Italian freedom could be won only if Italians themselves expelled the Fascist crew which had seized their Government, and, as Italians, joined the common fight against the Nazi oppressors, enemies of Italy and of mankind.

In the months which followed, armies of the United Nations entered Sicily and Italy as liberators and as friends of the Italian people. The common and kindly folk of the streets, the villages, and the farms were swift to welcome them as friends. From Lombard and Piedmont cities to the Campania, old groups in Italy arose in wrath; labor unions, democratic organizations, simple neighborhoods spoke with the new voice of popular authority. A timid crew of Fascist leaders meeting in council knew at long last that their day was done. On July 25, under pressure from the people, they deposed the Duce. Immediately after, many of them fled to Germany. Marshal Badoglio, placing himself in charge, promptly abolished the Fascist government, imprisoned Mussolini, dissolved the Fascist party, released the political prisoners of the Fascist regime, and opened negotiations with the American and British commanders of the Allied forces.

The Nazi generals realized little of the true significance of those

[1] Department of State, *Bulletin*, IX, p. 256.

flaming days. Hitler had forgotten that Italy was or could be an independent nation. But the little people of the streets who demanded peace
with the Allies knew better. They knew that peace with the United Nations inevitably meant war with the Nazis. Actually, the putting into
effect of Marshal Badoglio's surrender was delayed for the sole purpose
of giving him time to provide, as far as possible, against the German
attack on Italian troops which was sure to follow, as it did. For the
Italian people were not asking neutrality. They were asking freedom;
and no group could hope to lead Italy which did not at once make expulsion of the German invader its immediate task.

What followed is part of the known history of these brave and passionate times. The Allied armies landed at Salerno with Italian help;
they beat off in mass attack the German divisions in the south. The
American Fifth and the British Eighth Armies established contact,
moved northward, freed Naples. The Germans, retiring, sacked the
city, killing hostages and murdering women and children in what seems
to have been a sadistic lust for killing.

Meanwhile, German S.S. irregulars claimed to have recaptured Mussolini. After some bickering, he was named as a Quisling. A handful of
traitors, miscalled a "government," were set to dangle on the outskirts
of the Nazi military headquarters. Frenzied appeals in the Italian
language, written in Goebbels' best style, asking other Italians to turn
Quisling, found little response.

Badoglio, in command of the Italian forces, recognized the relentless
logic of the situation. He called on all Italians to make common front
against the Nazi tyranny. Many sincere anti-Fascists have differed with
the Marshal during his long career. But their best thinking was summed
up by Count Carlo Sforza, who promptly and forthrightly declared that
so long as Badoglio was fighting the common enemy, it would be criminal
for any Italian to weaken his hand: politics and constitutional questions
should be adjourned, to be dealt with after the liberation; all hands, now,
must join the common front against the common enemy.

Clearly, Italian people can be trusted to deal with the reorganization of
Italy when it is cleared of invading bayonets. Today the pressing task is
to mobilize every Italian from the Alps to the Ionian Sea as a mighty
army to repel these modern barbarians who seek to make of Italy a
Nazi gau.

Properly, tonight, you are thinking of the reestablishment of the institutions on which free Italy was based. Particularly you are interested
in the re-creation of the free trades unions. This is right. Any informed
student of Europe knows that no rebuilding is possible which does not
include recognition of the far greater place of labor in the world to come.
Plainly this must mean reconstituting labor organizations as free and
self-governing bodies capable of speaking once more for the workers,

by whom the brunt of this fearful struggle has been borne and for whom the peace must be made. God speed you all.

In frankness you should be told that this work has of necessity to abide military possibilities. Tonight, the great industrial centers are within German lines. The men who seek to reconstitute free trades unions must do so at fearful risk of life, family, reputation, even memory. Already many have died unknown, unsung, in this terrible task of bringing dynamic freedom back to their people. Before free trades unions can be constituted, all of us, and all of Italy, will have to fight — to fight side by side with all who likewise risk their lives in common cause to make an Italy capable of restoring to every Italian his rightful part in free institutions of labor and in politics. Let us leave aside political quarrels, stand fast in the mighty and growing work of liberation, salute the struggle — and salute the men.

Happily the barriers which Mussolini and the Nazis built between Italy and the world of freedom are gradually being broken down. I believe the time will not be long when it will be possible for Americans to have limited communication by mail with their friends and relatives in Sicily and on the liberated mainland. Provision for supplies for the peoples of the liberated areas was included in the allied military plan, and allied civilian agencies have been preparing such other economic support as may be needed. The elimination of Fascists in these liberated areas, according to our reports, is now being taken care of quite thoroughly by the Italian people. As the military lines move northward, the frontier of freedom moves with them.

. . . .

(2) *Message from Marshal Badoglio to the Commander-in-Chief of the Allied Forces (Eisenhower), Communicating Italy's Declaration of War Against Germany, October 13, 1943* [1]

I take great pleasure in informing you that His Majesty the King of Italy has declared war on Germany. The declaration will be handed by our Ambassador in Madrid to the German Ambassador, at 3 o'clock P.M. (Greenwich time) on October thirteenth. By this act all ties with the dreadful past are broken and my Government will be proud to be able to march with you on to the inevitable victory. Will you be good enough, my dear General, to communicate the foregoing to the Anglo-American, Russian and other United Nations Governments. I should also be grateful to you if you would be kind enough to inform the Italian Embassies in Ankara, in Buenos Aires, and the Legations in Bern, Stockholm, Dublin and Lisbon.

[1] *Ibid.*, p. 253.

(a) *Instruction from Marshal Badoglio to the Italian Ambassador in Madrid, October 13, 1943* [1]

[Translation]

Your Excellency, you are instructed by His Majesty the King to communicate to the German Ambassador in Madrid, in order that he may inform his Government, that "in the face of the repeated and intensified acts of war committed against the Italians by the armed forces of Germany, from 1500 hours (GMT) 11 A.M. EWT of the 13th day of October, Italy considers herself in a state of war with Germany."

(3) *Proclamation by Marshal Badoglio to the Italian People, October 13, 1943* [2]

[Translation]

Italians, with the declaration made September 8th, 1943, the Government headed by me, in announcing that the Commander-in-Chief of the Anglo-American Forces in the Mediterranean had accepted the Armistice requested by us, ordered the Italian troops to remain with their arms at rest but prepared to repel any act of violence directed at them from whatever other source it might come. With a synchronized action, which clearly reversed an order previously given by some high authority, German troops compelled some of our units to disarm, while, in most cases, they proceeded to a decisive attack against our troops. But German arrogance and ferocity did not stop here. We had already seen some examples of their behavior in the abuses of power, robbery, and violence of all kinds perpetrated in Catania while they were still our allies. Even more savage incidents against our unarmed populations took place in Calabria, in the Puglie and in the area of Salerno. But where the ferocity of the enemy surpassed every limit of the human imagination was at Naples. The heroic population of that city, which for weeks suffered every form of torment, strongly cooperated with the Anglo-American troops in putting the hated Germans to flight. Italians! There will not be peace in Italy as long as a single German remains upon our soil. Shoulder to shoulder, we must march forward with our friends of the United States, of Great Britain, of Russia, and of all the other United Nations. Wherever Italian troops may be, in the Balkans, Yugoslavia, Albania, and in Greece, they have witnessed similar acts of aggression and cruelty and they must fight against the Germans to the last man. The Government headed by me will shortly be completed. In order that it may constitute a true expression of democratic government in Italy, the representatives of every political party will be asked

[1] *New York Times*, October 14, 1943.
[2] Department of State, *Bulletin*, IX, p. 253.

to participate. The present arrangement will in no way impair the untrammelled right of the people of Italy to choose their own form of democratic government when peace is restored. Italians! I inform you that His Majesty the King has given me the task of announcing today, the thirteenth day of October, the Declaration of War against Germany.

(4) Joint Statement of the President (Roosevelt), the Prime Minister of the United Kingdom (Churchill) and the Premier of the Soviet Union (Stalin) Concerning Declaration of War by Italy Against Germany, October 13, 1943 [1]

The Governments of Great Britain, the United States and the Soviet Union acknowledge the position of the Royal Italian Government as stated by Marshal Badoglio and accept the active cooperation of the Italian nation and armed forces as a cobelligerent in the war against Germany. The military events since September eighth and the brutal maltreatment by the Germans of the Italian population, culminating in the Italian declaration of war against Germany have in fact made Italy a cobelligerent and the American, British and Soviet Governments will continue to work with the Italian Government on that basis. The three Governments acknowledge the Italian Government's pledge to submit to the will of the Italian people after the Germans have been driven from Italy, and it is understood that nothing can detract from the absolute and untrammelled right of the people of Italy by constitutional means to decide on the democratic form of government they will eventually have.

The relationship of cobelligerency between the Government of Italy and the United Nations governments cannot of itself affect the terms recently signed, which retain their full force and can only be adjusted by agreement between the allied governments in the light of the assistance which the Italian Government may be able to afford to the United Nations' cause.

(5) Statement of Marshal Badoglio Regarding Future Intentions of His Government, November 13, 1943 [2]

[Translation]

In the proclamation to the Italian people last October 13 in which I announced that, by order of His Majesty the King, war had been declared against Germany, I also laid down proposals regarding the constitution of the Government headed by me. It was my intention to call on the more outstanding representatives of all political parties, none excluded, so that the Government could assume a completely democratic aspect.

[1] *Ibid.*, p. 254.   [2] *New York Times*, November 15, 1943.

I submitted to the Allied Commission that the formation of this Government had to be brought about gradually, since many of those representatives were not in the liberated zones and therefore not available for the time being. I gave assurance then that I would communicate with statesmen in the liberated zones to initiate a partial completion of the Government. In fact, I went to Naples, where I conferred with Count Sforza, Benedetto Croce and others.

Sforza stated that he was ready to give all possible support to my Government but that he would not take part in the same since it was his belief that the King should abdicate, the Crown Prince should renounce his succession and his son, the Prince of Naples, should be made King with a regency appointed because of his minority. Benedetto Croce voiced the same belief.

I pointed out to them that the most important problem was freeing Italy from Germany; that we should avoid any act, especially one of so radical a nature, that would cause a disturbance in the liberated zone, which must be avoided in our interest and that of the Allies at all cost, and that in any case we should await the liberation of Italy as a whole so that the Italian people as a whole, not merely a fraction thereof, could openly decide what form of government they preferred.

Since both Sforza and Croce remained firm in their opinion, and as the other political leaders to whom I talked did not agree to take part in the Government, I returned here without having reached a final settlement. Meanwhile the head of the Allied Commission informed me that various sections of the Commission were on the way, destined to start working with different Ministries, in order to start a new administration rolling. It was, therefore, indispensable to proceed with the forming of at least an executive part of the Ministries so that work with various sections of the Commission should not be delayed.

Now a new matter appeared. The heads of each party made known to me that, once the capital had been liberated, they favored the establishment of a completely constitutional Government composed of political personages, leaving to me only the military. I then submitted a solution to the King: to form a Government for the present by placing technical experts in each Ministry, thereby starting work with the Commission and, when Rome had been liberated, I would present my resignation as head of the Government and retire.

The new political Government formed by the King would in this manner find for itself a group of experts and an amount of work already in progress in each Ministry. Regardless of prevailing conditions in Rome at that time, it would be able to continue without interruption its work with the Allied Commission.

The King approved this plan. I will now complete the Government with Under-Secretaries who will possess, by means of proper decrees, the authority intended to consider and deal with matters pertaining to each Ministry, including the authority to sign all documents within the competence of the respective Ministers.

In this manner, the necessary administrative work will not be held in abeyance; the causes for disturbances in liberated zones will be avoided and the desires manifested by the heads of all political parties will be fully met.

Regarding myself, once we have reached Rome, I shall be delighted to unload so heavy a burden into more expert hands and more youthful energies. I am happy to have assumed, by order of the King, the responsibility of the armistice and the declaration of war against Germany and to have in every way and with all my power collaborated with the efforts that the Anglo-American forces have put and are still putting forth to free Italy.

(6) *Statement of the King of Italy (Victor Emmanuel III), April 12, 1944* [1]

[Translation]

The Italian people know that I have always been at their side in difficult times and happy ones. They know that eight months ago I put an end to the Fascist regime and brought Italy, notwithstanding every danger and risk, to the side of the United Nations in the struggle for liberation against Nazism.

The Italian Navy, Air Force and Army, obedient to my call, during the past eight months have been fighting undauntedly against the enemy, shoulder to shoulder with the Allied forces. The Italian contribution to victory is and shall ever be more great. The day will come when, our deep wounds healed, we shall once more take our place as a free people among free nations.

Putting into effect what I have suggested to the Allied authorities and to my Government, I have decided to withdraw from public affairs by appointing my son, the Prince of Piedmont, Lieutenant General of the Realm. This appointment will become effective by a formal transfer of power on the day on which the Allied troops enter Rome. This decision, which I and my family firmly believe furthers national unity, is final and irrevocable.

3. LIBERATION OF ROME

King Victor Emmanuel signed a decree on June 5, 1944 on the advice of the Prime Minister and in agreement with the Cabinet Council nominating the Prince of Piedmont Lieutenant General and giving him the right to exercise all royal prerogatives without exception. The next day the Prince accepted the resignation of the Badoglio Government and asked the Marshal to form a new one.

[1] *New York Times*, April 12, 1944.

The American Fifth Army had entered Rome on June 4, meeting only sporadic resistance. The German General Kesselring had proposed to the Vatican authorities that the belligerents should recognize Rome as an open city and requesting that this proposal should be conveyed to the Anglo-American command.

On June 9 at a meeting in Rome of groups of politicians a resolution against acceptance of office under Badoglio was carried unanimously, and he resigned. The Crown Prince summoned Signor Bonomi who, before accepting the charge, asked for a guarantee that a constituent assembly would be summoned at the end of the war, and also requested a new oath of allegiance that would not commit Ministers to support the House of Savoy. Both conditions were accepted and Bonomi formed a Government representing all parties. The Bonomi Government assumed its functions on June 18, after consultations in Naples with the Allied Advisory Council. Signor Bonomi pledged himself to entrust the solution of the constitutional issue to a popular assembly which would be summoned as soon as the whole of Italy was liberated. The Cabinet held its first meeting in Rome on July 15.

(1) *Radio Address by the President (Roosevelt), June 5, 1944* [1]

[Excerpts]

Yesterday, June fourth, 1944, Rome fell to American and Allied troops. The first of the Axis capitals is now in our hands. One up and two to go!

It is perhaps significant that the first of these capitals to fall should have the longest history of all of them. The story of Rome goes back to the time of the foundations of our civilization. We can still see there monuments of the time when Rome and the Romans controlled the whole of the then known world. That, too, is significant, for the United Nations are determined that in the future no one city and no one race will be able to control the whole of the world.

.   .   .   .

In Italy the people had lived so long under the corrupt rule of Mussolini that, in spite of the tinsel at the top, their economic condition had grown steadily worse. Our troops have found starvation, malnutrition, disease, a deteriorating education, and lowered public health — all by-products of the Fascist misrule.

The task of the Allies in occupation has been stupendous. We have had to start at the very bottom, assisting local governments to re-form on democratic lines. We have had to give them bread to replace that which was stolen out of their mouths by the Germans. We have had to make it possible for the Italians to raise and use their own local crops. We have to help them cleanse their schools of Fascist trappings.

The American people as a whole approve the salvage of these human beings, who are only now learning to walk in a new atmosphere of freedom.

[1] Department of State, *Bulletin*, X, p. 526.

Some of us may let our thoughts run to the financial cost of it. Essentially it is what we can call a form of relief. At the same time we hope that this relief will be an investment for the future — an investment that will pay dividends by eliminating Fascism and ending any Italian desires to start another war of aggression in the future. They are dividends which justify such an investment, because they are additional supports for world peace.

The Italian people are capable of self-government. We do not lose sight of their virtues as a peace-loving nation.

We remember the many centuries in which the Italians were leaders in the arts and sciences, enriching the lives of all mankind.

We remember the great sons of the Italian people — Galileo and Marconi, Michelangelo and Dante — and that fearless discoverer who typifies the courage of Italy, Christopher Columbus.

Italy cannot grow in stature by seeking to build up a great militaristic empire. Italians have been overcrowded within their own territories, but they do not need to try to conquer the lands of other peoples in order to find the breath of life. Other peoples may not want to be conquered.

In the past Italians have come by the millions to the United States. They have been welcomed, they have prospered, they have become good citizens, community and governmental leaders. They are not Italian-Americans. They are Americans — Americans of Italian descent.

Italians have gone in great numbers to the other Americas — Brazil and the Argentine, for example — and to many other nations in every continent of the world, giving of their industry and their talents, and achieving success and the comfort of good living.

Italy should go on as a great mother nation, contributing to the culture and progress and goodwill of all mankind — and developing her special talents in the arts, crafts, and sciences, and preserving her historic and cultural heritage for the benefit of all peoples.

We want and expect the help of the future Italy toward lasting peace. All the other nations opposed to Fascism and Nazism should help give Italy a chance.

The Germans, after years of domination in Rome, left the people in the Eternal City on the verge of starvation. We and the British will do everything we can to bring them relief. Anticipating the fall of Rome, we made preparations to ship food supplies to the city, but it should be borne in mind that the needs are so great and the transportation requirements of our armies so heavy that improvement must be gradual. We have already begun to save the lives of the men, women, and children of Rome.

This is an example of the efficiency of your machinery of war. The magnificent ability and energy of the American people in growing the crops, building the merchant ships, making and collecting the cargoes, getting the supplies over thousands of miles of water, and thinking ahead to meet emergencies — all this spells, I think, an amazing efficiency on the part of our armed forces, all the various agencies working with them, and American industry and labor as a whole.

No great effort like this can be a hundred per cent perfect, but the batting average is very, very high.

I extend the congratulations and thanks of the American people to General Alexander, who has been in command of the whole Italian operation; to General Clark and General Leese of the Fifth and the Eighth Armies; to General Wilson, the Supreme Allied Commander of the Mediterranean theater, and General Devers, his American Deputy; to General Eaker; to Admirals Cunningham and Hewitt; and to all their brave officers and men.

May God bless them and watch over them and over all of our gallant, fighting men.

(2) Decree of the King of Italy (Victor Emmanuel III), Appointing Humbert, Prince of Piedmont, Lieutenant General, June 5, 1944 [1]

[Translation]

I, Victor Emmanuel III, by the grace of God and by the will of the nation King of Italy, in collaboration with the President of the Council of Ministers and with the agreement of the Council, have ordered and order as follows:

My beloved son, Humbert of Savoy, Prince of Piedmont, is nominated our Lieutenant General. In collaboration with responsible Ministers he will in our name superintend all matters of administration and exercise all royal prerogatives without exception, signing royal decrees which will be countersigned and authenticated in the usual way.

We order all concerned to observe this decree and to see that it is observed as the law of the State.

Given at Ravello June 5, 1944.

C. Germany

During the period under review, there were no particularly significant developments in declared United States policy regarding the treatment of Germany. By the Declaration on Austria (see p. 231), agreed to at the Moscow Conference ending October 30, 1943, the Government of the United States joined with the British and Soviet Governments in agreeing that Austria "shall be liberated from German domination." At the same time, by the Declaration of German Atrocities (see p. 231), the three governments declared that at the time of the granting of any armistice to any German government "those German officers and men and members of the Nazi party who have been responsible for, or have taken a consenting part in the above atrocities, massacres and executions, will be sent back to the countries in which their abominable deeds were done in

[1] New York Times, June 6, 1944.

order that they may be judged and punished according to the laws of those liberated countries and of the free governments which will be created therein." It was also stated that "major criminals, whose offenses have no particular geographic location" "will be punished by the joint decision of the Governments of the Allies."

At the Moscow Conference, it was also agreed to establish a European Advisory Commission, one of whose functions was to consider the treatment of Germany and formulate proposals for the consideration of the Governments represented.

In his address to the House of Commons on February 22, 1944, Prime Minister Churchill stated that the Allies would not be bound to Germany at the time of surrender "by any pact or obligation," that there would be no question "of the Atlantic Charter applying to Germany as a matter of right" (see p. 210). In his radio address of April 9, Secretary of State Hull stated the United States' position to be that "the Charter is an expression of fundamental objectives toward which we and our Allies are directing our policies." He emphasized that the Charter "does not prevent any steps, including those relating to enemy states, necessary to achieve these purposes." There was no more specific reference to the Charter's application to Germany.

D. Japan

(1) Radio Address by the Former American Ambassador to Japan (Grew), August 28, 1943 [1]

[Excerpt]

. . . .

Now, what shall be done with Japan after we have achieved final victory? Here again a good many imponderable factors enter into the problem. Among these factors will of course be the extent of the impact on the Japanese people of their losses, their defeat, and their final unconditional surrender, as well as the attitude toward Japan at that time of the other United Nations.

Our Government is constantly studying post-war problems but I do not know what the outcome of those studies will be.

In any discussion of post-war policy it should be borne in mind that one fundamental principle set forth in the Atlantic Charter is respect for the right of all peoples to choose the form of government under which they will live. The Charter, however, contains, *inter alia*, another principle of equal fundamental importance, namely, abandonment of the use of force and, pending the establishment of a wider and permanent system of general security, the disarmament of nations which threaten, or may threaten, aggression outside of their frontiers. In the light of that latter provision, common sense dictates that the military terms of settlement shall prevent Japan from again becoming a menace

---

[1] Mr. Grew was at the time Special Assistant to the Secretary. The address was given on the weekly program "For This We Fight" under the Auspices of the Commission to Study the Organization of Peace. Department of State, *Bulletin*, IX, p. 126.

to international peace. This of course presupposes disarmament and the denial to Japan of certain strategic islands, quite apart from the restitution by Japan of other territories seized by force. It presupposes too the condign punishment of Japan's military leaders responsible for her aggression, as well as of those guilty of the hideous and utterly barbarous cruelties practiced alike upon prisoners and wounded and upon noncombatant civilians of the United Nations.

But that would solve only a part of the problem. Effective steps will undoubtedly have to be taken to rid the Japanese permanently of the cult of militarism of which, in varying degrees, they have been the unresisting pawns throughout their history. This will of course mean a substantial reorientation of their domestic life and outlook through the process of re-education in all their institutions of learning from the kindergarten to the university.

My own opinion, based upon my 10 years of experience in Japan,[1] is that this process will present no insuperable obstacles. At least a part of that process will come about automatically with the defeat of the Japanese nation. First of all, we must remember that in Japanese life and thought a loss of "face" plays an important role. When the Japanese people witness the complete defeat and discomfiture of their army and navy and air force — which they have been told have never yet lost a war and, being allegedly protected by their sun goddess, can never be beaten — that military machine will be discredited throughout the length and breadth of the land. Within the last generation there have been times when the prestige of the Japanese Army was so low that army officers were reluctant to wear uniform in public when off duty; and the incursion into Manchuria in 1931 was undoubtedly stimulated if not impelled among other considerations by the desire of the army to recover its former influence and prestige. What has happened before can happen again. Throughout Japanese history the pendulum has swung to and fro between aggressive and peace-seeking policies and action.

Furthermore, ever since the Manchuria venture, and especially since the commencement of the China war in 1937, the Japanese people have suffered acutely. Living conditions have become harder; the standard of living has steadily deteriorated, and periodically Japanese families have received from overseas in ever-increasing numbers the little white boxes containing the ashes of their loved ones. They are taught the glories of such sacrifice, but human nature and human sorrow are fundamentally much the same everywhere. Weariness of war is just as current among the Japanese as among any other people.

It is my belief that when Japan's war with the United Nations is over, even in their defeat, the great majority of the Japanese people will give a

---

[1] See Grew, Joseph C. *Ten Years in Japan.* N.Y., Simon and Schuster, 1944.

sigh of profound relief and will welcome a new orientation and outlook so long as they are not deprived of the hope of better things to come.

Just as we must not deny to ourselves hope of better things to come, so we must not deny them or any one else, that hope. I have no sympathy whatever with those who hold, as some people hold, that before we can find permanent peace in the Orient, the Japanese common people will have to be decimated. Man for man, the Japanese people at home in their own land are not inherently the wolves in human form which some of our own people who do not know them believe. Once caught in the military machine they are taught brutality, cruelty, trickery, and ruthlessness as a matter of high strategy — in the mistaken belief of their leaders that these things will break the morale of their enemies and lead to victory. Little do those Japanese leaders seem to realize that such methods of warfare have an effect precisely the reverse of that intended. The Japanese people are going to learn to their sorrow that crime and brutality do not pay, and once they have learned that lesson, the finer qualities which I know that many of them possess will have opportunity to come to the fore. The Japanese in their own Japan are naturally a thrifty, hard-working, progressive people with great recuperative powers. Throughout their history they have become inured to and have surmounted great disasters — disasters wreaked by fire and flood, by earthquake and typhoon. Given the opportunity, they will likewise overcome the ravages of war, even with their substance spent and their cities destroyed. Those recuperative powers must be wisely directed into the healthy channels of peaceful economic and cultural pursuits and away, forever, from military enterprise.

But many difficult problems will confront us in the post-war settlement with Japan, problems of industry, commerce, agriculture, and finance, of education and government. We are already preparing against the day when those problems will arise but the time has not yet come when their solution can be decided upon in detail. As a fundamental conception, I personally believe that the healthy growth, wisely guided in its initial stages, will have to come — through re-education — from within. If an ancient tree is torn up by the roots and remodeled it will not live, but if the healthy trunk and roots remain the branches and foliage can, with care, achieve regeneration. Whatever is found to be healthy in the Japanese body politic should be preserved; the rotten branches must be ruthlessly cut away.

Only skilled hands should be permitted to deal with that eventual problem upon the happy solution of which so very much in the shaping of our post-war world will depend.

.   .   .   .

(2) *Joint Statement of President Roosevelt, Generalissimo Chiang Kai-shek and Prime Minister Churchill, Cairo, December 1, 1943*

[See p. 232.]

(3) *Proclamation No. 1 of the Commander-in-Chief of the United States Pacific Fleet and Pacific Ocean Areas (Nimitz) to the People of the Marshall Islands, January 31, 1944* [1]

TO THE PEOPLE OF THE MARSHALL ISLANDS:

In prosecuting their war against the Japanese it has become necessary for the armed forces of the United States under my command to occupy this and other islands of the Marshall Islands.

It is the policy of the United States Forces not to make war upon the civilian inhabitants of these islands but to permit them to continue their normal lives and occupations in a peaceable manner, so far as war necessities and their own behavior permit.

In order to preserve law and order and provide for the safety and welfare both of my forces and of yourselves, it is necessary to establish Military Government in the islands occupied by United States Forces.

THEREFORE, I, C. W. Nimitz, Admiral, United States Navy, Commander-in-Chief, United States Pacific Fleet and Pacific Ocean Areas and Military Governor of the Marshall Island Areas occupied by United States Forces, do hereby proclaim as follows:

I

All powers of government and jurisdiction in the occupied territory and over the inhabitants therein, and final administrative responsibility, are vested in me as Admiral, United States Navy, Commanding the United States Forces of Occupation, and Military Governor, and will be exercised through subordinate commanders by my direction.

II

The exercise of the powers of the Emperor of Japan shall be suspended during the period of military occupation.

III

All persons will obey promptly all orders given by me or under my authority; must not commit acts hostile to the United States Forces under my command or in any way helpful to the Japanese; must not commit acts of violence or any act which may disturb public safety in any way.

[1] From Navy Department, Headquarters of Commander-in-Chief, United States Fleet.

IV

Your existing personal and property rights will be respected and your existing laws and customs remain in force and effect, except to the extent that it is necessary for me in the exercise of my powers and duties to change them.

V

Until further notice, United States dollar currency, overprinted "Hawaii" and United States coins will be legal tender in the occupied territory and all persons are warned against accepting or dealing in any other currency whatever, except as permitted under my orders.

VI

So long as you remain peaceable and comply with the orders of the United States Forces of occupation, you will be subject to no greater interference than is made necessary by war conditions, and may go about your normal occupations without fear.

VII

Further proclamations and orders will be issued by me or under my authority from time to time. They will state what is required of you and what you are forbidden to do and will be displayed at police stations and in your villages.

C. W. NIMITZ,
Admiral, United States Navy,
Commander-in-Chief,
United States Pacific Fleet and
Pacific Ocean Areas
MILITARY GOVERNOR OF THE MARSHALL ISLANDS

E. Other Enemy States

(1) *Statement of the Secretary of State (Hull) on the Second Anniversary of the Declarations of War Against the United States by Bulgaria, Hungary, and Rumania, December 11, 1943* [1]

It is just two years since the Governments of Bulgaria, Hungary, and Rumania, having already become servile puppets of Hitler, obedient to the orders of their master, declared war against the United States. To what degree they had been counting on our magnanimity to spare their peoples the consequences of this rash step foredoomed to disaster we do not know. The fact is that whatever may be the sentiments of their peoples, the governments in power in these three countries have recklessly continued their participation in the war against us, strengthening

[1] Department of State, *Bulletin*, IX, p. 413.

with men and material resources the Nazi war-machine. They must by this time realize that they will have to share the responsibility for and consequences of the terrible defeat that United Nations arms are so surely bringing to Nazi Germany.

(2) *German Invasion of Hungary. Statement of the Secretary of State (Hull), March 24, 1944* [1]

The rapid decline of Nazi tyranny has never been so apparent as today, when Hitler, in growing awareness that he cannot withstand the united efforts of the freedom-loving peoples of the world, has shown his desperation by turning with his accustomed treachery upon a former ally.

Only by firm resistance to the hated invader can Hungary, the first of the Axis satellites to feel the Nazi whip, hope to regain the respect and friendship of free nations and demonstrate its right to independence.

(3) *Declaration by the American, British, and Soviet Governments Regarding the Four Axis Satellites, May 12, 1944* [2]

Through the fateful policy of their leaders, the people of Hungary are suffering the humiliation of German occupation. Rumania is still bound to the Nazis in a war now bringing devastation to its own people. The Governments of Bulgaria and Finland have placed their countries in the service of Germany and remain in the war at Germany's side.

The Governments of Great Britain, the Soviet Union, and the United States think it right that these peoples should realize the following facts:

1. The Axis satellites, Hungary, Rumania, Bulgaria, and Finland, despite their realization of the inevitability of a crushing Nazi defeat and their desire to get out of the war are by their present policies and attitudes contributing materially to the strength of the German war-machine.

2. These nations still have it within their power, by withdrawing from the war and ceasing their collaboration with Germany and by resisting the forces of Nazism by every possible means, to shorten the European struggle, diminish their own ultimate sacrifices, and contribute to the Allied victory.

3. While these nations cannot escape their responsibility for having participated in the war at the side of Nazi Germany, the longer they continue at war in collaboration with Germany the more disastrous will be the consequences to them and the more rigorous will be the terms which will be imposed upon them.

4. These nations must therefore decide now whether they intend to persist in their present hopeless and calamitous policy of opposing the inevitable Allied victory, while there is yet time for them to contribute to that victory.

[1] *Ibid.*, X, p. 278.   [2] *Ibid.*, p. 425.

2. PUNISHMENT OF WAR CRIMINALS

(1) *Refuge in Neutral Countries for Axis Leaders. Statement of the President (Roosevelt), July 30, 1943* [1]

On August 21, 1942 I issued a statement to the press in which after referring to the crimes against innocent people committed by the Axis powers I stated:

"The United Nations are going to win this war. When victory has been achieved, it is the purpose of the Government of the United States, as I know it is the purpose of each of the United Nations, to make appropriate use of the information and evidence in respect to these barbaric crimes of the invaders, in Europe and in Asia. It seems only fair that they should have this warning that the time will come when they shall have to stand in courts of law in the very countries which they are now oppressing and answer for their acts." [2]

On October 7, 1942 I stated that it was "the intention of this Government that the successful close of the war shall include provision for the surrender to the United Nations of war criminals." [3]

The wheels of justice have turned constantly since those statements were issued and are still turning. There are now rumors that Mussolini and members of his Fascist gang may attempt to take refuge in neutral territory. One day Hitler and his gang and Tojo and his gang will be trying to escape from their countries. I find it difficult to believe that any neutral country would give asylum to or extend protection to any of them. I can only say that the Government of the United States would regard the action by a neutral government in affording asylum to Axis leaders or their tools as inconsistent with the principles for which the United Nations are fighting and that the United States Government hopes that no neutral government will permit its territory to be used as a place of refuge or otherwise assist such persons in any effort to escape their just deserts.

(a) *Instructions to American Diplomatic Representatives in Neutral Countries. Press Release of the Department of State, July 31, 1943* [4]

The diplomatic representatives of the United States in Stockholm, Ankara, Madrid, Lisbon, Bern, Vatican City, and Buenos Aires have been instructed by the Department of State to bring the President's statement to the attention of the Governments to which they are accredited.

[1] *Ibid.*, IX, p. 62.
[2] *Ibid.*, VII, p. 663; *Documents, V, 1942–43*, p. 176.
[3] Department of State, *Bulletin*, VII, p. 797; *Documents, V, 1942–43*, p. 177.
[4] Department of State, *Bulletin*, IX, p. 62.

The British representatives at the above places and the representatives of the Union of Soviet Socialist Republics in Stockholm and Ankara are making similar representations.

———

In a note delivered to the United States Chargé d'Affaires on August 31, the Argentine Government upheld its right to grant asylum to any person accused of political crimes but undertook to consider each individual case on its merits in the event that any fleeing Fascist or Nazi leader should seek sanctuary in Argentina.

(2) *Declaration of the President (Roosevelt) on German Crimes in Poland, August 30, 1943* [1]

Trustworthy information has reached the United States Government regarding the crimes committed by the German invaders against the population of Poland. Since the autumn of 1942 a belt of territory extending from the province of Bialystok southward along the line of the River Bug has been systematically emptied of its inhabitants. In July 1943 these measures were extended to practically the whole of the province of Lublin, where hundreds of thousands of persons have been deported from their homes or exterminated.

These measures are being carried out with the utmost brutality. Many of the victims are killed on the spot. The rest are segregated. Men from 14 to 50 are taken away to work for Germany. Some children are killed on the spot; others are separated from their parents and either sent to Germany to be brought up as Germans or sold to German settlers or dispatched with the women and old men to concentration camps.

The United States Government reaffirms its resolve to punish the instigators and actual perpetrators of these crimes. It further declares that, so long as such atrocities continue to be committed by the representatives and in the name of Germany, they must be taken into account against the time of the final settlement with Germany. Meanwhile the war against Germany will be prosecuted with the utmost vigor until the barbarous Hitlerite tyranny has been finally overthrown.

(3) *Declaration of the United Kingdom, the United States and the Soviet Union on German Atrocities, Moscow, October 30, 1943*

[See p. 231.]

(4) *War Refugees. Statement of the President (Roosevelt), March 24, 1944* [2]

[Excerpt]

The United Nations are fighting to make a world in which tyranny and aggression cannot exist; a world based upon freedom, equality, and justice; a world in which all persons regardless of race, color, or creed may live in peace, honor, and dignity.

[1] *Ibid.*, p. 150.   [2] *Ibid.*, X, p. 277.

In the meantime in most of Europe and in parts of Asia the systematic torture and murder of civilians — men, women, and children — by the Nazis and the Japanese continue unabated. In areas subjugated by the aggressors innocent Poles, Czechs, Norwegians, Dutch, Danes, French, Greeks, Russians, Chinese, Filipinos — and many others — are being starved or frozen to death or murdered in cold blood in a campaign of savagery.

The slaughters of Warsaw, Lidice, Kharkov, and Nanking — the brutal torture and murder by the Japanese, not only of civilians but of our own gallant American soldiers and fliers — these are startling examples of what goes on day by day, year in and year out, wherever the Nazis and the Japs are in military control, free to follow their barbaric purpose.

In one of the blackest crimes of all history — begun by the Nazis in the day of peace and multiplied by them a hundred times in time of war — the wholesale systematic murder of the Jews of Europe goes on unabated every hour. As a result of the events of the last few days, hundreds of thousands of Jews, who while living under persecution have at least found a haven from death in Hungary and the Balkans, are now threatened with annihilation as Hitler's forces descend more heavily upon these lands. That these innocent people, who have already survived a decade of Hitler's fury, should perish on the very eve of triumph over the barbarism which their persecution symbolizes, would be a major tragedy.

It is therefore fitting that we should again proclaim our determination that none who participate in these acts of savagery shall go unpunished. The United Nations have made it clear that they will pursue the guilty and deliver them up in order that Justice be done. That warning applies not only to the leaders but also to their functionaries and subordinates in Germany and in the satellite countries. All who knowingly take part in the deportation of Jews to their death in Poland, or Norwegians and French to their death in Germany, are equally guilty with the executioner. All who share the guilt shall share the punishment.

Hitler is committing these crimes against humanity in the name of the German people. I ask every German and every man everywhere under Nazi domination to show the world by his action that in his heart he does not share these insane criminal desires. Let him hide these pursued victims, help them to get over their borders, and do what he can to save them from the Nazi hangman. I ask him also to keep watch and to record the evidence that will one day be used to convict the guilty.

.   .   .   .

3. TREATMENT BY ENEMY COUNTRIES OF AMERICAN NATIONALS

(1) *Summary of Steps Taken by the Department of State in Behalf of American Nationals in Japanese Custody. Department of State Release, January 13, 1944* [1]

1. *Treatment of prisoners of war and civilian internees*

Upon the outbreak of war between the United States and Japan, the United States Government, in an endeavor to insure humane treatment for American nationals in Japanese hands, confirmed its intention to observe the Geneva Prisoners of War Convention (convention relative to the treatment of prisoners of war, signed at Geneva on July 27, 1929 and ratified by the United States in 1932),[2] and to apply its provisions to prisoners of war and, so far as its provisions might be adaptable, to civilian internees. The Japanese Government, which had signed but had not ratified the convention, thereupon notified the United States Government that it would apply the provisions of the convention, *mutatis mutandis*, to the treatment of American prisoners of war and to the treatment of American civilian internees so far as its provisions might be adaptable to civilian internees.

The United States Government has also obtained assurances from the Japanese Government that it is applying the Geneva Red Cross Convention (convention for the amelioration of the condition of the wounded and the sick of armies in the field, which was also signed at Geneva on July 27, 1929 and which was ratified by the United States in 1932 and by Japan in 1934).[3]

The conventions named above provide a humanitarian standard of treatment for prisoners of war. Specifically, they provide that prisoners of war shall be treated humanely and held in honorable captivity — not imprisoned as criminals. They establish as the standard for the shelter and diet of prisoners of war, the corresponding treatment of the garrison troops of the detaining power, and they establish fundamental rights regarding correspondence, medical care, clothing, pay for labor, satisfaction of intellectual, recreational, and religious needs, and the continued enjoyment of full civil status. For persons generally referred to as "protected personnel" — that is, doctors, nurses, and other sanitary (medical) personnel and chaplains — they provide certain special rights and protection.

The Department of State is constantly alert to insure observance of the conventions. Whenever it is learned through the Swiss Government, which represents American interests in Japan and Japanese-occupied territories, through the International Red Cross, or otherwise, that the terms of the conventions are not being observed, the United States Government draws to the attention of the Japanese Government that Government's obligations under the Red Cross Convention and under its agreement to apply to the treatment of interned American nationals in Japanese hands the provisions of the Prisoners of War Convention.

2. *Exchange of civilians*

Negotiations between the United States Government and the Japanese Government lasting more than a year culminated in a second exchange of civilians

---

[1] *Ibid.*, p. 78.
[2] *Treaties, Conventions, etc., 1923–1937*, IV, p. 5224.
[3] *Ibid.*, p. 2074.

resulting in the repatriation of approximately 1,240 nationals of the United States, including a small number from the Philippine Islands, and 260 nationals of the other American Republics and Canada. In the first exchange, which took place in the summer of 1942, over 1,300 United States officials and non-officials were repatriated from the Far East.

The Japanese Government refused to apply the provisions of the civilian-exchange arrangements to American civilians who were captured in the Philippine Islands, Guam, and Wake Island. After protracted negotiations it finally agreed to permit the repatriation of only a small number of American civilians from the Philippines in the second exchange. The repatriates were thus drawn almost entirely from Japan, Japanese-occupied China, Hong Kong, and Indo-China.

The Swiss representatives in the Far East, under broad directives issued by the United States Government, compiled the list of those to be repatriated, giving preference to the following categories of American civilians in Japanese hands: (1) those under close arrest; (2) interned women and children; (3) the seriously ill; and (4) interned men, with preference being given, other things being equal, to married men long separated from their families in the United States.

The second exchange of American and Japanese nationals having been completed by the return of the motorship *Gripsholm* to the United States on December 1, 1943, the Department is now endeavoring to negotiate a third exchange of American and Japanese nationals and will continue its endeavors to induce the Japanese Government to agree to the general release for repatriation of all American civilians in its custody. The Department hopes eventually to obtain Japanese agreement to further exchanges at an accelerated rate so that all American civilians remaining in Japanese custody, numbering about 10 thousand, may have an opportunity to be repatriated at the earliest practicable date.

3. *Repatriation of sick and wounded prisoners of war*

Article 68 of the Prisoners of War Convention provides that:

"Belligerents are bound to send back to their own country, regardless of rank or number, seriously sick and seriously injured prisoners of war, after having brought them to a condition where they can be transported.

"Agreements between belligerents shall accordingly settle as soon as possible the cases of invalidity or of sickness entailing direct repatriation, as well as the cases entailing possible hospitalization in a neutral country. While awaiting the conclusion of these agreements, belligerents may have reference to the model agreement annexed, for documentary purposes, to the present Convention."

The model agreement defines the degree of incapacity that shall be considered sufficient to qualify a prisoner of war for repatriation. This Government proposed to the Japanese Government that the model agreement be observed on a reciprocal basis and made insistent demands that the Japanese Government honor the obligation imposed by the convention to repatriate sick and wounded prisoners. The Japanese Government replied, after long delay, that it could not make a favorable response to the United States Government's proposal. The Department of State has formulated, in consultation with other agencies of the Government, further proposals in an effort to induce the Japanese Government to enter into negotiations for the exchange of sick and wounded prisoners of war, and these proposals are being transmitted to the Japanese Government in connection with proposals for the continuation of the repatriation of civilians.

4. *Repatriation of sanitary personnel*

Article 9 of the Red Cross Convention provides, in part:

"The personnel charged exclusively with the removal, transportation, and treatment of the wounded and sick, as well as with the administration of sanitary formations and establishments, and the chaplains attached to armies, shall be respected and protected under all circumstances. If they fall into the hands of the enemy they shall not be treated as prisoners of war."

Article 12 of the same convention provides, in part:

"The persons described in Articles 9, 10 and 11 may not be detained after they have fallen into the power of the adversary.

"Unless there is an agreement to the contrary, they shall be sent back to the belligerent to whose service they are attached as soon as a way is open for their return and military exigencies permit.

"While waiting to be returned, they shall continue in the exercise of their functions under the direction of the adversary; they shall be assigned preferably to the care of the wounded and sick of the belligerent to whose service they are attached."

Pursuant to the provisions of Article 12 of the Red Cross Convention, it was proposed to the Japanese Government that the repatriation of the personnel protected under the convention be begun, since facilities for their return to the United States could be made available on the vessels employed for the exchange of civilian nationals. In order, however, not to deprive American prisoners of war of the care that they may require and might not otherwise receive, the United States Government also proposed to the Japanese Government, on a basis of reciprocity, that the right of repatriation be waived for protected personnel needed and permitted in prisoner-of-war camps or hospitals to render spiritual and medical assistance to compatriots who were in the care of that personnel at the time of capture. This Government further proposed that the selection of protected personnel to be repatriated be made by the senior officer of the unit captured.

The Japanese Government agreed in principle to the repatriation of protected personnel in connection with exchanges of civilians but reserved to itself the decision whether the retention of that personnel was necessary for the care of American prisoners of war and civilian internees under Japanese control. The Department accordingly requested the Swiss Government to endeavor to arrange for the accommodation of American protected personnel in future American-Japanese civilian exchange operations.

Although it repatriated five nurses from Guam at the time of the first civilian exchange, the Japanese Government apparently did not find that it had in its power surplus American protected personnel available for repatriation in the second exchange as no such personnel was included in the lists for that exchange. However, the Department intends, when conducting negotiations for further exchanges of civilians, to convey again to the Japanese Government the expectation of the United States Government that protected personnel whose repatriation proves possible will be included in future exchange operations.

5. *Exchange of able-bodied prisoners of war*

As indicated in a statement to the press dated May 25, 1943,[1] there is no customarily accepted practice among nations or provision of international law

---

[1] Department of State, *Bulletin*, VIII, p. 472.

or conventions for the return or exchange during hostilities of able-bodied members of the armed forces of one belligerent who may be captured by the forces of an opposing belligerent. In the circumstances, there is no immediate prospect of obtaining the release and return to the United States of able-bodied members of the American armed forces taken prisoners of war by the Japanese.

6. *Shipment of relief supplies to the Far East*

Early in 1942 the American Red Cross, in conjunction with the interested agencies of the United States Government, made efforts to find a means acceptable to the Japanese Government of forwarding to our prisoners of war and civilian internees in the Far East necessary supplies of food, medicine, clothing, and comforts such as are regularly sent to American citizens in corresponding circumstances in other enemy-held areas. A neutral vessel to carry such supplies to Japan was obtained and chartered in the summer of 1942. The Japanese Government, however, refused to give its safe-conduct for the voyage of the vessel to the Far East. In response to repeated representations the Japanese Government indicated that it was unwilling for strategic reasons to grant any non-Japanese vessel safe-conduct to move in Japanese waters and that it had no intention of sending one of its own vessels to any neutral area in order to pick up relief supplies for United States and Allied prisoners of war and civilians as was suggested by the United States Government. Upon the receipt of this Japanese reply the United States Government pointed out its expectation that the Japanese would modify their position as soon as strategic reasons would permit and suggested for the interim the immediate appointment of International Red Cross delegates to Japanese-occupied territory who might receive and distribute funds in behalf of American nationals. This suggestion was eventually accepted by the Japanese only for Hong Kong and certain areas in occupied China. They have not accepted it so far for the Philippine Islands, Malaya, and the Netherlands Indies. Efforts to induce the Japanese Government to abandon its position against the use of neutral ships to carry relief supplies into its waters were continued and new avenues of approach were fully canvassed, including the possibility of sending relief supplies to transit through Soviet territory. One suggestion proposed the sending of supplies by air to some point where the Japanese might lift them, with particular reference to medical supplies which might be scarce in Japan. No reply to this particular proposal was ever received. Another proposal was that the American Red Cross would provide a cargo ship to go to some point in the Pacific where a Japanese crew might take it over in order to conduct it to the ports where relief cargo should be discharged. This proposal was rejected by the Japanese. Numerous other proposals were considered but were either abandoned because of obstacles interposed by other enemy governments or were found to be otherwise impossible of accomplishment.

In March 1943 the Japanese Government, in response to repeated representations stressing its responsibility to cooperate in solving the problem, stated that strategic reasons still prevented neutral vessels from plying the Pacific waters but that it would explore other means of permitting the delivery of relief supplies. In the following month the Japanese Government stated that it might consent to receive supplies overland or by sea from Soviet territory. There have ensued since that time long and complicated negotiations with the Japanese and Soviet Governments. Each detail of the negotiations had to be dealt with through a long and complicated procedure involving the handling of communications at Tokyo, Bern, Washington, and Moscow and in reverse direction through the same channels. Despite these difficulties, it has now been possible with the Soviet Government's cooperation to create a stockpile of prisoner-of-war relief supplies on Soviet territory. Moreover, the Soviet Government has given assurances that it will facilitate the transit through the Soviet Union of such relief supplies on a continuing basis when a satisfactory arrangement for the onward shipment of these supplies is reached between the Japanese and American Governments. In spite of the Department's repeated endeavors to bring this matter to a conclusion, the Japanese Government has not thus far indicated the means by which it is prepared to receive these supplies. The Department is continuing its efforts in this regard, and it is hoped that a definite arrangement can soon be made whereby relief supplies will move on a continuing basis to all American nationals detained by the Japanese.

While the foregoing negotiations have been in progress it has fortunately been possible to take advantage of the two exchanges of civilians with the Japanese Government, one in July 1942 and the other in October 1943, to send to our nationals in the Far East an important quantity of relief supplies by means of the exchange vessels.

Reports of the distribution of relief supplies which left the United States on the first exchange vessel in 1942 were in due course received from the Far East. There was placed on the motor vessel *Gripsholm* when it left this country to effect the second exchange of civilian nationals another large cargo of assorted relief supplies, American Red Cross standard food parcels, next-of-kin parcels, and mail for distribution to American prisoners of war and American civilians interned in the Philippine Islands, occupied China, Hong Kong, Japan, the Netherlands East Indies, and Malaya. Valued at over $1,300,000 and weighing 1,600 short tons, these supplies included 140,000 food parcels of approximately 13 pounds each; 2,800 cases of medical supplies, including surgical instruments, dressings, 7,000,000 vitamin capsules, etc.; 950 cases of comfort articles for men and women; 24,000,000 cigarettes; from 20,000 to 25,000 next-of-kin parcels; and important supplies of clothing for men and women. This entire cargo was transferred to the Japanese exchange vessel at Mormugão and dispatched eastward.

In addition to the shipment of relief supplies on the exchange vessels and the other measures mentioned above, the Department of State and the American Red Cross are continuing to give close attention to all other phases of the subject.

7. *Provision of financial assistance to American nationals in the Far East*

Since the Trading With the Enemy Act as amended prohibits, among other things, individual remittances to enemy and enemy-occupied or enemy-controlled territory, unless licensed, and since the issuance of such licenses is contrary to the policy of the Government, the Department of State, shortly after this country's entry into the war, made provision for the extension of financial assistance from public funds in the form of loans to Americans in such territories through representatives of the Swiss Government representing American interests there. An information sheet explaining how such assistance is extended and how funds so advanced may be reimbursed to the United States Government is printed below. With certain exceptions in territories occupied or controlled by Japan, the enemy governments have permitted payments to be made to qualified American nationals in the manner described. The Japanese authorities, however, have thus far refused to permit the Swiss Government's representatives, in certain areas under Japanese control, to extend financial assistance to American nationals in those areas on the same basis as elsewhere. The Department, therefore, has had to find other means of making funds available to Americans in such areas.

At Hong Kong, where the Swiss Government has not been permitted by the Japanese Government to act in behalf of American nationals, the International Red Cross delegate has been authorized to provide assistance to qualified American nationals there from public funds made available for the purpose by the Department.

Immediately after the fall of the Philippine Islands, the Department endeavored to arrange for the extension of financial assistance to qualified American nationals there. In June 1943, the Japanese Government permitted the transfer of $25,000, representing a contribution by the American Red Cross, to be made to the Executive Committee of the Santo Tomas internment camp at Manila, and later allowed the transfer of a second Red Cross contribution of $25,000 for the relief of American nationals interned in Manila.

It was not until July 1943 that the Japanese Government indicated that it would agree in principle to permit payments to American nationals interned in other parts of the Philippine Islands, and to allow further payments to the internees at Manila. Accordingly, the Department in August 1943 authorized the Swiss Government to make remittances, in accordance with the need and the number of eligible individuals, to the executive committees of the American internment camps in the Philippine Islands beginning with the month of August or as soon as feasible thereafter. Funds delivered to the executive committees under this authorization may be used (1) for the purchase of available supplies considered necessary to supplement the diet provided by the Japanese authorities, (2) to pay for essential services obtained outside camp, (3) to provide each internee with a small amount of money for personal use, and (4) to advance funds, against promissory notes if possible, to indigent internees for delivery to such members of their families as may be at liberty.

The Japanese Government has recently consented to monthly transfers of United States Government funds to the Executive Committee of the Santo Tomas internment camp to be used for the relief of American nationals at Santo Tomas, Los Banos, Baguio, and Davao which, according to latest available information, are the only civilian internment camps now maintained by the Japanese in the Philippine Islands. These transfers are now being effected from such funds on deposit with the Swiss Government for the purposes mentioned above.

The Department's standing instructions to the Swiss representatives in charge of American interests in enemy-held areas are that funds provided by this Government may be made available to American prisoners of war as well as to interned American civilians for necessary personal expenditures in accordance with their established needs over and above the food, shelter, and other necessities provided them by the detaining power. Such assistance has already been made available through the local International Red Cross delegates to American prisoners of war near Shanghai and Hong Kong. The Department of State is pressing for the extension to American prisoners of war in the Philippine Islands of the system of financial assistance referred to above which the Japanese have agreed to make available to civilian internees.

(a) Procedure To Be Followed in Extending Financial Assistance to American Nationals in Territories Where the Interests of the United States Are Represented by Switzerland. Department of State Release, January 13, 1944 [1]

The Department of State has completed arrangements for financial assistance to American nationals in territories where the interests of the United States are represented by Switzerland.[2] Those able to qualify for such assistance will be entitled to receive from the Swiss representatives monthly payments corresponding to their established needs and the prevailing cost of living in the country concerned. All recipients will be limited to the monthly payments established for their place of residence, regardless of their ability or the ability of others interested in their welfare to repay amounts greater than the sums advanced. It is realized that a limitation upon the amount that American nationals may expend in enemy territory, even from their own resources, will entail some hardship. The conservation of foreign exchange, however, is an essential factor in the present economic policy of the United States and it is expected that Americans everywhere will willingly share with those in the armed forces the sacrifices that must be made in winning the war.

Based upon the latest ascertained cost of living in the various countries concerned, the maximum monthly payment for the head of a household will range from $60 to $130, with smaller allowances for additional members of the household. The monthly payments are subject to revisions from time to time to meet changing living cost. In addition, the Swiss representatives are authorized to make special advances for such extraordinary expenditures as may be essential to the health or safety of American nationals for medical, surgical, or dental care, for hospitalization, for reasonable legal defense against political or criminal charges, or for a decent though modest burial where such is not provided by friends or relatives locally nor by the local authorities.

Wherever prisoners of war and interned civilians are supported by the detaining power, it is expected that payments made to them will generally not exceed a small sum sufficient to provide spending money for miscellaneous personal needs not supplied by the detaining power. However, no payments will be made to officers or to persons of equivalent status held as prisoners of war, who receive pay under the convention relative to the treatment of prisoners of war, signed at Geneva on July 27, 1929.

Swiss representatives charged with the representation of the interests of the United States will explain to the recipients that such financial assistance should not be considered as public bounty but as loans from public funds to American nationals finding themselves in an abnormal position by reason of the war. It is accordingly expected that all sums advanced will be repaid either by the recipients themselves or by relatives, friends, business associates, employers, or legal representatives in the United States.

Receipts embodying promises to repay without interest the sums advanced will be taken for all payments. Private deposits to reimburse the Government for sums advanced shall be made with the Department of State. Persons wishing to make such deposits should indicate the names of the beneficiaries and should remit by postal money orders or certified checks payable to "The Secretary of State of the United States."

[1] *Ibid.*, X, p. 84.
[2] Switzerlend represents the interests of the United States in Germany, Italy, and Japan, in territories occupied by those countries, and in Bulgaria, Hungary and Rumania.

(2) *Telegram from the Secretary of State (Hull) to American Legation in Bern, Switzerland, for Communication to the Japanese Government, January 27, 1944* [1]

Immediately after the attack on Pearl Harbor the Department of State took up with Japan the matter of according proper treatment for American nationals in Japanese hands. Although Japan was not a party to the Geneva Prisoners of War Convention the Department obtained from the Japanese Government a commitment to apply the provisions of that convention to American prisoners of war, and, so far as adaptable, to civilian internees held by Japan. Since the very beginning of the war, by repeated protests and representations through the protecting power, the Department again and again called to the Japanese Government's attention failures on the part of Japanese authorities to live up to their Government's undertakings.

Following the first exchange voyage of the *Gripsholm*, the Department made accounts of repatriates the basis of a vigorous and comprehensive protest to the Japanese Government.

The execution of American aviators, who fell into Japanese hands after General Doolittle's raid over Tokyo, evoked a protest in which the Department again called upon the Japanese Government to carry out its agreement to observe the provisions of the convention and warned the Japanese Government that the American Government would hold personally and officially responsible for their acts of depravity and barbarity all officers of the Japanese Government who had participated in their commission and, with the inexorable and inevitable conclusion of the war, would visit upon such Japanese officers the punishment they deserved for their uncivilized and inhuman acts against American prisoners of war.

When it received from the military authorities reports of the brutal atrocities and depraved cruelties inflicted by the Japanese upon American prisoners of war in the Philippines the Department again called upon the Japanese Government to honor its undertaking to apply the provisions of the Geneva Prisoners of War Convention and to observe in its treatment of American nationals held by it the international common law of decency.

These protests were but three of the many that have been sent by the Department to Japan.

In order that the public might be familiar with the Department's efforts to obtain from Japan fulfilment of its undertakings to treat American nationals in its hands in accordance with humane and civilized principles, the Department released to the press on January 31, 1944 [2] a statement giving the dates of the principal representations and protests made by the Department, with a brief résumé of their purpose. The latest of these, representations comprehensively citing categories of abuse and of neglect to which American prisoners in the hands of the Japanese have been subjected and calling for amelioration of the treatment accorded to American nationals, both prisoners of war and civilian internees, went forward on January 27, and is given below.

Please request Swiss Legation Tokyo to deliver the following textually to the Japanese Government:

The Government of the United States refers to its communication delivered to the Japanese Government on December 23, 1942 by the Swiss Legation in Tokyo in charge of American interests in Japan and Japanese-occupied territory concerning reports that the Government of the United States had received of the mistreatment of American nationals in Japanese hands. The Swiss Legation in Tokyo on May 28, 1943 forwarded to the Government of the United States a preliminary reply from the Japanese Government to this communication in which that Government stated that it would communicate in due course the results of investigations concerning each instance referred to in the note of the Government of the United States. No reports of investigations regarding these instances have yet been received.

The Government of the United States has taken due note of the statements of the Japanese Government "concerning the special circumstances prevailing in areas which have until recently been fields of battle" and concerning "the manifold difficulties which exist in areas occupied by the Japanese forces or where military operations are still being carried on." The Government of the United States points out, however, that the regions in which Americans have been taken prisoner or interned have long ceased to be scenes of active military operations and that the Japanese holding authorities have therefore had ample opportunity to establish an orderly and humane internment program in accordance with their Government's undertakings. Despite this fact the Government of the United States continues to receive reports that the great proportion of American nationals are the victims either of inhuman cruelty or of callous failure to provide the necessities of life on the part of the Japanese holding authorities, in violation of the common laws of civilization and of the Japanese Government's undertaking to apply to American nationals the humane provisions of the Geneva Prisoners of War Convention.

There follows a statement of the principal categories of the deprivation of rights, cruelties, wanton neglect, mistreatment and hardships to which, according to information received by the Government of the United States from many sources, Americans in Japanese custody have been subjected.

I. Representatives of the Swiss Government entrusted with the protection of American interests in Japan and Japanese-occupied territory have not been permitted to go to every place without exception where prisoners of war and civilian internees are interned, have not been permitted to interview without witnesses the persons held, and have not had access to all places occupied by the prisoners (Article 86 of the Geneva Prisoners of War Convention).

II. Representatives of the International Red Cross Committee have been refused permission to visit most of the places where American nationals are held by the Japanese authorities (Articles 79 and 88).

III. American nationals have not been permitted to forward complaints to the Japanese holding authorities or to representatives of the protecting power (Article 42).

IV. The Japanese authorities have punished and have threatened to punish American nationals for complaining concerning the conditions of captivity (Article 42).

V. The Japanese Government has failed to furnish needed clothing to American nationals (Article 12).

VI. The Japanese authorities have confiscated personal effects from American civilian internees and prisoners of war (Article 6).

VII. American prisoners of war and civilian internees have been subjected to insults and public curiosity (Article 2).

VIII. Civilians and prisoners of war interned by Japan are suffering from malnutrition and deficiency diseases because of the failure and refusal of the detaining authorities to provide health sustaining food for their charges, or to permit the United States to make regular shipments on a continuing basis under appropriate neutral guarantees of supplemental food and medical supplies.

(Article 11 and the specific reciprocal undertaking of Japan to take into account national differences in diet.)

IX. The Japanese authorities have devoted to improper and forbidden uses the profits of the sale of goods in camp canteens instead of devoting them to the welfare of the persons held in the camps (Article 12).

X. Contrary to the specific undertaking of the Japanese Government, the detaining authorities have compelled civilians to perform labor other than that connected with the administration, maintenance and management of internment camps. Officer prisoners of war have been forced to labor and noncommissioned officers to do other than supervisory labor (Article 27).

XI. Prisoners of war have been required to perform labor that has a direct relation with war operations (Article 31).

XII. Medical care has in many instances been denied to prisoners of war and civilian internees and when given has been generally so poor as to cause unnecessary suffering and unnecessary deaths (Article 14).

XIII. The Japanese Government has reported the names of only a part of the American prisoners of war and civilian internees in its hands (Article 77) and of American combatants found dead by Japanese forces (Article 4 of the Convention for the Amelioration of the Condition of the Sick and Wounded of Armies in the Field, to which Japan is a contracting party).

XIV. The Japanese Government has not permitted internees and prisoners of war freely to exercise their religion (Article 16).

XV. The Japanese Government has not posted the Convention in camps in English translation, thus depriving American prisoners of war and civilian internees of knowledge of their rights thereunder (Article 84).

XVI. The Japanese Government has failed to provide adequate equipment and accommodations in prisoner of war and civilian internment camps and transports, but on the contrary forced them to subsist in inhumane conditions (Article 10).

XVII. The Japanese Government has completely failed to apply the provisions of the Geneva Prisoners of War Convention (Title III, Section V, Chapter 3) with regard to trial and punishment of prisoners of war despite the fact that violations of its undertaking in this respect have repeatedly been called to its attention, but on the contrary has imposed cruel and inhuman punishments without trial.

XVIII. The Japanese authorities have inflicted corporal punishment and torture upon American nationals (Article 46).

The Government of the United States emphasizes that it has based the foregoing charges only on information obtained from reliable sources. Many well-authenticated cases can be cited in support of each of the charges.

The Government of the United States also desires to state most emphatically that, as the Japanese Government can assure itself from an objective examination of the reports submitted to it by the Spanish, Swedish, and International Red Cross representatives who have repeatedly visited all places where Japanese are held by the United States, the United States has consistently and fully applied the provisions of the Geneva Prisoners of War Convention in the treatment of all Japanese nationals held by it as prisoners of war or (so far as they are adaptable) as civilian internees, detainees or evacuees in relocation centers. Japanese nationals have enjoyed high standards of housing, food, clothing, and medical care. The American authorities have furthermore freely and willingly accepted from the representatives of the protecting Powers and the International Red Cross Committee suggestions for the improvement of conditions under which Japanese nationals live in American camps and centers and have given effect to many of these suggestions, most of which, in view of the high standards normally maintained, are directed toward the obtaining of extraordinary benefits and privileges of a recreational, educational or spiritual nature.

The Government of the United States demands that the Japanese Government immediately take note of the charges made above and take immediate steps to raise the treatment accorded American nationals held by Japan to the standard provided by the Geneva Prisoners of War Convention, which the United States and the Japanese Governments have mutually undertaken to apply. The Government of the United States also expects the Japanese Government to take proper disciplinary or penal action with regard to those of its officials, employees, and agents who have violated its undertakings with respect to the Geneva Convention and the international Common Laws of decency.

The Government of the United States again directs the attention of the Japanese Government to the system of neutral supervision provided in Article 86 of the Geneva Convention. The Government of the United States again reminds the Japanese Government of the complete fulfillment of the provisions of this Article as respects the activities of the Government of Spain acting as protecting Power for Japanese interests in the continental United States and of the Government of Sweden as protecting Power for Japanese interests in Hawaii.

The Government of the United States therefore expects the Japanese Government, in accordance with recognized practice of civilized states, fully to implement the provisions of the Geneva Prisoners of War Convention. The United States Government demands that the Japanese Government will, among other things, promptly implement the provisions of Article 86 in respect to the activities of the Government of Switzerland as protecting Power for American interests in Japan and Japanese-controlled territory and will make it possible for the Government of Switzerland to give to the Government of the United States assurances to the effect that Swiss representatives have been able to convince themselves by the full exercise of the rights granted under Article 86 that the abuses set forth in the foregoing statement have been completely rectified or that steps have been taken in that direction that are considered by Switzerland to be adequate.

The United States Government until the present has refrained from publishing in this country the facts known to it regarding outrages perpetrated upon its nationals, both prisoners of war and civilian internees, by the Japanese. The United States Government hopes that as these facts are now again officially called to the Japanese Government's attention that Government will adopt a policy of according to United States nationals in its hands the treatment to which they are entitled, and will permit representatives of the protecting Power to make such investigations and inspections as are necessary in order to give assurances to this Government that improved treatment is in fact being accorded to American nationals. In such case this Government would be in a position to assure the American people that the treatment of American nationals by the Japanese authorities had been brought into conformity with the standards recognized by civilized nations.

In a companion telegram of the same date,[1] there were recited in numbered sections, the numbers of which corresponded to the numbered charges in the telegram above, examples of some of the specific incidents upon which the United States Government based the charges made by it against the Japanese Government in the telegram above. The specific incidents were selected from the numerous ones that had been reported from many reliable sources to this Government.

[1] *Ibid.*, p. 171.

(3) *Statement of the American Red Cross on Efforts to Get Relief to American War Prisoners in Japanese Hands, Department of State Release, February 13, 1944* [1]

The American Red Cross has spared and will continue to spare no effort to effect Japan's full compliance with the Geneva Prisoners of War Convention of 1929 and to establish a regular route for the shipment of supplies to prisoners of war and internees in the Far East. A chronological summary of steps which have been taken to date in this regard in full cooperation with the International Committee of the Red Cross and all the national Red Cross societies of the United Nations directly involved, follows:

From December 7, 1941 to the end of January 1943, 167 cables were sent by the American Red Cross to Geneva, Switzerland, pertaining to the shipment of relief to American prisoners of war and civilian internees in the Far East and related subjects. Many of these cables dealt with mail and communications facilities, while others were concerned with the local procurement of supplementary relief supplies by means of cash from the American Red Cross.

As the Department of State has recently pointed out, although Japan is not a party to the Geneva Prisoners of War Convention, the Department, immediately after the outbreak of hostilities in the Far East, obtained from the Japanese Government a commitment to apply the provisions of the convention to American prisoners of war, and, so far as adaptable, to civilian internees held by Japan. Following this, the Japanese Government approved the appointment of International Committee delegates for permanent station in Japan, Shanghai, and Hong Kong. Despite repeated representations by the American Red Cross, however, the Japanese Government has yet to approve the appointment of an International Committee delegate to function in the Philippines or even to visit the islands.

On December 31, 1941 the International Committee was asked to obtain Japanese approval for a relief ship to carry supplies to prisoners of war and civilian internees in the Far East. When the American Red Cross was informed by the Committee that negotiations to that end were in progress, the *Kanangoora*, a Swedish ship then berthed at San Francisco, was chartered and loaded in the summer of 1942 with Canadian and American Red Cross supplies valued at over one million dollars. In August 1942 the Japanese authorities finally refused safeconduct for this ship and stated that no neutral vessel would be permitted in waters controlled by Japan. The charter of the *Kanangoora* consequently was canceled and the ship unloaded.

While these negotiations were under way the Japanese agreed to accept relief supplies shipped on diplomatic exchange vessels. The *Gripsholm*, which was about to sail from New York on its first exchange voyage in June 1942, was accordingly loaded with more than 100 tons of American Red Cross supplies and an equal amount of Canadian, which eventually reached Yokohama in August 1942. It was expected that a second exchange would follow immediately upon the return of the *Gripsholm*, and in September 1942 a second cargo was loaded. Because of the delay in concluding the exchange negotiations, however, these supplies were discharged from the *Gripsholm* early in 1943.

Fully realizing that diplomatic exchange ships alone were at best nothing more than a temporary expedient, and that a regular route should be established for the flow of relief supplies to United Nations prisoners of war and civilian internees in the Far East, the American Red Cross, through the State Depart-

[1] *Ibid.*, p. 189.

ment and the International Committee, undertook a series of steps in an effort to reach some understanding with the Japanese authorities as to how this might be brought about.

It was suggested in turn (1) that a neutral port be selected to which a neutral ship might carry relief supplies from the United States, the suppliers to be picked up at this neutral port by Japanese ships; (2) that the American Red Cross turn over to the Japanese a fully loaded ship in mid-Pacific or at any other point acceptable to the Japanese; (3) that supplies be flown from the United States to a neutral point for relay to Japan; (4) that, if the necessary arrangements could be made with the Soviet Union, supplies be shipped on Soviet vessels to Vladivostok and then transshipped to Japanese-controlled territory.

The most far-reaching proposal was made in February 1943 when the American Red Cross, with the approval of the United States Government, offered to furnish to the Japanese Red Cross a ship to carry relief supplies to the Far East. The proposal then made was that a fully loaded ship be turned over to the Japanese at any point specified by them — even in mid-Pacific if necessary — from there be manned by a Japanese crew, and, after the distribution of the supplies, be returned empty. The Japanese crew would then pick up a second fully loaded ship and the process would be repeated.

The Japanese never even replied to this proposal. Instead, in April 1943 they suggested that they would consider accepting supplies sent by Soviet ships from a West Coast port to Vladivostok. The State Department secured the approval of the Soviet Union to this suggestion, and at the end of May 1943 the State Department advised the Japanese of the Soviet agreement, at the same time asking them to specify the means they proposed to use in getting the supplies from Vladivostok to the camps. While awaiting the Japanese answer, the United States Government asked the Russians to start carrying supplies to Vladivostok at once. In late August the Soviet Union agreed to carry 1,500 tons of supplies monthly on Soviet ships to Vladivostok.

Although no definite agreement had been reached with the Japanese that supplies shipped to Vladivostok would be accepted by them and in due course be distributed to the prison camps, the American Red Cross and interested governmental agencies decided that, despite the risks involved, it was highly desirable to lose no more time in accumulating a stockpile of food, medicines, and clothing at the nearest point possible to the Far Eastern camps. The aim was to avoid any further delay in the distribution of supplies in the event of Japanese agreement. Consequently, some 1,500 tons of urgently needed supplies were assembled and shipped from the West Coast and are now warehoused in Vladivostok. Further substantial amounts are ready in this country for immediate shipment as soon as the Japanese begin accepting the supplies already in Vladivostok. While the actual movement of goods was taking place, a series of cables were sent through Geneva to the Japanese Red Cross urging a definite Japanese proposal for the distribution of the supplies. There has still been no definite plan from the Japanese side, but further steps to obtain a solution to this problem are receiving continuous consideration.

The second shipment of American relief supplies on diplomatic exchange vessels was made in September 1943. The *Gripsholm* then left New York with a cargo valued at over $1,300,000, including 140,000 specially prepared 13-pound food packages, 2,800 cases of medical supplies, including drugs, surgical instruments, and dressings, 7 million vitamin capsules; and large quantities of clothing and comfort articles for men, women, and children. The entire cargo was transferred to the Japanese exchange vessel *Teia Maru*, which sailed eastward from Mormugão on October 21, 1943. About one half of these supplies, including 78,000 food parcels and 73 tons of drugs and medicine, were unloaded at Manila on November 8, 1943 for distribution to camps in the Philippines. About a week later several hundred tons were unloaded at Yokohama for distribution in Japan and elsewhere in the Far East.

The Department of State announced on May 23, 1944 [1] that the War Prisoners' Aid of the Young Men's Christian Association had recently been informed by its Stockholm office that the Japanese authorities in the Philippine Islands had extended permission to the neutral delegate there of the War Prisoners' Aid to purchase locally relief supplies to an amount not exceeding $25,000 monthly for shipment to civilian internment and prisoner-of-war camps in the Philippine Islands. United States Government funds were made available for expenditure by the War Prisoners' Aid delegate for this purpose.

In a communication dated May 10, 1944,[1] sent through Swiss Government channels, the Japanese Government offered to send to a Soviet port at regular intervals a Japanese ship to pick up relief supplies which were shipped to Vladivostok last fall — and additional relief supplies and mail intended for distribution to Allied nationals interned in the Far East which would be sent subsequently via Soviet territory with the cooperation of the Soviet Government — and to transport them to Japan. The Soviet Government expressed its willingness to cooperate and named a convenient Soviet Pacific port adjacent to Vladivostok where the relief supplies already on Soviet territory may be picked up by a Japanese ship. The Soviet Government suggested, alternatively, that these supplies might be sent overland and offered to deliver them to the Japanese authorities at a convenient border railroad station. The Soviet Government named an equally accessible port where such mail and relief supplies as may be shipped in the future for distribution to Allied nationals in Japanese custody may be picked up by Japanese ships. The Japanese Government was informed of the foregoing through the Swiss Government.

4. RESPECT FOR RELIGIOUS SHRINES AND HISTORIC MONUMENTS IN COURSE OF MILITARY OPERATIONS

(1) *Statement of the President (Roosevelt), March 14, 1944* [2]

Everyone knows the Nazi record on religion. Both at home and abroad, Hitler and his followers have waged a ruthless war against the churches of all faiths.

Now the German army has used the Holy City of Rome as a military center. No one could have been surprised by this — it is only the latest of Hitler's many affronts to religion. It is a logical step in the Nazi policy of total war — a policy which treats nothing as sacred.

We on our side have made freedom of religion one of the principles for which we are fighting this war. We have tried scrupulously — often at considerable sacrifice — to spare religious and cultural monuments, and we shall continue to do so.

(2) *Statement of the Secretary of State (Hull), March 14, 1944* [2]

I think we all understand that the Allied military authorities in Italy are dealing primarily with considerations of military necessity forced on

---

[1] *Ibid.*, p. 496, 536.　　　　　　　　　[2] *Ibid.*, p. 253.

them by the activities and attitude of the German military forces. Naturally we are as much interested as any government or any individual in the preservation of religious shrines, historic structures, and human lives. I am sure that our military people have that same view. It is my understanding that the Allied military authorities are pursuing a policy of avoiding damage to such shrines and monuments to the extent humanly possible in modern warfare and in the circumstances which face them. If the Germans were not entrenched in these places or were they as interested as we are in protecting religious shrines and monuments and in preserving the lives of innocent civilians and refugees, no question would arise.

(3) Communication from the President (Roosevelt) to the Prime Minister of Eire (de Valera), April 3, 1944 [1]

I have received through your Minister your recent communication concerning the danger which now threatens the city of Rome. I share your concern for the preservation of that ancient monument of our common civilization and faith.

It is well known that American military authorities in Italy are committed to a policy of avoiding damage to religious shrines and historical monuments to the extent humanly possible in modern warfare. This applies to the city of Rome as well as to other parts of Italy where the forces of the United Nations are engaged in active fighting. We have tried scrupulously — often at considerable sacrifice — to spare religious and cultural monuments and we shall continue to do so.

However, in addressing an appeal to the Government of the United States to preserve Rome from destruction, you are, of course, aware that the Germans, occupying the Italian capital by force, are using to the limit of its capacities the communication network and other facilities of Rome to further a purely German military operation. If the German forces were not entrenched in Rome, no question would arise concerning the city's preservation.

I note that you have sent a similar communication to the German Government. The fate of Rome rests in that quarter.

(a) The Prime Minister of Eire (de Valera) to the President (Roosevelt), March 15, 1944 [2]

As head of the Government of a State whose citizens in a great majority belong to the Holy Catholic Apostolic and Roman Church, I think it my duty to express on their behalf the deep distress which they feel —

[1] *Ibid.*, p. 371.
[2] *New York Times*, April 20, 1944.

distress shared by 300,000,000 Catholics throughout the whole world — at the danger now threatening the city of Rome and at the absence of any measures by the belligerent powers to insure its safety.

It is clear to all that, if the city is to be militarily defended by one side and by the other attacked, its destruction is inevitable.

The destruction of this holy city which for almost 2,000 years has been the seat of the sovereign authority of the Catholic Church and contains the great central temples of Catholic religion and the great central seminaries and libraries of Christian faith would be a major calamity for the human race, robbing man for all time of the noblest memorials of his supreme religious and cultural heritage whose origins teach of our divine Saviour, Jesus Christ.

Millions of Catholics would risk their lives to save these memorials, symbols of eternal things which alone give meaning to human life.

I request you to listen to the voice of millions from every land praying the belligerents to seek, through appropriate intermediary channels, an agreement by which Rome may be saved.

Future generations will forget the military considerations which may now seem to dictate the occupation or possession of Rome, but should the city be destroyed the fact of its destruction will be remembered forever.

So, too, should the city by agreement be spared, future generations will remember with enduring gratitude those States and their leaders who will have preserved for the ennoblement of mankind this great center of Christian faith and civilization.

CHAPTER V

THE UNITED NATIONS

1. MEMBERSHIP AND BASIC PRINCIPLES OF COLLABORATION

[See *Documents, IV, 1941–42,* p. 198; *V, 1942–43,* p. 199.]

A. Unilateral Reaffirmations and Interpretations

(1) *Statement of the President (Roosevelt) on the Second Anniversary of the Signing of the Atlantic Charter, August 14, 1943* [1]

Today, on the second anniversary of the signing of the Atlantic Charter, I would cite particularly two of its purposes and principles on which we base our "hopes for a better future for the world":

First — respect for the right of all peoples to choose the form of government under which they will live. When the Atlantic Charter was first signed, there were those who said that this was impossible of achievement. And yet today, as the forces of liberation march on, the right of self-determination is becoming once more a living reality.

Second — world-wide collaboration with the object of security for all, of improved labor standards, economic adjustment, and social security.

It happens that today is also the anniversary of the day in 1935 when our own American Social Security Act became law.

That humanitarian law made a real beginning toward the abolition of want in this country. More than 60 million workers with their own contributions are building security for their old age and for their families in case of death. Several million are already enjoying benefits. However, in all fairness and in all equity, we should extend these benefits to farmers, farm laborers, small businessmen, and others working for themselves or in occupations specifically excluded by law. We should extend social security to provide protection against the serious economic hazard of ill-health.

We are now fighting a great war. We fight on the side of the United Nations, each and every one of whom has subscribed to the purposes and principles of the Atlantic Charter.

Today, we stand upon the threshold of major developments in this war. We are determined that we shall gain total victory over our enemies, and we recognize the fact that our enemies are not only Germany, Italy and Japan: they are all the forces of oppression, intolerance, insecurity, and injustice which have impeded the forward march of civilization.

[1] Department of State, *Bulletin,* IX, p. 92.

(2) *Address by the Prime Minister of the United Kingdom (Churchill) before the House of Commons, February 22, 1944* [1]

[Excerpt]

The liberation of Poland may presently be achieved by the Russian armies after these armies have suffered millions of casualties in breaking the German military war machine. I cannot feel that the Russian demand for reassurances about her western frontiers goes beyond the limits of what is reasonable or just. Marshal Stalin and I also spoke and agreed upon the need for Poland to obtain compensation at the expense of Germany both in the north and in the west.

Here I may point out that the term "unconditional surrender" does not mean that the German people will be enslaved or destroyed. It means, however, that the Allies will not be bound to them at the moment of surrender by any pact or obligation. There will be no question, for instance, of the Atlantic Charter applying to Germany as a matter of right and barring territorial transferences or adjustments in enemy countries. No such arguments will be admitted by us as were used by Germany after the last war, saying that they surrendered in consequence of President Wilson's Fourteen Points.

Unconditional surrender means that the victors have a free hand. It does not mean that they are entitled to behave in a barbarous manner nor that they wish to blot out Germany from among the nations of Europe. If we are bound, we are bound by our own consciences to civilization. We are not to be bound to the Germans as a result of a bargain struck. That is the meaning of "unconditional surrender."

(3) *Radio Address by the Secretary of State (Hull), April 9, 1944* [2]

[Excerpt]

There has been discussion recently of the Atlantic Charter and of its application to various situations. The Charter is an expression of fundamental objectives toward which we and our allies are directing our policies. It states that the nations accepting it are not fighting for the sake of aggrandizement, territorial or otherwise. It lays down the common principles upon which rest the hope of liberty, economic opportunity, peace and security through international cooperation. It is not a code of law from which detailed answers to every question can be distilled by painstaking analysis of its words and phrases. It points the direction in which solutions are to be sought; it does not give solutions. It charts the course upon which we are embarked and shall continue. That course includes the prevention of aggression and the establishment of world security. The Charter certainly does not prevent any steps, including those relating to enemy states, necessary to achieve these objectives.

[1] *Parliamentary Debates, Commons*, vol. 397, p. 690–701.
[2] Senate Doc. No. 181, 78th Cong., 2d sess., p. 6–7; for full text see this volume, p. 25.

What is fundamental are the objectives of the Charter and the determination to achieve them.

B. Supplementary Agreements between All or Certain of the United Nations

[See *Documents, IV, 1941–42*, p. 235; *V, 1942–43*, p. 208, 217.]

The Moscow Tripartite Conference of Foreign Ministers of October 19–30, 1943, the Cairo Conference of November 22–26, and the Tehran Conference of November 28–December 1 resulted in important declarations of policy supplementing the agreements already entered into by the United Nations directly concerned. For texts of these declarations, see p. 229, 232 and 234.

C. Adherences to the Declaration by United Nations

(1) *Adherence of Iran. Exchange of Communications between the Minister of Iran (Shayesteh) and the Secretary of State (Hull), September 10, 1943* [1]

(a) *The Minister of Iran (Shayesteh) to the Secretary of State (Hull)*

MR. SECRETARY:

I have the honor to communicate to Your Excellency, in compliance with instructions received from my Government, that by act of the 9th day of this month, Iran declares the existence of a state of war with Germany and formally adheres to the Declaration of the United Nations:

The Iranian people and their Government, sincerely believing in the principles of the Atlantic Charter, have already contributed by all ways and means at their disposal to the common cause of the Allies and to the prosecution of the war against aggressors. Now, interpreting this obvious policy, they have decided to adhere formally to the Declaration of the United Nations dated January 1, 1942.

In conveying the advice to Your Excellency of this decision of the Iranian Government, and also in accordance with the above instructions, I should very much appreciate the favor of your good offices to the end that the same be transmitted to the other signatory nations of the foregoing Declaration.

(b) *The Secretary of State (Hull) to the Minister of Iran (Shayesteh)*

SIR:

I have the honor to acknowledge the receipt of your note of September 10, 1943 in which you state, in compliance with instructions from your Government, that by act of September 9, 1943 Iran declared the existence of a state of war with Germany and formally adhered to the Declaration by United Nations.

This action of the Government of Iran is a new manifestation of the determination of Iran to contribute to the cause of the freedom-loving

[1] Department of State, *Bulletin*, IX, p. 166, 167.

nations in their struggle for victory over Hitlerism. The Government of the United States, as depository for the Declaration, is indeed gratified to welcome Iran into the ranks of the United Nations.

This was followed by an exchange of communications between the Secretary of State and the Iranian Minister of Foreign Affairs, initiated by a communication dated September 10, from the Iranian Foreign Minister (Saed) advising the Secretary that his Government "with the approval of the Parliament, has just declared its adherence to the Declaration of United Nations of January 1, 1942" and that Mr. Shayesteh, the Iranian Minister in Washington, "has just been authorized to sign the above-mentioned declaration." [1]

(2) Adherence of Colombia. Exchange of Communications between the Minister of Foreign Affairs (Lozano y Lozano) and the Secretary of State (Hull), December 22 and 27, 1943 [2]

(a) The Minister of Foreign Affairs (Lozano y Lozano) to the Secretary of State (Hull), December 22, 1943

I have the honor to inform Your Excellency that the Government of Colombia has decided to adhere to the Declaration by the United Nations signed at Washington on January 1, 1942. This Government has sent full powers for signing this document to His Excellency Alfonso Lopez, titular President of the Republic, who is at present in New York. In taking this step, which constitutes a logical and natural evolution of her preceding international attitudes, Colombia ratifies her willingness to cooperate by all means within her power with the free nations of the world, involved, like herself, in a decisive combat against the totalitarian political system. In defense of the right and liberty of the peoples unjustly attacked on various occasions by the German Reich, my country has been compelled to proclaim a state of belligerency towards that power and desires to bind itself closely to the bloc of nations united in the solidary effort against the common enemy and to collaborate more closely with the United States and the other belligerent nations of America in the defense of this continent. I request Your Excellency to take the necessary steps so that our plenipotentiary can sign the declaration to which I have referred, and I ask likewise that this action be made known to the Governments interested. I express cordial wishes for the victory of the United Nations and for the increasing prosperity and greatness of the United States and I repeat to Your Excellency at this opportunity the assurances of my highest consideration.

(b) The Secretary of State (Hull) to the Minister of Foreign Affairs (Lozano y Lozano), December 27 1943

I have received your telegram of December 22, 1943 stating that in defense of the right and liberty of peoples unjustly attacked by the German Reich, Colombia had been compelled to proclaim a state of belliger-

[1] *Ibid.*, p. 180.   [2] *Ibid.*, X, p. 108.

ency toward that nation; that Colombia desires to bind itself closely to the nations united against the common enemy and to collaborate more closely with the United States and the other belligerent nations of America in the defense of this continent; and that the Government of Colombia has decided to adhere to the Declaration by United Nations and has sent full powers for signing this document to His Excellency, President Alfonso Lopez, who is now in New York.

Colombia's action in thus formally aligning itself with the United Nations brings to thirty-four the number of freedom-loving nations which have pledged themselves to employ their full resources in the struggle against the common enemy. On behalf of this Government, as depository for the Declaration by United Nations, I take great pleasure in welcoming Colombia into the ranks of the United Nations.

Appropriate arrangements are being made for President Lopez to sign the Declaration.

(3) *Adherence of Liberia. Exchange of Communications between the Secretary of State of Liberia (Dennis) and the Secretary of State of the United States (Hull), February 26 and April 6, 1944* [1]

(a) *The Secretary of State of Liberia (Dennis) to the Secretary of State of the United States (Hull), February 26, 1944*

YOUR EXCELLENCY,

The Government of Liberia declared by Proclamation on the 27th day of January 1944, a state of war existing between Liberia on the one hand, and Germany and Japan on the other. Motivated by the principles of human freedom and the right of self-determination, the Government subscribes and endorses the purposes and principles as enunciated by, and embodied in, the Joint Declaration of the President of the United States of America and the Prime Minister of the United Kingdom of Great Britain and Northern Ireland, dated August 14, 1941, known as the Atlantic Charter, and adheres by this communication to the Declaration by United Nations, dated January 1, 1942.

The Honorable Walter F. Walker, Consul-General of Liberia at New York City, has been authorized to sign the above mentioned Declaration.

(b) *The Secretary of State of the United States (Hull) to the Secretary of State of Liberia (Dennis), April 6, 1944*

I have received your communication of February 26, 1944, stating that the Government of Liberia declared by proclamation on January 27, 1944 a state of war existing between Liberia on the one hand and Germany and Japan on the other; that motivated by the principles of human freedom and the right of self-determination, the Government subscribes to and endorses the purposes and principles of the Atlantic Charter; that

[1] *Ibid.*, p. 346.

the Government of Liberia adheres to the Declaration by United Nations and has authorized Walter F. Walker, Consul General at New York City, to sign the Declaration.

The Government of the United States, as depository for the Declaration, is gratified to welcome Liberia into the ranks of the United Nations. This action of Liberia brings to thirty-five the number of United Nations, all of which have pledged themselves to employ their full resources in the struggle for victory over Hitlerism.

Arrangements are being made for Consul General Walker to sign the Declaration.

D. Adherences to the Principles of the Atlantic Charter

(1) *Adherence of Egypt. Exchange of Communications between the Minister of Egypt (Hassan) and the Secretary of State (Hull), November 20 and 27, 1943* [1]

(a) *The Minister of Egypt (Hassan) to the Secretary of State (Hull), November 20, 1943*

SIR:

Acting on instructions of my Government, I have the honor to transmit to Your Excellency the following communication:

"Ever since the Joint Declaration of President Roosevelt and Prime Minister Churchill published to the world on August 14, 1941 and since known as the Atlantic Charter, the Egyptian Government has publicly expressed its entire approval of the principles, and the lofty ideals this Pact engenders as a basis for the reconstruction of a future world.

"Both through respect of her treaty obligations with Great Britain, and taking into consideration the objectives to which the democratic powers have dedicated their efforts for the attainment of a just and lasting peace, Egypt has not failed to extend to her ally, and consequently, the United Nations, every help provided for by the treaty of Amity and Alliance between her and Great Britain. It is because of this that Egypt hereby declares its adherence to the principles enunciated in the Atlantic Charter, which holds forth the promise of a universal peace; for Egypt is convinced that the sole peace capable of covering all nations, and providing them with security and justice, is a peace which recognizes the sovereign rights of all peoples, and sets forth the essential principle of human liberty as a basis for a highly civilized world. Egypt is, therefore, glad to be able to contribute its share, and associate in such a system and order, as evolved and provided for by the Atlantic Charter, which stands as much for the Orient as for the Occident, and for the New World as for the Old in bringing forward the trend for a modern life of a high order. In this connection, Egypt highly appreciates the decision that no discrimination whatsoever be tolerated, that would divide races and peoples.

[1] *Ibid.*, IX, p. 382.

"By her adherence to the principles enunciated in the Atlantic Charter, Egypt endorses her traditional liberal policy of justice and amity towards all nations, inasmuch as this policy cannot but strengthen and cement all the more firmly the ties of Egypt with the other nations animated with the desire of creating and establishing a happier future for the world."

(b) *The Secretary of State (Hull) to the Minister of Egypt (Hassan), November 27, 1943*

SIR:

I have the honor to acknowledge the receipt of your note of November 20, 1943, in which you state, under instructions from your Government, that Egypt declares its adherence to the principles enunciated in the Atlantic Charter and that by adhering to those principles Egypt endorses her traditional liberal policy of justice and amity toward all nations.

I wish to thank you for informing me of this action of the Egyptian Government which constitutes new evidence of Egypt's firm devotion to the ideals and principles for which the United Nations are fighting.

E. United Nations and Associated Nations

(1) *List of United Nations and Associated Nations, as of June 30, 1944* [1]

[See *Documents, V, 1942–43*, p. 214.]

UNITED NATIONS

Original Signatories of Declaration by United Nations, January 1, 1942:

Australia	India
Belgium	Luxemburg
Canada	Netherlands
China	New Zealand
Costa Rica	Nicaragua
Cuba	Norway
Czechoslovakia	Panama
Dominican Republic	Poland
El Salvador	Union of South Africa
Greece	Union of Soviet Socialist Republics
Guatemala	United Kingdom
Haiti	United States
Honduras	Yugoslavia

[1] The above is the list of governments and authorities invited to participate in the United Nations Monetary and Financial Conference at Bretton Woods, N. H., July 1–22, 1944. The French Committee of National Liberation was also extended an invitation and was represented, even though the Committee was not at that time recognized as the Government of France. (*Ibid.*, X, p. 498.)

Nations that Subsequently Adhered to Declaration by United Nations:

Bolivia	April 27, 1943
Brazil	February 6, 1943
Colombia	January 17, 1944
Ethiopia	October 9, 1942
Iran	September 9, 1943
Iraq	January 16, 1943
Liberia	April 10, 1944
Mexico	June 5, 1942
Philippine Commonwealth . . .	June 10, 1942

ASSOCIATED NATIONS

Chile	Paraguay
Ecuador	Peru
Egypt	Uruguay
Iceland	Venezuela

2. LEND-LEASE

[See *Documents, III, 1940–41*, p. 711; *IV, 1941–42*, p. 169, 225; *V, 1942–43*, p. 105, 215; this volume, p. 118.]

A. Countries Eligible for Lend-Lease Assistance

(1) *Lend-Lease Countries and United Nations, as of June 30, 1944* [1]

COUNTRY	DECLARED ELIGIBLE FOR LEND-LEASE AID	LEND-LEASE AGREEMENT SIGNED	RECIPROCAL AID AGREEMENT SIGNED	UNITED NATIONS DECLARATION SIGNED
Argentina. . . .	May 6, 1941	——	——	——
Australia . . .	Nov. 11, 1941	([2])	Sept. 3, 1942	Jan. 1, 1942
Belgium	Jun. 13, 1941	Jun. 16, 1942	Jan. 30, 1943	Jan. 1, 1942
Bolivia	May 6, 1941	Dec. 6, 1941	——	Apr. 27, 1943
Brazil	May 6, 1941	Mar. 3, 1942	——	Feb. 6, 1943
Canada	Nov. 11, 1941	([3])	——	Jan. 1, 1942
Chile	May 6, 1941	Mar. 2, 1943	——	——
China	May 6, 1941	Jun. 2, 1942	——	Jan. 1, 1942
Colombia . .	May 6, 1941	Mar. 17, 1942	——	Jan. 17, 1944
Costa Rica . .	May 6, 1941	Jan. 16, 1942	——	Jan. 1, 1942
Cuba	May 6, 1941	Nov. 7, 1941	——	Jan. 1, 1942
Czechoslovakia . .	Jan. 5. 1942	Jul. 11, 1942	——	Jan. 1, 1942
Dominican Republic	May 6, 1941	Aug. 2, 1941	——	Jan. 1, 1942
Ecuador	May 6, 1941	Apr. 6, 1942	——	——
Egypt	Nov. 11, 1941	——	——	——

[1] *Sixteenth Report to Congress on Lend-Lease Operations for the Period Ended June 30, 1944*, p. 64.

Country	Declared Eligible for Lend-Lease Aid	Lend-Lease Agreement Signed	Reciprocal Aid Agreement Signed	United Nations Declaration Signed
El Salvador . . .	May 6, 1941	Feb. 2, 1942	——	Jan. 1, 1942
Ethiopia	Dec. 7, 1942	Aug. 9, 1943	——	Jul. 28, 1942
French Committee of National Lib-. eration [4] . . .	{ Nov. 11, 1941 { Nov. 13, 1942	—— Sept. 25, 1943	Sept. 3, 1942 Sept. 25, 1943	—— ——
Greece	Mar. 11, 1941	Jul. 10, 1942	——	Jan. 1, 1942
Guatemala . . .	May 6, 1941	Nov. 16, 1942	——	Jan. 1, 1942
Haiti	May 6, 1941	Sept. 16, 1941	——	Jan. 1, 1942
Honduras . . .	May 6, 1941	Feb. 28, 1942	——	Jan. 1, 1942
Iceland	Jul. 1, 1941	Nov. 21, 1941	——	——
India	Nov. 11, 1941	——	——	Jan. 1, 1942
Iran	Mar. 10, 1942	——	——	Sept. 9, 1943
Iraq	May 1, 1942	——	——	Jan. 16, 1942
Liberia	Mar. 10, 1942	Jun. 8, 1943	Apr. 10, 1944	Apr. 10, 1944
Luxemburg . . .	——	——	——	Jan. 1, 1942
Mexico	May 6, 1941	Mar. 18, 1943	——	Jun. 5, 1942
Netherlands. . .	Aug. 21, 1941	Jul. 8, 1942	Jun. 14, 1943	Jan. 1, 1942
New Zealand . .	Nov. 11, 1941	([2])	Sept. 3, 1942	Jan. 1, 1942
Nicaragua . . .	May 6, 1941	Oct. 16, 1941	——	Jan. 1, 1942
Norway	Jun. 4, 1941	Jul. 11, 1942	——	Jan. 1, 1942
Panama	May 6, 1941	——	——	Jan. 1, 1942
Paraguay . . .	May 6, 1941	Sept. 20, 1941	——	——
Peru	May 6, 1941	Mar. 11, 1942	——	——
Philippines . . .	——	——	——	Jun. 10, 1942
Poland.	Aug. 28, 1941	Jul. 1, 1942	——	· Jan. 1, 1942
Saudi Arabia . .	Feb. 18, 1943	——	——	——
South Africa . .	Nov. 11, 1941	——	——	Jan. 1, 1942
Turkey	Nov. 7, 1941	——	——	——
United Kingdom .	Mar. 11, 1941	Feb. 23, 1942	Sept. 3, 1942	Jan. 1, 1942
United States . .	——	——	——	Jan. 1, 1942
U.S.S.R.	Nov. 7, 1941	June 11, 1942	——	Jan. 1, 1942
Uruguay	May 6, 1941	Jan. 13, 1942	——	——
Venezuela . . .	May 6, 1941	Mar. 18, 1942	——	——
Yugoslavia . . .	Nov. 11, 1941	Jul. 24, 1942	——	Jan. 1, 1942

[2] No Master Lend-Lease Agreement has been concluded with either Australia or New Zealand, but in the Reciprocal Aid Agreements entered into with these countries, they accepted the principles of the Lend-Lease Agreement with the United Kingdom as applicable to their lend-lease relations with the United States.

[3] In an exchange of notes dated November 30, 1942, Canada accepted the underlying principles of Article VII of the Master Agreement.

[4] Territory under the jurisdiction of the French National Committee was declared eligible to receive lend-lease aid on November 11, 1941, and a reciprocal aid agreement was entered into with the Committee on September 3, 1942. French North and West Africa were declared eligible to receive lend-lease aid on November 13, 1942. On September 25, 1943, a Modus Vivendi Agreement governing lend-lease aid and reciprocal aid was entered into with the French Committee of National Liberation, successor to the French National Committee and to the Haut Commandement en Chef Civile et Militaire established in French North and West Africa after the events of November 1942. See p. 219.

B. Agreements Regarding Lend-Lease Aid

[See *Documents, IV, 1941–42*, p. 235; *V, 1942–3*, p. 217.]

(1) *Exchange of Notes Relating to Agreement between the Governments of the United States and Ethiopia, Signed at Washington, August 9, 1943* [1]

The text of the main agreement was the same in all important respects as that of the agreement with the United Kingdom (see *Documents, IV, 1941–42*, p. 235) and for that reason is not reprinted here. There was, however, a supplementary exchange of notes, given below. The reply of the Vice Minister of Finance (Deressa) is not reprinted, as it is an identic note.

(a) *The Secretary of State (Hull) to the Vice Minister of Finance of Ethiopia (Deressa)*

EXCELLENCY:

I have the honor to refer to the conversations that have occurred between the representatives of our two Governments in connection with the agreement signed at Washington on this day, between the Government of the United States of America and the Government of Ethiopia on the principles applying to aid under the Act of March 11, 1941, and to set forth my understanding of the accord reached with particular reference to Articles V and VII of the agreement as follows:

1. It is agreed that if substantial amounts of materials or assistance furnished or to be furnished under the Act of Mar 11, 1941 or otherwise, by any Agency of the United States Government without current payment by the Government of Ethiopia have been or shall be employed by either of our two Governments, during the present war, in the construction of any installations on Ethiopian territory, the disposition of such installations remaining on Ethopian territory after the present war shall be governed by an agreement or agreements to which both our Governments shall be parties. Such agreement or agreements shall make appropriate provision for the future ownership and operation of the installation or installations in question, and for the payments or other benefits to be received by the Government of the United States on account of its contribution to their cost. The governing purpose of such agreement or agreements shall be to carry out in practice, in whatever way may then appear to be the most effective, the principles of the Joint Declaration of August 14, 1941, known as the Atlantic Charter, and in particular point Fourth thereof relating to the enjoyment by all States of access on equal terms to the trade and to the raw materials of the world. If such agreement in the case of any installation is not reached within a reasonable time after the end of the present emergency, as determined

---

[1] *Executive Agreement Series* 334; Department of State, *Bulletin*, IX, p. 95.

by the President of the United States of America, the Government of the United States may withdraw that installation, or the parts thereof which it shall have contributed, whether located on private or on public land, doing no unnecessary damage in the process, and leaving the land involved in a safe condition.

2. The other obligations of our two Governments in respect of mutual aid will be satisfied in accordance with the provisions of the agreement signed this day.

(2) *Modus Vivendi between the Government of the United States and the French Committee of National Liberation on Reciprocal Aid in French North and West Africa, Signed September 25, 1943* [1]

The Government of the United States and the French Committee of National Liberation, desirous of lending each other the reciprocal aid necessary to the prosecution of the joint war effort, are agreed upon the following provisional Modus Vivendi which will, following signature, be applicable in French North and West Africa:

I. With reference to supplies and services urgently needed to maintain the French war effort, which the United States has furnished to the French authorities and will continue to furnish, within limitations of need and supply, it is understood that:

(*a*) Military aid, including supplies for railroads, docks, public utilities, and other facilities to the extent that such supplies are determined to be military aid is made available on a straight Lend-Lease basis, in the light of the considerations set forth in Paragraph V. Such aid does not include the pay and allowances of French forces. The United States reserves the right to require the return of any articles furnished under this paragraph and not lost, destroyed or consumed,

(*i*) if at any time it is decided that such restitution would be an advantage in the conduct of the war, or

(*ii*) if at the end of the present emergency as determined by the President of the United States, the President shall determine that such articles are useful in the defense of the United States or of the Western Hemisphere, or to be otherwise of use to the United States.

(*b*) For all civilian supplies imported from the United States, the French authorities will pay upon the basis of prices to be agreed. Payment will be made, currently at convenient intervals, in dollars, to an appropriately designated account in the United States.

(*c*) The distinction between civilian and military aid, supplies and services, where such distinction may be necessary, will be made by agreement.

[1] House Doc. No. 497, 78th Cong., 2d sess. [*Report to Congress on Lend-Lease Operations*], p. 79.

(d) All aid furnished under Paragraph I (a) and I (b) will be made available by the United States under the authority and subject to the terms and conditions provided for in the Act of Congress of 11 March, 1941, as amended (Public Law 11, 77th Cong., 1st sess.).

II. With reference to supplies and services urgently needed to maintain the United States war effort, which the French authorities have furnished to the United States and will continue to furnish, within limitations of need and supply, it is understood that:

(a) The French authorities undertake to make available to or for the use of the armed forces and other governmental agencies of the United States, as reverse Lend-Lease aid to the United States, on a straight Lend-Lease basis, when it is found that such aid can most effectively be procured in territory under their control.

(i) military equipment, munitions, and military and naval stores;

(ii) other supplies, materials, facilities and services for United States forces, including the use of railway and port facilities, but not including the pay and allowances of such forces nor the administrative expenses of American missions;

(iii) supplies, materials, facilities and services, except for the wages and salaries of United States citizens, needed in the construction of military projects, tasks and similar capital works required in the common war effort, to the extent that French North or West Africa is the most practicable source of such supplies, materials, facilities or services;

(iv) such other supplies, materials, services or facilities as may be agreed upon as necessary in the prosecution of the war, but not including exports of civilian supplies to the United States from North and West Africa.

While the French authorities retain, of course, the right of final decision, subject to the obligations and arrangements they have entered into for the prosecution of the war, decisions as to the most effective use of resources shall, so far as possible, be made in common, pursuant to common plans for winning the war.

(b) All civilian supplies exported from French North and West Africa to the United States will be paid for on the basis of prices to be agreed. Payment will be made currently, at convenient intervals, in dollars, to an appropriate designated account in the United States.

(c) The distinction between civilian and military aid, supplies and services, where such distinction may be necessary, will be made by agreement.

(d) In order to obtain the supplies and services included within the scope of Paragraph II (a), duly authorized United States officers or other officials will submit their requests to the official services duly designated by the French authorities. These services will be established in Algiers, Casablanca, Oran, Tunis, Dakar, and other places where it may be found practicable and convenient to establish organizations for facilitating the transfer of reciprocal aid.

(e) For use in those exceptional cases, and particularly in cases of local procurement of supplies, in which it is agreed to be more practicable to secure such reverse Lend-Lease supplies, facilities and services by direct purchase, rather than by the method of procurement set forth in Paragraph II (b), it is agreed that the French authorities establish a franc account in convenient banking institutions and in the name of a designated officer of the United States to facilitate the provision of reverse Lend-Lease aid as contemplated by Paragraph II (a). The French contributions to this account will be mutually agreed upon from time to time in the light of the changing needs of the American forces, and other appropriate factors. Such an account will not be used for the payment of wages and salaries of American military or civilian personnel, nor for administrative expenses of American missions. Estimates of the franc requirements of the United States will be submitted to designated French authorities from time to time, as may be found convenient. The French authorities will be kept fully and currently informed of all transactions in this account.

III. In exceptional cases, and when they deem it preferable, the American military forces, or other agencies of the United States Government, may continue to use their present practice of acquiring francs against dollars from the French authorities.

IV. Adequate statistical records will be kept of all goods and services exchanged as mutual aid under paragraphs I and II above.

V. The provisions of this modus vivendi correspond to a desire to reduce to an appropriate minimum the need of either party for currency of the other party. Provisions which call for payments in dollars have been decided upon in view of the special situation arising from accumulated dollar balances and availabilities of dollar funds due to the presence of United States troops in French North and West Africa. Revision of the payment provisions of this modus vivendi will be made should the situation require.

Signed at Algiers this 25th day of September, A.D. 1943.

For the Government of the United States of America:

ROBERT MURPHY

For the French Committee of National Liberation:

MASSIGLI
JEAN MONNET

(3) *Protocol Regarding Military Supplies to the Soviet Union. Department of State Release, October 19, 1943* [1]

A third agreement for the provision of supplies to the Union of Soviet Socialist Republics was signed in London on October 19, 1943, by the United States, United Kingdom, Canadian, and Soviet Governments by which the first three Governments undertake to supply armaments, equipment, materials, and food-stuffs to the Union of Soviet Socialist Republics. Two former agreements of this kind were signed — the first in Moscow in October 1941 and the second in Washington in October 1942,[2] the present agreement represents a continuation of existing arrangements. This is the first time, however, that Canada has taken part as a signatory, though supplies from Canada have previously formed part of the commitment of the United Kingdom and in some cases of that of the United States. The period covered by the second agreement ended on June 30, but, although the third agreement has only now been signed, its provisions have been effective for the past three months and the flow of supplies of all kinds to the Union of Soviet Socialist Republics has continued without interruption. The present agreement was signed by Ambassador John G. Winant on behalf of the United States, by Mr. Oliver Lyttelton and Sir Alexander Cadogan on behalf of the United Kingdom, by Mr. Vincent Massey on behalf of Canada, and by Ambassador Feodor Gusev and Mr. Dmitri Borisenko on behalf of the Union of Soviet Socialist Republics.

From the beginning of the Soviet lend-lease program in October 1941 through June 30, 1944, total United States lend-lease exports to the U.S.S.R. have amounted to $5,900,000,000. Of that amount, more than $1,650,000,000 was shipped in the first six months of 1944.[3]

(4) *Agreement With Liberia Relating to Construction of a Port and Port Works on the Coast of Liberia. Department of State Release, January 8, 1944* [4]

According to information received by the Secretary of State from the American Minister at Monrovia, there was signed on December 31, 1943 at Monrovia, by the American Minister and the Secretary of State of Liberia, an agreement relating to the construction of a port and port works on the coast of Liberia.

This agreement was made in pursuance of principles laid down by the mutual-aid agreement of June 8, 1943 [5] between the United States and Liberia, which was negotiated under the authority of and in conformity with the Lend-Lease Act of March 11, 1941.

Under this agreement, which became effective upon signature, the Government of the United States makes certain funds available, upon specified conditions, for the construction of a port and port works at a mutually agreed-upon site on the coast of the Republic of Liberia.

Provision is made for the payment, from revenues of the port, of the administrative and other costs of operating the port and for annual payments in amortization of the funds made available by the Government of the United States. The agreement contains provisions relating to joint operating control by the United States and Liberia pending amortization of the cost of the port, port works, and access roads.

[1] Department of State, *Bulletin*, IX, p. 272.   [2] *Ibid.*, V, p. 364 and VII, p. 805.
[3] *Sixteenth Report to Congress on Lend-Lease Operations for the Period Ended June 30, 1944*, p. 31.
[4] Department of State, *Bulletin*, X, p. 38, 39.
[5] *Ibid.*, VIII, p. 515; *Executive Agreement Series* 324.

(5) *Distribution of Lend-Lease Material. Joint Statement of the Secretary of State (Hull) and the Foreign Economic Administrator (Crowley), March 18, 1944* [1]

Our attention has been called to recent newspaper reports to the effect that the British White Paper of September 10, 1941,[2] was being scrapped to give British exporters freedom in the commercial export of articles and materials received under lend-lease, or similar goods. These reports are entirely untrue.

The White Paper was a unilateral declaration of policy by the British Government that it would not permit the re-export of lend-lease goods or similar goods in short supply in the United States except under certain specified circumstances where war-supply considerations made it necessary. That policy has been successfully administered for more than two years, and valuable experience has been gained in its administration.

With the expansion of reverse-lend-lease aid from Britain to the United States to include raw materials, discussions have been undertaken between representatives of the British and American Governments looking toward the formulation of an agreed set of principles on a bilateral basis governing the re-export of lend-lease and mutual-aid goods and similar goods. The discussions have proceeded on the lines of the same basic policy followed under the original White Paper. It has also been attempted to work out improved administrative procedures for the effectuation of these policies, based on the experience acquired in this field in the last two years.

Discussions with the British representatives have not yet been concluded and may continue for some time. As soon as it is possible to do so, the appropriate committees of Congress will be consulted. Whatever arrangement is finally adopted will protect the interests of American industry and trade to the fullest extent consistent with the requirements of war and will be made public as soon as an agreement is reached.

(6) *Joint Statement on Special Lend-Lease Agreement with India of Secretary of the Treasury (Morgenthau) and Foreign Economic Administrator (Crowley), June 15, 1944* [3]

The United States Government has agreed to supply the Government of India under a special lend-lease agreement with 100 million ounces of silver to be used to maintain an adequate supply of coinage for the large numbers of United Nations forces there and for India's expanded war production, and to help to keep prices stable in this important United Nations supply base and war theater.

The Government of India has agreed to return the silver to the United States after the end of the war on an ounce-for-ounce basis.

---

[1] Department of State, *Bulletin*, X, p. 256.

[2] *Ibid.*, V, p. 204; *Documents, IV, 1941–42*, p. 592.

[3] Treasury Department, Press Service Release, No. 42–27.

The silver bullion will be supplied to India from the large stocks of United States Treasury free silver. The shipments of silver will not impair in any way the supply of silver required for domestic purposes in the United States.

Silver has been supplied under lend-lease from time to time to a number of other countries for industrial and coinage purposes essential to the war. The total amount of silver shipped under lend-lease to date to all countries is approximately 4,000 short tons.

At the Moscow Conference of October 1943, the Soviet Union is reported to have raised the question of Turkey's position in relation to the Allies, and urged that neither ships nor war materials should be sent to Turkey unless the Turkish Government was prepared to use them against the Germans. Conversations were held later by British, American and Soviet officials on the subject and strong notes of protest were delivered by the British and American Ambassadors on April 14 on the continuance of Turkish-German trade. These notes were in accord with the request in Secretary of State Hull's speech of April 9, 1944 that neutral countries cease trading with Germany. A German commercial mission was then in Ankara negotiating a renewal of the trade pact.

On April 1, the United States suspended lend-lease assistance to Turkey, pending a survey of her attitude toward the Allied cause.[1] The British Government had announced on March 2 that it had ordered the shipment of all military supplies to Turkey stopped. The Allied suspension of supplies to Turkey brought about a reconsideration of Turkish-German relations.

The Turkish Foreign Minister announced in the National Assembly on April 20 that all exports of chrome to Germany would cease on the next day. He said that "according to our pact with Great Britain signed in 1939 we are not neutrals. It is necessary for us to consider the Allied note as being not to a neutral, but to an ally of the British and their allies." The Turkish Government maintained diplomatic relations with Germany until August 2, 1944, when they were formally severed.

3. COORDINATION OF POLICIES AND MILITARY PLANS

During the period under review, important progress was made in bringing the Soviet Union into active participation in conferences intended to discuss and produce agreement on questions of policy and over-all strategy. Until the Moscow Conference, there had been close cooperation between the British and American Governments (see *Documents, IV, 1941–42*, p. 239; *V, 1942–43*, p. 248), but it had apparently been impossible to bring the Soviet Government into these discussions on a comparable basis. The Tripartite Conference at Moscow was an important milestone in the development of cooperative relations between the three major military powers allied in war against the Axis powers.

A. The Quebec Conference, August 11–24, 1943

(1) *Joint Statement of the President (Roosevelt) and the Prime Minister of the United Kingdom (Churchill), August 24, 1943*[2]

This was the fifth meeting of President Roosevelt and Prime Minister Churchill, with their top political and military advisers. The meeting was

----

[1] Royal Institute of International Affairs, London, *Bulletin of International News*, XXI (1944), p. 327.　　　　　　　[2] Department of State, *Bulletin*, IX, p. 121.

held at the time when the campaign in Sicily was coming to its close and when the invasion of continental Europe appeared to be the next step in the European area.

The Soviet Government was not represented. In a broadcast from Moscow, it had been stated that because of the nature of the proposed discussions, Soviet participation "was not and is not envisaged." [1] Prime Minister Churchill stated, however, in his broadcast from Quebec on August 31, that while he and President Roosevelt were willing to undertake every possible means to achieve a three-power meeting, Marshal Stalin, in direct command of the victorious Russian armies, could not at that time leave the battlefront where operations of vital consequence were going on. [2] The Conference was apparently held to discuss military and political questions. The military topics given first consideration were the planning of future European military operations and the stepping-up of the tempo of military operations in the Far East. The appointment of Lord Louis Mountbatten, Chief of British Combined Operations, to the newly created Southeastern Asia Command was a direct consequence of the discussions. Of the major political problems considered, first consideration was probably given to the improvement of relations with the Soviet Union, still considered unsatisfactory because of Soviet dissatisfaction with the Allied failure to open a military front in western Europe. The recall of Maxim Litvinov as Ambassador to Washington was interpreted by some as a sign of Soviet displeasure. Other questions apparently discussed were relations with the French Committee of National Liberation (for statements of United States and British Governments, see p. 668) and the treatment of Italy. [3]

Following the Conference, President Roosevelt delivered an address on August 25 to the Canadian Parliament in which he spoke generally of the results achieved (see p. 1). Prime Minister Churchill, in his broadcast from Quebec on August 31, [4] was somewhat more specific. He said that the President and he would "persevere in our efforts to meet Marshal Stalin. And in the meantime it seems most necessary and urgent that a conference of the British, United States and Russian Foreign Ministers, or their responsible representatives, should be held." He added: "We shall also be very glad to associate Russian representatives with us in the political decisions which arise out of the victories the Anglo-American forces have gained in the Mediterranean. In fact, there is no step which we may take, or which may be forced upon us by the unforeseeable course of this war, about which we should not wish to consult with our Russian friends and allies in the fullest confidence and candor. It will be a very great advantage to everyone, and indeed to the whole free world, if a unity of thought and decision upon practical measures for the longer future, as well as upon strategic problems, could be reached between the three great opponents of the Hitlerite tyranny."

The Anglo-American war conference, which opened at Quebec on August 11, under the hospitable auspices of the Canadian Government, has now concluded its work.

The whole field of world operations has been surveyed in the light of the many gratifying events which have taken place since the meeting of the President and the Prime Minister in Washington at the end of May,

[1] *New York Times*, section 4, August 15, 1943.
[2] *Bulletin of International News*, XX (1943), p. 820.
[3] *New York Times*, section 4, August 29, 1943.
[4] *New York Times*, September 1, 1943; British Information Services, *British Speeches of the Day*, No. 7, September 1943, p. 22.

and the necessary decisions have been taken to provide for the forward action of the fleets, armies, and air forces of the two nations.

Considering that these forces are intermingled in continuous action against the enemy in several quarters of the globe, it is indispensable that entire unity of aim and method should be maintained at the summit of the war direction.

Further conferences will be needed, probably at shorter intervals than before, as the war effort of the United States and British Commonwealth and Empire against the enemy spreads and deepens.

It would not be helpful to the fighting troops to make any announcement of the decisions which have been reached. These can only emerge in action.

It may, however, be stated that the military discussions of the chiefs of staff turned very largely upon the war against Japan and the bringing of effective aid to China. Dr. T. V. Soong, representing the Generalissimo Chiang Kai-shek, was a party to the discussions. In this field, as in the European, the President and the Prime Minister were able to receive and approve the unanimous recommendation of the Combined Chiefs of Staff. Agreements were also reached upon the political issues underlying or arising out of the military operations.

It was resolved to hold another conference before the end of the year between the British and American authorities, in addition to any tripartite meeting which it may be possible to arrange with Soviet Russia. Full reports of the decisions so far as they affect the war against Germany and Italy will be furnished to the Soviet Government.

Consideration has been given during the Conference to the question of relations with the French Committee of Liberation, and it is understood that an announcement by a number of governments will be made in the latter part of the week.

B. The Moscow Tripartite Conference, October 19–30, 1943

The Moscow Conference was of historic significance as the first meeting of foreign ministers and military leaders of the United States, the United Kingdom and the Soviet Union for the discussion of common political and military problems. It came at a time when the Soviet forces were triumphantly advancing in the East and Italy had finally surrendered to Allied forces. As President Roosevelt stated at his press conference on October 29, the Conference provided the opportunity for an exchange of views, agreement on important questions, and a better coordination of military efforts. The Conference presumably covered a wide range of military and political questions, the question of a large-scale second front in Western Europe, the question of Eastern European boundaries, the treatment of defeated Germany and the development of procedures for more effective collaboration for common purposes.[1]

After his return, Secretary Hull addressed the two Houses of Congress in joint session on the results of the Conference (see p. 11).

[1] *New York Times*, section 4, October 24, 1943.

(1) *Anglo-Soviet-American Communiqué, Released November 1, 1943* [1]

The Conference of Foreign Secretaries of the United States of America, Mr. Cordell Hull, of the United Kingdom, Mr. Anthony Eden, and of the Soviet Union, Mr. V. M. Molotov, took place at Moscow from the 19th to 30th of October 1943. There were twelve meetings.

In addition to the Foreign Secretaries the following took part in the Conference:

For the United States of America: Mr. W. Averell Harriman, Ambassador of the United States, Major General John R. Deane, United States Army, Mr. Green H. Hackworth, Mr. James C. Dunn, and experts.

For the United Kingdom: Sir Archibald Clerk Kerr, His Majesty's Ambassador, Mr. William Strang, Lt. General Sir Hastings Ismay, and experts.

For the Soviet Union: Marshal K. E. Voroshilov, Marshal of the Soviet Union, Mr. A. Y. Vyshinski, Mr. M. M. Litvinov, Deputy People's Commissars for Foreign Affairs, Mr. V. A. Sergeyev, Deputy People's Commissar for Foreign Trade, Major-General A. A. Gryslov, of the General Staff, Mr. G. F. Saksin, Senior Official of the People's Commissariat for Foreign Affairs, and experts.

The agenda included all the questions submitted for discussion by the three Governments. Some of the questions called for final decisions and these were taken. On other questions, after discussion, decisions of principle were taken: these questions were referred for detailed consideration to commissions specially set up for the purpose, or reserved for treatment through diplomatic channels. Other questions again were disposed of by an exchange of views.

The Governments of the United States, the United Kingdom and the Soviet Union have been in close cooperation in all matters concerning the common war effort. But this is the first time that the Foreign Secretaries of the three Governments have been able to meet together in conference.

In the first place there were frank and exhaustive discussions of measures to be taken to shorten the war against Germany and her satellites in Europe. Advantage was taken of the presence of military advisers, representing the respective Chiefs of Staff, in order to discuss definite military operations, with regard to which decisions had been taken and which are already being prepared, and in order to create a basis for the closest military cooperation in the future between the three countries.

Second only to the importance of hastening the end of the war was the unanimous recognition by the three Governments that it was essential in their own national interests and in the interest of all peace-loving nations to continue the present close collaboration and cooperation in

[1] Department of State, *Bulletin*, IX, p. 307.

the conduct of the war into the period following the end of hostilities, and that only in this way could peace be maintained and the political, economic and social welfare of their peoples fully promoted.

This conviction is expressed in a declaration in which the Chinese Government joined during the Conference and which was signed by the three Foreign Secretaries and the Chinese Ambassador at Moscow on behalf of their governments. This declaration, published today provides for even closer collaboration in the prosecution of the war and in all matters pertaining to the surrender and disarmament of the enemies with which the four countries are respectively at war. It sets forth the principles upon which the four governments agree that a broad system of international cooperation and security should be based. Provision is made for the inclusion of all other peace-loving nations, great and small, in this system.

The Conference agreed to set up machinery for ensuring the closest cooperation between the three Governments in the examination of European questions arising as the war develops. For this purpose the Conference decided to establish in London a European Advisory Commission to study these questions and to make joint recommendations to the three Governments.

Provision was made for continuing, when necessary, tripartite consultations of representatives of the three Governments in the respective capitals through the existing diplomatic channels.

The Conference also agreed to establish an Advisory Council for matters relating to Italy, to be composed in the first instance of representatives of their three governments and of the French Committee of National Liberation. Provision is made for the addition to this council of representatives of Greece and Yugoslavia in view of their special interests arising out of the aggressions of Fascist Italy upon their territory during the present war. This Council will deal with day-to-day questions, other than military operations, and will make recommendations designed to coordinate Allied policy with regard to Italy.

The three Foreign Secretaries considered it appropriate to reaffirm, by a declaration published today, the attitude of their Governments in favor of restoration of democracy in Italy.

The three Foreign Secretaries declared it to be the purpose of their Governments to restore the independence of Austria. At the same time they reminded Austria that in the final settlement account will be taken of efforts that Austria may make towards its own liberation. The declaration on Austria is published today.

The Foreign Secretaries issued at the Conference a declaration by President Roosevelt, Prime Minister Churchill and Premier Stalin containing a solemn warning that at the time of granting any armistice to any German Government those German officers and men and members of the Nazi party who have had any connection with atrocities and executions in countries overrun by German forces will be taken back to the countries in which their abominable crimes were committed to be charged and punished according to the laws of those countries.

In the atmosphere of mutual confidence and understanding which characterized all the work of the Conference, consideration was also given to other important questions. These included not only questions of a current nature, but also questions concerning the treatment of Hitlerite Germany and its satellites, economic cooperation and the assurance of general peace.

(2) *Declaration of Four Nations on General Security, October 30, 1943*

The Governments of the United States of America, the United Kingdom, the Soviet Union and China: united in their determination, in accordance with the Declaration by the United Nations of January 1, 1942, and subsequent declarations, to continue hostilities against those Axis powers with which they respectively are at war until such powers have laid down their arms on the basis of unconditional surrender;

conscious of their responsibility to secure the liberation of themselves and the peoples allied with them from the menace of aggression;

recognizing the necessity of ensuring a rapid and orderly transition from war to peace and of establishing and maintaining international peace and security with the least diversion of the world's human and economic resources for armaments;

jointly declare:

1. That their united action, pledged for the prosecution of the war against their respective enemies, will be continued for the organization and maintenance of peace and security.

2. That those of them at war with a common enemy will act together in all matters relating to the surrender and disarmament of that enemy.

3. That they will take all measures deemed by them to be necessary to provide against any violation of the terms imposed upon the enemy.

4. That they recognize the necessity of establishing at the earliest practicable date a general international organization, based on the principle of the sovereign equality of all peace-loving states, and open to membership by all such states, large and small, for the maintenance of international peace and security.

5. That for the purpose of maintaining international peace and security pending the reestablishment of law and order and the inauguration of a system of general security, they will consult with one another and as occasion requires with other members of the United Nations with a view to joint action on behalf of the community of nations.

6. That after the termination of hostilities they will not employ their military forces within the territories of other states except for the purposes envisaged in this declaration and after joint consultation.

7. That they will confer and cooperate with one another and with other members of the United Nations to bring about a practicable general agreement with respect to the regulation of armaments in the post-war period.

V. Molotov
Anthony Eden
Cordell Hull
Foo Ping-sheung

(3) Declaration Regarding Italy, October 30, 1943 [1]

The Foreign Secretaries of the United States of America, the United Kingdom and the Soviet Union have established that their three Governments are in complete agreement that Allied policy towards Italy must be based upon the fundamental principle that Fascism and all its evil influences and emanations shall be utterly destroyed and that the Italian people shall be given every opportunity to establish governmental and other institutions based upon democratic principles.

The Foreign Secretaries of the United States of America and the United Kingdom declare that the action of their Governments from the inception of the invasion of Italian territory, in so far as paramount military requirements have permitted, has been based upon this policy.

In the furtherance of this policy in the future the Foreign Secretaries of the three Governments are agreed that the following measures are important and should be put into effect:

1. It is essential that the Italian Government should be made more democratic by the introduction of representatives of those sections of the Italian people who have always opposed Fascism.

2. Freedom of speech, of religious worship, of political belief, of the press and of public meeting shall be restored in full measure to the Italian people, who shall also be entitled to form anti-Fascist political groups.

3. All institutions and organizations created by the Fascist regime shall be suppressed.

4. All Fascist or pro-Fascist elements shall be removed from the administration and from the institutions and organizations of a public character.

5. All political prisoners of the Fascist regime shall be released and accorded a full amnesty.

6. Democratic organs of local government shall be created.

[1] For description of relations of Italy with the Allied Governments see this volume, p. 160.

7. Fascist chiefs and other persons known or suspected to be war criminals shall be arrested and handed over to justice.

In making this declaration the three Foreign Secretaries recognize that so long as active military operations continue in Italy the time at which it is possible to give full effect to the principles set out above will be determined by the Commander-in-Chief on the basis of instructions received through the Combined Chiefs of Staff. The three Governments parties to this declaration will at the request of any one of them consult on this matter.

It is further understood that nothing in this resolution is to operate against the right of the Italian people ultimately to choose their own form of government.

(4) *Declaration on Austria, October 30, 1943*

The Governments of the United Kingdom, the Soviet Union and the United States of America are agreed that Austria, the first free country to fall a victim to Hitlerite aggression, shall be liberated from German domination.

They regard the annexation imposed upon Austria by Germany on March 15, 1938, as null and void. They consider themselves as in no way bound by any changes effected in Austria since that date. They declare that they wish to see reestablished a free and independent Austria, and thereby to open the way for the Austrian people themselves, as well as those neighboring states which will be faced with similar problems, to find that political and economic security which is the only basis for lasting peace.

Austria is reminded, however, that she has a responsibility which she cannot evade for participation in the war on the side of Hitlerite Germany, and that in the final settlement account will inevitably be taken of her own contribution to her liberation.

(5) *Declaration on German Atrocities, October 30, 1943*

The United Kingdom, the United States and the Soviet Union have received from many quarters evidence of atrocities, massacres and cold-blooded mass executions which are being perpetrated by the Hitlerite forces in the many countries they have overrun and from which they are now being steadily expelled. The brutalities of Hitlerite domination are no new thing and all the peoples or territories in their grip have suffered from the worst form of government by terror. What is new is that many of these territories are now being redeemed by the advancing armies of the liberating Powers and that in their desperation, the recoiling Hitlerite Huns are redoubling their ruthless cruelties.

This is now evidenced with particular clearness by monstrous crimes of the Hitlerites on the territory of the Soviet Union which is being liberated from the Hitlerites, and on French and Italian territory.

Accordingly, the aforesaid three allied Powers, speaking in the interests of the thirty-two [thirty-three] United Nations, hereby solemnly declare and give full warning of their declaration as follows:

At the time of the granting of any armistice to any government which may be set up in Germany, those German officers and men and members of the Nazi party who have been responsible for, or have taken a consenting part in the above atrocities, massacres and executions, will be sent back to the countries in which their abominable deeds were done in order that they may be judged and punished according to the laws of these liberated countries and of the free governments which will be created therein. Lists will be compiled in all possible detail from all these countries having regard especially to the invaded parts of the Soviet Union, to Poland and Czechoslovakia, to Yugoslavia and Greece, including Crete and other islands, to Norway, Denmark, the Netherlands, Belgium, Luxemburg, France and Italy.

Thus, the Germans who take part in wholesale shootings of Italian officers or in the execution of French, Dutch, Belgian or Norwegian hostages or of Cretan peasants, or who have shared in the slaughters inflicted on the people of Poland or in territories of the Soviet Union which are now being swept clear of the enemy, will know that they will be brought back to the scene of their crimes and judged on the spot by the peoples whom they have outraged. Let those who have hitherto not imbrued their hands with innocent blood beware lest they join the ranks of the guilty, for most assuredly the three allied powers will pursue them to the uttermost ends of the earth and will deliver them to their accusers in order that justice may be done.

The above declaration is without prejudice to the case of the major criminals, whose offenses have no particular geographical localization and who will be punished by the joint decision of the Governments of the Allies.

(Signed):

ROOSEVELT
CHURCHILL
STALIN

C. The Cairo Conference, November 22–26, 1943

(1) Statement Issued Following the Conference of President Roosevelt, Generalissimo Chiang Kai-shek and Prime Minister Churchill [1]

This Conference was held to consider war and peace problems of the Far East. Since the Soviet Union was not engaged in war with Japan, no representative of

[1] Department of State, Bulletin, IX, p. 393. The statement was released to the press by the White House on December 1, 1943.

that government was present. President Roosevelt, Generalissimo Chiang Kai-shek and Prime Minister Churchill were accompanied by their respective military and diplomatic advisers. China had not been represented at the Moscow Conference, though the Chinese Ambassador did join in signing the Declaration of Four Nations on General Security.

The several military missions have agreed upon future military operations against Japan. The Three Great Allies expressed their resolve to bring unrelenting pressure against their brutal enemies by sea, land, and air. This pressure is already rising.

The Three Great Allies are fighting this war to restrain and punish the aggression of Japan. They covet no gain for themselves and have no thought of territorial expansion. It is their purpose that Japan shall be stripped of all the islands in the Pacific which she has seized or occupied since the beginning of the first World War in 1914, and that all the territories Japan has stolen from the Chinese, such as Manchuria, Formosa, and the Pescadores, shall be restored to the Republic of China. Japan will also be expelled from all other territories which she has taken by violence and greed. The aforesaid three great powers, mindful of the enslavement of the people of Korea, are determined that in due course Korea shall become free and independent.

With these objects in view the three Allies, in harmony with those of the United Nations at war with Japan, will continue to persevere in the serious and prolonged operations necessary to procure the unconditional surrender of Japan.

(a) Radio Address by the President (Roosevelt), December 24, 1943 [1]

[Excerpt]

At Cairo, Prime Minister Churchill and I spent four days with the Generalissimo, Chiang Kai-shek. It was the first time that we had had an opportunity to go over the complex situation in the Far East with him personally. We were able not only to settle upon definite military strategy but also to discuss certain long-range principles which we believe can assure peace in the Far East for many generations to come.

Those principles are as simple as they are fundamental. They involve the restoration of stolen property to its rightful owners and the recognition of the rights of millions of people in the Far East to build up their own forms of self-government without molestation. Essential to all peace and security in the Pacific and in the rest of the world is the permanent elimination of the Empire of Japan as a potential force of aggression. Never again must our soldiers and sailors and marines be compelled to fight from island to island as they are fighting so gallantly and so successfully today.

(b) Message of Generalissimo Chiang Kai-shek to the Chinese People, January 1, 1944 [2]

[Excerpt]

Here I wish to report to the Army and people of our country the impressions I received during my participation in the Cairo Conference, which, I am sure,

[1] *Ibid.*, X, p. 4.   [2] *United Nations Review*, IV (1944), p. 58.

you will be glad to hear. In 1938 I pointed out that ever since the Meiji reform Japan had consistently followed a policy of continental aggression to satisfy her ambition for the enslavement of China and domination of East Asia as a first step toward world conquest. To crush such ambitious designs of Japan, we must strive to liberate the Korean people and regain Formosa as one of the aims of our resistance.

At the Cairo Conference, America, Great Britain, and China unanimously agreed to strip Japan of all the Pacific Islands she has seized or occupied since the first World War and to drive her out of all the territories which she has despoiled by force or out of greed. She has to restore to us the four Northeastern Provinces, Formosa, and the Pescadores. She has to permit Korea to be free and independent. Thus we have received absolute assurances of attaining the aims of our sacred war of resistance. This will not only cheer our fellow country-men in Formosa, the Pescadores, and the Northeast, as well as the people of Korea, but all the oppressed and maltreated Asiatic peoples both in the Pacific and Asia mainland may look forward with hope for liberation.

In the intimate talks I had with President Roosevelt and Prime Minister Churchill at Cairo, we considered steps for mutual cooperation and agreed upon certain plans for the prosecution of the war. We also touched upon the question of the disposal of the enemy after the war.

One important problem in this connection concerns Japan's form of government. When President Roosevelt asked my views, I frankly replied: "It is my opinion that all the Japanese militarists must be wiped out and the Japanese political system must be purged of every vestige of aggressive elements. As to what form of government Japan should adopt, that question can better be left to the awakened and repentant Japanese people to decide for themselves."

I also said: "If the Japanese people should rise in a revolution to punish their warmongers and to overthrow their militarist government, we should respect their spontaneous will and allow them to choose their own form of government." President Roosevelt fully approved of my idea. This opinion of ours is entirely based on the spirit of the Joint Declaration of the United Nations in 1942.

Today I make public this conversation with President Roosevelt at Cairo in order to impress upon our Army and people that after victory we hope not only to set free all the peoples who have been oppressed and enslaved by the enemy, but also to give a helping hand to the innocent and harmless people in Japan.

I have returned from the Cairo Conference with renewed devotion to the ideals of justice and peace. I may tell you that the deepest impressions I have of President Roosevelt are of his unflinching faith, his firm determination to emancipate all the world's oppressed peoples, and his sincere desire to help China become a truly free and independent nation. His basic policy is the attainment of real peace in the world and genuine equality among men, and he thinks that in such a future world as he visualizes China must be one of the pillars. This spirit of his arises from his innate love of justice and righteousness and his policy is based upon the peaceful relations of mutual trust between the American and Chinese peoples during the last 150 years.

D. The Tehran Conference, November 28–December 1, 1943

The Conference was attended by President Roosevelt, Prime Minister Churchill and Marshal Stalin, with their principal military and diplomatic advisers. It was understood that the discussion would cover a range of political and military questions. A question of primary concern was understood to be the coordination of Allied and Soviet military operations for a major assault upon Hitler's Europe.[1]

[1] *New York Times*, section 4, December 5, 1943.

(1) *Declaration of the Three Powers, December 1, 1943* [1]

We — The President of the United States, the Prime Minister of Great Britain, and the Premier of the Soviet Union, have met these four days past, in this, the Capital of our Ally, Iran, and have shaped and confirmed our common policy.

We express our determination that our nations shall work together in war and in the peace that will follow.

As to war — our military staffs have joined in our round table discussions, and we have concerted our plans for the destruction of the German forces. We have reached complete agreement as to the scope and timing of the operations to be undertaken from the east, west and south.

The common understanding which we have here reached guarantees that victory will be ours.

And as to peace — we are sure that our concord will win an enduring Peace. We recognize fully the supreme responsibility resting upon us and all the United Nations to make a peace which will command the goodwill of the overwhelming mass of the peoples of the world and banish the scourge and terror of war for many generations.

With our diplomatic advisors we have surveyed the problems of the future. We shall seek the cooperation and active participation of all nations, large and small, whose peoples in heart and mind are dedicated, as are our own peoples, to the elimination of tyranny and slavery, oppression and intolerance. We will welcome them, as they may choose to come, into a world family of Democratic Nations.

No power on earth can prevent our destroying the German armies by land, their U-Boats by sea, and their war plants from the air.

Our attack will be relentless and increasing.

Emerging from these cordial conferences we look with confidence to the day when all peoples of the world may live free lives, untouched by tyranny, and according to their varying desires and their own consciences.

We came here with hope and determination. We leave here, friends in fact, in spirit and in purpose.

ROOSEVELT, CHURCHILL AND STALIN

．　．　．　．　．　．　．　．

(2) *Declaration Regarding Iran, December 1, 1943* [2]

For texts of statements of British and Soviet Governments, dated August 25, 1941, at time of decisions to send military forces into Iran, and of the Treaty of Alliance between the United Kingdom, the Union of Soviet Socialist Republics and Iran, signed at Tehran, January 29, 1942, see *Documents, IV, 1941–42,* p. 674 et seq.

[1] Department of State, *Bulletin,* IX, p. 409. The text was given to the press at the White House, December 6, 1943.

[2] *Ibid.* The text was issued in Tehran on December 6.

The President of the United States of America, the Premier of the Union of Soviet Socialist Republics, and the Prime Minister of the United Kingdom, having consulted with each other and with the Prime Minister of Iran, desire to declare the mutual agreement of their three Governments regarding their relations with Iran.

The Governments of the United States of America, the Union of Soviet Socialist Republics and the United Kingdom recognize the assistance which Iran has given in the prosecution of the war against the common enemy, particularly by facilitating transportation of supplies from overseas to the Soviet Union. The three Governments realize that the war has caused special economic difficulties for Iran and they are agreed that they will continue to make available to the Government of Iran such economic assistance as may be possible, having regard to the heavy demands made upon them by their world-wide military operations and to the world-wide shortage of transport, raw materials and supplies for civilian consumption.

With respect to the post-war period, the Governments of the United States of America, the Union of Soviet Socialist Republics and the United Kingdom are in accord with the Government of Iran that any economic problem confronting Iran at the close of hostilities should receive full consideration along with those of the other members of the United Nations by conferences or international agencies held or created to deal with international economic matters.

The Governments of the United States of America, the Union of Soviet Socialist Republics and the United Kingdom are at one with the Government of Iran in their desire for the maintenance of the independence, sovereignty and territorial integrity of Iran. They count upon the participation of Iran together with all other peace-loving nations in the establishment of international peace, security and prosperity after the war in accordance with the principles of the Atlantic Charter, to which all four governments have continued to subscribe.

(a) Radio Address by the President (Roosevelt), December 24, 1943 [1]

[Excerpt]

After the Cairo conference, Mr. Churchill and I went by airplane to Tehran. There we met with Marshal Stalin. We talked with complete frankness on every conceivable subject connected with the winning of the war and the establishment of a durable peace after the war.

During the last two days at Tehran, Marshal Stalin, Mr. Churchill, and I looked ahead to the days and months and years which will follow Germany's defeat. We were united in determination that Germany must be stripped of her military might and be given no opportunity within the foreseeable future to regain that might.

[1] Ibid., X, p. 5.

The United Nations have no intention to enslave the German people. We wish them to have a normal chance to develop, in peace, as useful and respectable members of the European family. But we most certainly emphasize that word "respectable" — for we intend to rid them once and for all of Nazism and Prussian militarism and the fantastic and disastrous notion that they constitute the "master race."

We did discuss international relationships from the point of view of big, broad objectives, rather than details. But on the basis of what we did discuss, I can say even today that I do not think any insoluble differences will arise among Russia, Great Britain, and the United States.

In these conferences we were concerned with basic principles — principles which involve the security and the welfare and the standard of living of human beings in countries large and small.

To use an American and ungrammatical colloquialism, I may say that I "got along fine" with Marshal Stalin. He is a man who combines a tremendous, relentless determination with a stalwart good humor. I believe he is truly representative of the heart and soul of Russia; and I believe that we are going to get along well with him and the Russian people — very well indeed.

E. Second Cairo Conference, December 4–6, 1943

(1) *Communiqué Issued by the President (Roosevelt), the Prime Minister of the United Kingdom (Churchill), and the President of Turkey (Inonu), December 7, 1943* [1]

This Conference, held following the Tehran Conference, presumably had as its purpose to inform the Turkish President of the nature of the decisions taken and to reassure Turkey, to which Great Britain was bound by a treaty of alliance, as to the policy and intentions of the Soviet Union.

Mr. Roosevelt, President of the United States; M. Ismet Inonu, President of the Turkish Republic; and Winston Churchill, Prime Minister of the United Kingdom, met in Cairo on December 4, 5, and 6, 1943. Anthony Eden, His Britannic Majesty's principal Secretary of State for Foreign Affairs; Numan Menemencioglu, Minister of Foreign Affairs for Turkey; and Harry Hopkins took part in their deliberations. Participation in this conference of the head of the Turkish state in response to a cordial invitation addressed to him by the United States, the British and the Soviet Governments bears striking testimony to the strength of the alliance which unites Great Britain and Turkey and to the firm friendship existing between the Turkish people and the United States of America and the Soviet Union.

Presidents Roosevelt and Inonu and Prime Minister Churchill reviewed the general political situation and examined at length the policy

[1] *Ibid.*, IX, p. 412.

to be followed, taking into account the joint and several interests of the three countries. A study of all the problems in a spirit of understanding and loyalty showed that the closest unity existed between the United States of America, Turkey and Great Britain in their attitude to the world situation. The conversations in Cairo consequently have been most useful and most fruitful for the future of the relations between the four countries concerned. The identity of interests and of views of the great American and British democracies with those of the Soviet Union, as also the traditional relations of friendship existing between these three powers and Turkey, have been reaffirmed throughout the proceedings of the Cairo conference.

4. INTERNATIONAL AGENCIES DEALING WITH THE PROSECUTION OF THE WAR, AS OF JUNE 30, 1944

[See *Documents, IV, 1941–42,* p. 248, 351, 426; *V, 1942–43,* p. 261.]

To facilitate the conduct of the war numerous war agencies have been set up by the Allied Governments. The list of those functioning on June 30, 1944 is given below. In addition the United States is participating in the work of a number of United Nations organizations, such as the United Nations Relief and Rehabilitation Administration (see p. 248), and the United Nations Interim Commission on Food and Agriculture (see p. 415) primarily concerned with post-war problems.

Advisory Council for Italy

The Moscow Conference on October 30, 1943 agreed to establish an Advisory Council [1] for matters relating to Italy, to be composed in the first instance of representatives of Governments of the United Kingdom, the United States, the Soviet Union and of the French Committee of National Liberation. Provision was made for the addition of representatives of Greece and Yugoslavia in view of their special interests arising out of the aggressions of Fascist Italy upon their territory during the present war. This Council deals primarily with non-military questions and makes recommendations designed to coordinate Allied policy with regard to Italy. Its second function is to watch the operation of the machinery for enforcing the armistice terms.

The Council was established on November 30, 1943 with headquarters in Algiers. It was composed originally of the following representatives of the Allies: René Massigli (France), the President; Robert Murphy (U.S.A.), Harold Macmillan (United Kingdom) and Andrey J. Vyshinsky (U.S.S.R.). Mils Krek was appointed Yugoslav representative early in January 1944 and a little later M. Politis was appointed to represent Greece.

Allied Control Commission for Italy [2]

General Eisenhower announced on November 10, 1943 the formation of the Commission, which represented the United Nations. It was charged with the duty of carrying out the terms of the Italian Armistice of September 3, 1943 and of aligning Italian economy in support of the fight against Germany.

The Control Commission was divided into four sections: military, political, economic and administrative, and communications.

[1] *Ibid.,* p. 308; *Bulletin of International News,* XXI (1944), p. 718.
[2] *Bulletin of International News,* XX (1943), p. 1059.

Allied Supply Council — United States and Australia [1]

Upon the invitation of the Australian Government, this council was set up to coordinate plans and advise on the present and potential supplies, of all sorts, available from Australian sources.

Anglo-American Caribbean Commission [2]

A joint *communiqué* released simultaneously in Washington and London on March 9, 1942 announced the creation of the Anglo-American Caribbean Commission to encourage and strengthen "social and economic cooperation between the United States of America and its possessions and bases in the area known geographically and politically as the Caribbean, and the United Kingdom and the British colonies in the same area, and to avoid unnecessary duplication of research in these fields." According to the announcement, "members of the Commission will concern themselves primarily with matters pertaining to labor, agriculture, housing, health, education, social welfare, finance, economics and related subjects in the territories under the British and United States flags within this territory."

British-American Joint Patent Interchange Committee [3]

The British-American Joint Patent Interchange Committee was created pursuant to Article XIII of Executive Agreement Series 268 (British-American Patent Interchange Agreement) as a result of an exchange of notes between the two governments. The Agreement, signed at Washington on August 24, 1942, is effective as of January 1, 1942, and may be terminated by either government on any date not less than 6 months after the giving of notice of such termination.

It is the function of the Joint Committee to deal with problems arising in connection with operations under the British-American Patent Interchange Agreement and to make appropriate recommendations to proper authorities with respect thereto. The Agreement has for its purpose facilitating the interchange of patent rights, inventions, technical information, designs, and processes between the two governments under the lend-lease mutual-aid programs.

In dealing with problems arising as a result of the operations under the Agreement, the Committee meets jointly as well as in its American and British sections. Problems pertaining to both governments are finally resolved by the Joint Committee and appropriate recommendations are made to the proper authorities of both governments. Problems that arise which affect only one government are dealt with by that section of the Joint Committee which represents the interested government, and when such problems are finally concluded, appropriate recommendations are made to the proper authorities of that government.

Combined Chiefs of Staff — United States and United Kingdom [4]

Establishment of the Combined Chiefs of Staff was announced by the War Department on February 6, 1942. Under the direction of the heads of the United Nations, the Combined Chiefs of Staff collaborate in the formulation and execution of policies and plans concerning (a) the strategic conduct of the war; (b) the broad program of war requirements, based on approved strategic

[1] Department of State, *Bulletin*, VIII, p. 66.
[2] *Ibid.*; see also this volume, p. 597.
[3] *United States Government Manual, Summer, 1944*, p. 171.   [4] *Ibid.*, p. 166.

policy; (c) the allocation of munition resources, based on strategic needs and the availability of means of transportation; (d) the requirements for overseas transportation for the fighting services of the United Nations, based on approved strategic priority.

Combined Food Board — United States, United Kingdom, and Canada [1]

Acting jointly, the President of the United States and the Prime Minister of Great Britain on June 9, 1942 authorized the creation of the Combined Food Board to obtain a planned and expeditious utilization of the food resources of the United Nations, in order to coordinate further the prosecution of the war effort. In October 1943, Canadian Prime Minister W. L. Mackenzie King accepted membership on behalf of the Government of Canada.[2]

The Board considers, investigates, and formulates plans with regard to any question relating to the supply, production, transportation, disposal, allocation or distribution, in or to any part of the world, of foods, agricultural materials from which foods are derived, and equipment and nonfood materials ancillary to the production of such foods and agricultural materials.

It works in collaboration with others of the United Nations toward the best utilization of their food resources, and, in collaboration with the interested nation or nations, formulates plans and recommendations for the development, expansion, purchase, or other effective use of their food resources.[3]

Combined Production and Resources Board — United States, United Kingdom, and Canada [4]

The creation of the Combined Production and Resources Board was announced by the President on June 9, 1942. The Board was established by the President of the United States and the Prime Minister of Great Britain, in order to complete the organization needed for the most effective use of the combined resources of the United States and the United Kingdom for the prosecution of the war.

On November 10, 1942, by agreement of the President of the United States, the Prime Minister of Great Britain, and the Prime Minister of Canada, the Board was expanded to include a Canadian member.

The Board combines the production programs of the United States, the United Kingdom, and Canada into a single integrated program, adjusted to the strategic requirements of the war, as indicated to the Board by the Combined Chiefs of Staff, and to all relevant production factors. The board takes account of the need for maximum utilization of the productive resources available to the United States, the British Commonwealth of Nations, and the United Nations, the need to reduce demands on shipping to a minimum, and the essential needs of the civilian populations.

In close collaboration with the Combined Chiefs of Staff, the Board works to assure the continuous adjustment of the combined production program to meet

---

[1] Ibid., p. 167.

[2] For message of President Roosevelt and Prime Minister Churchill to Prime Minister Mackenzie King, and his reply, see Department of State, *Bulletin*, IX, p. 292.

[3] Claude R. Wickard, United States Secretary of Agriculture, was named neutral chairman and Marvin Jones, War Food Administrator, became United States member of the Board. (*Ibid.*, p. 293.) The War Food Administration was strengthened by Executive Order No. 9392, 8 *Fed. Reg.*, p. 14783.

[4] *United States Government Manual, Summer, 1944*, p. 167.

changing military requirements. The Combined Chiefs of Staff and the Munitions Assignments Board keep the Combined Production and Resources Board currently informed concerning military requirements, and the Combined Production and Resources Board keeps the Combined Chiefs of Staff and the Munitions Assignments Board currently informed concerning the facts and possibilities of production.

Combined Raw Materials Board — United States and United Kingdom [1]

The establishment of the Combined Raw Materials Board was announced by the President of the United States and the Prime Minister of Great Britain on January 26, 1942. The Board was given a comprehensive responsibility for the planning of the raw materials effort of the two countries and for collaborating with the other United Nations to provide for the most effective utilization of all raw material resources at their disposal.

The activities of the Board include over-all review of the supply and requirements position of the United Nations for the major critical and essential raw materials, allocation of supplies of scarce raw materials among the United Nations when necessary, recommendations aimed at expanding supplies and conserving the use of raw materials in short supply, coordinating the purchasing activities of the United States and Great Britain in foreign raw material markets, and the adjustment of the day-to-day raw materials problems which have been referred to or initiated by the Board.

The Board's decisions are made after consultation with the appropriate government agencies in the two countries, and it relies on the operating agencies of both countries to implement its decisions. Through the Board's Advisory Operating Committee, on which are represented American and British agencies concerned with raw material and shipping problems, a machinery is provided for discussion of raw material problems requiring cooperative action by the operating agencies of the two countries.

Combined Shipping Adjustment Board — United States and United Kingdom [2]

Creation of the Combined Shipping Adjustment Board was announced by the President of the United States and the Prime Minister of Great Britain on January 26, 1942. The function of the Board is to adjust and concert in one harmonious policy the work of the British Ministry of War Transport and the War Shipping Administration.

The Emergency Advisory Committee for Political Defense [3]
(Inter-American)

The Emergency Advisory Committee for Political Defense was established pursuant to a resolution of the Third Meeting of Ministers of Foreign Affairs of the American Republics, held at Rio de Janeiro in January 1942. The Committee studies and recommends to each of the American governments members of the Pan American Union appropriate measures for the control of sabotage and all other types of subversive activities directed by extracontinental forces against the ideals and security of the Western Hemisphere. The Committee is made up of seven members, each representing the entire inter-American community rather than any one nation exclusively. The first meeting was held on April 15, 1942.

[1] *Ibid.*, p. 169.   [2] *Ibid.*, p. 171.   [3] Department of State, *Bulletin*, VIII, p. 69; XII, p. 3.

European Advisory Commission

The Commission was established following a decision taken at the Moscow Conference on October 30, 1943. Its purpose is to assist the governments of the United States,[1] the United Kingdom and the Soviet Union in reaching a joint policy on European political problems. It attempts to achieve this purpose by studying questions as they arise and making joint recommendations to the three governments.

Three permanent delegates, the American Ambassador to London John G. Winant,[2] Sir William Strong of Great Britain and the Soviet Ambassador to London, Foydor Guseff, attended the preliminary meeting on December 15, 1943 at the headquarters of the Commission at Lancaster House, St. James's Palace, London. The first formal meeting was held on January 14, 1944, with Ambassador Winant in the chair.

Inter-American Commission for Territorial Administration [3]

The Inter-American Commission for Territorial Administration was established under the provisions of the Convention on the Provisional Administration of European Colonies and Possessions in the Americas, which entered into force on January 8, 1942. The Commission, composed of a representative from each of the ratifying states, undertakes the provisional administration of any territory located in the Americas, should a non-American state directly or indirectly attempt to replace another non-American state in the sovereignty or control which it exercised over such territory.

Inter-American Defense Board [4]

The Inter-American Defense Board is a permanently constituted organization composed of military, naval, and aviation technical delegates appointed by each of the governments of the 21 American Republics. It was established in accordance with Resolution XXXIX of the Meeting of Foreign Ministers at Rio de Janeiro in January 1942. The Board meets regularly in the City of Washington and is an autonomous international organization under the auspices of the Pan American Union. The Board studies and recommends to the governments of the American Republics measures necessary for the defense of the Western Hemisphere.

Inter-American Development Commission [5]

The Inter-American Development Commission, of which the Coordinator of Inter-American Affairs is Chairman, is a permanent international body set up by the Inter-American Financial and Economic Advisory Committee. The aim of the Commission is to encourage development of natural resources and industry in the other American Republics. The Office of Inter-American Affairs collaborates closely with the Commission.

National Development Commissions have been established to cooperate in the work.

[1] *Ibid.*, IX, p. 308.

[2] Ambassador Winant was appointed as the representative of the United States, according to a press release of the Department of State, December 4, 1943. (*Ibid.*, p. 393.)

[3] *Ibid.*, VIII, p. 70.

[4] *United States Government Manual, Summer 1944*, p. 176.

[5] *Ibid.*, p. 82. See this volume, p. 501.

Inter-American Financial and Economic Advisory Committee [1]

The Committee was established in accordance with a resolution of the Meeting of Ministers of Foreign Affairs of the American Republics, held at Panamá, September to October 1939, that an Inter-American Financial and Economic Advisory Committee be created to consider means of establishing a close cooperation between the American Republics in order that they may protect their economic and financial structure, maintain their fiscal equilibrium, safeguard the stability of their currencies, promote and expand their industries, intensify their agriculture and develop their commerce. The Committee was installed at the Pan American Union on November 15, 1939.

Inter-American Juridical Committee [2]

The Inter-American Juridical Committee came into being as a result of a resolution of the Third Meeting of Ministers of Foreign Affairs of the American Republics held at Rio de Janeiro in January 1942, which stated that "the Inter-American Neutrality Committee at present existing will continue to function in its present form under the name of 'Inter-American Juridical Committee.'" The Committee has as its objects: (a) to study juridical problems created by the war and those which are submitted to it in accordance with the resolutions approved at the Meetings of the Ministers of Foreign Affairs or at the International Conferences of American States; (b) to continue the studies on the subject of contraband of war and on the project of a code relating to the principles and rules of neutrality; (c) to report on possible claims arising from the requisition or use of immobilized merchant vessels or those under the flag of a non-American enemy, or belonging to states whose territories are occupied by a non-American enemy, as well as on possible claims by any American republic against a non-American enemy state for unlawful acts committed to the detriment of such republic, its nationals or their property; (d) to develop and coordinate the work of codifying international law; and (e) to formulate recommendations with regard to the manner of solving the problems mentioned under (a) above. The Committee is made up of seven members, each representing the entire inter-American community rather than any one nation exclusively.

Inter-American Maritime Technical Commission [3]

The Inter-American Maritime Technical Commission was established pursuant to a resolution of the Inter-American Financial and Economic Advisory Committee of November 14, 1941, which recommended the organization of a commission that would be a dependency of the Inter-American Financial and Economic Advisory Committee and would formulate plans for the efficient use of all the merchant vessels of the American Republics available for service between the American Republics and would recommend to the maritime authorities the allocation of such vessels to particular routes or to the carrying of articles of a specific nature.

Intergovernmental Committee on Political Refugees [4]

The Intergovernmental Committee on Political Refugees is the Committee of the whole of the continuing conference of representatives of 32 governments which met in Évian, France, in July 1938 on the initiative of President Roosevelt

---

[1] Department of State, *Bulletin*, VIII, p. 71.
[2] *Ibid.*, p. 72.   [3] *Ibid.*, p. 73.   [4] *Ibid.*

for the purpose of ascertaining what constructive steps the governments might take in common to cope with the urgent problem of the resettlement of political refugees. Radical internal developments in a number of European countries had rendered it necessary that some concerted humanitarian effort be made to consider all possible opportunities for relief through permanent resettlement of as many oppressed individuals as possible. The Committee held its first meeting at Évian, France; in July 1938, and shortly thereafter established permanent headquarters at London under the supervision of a Director.

Joint Brazil-United States Defense Commission [1]

The Commission, composed of military delegates — Army, Navy, and Air — of the two countries, was established in August 1942. Meetings are held in Washington for the purpose of making staff plans for the mutual defense of the Western Hemisphere.

Joint Economic Committees — United States and Canada [2]

Joint Hide Control Office — United States, United Kingdom and Canada

On October 28, 1943 [3] it was announced that a Joint Hide Control Office had been set up, in which the United States and the United Kingdom will have equal representation and in which Canada will participate as its interests dictate. The function of this agency will be to receive offers of hides through the usual channels in the respective countries, to determine upon purchases and allocations of such offers, and to inform the appropriate governmental purchasing agencies in each country of the offers they might accept. The Import Division of the Foreign Economic Administration is the agency designated to purchase foreign hides for the United States.

Joint Mexican-United States Defense Commission [4]

The Governments of Mexico and the United States announced on January 12, 1942 the organization of a mixed defense commission. The United States Section of the Joint Mexican-United States Defense Commission was officially established by Executive Order 9080 of February 27, 1942.

The purposes of the Commission are to study problems relating to the common defense of the United States and Mexico, to consider broad plans for the defense of Mexico and adjacent areas of the United States, and to propose to the respective governments the cooperative measures which, in its opinion, should be adopted.

[1] *United States Government Manual, Summer 1944*, p. 175.

[2] It was announced on March 14, 1944 that the Governments of Canada and the United States have agreed to dissolve the Joint Economic Committees which were established on June 17, 1941 to assist in the collaboration of the two countries in the utilization of their combined resources for the requirements of war. (Department of State, *Bulletin*, IX, p. 264.)

[3] *New York Times*, October 29, 1943.

[4] *United States Government Manual, Summer 1944*, p. 175.

Joint War Production Committee — United States and Canada [1]

The Joint Defense Production Committee was set up on November 5, 1941, by the President of the United States and the Prime Minister of Canada, to coordinate the capacities of the two countries for the production of defense matériel. This action puts into effect a recommendation of the Joint Economic Committees of Canada and the United States. The name "Joint Defense Production Committee" was later changed to Joint War Production Committee.

On December 22 the Joint War Production Committee, United States and Canada, adopted a statement of war production policy for Canada and the United States.[2]

The Joint War Production Committee has in the main functioned through the organization of 10 joint technical subcommittees composed chiefly, on the Canadian side, of Government production executives and, on the United States side, of War Production Board officials and procurement officers from the armed services. These 10 joint technical subcommittees are: Tank-Automotive, Artillery, Artillery Ammunition, Small Arms and Small Arms Ammunition, Chemicals and Explosives, Signal Corps Equipment, Conservation, Aircraft, Naval Shipbuilding, and Merchant Shipbuilding.

Material Coordinating Committee — United States and Canada [3]

Announcement of establishment was made on May 14, 1941 by the Director General of the Office of Production Management (now the War Production Board). The primary purpose of the Committee is to make possible the free exchange of vital information between responsible officials of the two governments relating to their supplies of strategic raw materials required for defense production. The exchange of such information, it was felt, would be of assistance to each government in planning its defense program, especially in relationship to questions concerning war material supplies needed for the production of military items.

The Mediterranean Commission

An announcement that the Commission had been set up was made on September 4, 1943,[4] the day after the signature of the armistice with Italy. It was stated that representatives of the United States, the United Kingdom and the Soviet Union would serve on the Commission which would deal with economic and political questions touching Italy and the entire Mediterranean basin.

Middle East Supply Center [5]

The Middle East Supply Center was first set up in Cairo by the British Government in April 1941 when the shipping problem was acute and it had become impossible for unrestricted imports to be sent to the Middle East, or conversely

[1] *Ibid.*, p. 163.

[2] *Documents, IV, 1941–42*, p. 438; Department of State, *Bulletin*, V, p. 578.

[3] *United States Government Manual, Summer 1944*, p. 164.

[4] *New York Times*, September 10, 1943.

[5] For a general description of Middle East Supply Program, see speech of Frederick Winant, chairman of Middle East Supplies Committee, Washington, at New York City, February 24, 1944. (Department of State, *Bulletin*, X, p. 199.) James M. Landis was appointed to serve as American Director of Economic Operations on September 10, 1943. (*Ibid.*, IX, p. 167.)

for exports to be sent to overseas markets. From 1942 the United States cooperated and the organization now operates under a joint Anglo-American policy. In Cairo this policy is the concern of a small Executive Committee. On questions of policy requiring coordination of other civil or military administrations in the Middle East the Center consults with the Supply and Transportation Committee of the Middle East War Council, which is under the chairmanship of the British Minister Resident in the Middle East. Although the functions of the Middle East Supply Center are purely those of an advisory and coordinating body, for it has no executive powers, it is the sole agency whose recommendations as to supplies for the Middle East countries are accepted by the official bodies responsible in London and Washington, where final decisions as to the allocation of supply requirements are taken by the various Combined Boards and other agencies concerned.

The area within the scope of the Center includes Egypt, the Sudan, Tripolitania, Cyrenaica, Eritrea, Ethiopia, British and French Somaliland, Aden, Palestine, Syria, the Lebanon, Transjordan, Saudi Arabia, the Arab Sheikdoms, Iraq, Iran and Cyprus.

The activities now cover a very wide field of economic problems and the whole position in the Middle East is kept under continuous review by the Intelligence and Statistical Sections of the Center.

Another important undertaking is the destruction of pests, in particular locusts, from which agriculture in the Middle East suffers badly. In the industrial field the Center has made available scientific knowledge in the development of industrial plans and also the services of international technical experts.

On the medical side the center has been responsible for the importation of essential drugs and other medical necessities. In association with the center, a Middle East Medical Advisory Committee has been established in Cairo.

In January 1943, a conference was held in Cairo to discuss agricultural problems and in November 1943 a Middle East Statistical Bureau was established following a conference on statistics.

A conference on agricultural development was convened in Cairo in February 1944 under the auspices of the Center, and in April 1944 financial problems were discussed at a conference called by the British Resident Minister's Supply Council. This conference was attended by experts representing eleven Middle East Governments, together with representatives of the Government of India, the British, American and French treasuries, the Administration of occupied enemy territories, and the Economic and Financial Department of the League of Nations.

Munitions Assignments Board — United States and United Kingdom [1]

Creation of the Munitions Assignments Board was announced by the President of the United States and the Prime Minister of Great Britain on January 26, 1942.

The United States Section of the Board, working in close collaboration with the corresponding London organization, maintains full information of the entire munitions resources of Great Britain and the United States and translates such resources into terms of combat forces of their material reserves. It submits such statements to the Combined Chiefs of Staff, keeping the estimate up to date in the light of war developments and variations in production achievements and prospects, as ascertained through effective liaison with supply authorities. It

[1] *United States Government Manual, Winter 1943–44,* p. 171.

keeps the Combined Chiefs of Staff informed and recommends measures necessary that planned requirements programs may be in line with (*a*) strategic policy, (*b*) changing operations conditions in their effect on war material, and (*c*) the realities of production. Under strategic policies, directives, and priorities as approved in agreement with the corresponding London organization, the United States section is responsible for making assignments of stocks and production of finished war material to the United States and Great Britain, and to others of the United Nations.

Pacific War Council [1]

Formation of the Pacific War Council was announced by the President on March 30, 1942. The Council considers matters of policy relating to the joint war effort. Meetings are held at the White House. A diplomatic representative of each of the following nations attends meetings of the Council: United States, Great Britain, China, Netherlands, Australia, Canada, New Zealand, and the Commonwealth of the Philippines.

Permanent Joint Board on Defense — United States and Canada [2]

The Permanent Joint Board on Defense was set up by the United States and Canada in pursuance of a joint announcement of the President and Prime Minister W. L. Mackenzie King, dated August 17, 1940, at Ogdensburg, N. Y., for the purpose of carrying out studies relating to sea, land, and air problems, including personnel and matériel, and to consider, in the broad sense, the defense of the northern half of the Western Hemisphere.

United Nations Information Board [3]

The United Nations Information Board, membership of which is open to all United Nations, has held regular sessions under this name since November 1942; it grew, however, out of the Inter-Allied Information Committee which was created in September 1940. Representatives of 19 nations now sit on the Board, which controls and finances the United Nations Information Office, a limited international secretariat working for common interests in the field of information. Associated with the Board is a parallel organization in London, England.

The United Nations Information Office provides a clearing house for information on the United Nations, individually and collectively. For this purpose close cooperation has been established both with national information services and with other United Nations organizations. Inquiries regarding individual member nations are referred to the information service of the country concerned, but information about joint activities and matters of joint interest are dealt with by the Office itself. The Office acts as a service agency for representatives of newspapers and periodicals, authors, moving picture and radio organizations, and the public generally. It maintains a reference library dealing with matters which concern the United Nations, including a special section for information on postwar planning.

[1] *Ibid., Summer 1944*, p. 178.
[2] *Ibid.*, p. 165.
[3] *Ibid.*, p. 183.

CHAPTER VI

RELIEF AND REHABILITATION

1. UNITED NATIONS RELIEF AND REHABILITATION ADMINISTRATION

The United Nations Relief and Rehabilitation Administration is an international agency, created on November 9, 1943, through the signing of an Agreement at the White House by the United Nations and other nations associated with them in the war. The Administration was created with a view to giving effect to the determination of the United Nations and the other nations associated with them in the war that, as stated in the preamble of the Agreement, "immediately upon the liberation of any area by the armed forces of the United Nations or as a consequence of retreat of the enemy the population thereof shall receive aid and relief from their sufferings, food, clothing and shelter, aid in the prevention of pestilence and in the recovery of the health of the people, and that preparation and arrangement shall be made for the return of prisoners and exiles to their homes and for assistance in the resumption of urgently needed agricultural and industrial production and the restoration of essential services."

The United Nations Relief and Rehabilitation Administration had its beginnings in September 1941, when the European Governments-in-Exile met with the British Government in London to form an organization known as the Inter-Allied Post-War Requirements Committee (Leith-Ross Committee) for the purpose of surveying the situation of the occupied countries of Europe at the end of the war, and of determining the requirements for reestablishing production and civilian life.[1] Eventually the Soviet Union and the United States were invited to join as observers, but the committee had neither operating powers nor an executive and the Secretariat was a department of the British Government and not international in character.[2]

As the work continued, both the United States and Soviet Governments made suggestions looking toward the establishment of a truly international organization with an international civil service. These suggestions led to discussions in 1942 among the Governments of China, the Soviet Union, the United Kingdom and the United States, which lasted into the summer of 1943. On June 10, 1943, the United States Government, with the consent and agreement of the other three powers, put out for discussion a draft document proposing a United Nations Relief and Rehabilitation Organization.[3]

A thorough discussion within the American Government and among the governments of the forty-four countries which eventually became signatories resulted in a revised draft [4] (September 20, 1943), which was then recirculated among the countries involved and received unanimous agreement.

Analyzing the changes made in the original draft agreement of June 10, we find that the principal change had the effect of reducing the power of the Central Committee so that there would be no question of its functioning as an omnipotent "Big Four" behind the Council. This apparently was the original idea but some of the smaller nations objected for fear that a "big-four" precedent might

[1] *Documents, IV, 1941–42*, p. 262.
[2] Statement by Dean Acheson from *Hearings before House Committee on Foreign Affairs on H. J. Res. 192*, 78th Cong., 1st sess., p. 8.
[3] Department of State, *Bulletin*, VIII, p. 523.
[4] *Ibid.*, IX, p. 211.

be set in the establishment of future organizations of the United Nations. Other changes defined the powers of the Council more in detail and made it clear that financial contributions to the organization should be made by governments only, in accordance with their constitutional procedures. This last change together with the addition of an article (X) providing a means of withdrawal from UNRRA came principally as a result of conferences between a subcommittee of the Senate Committee on Foreign Relations and representatives of the State Department.

More specifically, Article V, section 1 originally read: "Each member government pledges its full support to the Administration, within the limits of its available resources and subject to the requirements of its constitutional procedure, through contributions of funds, materials, equipment, supplies and services, for use in its own, adjacent or other areas in need . . ." The revised text changed the article to read: "In so far as its appropriate constitutional bodies shall authorize, each member government will contribute to the support of the administration. . . . The amount and character of the contributions of each member government under the provision [Article I, paragraph 2 (a)] will be determined from time to time by its appropriate constitutional bodies."

In the formulation and recommendation to member governments of various measures under Article I, 2 (c) the recommendations required approval by vote of the Council, in the revised draft, as well as unanimous vote of the Central Committee. In the admission of new members (Article II) the Council "may, if it desires, authorize the Central Committee to accept new members between sessions of the Council," but the Central Committee cannot act without this authorization. In the exercise of powers of the Council between its sessions by the Central Committee (Article III, 3) the Committee "shall when necessary make policy decisions of an emergency nature" . . . "which shall be promptly communicated to each member government. All such decisions shall be open to reconsideration by the Council at any regular session or at any special session." The revision constituted a limitation of the powers of the Central Committee. It was also specified that the Director General would preside but without a vote. For the appointment of members to the various committees (Article III, 4, 5, 6), the Council was designated in the revised draft, the powers of the Central Committee being limited to emergency appointments between sessions of the Council, such appointments to continue until the next session of the Council. Other changes provided that the Council should vote by a simple (rather than two-thirds) majority (Article II, 1); that the Council should be convened within thirty days after request therefor by one-third of the members instead of by a majority (Article II, 2); and that if a report on the progress of UNRRA's activities should affect the interests of a member government in such a way as to render it questionable whether it should be published, such government should have an opportunity of expressing its views on the question of publication (Article IV, 5). Also, Article VIII, originally providing that the provisions of the Agreement could be amended by a unanimous vote of the Central Committee and a two-thirds vote of the Council, was entirely changed to omit the rule of unanimity and to include three alternative methods of amendment: new obligations require two-thirds vote of Council and shall take effect for each member government on acceptance by it; modifications of Articles III or IV require two-thirds vote of Council, including all members of Central Committee; other amendments shall take effect by two-thirds vote of the Council. Article X, providing a means of withdrawal, was a completely new addition.

At a ceremony in the White House on November 9, 1943, representatives of the forty-four United and Associated Nations signed the agreement. On November 10 the UNRRA Council, provided for in the Agreement, met at Atlantic City, New Jersey, and continued in session until December 1, 1943.[1]

[1] *First Session of the Council of the United Nations Relief and Rehabilitation Administration. Selected Documents. Atlantic City, N. J., November 10–December 1, 1943* (Department of State Publication 2040. Conference Series 53).

The Administration is composed of (1) a Council, consisting of one member from each nation signatory to the Agreement; (2) a Central Committee consisting of the members for China, the Union of Soviet Socialist Republics, the United Kingdom, and the United States; (3) a Committee of the Council for Europe; (4) a Committee of the Council for the Far East; (5) a Committee on Supplies; (6) a Committee on Financial Control; (7) standing technical Committees on Agriculture, Displaced Persons, Health, Industrial Rehabilitation and Welfare; (8) and an administrative staff under a Director General, who is the executive officer of the Administration. Herbert H. Lehman, Director of the Office of Foreign Relief and Rehabilitation Operations in the government of the United States, was unanimously elected Director General of UNRRA by the Council on November 11.

Under the chairmanship of Assistant Secretary of State Acheson, member of the Council for the United States, the Council proceeded to provide for the organization of the administration and to lay down the broad policies to guide its activities. Not only did the Council consider the scope of activities to be undertaken by the Administration, but also the procedures for obtaining supplies and distributing the financial burden as equitably as possible, the methods for assuring equitable distribution of supplies, and other questions relating more particularly to the administration of relief and rehabilitation measures in the field and to relations with other governments and organizations. Finally, rules were laid down "to govern the conduct of the Administration itself, so as to secure effective representation of the interested nations in the formulation of the policies of the Administration and to facilitate the operations of the Director General in carrying out these policies.

The operating funds of the organization are contributed by the member nations which have not been invaded. The Council has recommended as a basis for the contribution of such nations one percent of their national income for the year ending June 30, 1943. Administrative expenses, on the other hand, are shared by all member governments.

The Administration seeks to insure to the peoples in areas liberated from the enemy the provision of the following:

Relief supplies of essential consumer goods to meet immediate needs, such as food, fuel, clothing, shelter, and medical supplies.

Relief services such as health and welfare; assistance in caring for, and maintaining records of, persons found in any areas under the control of any of the United Nations who by reason of war have been displaced from their homes, and in agreement with the appropriate governments, military authorities, or other agencies, in securing their repatriation or return; and such technical services as may be necessary for these purposes.

Rehabilitation supplies and services — materials (such as seeds, fertilizers, raw materials, fishing equipment, machinery, and spare parts) needed to enable a recipient country to produce and transport relief supplies for its own and other liberated areas, and such technical services as may be necessary for these purposes.

Rehabilitation of public utilities and services so far as they can be repaired or restored to meet immediate needs, such as light, water, sanitation, power, transport, temporary shortage, communications, and assistance in procuring material equipment for the rehabilitation of educational institutions.

Shortly after the ceremony at the White House on November 9, Representative Bloom, chairman of the House Committee on Foreign Affairs, introduced into the House of Representatives on November 15 a joint resolution (H. J. Res. 192) "to enable the United States to participate in the work of the United Nations relief and rehabilitation organization." For legislative history of the resolution, see p. 37. The bill was signed by President Roosevelt on March 28, 1944.

(1) *Agreement for United Nations Relief and Rehabilitation Adminis-*
tration, Signed at Washington, November 9, 1943 [1]

For text of the address of President Roosevelt on the occasion of the signature
of the Agreement, see Department of State, *Bulletin,* IX, p. 317.

The Governments or Authorities whose duly authorized representatives have subscribed hereto,

Being United Nations or being associated with the United Nations
in this war,

Being determined that immediately upon the liberation of any area
by the armed forces of the United Nations or as a consequence of retreat
of the enemy the population thereof shall receive aid and relief from their
sufferings, food, clothing and shelter, aid in the prevention of pestilence
and in the recovery of the health of the people, and that preparation and
arrangements shall be made for the return of prisoners and exiles to their
homes and for assistance in the resumption of urgently needed agricultural and industrial production and the restoration of essential services,

Have agreed as follows:

ARTICLE I. There is hereby established the United Nations Relief and
Rehabilitation Administration.

1. The Administration shall have power to acquire, hold and convey
property, to enter into contracts and undertake obligations, to designate
or create agencies and to review the activities of agencies so created, to
manage undertakings and in general to perform any legal act appropriate
to its objects and purposes.

2. Subject to the provisions of Article VII, the purposes and functions
of the Administration shall be as follows:

(*a*) To plan, coordinate, administer or arrange for the administration
of measures for the relief of victims of war in any area under the control
of any of the United Nations through the provision of food, fuel, clothing,
shelter and other basic necessities, medical and other essential services;
and to facilitate in such areas, so far as necessary to the adequate provision of relief, the production and transportation of these articles and
the furnishing of these services. The form of activities of the Administration within the territory of a member government wherein that government exercises administrative authority and the responsibility to be
assumed by the member government for carrying out measures planned
by the Administration therein shall be determined after consultation
with and with the consent of the member government.

(*b*) To formulate and recommend measures for individual or joint
action by any or all of the member governments for the coordination of
purchasing, the use of ships and other procurement activities in the
period following the cessation of hostilities, with a view to integrating

[1] *Executive Agreement Series* 352; Department of State Publication 2075.

the plans and activities of the Administration with the total movement of supplies, and for the purpose of achieving an equitable distribution of available supplies. The Administration may administer such coordination measures as may be authorized by the member governments concerned.

(c) To study, formulate and recommend for individual or joint action by any or all of the member governments measures with respect to such related matters, arising out of its experience in planning and performing the work of relief and rehabilitation, as may be proposed by any of the member governments. Such proposals shall be studied and recommendations formulated if the proposals are supported by a vote of the Council, and the recommendations shall be referred to any or all of the member governments for individual or joint action if approved by unanimous vote of the Central Committee and by vote of the Council.

ARTICLE II. *Membership.* The members of the United Nations Relief and Rehabilitation Administration shall be the governments or authorities signatory hereto and such other governments or authorities as may upon application for membership be admitted thereto by action of the Council. The Council may, if it desires, authorize the Central Committee to accept new members between sessions of the Council.

Wherever the term "member government" is used in this Agreement it shall be construed to mean a member of the Administration whether a government or an authority.

ARTICLE III. *The Council.* 1. Each member government shall name one representative, and such alternates as may be necessary, upon the Council of the United Nations Relief and Rehabilitation Administration, which shall be the policy-making body of the Administration. The Council shall, for each of its sessions, select one of its members to preside at the session. The Council shall determine its own rules of procedure. Unless otherwise provided by the Agreement or by action of the Council, the Council shall vote by simple majority.

2. The Council shall be convened in regular session not less than twice a year by the Central Committee. It may be convened in special session whenever the Central Committee shall deem necessary, and shall be convened within thirty days after request therefor by one-third of the members of the Council.

3. The Central Committee of the Council shall consist of the representatives of China, the Union of Soviet Socialist Republics, the United Kingdom and the United States of America, with the Director General presiding, without vote. Between sessions of the Council it shall when necessary make policy decisions of an emergency nature. All such decisions shall be recorded in the minutes of the Central Committee which shall be communicated promptly to each member government. Such decisions shall be open to reconsideration by the Council at any

regular session or at any special session called in accordance with Article III, paragraph 2. The Central Committee shall invite the participation of the representative of any member government at those of its meetings at which action of special interest to such government is discussed. It shall invite the participation of the representative serving as Chairman of the Committee on Supplies of the Council at those of its meetings at which policies affecting the provision of supplies are discussed.

4. The Committee on Supplies of the Council shall consist of the members of the Council, or their alternates, representing those member governments likely to be principal suppliers of materials for relief and rehabilitation. The members shall be appointed by the Council, and the Council may authorize the Central Committee to make emergency appointments between sessions of the Council, such appointments to continue until the next session of the Council. The Committee on Supplies shall consider, formulate and recommend to the Council and the Central Committee policies designed to assure the provision of required supplies. The Central Committee shall from time to time meet with the Committee on Supplies to review policy matters affecting supplies.

5. The Committee of the Council for Europe shall consist of all the members of the Council, or their alternates, representing member governments of territories within the European area and such other members of the Council representing other governments directly concerned with the problems of relief and rehabilitation in the European area as shall be appointed by the Council; the Council may authorize the Central Committee to make these appointments in cases of emergency between sessions of the Council, such appointments to continue until the next session of the Council. The Committee of the Council for the Far East shall consist of all the members of the Council, or their alternates, representing member governments of territories within the Far Eastern area and such other members of the Council representing other governments directly concerned with the problems of relief and rehabilitation in the Far Eastern area as shall be appointed by the Council; the Council may authorize the Central Committee to make these appointments in cases of emergency between sessions of the Council, such appointments to continue until the next session of the Council. The regional committees shall normally meet within their respective areas. They shall consider and recommend to the Council and the Central Committee policies with respect to relief and rehabilitation within their respective areas. The Committee of the Council for Europe shall replace the Inter-Allied Committee on European post-war relief established in London on September 24, 1941 and the records of the latter shall be made available to the Committee for Europe.

6. The Council shall establish such other standing regional committees as it shall consider desirable, the functions of such committees and the

method of appointing their members being identical to that provided in Article III, paragraph 5 with respect to the Committees of the Council for Europe and for the Far East. The Council shall also establish such other standing committees as it considers desirable to advise it, and, in intervals between sessions of the Council, to advise the Central Committee. For such standing technical committees as may be established, in respect of particular problems such as nutrition, health, agriculture, transport, repatriation, and finance, the members may be members of the Council or alternates nominated by them because of special competence in their respective fields of work. The members shall be appointed by the Council, and the Council may authorize the Central Committee to make emergency appointments between sessions of the Council, such appointments to continue until the next session of the Council. Should a regional committee so desire, subcommittees of the standing technical committees shall be established by the technical committees in consultation with the regional committees, to advise the regional committees.

7. The travel and other expenses of members of the Council and of members of its committees shall be borne by the governments which they represent.

8. All reports and recommendations of committees of the Council shall be transmitted to the Director General for distribution to the Council and the Central Committee by the secretariat of the Council established under the provisions of Article IV, paragraph 4.

ARTICLE IV. *The Director General.* 1. The executive authority of the United Nations Relief and Rehabilitation Administration shall be in the Director General, who shall be appointed by the Council on the nomination by unanimous vote of the Central Committee. The Director General may be removed by the Council on recommendation by unanimous vote of the Central Committee.

2. The Director General shall have full power and authority for carrying out relief operations contemplated by Article I, paragraph 2 (*a*), within the limits of available resources and the broad policies determined by the Council or its Central Committee. Immediately upon taking office he shall in conjunction with the military and other appropriate authorities of the United Nations prepare plans for the emergency relief of the civilian population in any area occupied by the armed forces of any of the United Nations, arrange for the procurement and assembly of the necessary supplies and create or select the emergency organization required for this purpose. In arranging for the procurement, transportation, and distribution of supplies and services, he and his representatives shall consult and collaborate with the appropriate authorities of the United Nations and shall, wherever practicable, use the facilities made available by such authorities. Foreign voluntary relief agencies may not engage in activity in any area receiving relief from the Administration

without the consent and unless subject to the regulation of the Director General. The powers and duties of the Director General are subject to the limitations of Article VII.

3. The Director General shall also be responsible for the organization and direction of the functions contemplated by Article I, paragraphs 2 (b) and 2 (c).

4. The Director General shall appoint such Deputy Directors General, officers, expert personnel, and staff at his headquarters and elsewhere, including field missions, as he shall find necessary, and he may delegate to them such of his powers as he may deem appropriate. The Director General, or upon his authorization the Deputy Directors General, shall supply such secretariat and other staff and facilities as shall be required by the Council and its committees, including the regional committees and subcommittees. Such Deputy Directors General as shall be assigned special functions within a region shall attend meetings of the regional standing committee whenever possible and shall keep it advised on the progress of the relief and rehabilitation program within the region.

5. The Director General shall make periodic reports to the Central Committee and to the Council covering the progress of the Administration's activities. The reports shall be made public except for such portions as the Central Committee may consider it necessary, in the interest of the United Nations, to keep confidential; if a report affects the interests of a member government in such a way as to render it questionable whether it should be published, such government shall have an opportunity of expressing its views on the question of publication. The Director General shall also arrange to have prepared periodic reports covering the activities of the Administration within each region and he shall transmit such reports with his comments thereon to the Council, the Central Committee and the respective regional committees.

ARTICLE V. *Supplies and Resources.* 1. In so far as its appropriate constitutional bodies shall authorize, each member government will contribute to the support of the Administration in order to accomplish the purposes of Article I, paragraph 2 (a). The amount and character of the contributions of each member government under this provision will be determined from time to time by its appropriate constitutional bodies. All such contributions received by the Administration shall be accounted for.

2. The supplies and resources made available by the member governments shall be kept in review in relation to prospective requirements by the Director General, who shall initiate action with the member governments with a view to assuring such additional supplies and resources as may be required.

3. All purchases by any of the member governments, to be made outside their own territories during the war for relief or rehabilitation pur-

poses, shall be made only after consultation with the Director General, and shall, so far as practicable, be carried out through the appropriate United Nations agency.

ARTICLE VI. *Administrative Expenses.* The Director General shall submit to the Council an annual budget, and from time to time such supplementary budgets as may be required, covering the necessary administrative expenses of the Administration. Upon approval of a budget by the Council the total amount approved shall be allocated to the member governments in proportions to be determined by the Council. Each member government undertakes, subject to the requirements of its constitutional procedure, to contribute to the Administration promptly its share of the administrative expenses so determined.

ARTICLE VII. Notwithstanding any other provision herein contained, while hostilities or other military necessities exist in any area, the Administration and its Director General shall not undertake activities therein without the consent of the military command of that area, and unless subject to such control as the command may find necessary. The determination that such hostilities or military necessities exist in any area shall be made by its military commander.

ARTICLE VIII. *Amendment.* The provisions of this Agreement may be amended as follows:

a. Amendments involving new obligations for member governments shall require the approval of the Council by a two-thirds vote and shall take effect for each member government on acceptance by it;

b. Amendments involving modification of Article III or Article IV shall take effect on adoption by the Council by a two-thirds vote, including the votes of all the members of the Central Committee;

c. Other amendments shall take effect on adoption by the Council by a two-thirds vote.

ARTICLE IX. *Entry into Force.* This Agreement shall enter into force with respect to each signatory on the date when the Agreement is signed by that signatory, unless otherwise specified by such signatory.

ARTICLE X. *Withdrawal.* Any member government may give notice of withdrawal from the Administration at any time after the expiration of six months from the entry into force of the Agreement for that government. Such notice shall take effect twelve months after the date of its communication to the Director General subject to the member government having met by that time all financial, supply or other material obligations accepted or undertaken by it.

IN WITNESS WHEREOF, this Agreement is signed by the following representatives, duly authorized for that purpose by their respective Governments or Authorities.

DONE in Washington this ninth day of November, one thousand nine hundred forty-three, in the English language, the original to be deposited in the archives of the Department of State of the United States of America, and certified copies thereof to be furnished by the Government of the United States of America to each of the Governments and Authorities on whose behalf this Agreement is signed.

[Here follow signatures.]

The Agreement was signed by: The Commonwealth of Australia, Belgium, Bolivia, the United States of Brazil, Canada, Chile, China, Colombia, Costa Rica, Cuba, Czechoslovakia, the Dominican Republic, Ecuador, Egypt, El Salvador, Ethiopia, the French Committee of National Liberation, Greece, Guatemala, Haiti, Honduras, Iceland, India, Iran, Iraq, Liberia, Luxemburg, the United Mexican States, the Netherlands, New Zealand, Nicaragua, Norway, Panama, Paraguay, Peru, the Philippine Commonwealth, Poland, the Union of South Africa, the Union of Soviet Socialist Republics, the United Kingdom of Great Britain and Northern Ireland, the United States of America, Uruguay, Venezuela, Yugoslavia.

It is provided in Article IX of the Agreement that it shall enter into force with respect to each signatory on the date when signed by that signatory, unless otherwise specified by such signatory. The Agreement was signed on behalf of 14 Governments (Chile, Colombia, Cuba, Ecuador, Ethiopia, Guatemala, India, Iran, Iraq, Mexico, Nicaragua, Peru, Uruguay, and Venezuela) with a reservation or statement to the effect, in each case, that the Agreement was signed subject to ratification or legislative approval.[1]

(2) Resolutions on Policy of the First Session of the Council, Held at Atlantic City, New Jersey, November 10–December 1, 1943 [2]

PART I. GENERAL POLICIES

No. 1 — Scope of the Activities of the Administration

RESOLVED

That the following shall be the broad policies of the Administration with respect to the scope of its activities:

I. Areas in Which the Administration Will Operate

The exact geographical areas in which the Administration will operate and the kind of operations it will undertake in each case must be determined by the Director General (in the light of policies laid down from time to time by the Council) only after consultation with, and with the consent of, the government or authority (military or civil) which exercises administrative authority in the area. The Administration's activities in

---

[1] Department of State, *Bulletin*, IX, p. 336.

[2] *First Session of the Council of the United Nations Relief and Rehabilitation Administration. Selected Documents, Atlantic City, New Jersey, November 10–December 1, 1943.* Washington, Govt. Printing Office, 1944 (Department of State Publication 2040, Conference Series 55), p. 27–68.

seeking to achieve the objectives referred to in the preamble of the Agreement setting it up will be governed as follows:

1. In the case of a liberated area in which a government or recognized national authority does not yet exercise administrative authority, the Administration will operate from such a time and for such purposes as may be agreed upon between the military command and the Administration, and subject to such control as the military command may find necessary. The Administration shall, so far as circumstances permit, seek the advice of the government or recognized national authority concerned.

2. In the case of a liberated area in which a government or recognized national authority exercises administrative authority, the Administration will operate only after consultation with, and with the consent of, the government or recognized national authority concerned regarding the form of activities to be undertaken by the Administration within the whole or part of such area.

3. If it appears necessary for the Administration to operate in an enemy or ex-enemy area in carrying out the purposes of the Agreement, it will do so only from such a time and for such purposes as may be agreed upon between the military command, the established control authority or duly recognized administration of the area on the one hand and the Administration on the other, and subject to such control as the military command or the established control authority may find necessary; provided that the Council approve the scale and nature of the operations it is proposed to undertake and the standard of provision, and that all expenses connected with such possible operations in an enemy or ex-enemy area should be carried by the enemy or ex-enemy country concerned. The Director General will consult with the military command or established control authorities having control of enemy or ex-enemy areas with a view to securing information as to any surpluses of supplies from time to time available in such enemy or ex-enemy areas from which relief and rehabilitation import requirements of liberated areas might be met.

Nothing in the above should be taken as preventing the Administration from carrying on activities in other areas in order to perform the tasks laid upon it in the Agreement, provided that the government or authority (military or civil) exercising administrative authority in the area concerned agrees.

II. The Range of Services Which the Administration Will Provide

The supplies and services of which the Administration will seek to insure the provision fall under four heads:

1. *Relief supplies:* essential consumer goods to meet immediate needs, such as food, fuel, clothing, shelter, medical supplies.

2. *Relief services:* such as health and welfare; assistance in caring for, and maintaining records of, persons found in any areas under the control of any of the United Nations who by reason of war have been displaced from their homes and, in agreement with the appropriate governments, military authorities or other agencies, in securing their repatriation or return; and such technical services as may be necessary for these purposes.

3. *Rehabilitation supplies and services:* materials (such as seeds, fertilizers, raw materials, fishing equipment, machinery and spare parts) needed to enable a recipient country to produce and transport relief supplies for its own and other liberated areas, and such technical services as may be necessary for these purposes.

4. *Rehabilitation of public utilities and services:* so far as they can be repaired or restored to meet immediate needs: such as light, water, sanitation, power, transport, temporary storage, communications, and assistance in procuring material equipment for the rehabilitation of educational institutions.

III. Relation of the Administration With Existing Intergovernmental Authorities and Agencies Established to Deal With Supplies, Shipping, and Related Questions

1. The activities of the Administration in bringing assistance to the victims of war will be so conducted that they do not impede the effective prosecution of the war. The prosecution of the war demands that scarce supplies and shipping tonnage shall be carefully controlled and allocated in order to assure not only that the supplies and shipping requirements of the armed forces are fully met, but also that a fair distribution of supplies is made between the civil populations of the various areas having due regard to their actual or potential contribution to the war effort. It will therefore be essential, both for the conduct of the war and in order to promote a fair distribution of supplies between the inhabitants of areas with which the Administration is concerned and those of other areas, that demands upon supplies and shipping presented by the Administration should be coordinated with other demands through the use of the existing intergovernmental agencies concerned with the allocation of supplies and shipping.

2. It will be an essential part of the functions of the Administration to secure a fair distribution of goods which are in short supply and of shipping services to and among the various areas liberated or to be liberated. For this purpose the Administration must have full knowledge of all the relief and rehabilitation import requirements of such areas, whatever arrangements may be contemplated for procurement or finance. Therefore, member governments shall keep the Administration

fully informed of their requirements and programs of intended purchases. The Director General may present to the intergovernmental allocating agencies such recommendations or objections as he may deem necessary to obtain a fair distribution to and among both liberated and to be liberated areas. The Director General will present before the intergovernmental allocating agencies the over-all requirements for relief and rehabilitation of all areas liberated and to be liberated in order to permit a global consideration of these needs with all other needs. He may also present the particular requirements of any country for which the assistance of the Administration has been requested. It is anticipated that the Director General and, where necessary, the Chairman of the Committee on Supplies, will be fully consulted by the intergovernmental allocating agencies when any matter touching the interests of the Administration is under discussion.

3. In order that the supplies allocated by the appropriate intergovernmental agency against requirements presented and supported by the Administration may be procured expeditiously and without duplication of effort, the Director General, after consultation, where necessary, with the appropriate intergovernmental agency, will make use wherever possible of the established national agencies concerned with the procurement, handling, storage, and transport of supplies. The member governments to which such national agencies are responsible would agree on their part to put the services of such agencies at the disposal of the Administration. Such additional responsibilities would form part of those already undertaken in prosecuting the war effort of the United Nations.

IV. Relationship of the Administration With the Military Command

1. Before an area is liberated, the Administration will, when requested by the military authorities,

> (a) consult with them in the planning of supplies for the relief and rehabilitation of the area during the period of military control;
>
> (b) arrange for the advance procurement of such supplies as may be agreed on to supplement supplies to be provided by the military authorities.

2. During the period when a liberated area is under military control, the Administration, so far as the Director General deems practicable, will, when requested by the military authorities,

> (a) arrange for the procurement of supplies to supplement supplies being provided by the military authorities;
>
> (b) furnish expert personnel and services, and advise on the conservation and utilization for relief purposes of stocks and productive resources;

(c) assist in the carrying out of policies with regard to the re-
     patriation or return of displaced persons as formulated in
     paragraph II, 2, above;

(d) undertake other relief and rehabilitation activities;

(e) assume responsibility in whole or in part for such activities.

In undertaking any of these functions the Administration shall, so far
as circumstances permit, seek the advice of the government or recognized
national authority concerned.

3. It is recommended to the member governments that the Administration be kept informed so far as is practicable of the operations of the
civil affairs branches of the military command and control authorities,
in order that the Director General may make the necessary preparations
for the provision of staff and facilities so that a smooth transition from
the period of military control may be insured and the flow of supplies
maintained.

4. It is recommended to member governments that the transition in
each area from military to civilian relief and rehabilitation operations
be consummated at the earliest date that military considerations permit.

No. 2 — Non-discrimination

RESOLVED

1. That, in any area where relief and rehabilitation operations are
being conducted through the employment, in whole or in part, of the
Administration's resources, relief and rehabilitation in all its aspects shall
be distributed or dispensed fairly on the basis of the relative needs of the
population in the area, and without discrimination because of race, creed,
or political belief.

2. That, in determining the relative needs of the population, there
may be taken into account the diverse needs caused by discriminatory
treatment by the enemy during its occupation of the area.

No. 3 — Assistance From Member Governments

RESOLVED

That the Council recommends that member governments take such
steps as may be necessary and feasible to facilitate any operations of the
Administration within areas under their control, assisting the Administration in obtaining such services, facilities, and personnel as may be
required to carry on such operations, and arranging to the extent possible that the Administration's expenditures for services, facilities, supplies, equipment, and personnel be minimized so that its resources may
be devoted directly to relief and rehabilitation.

No. 4 — Administration Publicity

RESOLVED

That the Council recommends that member governments, consistently with such measures as they consider necessary to regulate the dissemination of information while hostilities or other military necessities exist, afford the Administration opportunity to make public information with regard to its operations, and that they permit the use of special labels or other designations on supplies and equipment belonging to or furnished by the Administration.

No. 5 — Relations of the Administration With Intergovernmental Agencies Other Than Those Established to Deal With Supplies, Shipping, and Related Questions

RESOLVED

1. That the Council reaffirms the principle of cooperation between the Administration and other intergovernmental agencies as set forth in the report of the Temporary Committee on Admission of Observers adopted by the Council on November 12, 1943.

2. That the Council invite representatives of the League of Nations Technical Organizations, the International Labor Organization, the Intergovernmental Committee on Refugees, and the United Nations Interim Commission on Food and Agriculture (or representatives from the Permanent Organization for Food and Agriculture now represented by the Interim Commission), to attend as observers and to participate in the meetings of the Council, its committees, and subcommittees, and in the meetings of regional committees and technical standing committees, in accordance with appropriate provisions in the Permanent Rules of Procedure.

3. That the Director General avail himself of the organizations mentioned in paragraph 2 above as the nature of the work and other circumstances make appropriate.

4. That the Director General, in pursuance of the principle set forth in paragraph 1 above, cooperate to such a degree and to such extent as he may deem desirable in the interests of the Administration with all other intergovernmental agencies whose operations and specialized services may be of value to the Administration, including the sending of his representatives as observers to the meetings of other intergovernmental agencies, as well as those mentioned in paragraph 2 above.

No. 6 — Collaboration With Regard to Economic Measures

RESOLVED

That the Council recommends that member governments consult with the Director General with a view to avoiding, so far as possible, the subjection of the funds, supplies, equipment, and services of the Administration to economic measures which might diminish the effectiveness of such activities or impose financial burdens on the Administration.

PART II. RELIEF AND REHABILITATION POLICIES

No. 7 — Relief Distribution Policies

RESOLVED

That the Council approves the following statement as a guide to activities with respect to relief and rehabilitation distribution:

1. That at no time shall relief and rehabilitation supplies be used as a political weapon, and no discrimination shall be made in the distribution of relief supplies because of race, creed, or political belief.

2. That in general the responsibility for the distribution, within an area, of relief and rehabilitation supplies should be borne by the government or recognized national authority which exercises administrative authority in the area.

3. That distribution should be so conducted that all classes of the population, irrespective of their purchasing power, shall receive their equitable shares of essential commodities. When supplies are sold to consumers, prices should be set at such levels as to facilitate the flow of supplies into the proper hands, and to avoid maladjustments in the price structure of the areas.

4. That distribution of relief and rehabilitation supplies should take place under effective rationing and price controls. The suppression of black markets should not be left to general pronouncements and decrees, but should be the subject of active measures of enforcement applied vigorously and unremittingly.

5. That the government or recognized national authority which exercises administrative authority in the area should take appropriate measures to insure that so far as the distribution within a liberated territory of relief and rehabilitation goods is done through private trade, the remuneration earned by private traders for their services is no more than is fair and reasonable.

6. That use should be made to the maximum practicable extent of normal agencies of distribution (governmental, commercial, cooperative), to the particular ends of combating inflation and restoring normal economic activity. This principle, however, cannot be pursued at the expense of measures found necessary under emergency conditions to insure an adequate control of the distribution of supplies and their direction to the appropriate consumers.

7. That if the Administration is called on by the military authority to furnish distribution services through its own organization and per-

sonnel in a liberated territory in which a government or recognized national authority does not yet exercise administrative authority, the Administration should, subject to the general provisions governing the relation of the Administration to the military authority and the government or recognized national authority concerned, make the fullest possible use of local authorities and of local organizations.

8. That the Administration be prepared to render direct assistance in distribution whenever, because of unusual circumstances, the government or recognized national authority concerned requests such aid within its territory. Wherever as a consequence of such request, the Administration is directly concerned with internal distribution, it should follow, in cooperation with the national or local authorities, the same general principles as those recommended above.

9. That the Director General should be kept fully informed concerning the distribution of relief and rehabilitation supplies within any recipient areas, and under all circumstances there should be the fullest working cooperation between the governments or recognized national authorities concerned and the Administration for this purpose.

No. 8 — Health and Medical Care

RESOLVED

1. That the Council urge its members, when nominating alternates for membership of [1] the standing technical Committee on Health, to designate as such alternates accredited and technically competent representatives of their respective national health services.

2. That the Council recommends that governments and recognized national authorities cooperate fully with the Administration in establishing at the earliest possible date regional and other emergency agreements and arrangements for the notification within the limits of military security, of diseases likely to become epidemic, uniformity in quarantine regulations, and for other measures of prevention.

3. That the Council recommends that governments and recognized national authorities, whenever so requested by the Administration, offer all facilities in making available to the Administration suitable personnel for its health organization, including the temporary loan of technical experts and the services of scientific institutions.

4. That the Council recommends the closest collaboration at the earliest possible time between the Administration and the Allied Military Authorities, particularly in relation to the notification of infectious diseases, within the limits of military security, and to the orderly transfer to the Administration of the epidemic control and other public-health measures put into operation by the military authorities.

[1] So in original.

5. That the Council recommends that governments and recognized national authorities whenever so requested by the Administration, facilitate in every way possible the assignment of their nationals from the occupied countries for technical training especially in the newer aspects of medical and sanitary sciences in the countries where such training is available; under the condition that the request be filed by the government concerned.

No. 9 — Welfare Services and Voluntary Relief Agencies

RESOLVED

1. That welfare services administered by or in cooperation with the Administration shall be provided without discrimination because of race, creed, or political belief.

2. That it shall be the policy of the Administration to enlist the cooperation and seek the participation of appropriate foreign voluntary relief agencies, to the extent that they can be effectively utilized in relief activities for which they have special competence and resources, subject to the consent and regulation of the Director General in accordance with Article IV, paragraph 2, of the Agreement.

3. That the extent to which foreign voluntary relief agencies should be used for assistance in the relief and rehabilitation of distressed people in any country should be a matter to be determined by the Director General in consultation with the government or recognized national authority concerned.

4. That within the framework of its total program and with the closest collaboration between the health, welfare, and other appropriate organization units, the Administration should make specific provision for welfare services for victims of war — in particular for children, expectant and nursing mothers, the aged, and the disabled.

5. That, in general, welfare services should be administered, so far as possible, by the government or recognized national authority concerned and the Administration should make its resources available to the appropriate agency in accordance with plans agreed upon between the Administration and the national agency.

Continuous cooperation should be maintained and information exchanged between the government or recognized national authority concerned and the Administration.

6. That the Administration should be prepared to administer welfare services directly, either in part or in whole, when called upon by a government or recognized national authority, which for any reason is unable itself to administer these services.

7. That because of already prolonged suffering due to war and because of critical needs, the Administration should arrange to provide, as

promptly as possible, the necessary welfare services, to be available when countries are liberated or occupied by the United Nations.

8. That welfare services should be designed to help people to help themselves. Wherever possible constructive work opportunities and measures for self-help should be provided to permit those receiving relief to produce at least some of their own basic requirements.

9. That because of the magnitude and complexity of the welfare problems confronting the Administration, and the necessity for effective technical guidance, there should be established a standing technical Committee on Welfare.

No. 10 — Policies With Respect to Displaced Persons

RESOLVED

1. That the Council recommends that member governments and the Director General exchange information on all phases of the problem, including such matters as the numbers and places of temporary residence of their nationals in other countries, and of the presence of the nationals of other countries, or stateless persons, within their territories.

2. That the Council recommends that member governments consult with and give full aid to the Director General in order that he may, in concert with them, plan, coordinate, administer or arrange for the administration of orderly and effective measures for the return to their homes of prisoners, exiles, and other displaced persons.

3. That the Council recommends that member governments consult with the Director General for the purpose of carrying out measures with respect to the repatriation or return of displaced persons; and that the classes of persons to be repatriated be those referred to in paragraphs 5 and 6 of the report of Subcommittee 4 of Committee IV.

4. That the question of the assistance to be given by the Administration in the return to their homes of displaced persons of enemy or ex-enemy nationality who have been intruded into homes from which nationals of the United Nations have been expelled should be considered as a separate issue to be dealt with in accordance with the provisions of paragraphs 11 and 12 of the report of Subcommittee 4 of Committee IV.

5. That steps be taken to insure the closest cooperation with the Committee on Health, as well as with the national health authorities of the various countries concerned, with a view to preventing and controlling any epidemics which may be expected to arise in connection with repatriation of large groups of displaced persons.

6. That the Director General take steps to insure the closest cooperation with such agencies as the International Red Cross and the Intergovernmental Committee on Refugees and any other appropriate bodies of suitable standing whose assistance may be of value, with a view to

invoking their collaboration in the work of the repatriation of displaced persons.

7. That the Director General should establish the earliest possible contact with the military authorities of the United Nations with a view to concerting plans for dealing in a uniform and closely coordinated manner with any large groups of displaced persons which may be found in any liberated or occupied territory on the entry of the forces of the United Nations into that territory.

No. 11 — Policies With Respect to Agricultural Rehabilitation and Other Means of Increasing Food Essential to Relief

RESOLVED

That the Council approves the following statement as a guide to activities with respect to agricultural rehabilitation and other methods of increasing food essential to relief:

1. That for the first crop year after liberation in any area the Administration, through its agricultural rehabilitation and food production program, should give priority to the production of food for direct human consumption. For that year the war production pattern in liberated areas should generally be continued with emphasis upon maximum output both from the soil and from fisheries. In certain areas, however, modification in this policy may be undertaken where a continuance of the war production pattern results in a disproportionate sacrifice in productivity, provided essential foods are otherwise available.

2. That it shall be the responsibility of the Administration to assist governments and recognized national authorities in the liberated areas immediately to take the necessary steps in providing the supplies and services needed to enable farmers to sow and harvest essential crops during the first crop year, to maintain their dairy herds, and to rehabilitate their farms for immediate food production. It shall also be the responsibility of the Administration to assist in restoring necessary processing facilities; in providing for the early expansion of fisheries and of the whaling industry; in reinstating the agricultural labor needed to carry out the production program; and, to the extent that they can contribute to the solution of relief problems, in reestablishing experimental stations and essential agricultural institutions, organizations, and services, in making the necessary technical surveys to determine agricultural requirements and to lay the basis for production programs.

3. That it shall be the policy of the Administration to integrate to the fullest possible extent its short-run agricultural rehabilitation and food production efforts with the longer-run reconstruction objectives of the United Nations Organization for Food and Agriculture, and to shape its policies so as not to hamper the achievement of those objectives, which

call for the progressive realization in all countries of diets adequate both in quantity and quality.

4. That since priorities between various agricultural items will vary from area to area, such priorities shall be determined by the government or recognized national authority concerned in conjunction with the Director General in accordance with the general policy outlined above. In determining such priority for agriculture and fishing requirements the test should be applied whether the supply of these requirements will bring early and large returns in the form of crops and fish for direct human consumption.

5. The Administration should be prepared when requested by a government or recognized national authority to assist them in making technical field surveys in establishing priority on the need for supplies in making available information concerning production surpluses in nearby areas, and in providing such other technical assistance as is required.

No. 12 — Policies With Respect to the Rehabilitation of Such Industries, Transport, and Other Services as Are Essential to Relief

WHEREAS

The preamble of the Agreement states that preparations and arrangements shall be made for assistance in the resumption of urgently needed industrial production and the restoration of essential services, it is therefore

RESOLVED

That, subject to the provisions of Resolutions Nos. 1 and 17 of this Session, the Council approves the following statement as a guide to activities with respect to the rehabilitation of such industries, transport and other services as are essential to relief:

1. Rehabilitation supplies are to consist of materials, such as raw materials, machinery, and spare parts needed to enable a recipient country to produce and transport relief supplies for its own and other liberated territories; and, within the scope of the Administration, the rehabilitation of public utilities and services, so far as they can be repaired and restored to meet immediate, basic needs, such essentials as light and water, power, transportation, and communication. These needs include rehabilitation of essential relief industries, such as those which provide food, shelter, clothing, medical supplies.

2. Raw materials may be supplied by (*a*) the liberated country in which the industry is situated and in which the materials are to be used, (*b*) another liberated country, or (*c*) any other country. The task of the Administration in cases (*a*) and (*b*) should be the rehabilitation of the

raw material producing industries such as coal mines, mineral mines, construction materials industries, etc.

3. If the raw materials required must be imported from overseas, it should be the responsibility of the Administration, through the appropriate national or intergovernmental agencies, to arrange for necessary allocation and procurement of supplies, so that there may be created as promptly as possible, reserves to be available at the request of the Director General when and wherever the need arises.

4. It is recommended that pools be created of materials such as processing materials, machine tools, mobile power units, maintenance equipment, industrial machinery of both standard and special types, and spare parts.

5. It is recommended that in cases where home production exceeds home consumption, the government or recognized national authority concerned should take all steps necessary to enable the excess of production available in a country to be put at the disposal of other liberated areas which may need such supplies to cover their deficits.

6. It should be the policy of the Administration to help those countries whose industries can be rehabilitated for production of relief and rehabilitation goods urgently required in other liberated areas. It is recommended that in attainment of these objectives the following be considered: special allocations of raw materials, machinery, and spare parts, by placing at the disposal of those countries, at the request of their governments, an experienced staff, and by providing special priorities for the return of skilled personnel awaiting repatriation.

7. It is recommended that the governments or recognized national authorities having administrative authority in a liberated area will keep the Director General and the appropriate regional committee fully informed as to any surplus of supplies from time to time available in such area, to meet, when circumstances permit, relief and rehabilitation import requirements of other liberated areas.

8. It is recommended that the Administration should, in consultation with the governments or recognized national authorities concerned and the appropriate international coordinating authority, assist liberated areas in restoring the transport and communications system to satisfactory working condition; it should also help to restore equipment, repair shops, workshops, shipyards, etc. It is recommended that a pool of transportation equipment both fixed and mobile should be created either from stocks manufactured overseas or in Allied or in neutral countries. Equipment which has been the property of the enemy may also form part of the pool.

9. It should be the task of the Administration to participate in conjunction with military and other appropriate authorities in the organization and coordination of the transportation of relief and rehabilitation supplies during the relief and rehabilitation period.

10. It is recommended that the requirements for raw materials, machinery, spare parts and processing materials should be established within each country and that a definite order of priority be established taking into consideration: (*a*) technical factors, such as, on the one hand, the necessity of restoring the public services (gas, water, electricity), and, on the other, the needs of various types of consumer goods; (*b*) social factors, such as the necessity of providing reemployment; (*c*) temporary economic factors, such as scarcity of certain raw materials and shipping.

11. The task of rehabilitation must not be considered as the beginning of reconstruction — it is coterminous with relief. No new construction or reconstruction work is contemplated, but only rehabilitation as defined in the preamble of the Agreement. Problems, such as unemployment, are important, but not determining factors. They are consequences and, at the same time, motives of action. The Administration cannot be called upon to help restore continuous employment in the world.

No. 13 — Policies With Respect to Shelter

RESOLVED

That the Council approves the following statement as a guide to activities with respect to shelter:

1. Any general rebuilding policy for the areas to be liberated is in the sphere of long-term reconstruction and does not, therefore, come within the purview of the Administration.

2. In the relief period priority in the rehabilitation of essential shelter or accommodation in the liberated areas should be given to:

> hospitals and schools;
> habitations for homeless persons, especially for workers engaged in essential public services and in industries having high priority in relief, as well as for farmers and agricultural workers.

3. Where it may be necessary, however, there should be imported construction tools such as hand tools, building supplies and equipment, including excavating machinery, should essential materials and equipment not be found available, or be in short supply.

4. As regards the problem of shelter for displaced persons, which falls into two parts — temporary accommodation at collecting points and at frontiers, and accommodation of a more permanent, though not necessarily final character, for persons who cannot be returned to their homes either because their homes have been destroyed or because these are in territories still occupied by the enemy — wherever possible existing buildings, camps, barracks, and other buildings, should be used as they are or can be made suitable.

5. Where, in some enemy-occupied territories, extensive enemy colonization has taken place, and where consolidation of holdings and construction of military installations has been accompanied by destruction of farmhouses and buildings, there should be provided camp accommodations for farmers and agricultural workers upon return to their own country. Any large-scale permanent reconstruction of holdings and the rebuilding of farmhouses and other structures should not be undertaken by the Administration. Pools of building materials shall be promptly created so that advance arrangements can be made for the accommodation of farmers and agricultural workers.

6. Where prefabricated housing is a specialized industry in any of the territories of a member government, the importance of making these supplies available as a part of the contribution of these governments should be recognized.

7. Where there is widespread destruction of particular areas caused by military operations or of a deliberate "scorched earth" policy on the part of the enemy, although priority should be given to housing repairs as indicated in paragraph 2, accommodation or shelter for workers in the food processing industries should be provided.

8. It is of importance that arrangements should be made, with the consent of the government concerned, for an export assessment of this damage, so that detailed and accurate specifications of the equipment required in the reconstruction of factories providing essential relief requirements and the shelter or accommodations for the workers engaged in those industries may be obtained at as early a date as possible. In order that this work may be started, if possible, during the period of military responsibility for civilian relief and rehabilitation, the Council recommends to its member governments that the military authorities be invited to advise the Administration, to the fullest extent consistent with military security, of conditions found in the area affecting civilian relief and rehabilitation requirements and supplies.

PART III. FINANCE AND SUPPLIES

No. 14 — Financial Plan for the Administration

RESOLVED

That the following Financial Plan for the Administration be adopted:

Administrative Budget and Program of Operations

Section 1. Program of Operations

The Director General shall prepare as soon as possible, and submit to the next session of the Council, a program of operations covering proposed activities of the Administration in connection with relief and rehabilitation including the care and transportation of displaced persons. This program may cover the entire period of contemplated operations of the Administration, or any part thereof. The operating program shall serve as a guide to the activities of the Director General; but, except as provided in Article IV, paragraph 2 of the Agreement, shall not limit his action when the situation requires other action. From time to time, the Director General shall submit to the Council revisions of, or supplements to the operating program which experience may show to be desirable.

Section 2. Annual Administrative Budget

The Director General shall prepare annually a budget covering the estimated administrative expense of the Administration for a calendar year. The budget shall be accompanied by an explanation and justification of the amount required. The proposed budget shall be submitted to the Council in accordance with the regulations of the Council with respect to administrative expenditures and receipts.

Section 3. Supplementary Administrative Budgets

The Director General may submit supplementary budgets to the Council covering the necessary administrative expenses not provided for in the annual budget.

Contributions

Section 4. General Contributions

As to the amount and character of the contribution of each member government, to be determined by its constitutional bodies as provided for in Article V of the Agreement, the Council recommends that each member government whose home territory has not been occupied by the enemy shall make a contribution for participation in the work of the Administration, approximately equivalent to one per cent of the national income of the country for the year ending June 30, 1943 as determined by the member government.

The Council recognizes that there are cases in which the recommendation above may conflict with particular demands arising from the continuance of the war or may be excessively burdensome because of peculiar situations, and therefore recognizes that the amount and character of the contribution recommended is subject to such conditions.

Section 5. Character of Contribution

Subject to the provisions of Article V, paragraph 1, of the Agreement the Council recommends that as much as possible, but not less than 10 per cent, of the amount contributed by each member government as recommended in section 4 hereof, shall be in such form of currency as can be expended in areas outside of the contributing country; and that the balance thereof shall be in the form of a credit in local currency which shall be available for the purchase of the contributing country's supplies and services.

Section 6. Contributions Toward Administrative Expenses

A member government may treat its share of the administrative expenses, as determined by the Council under Article VI of the Agreement, as included in its contribution made under sections 4 and 5 hereof.

Section 7. Contributions by Other Member Governments

The Council recommends that member governments other than a member government referred to in section 4 hereof, which are able to contribute to the work of the Administration for relief and rehabilitation outside its own territory (in addition to its annual contribution for allocated administrative expenses), should do so.

Section 8. Additional Contributions by Member Governments

The Council recommends that member governments desiring to make contributions in addition to those recommended in section 4 hereof should do so.

Section 9. Contributions by Non-member Governments and Non-governmental Sources

The Council expects that contributions will be received to the work of the Administration from non-member governments or non-governmental sources. Such contributions may be accepted in accordance with rules and regulations established by the Director General in conformity with general policies of the Administration.

Section 10. Action on Contributions

The Council recommends that each member government take at the earliest possible time such constitutional budgetary, administrative, or legislative steps as may be necessary to make its contribution available when needed for the purposes of the Administration.

Section 11. Direct Contributions to Liberated Areas

The Council recommends that member governments giving to or receiving from foreign sources, direct contributions or other direct aid in the nature of relief and rehabilitation in addition to contributions to or from the Administration, shall do so only after prior notification and consultation with the Director General.

Section 12. Immediate Administrative Expenses

In order to meet immediate administrative expenses, the Director General may ask such of the member governments as may be in a position to do so to make immediate advance payments in the amounts necessary, with appropriate credit toward the general amounts recommended in sections 4 and 5 hereof.

Expenditures: Administrative and Operational

Section 13. Rate of Contributions

The Council recommends that, so far as is consistent with efficient operation, contributions of all member governments for the work of the Administration shall be called upon at an approximately equal rate.

Section 14. Administrative Expenses

The Director General may incur obligations and make expenditures for administrative purposes from the general resources of the Administration, in accordance with approved administrative budgets.

Section 15. Use of Currency

The Director General may use so much of the foreign exchange available to the Administration as he may deem necessary for defraying administrative and operational expenses which cannot be met from local currency credits. Such expenditures may be made in any country, whether or not the government thereof is a member government. The consent of a member government must be secured for the use of any of its local currency to finance expenditures in any other country.

Distribution

Section 16. Governments in a Position to Pay With Suitable Means of Foreign Exchange

It shall be the policy of the Administration not to deplete its available resources for the relief and rehabilitation of any area whose government is in a position to pay with suitable means of foreign exchange.

Section 17. Determination of Whether a Government is in a Position to Pay With Suitable Means of Foreign Exchange

When a member government considers that it is not in a position to pay as in the foregoing section, the Director General, in consultation with the member government involved and on the advice of the appropriate committee or subcommittee of the Council, shall determine whether the government or country is not in a position to pay for relief and rehabilitation supplies and services. In case of disagreement, either the member government or the Director General may refer the matter to the Council.

In making the determination the applicant's foreign exchange assets and its sources of foreign exchange shall be taken into account. Although payment for relief and rehabilitation supplies and services shall be considered to have a strong claim on the foreign exchange assets of the applicant country, due consideration shall be given also to its need of foreign exchange for other purposes.

The Director General, from time to time, shall review such determination in the light of changing circumstances.

Section 18. Policy on Relief Debt Burdens

It shall be the policy of the Administration that an applicant government shall not be required to assume the burden of an enduring foreign exchange debt for the procurement of relief and rehabilitation supplies and services.

Section 19. Supplies and Services for Which Member Governments Are Not in a Position to Pay With Suitable Means of Foreign Exchange

The Council recommends that governments not in a position to pay in suitable means of foreign exchange for necessary relief and rehabilitation supplies or services make available to the Administration in whole or in part the local currency proceeds from the sale of supplies furnished by the Administration. It shall be the policy of the Administration to use any such local currency for relief and rehabilitation work, including the care and movement of displaced persons, and for such other purposes as may be agreed upon with the government. Programs for the utilization of such local currency shall be formulated by the Director General and the member government involved.

Section 20. Expenses Met With Local Currency

The Council recommends that so far as possible all expenses of the Administration within a liberated area shall be borne by the government of such area, and shall be paid in local currency made available by the government of the area or derived from the proceeds of the sale of supplies.

Section 21. Distribution of Gold or Convertible Currency Forbidden

Under no circumstances shall any distribution of gold or convertible currency resources be made by the Administration to any member or non-member government except for purchases of essential supplies and services.

Custody and Management of Funds

Section 22. Form of Assets

All funds and currency credits of the Administration shall be retained, so far as advisable, in the form in which they are received until needed.

Section 23. Fiscal Agents

The Director General shall in consultation with the appropriate member government, select such fiscal agents for the Administration as he may require.

Section 24. Accounting

The Director General shall prescribe a procedure to secure careful accounting for all funds and other property of the Administration and shall require all officials, employees, and agents of the Administration to comply with such procedure.

Section 25. Audit

All financial transactions of the Administration shall be audited annually by an auditor selected by the Council upon the recommendation of the appropriate committee of the Council.

No. 15 — Insurance

RESOLVED

That if it appears to the Director General conducive to the efficient and economical discharge of the business of the Administration, the Administration may carry its own risks without insurance except as may be otherwise directed by the Council.

No. 16 — Taxation of Relief and Rehabilitation Supplies

RESOLVED

1. That the Council recommends that all member governments make appropriate measures according to their constitutional procedures to insure that relief and rehabilitation supplies and services furnished by the Administration are not subjected to taxation in a manner which reduces the resources of the Administration.

2. That so far as may be required for the attainment of the above purpose, the Council recommends to all member governments that, *inter alia,*

    (a) export taxes on supplies to be furnished by the Administration to a member government for relief and rehabilitation be waived, or other equivalent action taken; and such supplies be exempted from any new or additional export taxes. The

Council recognizes that such action on existing export taxes may be equivalent to a part of a member government's general contribution under Section 4 of the Financial Plan, but urges that such contribution be made under Section 8 of the said Plan;

(b) appropriate action be taken where the necessary arrangements do not already exist to provide that supplies of the Administration in transit through a member government's country are not subjected to any burden of taxation;

(c) relief and rehabilitation supplies furnished by the Administration be not subjected in liberated areas to the burden of any form of taxation in a manner which reduces the resources of the Administration.

3. That the appropriate Committee of the Council concern itself with the relationship of customs duties and other taxes in liberated areas to relief and rehabilitation work, and that a study of the problem and the preparation of recommendations be undertaken for the future guidance of the Council with regard to relief and rehabilitation work.

No. 17 — Procedures for Ascertaining and Meeting Deficits in Supplies Requiring Importation

RESOLVED

That the following shall be the policies of the Administration with regard to procedures for ascertaining and meeting deficits in supplies requiring importation:

A. Policies Relating to Procedures for Estimating and Meeting Import Requirements

I. Preparation and Presentation of Over-all Requirements

1. The Committee of the Council for Europe and the Committee of the Council for the Far East will recommend, from time to time, as policies to be adopted by the Council whatever basis or bases the Committees think appropriate for the whole or parts of their respective areas.

2. The Council will consider these recommendations and, from time to time, determine the policies to be adopted, on the basis of which over-all estimates of relief and rehabilitation requirements shall be made.

3. The Director General, in consultation with the appropriate regional committees, will compute estimates of over-all requirements for their respective areas in conformity with the bases and policies approved by the Council.

4. The Director General will present before the intergovernmental allocating agencies estimates of over-all requirements for relief and rehabilitation of all areas, liberated and to be liberated, in order to permit a global consideration of these requirements and all other requirements.

II. Preparation and Presentation of National Requirements

1. The Director General may present to the intergovernmental allocating agencies the particular requirements of any country for which the assistance of the Administration has been requested.

2. In cases where requirements or programs of intended purchases are presented directly to the intergovernmental allocating agencies by the government of a country liberated or to be liberated, such government, in advance of their presentation, shall keep the Director General fully informed of such requirements or programs. The Director General may present to these agencies such recommendations or objections in respect of these requirements or programs as he may deem necessary to obtain a fair distribution of relief and rehabilitation supplies to and among the various areas liberated or to be liberated.

3. In determining what requirements he should present to the intergovernmental allocating agencies in respect of countries for which the assistance of the Administration has been requested, and what recommendations or objections he should make in respect of requirements presented by member governments directly to such agencies in order to obtain a fair distribution of relief and rehabilitation supplies, as provided in paragraphs 1 and 2 immediately preceding, the Director General shall pay due regard to the degree of urgency of particular relief and rehabilitation requirements and to the extent of damage suffered by member governments in a part or the whole of their respective areas as a result of hostilities or of occupation by the enemy.

4. It is expected that the Director General will be fully consulted by the intergovernmental allocating agencies when any matter touching the interests of the Administration is under discussion, and where necessary the chairman of the Committee on Supplies will likewise be consulted.

III. Procedures for Obtaining Supplies

1. Subject to Article I, paragraph 2, of the Agreement, the Director General, after consultation when necessary with the appropriate intergovernmental agency, will make use whenever possible of the established national agencies concerned with procurement, handling, storage, and transport of supplies; such use to be subject to the general agreement of the government concerned. By consultation with the government concerned, or otherwise, every effort will be made to prevent any dislocation of the economy of a supplying country resulting from procurement by or on behalf of the Administration.

2. The Director General will consider it one of his first and most important tasks to seek, through the appropriate national and intergovernmental agencies, to arrange for necessary allocations and procurement of supplies and their storage, shipping, and handling, so that there

shall be created as promptly as possible balanced reserves which shall be available at the request of the Director General whenever and wherever the need arises.

3. Member governments having administrative authority in a liberated area will keep the Director General and the appropriate regional committee fully informed as to any surplus of supplies from time to time available in such area, to meet, when circumstances permit, relief and rehabilitation import requirements of other liberated areas.

4. The Director General will consult with the military command or other established control authorities responsible for enemy or ex-enemy territories, with a view to securing information as to any surplus of supplies from time to time available in such enemy or ex-enemy territories, from which relief and rehabilitation import requirements of liberated areas might be met.

B. Recommendations Relating to Period of Military Responsibility for Civilian Relief and Rehabilitation

With regard to the period when a liberated area is under military control, the Council recommends to member governments that:

1. The military authorities be invited to advise the Administration, to the fullest extent consistent with military security, of conditions found in the area affecting civilian relief and rehabilitation requirements and supplies, so that planning and estimating may be as accurate as possible.

2. Representatives of the Administration enter the area at the earliest possible date to assist in preparations for the transition from military to civilian responsibility, after having first secured the permission of the appropriate military command, and, whenever practicable, after consultation with the national government or recognized national authority concerned.

PART IV. ORGANIZATION AND ADMINISTRATION

No. 18 — Composition of the Committee of the Council for Europe

WHEREAS

In paragraph 5 of Article III of the Agreement there is established a standing Committee of the Council for Europe and,

WHEREAS

The Agreement further provides that the said Committee "shall consist of all the members of the Council, or their alternates, representing member governments of territories within the European area and such other members of the Council representing other governments directly concerned with the problems of relief and rehabilitation in the European area as shall be appointed by the Council"; and,

WHEREAS

The terms "Europe" and "European area" are not defined in the Agreement; it is therefore

RESOLVED

1. That for the purposes of the Committee of the Council for Europe, the terms "Europe" and "European area" shall be construed to include the entire continent of Europe, the British Isles, Iceland, and all islands in the Mediterranean.

2. That the Committee of the Council for Europe shall consist of the members of the Council or their alternates representing Belgium, Czechoslovakia, the French Committee of National Liberation, Greece, Iceland, Luxemburg, the Netherlands, Norway, Poland, the Union of Soviet Socialist Republics, the United Kingdom, and Yugoslavia, being countries included within the European area, and in addition the members of the Council or their alternates representing Brazil, Canada, and the United States of America.

3. That the Central Committee is authorized to appoint additional members to the Committee in cases of emergency between sessions of the Council, such appointments to continue until the next session of the Council.

No. 19 — Composition of the Committee of the Council for the Far East

WHEREAS

In paragraph 5 of Article III of the UNRRA Agreement there is established a "Committee of the Council for the Far East"; and,

WHEREAS

The Agreement further provides that the said Committee "shall consist of all the members of the Council, or their alternates, representing member governments of territories within the Far Eastern area and such other members of the Council representing other governments directly concerned with the problems of relief and rehabilitation in the Far Eastern area as shall be appointed by the Council"; and,

WHEREAS

The terms "Far East" and "Far Eastern area" are not defined in the Agreement; it is therefore

RESOLVED

1. That for the purposes of the Committee of the Council for the Far East the terms "Far East" and "Far Eastern area" shall be construed to include eastern continental Asia, the East Indies, Philippine Islands, Australia, New Zealand, and the islands of the eastern Indian and western Pacific Oceans.

2. That the Committee of the Council for the Far East shall consist of the members of the Council or their alternates, representing Australia, China, the French Committee of National Liberation, India, the Netherlands, New Zealand, the Philippine Commonwealth, the United Kingdom, and the United States of America; and

3. That the Central Committee is authorized to appoint additional members to the Committee in cases of emergency between sessions of the Council, such appointments to continue until the next session of the Council.

No. 20 — Functions of the Committees of the Council for Europe and the Far East

RESOLVED

That the functions of the Committee of the Council for Europe and the Committee of the Council for the Far East shall be:

1. In the light of conditions prevailing in Europe and the Far East, and with the advice of such technical or special subcommittees as may be created, to recommend from time to time, as policies to be adopted by the Council, whatever basis or bases for over-all requirements the committees think appropriate for the whole or parts of their respective areas; and to advise the Director General with respect to the computation of over-all requirements for their respective areas in conformity with the bases and policies approved by the Council.

2. To advise the Director General with respect to the fair and equitable apportionment of relief and rehabilitation supplies available to areas within the European and Far Eastern regions respectively where the Administration may operate; and to assist him in securing the maximum production and interchange of any surplus supplies which can be made available within each region, by promoting appropriate national or intergovernmental action on the part of member governments.

3. To receive and discuss the periodic reports covering the programs and activities of the Administration in Europe and the Far East, respectively; and to advise the Director General on the organization of measures to assist displaced persons and the coordination of national action in regard to medical and other relief and rehabilitation problems common to each region; and

4. Generally to consider relief and rehabilitation policies in Europe and the Far East, respectively; to formulate recommendations on such policies,[1] and to discuss such recommendations with the Director General or his representative; and to transmit such recommendations to the Director General for distribution to the Council and the Central Committee.

[1] So in original.

No. 21 — Composition of the Committee on Supplies

RESOLVED

1. That the Committee on Supplies shall consist of members of the Council or their alternates representing Australia, Belgium, Brazil, Canada, China, the French Committee of National Liberation, the Netherlands, New Zealand, the Union of Soviet Socialist Republics, the United Kingdom, and the United States of America.

2. That the Central Committee is authorized to make emergency appointments between sessions of the Council, such appointments to continue until the next session of the Council.

No. 22 — Functions of the Committee on Supplies

WHEREAS

Article III, paragraph 4, of the Agreement provides that "The Committee on Supplies shall consider, formulate and recommend to the Council and the Central Committee policies designed to assure the provision of required supplies," it is therefore

RESOLVED

That the functions of the Committee on Supplies shall be:

1. To advise the Council, the Central Committee, and the Director General on general policies regarding the provision, financing, and transport of supplies.

2. To discuss with the Director General broad programs for securing the provision of supplies, as such programs affect the supplying countries.

3. To cooperate with the Director General and the established intergovernmental supply and shipping agencies regarding supply policies and, when necessary, make recommendations to supplement the actions of such agencies and to assure the availability of required supplies.

4. To cooperate with the Director General and the established intergovernmental and governmental agencies in efforts to increase production and the availability of supplies.

5. To cooperate with the Director General and the intergovernmental supply and shipping agencies concerned, so that as between contributing countries, their supplies and services shall be drawn upon in an equitable manner; and that any necessary financial adjustments among them may be arranged.

6. To consider whether there are unjustifiable differences in the valuations placed by the contributing countries upon the supplies and services purchased by or made available to the Administration, and make necessary recommendations regarding the adjustment of such valuations. These recommendations would be made after having given due regard to the points of view expressed by the representative of the contributing country concerned.

No. 23 — Appointment of a Subcommittee of the Committee on Supplies

RESOLVED

That the Council approve the appointment by the Chairman of the Committee on Supplies, after consultation with the Chairman of the Committee on Financial Control, of a subcommittee of not more than five members, of whom a majority would be drawn from the Committee on Supplies with the other member or members drawn from the Committee on Financial Control, and that this subcommittee be considered the appropriate subcommittee to advise the Director General relative to determining whether a government is in a position to pay, as provided in section 17 of the Financial Plan.

No. 24 — Composition of the Committee on Financial Control

RESOLVED

1. That the Committee on Financial Control shall consist of the members of the Council or their alternates representing China, Greece, Mexico, Norway, the Union of South Africa, the Union of Soviet Socialist Republics, the United Kingdom, and the United States of America.

2. That the Central Committee is authorized to make emergency appointments between sessions of the Council, such appointments to continue until the next session of the Council.

No. 25 — Functions of the Committee on Financial Control

RESOLVED

1. That the functions of the Committee on Financial Control shall be:

   (a) To review the annual budgets and any supplementary budgets of the Director General and to make reports, comments, and recommendations to the Council on these budgets.

   (b) To receive the quarterly reports of the Director General on Administrative expenditures and receipts and to make reports to the Council regarding them.

   (c) To recommend auditors to the Council and to advise the Council regarding the scope and frequency of the reports to be obtained from the auditors. Such auditors' reports shall cover, in particular, the system of accounting employed by the Administration, the funds expended in the purchase and received from the sale of supplies, the liabilities of the Administration and, generally, any matters of substance which the auditors may raise on examination of the Administration's accounts.

   (d) To make recommendations to the Council regarding the share of the Administrative expense of the Administration to be provided by each member government.

(e) To give attention to the effect, if any, which the receipt and expenditure by the Administration of local currency proceeds, referred to in section 19 of the Financial Plan, may have upon inflation in any country in which the Administration may operate, and make recommendations as to procedures in relation to such receipts or expenditures which may aid in counteracting inflationary trends.

(f) Generally to advise the Council on all financial matters within the competency of the Administration other than those falling within the scope of the Committee on Supplies.

(g) To advise the Director General upon any of the foregoing matters when he so requests.

2. That the Central Committee is hereby authorized to make any further arrangements necessary in regard to the work of the Committee on Financial Control.

No. 26 — Creation and Composition of Standing Technical Committees

WHEREAS
Many of the policy problems of the Council and of its regional committees are highly technical in character; and,

WHEREAS
In paragraph 6 of Article III of the Agreement, the creation of standing technical committees is authorized; it is therefore

RESOLVED
1. That the Council hereby creates standing technical committees on:

> Agriculture
> Displaced Persons
> Health
> Industrial Rehabilitation
> Welfare

2. That such committees shall consist of such members of the Council as indicate to the Director General their intention to participate in the work of a committee or committees, or of alternates nominated by such members of the Council as shall elect to do so, such alternates to possess special competence in the problems relating to the work of the committee to which they are nominated.

3. That the Central Committee is hereby authorized to make any further arrangements necessary in regard to the work of these committees and to make emergency appointments between sessions of the Council, such appointments to continue until the next session of the Council.

No. 27 — Functions of the Committee on Agriculture

RESOLVED

That the functions of the standing technical Committee on Agriculture shall be:

1. To advise the Council, the Central Committee, and the Director General as to the nature of and scope of problems relating to agriculture, fisheries, and food production and the rehabilitation of industries concerned therewith in areas in which the Administration will operate.

2. Periodically to review the programs of the Administration with regard to agriculture, fisheries, food production, and related subjects, and consult with the Director General thereon with respect to any suggested modifications.

3. To formulate proposals on technical policies in regard to agriculture, fisheries, and food production and the rehabilitation of the industries concerned therewith and related subjects, discuss such proposals with the Director General, and transmit such proposals to the Director General for distribution to the Council and the Central Committee; and

4. When requested by and in consultation with the Committees of the Council for Europe or for the Far East or such other regional committees as may hereafter be established, to appoint subcommittees to advise the regional committee and the chief representative of the Director General in the region concerned with respect to agriculture, fisheries, and food production and the rehabilitation of the industries concerned therewith and related subjects.

No. 28 — Functions of the Committee on Displaced Persons

RESOLVED

That the functions of the standing technical Committee on Displaced Persons shall be:

1. To advise the Council, the Central Committee, and the Director General on the organization of the work of the Administration in assisting in the repatriation and return of persons who have been obliged to leave their homes as a result of the war.

2. Periodically to review the programs of the Administration with respect to displaced persons with a view to calling the attention of the Council to any features in those programs which in their view require modification; and

3. When requested by, and in consultation with, the Committees of the Council for Europe or for the Far East or such other regional committees as may hereafter be established, to appoint subcommittees to advise the regional committee and the chief representative of the Director General in the region concerned, with respect to problems of displaced persons.

No. 29 — Functions of the Committee on Health

RESOLVED

That the functions of the standing technical Committee on Health shall be:

1. To advise the Council, the Central Committee, and the Director General as to the nature and scope of problems relating to health, medicine, and nutrition in areas in which the Administration will operate.

2. Periodically to review the programs of the Administration in the health, medical, nutrition, and related fields, and consult with the Director General thereon with respect to any suggested modifications.

3. To formulate proposals on technical policies relating to health, medical, nutrition, and related fields, discuss such proposals with the Director General, and transmit such proposals to the Director General for transmission to the Council and to the Central Committee; and

4. When requested by, and in consultation with, the Committees of the Council for the Far East or for Europe, or such other regional committees as may hereafter be established, to appoint subcommittees to advise the regional committee and the chief representative of the Director General in the region concerned, with respect to health and related special problems.

No. 30 — Functions of the Committee on Industrial Rehabilitation

RESOLVED

That the functions of the standing technical Committee on Industrial Rehabilitation shall be:

1. To advise the Council, the Central Committee, and the Director General as to the nature of and scope of problems in fields relating to the rehabilitation of public utilities and services, to the rehabilitation of industries producing urgently needed goods, and to rehabilitation supplies in areas in which the Administration will operate.

2. Periodically to review the programs of the Administration in such fields of industrial rehabilitation, and consult with the Director General thereon with respect to any suggested modifications.

3. To formulate proposals on technical policies relating to the rehabilitation of public utilities and services, to the rehabilitation of industries producing urgently needed goods, and to rehabilitation supplies, to discuss such proposals with the Director General, and transmit such proposals to the Director General for distribution to the Council and to the Central Committee; and

4. When requested by, and in consultation with the Committees of the Council for Europe or for the Far East or such other regional committees as may hereafter be established, to appoint subcommittees to

advise the regional committee and the chief representative of the Director General in the region concerned, with respect to problems of industrial rehabilitation.

No. 31 — Functions of the Committee on Welfare

RESOLVED

That the functions of the standing technical Committee on Welfare shall be:

1. To advise the Council, the Central Committee, and the Director General as to the nature and scope of welfare problems in areas in which the Administration will be operating; including the direct provision to victims of war of relief through other than normal economic channels of distribution; emergency measures for the care of children, expectant and nursing mothers, the aged and disabled, and other victims of war; and the measures necessary to secure the effective cooperation in this work of voluntary relief organizations.

2. Periodically to review the programs of the Administration in the above fields and consult with the Director General with respect to any suggested modifications.

3. To formulate proposals on technical policies relating to welfare problems, discuss such proposals with the Director General, and transmit such proposals to the Director General for distribution to the Council and the Central Committee; and

4. When requested by and in consultation with the committees of the Council for Europe or for the Far East or for such other regional committees as may hereafter be established, to appoint subcommittees to advise the regional committee and the chief representative of the Director General in the region concerned, with respect to welfare problems.

No. 32 — Facilities and Immunities for the Administration, Its Council and Committee Members and Its Staff

WHEREAS

The Council is desirous of insuring to the Administration and its agents the independence necessary for the efficient performance of the duties entrusted to them, and of avoiding the imposition of financial burdens upon the funds contributed by member governments to the Administration; it is therefore

RESOLVED

I. That the Council recommends:

1. That the member governments accord to the Administration the facilities, privileges, immunities, and exemptions which they accord to each other.

(a) Immunity from suit and legal process except with the

consent of, or so far as is provided for in any contract entered into by or on behalf of, the Administration;

(b) Inviolability of premises occupied by and of the archives of the Administration;

(c) Exemptions from taxation, including customs duties;

(d) Exemptions from or facilities in respect of foreign exchange controls.

2. That member governments take any steps that they may consider necessary to enable the Administration to exercise within their jurisdiction the powers conferred on it by Article I, paragraph 1, of the Agreement.

3. That member governments accord to representatives of member governments on the Council and its committees and to the officials and employees of the Administration when engaged on the business of the Administration, the following privileges and immunities in their respective territories:

(a) immunity from legal process of any kind in respect of acts performed by them in their official capacity and falling within their functions as such;

(b) immunity from taxation on official salaries, allowances, or other emoluments as representatives, officials, or employees of the Administration;

(c) the same immunities from immigration restrictions, alien registration and military service obligations and the same facilities as regards exchange restrictions as are accorded to representatives, officials, and employees of similar rank of other member governments;

(d) any further privileges and immunities that the Director General may request as necessary to safeguard representatives, officials, or employees in the territories of any member government where they are engaged and particularly those engaged in field operations in the areas in which the Administration may be undertaking relief and rehabilitation.

Provided that each member government shall determine to what extent the above recommendations shall apply to its own nationals, and to non-nationals in permanent residence in its territories.

4. That the member governments make any necessary arrangements with the Director General for the application of the foregoing recommendations.

II. That the Council requests the Director General

1. To initiate immediate negotiations with member governments to bring such arrangements into operation as rapidly as possible.

2. Wherever appropriate, to approach non-member governments with a view to their granting such of the above-mentioned facilities, privileges, immunities, and exemptions as may be desirable to facilitate the work of the Administration.

No. 33 — Immunities and Priorities for Transit Goods

RESOLVED

That the Council recommends that each member government expedite to the extent possible supplies and equipment of the Administration in transit, and that it exempt such supplies and equipment of the Administration from adverse legal action or seizure.

No. 34 — Official Correspondence of the Administration

WHEREAS

The Council recognizes the need for expedition, economy, and secrecy in the transmission of the official correspondence of the Administration; it is therefore

RESOLVED

I. That the Council recommends:

1. That the member governments accord to the official correspondence of the Administration

(a) the same treatment as is accorded by them to the official correspondence of other member governments, including:

(i) Priorities for telephone and telegraph communications, whether cable or radio, and for mail transmitted by pouch or by courier.

(ii) Government rebates for official telegrams.

(iii) Diplomatic status for couriers and pouches of the Administration.

(iv) Under appropriate safeguards, exemption from censorship of the official correspondence of the Administration.

(v) Appropriate arrangements for the use of codes and of cable addresses for the telegraphic correspondence of the Administration.

(b) Appropriate postal facilities, including such franking privileges or arrangements for the use of specially printed or overprinted stamps as may be possible.

2. That the member governments make any necessary arrangements with the Director General for the application of the foregoing recommendations.

II. That the Council requests the Director General:

1. To initiate immediate negotiations with member governments to bring such arrangements into operation as rapidly as possible.

2. Wherever appropriate, to approach non-member governments with a view to their granting such of the above-mentioned facilities, privileges, immunities, and exemptions as may be desirable to facilitate the work of the Administration.

No. 35 — Communications With Neutral Governments

RESOLVED

That the Council recommends that member governments extend to the Director General technical facilities for communicating with governments neutral in the present conflict.

No. 36 — Travel Facilities for the Staff of the Administration

WHEREAS

The Council has in mind the importance of securing the expeditious and unhindered travel of officials and employees of the Administration necessary to permit the prompt fulfillment by the Administration of the urgent tasks entrusted to it; it is therefore

RESOLVED

I. That the Council recommends:

1. That the Director General issue to officials and employees of the Administration for use when traveling on official business a document identifying the official or employee and requesting in the name of the Administration that all appropriate facilities be granted to the bearer.

2. That all member governments give full recognition to such documents and instruct their diplomatic, consular, customs, and immigration services and any other services which may be concerned to recognize such documents as entitling the bearer to all appropriate facilities.

3. That in respect to passports and visas the member governments accord to the officials and employees of the Administration the same treatment as is accorded to the officials and employees of comparable rank of their own or other governments.

4. That all member governments take the necessary steps to grant all appropriate and possible priorities for the travel of the officials of the Administration on official business and government rebates for such travel.

5. That the member governments make any necessary arrangements with the Director General for the application of the foregoing recommendations.

II. That the Council requests the Director General:

1. To initiate immediate negotiations with member governments to bring such arrangements into operation as rapidly as possible.

2. Wherever appropriate, to approach non-member governments with a view to their granting such of the above-mentioned facilities, privileges, immunities, and exemptions as may be desirable to facilitate the work of the Administration.

No. 37 — Personnel Policies

WHEREAS

The Council desires to promote the concept of a truly international civil service; and,

WHEREAS

It recognizes that the success of the Administration will in large part depend upon the vision, competence, integrity, and loyalty of the men and women who will become its administrative officers, and comprise its technical staff; and that the vesting, by the Agreement, of full executive authority and responsibility in the Director General, requires that he act with the greatest possible freedom in the selection of personnel and the establishment of personnel standards; it is therefore

RESOLVED

1. That the staff of the Administration should be of an international character, selected upon the basis of individual competence, character, and integrity, without discrimination on the grounds of sex, race, nationality, or creed, and recruited upon as wide a geographic basis as is possible, compatible with efficient administration; and that salary standards be established at a sufficiently high level to make it possible for the Administration to secure the employment of persons possessing the highest qualifications within their own particular field of endeavor; and that due consideration should be given to the special problems which will arise because of the varying salary standards that will prevail in the different countries in which the Administration will operate.

2. That the Council recommends:

(a) That all member governments endeavor to make available to the Administration such persons in their own civil service as the Director General may invite to join the staff of the Administration; and to take proper steps to insure that the established rights and status of such persons shall be in no way adversely affected by their temporary employment by the Administration.

(*b*) That international agencies be urged to adopt the same policy with respect to such of their employees as may be invited to join the staff of the Administration.

No. 38 — *Administrative Budget and the Allocation of Administrative Expenses*

RESOLVED

1. That the annual budget covering the necessary administrative expenses of the Administration for the calendar year 1944 and the unelapsed part of the year 1943 submitted by the Director General in the amount of $10,000,000 is hereby approved.

2. That the total amount of $10,000,000 approved in the preceding paragraph is allocated to the member governments in the following proportions:

Australia	1.50	India	4.00
Belgium	1.00	Iran	.10
Bolivia	.10	Iraq	.10
Brazil	1.50	Liberia	.05
Canada	3.00	Luxemburg	.05
Chile	.20	Mexico	.70
China	5.00	Netherlands	1.50
Colombia	.30	New Zealand	.30
Costa Rica	.05	Nicaragua	.05
Cuba	.20	Norway	.30
Czechoslovakia	1.00	Panama	.05
Dominican Republic	.05	Paraguay	.05
Ecuador	.05	Peru	.25
Egypt	.70	Philippines	.05
El Salvador	.05	Poland	1.00
Ethiopia	.05	Union of South Africa	1.00
French Committee of National		U.S.S.R.	15.00
Liberation	4.00	United Kingdom	15.00
Greece	.50	U. S. A.	40.00
Guatemala	.05	Uruguay	.20
Haiti	.05	Venezuela	.10
Honduras	.05	Yugoslavia	.70
Iceland	.05		100.00

No. 39 — *Salary of the Director General*

RESOLVED

That the salary of the Director General be the salary of the members of the Cabinet of the President of the United States of America.

No. 40 — *Rules of Procedure of the Council and the Rules of Standing Committees of the Council*

RESOLVED

That the Rules of Procedure of the Council attached hereto, together with Annex I thereto, Rules of Standing Committees of the Council, shall be the rules of procedure of the Council and the rules of Standing Committees of the Council.[1]

[1] Rules of Procedure of the Council, *ibid.*, p. 69; Annex I, p. 76.

No. 41 — Regulations With Respect to Expenditures and Receipts of the Administration

RESOLVED

That the Council adopts the regulations attached hereto which shall be considered as Annex II to the Rules of Procedure of the Council.[1]

(3) Joint Resolution (H. J. Res. 192) to Enable the United States to Participate in the Work of the United Nations Relief and Rehabilitation Administration, Approved March 28, 1944 [2]

Resolved by the Senate and House of Representatives of the United States of America in Congress assembled, That there is hereby authorized to be appropriated to the President such sums, not to exceed $1,350,000,000 in the aggregate, as the Congress may determine from time to time to be appropriate for participation by the United States (including contributions in funds or otherwise and all necessary expenses related thereto) in the work of the United Nations Relief and Rehabilitation Administration, established by an agreement concluded by the United Nations and Associated Governments on November 9, 1943, reading as follows:

[Text of agreement omitted.[3]]

SEC. 2. Amounts appropriated under this resolution shall be expended under the direction of the President pursuant to section 1 hereof. The President shall submit to the Congress quarterly reports of expenditures made under any such appropriations and of operations under the Agreement.

SEC. 3. In the adoption of this joint resolution the Congress expresses its approval of and reliance upon the policy adopted by the United Nations Relief and Rehabilitation Administration at the first session of the Council, summarized in paragraph 11 of Resolution Numbered 12, and reading as follows:

"11. The task of rehabilitation must not be considered as the beginning of reconstruction — it is coterminous with relief. No new construction or reconstruction work is contemplated, but only rehabilitation as defined in the preamble of the Agreement. Problems, such as unemployment, are important, but not determining factors. They are consequences and, at the same time, motives of action. The Administration cannot be called upon to help restore continuous employment in the world."

SEC. 4. In expressing its approval of this joint resolution, it is the recommendation of Congress that insofar as funds and facilities permit, any area (except within enemy territory and while occupied by the enemy) important to the military operations of the United Nations which is stricken by famine or disease may be included in the benefits to be

[1] Annex II appears, *ibid.*, p. 80.   [2] Public Law 267, 78th Cong.   [3] See p. 251.

294 DOCUMENTS ON AMERICAN FOREIGN RELATIONS

made available through the United Nations Relief and Rehabilitation Administration.

SEC. 5. No amendment under Article VIII (*a*) of the agreement involving any new obligation for the United States shall be binding upon the United States without approval by joint resolution of Congress.

SEC. 6. In adopting this joint resolution the Congress does so with the following reservation:

That in the case of the United States the appropriate constitutional body to determine the amount and character and time of the contributions of the United States is the Congress of the United States.

SEC. 7. In adopting this joint resolution the Congress does so with the following reservation:

That it is understood that the provision in paragraph 11 of Resolution Numbered 12 adopted at the first session of the council, referred to in section 3 of this joint resolution and reading "The task of rehabilitation must not be considered as the beginning of reconstruction — it is coterminous with relief," contemplates that rehabilitation means and is confined only to such activities as are necessary to relief.

SEC. 8. In adopting this joint resolution the Congress does so with the following reservation:

That the United Nations Relief and Rehabilitation Administration shall not be authorized to enter into contracts or undertake or incur obligations beyond the limits of appropriations made under this authorization and by other countries and receipts from other sources.

SEC. 9. The authorization contained in this joint resolution shall expire on June 30, 1946.

(a) *Message of the President (Roosevelt) to Congress on United States Participation, November 15, 1943* [1]

TO THE CONGRESS OF THE UNITED STATES:

I am happy to inform the Congress that on November 9, 1943, representatives of 43 nations and peoples joined with our own Government in signing the accompanying UNRRA agreement,[2] setting up an international Relief and Rehabilitation Administration to give first aid in the liberated areas. This agreement provides only the framework. The implementation is left to the constitutional lawmaking body of the member states.

The task of the organization will be to assist in furnishing the medicine, food, clothing, and other basic necessities and essential services which are required to restore the strength of the liberated peoples. They have been deliberately stripped by the enemy in order to support the Axis war-machine. More than that, the Axis leaders have boasted that as they withdraw, they will leave only devastation — what they have not stolen, they will destroy. As our American soldiers fight their way up the Italian boot, they are discovering at first-hand that the barbarism of the Nazis is equal to their boasts. Their only rivals in this respect are the Japanese.

[1] *Congressional Record*, vol. 89, p. 9593 (daily edition, November 15, 1943).
[2] See this volume, p. 251.

UNRRA will be able to make only a beginning in the vast task of aiding the victims of war. The greatest part of the job will have to be done by the liberated peoples themselves. What UNRRA can do is to help the liberated peoples to help themselves, so that they may have the strength to undertake the task of rebuilding their destroyed homes, their ruined factories, and their plundered farms.

The length of the war may be materially shortened if, as we free each occupied area, the people are enlisted in support of the United Nations' armies.

Already, for example, a new French Army has been created, and, as we strike toward Berlin, increasing numbers in Sicily and Italy are falling in step beside the soldiers of the United Nations. Others construct roads and military installations required for our military operations. Millions more are waiting for the moment when they, too, can strike a blow against the enemy.

They do not want charity. They seek the strength to fight, and to do their part in securing the peace. Aid to the liberated peoples during the war is thus a matter of military necessity as well as of humanity.

UNRRA will not, of course, be expected to solve the long-range problems of reconstruction. Other machinery and other measures will be necessary for this purpose. What UNRRA can do is to lay the necessary foundation for these later tasks of reconstruction.

The devastation and disorganization caused by the Nazi and Japanese war machines is so great that this world disaster can be met only by the united action of the 44 United Nations and associated nations. Accordingly, under the agreement establishing UNRRA, it is proposed that each nation will contribute in accordance with its ability. Each will determine for itself the amount and character of the contribution which it can make.

A small fraction of the national income of the contributing member states will, it is hoped, be sufficient to meet the needs. Some of the liberated nations may be able to make payment for the supplies and services rendered. But only by bringing to bear the resources of all the United Nations will we be able to relieve a substantial part of the suffering of the millions who will need help.

The nature and the amount of the contribution to be made by the United States will, in accordance with the terms of the UNRRA agreement, be determined by the Congress of the United States under its constitutional procedure.

At this time I recommend to the Congress the enactment of a bill authorizing the appropriation of funds as Congress may from time to time determine to permit the participation by the United States in the work of UNRRA. I am not now recommending the appropriation of a specific sum. At a later date after the conclusion of the Atlantic City meeting, I shall send to you a further recommendation, informing you of the result of the meeting and requesting the appropriation of specific funds.[1]

FRANKLIN D. ROOSEVELT

(b) Letter of the Secretary of State (Hull) to the Chairman of the House Foreign Affairs Committee (Bloom), December 7, 1943 [2]

MY DEAR MR. BLOOM:

I understand that H. J. Res. 192, a bill to authorize appropriations to enable the United States to participate in the work of the United Nations Relief and Rehabilitation Administration, is now before your Committee. I wish to endorse

[1] *Ibid.*, p. 302.

[2] Department of State, *Bulletin*, IX, p. 416; *Hearings before the Committee on Foreign Affairs, House of Representatives, on H. J. Res. 192* [*To Enable the United States to Participate in the Work of the United Nations Relief and Rehabilitation Administration*], 78th Cong., 1st and 2d sess., p. 5.

this Bill and strongly commend it to the favorable consideration of the Committee.

The UNRRA Agreement itself was carefully worked out after consultations with members of Congress, and especially with the Foreign Affairs and Foreign Relations Committees. This Agreement, as you know, was signed on November 9 and the first meeting of the UNRRA Council was held at Atlantic City. The Council elected a distinguished American, the Honorable Herbert H. Lehman, to be Director General of the Administration. It laid the groundwork for the organization of UNRRA and adopted sound and useful resolutions on the policies which it should follow. It now remains for this organization to begin its important operations. All the forty-four United and Associated Nations are joining in its work and I know that Congress will wish the United States to play its proper part. As the President said:[1]

". . . it is hard for us to grasp the magnitude of the needs in occupied countries.

"The Germans and the Japanese have carried on their campaigns of plunder and destruction with one purpose in mind: that in the lands they occupy there shall be left only a generation of half-men — undernourished, crushed in body and spirit, without strength or incentive to hope — ready, in fact, to be enslaved and used as beasts of burden by the self-styled master races.

"The occupied countries have been robbed of their foodstuffs and raw materials, and even of the agricultural and industrial machinery upon which their workers must depend for employment. The Germans have been planning systematically to make the other countries economic vassals, utterly dependent upon and completely subservient to the Nazi tyrants. . . .

"It is not only humane and charitable for the United Nations to supply medicine, food and other necessities to the peoples freed from Axis control; it is a clear matter of enlightened self-interest and of military strategic necessity."

The broad plans growing out of the Moscow Conference, which Congress has so warmly endorsed, will need the work of this great organization to ensure, in the words of the Four-Nation Declaration, "a rapid and orderly transition from war to peace" so that we may proceed to our announced purpose of "maintaining international peace and security with the least diversion of the world's human and economic resources for armaments."

It is as essential to be prepared for the emergency which will follow the end of the war as it is to be prepared for the great operations which will bring the victorious peace. This organization must begin its work close upon the heels of the armies of the United Nations, not only to assure that the liberated peoples will live and be strengthened for the tasks of peace, but to assure that the end of the fighting brings peace and not disorganization and further conflict. An instrument of great promise has been forged for this purpose by all the United and Associated Nations. That instrument is ready; the task is imminent. I earnestly recommend that the Congress authorize the funds for full and effective participation by this country.

(c) Report from the Senate Committee on Foreign Relations, to Accompany H. J. Res. 192, February 14, 1944 [2]

[Excerpts]

In the discussions in Congress, major emphasis was given to the desirability of limiting the scope of UNRRA'S activities to the fields of relief and rehabilitation, to the exclusion of all pertaining to long-range reconstruction. This excerpt

[1] Address on the Occasion of the Signature of the Agreement for United Nations Relief and Rehabilitation Administration, November 9, 1943, Department of State, *Bulletin*, IX, p. 317.   [2] Senate Report No. 688, 78th Cong., 2d sess.

from the Senate Committee's report expresses this point of view and the under-standing of the Committee as to how the work of UNRRA was to be limited in practice. A letter, recommending passage of the resolution was received by the committee from Secretary of State Cordell Hull, identical with the letter quoted above at p. 296.

THE SCOPE OF THE UNITED NATIONS RELIEF AND REHABILITATION ADMINISTRATION'S OPERATIONS

The task of the United Nations Relief and Rehabilitation Administration is international in scope, directly involving and affecting many countries. It cannot be solved except through cooperative international action.

The agreement itself defines the job in these terms: That the signatory na-tions are determined —

that immediately upon the liberation of any area by the armed forces of the United Nations or as a consequence of retreat of the enemy the population thereof shall receive aid and relief from their sufferings, food, clothing, and shelter, aid in the prevention of pestilence and in the recovery of the health of the people, and that preparation and arrangements shall be made for the return of prisoners and exiles to their homes and for assistance in the resumption of urgently needed agricultural and industrial production and the restoration of essential services.

The United Nations Relief and Rehabilitation Administration is therefore directed in Article I of the Agreement —

To plan, coordinate, administer or arrange for the administration of measures for the relief of victims of war in any areas under the control of any of the United Nations through the provision of food, fuel, clothing, shelter, and other basic necessities, medical and other essential services; and to facilitate in such areas, so far as necessary to the adequate provision of relief, the production and trans-portation of these articles and the furnishing of these services.

The language quoted from the preamble and Article I of the Agreement was carefully worked over by the members of the subcommittee of the Foreign Relations Committee and, with the cooperation of the representatives of the executive branch of the Government, important changes were made therein before the execution of the agreement, to limit the activities of the organization to relief and to rehabilitation operations incident to relief.

After the cessation of hostilities in a liberated area, the United Nations Relief and Rehabilitation Administration will thus be concerned with the emergency task of providing relief to the victims of war in that area. But the United Nations Relief and Rehabilitation Administration is not to be responsible for the whole of the vast job of relief and rehabilitation. It will not be concerned with plans for rebuilding bombed cities, or reestablishing the economic life of devastated areas. The program of the United Nations Relief and Rehabilitation Adminis-tration is a relief program, designed to provide relief supplies, and such emer-gency industrial or agricultural supplies as are needed to facilitate at the earliest possible moment the flow of relief supplies.

There are four general categories of supplies and services which the United Nations Relief and Rehabilitation Administration will assist in furnishing to liberated areas: (1) Essential consumer goods, such as medical supplies, food, fuel, temporary shelter, and clothing; (2) health and welfare services, including the care and repatriation of displaced persons; (3) materials necessary to the resumption of the production of relief supplies within liberated areas, such as seed, fertilizer, fishing equipment, essential machinery and spare parts; and (4) materials and technical help to repair, so far as they can be repaired or restored to meet immediate needs, essential utilities, and public services. These matters are provided for in Resolution No. 1, adopted by the Council at the Atlantic City session, which resolution defines the scope of the Administration's functions and limits it to these activities. Other resolutions of the Council, such as Resolution No. 12 on industrial rehabilitation, which define in more detail the various types of operations to be carried on by this organization, are subject to the limitations contained in Resolution No. 1, and, of course, in the agreement itself. Resolution No. 12 is by its terms subject to the provisions of Resolution No. 1.

Thus, care has been taken to limit the scope of the rehabilitation operations of the Administration to work which will enable a recipient country to produce or transport relief supplies for its own and other liberated areas and to the repair or restoration of public utilities only to the extent necessary to meet immediate needs. In the field of agriculture it is limited to short-run agricultural rehabilitation and food-production efforts. Rehabilitation is stated in a resolution of the Council to be coterminous with relief, rather than the beginning of reconstruction, and is not to comprehend any general rebuilding program.

The problem of relief and relief rehabilitation is an emergency issue of high political and humanitarian importance. The victims of war must be fed as soon as possible. The permanent reconstruction of devastated areas and the reestablishment of currencies are different types of problems. These are long-term problems which should be considered separately from emergency relief; they have been left to agencies and arrangements other than the United Nations Relief and Rehabilitation Administration.

It has been reliably estimated that 80 to 85 percent of the needs of all the liberated areas will be produced within these areas, and an additional 5 to 10 percent will be paid for in gold or foreign exchange by those of the liberated areas having such gold or foreign exchange. In this connection, it should be clearly understood that the United Nations Relief and Rehabilitation Administration does not propose to finance even all such imports as may be necessary for relief within the liberated areas. Several of the countries now occupied by the enemy have funds in gold or foreign exchange with which they will pay for their imported relief supplies. The United Nations Relief and Rehabilitation Administration's job with respect to supplies for such countries is to make representations to insure that there will be an equitable division of goods in short supply to and among all the liberated areas, and to see to it that the necessary imports are available for those liberated areas the governments of which are too poor to buy such supplies themselves. That task must be accepted as a common responsibility of all nations fortunate enough not to have suffered the horror of invasion, and interested in restoring a world of trade and peace.

Apart from questions of supply, the United Nations Relief and Rehabilitation Administration will assist in caring for displaced persons and in coordinating and controlling their movements, in the interest of the health and economic life of all nations. The vast number of persons, both in Europe and in the Far East, who have been forced from their homes defies imagination. Contrary to the terms of the Geneva Convention, prisoners of war have been demobilized and put into factories. Millions of workmen have been transported to Germany, populations have been shifted to carry out Hitler's unbelievable policies of extermination. Refugees and evacuees are everywhere in enemy-held territory. If all these people were to start homeward without supervision as soon as the shooting stops, the dangers of epidemic and economic confusion would be overwhelming. An organized international program is essential, if many nations are not to suffer in this process, and if world recovery is not to be needlessly delayed. The United Nations Relief and Rehabilitation Administration's work in this connection does not extend beyond aid for the victims of war. It is exclusively a relief function; and the only matters of rehabilitation in this function are those which are indispensable to relief itself. It does not encompass the political questions presented to the Inter-Governmental Committee on Refugees, established by the Évian conference, nor does it deal with the vital and tragic problems considered at the recent Bermuda conference on the fate of refugees in Europe.

The United Nations Relief and Rehabilitation Administration will necessarily take an active part in the problem of public health within the liberated areas. It will provide for the organization of adequate measures to protect the public health of the countries which are now occupied by the enemy. Particularly in connection with the treatment of displaced persons, and with the quick restoration of adequate public-health services, an international problem of great magnitude will be presented in all liberated areas.

The United Nations Relief and Rehabilitation Administration promises a solution of these essentially international problems. It applies the spirit and principles of international cooperation enunciated by the Fulbright and Connally resolutions,[1] and of the Moscow Declaration,[2] in a most practical and encouraging way. It should provide the kind of experience in international cooperation, without which we cannot hope to maintain peace.

RELATIONSHIP WITH THE MILITARY AUTHORITIES

As noted above, provision has been made so that the activities of the Administration in any given areas shall be subject to the condition that such activities shall not interfere with military considerations. Article VII of the Agreement states that "while hostilities or other military necessities exist in any area, the Administration and its Director General shall not undertake activities therein without the consent of the military command of that area, and unless subject to such control as the command may find necessary. The determination that such hostilities or military necessities exist in any area shall be made by its military commander." This provision was inserted in the agreement to avoid any possibility that the United Nations Relief and Rehabilitation Administration's activities would interfere with military activities and the same policy has been elaborated in the resolutions of the Council. After hearing the views of the War Department on this point, the committee is satisfied that every precaution has been taken to subordinate the operations of this organization to military considerations.

It is understood that there will be relief and rehabilitation activities carried on by the military authorities during an initial period after liberation. These activities are necessary to discharge the responsibility imposed upon the military as a matter of international law and morality to protect the civilian populations in areas under their control; they are also required as a matter of military necessity to keep those civilian populations in repose.

During this military period, however, the United Nations Relief and Rehabilitation Administration will stand ready to act during the military period to the

---

[1] See this volume, p. 315–16.
[2] *Ibid.*, p. 229.

extent that the military authorities consent. For the purposes of planning, both the Army and the civilian side, a period of 6 months has been taken as the period of military responsibility for relief and rehabilitation. In actual operation there will of course be a considerable variation as to the length of that period, depending on the rapidity with which the armed forces move forward and other factors.

FIELD OPERATIONS

Relief and rehabilitation operations will take place in the territories of our allies in Europe and the Far East when they are liberated from Axis occupation. Aside from this, there will be certain operations in areas other than those which have been occupied, in connection with the United Nations Relief and Rehabilitation Administration's function of assisting in the care and movement of displaced persons. For example, many refugees from Poland, France, and other parts of Europe are now in North Africa and the Middle East. Similar problems exist in the Far East. The care of these displaced persons and the work of facilitating their return to their homes will come within the scope of the United Nations Relief and Rehabilitation Administration's operations. Aside from operations of this nature, however, the United Nations Relief and Rehabilitation Administration's relief activities are directed under the agreement to the relief of countries which have been liberated from enemy occupation.

Operations in the enemy or ex-enemy territories may also have to be carried on. Disease and epidemics know no boundaries, and their outbreak in any area may endanger all adjacent areas, as well as the health of our occupying troops. Millions of the citizens of the United Nations have been brought into Germany and put to forced labor; more millions of prisoners of war have been illegally demobilized and forced to work in enemy countries. It is the responsibility of the United Nations Relief and Rehabilitation Administration to assist in the repatriation of these people. All such activities will require operations in enemy or ex-enemy territories, subject, of course, to the consent of the military or other control authority set up in the area by the United Nations. The policy resolutions adopted by the Council specifically provide, furthermore, that the Council must approve the scale and nature of such operations and that all expenses of operations in an enemy or ex-enemy country should be borne by that country.

In all cases, the United Nations Relief and Rehabilitation Administration can operate in an area only after consultation with and with the consent of the government or authority (military or civilian) exercising administrative authority in the area. The United Nations Relief and Rehabilitation Administration will operate as a service agency, and it is expected that the primary responsibility for the distribution of relief supplies and for rehabilitation work will be borne by the government or recognized national authority which exercises administrative control in the area. It is planned that, to the maximum practicable extent, the supplies furnished by the United Nations Relief and Rehabilitation administration will be sold through the normal agencies of distribution (governmental, commercial, cooperative), within the liberated areas. Although it must closely supervise the distribution of its supplies, the Administration will have no facilities for large-scale distribution through its own agencies, no powers to control distribution through rationing or otherwise. It is not intended to be a governmental body, in other words, with powers of local administration which only a government can perform.

Care has been taken to see to it that relief supplies will not be used as a political weapon by any faction or group, and this firm policy is made clear in many of the Council's resolutions. The United Nations Relief and Rehabilitation Administration is an agency of limited powers, consecrated to the job of relief. It cannot recognize a government, nor otherwise engage in political activities or decisions.

.   .   .   .

Conclusion

The committee has amended the House text of section 5 so that this authorization comes to a specific end on June 30, 1946. This is not intended to indicate the withdrawal of the United States from the United Nations Relief and Rehabilitation Administration at that time if conditions require and justify subsequent American participation. But the committee believes that our heavy American share of this responsibility should be definitely reviewed by Congress at some definite period. Throughout the hearings of the committee, we have consistently emphasized the intention of the committee to approve the United Nations Relief and Rehabilitation Administration solely as a relief measure and not as a general reconstruction measure. The committee recognizes the fact that certain forms of immediate rehabilitation may be an indispensable part of relief. But it is the definite opinion of the committee that relief incident to the war effort is the sole objective to which we subscribe in this endorsement of the pending resolution.

It is for this controlling reason that the committee has put a definite time limit upon the authorization of funds. The United Nations Relief and Rehabilitation Administration agreement itself clearly and specifically spells out the fact that our fiscal obligations under the agreement are confined to such specific appropriations as Congress shall hereafter make for this purpose. This also applies to the commitments in respect to administrative expenses. It is appropriate that the whole matter should again pass in congressional review at the end of 2 years. We are prepared to accept our full share of responsibility in the great and essential functions served by the United Nations Relief and Rehabilitation Administration as an unavoidable part of the war effort, and in this indispensable preliminary aid to the liberated areas. At the same time our own resources are not without limitations and we desire to implement our congressional responsibility in this behalf.

The committee believes that participation by the United States in the work of the United Nations Relief and Rehabilitation Administration is of importance in our national interest and in the interest of the future well-being of the countries which have been overrun during the course of this war. The problems which confront us in the field of relief and rehabilitation in the occupied countries of Europe and Asia can best be solved by cooperative action among the nations in the manner envisaged in the creation of the United Nations Relief and Rehabilitation Administration. The problems are too great and too complex for any one nation to undertake alone. Such problems as the control of epidemics and the repatriation of the millions of homeless people in Europe and the Far East are problems which transcend national boundaries. The control and mobilization of available supplies and the equitable apportionment of these supplies according to the needs of the different areas can also be worked out satisfactorily through collective action. In this way the problems of the occupied countries can be handled in a way which will be fair to all concerned. Although the financial burden which will fall upon the United States under this authorization is large, it cannot seriously be maintained that it is excessive in view of the tremendous scope of the problems which lie ahead of this organization. It is believed that by participating actively in this work the United States can carry out in the field of international action the responsibilities of leadership that lie upon us.

(4) *An Act Making Appropriations . . . for the Participation by the United States in the Work of the United Nations Relief and Rehabilitation Administration . . . for the Fiscal Year Ending June 30, 1945, and for Other Purposes, Approved June 30, 1944* [1]

In a letter of May 3, 1944,[2] President Roosevelt transmitted to Speaker Rayburn of the House of Representatives an estimate of appropriation to enable the United States to participate in the work of UNRRA, as authorized by the Act of March 28, 1944 (Public Law 267), in the amount of $450,000,000, and a proposed provision authorizing the disposition or expenditure by the President of supplies, services, or funds available under the Lend-Lease Act of March 11, 1941, in the amount of $350,000,000.

In the United Nations Relief and Rehabilitation Administration Participation Appropriation Act of June 30, 1944, given below, the President is authorized to expend $450,000,000 and he may dispose of, or expend, supplies, services and funds to the total value of $350,000,000 available under the Lend-Lease Act. The authority to utilize lend-lease supplies, services or funds shall not be exercised until the United States Joint Chiefs of Staff shall certify that the state of the war permits such use. The utilization shall be upon the determination of the Administrator of the Foreign Economic Administration.

TITLE II — UNITED NATIONS RELIEF AND REHABILITATION
ADMINISTRATION

SEC. 201. To enable the President to carry out the provisions of the Act of March 28. 1944 (Public Law 267), and for each and every purpose incident thereto or necessary therefor, $450,000,000, not to exceed $21,790,000 shall be available for procurement of sixty-one million seven hundred thousand pounds of domestic raw wool, or such amount of domestic raw wool as the foregoing sum will purchase, from stock piles of the United States Government existing on the date of the approval of this Act and not to exceed $43,200,000 shall be available for procurement of three hundred and forty-five thousand five hundred bales of domestic cotton, or such amount of domestic cotton as the foregoing sum will purchase, owned by the Commodity Credit Corporation, to be available immediately and to remain available until June 30, 1946: *Provided,* That (1) any sums allocated by the President to any executive department, independent establishment, or agency for any of the purposes

---

[1] Public Law 382, 78th Cong.
[2] House Doc. No. 572, 78th Cong., 2d sess., p. 1.

hereof, from funds appropriated by or authorized to be expended under this title or from funds made available by the United Nations Relief and Rehabilitation Administration, may be expended without regard to those provisions of law waived by law with respect to the expenditure of Government funds by such department, independent establishment, or agency; (2) the appropriations, funds, or accounts of any executive department, independent establishment, or agency shall be reimbursed or credited from sums allocated hereunder, except as hereinafter provided, for any supplies or services procured from such appropriations or funds or by use of such accounts and furnished for any of the purposes hereof; and (3) any supplies or services procured from funds appropriated by or authorized to be expended under this title may be retained by or transferred to any executive department, independent establishment, or agency, and said funds shall be reimbursed from payments made in return therefor by such department, independent establishment, or agency: *Provided further*, That any officer or employee of any executive department, independent establishment, or agency who is detailed to the United Nations Relief and Rehabilitation Administration and compensated hereunder, either directly or by reimbursement of applicable appropriations or funds, shall, while so detailed, retain and be entitled to the rights, benefits, privileges, and status of an officer or employee of the United States and of the Department, independent establishment, or agency from which detailed.

SEC. 202. In addition to the sum appropriated by section 201 of this title, any supplies, services, or funds available for disposition or expenditure by the President under the Act of March 11, 1941, as amended (22 U. S. C. 411–419), and Acts supplementary thereto, may be disposed of or expended by the President to carry out the provisions of the Act of March 28, 1944, without reimbursement of the appropriations from which such supplies or services were procured or such funds were provided: *Provided*, That the supplies, services, and funds disposed of or expended under the authority of this section shall not exceed a total value, as determined under regulations to be approved by the President, of $350,000,000 and shall be charged to the amount authorized to be appropriated by said Act of March 28, 1944: *Provided further*, That the authority granted by this section shall not become effective until the United States Joint Chiefs of Staff shall have issued a certification that the state of war permits the exercise of such authority and the utilization of lend-lease supplies, services, or funds for the purposes of section 201 of this title; and after such certification such utilization shall be upon the determination of the Administrator of the Foreign Economic Administration.

SEC. 203. This title may be cited as "United Nations Relief and Rehabilitation Administration Participation Appropriation Act, 1945."

(5) *Joint Statement of War Department, State Department and Foreign Economic Administration to Subcommittee of House Committee on Appropriations on Relation between Activities of War Department and those of United Nations Relief and Rehabilitation Administration, May 10, 1944* [1]

The exact pattern of the operations which will follow the establishment of the second front in Europe is impossible to foretell. Whatever the eventualities preparation must be made as a matter of military or political necessity, as the case may be, to meet the essential needs of the civilian populations liberated from German control.

Because of the speculative character of military operations, it is not possible at the present time to present to the committee a precise program of the civilian requirements for the various countries in Europe. However, an indication can be given to the committee as to the outlines of the possible needs, to the nature of the several situations which may arise during the initial period, and to the mechanisms which will be available to meet those situations.

Insofar as the armies of the United States participate directly in military engagements, the War Department will provide as an integral part of its supply program this country's share of such supplies as are needed to maintain the civilian populations. The dictates of military necessity and the requirements of international law place upon invading armies the responsibility for the security of civilian populations which fall within their control. In conducting their military operations the armies must take such measures as are necessary to avoid disease, unrest, and interference with supply lines. The War Department is, therefore, including in its appropriation a request for funds to make available essential civilian supplies to the populations in areas which will most probably be affected by our own military operations. Since to a large extent these areas will be the scene of combined operations, the War Department's request for funds covers only the estimated United States' share of the responsibility.

If the opening of the second front precipitates the collapse of Axis resistance, the armies may be able to turn over the control of large sections of Europe to the indigenous governments. In such event the United Nations Relief and Rehabilitation Administration, in cooperation with those governments, or in certain appropriate cases those governments alone, should be able to shoulder the burden of civilian supply.

On the other hand, the Germans may withdraw from certain parts of Europe but continue fighting elsewhere. Military control may be neces-

---

[1] *Hearings before the Subcommittee of the Committee on Appropriations, House of Representatives, on Foreign Economic Administration Appropriation Bill for 1945*, 78th Cong., 2d sess. p. 245.

sary initially, and it will not be possible in practice for the United Nations Relief and Rehabilitation Administration to assume responsibility at the beginning, although it may be called upon at the outset by the military to assist in certain supply activities where the use of its trained personnel is advantageous. Furthermore, in certain areas the necessary military-control authorities may not include any substantial body of United States troops. Where these conditions prevail, it is proposed to procure essential civilian supplies for such areas out of funds appropriated to the Foreign Economic Administration for lend-lease purposes. Under these conditions and upon the request of the War Department, these supplies will be turned over to the War Department, which will assume the responsibility of shipment, and the goods will be distributed under the direction of a responsible allied military authority. It is not now possible to determine the precise areas in which it may prove necessary to use lend-lease funds in this manner to maintain the civilian economy at a minimum level for that presumably brief period in which military control will be necessary. Therefore, no amount has been budgeted for this purpose. Accordingly, this situation represents a contingent requirement for lend-lease funds.

The interested agencies have given careful study to the various situations under which it may be necessary to make civilian supplies available in Europe during the military period. Arrangements similar to those outlined herein are being developed for the Far East.

(a) Supplementary Statement by Assistant Secretary of State Acheson [1]

All the way through the negotiations on the United Nations Relief and Rehabilitation agreement, and all through the resolutions which were passsed at Atlantic City, we have had, under the instructions of the President and the War Department, one very clear rule, right from the very beginning: that no international organization or civilian organization of any sort should be allowed to go into any area which is a scene of military operations until asked to do so by the military authorities. They have no right, no privilege of any kind, of coming into a military area, or doing anything in such an area, where they would be getting in the way of troops in any possible way, unless and until the military commander asks them to come in. That is in the UNRRA agreement; it is in the resolutions, and it is an absolutely firm understanding and policy.

Everybody realizes fully that if military operations are going on, not only the control of the whole area where the operations exist, but in all of the supply lines leading to such military area, whether on the ocean or on land, and all port facilities and transportation facilities, must be in control of the military people, and nobody else should be shipping anything or administering anything or in any way interfering with those operations until they are asked to do so.

That is the underlying conception which goes all the way through here. I just wanted to make that clear to the committee.

[1] *Ibid.*, p. 246.

(6) *Executive Order 9453 on Participation by the United States in the Work of the United Nations Relief and Rehabilitation Administration, July 6, 1944* [1]

By virtue of the authority vested in me as President of the United States by the Constitution and statutes, and in order to facilitate the participation of the United States in the work of the United Nations Relief and Rehabilitation Administration, it is hereby ordered as follows:

1. Subject to such policies and directions as the President may from time to time prescribe, the Administrator of the Foreign Economic Administration is authorized and directed to exercise and perform, through any Executive department, independent establishment, or agency, all the functions and authority with respect to the expenditure of funds, and the provision of supplies and services related thereto, vested in the President by Public Law 267, approved March 28, 1944, and the United Nations Relief and Rehabilitation Administration Participation Appropriation Act, 1945.

2. Subject to the provisions of the Agreement for United Nations Relief and Rehabilitation Administration, concluded November 9, 1943, the United States representative on the Council of the United Nations Relief and Rehabilitation Administration, as named by the President, shall designate or arrange for the designation of United States alternates on the Council and of United States members and alternates on committees and subcommittees of the Council.

3. All activities of the United States Government pertaining to its participation and membership in the United Nations Relief and Rehabilitation Administration shall be carried on in conformity with the foreign policy of the United States as defined by the Secretary of State.

2. WAR REFUGEES

[See *Documents*, V, *1942–43*, p. 286.]

(1) *Executive Order 9417 Establishing a War Refugee Board, January 22, 1944* [2]

The War Refugee Board was set up to take action for the immediate rescue from the Nazis of as many as possible of the persecuted minorities of Europe — racial, religious, or political — all civilian victims of enemy savagery.

The Board is charged with direct responsibility to the President in seeing that the policy announced in the preamble to the order is carried out. The President indicated that while he would look directly to the Board for the successful execution of this policy, the Board, of course, would cooperate fully with the Intergovernmental Committee, the United Nations Relief and Rehabilitation Administration, and other interested international organizations.

[1] 9 *Fed. Reg.*, p. 7637.
[2] *Ibid.*, p. 935; Department of State, *Bulletin*, X, p. 95.

The President stated that he expected to obtain the cooperation of all members of the United Nations and other foreign governments in carrying out this difficult but important task. He stated that the existing facilities of the State, Treasury, and War Departments would be employed to aid Axis victims to the fullest extent possible. He stressed that it was urgent that action be taken at once to forestall the plan of the Nazis to exterminate all the Jews and other persecuted minorities in Europe.

It was announced that it would be the duty of a full-time Executive Director of the Board to arrange for the prompt execution of the plans and programs developed and the measures inaugurated by the Board.

WHEREAS it is the policy of this Government to take all measures within its power to rescue the victims of enemy oppression who are in imminent danger of death and otherwise to afford such victims all possible relief and assistance consistent with the successful prosecution of the war;

Now, THEREFORE, by virtue of the authority vested in me by the Constitution and the statutes of the United States, as President of the United States and as Commander in Chief of the Army and Navy, and in order to effectuate with all possible speed the rescue and relief of such victims of enemy oppression, it is hereby ordered as follows:

1. There is established in the Executive Office of the President a War Refugee Board (hereinafter referred to as the Board). The Board shall consist of the Secretary of State, the Secretary of the Treasury and the Secretary of War. The Board may request the heads of other agencies or departments to participate in its deliberations whenever matters specially affecting such agencies or departments are under consideration.

2. The Board shall be charged with the responsibility for seeing that the policy of the Government, as stated in the Preamble, is carried out. The functions of the Board shall include without limitation the development of plans and programs and the inauguration of effective measures for (a) the rescue, transportation, maintenance and relief of the victims of enemy oppression, and (b) the establishment of havens of temporary refuge for such victims. To this end the Board, through appropriate channels, shall take the necessary steps to enlist the cooperation of foreign governments and obtain their participation in the execution of such plans and programs.

3. It shall be the duty of the State, Treasury and War Departments, within their respective spheres, to execute at the request of the Board, the plans and programs so developed and the measures so inaugurated. It shall be the duty of the heads of all agencies and departments to supply or obtain for the Board such information and to extend to the Board such supplies, shipping and other specified assistance and facilities as the Board may require in carrying out the provisions of this Order. The State Department shall appoint special attaches with diplomatic status, on the recommendation of the Board, to be stationed abroad in places

where it is likely that assistance can be rendered to war refugees, the duties and responsibilities of such attaches to be defined by the board in consultation with the State Department.

4. The Board and the State, Treasury and War Departments are authorized to accept the services or contributions of any private persons, private organizations, State agencies, or agencies of foreign governments in carrying out the purposes of this Order. The Board shall cooperate with all existing and future international organizations concerned with the problems of refugee rescue, maintenance, transportation, relief, rehabilitation, and resettlement.

5. To the extent possible the Board shall utilize the personnel, supplies, facilities and services of the State, Treasury and War Departments. In addition the Board, within the limits of funds which may be made available, may employ necessary personnel without regard for the Civil Service laws and regulations and the Classification Act of 1923, as amended, and make provisions for supplies, facilities and services necessary to discharge its responsibilities. The Board shall appoint an Executive Director who shall serve as its principal executive officer. It shall be the duty of the Executive Director to arrange for the prompt execution of the plans and programs developed and the measures inaugurated by the Board, to supervise the activities of the special attaches and to submit frequent reports to the Board on the steps taken for the rescue and relief of war refugees.

6. The Board shall be directly responsible to the President in carrying out the policy of this Government, as stated in the Preamble, and the Board shall report to him at frequent intervals concerning the steps taken for the rescue and relief of war refugees and shall make such recommendations as the Board may deem appropriate for further action to overcome any difficulties encountered in the rescue and relief of war refugees.

(2) *Statement of the President* (*Roosevelt*) *March 24, 1944* [1]

[Excerpt]

The first part of the President's statement referred to the systematic torture and murder of civilians in occupied countries by the Nazis and Japanese and reasserted the criminal responsibility of those engaged in these acts. For this part of statement, see this volume p. 191.

In the meantime, and until the victory that is now assured is won, the United States will persevere in its efforts to rescue the victims of brutality of the Nazis and the Japs. In so far as the necessity of military operations permits, this Government will use all means at its command to aid the escape of all intended victims of the Nazi and Jap executioner — regard-

[1] *Ibid.*, p. 277.

less of race or religion or color. We call upon the free peoples of Europe and Asia temporarily to open their frontiers to all victims of oppression. We shall find havens of refuge for them, and we shall find the means for their maintenance and support until the tyrant is driven from their homelands and they may return.

In the name of justice and humanity let all freedom-loving people rally to this righteous undertaking.

(3) *Memorandum Sent by the President (Roosevelt) to the Secretaries of War (Stimson), Navy (Knox), and Interior (Ickes), the Director of the Budget (Smith), and the Executive Director of the War Refugee Board (Pehle), June 8, 1944* [1]

There is attached a cable which I have dispatched to Robert Murphy in Algiers, requesting that he make arrangements for the departure to the United States as rapidly as possible of approximately 1,000 refugees now in southern Italy.

These refugees will be brought into this country outside of the regular immigration procedure and placed in Fort Ontario near Oswego, New York. While the War Refugee Board is charged with the overall responsibility for this project, the Army shall take the necessary security precautions so that these refugees will remain in the camp and the actual administration of the camp is to be in the hands of the War Relocation Authority.

Accordingly, the following steps should be taken as expeditiously as possible:

(1) The War Department and the Navy Department shall send whatever instructions are necessary to the military authorities in Italy and North Africa to expedite the transportation of these refugees to the United States.

(2) The War Department shall arrange to furnish and properly equip Fort Ontario to receive these refugees; shall arrange for their transportation from the port of arrival to the camp; and shall arrange for the necessary security precautions.

(3) The War Relocation Authority shall make arrangements to handle the actual administration of the camp, which will be designated as an Emergency Refugee Shelter.

(4) Until UNRRA is in a position to assume the financial responsibilities involved, the Bureau of the Budget shall make arrangements for financing the project; using to the extent possible any available funds of the War Department, the War Relocation Authority, and the War Refugee Board, and from the Foreign War Relief appropriation, and if necessary drawing upon the President's Emergency Fund.

[1] *Ibid.*, p. 532.

(a) Cablegram from the President (Roosevelt) to Ambassador Robert Murphy in Algiers [1]

Information available to me indicates that there are real possibilities of saving human lives by bringing more refugees through Yugoslavia to southern Italy. I am also informed that the escape of refugees by this route has from time to time been greatly impeded because the facilities in southern Italy for refugees have been overtaxed. I am advised that this is the situation at the present moment and that accordingly possibilities of increasing the flow of refugees to Italy may be lost.

I understand that many of the refugees in southern Italy have been and are being moved to temporary havens in areas adjacent to the Mediterranean and that efforts are being made to increase existing refugee facilities in these areas. I am most anxious that this effort to take refugees from Italy to areas relatively close by be intensified.

At the same time I feel that it is important that the United States indicate that it is ready to share the burden of caring for refugees during the war. Accordingly, I have decided that approximately 1,000 refugees should be immediately brought from Italy to this country, to be placed in an Emergency Refugee Shelter to be established at Fort Ontario near Oswego, New York, where under appropriate security restrictions they will remain for the duration of the war. These refugees will be brought into this country outside of the regular immigration procedure just as civilian internees from Latin American countries and prisoners of war have been brought here. The Emergency Refugee Shelter will be well equipped to take good care of these people. It is contemplated that at the end of the war they will be returned to their homelands.

You may assume that the Emergency Refugee Shelter will be ready to receive these refugees when they arrive. I will appreciate it therefore if you will arrange for the departure to the United States as rapidly as possible, consistent with military requirements, of approximately 1,000 refugees in southern Italy. You may call upon representatives of the War Refugee Board in Algiers to assist you in this matter. The full cooperation of our military and naval authorities should be enlisted in effecting the prompt removal and transportation of the refugees.

In choosing the refugees to be brought to the United States, please bear in mind that to the extent possible those refugees should be selected for whom other havens of refuge are not immediately available. I should however like the group to include a reasonable proportion of various categories of persecuted peoples who have fled to Italy.

You should bear in mind that since these refugees are to be placed in a camp in the United States under appropriate security restrictions, the procedure for the selection of the refugees and arrangements for bringing them here should be as simple and expeditious as possible, uncomplicated by any of the usual formalities involved in admitting people to the United States under the immigration laws.

However, please be sure that the necessary health checks are made to avoid bringing here persons afflicted with any loathsome, dangerous or contagious disease.

If you encounter any difficulties in arranging for the prompt departure of these refugees please let me know.

[1] *Ibid.*

(4) *Removal of European Refugees to the United States. Message of the President (Roosevelt) to the Congress, June 12, 1944* [1]

To the Congress of the United States:

Congress has repeatedly manifested its deep concern with the pitiful plight of the persecuted minorities in Europe whose lives are each day being offered in sacrifice on the altar of Nazi tyranny.

This Nation is appalled by the systematic persecution of helpless minority groups by the Nazis. To us the unprovoked murder of innocent people simply because of race, religion or political creed is the blackest of all possible crimes. Since the Nazis began this campaign many of our citizens in all walks of life and of all political and religious persuasions have expressed our feeling of repulsion and our anger. It is a matter with respect to which there is and can be no division of opinion amongst us.

As the hour of the final defeat of the Hitlerite forces draws closer, the fury of their insane desire to wipe out the Jewish race in Europe continues undiminished. This is but one example: Many Christian groups also are being murdered. Knowing that they have lost the war, the Nazis are determined to complete their program of mass extermination. This program is but one manifestation of Hitler's aim to salvage from military defeat victory for Nazi principles — the very principles which this war must destroy unless we shall have fought in vain.

This Government has not only made clear its abhorrence of this inhuman and barbarous activity of the Nazis, but in cooperation with other governments has endeavored to alleviate the condition of the persecuted peoples. In January of this year I determined that this Government should intensify its efforts to combat the Nazi terror. Accordingly, I established the War Refugee Board, composed of the Secretaries of State, Treasury and War. This Board was charged with the responsibility of taking all action consistent with the successful prosecution of the war to rescue the victims of enemy oppression in imminent danger of death and to afford such victims all other possible relief and assistance. It was entrusted with the solemn duty of translating this Government's humanitarian policy into prompt action, thus manifesting once again in a concrete way that our kind of world and not Hitler's will prevail. Its purpose is directly and closely related to our whole war effort.

Since its establishment, the War Refugee Board, acting through a full time administrative staff, has made a direct and forceful attack on the problem. Operating quietly, as is appropriate, the Board, through its representatives in various parts of the world, has actually succeeded in

---

[1] *Congressional Record*, vol. 90, p. 5827 (daily edition, June 12, 1944); Department of State, *Bulletin*, X, p. 553.

saving the lives of innocent people. Not only have refugees been evacuated from enemy territory, but many measures have been taken to protect the lives of those who have not been able to escape.

Above all, the efforts of the Board have brought new hope to the oppressed peoples of Europe. This statement is not idle speculation. From various sources, I have received word that thousands of people, wearied by their years of resistance to Hitler and by their sufferings to the point of giving up the struggle, have been given the will and desire to continue by the concrete manifestation of this Government's desire to do all possible to aid and rescue the oppressed.

To the Hitlerites, their subordinates and functionaries and satellites, to the German people and to all other peoples under the Nazi yoke, we have made clear our determination to punish all participants in these acts of savagery. In the name of humanity we have called upon them to spare the lives of these innocent people.

Notwithstanding this Government's unremitting efforts, which are continuing, the numbers actually rescued from the jaws of death have been small compared with the numbers still facing extinction in German territory. This is due principally to the fact that our enemies, despite all our appeals and our willingness to find havens of refuge for the oppressed peoples, persist in their fiendish extermination campaign and actively prevent the intended victims from escaping to safety.

In the face of this attitude of our enemies we must not fail to take full advantage of any opportunity, however limited, for the rescue of Hitler's victims. We are confronted with a most urgent situation.

Therefore, I wish to report to you today concerning a step which I have just taken in an effort to save additional lives and which I am certain will meet with your approval. You will, I am sure, appreciate that this measure is not only consistent with the successful prosecution of the war, but that it was essential to take action without delay.

Even before the Allied landing in Italy there had been a substantial movement of persecuted peoples of various races and nationalities into that country. This movement was undoubtedly prompted by the fact that, despite all attempts by the Fascists to stir up intolerance, the warm-hearted Italian people could not forsake their centuries-old tradition of tolerance and humanitarianism. The Allied landings swelled this stream of fleeing and hunted peoples seeking sanctuary behind the guns of the United Nations. However, in view of the military situation in Italy, the number of refugees who can be accommodated there is relatively limited. The Allied military forces, in view of their primary responsibility, have not been able, generally speaking, to encourage the escape of refugees from enemy territory. This unfortunate situation has prevented the escape of the largest possible number of refugees. Furthermore, as the number of refugees living in southern Italy increases, their care constitutes an additional and substantial burden for the military authorities.

Recently the facilities for the care of refugees in southern Italy have become so overtaxed that unless many refugees who have already escaped to that area and are arriving daily, particularly from the Balkan countries, can be promptly removed to havens of refuge elsewhere, the escape of refugees to that area from German-occupied territory will be seriously impeded. It was apparent that prompt action was necessary to meet this situation. Many of the refugees in southern Italy have been and are being moved to temporary refuges in the territory of other United and friendly nations. However, in view of the number of refugees still in southern Italy, the problem could not be solved unless temporary havens of refuge were found for some of them in still other areas. In view of this most urgent situation it seemed indispensable that the United States in keeping with our heritage and our ideals of liberty and justice take immediate steps to share the responsibility for meeting the problem.

Accordingly, arrangements have been made to bring immediately to this country approximately 1,000 refugees who have fled from their homelands to southern Italy. Upon the termination of the war they will be sent back to their homelands. These refugees are predominantly women and children. They will be placed on their arrival in a vacated Army camp on the Atlantic Coast where they will remain under appropriate security restrictions.

The Army will take the necessary security precautions and the camp will be administered by the War Relocation Authority. The War Refugee Board is charged with over-all responsibility for this project.

FRANKLIN D. ROOSEVELT

(5) *Proposal for Rescue of Refugees from German Territory. Telegram from the Secretary of State (Hull) to the Chairman of the Emergency Advisory Committee for Political Defense in Montevideo (Dr. Alberto Guani), June 17, 1944* [1]

I have the honor to acknowledge Your Excellency's communication of May 31, transmitting to me a copy of the resolution adopted by the Committee on that date.[2]

I note that this resolution proposes that the American Republics concert and intensify their efforts to rescue from German hands some thousands of oppressed minorities holding non-European documentation; that this be done by joint proposals to exchange German nationals from

---

[1] *Ibid.*, p. 566.
[2] The text of Resolution XXIV has been printed in the *Bulletin of the Pan American Union*, LXXVIII (1944), p. 466.

the American Republics for these persecuted groups; and that such exchanges can be achieved consistently with security considerations surrounding exchanges previously formulated by your Committee in the interests of hemispheric defense.

My Government will be most happy to participate actively in such an inter-American program. In company with some of its sister republics and other governments it has been giving intensive consideration to this problem. The direction and stimulus the Committee's resolution provides for the development of a joint program of larger proportions is most welcome, and is in line with those great humanitarian concepts for which the American Republics stand.

I extend to you and your distinguished colleagues the assurances of my highest consideration.

CHAPTER VII

INTERNATIONAL PEACE AND SECURITY

(1) *Fulbright Resolution (House Concurrent Resolution 25), Passed by the House of Representatives, September 21, 1943* [1]

The resolution (H. Con. Res. 25, 78th Cong., 1st sess.), introduced in the House of Representatives on June 15, 1943, by Congressman J. William Fulbright (D), Arkansas, was an important step in the 78th Congress toward bringing about the establishment of a general international organization to maintain peace and security. The resolution did not commit the United States to take any action, but merely expressed congressional intention to support the idea of American participation. It was reported from the Foreign Affairs Committee on June 16, 1943 (Report No. 553); on September 20 it was debated under a resolution to suspend the rules, which did not permit amendments from the floor, and passed the House on September 21, 1943 by a vote of yeas 360, nays 29, "present" 1, not voting 40.[2]

In its unanimous report the Committee proposed an amendment, adding the words "through its constitutional processes" at the end of the resolution as introduced. The effect of the amendment was a reaffirmation that nothing would be done contrary to the Constitution. Mr. Fulbright stated its purpose on the floor during the debate as follows:[3] "This resolution is not a grant of power to the Executive; it is simply an expression by our people, through their representatives, that we intend to participate sincerely in an effort to bring order into the world. If this resolution is adopted, the Executive can negotiate as to details with assurance that the people are willing to support any reasonable system of collective security. But as the various components of the system are agreed upon by the different governments, they still must be approved by legislation in the nature of treaties or by joint resolution of the Senate and the House of Representatives. This is not a final acceptance now of any agreements that may be evolved."

On September 24 the resolution was referred to the Senate Committee on Foreign Relations. No action was taken by the Committee on House Concurrent Resolution 25, but its purpose was considered in the framing of the Connally Resolution (see p. 316).

Resolved by the House of Representatives (the Senate concurring), That the Congress hereby expresses itself as favoring the creation of appropriate international machinery with power adequate to establish and to maintain a just and lasting peace, among the nations of the world, and as favoring participation by the United States therein through its constitutional processes.

Passed the House of Representatives September 21, 1943.

---

[1] *Congressional Record*, vol. 89, p. 7737–9, 7810, 7813 (daily editions, September 20 and 21, 1943).

[2] *Ibid.*, p. 7810 (daily edition, September 21, 1943).

[3] *Ibid.*, p. 7743 (daily edition, September 20, 1943).

(2) *Connally Resolution* (*Senate Resolution 192, as Amended*), *Passed by the Senate, November 5, 1943* [1]

The legislative efforts to place the United States Congress on record in support of American participation in a general international organization began in the first session of the 78th Congress shortly after it convened on January 6, 1943. At least a dozen resolutions were introduced in the Senate, and several in the House, dealing generally with post-war international aims. The one most widely discussed by the American public was Senate Resolution 114, which was submitted on March 16, 1943 by Senators Joseph H. Ball of Minnesota, Harold H. Burton of Ohio, Lister Hill of Alabama and Carl A. Hatch of New Mexico, and which became popularly known as the "B_2H_2 resolution" because of the initials of its sponsors. The resolution was referred to the Committee on Foreign Relations (for text, see p. 319). The resolution, together with others before the Committee, was referred to a subcommittee of the Committee on Foreign Relations. The subcommittee did not hold public hearings, but the sponsors of the resolutions conferred with its members.

In the House of Representatives opportunity was given for an expression of its opinion on American participation in post-war organization by the introduction of House Concurrent Resolution 25 by Congressman J. William Fulbright of Arkansas (see p. 315).

On July 2, 1943, Senators Vandenberg of Michigan and White of Maine submitted Senate Concurrent Resolution 16 (see p. 319).

During the summer recess of Congress, the whole question of America's post-war aims was presented to the public in speeches by Senator Connally on August 27, by Vice President Wallace on September 11, by Secretary of State Hull on September 12, 1943 (see p. 2), and by some 10 teams of Congressmen, consisting of a member of the Senate and the House in each case, which toured the country explaining the purpose of the "B_2H_2 resolution."

Before Congress reconvened on September 14, some of the Senators who were members of the Senate Committee on Foreign Relations had been active in drafting the resolution on foreign policy adopted on September 7 at the meeting of the Republican Post-War Advisory Council at Mackinac Island. The Mackinac Declaration called for "responsible participation by the United States in post-war cooperative organization among sovereign nations to prevent military aggression and to attain permanent peace with organized justice in a free world."

When the Fulbright Resolution (see p. 315) was referred to the Senate, action was taken on Senate Resolution 192, submitted on October 14 by Senator Connally and referred to the Committee on Foreign Relations. The subcommittee of the Committee on Foreign Relations, appointed to consider the resolutions submitted, reported favorably on S. Res. 192. The Senators sponsoring the "B_2H_2 resolution" appeared before the Committee on Foreign Relations on October 19 and argued for an amendment to make the post-war peace enforcement commitments more definite.

---

[1] The definition of the effect of a Senate resolution as given by the parliamentarian of the Senate and read into the *Congressional Record* by Senator Danaher (Conn.) on October 29, 1943 reads as follows:

"Under the uniform practice of this body, Senate (or simple) resolutions are used in dealing with nonlegislative matters exclusively within the jurisdiction of the Senate, such as expressing opinions or facts, creating and appointing committees of the body, calling on departments for information, reports, etc. They have no legal effect, their passage being attested only by the Secretary of the Senate, and require no action by the House of Representatives. Containing no legislative provisions, they are not presented to the President of the United States for his approval, as in the case of bills and joint resolutions." (*Congressional Record*, vol. 89, p. 9006, daily edition, October 29, 1943.)

On October 21, the Senate Committee on Foreign Relations approved Senate Resolution 192 as introduced. Debate began in the Senate on October 25 and a series of amendments were proposed. Senator Pepper (Fla.) and 13 other Senators, who regarded the language of the Connally resolution as too vague, proposed to change the third paragraph to read:

"That the United States, acting through its constitutional processes, join with the other United Nations and such free and sovereign nations as may be duly admitted, in the establishment and maintenance of an international organization to promote cooperation among nations, with authority to settle international disputes peacefully, and with power, including military force, to suppress military aggression and to preserve the peace of the world." (For third paragraph of S. Res. 192, see p. 318).

On November 1, following the publication by the Department of State of the texts of the declarations signed on October 30 at the Moscow meeting of the Foreign Ministers of the United States, the United Kingdom and the Soviet Union, Senator Connally asked unanimous consent to have these declarations printed in the *Congressional Record*.[1] He stated that "the Moscow agreement in general comports with our war aims, and with our post-war peace aims." A brief statement on the Moscow declaration by the 14 authors of the Pepper amendment was read by Senator Ball (Minn.) in which the Senators said: "We are especially gratified and encouraged at the forthright declarations in the agreement, specifically mentioning the United Nations, reiterating the Atlantic Charter, and calling for 'a general international organization' to maintain peace after the war. These are the kind of clear declarations of principle which we have sought to write into the Connally resolution with our amendment. We hope that the Senate now will be at least as clear and forthright in its expression as the agreement signed at Moscow."[2]

Two days later, after extensive debate in the Senate on the meaning of the language and possible application of the terms used in the resolution, Senator Connally offered, as chairman of the Committee on Foreign Relations, a modification of the original resolution[3] by incorporating point 4 of the Moscow Declaration on General Security and adding a paragraph reiterating the treaty-making procedure of the Senate (see p. 318).

The amendment of Senator Danaher (Conn.) which proposed to add a new section defining all the key words in the resolution was voted down on November 4 by yeas 15, nays 70.

Senator Revercomb (W. Va.) proposed to insert at the end of the fourth paragraph of the resolution as modified, after the words "international peace and security," the following: "That participation by the United States of America in such an organization shall be by treaty only." The amendment was rejected by yeas 28, nays 54.

An amendment proposed by Senator Willis (Ind.) called for the insertion of the following paragraph at the end of the modified resolution:[4]

"That any treaty concluded in accordance with the provisions of this resolution, on behalf of the Government of the United States with any other nation or any association of nations, shall not be binding upon the Government of the United States until a proposal of such treaty shall have been submitted to the United States Senate and concurred in by two-thirds of the Senators present."

However, the amendment was withdrawn as the substance of it was incorporated in the last paragraph of the Connally resolution.

Senator McClellan (Ark.) offered as a substitute for the third paragraph of the resolution the insertion of the following:[5]

[1] *Ibid.*, p. 9025 (daily edition, November 1, 1943).
[2] *Ibid.*, p. 9026.
[3] *Ibid.*, p. 9175 (daily edition, November 3, 1943).
[4] *Congressional Record*, vol. 89, p. 9295 (daily edition, November 5, 1943).
[5] *Ibid.*, p. 9324.

"That the Congress hereby expresses itself as favoring the creation of appropriate international machinery with power adequate to establish and to maintain a just and lasting peace among the nations of the world and as favoring participation by the United States therein through its constitutional processes."

At the request of Senator Connally, who stated that the Committee on Foreign Relations had had the matter before it, the Senate rejected the amendment.

Senator Reynolds (N. C.) proposed to amend by inserting in line 4 after the word "peace" a comma and then the following: "including a guaranty of the independence and territorial integrity of Latvia, Lithuania, Estonia, Poland, Yugoslavia, Greece and other subjugated nations." He also offered an amendment to add the words "agreement, pact, compact, or understanding" as well as "treaty" so that the declarations of any meeting, such as the Moscow Declarations, would have to be adopted by the Senate, two-thirds of the members present approving. The Senator then proposed a substitute resolution setting forth what he termed a "declaration of principles" on which we are willing to proceed with other nations. These amendments and his resolution were rejected.

Senator Eastland (Miss.) proposed an amendment to change the period at the end of the resolution to a semicolon and to add the following: "and since it is recognized that trade and economic collaboration are necessary to assure the maintenance of peace, the United States will cooperate with other nations to promote trade and to remove impediments and restraints which tend to hinder the prosperity of the United States and other nations, and which prevent nations from access upon fair and equitable terms to the raw materials and trade necessary to their national well-being." The amendment was rejected.

The final vote on Senate Resolution 192, as modified, was taken on November 5 and the result was announced as yeas 85, nays 5, not voting 6. A copy was sent to the President for his information.

Resolved, That the war against all our enemies be waged until complete victory is achieved.

That the United States cooperate with its comrades-in-arms in securing a just and honorable peace.

That the United States, acting through its constitutional processes, join with free and sovereign nations in the establishment and maintenance of international authority with power to prevent aggression and to preserve the peace of the world.

That the Senate recognizes the necessity of there being established at the earliest practicable date a general international organization, based on the principle of the sovereign equality of all peace-loving states, and open to membership by all such states, large and small, for the maintenance of international peace and security.

That, pursuant to the Constitution of the United States, any treaty made to effect the purposes of this resolution, on behalf of the Government of the United States with any other nation or any association of nations, shall be made only by and with the advice and consent of the Senate of the United States, provided two-thirds of the Senators present concur.

(a) *Senate Resolution 114, Introduced by Senators Ball* (*Minnesota*), *Hill* (*Alabama*), *Hatch* (*New Mexico*) *and Burton* (*Ohio*), *March 16, 1943* [1]

Resolved, That the Senate advises that the United States take the initiative in calling meetings of representatives of the United Nations for the purpose of forming an organization of the United Nations with specific and limited authority —

(1) To assist in coordinating and fully utilizing the military and economic resources of all member nations in the prosecution of the war against the Axis.

(2) To establish temporary administrations for Axis-controlled areas of the world as these are occupied by United Nations forces, until such time as permanent governments can be established.

(3) To administer relief and assistance in economic rehabilitation in territories of member nations needing such aid and in Axis territory occupied by United Nations forces.

(4) To establish procedures and machinery for peaceful settlement of disputes and disagreements between nations.

(5) To provide for the assembly and maintenance of a United Nations military force and to suppress by immediate use of such force any future attempt at military aggression by any nation.

That the Senate further advises that any establishment of such United Nations organization provide machinery for its modification, for the delegation of additional specific and limited functions to such organization, and for admission of other nations to membership, and that member nations should commit themselves to seek no territorial aggrandizement.

(b) *Senate Concurrent Resolution1 6, Introduced by Senators Vandenberg* (*Michigan*) *and White* (*Maine*), *July 2, 1943* [2]

Resolved by the Senate (*the House of Representatives concurring*), That this Congress favors (1) the prosecution of the war to conclusive victory; (2) the participation by the United States in post-war cooperation between sovereign nations to prevent, by any necessary means, the recurrence of military aggression and to establish permanent peace with justice in a free world; (3) the present examination of these aims, so far as consistent with the united war effort, and their ultimate achievement by due constitutional process and with faithful recognition of American responsibilities and American interests.

(c) *Senate Resolution 192, Introduced by Senator Connally* (*Texas*), *October 14, 1943* [3]

Resolved, That the war against all our enemies be waged until complete victory is achieved.

That the United States cooperate with its comrades-in-arms in securing a just and honorable peace.

That the United States, acting through its constitutional processes, join with free and sovereign nations in the establishment and maintenance of international authority with power to prevent aggression and to preserve the peace of the world.

[1] *Ibid.*, p. 8946 (daily edition, October 28, 1943).
[2] *Ibid.*, p. 8947. This resolution was rejected by the subcommittee of the Committee on Foreign Relations.   [3] *Ibid.*, p. 9319 (daily edition, November 5, 1943).

(d) Report from the Senate Committee on Foreign Relations, to Accompany Senate Resolution 192, October 21, 1943 [1]

The Committee on Foreign Relations, to whom was referred the resolution (S. Res. 192) declaratory of war and peace aims of the United States, having considered the same, report favorably thereon without amendment and recommend that the resolution do pass.

The full text of the resolution is as follows: (See p. 293.)

Your committee have had before it the following resolutions dealing generally with post-war aims of the United States:

1. Senate Resolution 22 by Mr. Wiley: Inviting the President to join with the Senate in creation of a Foreign Relations Advisory Council.
2. Senate Resolution 76 by Mr. Pepper: Authorizing the appointment of a subcommittee of the Committee on Foreign Relations to be known as the Committee on Reoccupation and Reconstruction.
3. Senate Resolution 91 by Mr. Gillette: Approving the basic principles of the Atlantic Charter.
4. Senate Resolution 99 by Mr. Thomas of Utah: Favoring the calling of a conference to formulate a program of international economic cooperation.
5. Senate Resolution 114 by Mr. Ball, Mr. Hill, Mr. Burton and Mr. Hatch: Favoring organization of the United Nations to maintain peace.
6. Senate Concurrent Resolution 10 by Mr. Kilgore: Requesting the President to invite foreign governments to participate in an international constitutional convention to draft a constitution providing for an international government.
7. Senate Resolution 135 by Mr. Pepper: Relating to membership of the United States in the United Nations in order to implement the Atlantic Charter.
8. Senate Joint Resolution 56 by Mr. Thomas of Utah: Relating to the participation of the United States in the establishment of a just and lasting peace.
9. Senate Joint Resolution 60 by Mr. La Follette: Establishing a committee to provide for the formation of a Pan-American Legislative Union.
10. Senate Concurrent Resolution 16 by Mr. Vandenberg and Mr. White: Relating to America's post-war plan.
11. House Concurrent Resolution 25 by Mr. Fulbright: Declaring the sense of the Congress with respect to participation by the United States in prevention of future aggression and the maintenance of peace.
12. Senate Joint Resolution 84 by Mr. Wilson: Requesting the President to invite friendly nations to enter upon consultations with delegates of the United States with a view to the promotion of permanent international peace.

The ultimate objective of all these resolutions is post-war peace. Their authors have made a notable contribution by bringing to the attention of your committee and the country such a variety of approaches to this objective. The committee has also had the benefit of information furnished by numerous peace-loving citizens in the form of letters, briefs, and pamphlets bearing upon the subject matter of this resolution. The committee wishes to thank all these persons for their valuable contributions, which materially aided the committee in its consideration of all aspects of this question. It should also be stated that the committee has had the benefit of the views of members of the Senate not members of the committee who had shown particular interest in this question.

[1] Senate Report No. 478, 78th Cong., 1st sess.

Both in subcommittee and in the full committee this subject has received the most mature consideration. The special subcommittee [1] considering post-war resolutions has worked diligently and with painstaking zeal since its appointment on March 25, 1943. Your committee believes that the resolution reported embodies the objective of these resolutions and will contribute materially to its attainment. Some members of your committee would have preferred modifications in the wording of the resolution. By a large majority, however, the committee voted to report the resolution as introduced.

In reporting this resolution, your committee kept in mind the overwhelming fact of the situation — the fact that complete victory is yet to be won. It seemed proper to reaffirm on behalf of the Senate of the United States the Nation's determination to wage war until such victory is actually achieved. Just as we fight the war in close cooperation with our comrades-in-arms, so do we contemplate that we shall also cooperate with them in securing a just and honorable peace. Finally, the resolution comprehends the establishment of international authority to prevent aggression and preserve the peace of the world.

Your committee recognizes its responsibility in framing a declaration which deals with a subject so vital not only to the people of the United States but to the whole world. It is realized by the committee that it is impossible at this time to blueprint a plan for curing all the ills of the world. Three things, however, are implicit in the resolution — the achieving of complete victory in the present war, cooperation with our comrades-in-arms in securing a just and honorable peace, and finally the establishment and maintenance of international authority with power to prevent aggression and to preserve the peace of the world.

It is hoped that this resolution will be accepted as a forward step in the direction of those objectives by all who believe in peace, and that it will be a contribution to cooperation among the nations of the earth toward the establishment and maintenance of peace.

As an expression of the sentiment of the United States Senate it is highly significant of an advanced and responsible attitude toward foreign relationships.

(e) Amendment to Senate Resolution 192, Proposed by Senator Connally (Texas), and Statements Thereon of Senators Hill (Alabama), Vandenberg (Michigan) and Hatch (New Mexico), November 3, 1943 [2]

Mr. CONNALLY. As chairman of the Committee on Foreign Relations, I have been authorized and directed to offer an amendment to the original resolution, rather an addendum or supplement to it.

Mr. VANDENBERG. An annex.

Mr. CONNALLY. Or, as suggested by the Senator from Michigan, an annex. We do not propose any change in the language of the original resolution, either as to substance or form or punctuation. However, we do propose the following amendment:

Amendment intended to be proposed by Mr. Connally, in line 9 —

I believe it is, or at the end of the resolution to insert the following:

That the Senate recognizes the necessity of there being established at the earliest practicable date a general international organization, based on the

[1] Senators Connally of Texas, George of Georgia, Thomas of Utah, Barkley of Kentucky, Gillette of Iowa, La Follette of Wisconsin, Vandenberg of Michigan and White of Maine.

[2] *Congressional Record*, vol. 89, p. 9175 (daily edition, November 3, 1943).

principle of the sovereign equality of all peace-loving states, and open to membership by all such states, large and small, for the maintenance of international peace and security.

The second paragraph:

That, pursuant to the Constitution of the United States, any treaty made to effect the purposes of this resolution, on behalf of the Government of the United States with any other nation or any association of nations, shall be made only by and with the advice and consent of the Senate of the United States, provided two-thirds of the Senators present concur.

Mr. President, the amendment is not being offered with a view that it in any wise changes the purposes or the principles enunciated in the original resolution, but it is being offered upon the theory that the first paragraph of the present amendment is simply a restatement and a ratification and a confirmation of the language contained in the original resolution, which we think has met with the general approval not only of the people of the United States, but of foreign nations and their representatives.

With respect to the second paragraph, which refers to the necessity for the Senate acting upon any treaties, we do not think that that was legally necessary, because in the original resolution we used the language, "United States, through its constitutional processes." When that language was used, we used it with the specific intent of saying that this Government could act only through its constitutional processes, one of which is that any treaty negotiated by the Executive must be negotiated with the advice and consent of the Senate. That is still our view. We do not think it was necessary to add this supplement; but certain Senators were rather disturbed by some fear that this might be construed as a ratification in advance. We have seen fit to recognize their views in that respect, and to make perfectly clear what we intended in the original resolution. I hope that these views will meet with the approval of Members of the Senate.

.   .   .   .

Mr. HILL. Mr. President, I wish to congratulate the distinguished Senator from Texas (Mr. CONNALLY), chairman of the committee, and the Foreign Relations Committee, on this action modifying the resolution so as to embody the language proposed by the Senator from Texas. The language embodies, practically verbatim ad literatim, point 4 of the Moscow Conference declaration. It embodies the point of that declaration which deals with our post-war policy and plan.

Those of us who have supported Senate Resolution 114 ever since March 16 last have felt that the basis of our whole post-war policy should be a general international organization. A general international organization, open to all nations, has been the foundation and framework of all that we have contended for and all that we have fought for. In my opinion other provisions of Senate Resolution 114 must and will inevitably follow the establishment of a general international organization. I shall wholeheartedly support the resolution as now modified by the distinguished chairman of the committee. I hope that the resolution may be brought to a speedy vote.

.   .   .   .

Mr. VANDENBERG. The able Senator from Alabama has stated the theory upon which his group has accepted the composite whole which the Senator from Texas is now presenting. I simply wish to add, from the standpoint of the subcommittee which has been laboring with this subject for many months — and I think I speak for every member of the subcommittee — that we have accepted it because in our judgment there is absolutely nothing in it which was not comprehended and encompassed by the original resolution.

. . . .

Mr. HATCH. The point which the Senator from Michigan has just raised is one which I wish to stress. Of course this amendment or modification was worked out in consultation with those of us who have been advocating other amendments and other proposals. In accordance with the interpretationswhich have been given here on the floor of the Senate to Senate Resolution 192, I believe that what the Senator from Michigan has just said is correct. However, Mr. President, some of us have not always interpreted the resolution in just that way. The modification makes clear some of those things which we thought it was essential to make clear.

At least the offering of this modification by the chairman of the Committee on Foreign Relations gives to the resolution, as now modified, a common ground upon which all can stand who are truly desirous of having an expression of the United States Senate toward the general aims and objectives which the proponents of Senate Resolution 192 claim for it, and also the objectives which we who sponsored certain amendments claimed for our amendments.

Mr. President, I see no reason why we cannot all unite in support of the resolution as modified.

. . . .

(3) *Declaration of Four Nations on General Security, Moscow, October 30, 1943*

[See p. 229.]

(4) *Foreign Policy of the United States of America. Radio Address by the Secretary of State (Hull), April 9, 1944* [1]

[Excerpt]

In this way we are proceeding with the matter of an international organization to maintain peace and prevent aggression. Such an organization must be based upon firm and binding obligations that the member nations will not use force against each other and against any other nation except in accordance with the arrangements made. It must provide for the maintenance of adequate forces to preserve peace and it must provide the institutions and procedures for calling this force into action to preserve peace. But it must provide more than this. It must provide for an international court for the development and application of law to the settlement of international controversies which fall within the realm of law, for the development of machinery for adjusting controversies to which the field of law has not yet been extended, and for other institutions for the development of new rules to keep abreast of a changing world with new problems and new interests.

We are at a stage where much of the work of formulating plans for the organization to maintain peace has been accomplished. . . .

[1] Department of State, *Bulletin*, X, p. 340; for full text see this volume, p. 25.

(5) *Foreign Affairs of the United States in Wartime and After. Address by Assistant Secretary of State Long, April 12, 1944* [1]

[Excerpt]

I have emphasized the dominant part that the war and its winning must play in the application of our current foreign policy. But, essential as is the total defeat of the Axis, that is not and cannot be the sole great objective. There are two others with which American foreign policy must be concerned — the prevention of future wars and the promotion of conditions which will permit our people to attain the greatest possible measure of economic well-being.

I should like to speak briefly of our preparations for the future in these two broad fields, of the establishment of an effective system of international peace and security, and of the creation of conditions and agencies for the promotion of economic and social welfare.

For some time the Department of State, in cooperation with other agencies of the Government, in collaboration with individual members of the Congress, and in consultation with individuals of experience in private life, has been engaged in studying these questions and in formulating the bases for constructive programs of action.

A thorough analysis of the mistakes of the unhappy past, a study of current developments, and an examination of future possibilities have led us to the following conclusions as regards some of the basic problems involved in the future prevention of aggression and war:

1. The major nations together with the other law-abiding states should create an international organization for the maintenance of peace and security.

2. The major nations — and in due course all nations — should pledge themselves not to use force against each other or against any other nation, except on the basis of arrangements made in connection with such an international organization.

3. Each of the major nations, and any other nations to be agreed upon, should accept special responsibility for maintaining adequate forces and for using such forces, on the basis of arrangements made in connection with the international organization, to prevent or suppress all disturbances of the peace.

Our basic thought is that a general international organization of sovereign nations, having for its primary objective the maintenance of peace and security, should comprise effective agencies and arrangements for the pacific settlement of international controversies, for joint use of force to suppress disturbances of the peace, and for fostering cooperative effort among nations for the progressive improvement of the general

[1] Delivered before the American Federation of Labor Forum on Labor and the Post-war World, New York, N. Y., Department of State, *Bulletin*, X, p. 342.

welfare. The organization should at the outset provide the indispensable minimum of machinery of action and should be expected to develop and grow as time goes on and as circumstances may indicate to be wise. It is clear that there must be some general body on which all member states will be equally represented to serve as a world assembly of nations. There must be a court of international justice. And there must be a small body or council, representative of the large and small nations, endowed with adequate powers and means to arrange for maintaining the peace.

The step in the direction of creating an effective general international organization was taken at Moscow. The four-nation declaration signed there constitutes a solemn declaration of intention on the part of the four major countries to act in common for the preservation of peace and security and to take the lead in the establishment of a permanent international organization for this basic purpose. The next step had to be a joint examination of the problems involved in setting up such an organization.

Our studies in preparation for discussion with other governments, which were well advanced before the Moscow Conference, have been intensively carried forward since. They have involved a careful examination of the various alternatives with respect to the structure, powers, and procedures of an international organization. They have involved also an examination of our constitutional processes as regards participation by this country in the creation and functioning of such an organization, including especially the providing of armed forces for international action.

The next step involves additional conferences with representatives of both parties in the Congress and thereafter a full exchange of views with other governments and, in accordance with our constitutional provisions, discussions at home — all looking toward an agreed proposal for an effective international security organization.

.   .   .   .

(6) *Post-War Security Organization Program. Statement of the President (Roosevelt), June 15, 1944* [1]

The conference today with officials of the Department of State on the post-war security organization program is a continuation of conferences which have been held from time to time during the past 18 months. These conferences have enabled me to give personal attention to the development and progress of the post-war work the Department of State is doing.

All plans and suggestions from groups, organizations, and individuals have been carefully discussed and considered. I wish to emphasize the

[1] *Ibid.*, p. 552.

entirely non-partisan nature of these consultations. All aspects of the post-war program have been debated in a cooperative spirit. This is a tribute to the political leaders who realize that the national interest demands a national program now. Such teamwork has met the overwhelming approval of the American people.

The maintenance of peace and security must be the joint task of all peace-loving nations. We have, therefore, sought to develop plans for an international organization comprising all such nations. The purpose of the organization would be to maintain peace and security and to assist the creation, through international cooperation, of conditions of stability and well-being necessary for peaceful and friendly relations among nations.

Accordingly, it is our thought that the organization would be a fully representative body with broad responsibilities for promoting and facilitating international cooperation, through such agencies as may be found necessary, to consider and deal with the problems of world relations. It is our further thought that the organization would provide for a council, elected annually by the fully representative body of all nations, which would include the four major nations and a suitable number of other nations. The council would concern itself with peaceful settlement of international disputes and with the prevention of threats to the peace or breaches of the peace.

There would also be an international court of justice to deal primarily with justiciable disputes.

We are not thinking of a superstate with its own police forces and other paraphernalia of coercive power. We are seeking effective agreement and arrangements through which the nations would maintain, according to their capacities, adequate forces to meet the needs of preventing war and of making impossible deliberate preparation for war and to have such forces available for joint action when necessary.

All this, of course, will become possible once our present enemies are defeated and effective arrangements are made to prevent them from making war again.

Beyond that, the hope of a peaceful and advancing world will rest upon the willingness and ability of the peace-loving nations, large and small, bearing responsibility commensurate with their individual capacities, to work together for the maintenance of peace and security.

CHAPTER VIII

TRADE AND FINANCE

1. PRINCIPLES OF POST-WAR ECONOMIC POLICY

See also statements contained in the addresses by Secretary of State Hull on American foreign policy, delivered September 12, 1943 (p. 2) and April 9, 1944 (p. 25), and the Memorandum given to the press on March 21, 1944 with the title *"Bases of the Foreign Policy of the United States"* (p. 21).

(1) *Statement of the Secretary of State (Hull), May 19, 1944* [1]

Since National Foreign-Trade Week was observed last year the war against the aggressors has approached its most crucial stage. Ultimate collapse of the armed forces of our enemies is certain, and we can hasten that collapse if we continue to maintain, at every moment, our utmost effort in complete unity with the other nations associated with us in this war.

The coming victory throws into clearer and sharper focus some of the tremendous tasks and problems which we shall face at the end of hostilities. Without relaxing our war effort in the slightest degree, we must give profound thought to post-war problems and begin to take steps which will help to solve them. We must hold fast to a clear vision of the security and well-being for which we are fighting and work toward effective means to preserve them after they have been won.

National Foreign-Trade Week is a most appropriate occasion for taking stock of our situation. Employment on the home-front is at an all-time high. Many millions now employed in making the things with which war is waged will need good jobs after the war making peacetime products, as will many millions now serving in our armed forces. Private enterprise will, I believe, meet this challenge with courage and resourcefulness. I believe, also, that the great majority of American businessmen will recognize the need, as well as the unique opportunity, for utilizing our enormous capacity in the production of the kinds of peacetime goods best suited to our material and human resources; for choosing those lines of production that can stand on their own feet without heavy tariff protection or subsidies.

---

[1] Made in connection with the observance of National Foreign-Trade Week, May 21-27. Department of State, *Bulletin*, X, p. 479.

Only as people everywhere have opportunity to produce those things and perform those tasks for which they are best fitted and to exchange those products for the products of other people at home or abroad, will the world have the maximum supplies of things to be enjoyed. This can be achieved only as we cooperate with other like-minded nations, as we are cooperating now in war, to provide a basis for expanding trade and commerce among nations on a sound and equitable basis.

The shift from wartime to peacetime commerce will undoubtedly entail some rather difficult adjustments both in our domestic economy and in our economic relations with other countries. Those adjustments must not involve such blunders as occurred after World War I when we, as well as other nations, adopted commercial policies and took economic measures that disregarded and injured the citizens of other countries. Neither this country nor the world could stand a repetition of the bitter resentment among nations, the retaliatory actions, and the economic chaos and depression which finally helped to plunge us into this war.

After this war, international economic relations must be developed through cooperative measures. There must be international arrangement for currency stability as an aid to commerce and the settlement of international financial transactions. Through international investment, capital must be made available for the sound development of latent natural resources and productive capacity in relatively undeveloped areas. Above all, provision must be made for reduction or removal of unreasonable trade barriers and for the abandonment of trade discriminations in all forms.

Such an international system of trade and financial relations, embodying sound economic standards and the principles of justice, must be created and made effective in order to support any international organization that may be set up to keep and enforce the peace. Otherwise, the structure of international security would be threatened with collapse as a result of economic disorder and conflict.

Leadership toward a new system of international relationships in trade and other economic affairs will devolve very largely upon the United States because of our great economic strength. We should assume this leadership, and the responsibility that goes with it, primarily for reasons of pure national self-interest. We ourselves cannot live in prosperity and security in our own country while people in other countries are suffering want and being driven to despair by economic hardship. If we are to have jobs for all our workers and markets for all our goods people in other countries must likewise have opportunity to produce to their maximum capacity and to pay us, with the fruits of their efforts, for the things we want to sell them.

The Government of the United States and other United Nations Governments are endeavoring to make as rapid progress as possible toward the objectives set forth in the Atlantic Charter, and the mutual-aid agreements, and the Moscow and Tehran Declarations.[1] In carrying out this great task they need and must have the support of the people whose interests they serve.

In this matter foreign traders have a special responsibility extending far beyond the mere safe-guarding and enhancement of their own business interests. They have a special knowledge of foreign trade and its place as a necessary support of international prosperity and world security. They can contribute much to the establishment of a sound system of trade relations among nations by sharing their knowledge and understanding with other citizens and groups. Observance of National Foreign-Trade Week is one means of carrying out this responsibility.

2. TRADE AGREEMENTS

[See *Documents, I, 1938–39*, p. 334; *II, 1939–40*, p. 448; *III, 1940–41*, p. 459; *IV, 1941–42*, p. 693; *V, 1942–43*, p. 616.]

During the period July 1, 1943 to June 30, 1944, a reciprocal trade agreement, negotiated under the authority of the Trade Agreements Act, was signed with the Government of Iceland on August 27, 1943.[2] The President's proclamation of this trade agreement and the instrument of ratification of the Regent of Iceland were exchanged on October 20, 1943.[3] The agreement entered into force on November 19, 1943.[4]

On October 19, the Acting Secretary of State gave formal notice of intention to negotiate a supplementary trade agreement with the Government of Cuba,[5] but on December 16 the Secretary of State announced that, after consultation with the Government of Cuba, a decision had been reached not to conclude this proposed supplementary agreement.[6]

On May 29, 1944, the Secretary of State and the Minister of Iran in Washington exchanged the President's proclamation and the Iranian instrument of ratification of the reciprocal trade agreement of April 8, 1943.[7] This agreement entered into force on June 28, 1944.[8]

[1] See this volume, p. 229 and 235.
[2] Department of State, *Bulletin*, IX, p. 133. For analysis of provisions, see *ibid.*
[3] *Ibid.*, p. 283; *Executive Agreement Series* 342.
[4] *Ibid.*
[5] Department of State, *Bulletin*, IX, p. 281.
[6] *Ibid.*, p. 431.
[7] *Ibid.*, X, p. 521.
[8] *Ibid.*

(1) *Reciprocal Trade Agreements Entered into under the Trade Agreements Act of 1934, as of June 30, 1944* [1]

COUNTRY	DATE SIGNED	DATE EFFECTIVE	EXECUTIVE AGREEMENT SERIES
Cuba	Aug. 24, 1934	Sept. 3, 1934	67
Brazil	Feb. 2, 1935	Jan. 1, 1936	82
Belgium (and Luxemburg) . .	Feb. 27, 1935	May 1, 1935	75
Haiti	Mar. 28, 1935	Jun. 3, 1935	78
Sweden	May 25, 1935	Aug. 5, 1935	79
Colombia	Sept. 13, 1935	May 20, 1936	89
Canada (see revised agreement below)	Nov. 15, 1935	Jan. 1, 1936	91
Honduras	Dec. 18, 1935	Mar. 2, 1936	86
Kingdom of the Netherlands (Netherlands in Europe, Netherlands India, Surinam and Curaçao).	Dec. 20, 1935	Feb. 1, 1936	100
Switzerland	Jan. 9, 1936	Feb. 15, 1936	90, 193
Nicaragua [2]	Mar. 11, 1936	Oct. 1, 1936	95, 120
Guatemala	Apr. 24, 1936	Jun. 15, 1936	92
France and its colonies, dependencies and protectorates other than Morocco	May 6, 1936	Jun. 15, 1936	146
Finland	May 18, 1936	Nov. 2, 1936	97
Costa Rica	Nov. 28, 1936	Aug. 2, 1937	102
El Salvador	Feb. 19, 1937	May 31, 1937	101
Czechoslovakia [3]	Mar. 7, 1938	Apr. 16, 1938	147
Ecuador	Aug. 6, 1938	Oct. 23, 1938	133
United Kingdom, including Newfoundland and the British Colonial Empire	Nov. 17, 1938	Jan. 1, 1939	164
Canada (revision of agreement of 1935)	Nov. 17, 1938	Jan. 1, 1939	149, 170
Turkey	Apr. 1, 1939	May 5, 1939	163
Venezuela	Nov. 6, 1939	Dec. 16, 1939	180
Cuba (first supplementary agreement)	Dec. 18, 1939	Dec. 23, 1939	165
Canada (supplementary fox fur agreement) [4]	Dec. 13, 1940	Dec. 20, 1940	216
Argentina	Oct. 14, 1941	Nov. 15, 1941 [5]	277
Cuba (second supplementary agreement)	Dec. 23, 1941	Jan. 5, 1942	229
Peru	May 7, 1942	Jul. 29, 1942	256
Uruguay	Jul. 21, 1942	Jan. 1, 1943	276
Mexico	Dec. 23, 1942	Jan. 30, 1943	311
Iran	Apr. 8, 1943	Jun. 28, 1944	410
Iceland	Aug. 27, 1943	Nov. 19, 1943	342
Turkey (application of Art. I of agreement of Apr. 1, 1939) . .	Apr. 14 and 22, 1944	Apr. 22, 1944	406

[1] Based on information received from Department of State.

[2] The duty concessions and certain other provisions of the trade agreement ceased to be in force as of March 10, 1938.

[3] The operation of this agreement was suspended as of April 22, 1939.

[4] This replaced a previous supplementary agreement relating to fox furs, signed on December 30, 1939. (*Executive Agreement Series* 184).

[5] Effective definitively January 8, 1943.

(2) *Trade Agreements in Process of Negotiation as of June 30, 1944* [1]

COUNTRY	DATE OF ISSUANCE OF PUBLIC NOTICE	LATEST DATE FOR SUBMITTING WRITTEN STATEMENTS	OPENING DATE OF PUBLIC HEARINGS
Bolivia [2]	Apr. 4, 1942	May 4, 1942	May 18, 1942
Paraguay	Jun. 23, 1943	Jul. 23, 1943	Aug. 4, 1943

3. MONETARY AND FINANCIAL COOPERATION

(1) *Final Act of the United Nations Monetary and Financial Conference, Bretton Woods, New Hampshire, July 1–22, 1944* [3]

A "Preliminary Draft Outline of Proposal for a United and Associated Nations Stabilization Fund" [4] was drawn up by technical experts in the Treasury Department, under the direction of Mr. Harry D. White, and published April 7, 1943. On April 8 there was published a British proposal, drafted by Treasury experts in consultation with other departments, under the direction of Baron Keynes.[5]

On August 20, 1943, the United States Treasury Department made public a revised draft of a tentative proposal for an international stabilization fund, prepared by technical experts of the Treasury in cooperation with monetary experts from nearly 30 other countries.[6] The revised draft was regarded as a preliminary document. It was stated that it had not received the official approval of the Treasury Department or of the Government.[7] The revision had been preceded by exploratory discussions which had been continuing in Washington since March 1943, in response to an invitation from the Secretary of the Treasury to the finance ministers of the United Nations.[8]

As a result of these exploratory discussions, an agreement was reached at the expert level on a "Joint Statement" [9] recommending the establishment of an International Monetary Fund as the most practical method of ensuring international monetary cooperation. Secretary of the Treasury Morgenthau made a "program report" to seven committees of the Senate and the House of Representatives on April 21.[10] In a foreword to the Joint Statement, Secretary of the Treasury Morgenthau stated that the tentative proposals were "part of a broad program for cooperation on international economic problems among the United

---

[1] Based on information received from Department of State.

[2] Inactive.

[3] *United Nations Monetary and Financial Conference, Final Act, Bretton Woods, New Hampshire, July 1 to July 22, 1944*, Department of State Publication 2187 (Conference Series 55).

[4] Washington, U. S. Treasury, April 7, 1943.

[5] *International Clearing Union. Text of a Paper Containing Proposals by British Experts for an International Clearing Union*, British Information Services, N. Y., April 8, 1943.

[6] *Preliminary Draft Outline of a Proposal for an International Stabilization Fund of the United and Associated Nations*, Washington, U. S. Treasury. Revised July 10, 1943.

[7] Department of State, *Bulletin*, IX, p. 112.

[8] *Documents, V, 1942–43*, p. 652.

[9] *Joint Statement by Experts on the Establishment of an International Monetary Fund of the United and Associated Nations*. Washington, U. S. Treasury, April 21, 1944.

[10] *New York Times*, April 22, 1944.

Nations," the objectives of which are "the expansion and development of international trade, the revival of orderly and stable exchange rates, and the elimination of discriminatory exchange practices that hamper world trade." In a statement made on April 22, Secretary of State Hull commended the purposes of the proposed plan, and while he made it clear that no Government had as yet accepted this particular plan or these particular principles, he expressed the view that the proposed principles constituted a framework within which a workable plan could be developed.[1] He concluded:

"If such programs can be put in operation before the end of the war, we will save much time in the task of bringing about domestic and world-wide prosperity when hostilities cease, and immeasurably strengthen the prospects of an enduring peace."

Plans for a Bank for International Reconstruction and Development were somewhat later in developing. The first draft[2] was prepared by the technical staff of the United States Treasury in consultation with the technical staffs of other Departments of the Government. The proposal had neither official status nor the approval of any Department of this Government. It was in outline form, touching on the more important points, and was intended only to stimulate thoughtful discussion of the problem in the hope that such discussion would call forth constructive criticism, suggestions and alternative proposals for possible later submission to the appropriate authorities and to the public. A United Nations Bank for Reconstruction and Development was proposed as another international agency needed to help attain and maintain world-wide prosperity after the war. It was designed as a companion agency to an International Stabilization Fund.

Secretary of the Treasury Morgenthau told Congressional Committees about the plan at a joint secret session on October 5, 1943. A Treasury Department release dated October 4 on "Guiding Principles for a Proposed United Nations Bank for Reconstruction and Development" was given to the American press following the publication of a story by *The Financial News* (London).[3]

Invitations were extended to all the United Nations and the nations associated with them in the war by the Secretary of State on May 26, 1944,[4] requesting them to send official representatives to a conference at Bretton Woods, New Hampshire on July 1, 1944, for a discussion of precise proposals for an international monetary fund and a bank for reconstruction and development. The President on June 23 announced the names of the American delegates to the Conference as follows:[5] Henry Morgenthau, Jr., Secretary of the Treasury, *chairman;* Fred M. Vinson, Director, Office of Economic Stabilization, *vice chairman;* Dean Acheson, Assistant Secretary of State; Edward E. Brown, President, First National Bank of Chicago; Leo T. Crowley, Administrator, Foreign Economic Administration; Marriner S. Eccles, Chairman, Board of Governors of the Federal Reserve System; Miss Mabel Newcomer, Professor of Economics, Vassar College; Brent Spense, House of Representatives, Chairman, Committee on Banking and Currency; Charles W. Tobey, United States Senate, Member, Committee on Banking and Currency; Robert F. Wagner, United States Senate, Chairman, Committee on Banking and Currency; Harry D. White, Assistant to the Secretary of the Treasury; and Jesse P. Wolcott, House of Representatives, Member, Committee on Banking and Currency.

A preliminary conference of experts to get the drafts to be discussed at Bretton Woods into improved shape was held at Atlantic City immediately preceding the convening of the Bretton Woods Conference.

[1] Department of State, *Bulletin,* X, p. 371.

[2] *Preliminary Draft Outline of a Proposal for a Bank for Reconstruction and Development of the United and Associated Nations.* Washington, U. S. Treasury, November 29, 1943.

[3] *New York Times,* October 9, 1943.

[4] Department of State, *Bulletin,* X, p. 498.

[5] *Ibid.,* p. 587.

The Governments of Australia, Belgium, Bolivia, Brazil, Canada, Chile, China, Colombia, Costa Rica, Cuba, Czechoslovakia, Dominican Republic, Ecuador, Egypt, El Salvador, Ethiopia; the French Delegation; the Governments of Greece, Guatemala, Haiti, Honduras, Iceland, India, Iran, Iraq, Liberia, Luxemburg, Mexico, Netherlands, New Zealand, Nicaragua, Norway, Panama, Paraguay, Peru, Philippine Commonwealth, Poland, Union of South Africa, Union of Soviet Socialist Republics, United Kingdom, United States of America, Uruguay, Venezuela, and Yugoslavia;

Having accepted the invitation extended to them by the Government of the United States of America to be represented at a United Nations Monetary and Financial Conference;

Appointed their respective delegates, who are listed below by countries in the order of alphabetical precedence:

[Here follows list of delegates.]

Who met at Bretton Woods, New Hampshire, on July 1, 1944, under the Temporary Presidency of The Honorable Henry Morgenthau, Jr., Chairman of the Delegation of the United States of America.

The Honorable Henrik de Kauffmann, Danish Minister at Washington, attended the Inaugural Plenary Session in response to an invitation of the Government of the United States to be present in a personal capacity. The Conference, on the proposal of its Committee on Credentials, extended a similar invitation for the remaining sessions of the Conference.

The Economic, Financial, and Transit Department of the League of Nations, the International Labor Office, the United Nations Interim Commission on Food and Agriculture, and the United Nations Relief and Rehabilitation Administration were each represented by one observer at the Inaugural Plenary Session. Their representation was in response to an invitation of the Government of the United States, and either the observers or their alternates attended the subsequent sessions in accordance with the resolution presented by the Committee on Credentials and adopted by the Conference. The observers and their alternates are listed below:

[Here follows list of names.]

[The description of the organization of the Conference [1] is omitted.]

The Final Plenary Session was held on July 22, 1944. As a result of the deliberations, as recorded in the minutes and reports of the respective

[1] The important committees for the purpose of transacting the business of the Conference were the Steering Committee (Mr. Morgenthau, chairman), the Coordinating Committee (Mr. Vinson, U. S. A., chairman), and three Technical Commissions: Commission I — International Monetary Fund (Mr. White, U. S. A., chairman); Commission II — Bank for Reconstruction and Development (Lord Keynes, U. K., chairman); and Commission III — Other Means of International Financial Cooperation (M. Suárez, Mex., chairman).

Commissions and their Committees and of the Plenary Sessions, the following instruments were drawn up:

INTERNATIONAL MONETARY FUND

Articles of Agreement of the International Monetary Fund, which are attached hereto as Annex A.[1]

INTERNATIONAL BANK FOR RECONSTRUCTION AND DEVELOPMENT

Articles of Agreement of the International Bank for Reconstruction and Development, which are attached hereto as Annex B.[2]

Summary of the Agreements in Annex A and Annex B, which is attached hereto as Annex C.[3]

The following resolutions, statement, and recommendations were adopted:

I. PREPARATION OF THE FINAL ACT

The United Nations Monetary and Financial Conference

RESOLVES:

That the Secretariat be authorized to prepare the Final Act in accordance with the suggestions proposed by the Secretary General in *Journal* No. 19, July 19, 1944;

That the Final Act contain the definitive texts of the conclusions approved by the Conference in plenary session, and that no changes be made therein at the Closing Plenary Session;

That the Coordinating Committee review the text and, if approved, submit it to the Final Plenary Session.

II. PUBLICATION OF DOCUMENTATION

The United Nations Monetary and Financial Conference

RESOLVES:

That the Government of the United States of America be authorized to publish the Final Act of this Conference; the Reports of the Commissions; the Minutes of the Public Plenary Sessions; and to make available for publication such additional documents in connection with the work of this Conference as in its judgment may be considered in the public interest.

---

[1] See this volume, p. 338.

[2] *Ibid.*, p. 373.

[3] *United Nations Monetary and Financial Conference, Bretton Woods, N. H., July 1 to July 22, 1944. Final Act and Related Documents.* Washington, D. C., 1944, Department of State Publication 2187 (Conference Series 55), p. 98.

III. Notification of Signatures and Custody of Deposits

The United Nations Monetary and Financial Conference

Resolves:

To request the Government of the United States of America

(1) as depository of the Articles of Agreement of the International Monetary Fund, to inform the Governments of all countries whose names are set forth in Schedule A of the Articles of Agreement of the International Monetary Fund, and all Governments whose membership is approved in accordance with Article II, Section 2, of all signatures of the Articles of Agreement; and

(2) to receive and to hold in a special deposit account gold or United States dollars transmitted to it in accordance with Article XX, Section 2 (d), of the Articles of Agreement of the International Monetary Fund, and to transmit such funds to the Board of Governors of the Fund when the initial meeting has been called.

IV. Statement Regarding Silver

The problems confronting some nations as a result of the wide fluctuation in the value of silver were the subject of serious discussion in Commission III. Due to the shortage of time, the magnitude of the other problems on the agenda, and other limiting considerations, it was impossible to give sufficient attention to this problem at this time in order to make definite recommendations. However, it was the sense of Commission III that the subject should merit further study by the interested nations.

V. Liquidation of the Bank for International Settlements

The United Nations Monetary and Financial Conference

Recommends:

The liquidation of the Bank for International Settlements at the earliest possible moment.

VI. Enemy Assets and Looted Property

Whereas, in anticipation of their impending defeat, enemy leaders, enemy nationals and their collaborators are transferring assets to and through neutral countries in order to conceal them and to perpetuate their influence, power, and ability to plan future aggrandizement and world domination, thus jeopardizing the efforts of the United Nations to establish and permanently maintain peaceful international relations;

Whereas, enemy countries and their nationals have taken the property of occupied countries and their nationals by open looting and plunder, by forcing transfers under duress, as well as by subtle and complex devices, often operated through the agency of their puppet governments, to give the cloak of legality to their robbery and to secure ownership and control of enterprises in the post-war period;

Whereas, enemy countries and their nationals have also, through sales and other methods of transfer, run the chain of their ownership and control through occupied and neutral countries, thus making the problem of disclosure and disentanglement one of international character;

Whereas, the United Nations have declared their intention to do their utmost to defeat the methods of dispossession practiced by the enemy, have reserved their right to declare invalid any transfers of property belonging to persons within occupied territory, and have taken measures to protect and safeguard property, within their respective jurisdictions, owned by occupied countries and their nationals, as well as to prevent the disposal of looted property in United Nations markets; therefore

The United Nations Monetary and Financial Conference

1. Takes note of and fully supports steps taken by the United Nations for the purpose of:

(*a*) uncovering, segregating, controlling, and making appropriate disposition of enemy assets;

(*b*) preventing the liquidation of property looted by the enemy, locating and tracing ownership and control of such looted property, and taking appropriate measures with a view to restoration to its lawful owners;

2. RECOMMENDS:

That all Governments of countries represented at this Conference take action consistent with their relations with the countries at war to call upon the Governments of neutral countries

(*a*) To take immediate measures to prevent any disposition or transfer within territories subject to their jurisdiction of any

(1) assets belonging to the Government or any individuals or institutions within those United Nations occupied by the enemy; and

(2) looted gold, currency, art objects, securities, other evidences of ownership in financial or business enterprises, and of other assets looted by the enemy;

as well as to uncover, segregate and hold at the disposition of the post-liberation authorities in the appropriate country any such assets within territory subject to their jurisdiction;

(b) to take immediate measures to prevent the concealment by fraudulent means or otherwise within countries subject to their jurisdiction of any

(1) assets belonging to, or alleged to belong to, the Government of and individuals or institutions within enemy countries;

(2) assets belonging to, or alleged to belong to, enemy leaders, their associates and collaborators; and

to facilitate their ultimate delivery to the post-armistice authorities.

VII. International Economic Problems

Whereas, in Article I of the Articles of Agreement of the International Monetary Fund it is stated that one of the principal purposes of the Fund is to facilitate the expansion and balanced growth of international trade, and to contribute thereby to the promotion and maintenance of high levels of employment and real income and to the development of the productive resources of all members as primary objectives of economic policy;

Whereas, it is recognized that the complete attainment of this and other purposes and objectives stated in the Agreement cannot be achieved through the instrumentality of the Fund alone; therefore

The United Nations Monetary and Financial Conference

Recommends:

To the participating Governments that, in addition to implementing the specific monetary and financial measures which were the subject of this Conference, they seek, with a view to creating in the field of international economic relations conditions necessary for the attainment of the purposes of the Fund and of the broader primary objectives of economic policy, to reach agreement as soon as possible on ways and means whereby they may best:

(1) reduce obstacles to international trade and in other ways promote mutually advantageous international commercial relations;

(2) bring about the orderly marketing of staple commodities at prices fair to the producer and consumer alike;

(3) deal with the special problems of international concern which will arise from the cessation of production for war purposes; and

(4) facilitate by cooperative effort the harmonization of national policies of Member States designed to promote and maintain high levels of employment and progressively rising standards of living.

VIII

The United Nations Monetary and Financial Conference

RESOLVES:

1. To express its gratitude to the President of the United States, Franklin D. Roosevelt, for his initiative in convening the present Conference and for its preparation;

2. To express to its President, The Honorable Henry Morgenthau, Jr., its deep appreciation for the admirable manner in which he has guided the Conference;

3. To express to the Officers and Staff of the Secretariat its appreciation for their untiring services and diligent efforts in contributing to the attainment of the objectives of the Conference.

IN WITNESS WHEREOF, the following delegates sign the present Final Act.

DONE at Bretton Woods, New Hampshire, on the twenty-second day of July, nineteen hundred and forty-four, in the English language, the original to be deposited in the archives of the Department of State of the United States, and certified copies thereof to be furnished by the Government of the United States of America to each of the Governments and Authorities represented at the Conference.

[Signatures follow here.]

(a) Articles of Agreement of the International Monetary Fund

The Governments on whose behalf the present Agreement is signed agree as follows:

INTRODUCTORY ARTICLE

The International Monetary Fund is established and shall operate in accordance with the following provisions:

ARTICLE I. PURPOSES

The purposes of the International Monetary Fund are:

(i) To promote international monetary cooperation through a permanent institution which provides the machinery for consultation and collaboration on international monetary problems.

(ii) To facilitate the expansion and balanced growth of international trade, and to contribute thereby to the promotion and maintenance of high levels of employment and real income and to the development of the productive resources of all members as primary objectives of economic policy.

(*iii*) To promote exchange stability, to maintain orderly exchange arrangements among members, and to avoid competitive exchange depreciation.

(*iv*) To assist in the establishment of a multilateral system of payments in respect of current transactions between members and in the elimination of foreign exchange restrictions which hamper the growth of world trade.

(*v*) To give confidence to members by making the Fund's resources available to them under adequate safeguards, thus providing them with opportunity to correct maladjustments in their balance of payments without resorting to measures destructive of national or international prosperity.

(*vi*) In accordance with the above, to shorten the duration and lessen the degree of disequilibrium in the international balances of payments of members.

The Fund shall be guided in all its decisions by the purposes set forth in this Article.

ARTICLE II. MEMBERSHIP

Section 1. *Original members*

The original members of the Fund shall be those of the countries represented at the United Nations Monetary and Financial Conference whose governments accept membership before the date specified in Article XX, Section 2 (*e*).

Section 2. *Other members*

Membership shall be open to the governments of other countries at such times and in accordance with such terms as may be prescribed by the Fund.

ARTICLE III. QUOTAS AND SUBSCRIPTIONS

Section 1. *Quotas*

Each member shall be assigned a quota. The quotas of the members represented at the United Nations Monetary and Financial Conference which accept membership before the date specified in Article XX, Section 2 (*e*), shall be those set forth in Schedule A. The quotas of other members shall be determined by the Fund.

Section 2. *Adjustment of quotas*

The Fund shall at intervals of five years review, and if it deems it appropriate propose an adjustment of, the quotas of the members. It may also, if it thinks fit, consider at any other time the adjustment of any particular quota at the request of the member concerned. A four-fifths majority of the total voting power shall be required for any change in quotas and no quota shall be changed without the consent of the member concerned.

Section 3. *Subscriptions: time, place, and form of payment*

(*a*) The subscription of each member shall be equal to its quota and shall be paid in full to the Fund at the appropriate depository on or before the date when the member becomes eligible under Article XX, Section 4 (*c*) or (*d*), to buy currencies from the Fund.

(*b*) Each member shall pay in gold, as a minimum, the smaller of

(*i*) twenty-five percent of its quota; or

(*ii*) ten percent of its net official holdings of gold and United States dollars as at the date when the Fund notifies members under Article XX, Section 4 (*a*) that it will shortly be in a position to begin exchange transactions.

Each member shall furnish to the Fund the data necessary to determine its net official holdings of gold and United States dollars.

(*c*) Each member shall pay the balance of its quota in its own currency.

(*d*) If the net official holdings of gold and United States dollars of any member as at the date referred to in (*b*) (*ii*) above are not ascertainable because its territories have been occupied by the enemy, the Fund shall fix an appropriate alternative date for determining such holdings. If such date is later than that on which the country becomes eligible under Article XX, Section 4 (*c*) or (*d*), to buy currencies from the Fund, the Fund and the member shall agree on a provisional gold payment to be made under (*b*) above, and the balance of the member's subscription shall be paid in the member's currency, subject to appropriate adjustment between the member and the Fund when the net official holdings have been ascertained.

Section 4. *Payments when quotas are changed*

(*a*) Each member which consents to an increase in its quota shall, within thirty days after the date of its consent, pay to the Fund twenty-five percent of the increase in gold and the balance in its own currency. If, however, on the date when the member consents to an increase, its monetary reserves are less than its new quota, the Fund may reduce the proportion of the increase to be paid in gold.

(*b*) If a member consents to a reduction in its quota, the Fund shall, within thirty days after the date of the consent, pay to the member an amount equal to the reduction. The payment shall be made in the member's currency and in such amount of gold as may be necessary to prevent reducing the Fund's holdings of the currency below seventy-five percent of the new quota.

Section 5. *Substitution of securities for currency*

The Fund shall accept from any member in place of any part of the member's currency which in the judgment of the Fund is not needed for its operations, notes or similar obligations issued by the member or the depository designated by the member under Article XIII, Section 2, which shall be non-negotiable, non-interest bearing and payable at their par value on demand by crediting the account of the Fund in the designated depository. This Section shall apply not only to currency subscribed by members but also to any currency otherwise due to, or acquired by, the Fund.

ARTICLE IV. PAR VALUES OF CURRENCIES

Section 1. *Expression of par values*

(a) The par value of the currency of each member shall be expressed in terms of gold as a common denominator or in terms of the United States dollar of the weight and fineness in effect on July 1, 1944.

(b) All computations relating to currencies of members for the purpose of applying the provisions of this Agreement shall be on the basis of their par values.

Section 2. *Gold purchases based on par values*

The Fund shall prescribe a margin above and below par value for transactions in gold by members, and no member shall buy gold at a price above par value plus the prescribed margin, or sell gold at a price below par value minus the prescribed margin.

Section 3. *Foreign exchange dealings based on parity*

The maximum and the minimum rates for exchange transactions between the currencies of members taking place within their territories shall not differ from parity

      (i) in the case of spot exchange transactions, by more than one percent; and

     (ii) in the case of other exchange transactions, by a margin which exceeds the margin for spot exchange transactions by more than the Fund considers reasonable.

Section 4. *Obligations regarding exchange stability*

(a) Each member undertakes to collaborate with the Fund to promote exchange stability, to maintain orderly exchange arrangements with other members, and to avoid competitive exchange alterations.

(b) Each member undertakes, through appropriate measures consistent with this Agreement, to permit within its territories exchange transactions between its currency and the currencies of other members only within the limits prescribed under Section 3 of this Article. A member whose monetary authorities, for the settlement of international transactions, in fact freely buy and sell gold within the limits prescribed by the Fund under Section 2 of this Article shall be deemed to be fulfilling this undertaking.

Section 5. *Changes in par values*

(a) A member shall not propose a change in the par value of its currency except to correct a fundamental disequilibrium.

(b) A change in the par value of a member's currency may be made only on the proposal of the member and only after consultation with the Fund.

(c) When a change is proposed, the Fund shall first take into account the changes, if any, which have already taken place in the initial par value of the member's currency as determined under Article XX, Section 4. If the proposed change, together with all previous changes, whether increases or decreases,

(i) does not exceed ten percent of the initial par value, the Fund shall raise no objection,

(ii) does not exceed a further ten percent of the initial par value, the Fund may either concur or object, but shall declare its attitude within seventy-two hours if the member so requests,

(iii) is not within (i) or (ii) above, the Fund may either concur or object, but shall be entitled to a longer period in which to declare its attitude.

(d) Uniform changes in par values made under Section 7 of this Article shall not be taken into account in determining whether a proposed change falls within (i), (ii), or (iii) of (c) above.

(e) A member may change the par value of its currency without the concurrence of the Fund if the change does not affect the international transactions of members of the Fund.

(f) The Fund shall concur in a proposed change which is within the terms of (c) (ii) or (c) (iii) above if it is satisfied that the change is necessary to correct a fundamental disequilibrium. In particular, provided it is so satisfied, it shall not object to a proposed change because of the domestic social or political policies of the member proposing the change.

Section 6. *Effect of unauthorized changes*

If a member changes the par value of its currency despite the objection of the Fund, in cases where the Fund is entitled to object, the member shall be ineligible to use the resources of the Fund unless the Fund otherwise determines; and if, after the expiration of a reasonable period, the difference between the member and the Fund continues, the matter shall be subject to the provisions of Article XV, Section 2 (*b*).

Section 7. *Uniform changes in par values*

Notwithstanding the provisions of Section 5 (*b*) of this Article, the Fund by a majority of the total voting power may make uniform proportionate changes in the par values of the currencies of all members, provided each such change is approved by every member which has ten percent or more of the total of the quotas. The par value of a member's currency shall, however, not be changed under this provision if, within seventy-two hours of the Fund's action, the member informs the Fund that it does not wish the par value of its currency to be changed by such action.

Section 8. *Maintenance of gold value of the Fund's assets*

(*a*) The gold value of the Fund's assets shall be maintained notwithstanding changes in the par or foreign exchange value of the currency of any member.

(*b*) Whenever (*i*) the par value of a member's currency is reduced, or (*ii*) the foreign exchange value of a member's currency has, in the opinion of the Fund, depreciated to a significant extent within that member's territories, the member shall pay to the Fund within a reasonable time an amount of its own currency equal to the reduction in the gold value of its currency held by the Fund.

(*c*) Whenever the par value of a member's currency is increased, the Fund shall return to such member within a reasonable time an amount in its currency equal to the increase in the gold value of its currency held by the Fund.

(*d*) The provisions of this Section shall apply to a uniform proportionate change in the par values of the currencies of all members, unless at the time when such a change is proposed the Fund decides otherwise.

Section 9. *Separate currencies within a member's territories*

A member proposing a change in the par value of its currency shall be deemed, unless it declares otherwise, to be proposing a corresponding change in the par value of the separate currencies of all territories in respect of which it has accepted this Agreement under Article XX, Section 2 (*g*). It shall, however, be open to a member to declare that its proposal relates either to the metropolitan currency alone, or only to one or more specified separate currencies, or to the metropolitan currency and one or more specified separate currencies.

ARTICLE V. TRANSACTIONS WITH THE FUND

Section 1. *Agencies dealing with the Fund*

Each member shall deal with the Fund only through its Treasury, central bank, stabilization fund, or other similar fiscal agency and the Fund shall deal only with or through the same agencies.

Section 2. *Limitation on the Fund's operations*

Except as otherwise provided in this Agreement, operations on the account of the Fund shall be limited to transactions for the purpose of supplying a member, on the initiative of such member, with the currency of another member in exchange for gold or for the currency of the member desiring to make the purchase.

Section 3. *Conditions governing use of the Fund's resources*

(a) A member shall be entitled to buy the currency of another member from the Fund in exchange for its own currency subject to the following conditions:

  (i) The member desiring to purchase the currency represents that it is presently needed for making in that currency payments which are consistent with the provisions of this Agreement;

  (ii) The Fund has not given notice under Article VII, Section 3, that its holdings of the currency desired have become scarce;

  (iii) The proposed purchase would not cause the Fund's holdings of the purchasing member's currency to increase by more than twenty-five percent of its quota during the period of twelve months ending on the date of the purchase nor to exceed two hundred percent of its quota, but the twenty-five percent limitation shall apply only to the extent that the Fund's holdings of the member's currency have been brought above seventy-five percent of its quota if they had been below that amount;

  (iv) The Fund has not previously declared under Section 5 of this Article, Article IV, Section 6, Article VI, Section 1, or Article XV, Section 2 (a), that the member desiring to purchase is ineligible to use the resources of the Fund.

(b) A member shall not be entitled without the permission of the Fund to use the Fund's resources to acquire currency to hold against forward exchange transactions.

Section 4. *Waiver of conditions*

The Fund may in its discretion, and on terms which safeguard its interests, waive any of the conditions prescribed in Section 3 (a) of this Article, especially in the case of members with a record of avoiding large or continuous use of the Fund's resources. In making a waiver it shall take into consideration periodic or exceptional requirements of the member requesting the waiver. The Fund shall also take into consideration a member's willingness to pledge as collateral security gold, silver, securities, or other acceptable assets having a value sufficient in the opinion of the Fund to protect its interests and may require as a condition of waiver the pledge of such collateral security.

Section 5. *Ineligibility to use the Fund's resources*

Whenever the Fund is of the opinion that any member is using the resources of the Fund in a manner contrary to the purposes of the Fund, it shall present to the member a report setting forth the views of the Fund and prescribing a suitable time for reply. After presenting such a report to a member, the Fund may limit the use of its resources by the member. If no reply to the report is received from the member within the prescribed time, or if the reply received is unsatisfactory, the Fund may continue to limit the member's use of the Fund's resources or may, after giving reasonable notice to the member, declare it ineligible to use the resources of the Fund.

Section 6. *Purchases of currencies from the Fund for gold*

(a) Any member desiring to obtain, directly or indirectly, the currency of another member for gold shall, provided that it can do so with equal advantage, acquire it by the sale of gold to the Fund.

(b) Nothing in this Section shall be deemed to preclude any member from selling in any market gold newly produced from mines located within its territories.

Section 7. *Repurchase by a member of its currency held by the Fund*

(a) A member may repurchase from the Fund and the Fund shall sell for gold any part of the Fund's holdings of its currency in excess of its quota.

(b) At the end of each financial year of the Fund, a member shall repurchase from the Fund with gold or convertible currencies, as determined in accordance with Schedule B, part of the Fund's holdings of its currency under the following conditions:

    (i) Each member shall use in repurchases of its own currency from the Fund an amount of its monetary reserves equal in value to one-half of any increase that has occurred during the year in the Fund's holdings of its currency plus one-half of any increase, or minus one-half of any decrease, that has occurred during the year in the member's monetary reserves. This rule shall not apply when a member's monetary reserves have decreased during the year by more than the Fund's holdings of its currency have increased.

(*ii*) If after the repurchase described in (*i*) above (if required) has been made, a member's holdings of another member's currency (or of gold acquired from that member) are found to have increased by reason of transactions in terms of that currency with other members or persons in their territories, the member whose holdings of such currency (or gold) have thus increased shall use the increase to repurchase its own currency from the Fund.

(*c*) None of the adjustments described in (*b*) above shall be carried to a point at which

(*i*) the member's monetary reserves are below its quota, or

(*ii*) the Fund's holdings of its currency are below seventy-five percent of its quota, or

(*iii*) the Fund's holdings of any currency required to be used are above seventy-five percent of the quota of the member concerned.

Section 8. *Charges*

(*a*) Any member buying the currency of another member from the Fund in exchange for its own currency shall pay a service charge uniform for all members of three-fourths percent in addition to the parity price. The Fund in its discretion may increase this service charge to not more than one percent or reduce it to not less than one-half percent.

(*b*) The Fund may levy a reasonable handling charge on any member buying gold from the Fund or selling gold to the Fund.

(*c*) The Fund shall levy charges uniform for all members which shall be payable by any member on the average daily balances of its currency held by the Fund in excess of its quota. These charges shall be at the following rates:

(*i*) *On amounts not more than twenty-five percent in excess of the quota:* no charge for the first three months; one-half percent per annum for the next nine months; and thereafter an increase in the charge of one-half percent for each subsequent year.

(*ii*) *On amounts more than twenty-five percent and not more than fifty percent in excess of the quota:* an additional one-half percent for the first year; and an additional one-half percent for each subsequent year.

(*iii*) *On each additional bracket of twenty-five percent in excess of the quota:* an additional one-half percent for the first year; and an additional one-half percent for each subsequent year.

(*d*) Whenever the Fund's holdings of a member's currency are such that the charge applicable to any bracket for any period has reached the rate of four percent per annum, the Fund and the member shall consider means by which the Fund's holdings of the currency can be reduced. Thereafter, the charges shall rise in accordance with the provisions of (c) above until they reach five percent and failing agreement, the Fund may then impose such charges as it deems appropriate.

(e) The rates referred to in (c) and (d) above may be changed by a three-fourths majority of the total voting power.

(f) All charges shall be paid in gold. If, however, the member's monetary reserves are less than one-half of its quota, it shall pay in gold only that proportion of the charges due which such reserves bear to one-half of its quota, and shall pay the balance in its own currency.

ARTICLE VI. CAPITAL TRANSFERS

Section 1. *Use of the Fund's resources for capital transfers*

(a) A member may not make net use of the Fund's resources to meet a large or sustained outflow of capital, and the Fund may request a member to exercise controls to prevent such use of the resources of the Fund. If, after receiving such a request, a member fails to exercise appropriate controls, the Fund may declare the member ineligible to use the resources of the Fund.

(b) Nothing in this Section shall be deemed

    (i) to prevent the use of the resources of the Fund for capital transactions or reasonable amount required for the expansion of exports or in the ordinary course of trade, banking or other business, or

    (ii) to affect capital movements which are met out of a member's own resources of gold and foreign exchange, but members undertake that such capital movements will be in accordance with the purposes of the Fund.

Section 2. *Special provisions for capital transfers*

If the Fund's holdings of the currency of a member have remained below seventy-five percent of its quota for an immediately preceding period of not less than six months, such member, if it has not been declared ineligible to use the resources of the Fund under Section 1 of this Article, Article IV, Section 6, Article V, Section 5, or Article XV, Section 2 (a), shall be entitled, notwithstanding the provisions of Section 1 (a) of this Article, to buy the currency of another member from the Fund with its own currency for any purpose, including capital transfers. Purchases for capital transfers under this Section shall not, however, be permitted if they have the effect of raising the Fund's holdings of the currency of the member desiring to purchase above seventy-five percent of its quota, or of reducing the Fund's holdings of the currency desired below seventy-five percent of the quota of the member whose currency is desired.

Section 3. *Controls of capital transfers*

Members may exercise such controls as are necessary to regulate international capital movements, but no member may exercise these controls in a manner which will restrict payments for current transactions or which will unduly delay transfers of funds in settlement of commitments, except as provided in Article VII, Section 3 (*b*), and in Article XIV, Section 2.

ARTICLE VII. SCARCE CURRENCIES

Section 1. *General scarcity of currency*

If the Fund finds that a general scarcity of a particular currency is developing, the Fund may so inform members and may issue a report setting forth the causes of the scarcity and containing recommendations designed to bring it to an end. A representative of the member whose currency is involved shall participate in the preparation of the report.

Section 2. *Measures to replenish the Fund's holdings of scarce currencies*

The Fund may, if it deems such action appropriate to replenish its holdings of any member's currency, take either or both of the following steps:

(*i*) Propose to the member that, on terms and conditions agreed between the Fund and the member, the latter lend its currency to the Fund or that, with the approval of the member, the Fund borrow such currency from some other source either within or outside the territories of the member, but no member shall be under any obligation to make such loans to the Fund or to approve the borrowing of its currency by the Fund from any other source.

(*ii*) Require the member to sell its currency to the Fund for gold.

Section 3. *Scarcity of the Fund's holdings*

(*a*) If it becomes evident to the Fund that the demand for a member's currency seriously threatens the Fund's ability to supply that currency, the Fund, whether or not it has issued a report under Section 1 of this Article, shall formally declare such currency scarce and shall thenceforth apportion its existing and accruing supply of the scarce currency with due regard to the relative needs of members, the general international economic situation, and any other pertinent considerations. The Fund shall also issue a report concerning its action.

(*b*) A formal declaration under (*a*) above shall operate as an authorization to any member, after consultation with the Fund, temporarily to impose limitations on the freedom of exchange operations in the scarce currency. Subject to the provisions of Article IV, Sections 3 and 4, the member shall have complete jurisdiction in determining the nature of such limitations, but they shall be no more restrictive than is necessary to limit the demand for the scarce currency to the supply held by, or accruing to, the member in question; and they shall be relaxed and removed as rapidly as conditions permit.

(*c*) The authorization under (*b*) above shall expire whenever the Fund formally declares the currency in question to be no longer scarce.

Section 4. *Administration of restrictions*

Any member imposing restrictions in respect of the currency of any other member pursuant to the provisions of Section 3 (*b*) of this Article shall give sympathetic consideration to any representations by the other member regarding the administration of such restrictions.

Section 5. *Effect of other international agreements on restrictions*

Members agree not to invoke the obligations of any engagements entered into with other members prior to this Agreement in such a manner as will prevent the operation of the provisions of this Article.

ARTICLE VIII. GENERAL OBLIGATIONS OF MEMBERS

Section 1. *Introduction*

In addition to the obligations assumed under other articles of this Agreement, each member undertakes the obligations set out in this Article.

Section 2. *Avoidance of restrictions on current payments*

(*a*) Subject to the provisions of Article VII, Section 3 (*b*), and Article XIV, Section 2, no member shall, without the approval of the Fund, impose restrictions on the making of payments and transfers for current international transactions.

(*b*) Exchange contracts which involve the currency of any member and which are contrary to the exchange control regulations of that member maintained or imposed consistently with this Agreement shall be unenforceable in the territories of any member. In addition, members may, by mutual |accord, cooperate in measures for the purpose of making the exchange control regulations of either member more effective, provided that such measures and regulations are consistent with this Agreement.

Section 3. *Avoidance of discriminatory currency practices*

No member shall engage in, or permit any of its fiscal agencies referred to in Article V, Section 1, to engage in, any discriminatory currency arrangements or multiple currency practices except as authorized under this Agreement or approved by the Fund. If such arrangements and practices are engaged in at the date when this Agreement enters into force the member concerned shall consult with the Fund as to their progressive removal unless they are maintained or imposed under Article XIV, Section 2, in which case the provisions of Section 4 of that Article shall apply.

Section 4. *Convertibility of foreign-held balances*

(*a*) Each member shall buy balances of its currency held by another member if the latter, in requesting the purchase, represents

   (*i*) that the balances to be bought have been recently acquired as a result of current transactions; or

   (*ii*) that their conversion is needed for making payments for current transactions.

The buying member shall have the option to pay either in the currency of the member making the request or in gold.

(*b*) The obligation in (*a*) above shall not apply

   (*i*) when the convertibility of the balances has been restricted consistently with Section 2 of this Article, or Article VI, Section 3; or

   (*ii*) when the balances have accumulated as a result of transactions effected before the removal by a member of restrictions maintained or imposed under Article XIV, Section 2; or

   (*iii*) when the balances have been acquired contrary to the exchange regulations of the member which is asked to buy them; or

   (*iv*) when the currency of the member requesting the purchase has been declared scarce under Article VII, Section 3 (*a*); or

   (*v*) when the member requested to make the purchase is for any reason not entitled to buy currencies of other members from the Fund for its own currency.

Section 5. *Furnishing of information*

(*a*) The Fund may require members to furnish it with such information as it deems necessary for its operations, including, as the minimum necessary for the effective discharge of the Fund's duties, national data on the following matters:

   (*i*) Official holdings at home and abroad, of (1) gold, (2) foreign exchange.

(*ii*) Holdings at home and abroad by banking and financial agencies, other than official agencies, of (1) gold, (2) foreign exchange.

(*iii*) Production of gold.

(*iv*) Gold exports and imports according to countries of destination and origin.

(*v*) Total exports and imports of merchandise, in terms of local currency values, according to countries of destination and origin.

(*vi*) International balance of payments, including (1) trade in goods and services, (2) gold transactions, (3) known capital transactions, and (4) other items.

(*vii*) International investment position, *i.e.*, investments within the territories of the member owned abroad and investments abroad owned by persons in its territories so far as it is possible to furnish this information.

(*viii*) National income.

(*ix*) Price indices, *i.e.*, indices of commodity prices in wholesale and retail markets and of export and import prices.

(*x*) Buying and selling rates for foreign currencies.

(*xi*) Exchange controls, *i.e.*, a comprehensive statement of exchange controls in effect at the time of assuming membership in the Fund and details of subsequent changes as they occur.

(*xii*) Where official clearing arrangements exist, details of amounts awaiting clearance in respect of commercial and financial transactions, and of the length of time during which such arrears have been outstanding.

(*b*) In requesting information the Fund shall take into consideration the varying ability of members to furnish the data requested. Members shall be under no obligation to furnish information in such detail that the affairs of individuals or corporations are disclosed. Members undertake, however, to furnish the desired information in as detailed and accurate a manner as is practicable, and, so far as possible, to avoid mere estimates.

(*c*) The Fund may arrange to obtain further information by agreement with members. It shall act as a centre for the collection and exchange of information on monetary and financial problems, thus facilitating the preparation of studies designed to assist members in developing policies which further the purposes of the Fund.

Section 6. *Consultation between members regarding existing international agreements*

Where under this Agreement a member is authorized in the special or temporary circumstances specified in the Agreement to maintain or establish restrictions on exchange transactions, and there are other engagements between members entered into prior to this Agreement which conflict with the application of such restrictions, the parties to such engagements will consult with one another with a view to making such mutually acceptable adjustments as may be necessary. The provisions of this Article shall be without prejudice to the operation of Article VII, Section 5.

ARTICLE IX. STATUS, IMMUNITIES AND PRIVILEGES

Section 1. *Purposes of Article*

To enable the Fund to fulfill the functions with which it is entrusted, the status, immunities and privileges set forth in this Article shall be accorded to the Fund in the territories of each member.

Section 2. *Status of the Fund*

The Fund shall possess full juridical personality, and, in particular, the capacity:

(*i*) to contract;

(*ii*) to acquire and dispose of immovable and movable property;

(*iii*) to institute legal proceedings.

Section 3. *Immunity from judicial process*

The Fund, its property and its assets, wherever located and by whomsoever held, shall enjoy immunity from every form of judicial process except to the extent that it expressly waives its immunity for the purpose of any proceedings or by the terms of any contract.

Section 4. *Immunity from other action*

Property and assets of the Fund, wherever located and by whomsoever held, shall be immune from search, requisition, confiscation, expropriation or any other form of seizure by executive or legislative action.

Section 5. *Immunity of archives*

The archives of the Fund shall be inviolable.

Section 6. *Freedom of assets from restrictions*

To the extent necessary to carry out the operations provided for in this Agreement, all property and assets of the Fund shall be free from restrictions, regulations, controls and moratoria of any nature.

Section 7. *Privilege for communications*

The official communications of the Fund shall be accorded by members the same treatment as the official communications of other members.

Section 8. *Immunities and privileges of officers and employees*

All governors, executive directors, alternates, officers and employees of the Fund

 (*i*) shall be immune from legal process with respect to acts performed by them in their official capacity except when the Fund waives this immunity.

 (*ii*) not being local nationals, shall be granted the same immunities from immigration restrictions, alien registration requirements and national service obligations and the same facilities as regards exchange restrictions as are accorded by members to the representatives, officials, and employees of comparable rank of other members.

 (*iii*) shall be granted the same treatment in respect of travelling facilities as is accorded by members to representatives, officials and employees of comparable rank of other members.

Section 9. *Immunities from taxation*

(*a*) The Fund, its assets, property, income and its operations and transactions authorized by this Agreement, shall be immune from all taxation and from all customs duties. The Fund shall also be immune from liability for the collection or payment of any tax or duty.

(*b*) No tax shall be levied on or in respect of salaries and emoluments paid by the Fund to executive directors, alternates, officers or employees of the Fund who are not local citizens, local subjects, or other local nationals.

(*c*) No taxation of any kind shall be levied on any obligation or security issued by the Fund, including any dividend or interest thereon, by whomsoever held

 (*i*) which discriminates against such obligation or security solely because of its origin; or

 (*ii*) if the sole jurisdictional basis for such taxation is the place or currency in which it is issued, made payable or paid, or the location of any office or place of business maintained by the Fund.

Section 10. *Application of Article*

Each member shall take such action as is necessary in its own territories for the purpose of making effective in terms of its own law the principles set forth in this Article and shall inform the Fund of the detailed action which it has taken.

ARTICLE X. RELATIONS WITH OTHER INTERNATIONAL ORGANIZATIONS

The Fund shall cooperate within the terms of this Agreement with any general international organization and with public international organizations having specialized responsibilities in related fields. Any arrangements for such cooperation which would involve a modification of any provision of this Agreement may be effected only after amendment to this Agreement under Article XVII.

ARTICLE XI.   RELATIONS WITH NON-MEMBER COUNTRIES

Section 1. *Undertakings regarding relations with non-member countries*

Each member undertakes:

(*i*) Not to engage in, nor to permit any of its fiscal agencies referred to in Article V, Section 1, to engage in, any transactions with a non-member or with persons in a non-member's territories which would be contrary to the provisions of this Agreement or the purposes of the Fund;

(*ii*) Not to cooperate with a non-member or with persons in a non-member's territories in practices which would be contrary to the provisions of this Agreement or the purposes of the Fund; and

(*iii*) To cooperate with the Fund with a view to the application in its territories of appropriate measures to prevent transactions with non-members or with persons in their territories which would be contrary to the provisions of this Agreement or the purposes of the Fund.

Section 2. *Restrictions on transactions with non-member countries*

Nothing in this Agreement shall affect the right of any member to impose restrictions on exchange transactions with non-members or with persons in their territories unless the Fund finds that such restrictions prejudice the interests of members and are contrary to the purposes of the Fund.

ARTICLE XII.   ORGANIZATION AND MANAGEMENT

Section 1. *Structure of the Fund*

The Fund shall have a Board of Governors, Executive Directors, a Managing Director and a staff.

Section 2. *Board of Governors*

(*a*) All powers of the Fund shall be vested in the Board of Governors, consisting of one governor and one alternate appointed by each member in such manner as it may determine. Each governor and each alternate shall serve for five years, subject to the pleasure of the member appointing him, and may be reappointed. No alternate may vote except in the absence of his principal. The Board shall select one of the governors as chairman.

(*b*) The Board of Governors may delegate to the Executive Directors authority to exercise any powers of the Board, except the power to:

(*i*) Admit new members and determine the conditions of their admission.

(*ii*) Approve a revision of quotas.

(*iii*) Approve a uniform change in the par value of the currencies of all members.

(*iv*) Make arrangements to cooperate with other international organizations (other than informal arrangements of a temporary or administrative character).

(*v*) Determine the distribution of the net income of the Fund.

(*vi*) Require a member to withdraw.

(*vii*) Decide to liquidate the Fund.

(*viii*) Decide appeals from interpretations of this Agreement given by the Executive Directors.

(*c*) The Board of Governors shall hold an annual meeting and such other meetings as may be provided for by the Board or called by the Executive Directors. Meetings of the Board shall be called by the Directors whenever requested by five members or by members having one quarter of the total voting power.

(*d*) A quorum for any meeting of the Board of Governors shall be a majority of the governors exercising not less than two-thirds of the total voting power.

(*e*) Each governor shall be entitled to cast the number of votes allotted under Section 5 of this Article to the member appointing him.

(*f*) The Board of Governors may by regulation establish a procedure whereby the Executive Directors, when they deem such action to be in the best interests of the Fund, may obtain a vote of the governors on a specific question without calling a meeting of the Board.

(*g*) The Board of Governors, and the Executive Directors to the extent authorized, may adopt such rules and regulations as may be necessary or appropriate to conduct the business of the Fund.

(*h*) Governors and alternates shall serve as such without compensation from the Fund, but the Fund shall pay them reasonable expenses incurred in attending meetings.

(*i*) The Board of Governors shall determine the remuneration to be paid to the Executive Directors and the salary and terms of the contract of service of the Managing Director.

Section 3. *Executive Directors*

(*a*) The Executive Directors shall be responsible for the conduct of the general operations of the Fund, and for this purpose shall exercise all the powers delegated to them by the Board of Governors.

(b) There shall be not less than twelve directors who need not be governors, and of whom

    (i) Five shall be appointed by the five members having the largest quotas;

    (ii) Not more than two shall be appointed when the provisions of (c) below apply;

    (iii) Five shall be elected by the members not entitled to appoint directors, other than the American Republics; and

    (iv) Two shall be elected by the American Republics not entitled to appoint directors.

For the purposes of this paragraph, members means governments of countries whose names are set forth in Schedule A, whether they become members in accordance with Article XX or in accordance with Article II, Section 2. When governments of other countries become members, the Board of Governors may, by a four-fifths majority of the total voting power, increase the number of directors to be elected.

(c) If, at the second regular election of directors and thereafter, the members entitled to appoint directors under (b) (i) above do not include the two members, the holdings of whose currencies by the Fund have been, on the average over the preceding two years, reduced below their quotas by the largest absolute amounts in terms of gold as a common denominator, either one or both of such members, as the case may be, shall be entitled to appoint a director.

(d) Subject to Article XX, Section 3 (b) elections of elective directors shall be conducted at intervals of two years in accordance with the provisions of Schedule C, supplemented by such regulations as the Fund deems appropriate. Whenever the Board of Governors increases the number of directors to be elected under (b) above, it shall issue regulations making appropriate changes in the proportion of votes required to elect directors under the provisions of Schedule C.

(e) Each director shall appoint an alternate with full power to act for him when he is not present. When the directors appointing them are present, alternates may participate in meetings but may not vote.

(f) Directors shall continue in office until their successors are appointed or elected. If the office of an elected director becomes vacant more than ninety days before the end of his term, another director shall be elected for the remainder of the term by the members who elected the former director. A majority of the votes cast shall be required for election. While the office remains vacant, the alternate of the former director shall exercise his powers, except that of appointing an alternate.

(g) The Executive Directors shall function in continuous session at the principal office of the Fund and shall meet as often as the business of the Fund may require.

(*h*) A quorum for any meeting of the Executive Directors shall be a majority of the directors representing not less than one-half of the voting power.

(*i*) Each appointed director shall be entitled to cast the number of votes allotted under Section 5 of this Article to the member appointing him. Each elected director shall be entitled to cast the number of votes which counted towards his election. When the provisions of Section 5 (*b*) of this Article are applicable, the votes which a director would otherwise be entitled to cast shall be increased or decreased correspondingly. All the votes which a director is entitled to cast shall be cast as a unit.

(*j*) The Board of Governors shall adopt regulations under which a member not entitled to appoint a director under (*b*) above may send a representative to attend any meeting of the Executive Directors when a request made by, or a matter particularly affecting, that member is under consideration.

(*k*) The Executive Directors may appoint such committees as they deem advisable. Membership of committees need not be limited to governors or directors or their alternates.

Section 4. *Managing Director and staff*

(*a*) The Executive Directors shall select a Managing Director who shall not be a governor or an executive director. The Managing Director shall be chairman of the Executive Directors, but shall have no vote except a deciding vote in case of an equal division. He may participate in meetings of the Board of Governors, but shall not vote at such meetings. The Managing Director shall cease to hold office when the Executive Directors so decide.

(*b*) The Managing Director shall be chief of the operating staff of the Fund and shall conduct, under the direction of the Executive Directors, the ordinary business of the Fund. Subject to the general control of the Executive Directors, he shall be responsible for the organization, appointment and dismissal of the staff of the Fund.

(*c*) The Managing Director and the staff of the Fund, in the discharge of their functions, shall owe their duty entirely to the Fund and to no other authority. Each member of the Fund shall respect the international character of this duty and shall refrain from all attempts to influence any of the staff in the discharge of his functions.

(*d*) In appointing the staff the Managing Director shall, subject to the paramount importance of securing the highest standards of efficiency and of technical competence, pay due regard to the importance of recruiting personnel on as wide a geographical basis as possible.

Section 5. *Voting*

(*a*) Each member shall have two hundred fifty votes plus one additional vote for each part of its quota equivalent to one hundred thousand United States dollars.

(*b*) Whenever voting is required under Article V, Section 4 or 5, each member shall have the number of votes to which it is entitled under (*a*) above, adjusted:

    (*i*) by the addition of one vote for the equivalent of each four hundred thousand United States dollars of net sales of its currency up to the date when the vote is taken, or

    (*ii*) by the subtraction of one vote for the equivalent of each four hundred thousand United States dollars of its net purchases of the currencies of other members up to the date when the vote is taken

provided, that neither net purchases nor net sales shall be deemed at any time to exceed an amount equal to the quota of the member involved.

(*c*) For the purpose of all computations under this Section, United States dollars shall be deemed to be of the weight and fineness in effect on July 1, 1944, adjusted for any uniform change under Article IV, Section 7, if a waiver is made under Section 8 (*d*) of that Article.

(*d*) Except as otherwise specifically provided, all decisions of the Fund shall be made by a majority of the votes cast.

Section 6. *Distribution of net income*

(*a*) The Board of Governors shall determine annually what part of the Fund's net income shall be placed to reserve and what part, if any, shall be distributed.

(*b*) If any distribution is made, there shall first be distributed a two percent non-cumulative payment to each member on the amount by which seventy-five percent of its quota exceeded the Fund's average holdings of its currency during that year. The balance shall be paid to all members in proportion to their quotas. Payments to each member shall be made in its own currency.

Section 7. *Publication of reports*

(*a*) The Fund shall publish an annual report containing an audited statement of its accounts, and shall issue, at intervals of three months or less, a summary statement of its transactions and its holdings of gold and currencies of members.

(*b*) The Fund may publish such other reports as it deems desirable for carrying out its purposes.

Section 8. *Communication of views to members*

The Fund shall at all times have the right to communicate its views informally to any member on any matter arising under this Agreement. The Fund may, by a two-thirds majority of the total voting power, decide to publish a report made to a member regarding its monetary or economic conditions and developments which directly tend to produce a serious disequilibrium in the international balance of payments of members. If the member is not entitled to appoint an executive director, it shall be entitled to representation in accordance with Section 3 (*j*) of this Article. The Fund shall not publish a report involving changes in the fundamental structure of the economic organization of members.

ARTICLE XIII. OFFICES AND DEPOSITORIES

Section 1. *Location of offices*

The principal office of the Fund shall be located in the territory of the member having the largest quota, and agencies or branch offices may be established in the territories of other members.

Section 2. *Depositories*

(*a*) Each member country shall designate its central bank as a depository for all the Fund's holdings of its currency, or if it has no central bank it shall designate such other institution as may be acceptable to the Fund.

(*b*) The Fund may hold other assets, including gold, in the depositories designated by the five members having the largest quotas and in such other designated depositories as the Fund may select. Initially, at least one-half of the holdings of the Fund shall be held in the depository designated by the member in whose territories the Fund has its principal office and at least forty percent shall be held in the depositories designated by the remaining four members referred to above. However, all transfers of gold by the Fund shall be made with due regard to the costs of transport and anticipated requirements of the Fund. In an emergency the Executive Directors may transfer all or any part of the Fund's gold holdings to any place where they can be adequately protected.

Section 3. *Guarantee of the Fund's assets*

Each member guarantees all assets of the Fund against loss resulting from failure or default on the part of the depository designated by it.

ARTICLE XIV. TRANSITIONAL PERIOD

Section 1. *Introduction*

The Fund is not intended to provide facilities for relief or reconstruction or to deal with international indebtedness arising out of the war.

Section 2. *Exchange restrictions*

In the post-war transitional period members may, notwithstanding the provisions of any other articles of this Agreement, maintain and adapt to changing circumstances (and, in the case of members whose territories have been occupied by the enemy, introduce where necessary) restrictions on payments and transfers for current international transactions. Members shall, however, have continuous regard in their foreign exchange policies to the purposes of the Fund; and, as soon as conditions permit, they shall take all possible measures to develop such commercial and financial arrangements with other members as will facilitate international payments and the maintenance of exchange stability. In particular, members shall withdraw restrictions maintained or imposed under this Section as soon as they are satisfied that they will be able, in the absence of such restrictions, to settle their balance of payments in a manner which will not unduly encumber their access to the resources of the Fund.

Section 3. *Notification to the Fund*

Each member shall notify the Fund before it becomes eligible under Article XX, Section 4 (*c*) or (*d*), to buy currency from the Fund, whether it intends to avail itself of the transitional arrangements in Section 2 of this Article, or whether it is prepared to accept the obligations of Article VIII, Sections 2, 3, and 4. A member availing itself of the transitional arrangements shall notify the Fund as soon thereafter as it is prepared to accept the above-mentioned obligations.

Section 4. *Action of the Fund relating to restrictions*

Not later than three years after the date on which the Fund begins operations and in each year thereafter, the Fund shall report on the restrictions still in force under Section 2 of this Article. Five years after the date on which the Fund begins operations, and in each year thereafter, any member still retaining any restrictions inconsistent with Article VIII, Sections 2, 3, or 4, shall consult the Fund as to their further retention. The Fund may, if it deems such action necessary in exceptional circumstances, make representations to any member that conditions are favorable for the withdrawal of any particular restriction, or for the general abandonment of restrictions, inconsistent with the provisions of any other articles of this Agreement. The member shall be given a suitable time to reply to such representations. If the Fund finds that the member persists in maintaining restrictions which are inconsistent with the purposes of the Fund, the member shall be subject to Article XV, Section 2 (*a*).

Section 5. *Nature of transitional period*

In its relations with members, the Fund shall recognize that the post-war transitional period will be one of change and adjustment and in making decisions on requests occasioned thereby which are presented by any member it shall give the member the benefit of any reasonable doubt.

ARTICLE XV. WITHDRAWAL FROM MEMBERSHIP

Section 1. *Right of members to withdraw*

Any member may withdraw from the Fund at any time by transmitting a notice in writing to the Fund at its principal office. Withdrawal shall become effective on the date such notice is received.

Section 2. *Compulsory withdrawal*

(*a*) If a member fails to fulfill any of its obligations under this Agreement, the Fund may declare the member ineligible to use the resources of the Fund. Nothing in this Section shall be deemed to limit the provisions of Article IV, Section 6, Article V, Section 5, or Article VI, Section 1.

(*b*) If, after the expiration of a reasonable period the member persists in its failure to fulfill any of its obligations under this Agreement, or a difference between a member and the Fund under Article IV, Section 6, continues, that member may be required to withdraw from membership in the Fund by a decision of the Board of Governors carried by a majority of the governors representing a majority of the total voting power.

(*c*) Regulations shall be adopted to ensure that before action is taken against any member under (*a*) or (*b*) above, the member shall be informed in reasonable time of the complaint against it and given an adequate opportunity for stating its case, both orally and in writing.

Section 3. *Settlement of accounts with members withdrawing*

When a member withdraws from the Fund, normal transactions of the Fund in its currency shall cease and settlement of all accounts between it and the Fund shall be made with reasonable despatch by agreement between it and the Fund. If agreement is not reached promptly, the provisions of Schedule D shall apply to the settlement of accounts.

ARTICLE XVI. EMERGENCY PROVISIONS

Section 1. *Temporary suspension*

(*a*) In the event of an emergency or the development of unforeseen c rcumstances threatening the operations of the Fund, the Executive

Directors by unanimous vote may suspend for a period of not more than one hundred twenty days the operation of any of the following provisions:

    (*i*) Article IV, Sections 3 and 4 (*b*)
    (*ii*) Article V, Sections 2, 3, 7, 8 (*a*) and (*f*)
    (*iii*) Article VI, Section 2
    (*iv*) Article XI, Section 1

(*b*) Simultaneously with any decision to suspend the operation of any of the foregoing provisions, the Executive Directors shall call a meeting of the Board of Governors for the earliest practicable date.

(*c*) The Executive Directors may not extend any suspension beyond one hundred twenty days. Such suspension may be extended, however, for an additional period of not more than two hundred forty days, if the Board of Governors by a four-fifths majority of the total voting power so decides, but it may not be further extended except by amendment of this Agreement pursuant to Article XVII.

(*d*) The Executive Directors may, by a majority of the total voting power, terminate such suspension at any time.

Section 2. *Liquidation of the Fund*

(*a*) The Fund may not be liquidated except by decision of the Board of Governors. In an emergency, if the Executive Directors decide that liquidation of the Fund may be necessary, they may temporarily suspend all transactions, pending decision by the Board.

(*b*) If the Board of Governors decides to liquidate the Fund, the Fund shall forthwith cease to engage in any activities except those incidental to the orderly collection and liquidation of its assets and the settlement of its liabilities, and all obligations of members under this Agreement shall cease except those set out in this Article, in Article XVIII, paragraph (*c*), in Schedule D, paragraph 7, and in Schedule E.

(*c*) Liquidation shall be administered in accordance with the provisions of Schedule E.

ARTICLE XVII. AMENDMENTS

(*a*) Any proposal to introduce modifications in this Agreement, whether emanating from a member, a governor or the Executive Directors, shall be communicated to the chairman of the Board of Governors who shall bring the proposal before the Board. If the proposed amendment is approved by the Board the Fund shall, by circular letter or telegram, ask all members whether they accept the proposed amendment. When three-fifths of the members, having four-fifths of the total voting power, have accepted the proposed amendment, the Fund shall certify the fact by a formal communication addressed to all members.

(b) Notwithstanding (a) above, acceptance by all members is required in the case of any amendment modifying

    (i) the right to withdraw from the Fund (Article XV, Section 1);

    (ii) the provision that no change in a member's quota shall be made without its consent (Article III, Section 2);

    (iii) the provision that no change may be made in the par value of a member's currency except on the proposal of that member (Article IV, Section 5 (b)).

(c) Amendments shall enter into force for all members three months after the date of the formal communication unless a shorter period is specified in the circular letter or telegram.

Article XVIII. Interpretation

(a) Any question of interpretation of the provisions of this Agreement arising between any member and the Fund or between any members of the Fund shall be submitted to the Executive Directors for their decision. If the question particularly affects any member not entitled to appoint an executive director it shall be entitled to representation in accordance with Article XII, Section 3 (j).

(b) In any case where the Executive Directors have given a decision under (a) above, any member may require that the question be referred to the Board of Governors, whose decision shall be final. Pending the result of the reference to the Board the Fund may, so far as it deems necessary, act on the basis of the decision of the Executive Directors.

(c) Whenever a disagreement arises between the Fund and a member which has withdrawn, or between the Fund and any member during liquidation of the Fund, such disagreement shall be submitted to arbitration by a tribunal of three arbitrators, one appointed by the Fund, another by the member or withdrawing member and an umpire who, unless the parties otherwise agree, shall be appointed by the President of the Permanent Court of International Justice or such other authority as may have been prescribed by regulation adopted by the Fund. The umpire shall have full power to settle all questions of procedure in any case where the parties are in disagreement with respect thereto.

Article XIX. Explanation of Terms

In interpreting the provisions of this Agreement the Fund and its members shall be guided by the following:

(a) A member's monetary reserves means its net official holdings of gold, of convertible currencies of other members, and of the currencies of such non-members as the Fund may specify.

(b) The official holdings of a member means central holdings (that is, the holdings of its Treasury, central bank, stabilization fund, or similar fiscal agency).

(*c*) The holdings of other official institutions or other banks within its territories may, in any particular case, be deemed by the Fund, after consultation with the member, to be official holdings to the extent that they are substantially in excess of working balances; provided that for the purpose of determining whether, in a particular case, holdings are in excess of working balances, there shall be deducted from such holdings amounts of currency due to official institutions and banks in the territories of members or non-members specified under (*d*) below.

(*d*) A member's holdings of convertible currencies means its holdings of the currencies of other members which are not availing themselves of the transitional arrangements under Article XIV, Section 2, together with its holdings of the currencies of such non-members as the Fund may from time to time specify. The term currency for this purpose includes without limitation coins, paper money, bank balances, bank acceptances, and government obligations issued with a maturity not exceeding twelve months.

(*e*) A member's monetary reserves shall be calculated by deducting from its central holdings the currency liabilities to the Treasuries, central banks, stabilization funds, or similar fiscal agencies of other members or non-members specified under (*d*) above, together with similar liabilities to other official institutions and other banks in the territories of members, or non-members specified under (*d*) above. To these net holdings shall be added the sums deemed to be official holdings of other official institutions and other banks under (*c*) above.

(*f*) The Fund's holdings of the currency of a member shall include any securities accepted by the Fund under Article III, Section 5.

(*g*) The Fund, after consultation with a member which is availing itself of the transitional arrangements under Article XIV, Section 2, may deem holdings of the currency of that member which carry specified rights of conversion into another currency or into gold to be holdings of convertible currency for the purpose of the calculation of monetary reserves.

(*h*) For the purpose of calculating gold subscriptions under Article III, Section 3, a member's net official holdings of gold and United States dollars shall consist of its official holdings of gold and United States currency after deducting central holdings of its currency by other countries and holdings of its currency by other official institutions and other banks if these holdings carry specified rights of conversion into gold or United States currency.

(*i*) Payments for current transactions means payments which are not for the purpose of transferring capital, and includes, without limitation:

    (1) All payments due in connection with foreign trade, other current business, including services, and normal short-term banking and credit facilities;

(2) Payments due as interest on loans and as net income from other investments;

(3) Payments of moderate amount for amortization of loans or for depreciation of direct investments;

(4) Moderate remittances for family living expenses.

The Fund may, after consultation with the members concerned, determine whether certain specific transactions are to be considered current transactions or capital transactions.

Article XX. Final Provisions

Section 1. *Entry into force*

This Agreement shall enter into force when it has been signed on behalf of governments having sixty-five percent of the total of the quotas set forth in Schedule A and when the instruments referred to in Section 2 (*a*) of this Article have been deposited on their behalf, but in no event shall this Agreement enter into force before May 1, 1945.

Section 2. *Signature*

(*a*) Each government on whose behalf this Agreement is signed shall deposit with the Government of the United States of America an instrument setting forth that it has accepted this Agreement in accordance with its law and has taken all steps necessary to enable it to carry out all of its obligations under this Agreement.

(*b*) Each government shall become a member of the Fund as from the date of the deposit on its behalf of the instrument referred to in (*a*) above, except that no government shall become a member before this Agreement enters into force under Section 1 of this Article.

(*c*) The Government of the United States of America shall inform the governments of all countries whose names are set forth in Schedule A, and all governments whose membership is approved in accordance with Article II, Section 2, of all signatures of this Agreement and of the deposit of all instruments referred to in (*a*) above.

(*d*) At the time this Agreement is signed on its behalf, each government shall transmit to the Government of the United States of America one one-hundredth of one percent of its total subscription in gold or United States dollars for the purpose of meeting administrative expenses of the Fund. The Government of the United States of America shall hold such funds in a special deposit account and shall transmit them to the Board of Governors of the Fund when the initial meeting has been called under Section 3 of this Article. If this Agreement has not come into force by December 31, 1945, the Government of the United States of America shall return such funds to the governments that transmitted them.

(*e*) This Agreement shall remain open for signature at Washington on behalf of the governments of the countries whose names are set forth in Schedule A until December 31, 1945.

(*f*) After December 31, 1945, this Agreement shall be open for signature on behalf of the government of any country whose membership has been approved in accordance with Article II, Section 2.

(*g*) By their signature of this Agreement, all governments accept it both on their own behalf and in respect of all their colonies, overseas territories, all territories under their protection, suzerainty, or authority and all territories in respect of which they exercise a mandate.

(*h*) In the case of governments whose metropolitan territories have been under enemy occupation, the deposit of the instrument referred to in (*a*) above may be delayed until one hundred eighty days after the date on which these territories have been liberated. If, however, it is not deposited by any such government before the expiration of this period the signature affixed on behalf of that government shall become void and the portion of its subscription paid under (*d*) above shall be returned to it.

(*i*) Paragraphs (*d*) and (*h*) shall come into force with regard to each signatory government as from the date of its signature.

Section 3. *Inauguration of the Fund*

(*a*) As soon as this Agreement enters into force under Section 1 of this Article, each member shall appoint a governor and the member having the largest quota shall call the first meeting of the Board of Governors.

(*b*) At the first meeting of the Board of Governors, arrangements shall be made for the selection of provisional executive directors. The governments of the five countries for which the largest quotas are set forth in Schedule A shall appoint provisional executive directors. If one or more of such governments have not become members, the executive directorships they would be entitled to fill shall remain vacant until they become members, or until January 1, 1946, whichever is the earlier. Seven provisional executive directors shall be elected in accordance with the provisions of Schedule C and shall remain in office until the date of the first regular election of executive directors which shall be held as soon as practicable after January 1, 1946.

(*c*) The Board of Governors may delegate to the provisional executive directors any powers except those which may not be delegated to the Executive Directors.

Section 4. *Initial determination of par values*

(*a*) When the Fund is of the opinion that it will shortly be in a position to begin exchange transactions, it shall so notify the members and shall request each member to communicate within thirty days the par value of its currency based on the rates of exchange prevailing on the sixtieth day before the entry into force of this Agreement. No member whose metropolitan territory has been occupied by the enemy shall be required to make such a communication while that territory is a theater of major hostilities or for such period thereafter as the Fund may determine. When such a member communicates the par value of its currency the provisions of (d) below shall apply.

(b) The par value communicated by a member whose metropolitan territory has not been occupied by the enemy shall be the par value of that member's currency for the purposes of this Agreement unless, within ninety days after the request referred to in (a) above has been received, (i) the member notifies the Fund that it regards the par value as unsatisfactory, or (ii) the Fund notifies the member that in its opinion the par value cannot be maintained without causing recourse to the Fund on the part of that member or others on a scale prejudicial to the Fund and to members. When notification is given under (i) or (ii) above, the Fund and the member shall, within a period determined by the Fund in the light of all relevant circumstances, agree upon a suitable par value for that currency. If the Fund and the member do not agree within the period so determined, the member shall be deemed to have withdrawn from the Fund on the date when the period expires.

(c) When the par value of a member's currency has been established under (b) above, either by the expiration of ninety days without notification, or by agreement after notification, the member shall be eligible to buy from the Fund the currencies of other members to the full extent permitted in this Agreement, provided that the Fund has begun exchange transactions.

(d) In the case of a member whose metropolitan territory has been occupied by the enemy, the provisions of (b) above shall apply, subject to the following modifications:

(i) The period of ninety days shall be extended so as to end on a date to be fixed by agreement between the Fund and the member.

(ii) Within the extended period the member may, if the Fund has begun exchange transactions, buy from the Fund with its currency the currencies of other members, but only under such conditions and in such amounts as may be prescribed by the Fund.

(iii) At any time before the date fixed under (i) above, changes may be made by agreement with the Fund in the par value communicated under (a) above.

(e) If a member whose metropolitan territory has been occupied by the enemy adopts a new monetary unit before the date to be fixed under (*d*) (*i*) above, the par value fixed by that member for the new unit shall be communicated to the Fund and the provisions of (*d*) above shall apply.

(*f*) Changes in par values agreed with the Fund under this Section shall not be taken into account in determining whether a proposed change falls within (*i*), (*ii*), or (*iii*) of Article IV, Section 5 (*c*).

(*g*) A member communicating to the Fund a par value for the currency of its metropolitan territory shall simultaneously communicate a value, in terms of that currency, for each separate currency, where such exists, in the territories in respect of which it has accepted this Agreement under Section 2 (*g*) of this Article, but no member shall be required to make a communication for the separate currency of a territory which has been occupied by the enemy while that territory is a theater of major hostilities or for such period thereafter as the Fund may determine. On the basis of the par value so communicated, the Fund shall compute the par value of each separate currency. A communication or notification to the Fund under (*a*), (*b*) or (*d*) above regarding the par value of a currency, shall also be deemed, unless the contrary is stated, to be a communication or notification regarding the par value of all the separate currencies referred to above. Any member may, however, make a communication or notification relating to the metropolitan or any of the separate currencies alone. If the member does so, the provisions of the preceding paragraphs (including (*d*) above, if a territory where a separate currency exists has been occupied by the enemy) shall apply to each of these currencies separately.

(*h*) The Fund shall begin exchange transactions at such date as it may determine after members having sixty-five percent of the total of the quotas set forth in Schedule A have become eligible, in accordance with the preceding paragraphs of this Section, to purchase the currencies of other members, but in no event until after major hostilities in Europe have ceased.

(*i*) The Fund may postpone exchange transactions with any member if its circumstances are such that, in the opinion of the Fund, they would lead to use of the resources of the Fund in a manner contrary to the purposes of this Agreement or prejudicial to the Fund or the members.

(*j*) The par values of the currencies of governments which indicate their desire to become members after December 31, 1945, shall be determined in accordance with the provisions of Article II, Section 2.

DONE at Washington, in a single copy which shall remain deposited in the archives of the Government of the United States of America, which shall transmit certified copies to all governments whose names are set forth in Schedule A and to all governments whose membership is approved in accordance with Article II, Section 2.

Schedule A

Quotas

(In millions of United States dollars)

Australia	200	India	400
Belgium	225	Iran	25
Bolivia	10	Iraq	8
Brazil	150	Liberia	.5
Canada	300	Luxemburg	10
Chile	50	Mexico	90
China	550	Netherlands	275
Colombia	50	New Zealand	50
Costa Rica	5	Nicaragua	2
Cuba	50	Norway	50
Czechoslovakia	125	Panama	.5
Denmark *	*	Paraguay	2
Dominican Republic	5	Peru	25
Ecuador	5	Philippine Commonwealth	15
Egypt	45	Poland	125
El Salvador	2.5	Union of South Africa	100
Ethiopia	6	Union of Soviet Socialist Re-	
France	450	publics	1200
Greece	40	United Kingdom	1300
Guatemala	5	United States	2750
Haiti	5	Uruguay	15
Honduras	2.5	Venezuela	15
Iceland	1	Yugoslavia	60

* The quota of Denmark shall be determined by the Fund after the Danish Government has declared its readiness to sign this Agreement but before signature takes place.

Schedule B

Provisions with Respect to Repurchase by a Member of Its Currency Held by the Fund

1. In determining the extent to which repurchase of a member's currency from the Fund under Article V, Section 7 (b), shall be made with each type of monetary reserve, that is, with gold and with each convertible currency, the following rule, subject to 2 below, shall apply:

(a) If the member's monetary reserves have not increased during the year, the amount payable to the Fund shall be distributed among all types of reserves in proportion to the member's holdings thereof at the end of the year.

(b) If the member's monetary reserves have increased during the year, a part of the amount payable to the Fund equal to one-half of the increase shall be distributed among those types of reserves which have increased in proportion to the amount by which each of them has increased. The remainder of the sum payable to the Fund shall be distributed among all types of reserves in proportion to the member's remaining holdings thereof.

(c) If after all the repurchases required under Article V, Section 7 (b), had been made, the result would exceed any of the limits specified in Article V, Section 7 (c), the Fund shall require such repurchases to be made by the members proportionately in such manner that the limits will not be exceeded.

2. The Fund shall not acquire the currency of any non-member under Article V, Section 7 (*b*) and (*c*).

3. In calculating monetary reserves and the increase in monetary reserves during any year for the purpose of Article V, Section 7 (*b*) and (*c*), no account shall be taken, unless deductions have otherwise been made by the member for such holdings, of any increase in those monetary reserves which is due to currency previously inconvertible having become convertible during the year; or to holdings which are the proceeds of a long-term or medium-term loan contracted during the year; or to holdings which have been transferred or set aside for repayment of a loan during the subsequent year.

4. In the case of members whose metropolitan territories have been occupied by the enemy, gold newly produced during the five years after the entry into force of this Agreement from mines located within their metropolitan territories shall not be included in computations of their monetary reserves or of increases in their monetary reserves.

SCHEDULE C

Election of Executive Directors

1. The election of the elective executive directors shall be by ballot of the governors eligible to vote under Article XII, Section 3 (*b*) (*iii*) and (*iv*).

2. In balloting for the five directors to be elected under Article XII, Section 3 (*b*) (*iii*), each of the governors eligible to vote shall cast for one person all of the votes to which he is entitled under Article XII, Section 5 (*a*). The five persons receiving the greatest number of votes shall be directors, provided that no person who received less than nineteen percent of the total number of votes that can be cast (eligible votes) shall be considered elected.

3. When five persons are not elected in the first ballot, a second ballot shall be held in which the person who received the lowest number of votes shall be ineligible for election and in which there shall vote only (*a*) those governors who voted in the first ballot for a person not elected, and (*b*) those governors whose votes for a person elected are deemed under 4 below to have raised the votes cast for that person above twenty percent of the eligible votes.

4. In determining whether the votes cast by a governor are to be deemed to have raised the total of any person above twenty percent of the eligible votes the twenty percent shall be deemed to include, first, the votes of the governor casting the largest number of votes for such person, then the votes of the governor casting the next largest number, and so on until twenty percent is reached.

5. Any governor part of whose votes must be counted in order to raise the total of any person above nineteen percent shall be considered as casting all of his votes for such person even if the total votes for such person thereby exceed twenty percent.

6. If, after the second ballot, five persons have not been elected, further ballots shall be held on the same principles until five persons have been elected, provided that after four persons are elected, the fifth may be elected by a simple majority of the remaining votes and shall be deemed to have been elected by all such votes.

7. The directors to be elected by the American Republics under Article XII, Section 3 (*b*) (*iv*) shall be elected as follows:

(*a*) Each of the directors shall be elected separately.

(*b*) In the election of the first director, each governor representing an American Republic eligible to participate in the election shall cast for one person all the votes to which he is entitled. The person receiving the largest number of votes shall be elected provided that he has received not less than forty-five percent of the total votes.

(c) If no person is elected on the first ballot, further ballots shall be held, in each of which the person receiving the lowest number of votes shall be eliminated, until one person receives a number of votes sufficient for election under (b) above.

(d) Governors whose votes contributed to the election of the first director shall take no part in the election of the second director.

(e) Persons who did not succeed in the first election shall not be ineligible for election as the second director.

(f) A majority of the votes which can be cast shall be required for election of the second director. If at the first ballot no person receives a majority, further ballots shall be held in each of which the person receiving the lowest number of votes shall be eliminated, until some person obtains a majority.

(g) The second director shall be deemed to have been elected by all the votes which could have been cast in the ballot securing his election.

SCHEDULE D

Settlement of Accounts with Members Withdrawing

1. The Fund shall be obligated to pay to a member withdrawing an amount equal to its quota, plus any other amounts due to it from the Fund, less any amounts due to the Fund, including charges accruing after the date of its withdrawal; but no payment shall be made until six months after the date of withdrawal. Payments shall be made in the currency of the withdrawing member.

2. If the Fund's holdings of the currency of the withdrawing member are not sufficient to pay the net amount due from the Fund, the balance shall be paid in gold, or in such other manner as may be agreed. If the Fund and the withdrawing member do not reach agreement within six months of the date of withdrawal, the currency in question held by the Fund shall be paid forthwith to the withdrawing member. Any balance due shall be paid in ten half-yearly installments during the ensuing five years. Each such installment shall be paid, at the option of the Fund, either in the currency of the withdrawing member acquired after its withdrawal or by the delivery of gold.

3. If the Fund fails to meet any installment which is due in accordance with the preceding paragraphs, the withdrawing member shall be entitled to require the Fund to pay the installment in any currency held by the Fund with the exception of any currency which has been declared scarce under Article VII, Section 3.

4. If the Fund's holdings of the currency of a withdrawing member exceed the amount due to it, and if agreement on the method of settling accounts is not reached within six months of the date of withdrawal, the former member shall be obligated to redeem such excess currency in gold or, at its option, in the currencies of members which at the time of redemption are convertible. Redemption shall be made at the parity existing at the time of withdrawal from the Fund. The withdrawing member shall complete redemption within five years of the date of withdrawal, or within such longer period as may be fixed by the Fund, but shall not be required to redeem in any half-yearly period more than one-tenth of the Fund's excess holdings of its currency at the date of withdrawal plus further acquisitions of the currency during such half-yearly period. If the withdrawing member does not fulfill this obligation, the Fund may in an

orderly manner liquidate in any market the amount of currency which should have been redeemed.

5. Any member desiring to obtain the currency of a member which has withdrawn shall acquire it by purchase from the Fund, to the extent that such member has access to the resources of the Fund and that such currency is available under 4 above.

6. The withdrawing member guarantees the unrestricted use at all times of the currency disposed of under 4 and 5 above for the purchase of goods or for payment of sums due to it or to persons within its territories. It shall compensate the Fund for any loss resulting from the difference between the par value of its currency on the date of withdrawal and the value realized by the Fund on disposal under 4 and 5 above.

7. In the event of the Fund going into liquidation under Article XVI, Section 2, within six months of the date on which the member withdraws, the account between the Fund and that government shall be settled in accordance with Article XVI, Section 2, and Schedule E.

SCHEDULE E

Administration of Liquidation

1. In the event of liquidation the liabilities of the Fund other than the repayment of subscriptions shall have priority in the distribution of the assets of the Fund. In meeting each such liability the Fund shall use its assets in the following order: —

(a) the currency in which the liability is payable;

(b) gold;

(c) all other currencies in proportion, so far as may be practicable, to the quotas of the members.

2. After the discharge of the Fund's liabilities in accordance with 1 above, the balance of the Fund's assets shall be distributed and apportioned as follows:

(a) The Fund shall distribute its holdings of gold among the members whose currencies are held by the Fund in amounts less than their quotas. These members shall share the gold so distributed in the proportions of the amounts by which their quotas exceed the Fund's holdings of their currencies.

(b) The Fund shall distribute to each member one-half the Fund's holdings of its currency but such distribution shall not exceed fifty percent of its quota.

(c) The Fund shall apportion the remainder of its holdings of each currency among all the members in proportion to the amounts due to each member after the distributions under (a) and (b) above.

3. Each member shall redeem the holdings of its currency apportioned to other members under 2 (c) above, and shall agree with the Fund within three months after a decision to liquidate upon an orderly procedure for such redemption.

4. If a member has not reached agreement with the Fund within the three-month period referred to in 3 above, the Fund shall use the currencies of other members apportioned to that member under 2 (c) above to redeem the currency of that member apportioned to other members. Each currency apportioned to a member which has not reached agreement shall be used, so far as possible, to redeem its currency apportioned to the members which have made agreements with the Fund under 3 above.

5. If a member has reached agreement with the Fund in accordance with 3 above, the Fund shall use the currencies of other members apportioned to that

member under 2 (*c*) above to redeem the currency of that member apportioned to other members which have made agreements with the Fund under 3 above. Each amount so redeemed shall be redeemed in the currency of tle member to which it was apportioned.

6. After carrying out the preceding paragraphs, the Fund shall pay to each member the remaining currencies held for its account.

7. Each member whose currency has been distributed to other members under 6 above shall redeem such currency in gold or, at its option, in the currency of the member requesting redemption, or in such other manner as may be agreed between them. If the members involved do not otherwise agree, the member obligated to redeem shall complete redemption within five years of the date of distribution, but shall not be required to redeem in any half-yearly period more than one-tenth of the amount distributed to each other member. If the member does not fulfill this obligation, the amount of currency which should have been redeemed may be liquidated in an orderly manner in any market.

8. Each member whose currency has been distributed to other members under 6 above guarantees the unrestricted use of such currency at all times for the purchase of goods or for payment of sums due to it or to persons in its territories. Each member so obligated agrees to compensate other members for any loss resulting from the difference between the par value of its currency on the date of the decision to liquidate the Fund and the value realized by such member on disposal of its currency.

[List of Articles and Schedules is omitted.]

(b) Articles of Agreement of the International Bank for Reconstruction and Development

The Governments on whose behalf the present Agreement is signed agree as follows:

INTRODUCTORY ARTICLE ·

The International Bank for Reconstruction and Development is established and shall operate in accordance with the following provisions:

ARTICLE I. PURPOSES

The purposes of the Bank are:

(*i*) To assist in the reconstruction and development of territories of members by facilitating the investment of capital for productive purposes, including the restoration of economies destroyed or disrupted by war, the reconversion of productive facilities to peacetime needs and the encouragement of the development of productive facilities and resources in less developed countries.

(*ii*) To promote private foreign investment by means of guarantees or participations in loans and other investments made by private investors; and when private capital is not available on reasonable terms, to supplement private investment by providing, on suitable conditions, finance for productive purposes out of its own capital, funds raised by it and its other resources.

(*iii*) To promote the long-range balanced growth of international trade and the maintenance of equilibrium in balances of payments by encouraging international investment for the development of the productive resources of members, thereby assisting in raising productivity, the standard of living and conditions of labor in their territories.

(*iv*) To arrange the loans made or guaranteed by it in relation to international loans through other channels so that the more useful and urgent projects, large and small alike, will be dealt with first.

(*v*) To conduct its operations with due regard to the effect of international investment on business conditions in the territories of members and, in the immediate post-war years, to assist in bringing about a smooth transition from a wartime to a peacetime economy.

The Bank shall be guided in all its decisions by the purposes set forth above.

Article II. Membership in and Capital of the Bank

Section 1. *Membership*

(*a*) The original members of the Bank shall be those members of the International Monetary Fund which accept membership in the Bank before the date specified in Article XI, Section 2 (*e*).

(*b*) Membership shall be open to other members of the Fund, at such times and in accordance with such terms as may be prescribed by the Bank.

Section 2. *Authorized capital*

(*a*) The authorized capital stock of the Bank shall be $10,000,000,000, in terms of United States dollars of the weight and fineness in effect on July 1, 1944. The capital stock shall be divided into 100,000 shares having a par value of $100,000 each, which shall be available for subscription only by members.

(*b*) The capital stock may be increased when the Bank deems it advisable by a three-fourths majority of the total voting power.

Section 3. *Subscription of shares*

(*a*) Each member shall subscribe shares of the capital stock of the Bank. The minimum number of shares to be subscribed by the original members shall be those set forth in Schedule A. The minimum number of shares to be subscribed by other members shall be determined by the Bank, which shall reserve a sufficient portion of its capital stock for subscription by such members.

(*b*) The Bank shall prescribe rules laying down the conditions under which members may subscribe shares of the authorized capital stock of the Bank in addition to their minimum subscriptions.

(c) If the authorized capital stock of the Bank is increased, each member shall have a reasonable opportunity to subscribe, under such conditions as the Bank shall decide, a proportion of the increase of stock equivalent to the proportion which its stock theretofore subscribed bears to the total capital stock of the Bank, but no member shall be obligated to subscribe any part of the increased capital.

Section 4. *Issue price of shares*

Shares included in the minimum subscriptions of original members shall be issued at par. Other shares shall be issued at par unless the Bank by a majority of the total voting power decides in special circumstances to issue them on other terms.

Section 5. *Division and calls of subscribed capital*

The subscription of each member shall be divided into two parts as follows:

(i) twenty percent shall be paid or subject to call under Section 7 (i) of this Article as needed by the Bank for its operations;

(ii) the remaining eighty percent shall be subject to call by the Bank only when required to meet obligations of the Bank created under Article IV, Sections 1 (a) (ii) and (iii).

Calls on unpaid subscriptions shall be uniform on all shares.

Section 6. *Limitation on liability*

Liability on shares shall be limited to the unpaid portion of the issue price of the shares.

Section 7. *Method of payment of subscriptions for shares*

Payment of subscriptions for shares shall be made in gold or United States dollars and in the currencies of the members as follows:

(i) under Section 5 (i) of this Article, two percent of the price of each share shall be payable in gold or United States dollars, and, when calls are made, the remaining eighteen percent shall be paid in the currency of the member;

(ii) when a call is made under Section 5 (ii) of this article, payment may be made at the option of the member either in gold, in United States dollars or in the currency required to discharge the obligations of the Bank for the purpose for which the call is made;

(iii) when a member makes payments in any currency under (i) and (ii) above, such payments shall be made in amounts equal in value to the member's liability under the call. This liability shall be a proportionate part of the subscribed capital stock of the Bank as authorized and defined in Section 2 of this Article.

Section 8. *Time of payment of subscriptions*

(*a*) The two percent payable on each share in gold or United States dollars under Section 7 (*i*) of this Article shall be paid within sixty days of the date on which the Bank begins operations, provided that

    (*i*) any original member of the Bank whose metropolitan territory has suffered from enemy occupation or hostilities during the present war shall be granted the right to postpone payment of one-half percent until five years after that date;

    (*ii*) an original member who cannot make such a payment because it has not recovered possession of its gold reserves which are still seized or immobilized as a result of the war may postpone all payment until such date as the Bank shall decide.

(*b*) The remainder of the price of each share payable under Section 7 (*i*) of this Article shall be paid as and when called by the Bank, provided that

    (*i*) the Bank shall, within one year of its beginning operations, call not less than eight percent of the price of the share in addition to the payment of two percent referred to in (*a*) above.

    (*ii*) not more than five percent of the price of the share shall be called in any period of three months.

Section 9. *Maintenance of value of certain currency holdings of the Bank*

(*a*) Whenever (*i*) the par value of a member's currency is reduced, or (*ii*) the foreign exchange value of a member's currency has, in the opinion of the Bank, depreciated to a significant extent within that member's territories, the member shall pay to the Bank within a reasonable time an additional amount of its own currency sufficient to maintain the value, as of the time of initial subscription, of the amount of the currency of such member, which is held by the Bank and derived from currency originally paid in to the Bank by the member under Article II, Section 7 (*i*), from currency referred to in Article IV, Section 2 (*b*), or from any additional currency furnished under the provisions of the present paragraph, and which has not been repurchased by the member for gold or for the currency of any member which is acceptable to the Bank.

(*b*) Whenever the par value of a member's currency is increased, the Bank shall return to such member within a reasonable time an amount of that member's currency equal to the increase in the value of the amount of such currency described in (*a*) above.

(*c*) The provisions of the preceding paragraphs may be waived by the Bank when a uniform proportionate change in the par values of the currencies of all its members is made by the International Monetary Fund.

Section 10. *Restriction on disposal of shares*

Shares shall not be pledged or encumbered in any manner whatever and they shall be transferable only to the Bank.

ARTICLE III. GENERAL PROVISIONS RELATING TO LOANS AND GUARANTEES

Section 1. *Use of resources*

(a) The resources and the facilities of the Bank shall be used exclusively for the benefit of members with equitable consideration to projects for development and projects for reconstruction alike.

(b) For the purpose of facilitating the restoration and reconstruction of the economy of members whose metropolitan territories have suffered great devastation from enemy occupation or hostilities, the Bank, in determining the conditions and terms of loans made to such members, shall pay special regard to lightening the financial burden and expediting the completion of such restoration and reconstruction.

Section 2. *Dealings between members and the Bank*

Each member shall deal with the Bank only through its Treasury, central bank, stabilization fund or other similar fiscal agency, and the Bank shall deal with members only by or through the same agencies.

Section 3. *Limitations on guarantees and borrowings of the Bank*

The total amount outstanding of guarantees, participations in loans and direct loans made by the Bank shall not be increased at any time, if by such increase the total would exceed one hundred percent of the unimpaired subscribed capital, reserves and surplus of the Bank.

Section 4. *Conditions on which the Bank may guarantee or make loans*

The Bank may guarantee, participate in, or make loans to any member or any political sub-division thereof and any business, industrial, and agricultural enterprise in the territories of a member, subject to the following conditions:

(i) When the member in whose territories the project is located is not itself the borrower, the member or the central bank or some comparable agency of the member which is acceptable to the Bank, fully guarantees the repayment of the principal and the payment of interest and other charges on the loan.

(ii) The Bank is satisfied that in the prevailing market conditions the borrower would be unable otherwise to obtain the loan under conditions which in the opinion of the Bank are reasonable for the borrower.

(*iii*) A competent committee, as provided for in Article V, Section 7, has submitted a written report recommending the project after a careful study of the merits of the proposal.

(*iv*) In the opinion of the Bank the rate of interest and other charges are reasonable and such rate, charges and the schedule for repayment of principal are appropriate to the project.

(*v*) In making or guaranteeing a loan, the Bank shall pay due regard to the prospects that the borrower, and, if the borrower is not a member, that the guarantor, will be in position to meet its obligations under the loan; and the Bank shall act prudently in the interests both of the particular member in whose territories the project is located and of the members as a whole.

(*vi*) In guaranteeing a loan made by other investors, the Bank receives suitable compensation for its risk.

(*vii*) Loans made or guaranteed by the Bank shall, except in special circumstances, be for the purpose of specific projects of reconstruction or development.

Section 5. *Use of loans guaranteed, participated in or made by the Bank*

(*a*) The Bank shall impose no conditions that the proceeds of a loan shall be spent in the territories of any particular member or members.

(*b*) The Bank shall make arrangements to ensure that the proceeds of any loan are used only for the purposes for which the loan was granted, with due attention to considerations of economy and efficiency and without regard to political or other non-economic influences or considerations.

(*c*) In the case of loans made by the Bank, it shall open an account in the name of the borrower and the amount of the loan shall be credited to this account in the currency or currencies in which the loan is made. The borrower shall be permitted by the Bank to draw on this account only to meet expenses in connection with the project as they are actually incurred.

ARTICLE IV. OPERATIONS

Section 1. *Methods of making or facilitating loans*

(*a*) The Bank may make or facilitate loans which satisfy the general conditions of Article III in any of the following ways:

(*i*) By making or participating in direct loans out of its own funds corresponding to its unimpaired paid-up capital and surplus and, subject to Section 6 of this Article, to its reserves.

(*ii*) By making or participating in direct loans out of funds raised in the market of a member, or otherwise borrowed by the Bank.

(*iii*) By guaranteeing in whole or in part loans made by private investors through the usual investment channels.

(b) The Bank may borrow funds under (a) (ii) above or guarantee loans under (a) (iii) above only with the approval of the member in whose markets the funds are raised and the member in whose currency the loan is denominated, and only if those members agree that the proceeds may be exchanged for the currency of any other member without restriction.

Section 2. *Availability and transferability of currencies*

(a) Currencies paid into the Bank under Article II, Section 7 (i), shall be loaned only with the approval in each case of the member whose currency is involved; provided, however, that if necessary, after the Bank's subscribed capital has been entirely called, such currencies shall, without restriction by the members whose currencies are offered, be used or exchanged for the currencies required to meet contractual payments of interest, other charges or amortization on the Bank's own borrowings, or to meet the Bank's liabilities with respect to such contractual payments on loans guaranteed by the Bank.

(b) Currencies received by the Bank from borrowers or guarantors in payment on account of principal of direct loans made with currencies referred to in (a) above shall be exchanged for the currencies of other members or reloaned only with the approval in each case of the members whose currencies are involved; provided, however, that if necessary, after the Bank's subscribed capital has been entirely called, such currencies shall, without restriction by the members whose currencies are offered, be used or exchanged for the currencies required to meet contractual payments of interest, other charges or amortization on the Bank's own borrowings, or to meet the Bank's liabilities with respect to such contractual payments on loans guaranteed by the Bank.

(c) Currencies received by the Bank from borrowers or guarantors in payment on account of principal of direct loans made by the Bank under Section 1 (a) (ii) of this Article shall be held and used, without restriction by the members, to make amortization payments, or to anticipate payment of or repurchase part or all of the Bank's own obligations.

(d) All other currencies available to the Bank, including those raised in the market or otherwise borrowed under Section 1 (a) (ii) of this Article, those obtained by the sale of gold, those received as payments of interest and other charges for direct loans made under Sections 1 (a) (i) and (ii), and those received as payments of commissions and other charges under Section 1 (a) (iii), shall be used or exchanged for other currencies or gold required in the operations of the Bank without restriction by the members whose currencies are offered.

(e) Currencies raised in the markets of members by borrowers on loans guaranteed by the Bank under Section 1 (a) (iii) of this Article, shall also be used or exchanged for other currencies without restriction by such members.

Section 3. *Provision of currencies for direct loans*

The following provisions shall apply to direct loans under Sections 1 (*a*) (*i*) and (*ii*) of this Article:

(*a*) The Bank shall furnish the borrower with such currencies of members, other than the member in whose territories the project is located, as are needed by the borrower for expenditures to be made in the territories of such other members to carry out the purposes of the loan.

(*b*) The Bank may, in exceptional circumstances when local currency required for the purposes of the loan cannot be raised by the borrower on reasonable terms, provide the borrower as part of the loan with an appropriate amount of that currency.

(*c*) The Bank, if the project gives rise indirectly to an increased need for foreign exchange by the member in whose territories the project is located, may in exceptional circumstances provide the borrower as part of the loan with an appropriate amount of gold or foreign exchange not in excess of the borrower's local expenditure in connection with the purposes of the loan.

(*d*) The Bank may, in exceptional circumstances, at the request of a member in whose territories a portion of the loan is spent, repurchase with gold or foreign exchange a part of that member's currency thus spent but in no case shall the part so repurchased exceed the amount by which the expenditure of the loan in those territories gives rise to an increased need for foreign exchange.

Section 4. *Payment provisions for direct loans*

Loan contracts under Section 1 (*a*) (*i*) or (*ii*) of this Article shall be made in accordance with the following payment provisions:

(*a*) The terms and conditions of interest and amortization payments, maturity and dates of payment of each loan shall be determined by the Bank. The Bank shall also determine the rate and any other terms and conditions of commission to be charged in connection with such loan.

In the case of loans made under Section 1 (*a*) (*ii*) of this Article during the first ten years of the Bank's operations, this rate of commission shall be not less than one percent per annum and not greater than one and one-half percent per annum, and shall be charged on the outstanding portion of any such loan. At the end of this period of ten years, the rate of commission may be reduced by the Bank with respect both to the outstanding portions of loans already made and to future loans, if the reserves accumulated by the Bank under Section 6 of this Article and out of other earnings are considered by it sufficient to justify a reduction. In the case of future loans the Bank shall also have discretion to increase the rate of commission beyond the above limit, if experience indicates that an increase is advisable.

(*b*) All loan contracts shall stipulate the currency or currencies in which payments under the contract shall be made to the Bank. At the option of the borrower, however, such payments may be made in gold, or subject to the agreement of the Bank, in the currency of a member other than that prescribed in the contract.

    (*i*) In the case of loans made under Section 1 (*a*) (*i*) of this Article, the loan contracts shall provide that payments to the Bank of interest, other charges and amortization shall be made in the currency loaned, unless the member whose currency is loaned agrees that such payments shall be made in some other specified currency or currencies. These payments, subject to the provisions of Article II, Section 9 (*c*), shall be equivalent to the value of such contractual payments at the time the loans were made, in terms of a currency specified for the purpose by the Bank by a three-fourths majority of the total voting power.

    (*ii*) In the case of loans made under Section 1 (*a*) (*ii*) of this Article, the total amount outstanding and payable to the Bank in any one currency shall at no time exceed the total amount of the outstanding borrowings made by the Bank under Section 1 (*a*) (*ii*) and payable in the same currency.

(*c*) If a member suffers from an acute exchange stringency, so that the service of any loan contracted by that member or guaranteed by it or by one of its agencies cannot be provided in the stipulated manner, the member concerned may apply to the Bank for a relaxation of the conditions of payment. If the Bank is satisfied that some relaxation is in the interests of the particular member and of the operations of the Bank and of its members as a whole, it may take action under either, or both, of the following paragraphs with respect to the whole, or part, of the annual service:

    (*i*) The Bank may, in its discretion, make arrangements with the member concerned to accept service payments on the loan in the member's currency for periods not to exceed three years upon appropriate terms regarding the use of such currency and the maintenance of its foreign exchange value; and for the repurchase of such currency on appropriate terms.

    (*ii*) The Bank may modify the terms of amortization or extend the life of the loan, or both.

Section 5. *Guarantees*

(*a*) In guaranteeing a loan placed through the usual investment channels, the Bank shall charge a guarantee commission payable periodically on the amount of the loan outstanding at a rate determined by the Bank. During the first ten years of the Bank's operations, this rate shall be not less than one percent per annum and not greater than one and one-half percent per annum. At the end of this period of ten years, the rate of commission may be reduced by the Bank with respect both to the outstanding portions of loans already guaranteed and to future loans if the reserves accumulated by the Bank under Section 6 of this Article and out of other earnings are considered by it sufficient to justify a reduction. In the case of future loans the Bank shall also have discretion to increase the rate of commission beyond the above limit, if experience indicates that an increase is advisable.

(b) Guarantee commissions shall be paid directly to the Bank by the borrower.

(c) Guarantees by the Bank shall provide that the Bank may terminate its liability with respect to interest if, upon default by the borrower and by the guarantor, if any, the Bank offers to purchase, at par and interest accrued to a date designated in the offer, the bonds or other obligations guaranteed.

(d) The Bank shall have power to determine any other terms and conditions of the guarantee.

Section 6. *Special reserve*

The amount of commissions received by the Bank under Sections 4 and 5 of this Article shall be set aside as a special reserve, which shall be kept available for meeting liabilities of the Bank in accordance with Section 7 of this Article. The special reserve shall be held in such liquid form, permitted under this Agreement, as the Executive Directors may decide.

Section 7. *Methods of meeting liabilities of the Bank in case of defaults*

In cases of default on loans made, participated in, or guaranteed by the Bank:

(a) The Bank shall make such arrangements as may be feasible to adjust the obligations under the loans, including arrangements under or analogous to those provided in Section 4 (c) of this Article.

(b) The payments in discharge of the Bank's liabilities on borrowings or guarantees under Sections 1 (a) (ii) and (iii) of this Article shall be charged:

  (i) first, against the special reserve provided in Section 6 of this Article.

  (ii) then, to the extent necessary and at the discretion of the Bank, against the other reserves, surplus and capital available to the Bank.

(c) Whenever necessary to meet contractual payments of interest, other charges or amortization on the Bank's own borrowings, or to meet the Bank's liabilities with respect to similar payments on loans guaranteed by it, the Bank may call an appropriate amount of the unpaid subscriptions of members in accordance with Article II, Sections 5 and 7. Moreover, if it believes that a default may be of long duration, the Bank may call an additional amount of such unpaid subscriptions not to exceed in any one year one percent of the total subscriptions of the members for the following purposes:

(*i*) To redeem prior to maturity, or otherwise discharge its liability on, all or part of the outstanding principal of any loan guaranteed by it in respect of which the debtor is in default.

(*ii*) To repurchase, or otherwise discharge its liability on, all or part of its own outstanding borrowings.

Section 8. *Miscellaneous operations*

In addition to the operations specified elsewhere in this Agreement, the Bank shall have the power:

(*i*) To buy and sell securities it has issued and to buy and sell securities which it has guaranteed or in which it has invested, provided that the Bank shall obtain the approval of the member in whose territories the securities are to be bought or sold.

(*ii*) To guarantee securities in which it has invested for the purpose of facilitating their sale.

(*iii*) To borrow the currency of any member with the approval of that member.

(*iv*) To buy and sell such other securities as the Directors by a three-fourths majority of the total voting power may deem proper for the investment of all or part of the special reserve under Section 6 of this Article.

In exercising the powers conferred by this Section, the Bank may deal with any person, partnership, association, corporation or other legal entity in the territories of any member.

Section 9. *Warning to be placed on securities*

Every security guaranteed or issued by the Bank shall bear on its face a conspicuous statement to the effect that it is not an obligation of any government unless expressly stated on the security.

Section 10. *Political activity prohibited*

The Bank and its officers shall not interfere in the political affairs of any member; nor shall they be influenced in their decisions by the political character of the member or members concerned. Only economic considerations shall be relevant to their decisions, and these considerations shall be weighed impartially in order to achieve the purposes stated in Article I.

ARTICLE V.   ORGANIZATION AND MANAGEMENT

Section 1.   *Structure of the Bank*

The Bank shall have a Board of Governors, Executive Directors, a President and such other officers and staff to perform such duties as the Bank may determine.

Section 2.   *Board of Governors*

(a) All the powers of the Bank shall be vested in the Board of Governors consisting of one governor and one alternate appointed by each member in such manner as it may determine. Each governor and each alternate shall serve for five years, subject to the pleasure of the member appointing him, and may be reappointed. No alternate may vote except in the absence of his principal. The Board shall select one of the governors as Chairman.

(b) The Board of Governors may delegate to the Executive Directors authority to exercise any powers of the Board, except the power to:

> (i) Admit new members and determine the conditions of their admission;
>
> (ii) Increase or decrease the capital stock;
>
> (iii) Suspend a member;
>
> (iv) Decide appeals from interpretations of this Agreement given by the Executive Directors;
>
> (v) Make arrangements to cooperate with other international organizations (other than informal arrangements of a temporary and administrative character);
>
> (vi) Decide to suspend permanently the operations of the Bank and to distribute its assets;
>
> (vii) Determine the distribution of the net income of the Bank.

(c) The Board of Governors shall hold an annual meeting and such other meetings as may be provided for by the Board or called by the Executive Directors. Meetings of the Board shall be called by the Directors whenever requested by five members or by members having one-quarter of the total voting power.

(d) A quorum for any meeting of the Board of Governors shall be a majority of the Governors, exercising not less than two-thirds of the total voting power.

(e) The Board of Governors may by regulation establish a procedure whereby the Executive Directors, when they deem such action to be in the best interests of the Bank, may obtain a vote of the Governors on a specific question without calling a meeting of the Board.

(f) The Board of Governors, and the Executive Directors to the extent authorized, may adopt such rules and regulations as may be necessary or appropriate to conduct the business of the Bank.

(*g*) Governors and alternates shall serve as such without compensation from the Bank, but the Bank shall pay them reasonable expenses incurred in attending meetings.

(*h*) The Board of Governors shall determine the remuneration to be paid to the Executive Directors and the salary and terms of the contract of service of the President.

Section 3. *Voting*

(*a*) Each member shall have two hundred fifty votes plus one additional vote for each share of stock held.

(*b*) Except as otherwise specifically provided, all matters before the Bank shall be decided by a majority of the votes cast.

Section 4. *Executive Directors*

(*a*) The Executive Directors shall be responsible for the conduct of the general operations of the Bank, and for this purpose shall exercise all the powers delegated to them by the Board of Governors.

(*b*) There shall be twelve Executive Directors, who need not be governors, and of whom:

(*i*) five shall be appointed, one by each of the five members having the largest number of shares;

(*ii*) seven shall be elected according to Schedule B by all the Governors other than those appointed by the five members referred to in (*i*) above.

For the purpose of this paragraph, "members" means governments of countries whose names are set forth in Schedule A, whether they are original members or become members in accordance with Article II, Section 1 (*b*). When governments of other countries become members, the Board of Governors may, by a four-fifths majority of the total voting power, increase the total number of directors by increasing the number of directors to be elected.

Executive directors shall be appointed or elected every two years.

(*c*) Each executive director shall appoint an alternate with full power to act for him when he is not present. When the executive directors appointing them are present, alternates may participate in meetings but shall not vote.

(*d*) Directors shall continue in office until their successors are appointed or elected. If the office of an elected director becomes vacant more than ninety days before the end of his term, another director shall be elected for the remainder of the term by the governors who elected the former director. A majority of the votes cast shall be required for election. While the office remains vacant, the alternate of the former director shall exercise his powers, except that of appointing an alternate.

(*e*) The Executive Directors shall function in continuous session at the principal office of the Bank and shall meet as often as the business of the Bank may require.

(*f*) A quorum for any meeting of the Executive Directors shall be a majority of the Directors, exercising not less than one-half of the total voting power.

(*g*) Each appointed director shall be entitled to cast the number of votes allotted under Section 3 of this Article to the member appointing him. Each elected director shall be entitled to cast the number of votes which counted toward his election. All the votes which a director is entitled to cast shall be cast as a unit.

(*h*) The Board of Governors shall adopt regulations under which a member not entitled to appoint a director under (*b*) above may send a representative to attend any meeting of the Executive Directors when a request made by, or a matter particularly affecting, that member is under consideration.

(*i*) The Executive Directors may appoint such committees as they deem advisable. Membership of such committees need not be limited to governors or directors or their alternates.

Section 5. *President and staff*

(*a*) The Executive Directors shall select a President who shall not be a governor or an executive director or an alternate for either. The President shall be Chairman of the Executive Directors, but shall have no vote except a deciding vote in case of an equal division. He may participate in meetings of the Board of Governors, but shall not vote at such meetings. The President shall cease to hold office when the Executive Directors so decide.

(*b*) The President shall be chief of the operating staff of the Bank and shall conduct, under the direction of the Executive Directors, the ordinary business of the Bank. Subject to the general control of the Executive Directors, he shall be responsible for the organization, appointment and dismissal of the officers and staff.

(*c*) The President, officers and staff of the Bank, in the discharge of their offices, owe their duty entirely to the Bank and to no other authority. Each member of the Bank shall respect the international character of this duty and shall refrain from all attempts to influence any of them in the discharge of their duties.

(*d*) In appointing the officers and staff the President shall, subject to the paramount importance of securing the highest standards of efficiency and of technical competence, pay due regard to the importance of recruiting personnel on as wide a geographical basis as possible.

Section 6. *Advisory Council*

(*a*) There shall be an Advisory Council of not less than seven persons selected by the Board of Governors including representatives of banking, commercial, industrial, labor, and agricultural interests, and with as wide a national representation as possible. In those fields where specialized international organizations exist, the members of the Council representative of those fields shall be selected in agreement with such organizations. The Council shall advise the Bank on matters of general policy. The Council shall meet annually and on such other occasions as the Bank may request.

(b) Councillors shall serve for two years and may be reappointed. They shall be paid their reasonable expenses incurred on behalf of the Bank.

Section 7. *Loan committees*

The committees required to report on loans under Article III, Section 4, shall be appointed by the Bank. Each such committee shall include an expert selected by the governor representing the member in whose territories the project is located and one or more members of the technical staff of the Bank.

Section 8. *Relationship to other international organizations*

(a) The Bank, within the terms of this Agreement, shall cooperate with any general international organization and with public international organizations having specialized responsibilities in related fields. Any arrangements for such cooperation which would involve a modification of any provision of this Agreement may be effected only after amendment to this Agreement under Article VIII.

(b) In making decisions on applications for loans or guarantees relating to matters directly within the competence of any international organization of the types specified in the preceding paragraph and participated in primarily by members of the Bank, the Bank shall give consideration to the views and recommendations of such organization.

Section 9. *Location of offices*

(a) The principal office of the Bank shall be located in the territory of the member holding the greatest number of shares.

(b) The Bank may establish agencies or branch offices in the territories of any member of the Bank.

Section 10. *Regional offices and councils*

(a) The Bank may establish regional offices and determine the location of, and the areas to be covered by, each regional office.

(b) Each regional office shall be advised by a regional council representative of the entire area and selected in such manner as the Bank may decide.

Section 11. *Depositories*

(*a*) Each member shall designate its central bank as a depository for all the Bank's holdings of its currency or, if it has no central bank, it shall designate such other institution as may be acceptable to the Bank.

(*b*) The Bank may hold other assets, including gold, in depositories designated by the five members having the largest number of shares and in such other designated depositories as the Bank may select. Initially, at least one-half of the gold holdings of the Bank shall be held in the depository designated by the member in whose territory the Bank has its principal office, and at least forty percent shall be held in the depositories designated by the remaining four members referred to above, each of such depositories to hold, initially, not less than the amount of gold paid on the shares of the member designating it. However, all transfers of gold by the Bank shall be made with due regard to the costs of transport and anticipated requirements of the Bank. In an emergency the Executive Directors may transfer all or any part of the Bank's gold holdings to any place where they can be adequately protected.

Section 12. *Form of holdings of currency*

The Bank shall accept from any member, in place of any part of the member's currency, paid in to the Bank under Article II, Section 7 (*i*), or to meet amortization payments on loans made with such currency, and not needed by the Bank in its operations, notes or similar obligations issued by the Government of the member or the depository designated by such member, which shall be non-negotiable, non-interest-bearing and payable at their par value on demand by credit to the account of the Bank in the designated depository.

Section 13. *Publication of reports and provision of information*

(*a*) The Bank shall publish an annual report containing an audited statement of its accounts and shall circulate to members at intervals of three months or less a summary statement of its financial position and a profit and loss statement showing the results of its operations.

(*b*) The Bank may publish such other reports as it deems desirable to carry out its purposes.

(*c*) Copies of all reports, statements and publications made under this section shall be distributed to members.

Section 14. *Allocation of net income*

(*a*) The Board of Governors shall determine annually what part of the Bank's net income, after making provision for reserves, shall be allocated to surplus and what part, if any, shall be distributed.

(*b*) If any part is distributed, up to two percent non-cumulative shall be paid, as a first charge against the distribution for any year, to each member on the basis of the average amount of the loans outstanding during the year made under Article IV, Section 1 (*a*) (*i*), out of currency corresponding to its subscription. If two percent is paid as a first charge, any balance remaining to be distributed shall be paid to all members in proportion to their shares. Payments to each member shall be made in its own currency, or if that currency is not available in other currency acceptable to the member. If such payments are made in currencies other than the member's own currency, the transfer of the currency and its use by the receiving member after payment shall be without restriction by the members.

ARTICLE VI. WITHDRAWAL AND SUSPENSION OF MEMBERSHIP: SUSPENSION OF OPERATIONS

Section 1. *Right of members to withdraw*

Any member may withdraw from the Bank at any time by transmitting a notice in writing to the Bank at its principal office. Withdrawal shall become effective on the date such notice is received.

Section 2. *Suspension of membership*

If a member fails to fulfill any of its obligations to the Bank, the Bank may suspend its membership by decision of a majority of the Governors, exercising a majority of the total voting power. The member so suspended shall automatically cease to be a member one year from the date of its suspension unless a decision is taken by the same majority to restore the member to good standing.

While under suspension, a member shall not be entitled to exercise any rights under this Agreement, except the right of withdrawal, but shall remain subject to all obligations.

Section 3. *Cessation of membership in International Monetary Fund*

Any member which ceases to be a member of the International Monetary Fund shall automatically cease after three months to be a member of the Bank unless the Bank by three-fourths of the total voting power has agreed to allow it to remain a member.

Section 4. *Settlement of accounts with governments ceasing to be members*

(*a*) When a government ceases to be a member, it shall remain liable for its direct obligations to the Bank and for its contingent liabilities to the Bank so long as any part of the loans or guarantees contracted before it ceased to be a member are outstanding; but it shall cease to incur liabilities with respect to loans and guarantees entered into thereafter by the Bank and to share either in the income or the expenses of the Bank.

(b) At the time a government ceases to be a member, the Bank shall arrange for the repurchase of its shares as a part of the settlement of accounts with such government in accordance with the provisions of (c) and (d) below. For this purpose the repurchase price of the shares shall be the value shown by the books of the Bank on the day the government ceases to be a member.

(c) The payment for shares repurchased by the Bank under this section shall be governed by the following conditions:

> (i) Any amount due to the government for its shares shall be withheld so long as the government, its central bank or any of its agencies remains liable, as borrower or guarantor, to the Bank and such amount may, at the option of the Bank, be applied on any such liability as it matures. No amount shall be withheld on account of the liability of the government resulting from its subscription for shares under Article II, Section 5 (ii). In any event, no amount due to a member for its shares shall be paid until six months after the date upon which the government ceases to be a member.

> (ii) Payments for shares may be made from time to time, upon their surrender by the government, to the extent by which the amount due as the repurchase price in (b) above exceeds the aggregate of liabilities on loans and guarantees in (c) (i) above until the former member has received the full repurchase price.

> (iii) Payments shall be made in the currency of the country receiving payment or at the option of the Bank in gold.

> (iv) If losses are sustained by the Bank on any guarantees, participations in loans, or loans which were outstanding on the date when the government ceased to be a member, and the amount of such losses exceeds the amount of the reserve provided against losses on the date when the government ceased to be a member, such government shall be obligated to repay upon demand the amount by which the repurchase price of its shares would have been reduced, if the losses had been taken into account when the repurchase price was determined. In addition, the former member government shall remain liable on any call for unpaid subscriptions under Article II, Section 5 (ii), to the extent that it would have been required to respond if the impairment of capital had occurred and the call had been made at the time the repurchase price of its shares was determined.

(d) If the Bank suspends permanently its operations under Section

5 (*b*) of this Article, within six months of the date upon which any government ceases to be a member, all rights of such government shall be determined by the provisions of Section 5 of this Article.

Section 5. *Suspension of operations and settlement of obligations*

(*a*) In an emergency the Executive Directors may suspend temporarily operations in respect of new loans and guarantees pending an opportunity for further consideration and action by the Board of Governors.

(*b*) The Bank may suspend permanently its operations in respect of new loans and guarantees by vote of a majority of the Governors, exercising a majority of the total voting power. After such suspension of operations the Bank shall forthwith cease all activities, except those incident to the orderly realization, conservation, and preservation of its assets and settlement of its obligations.

(*c*) The liability of all members for uncalled subscriptions to the capital stock of the Bank and in respect of the depreciation of their own currencies shall continue until all claims of creditors, including all contingent claims, shall have been discharged.

(*d*) All creditors holding direct claims shall be paid out of the assets of the Bank, and then out of payments to the Bank on calls on unpaid subscriptions. Before making any payments to creditors holding direct claims, the Executive Directors shall make such arrangements as are necessary, in their judgment, to insure a distribution to holders of contingent claims ratably with creditors holding direct claims.

(*e*) No distribution shall be made to members on account of their subscriptions to the capital stock of the Bank until

> (*i*) all liabilities to creditors have been discharged or provided for, and
>
> (*ii*) a majority of the Governors, exercising a majority of the total voting power, have decided to make a distribution.

(*f*) After a decision to make a distribution has been taken under (*e*) above, the Executive Directors may by a two-thirds majority vote make successive distributions of the assets of the Bank to members until all of the assets have been distributed. This distribution shall be subject to the prior settlement of all outstanding claims of the Bank against each member.

(*g*) Before any distribution of assets is made, the Executive Directors shall fix the proportionate share of each member according to the ratio of its shareholding to the total outstanding shares of the Bank.

(*h*) The Executive Directors shall value the assets to be distributed as at the date of distribution and then proceed to distribute in the following manner:

(*i*) There shall be paid to each member in its own obligations or those of its official agencies or legal entities within its territories, insofar as they are available for distribution, an amount equivalent in value to its proportionate share of the total amount to be distributed.

(*ii*) Any balance due to a member after payment has been made under (*i*) above shall be paid, in its own currency, insofar as it is held by the Bank, up to an amount equivalent in value to such balance.

(*iii*) Any balance due to a member after payment has been made under (*i*) and (*ii*) above shall be paid in gold or currency acceptable to the member, insofar as they are held by the Bank, up to an amount equivalent in value to such balance.

(*iv*) Any remaining assets held by the Bank after payments have been made to members under (*i*), (*ii*), and (*iii*) above shall be distributed *pro rata* among the members.

(*i*) Any member receiving assets distributed by the Bank in accordance with (*h*) above shall enjoy the same rights with respect to such assets as the Bank enjoyed prior to their distribution.

ARTICLE VII. STATUS, IMMUNITIES AND PRIVILEGES

Section 1. *Purposes of Article*

To enable the Bank to fulfill the functions with which it is entrusted, the status, immunities and privileges set forth in this Article shall be accorded to the Bank in the territories of each member.

Section 2. *Status of the Bank*

The Bank shall possess full juridical personality, and, in particular, the capacity:

(*i*) to contract;

(*ii*) to acquire and dispose of immovable and movable property;

(*iii*) to institute legal proceedings.

Section 3. *Position of the Bank with regard to judicial process*

Actions may be brought against the Bank only in a court of competent jurisdiction in the territories of a member in which the Bank has an office, has appointed an agent for the purpose of accepting service or notice of process, or has issued or guaranteed securities. No actions shall, however, be brought by members or persons acting for or deriving claims from members. The property and assets of the Bank shall, wheresoever located and by whomsoever held, be immune from all forms of seizure, attachment or execution before the delivery of final judgment against the Bank.

Section 4. *Immunity of assets from seizure*

Property and assets of the Bank, wherever located and by whomsoever held, shall be immune from search, requisition, confiscation, expropriation or any other form of seizure by executive or legislative action.

Section 5. *Immunity of archives*

The archives of the Bank shall be inviolable.

Section 6. *Freedom of assets from restrictions*

To the extent necessary to carry out the operations provided for in this Agreement and subject to the provisions of this Agreement, all property and assets of the Bank shall be free from restrictions, regulations, controls and moratoria of any nature.

Section 7. *Privilege for communications*

The official communications of the Bank shall be accorded by each member the same treatment that it accords to the official communications of other members.

Section 8. *Immunities and privileges of officers and employees*

All governors, executive directors, alternates, officers and employees of the Bank

      (*i*) shall be immune from legal process with respect to acts performed by them in their official capacity except when the Bank waives this immunity;

      (*ii*) not being local nationals, shall be accorded the same immunities from immigration restrictions, alien registration requirements and national service obligations and the same facilities as regards exchange restrictions as are accorded by members to the representatives, officials, and employees of comparable rank of other members;

      (*iii*) shall be granted the same treatment in respect of travelling facilities as is accorded by members to representatives, officials and employees of comparable rank of other members.

Section 9. *Immunities from taxation*

(*a*) The Bank, its assets, property, income and its operations and transactions authorized by this Agreement, shall be immune from all taxation and from all customs duties. The Bank shall also be immune from liability for the collection or payment of any tax or duty.

(*b*) No tax shall be levied on or in respect of salaries and emoluments paid by the Bank to executive directors, alternates, officials or employees of the Bank who are not local citizens, local subjects, or other local nationals.

(c) No taxation of any kind shall be levied on any obligation or security issued by the Bank (including any dividend or interest thereon) by whomsoever held —

   (i) which discriminates against such obligation or security solely because it is issued by the Bank; or

   (ii) if the sole jurisdictional basis for such taxation is the place or currency in which it is issued, made payable or paid, or the location of any office or place of business maintained by the Bank.

(d) No taxation of any kind shall be levied on any obligation or security guaranteed by the Bank (including any dividend or interest thereon) by whomsoever held —

   (i) which discriminates against such obligation or security solely because it is guaranteed by the Bank; or

   (ii) if the sole jurisdictional basis for such taxation is the location of any office or place of business maintained by the Bank.

Section 10. *Application of Article*

Each member shall take such action as is necessary in its own territories for the purpose of making effective in terms of its own law the principles set forth in this Article and shall inform the Bank of the detailed action which it has taken.

ARTICLE VIII.   AMENDMENTS

(a) Any proposal to introduce modifications in this Agreement, whether emanating from a member, a governor or the Executive Directors, shall be communicated to the Chairman of the Board of Governors who shall bring the proposal before the Board. If the proposed amendment is approved by the Board the Bank shall, by circular letter or telegram, ask all members whether they accept the proposed amendment. When three-fifths of the members, having four-fifths of the total voting power, have accepted the proposed amendment, the Bank shall certify the fact by a formal communication addressed to all members.

(b) Notwithstanding (a) above, acceptance by all members is required in the case of any amendment modifying

   (i) the right to withdraw from the Bank provided in Article VI, Section 1;

   (ii) the right secured by Article II, Section 3 (c);

   (iii) the limitation on liability provided in Article II, Section 6.

(c) Amendments shall enter into force for all members three months after the date of the formal communication unless a shorter period is specified in the circular letter or telegram.

Article IX. Interpretation

(*a*) Any question of interpretation of the provisions of this Agreement arising between any member and the Bank or between any members of the Bank shall be submitted to the Executive Directors for their decision. If the question particularly affects any member not entitled to appoint an executive director, it shall be entitled to representation in accordance with Article V, Section 4 (*h*).

(*b*) In any case where the Executive Directors have given a decision under (*a*) above, any member may require that the question be referred to the Board of Governors, whose decision shall be final. Pending the result of the reference to the Board, the Bank may, so far as it deems necessary, act on the basis of the decision of the Executive Directors.

(*c*) Whenever a disagreement arises between the Bank and a country which has ceased to be a member, or between the Bank and any member during the permanent suspension of the Bank, such disagreement shall be submitted to arbitration by a tribunal of three arbitrators, one appointed by the Bank, another by the country involved and an umpire who, unless the parties otherwise agree, shall be appointed by the President of the Permanent Court of International Justice or such other authority as may have been prescribed by regulation adopted by the Bank. The umpire shall have full power to settle all questions of procedure in any case where the parties are in disagreement with respect thereto.

Article X. Approval Deemed Given

Whenever the approval of any member is required before any act may be done by the Bank, except in Article VIII, approval shall be deemed to have been given unless the member presents an objection within such reasonable period as the Bank may fix in notifying the member of the proposed act.

Article XI. Final Provisions

Section 1. *Entry into force*

This Agreement shall enter into force when it has been signed on behalf of governments whose minimum subscriptions comprise not less than sixty-five percent of the total subscriptions set forth in Schedule A and when the instruments referred to in Section 2 (*a*) of this Article have been deposited on their behalf, but in no event shall this Agreement enter into force before May 1, 1945.

Section 2. *Signature*

(*a*) Each government on whose behalf this Agreement is signed shall deposit with the Government of the United States of America an instrument setting forth that it has accepted this Agreement in accordance with its law and has taken all steps necessary to enable it to carry out all of its obligations under this Agreement.

(b) Each government shall become a member of the Bank as from the date of the deposit on its behalf of the instrument referred to in (a) above, except that no government shall become a member before this Agreement enters into force under Section 1 of this Article.

(c) The Government of the United States of America shall inform the governments of all countries whose names are set forth in Schedule A, and all governments whose membership is approved in accordance with Article II, Section 1 (b), of all signatures of this Agreement and of the deposit of all instruments referred to in (a) above.

(d) At the time this Agreement is signed on its behalf, each government shall transmit to the Government of the United States of America one-one-hundredth of one percent of the price of each share in gold or United States dollars for the purpose of meeting administrative expenses of the Bank. This payment shall be credited on account of the payment to be made in accordance with Article II, Section 8 (a). The Government of the United States of America shall hold such funds in a special deposit account and shall transmit them to the Board of Governors of the Bank when the initial meeting has been called under Section 3 of this Article. If this Agreement has not come into force by December 31, 1945, the Government of the United States of America shall return such funds to the governments that transmitted them.

(e) This Agreement shall remain open for signature at Washington on behalf of the governments of the countries whose names are set forth in Schedule A until December 31, 1945.

(f) After December 31, 1945, this Agreement shall be open for signature on behalf of the government of any country whose membership has been approved in accordance with Article II, Section 1 (b).

(g) By their signature of this Agreement, all governments accept it both on their own behalf and in respect of all their colonies, overseas territories, all territories under their protection, suzerainty, or authority and all territories in respect of which they exercise a mandate.

(h) In the case of governments whose metropolitan territories have been under enemy occupation, the deposit of the instrument referred to in (a) above may be delayed until one hundred and eighty days after the date on which these territories have been liberated. If, however, it is not deposited by any such government before the expiration of this period, the signature affixed on behalf of that government shall become void and the portion of its subscription paid under (d) above shall be returned to it.

(i) Paragraphs (d) and (h) shall come into force with regard to each signatory government as from the date of its signature.

Section 3. *Inauguration of the Bank*

(*a*) As soon as this Agreement enters into force under Section 1 of this Article, each member shall appoint a governor and the member to whom the largest number of shares is allocated in Schedule A shall call the first meeting of the Board of Governors.

(*b*) At the first meeting of the Board of Governors, arrangements shall be made for the selection of provisional executive directors. The governments of the five countries, to which the largest number of shares are allocated in Schedule A, shall appoint provisional executive directors. If one or more of such governments have not become members, the executive directorships which they would be entitled to fill shall remain vacant until they become members, or until January 1, 1946, whichever is the earlier. Seven provisional executive directors shall be elected in accordance with the provisions of Schedule B and shall remain in office until the date of the first regular election of executive directors which shall be held as soon as practicable after January 1, 1946.

(*c*) The Board of Governors may delegate to the provisional executive directors any powers except those which may not be delegated to the Executive Directors.

(*d*) The Bank shall notify members when it is ready to commence operations.

DONE at Washington, in a single copy which shall remain deposited in the archives of the Government of the United States of America, which shall transmit certified copies to all governments whose names are set forth in Schedule A and to all governments whose membership is approved in accordance with Article II, Section 1 (*b*).

SCHEDULE A

Subscriptions

(Millions of dollars)

Australia	200	Denmark*	
Belgium	225	Dominican Republic	2
Bolivia	7	Ecuador	3.2
Brazil	105	Egypt	40
Canada	325	El Salvador	1
Chile	35	Ethiopia	3
China	600	France	450
Colombia	35	Greece	25
Costa Rica	2	Guatemala	2
Cuba	35	Haiti	2
Czechoslovakia	125	Honduras	1

* The quota of Denmark shall be determined by the Bank after Denmark accepts membership in accordance with these Articles of Agreement.

SCHEDULE A — *Continued*

Subscriptions

(Millions of dollars)

Iceland	1	Peru	17.5
India	400	Philippine Commonwealth	15
Iran	24	Poland	125
Iraq	6	Union of South Africa	100
Liberia	.5	Union of Soviet Socialist Republics	1200
Luxemburg	10		
Mexico	65	United Kingdom	1300
Netherlands	275	United States	3175
New Zealand	50	Uruguay	10.5
Nicaragua	.8	Venezuela	10.5
Norway	50	Yugoslavia	40
Panama	.2	Total	9100
Paraguay	.8		

SCHEDULE B

Election of Executive Directors

1. The election of the elective executive directors shall be by ballot of the Governors eligible to vote under Article V, Section 4 (*b*).

2. In balloting for the elective executive directors, each governor eligible to vote shall cast for one person all of the votes to which the member appointing him is entitled under Section 3 of Article V. The seven persons receiving the greatest number of votes shall be executive directors, except that no person who receives less than fourteen percent of the total of the votes which can be cast (eligible votes) shall be considered elected.

3. When seven persons are not elected on the first ballot, a second ballot shall be held in which the person who received the lowest number of votes shall be ineligible for election and in which there shall vote only (*a*) those governors who voted in the first ballot for a person not elected and (*b*) those governors whose votes for a person elected are deemed under 4 below to have raised the votes cast for that person above fifteen percent of the eligible votes.

4. In determining whether the votes cast by a governor are to be deemed to have raised the total of any person above fifteen percent of the eligible votes, the fifteen percent shall be deemed to include, first, the votes of the governor casting the largest number of votes for such person, then the votes of the governor casting the next largest number, and so on until fifteen percent is reached.

5. Any governor, part of whose votes must be counted in order to raise the total of any person above fourteen percent, shall be considered as casting all of his votes for such person even if the total votes for such person thereby exceed fifteen percent.

6. If, after the second ballot, seven persons have not been elected, further ballots shall be held on the same principles until seven persons have been elected, provided that after six persons are elected, the seventh may be elected by a simple majority of the remaining votes and shall be deemed to have been elected by all such votes.

[List of Articles and Schedules is omitted.]

[Annex C, the Summary of Agreements, is omitted.]

CHAPTER IX

TRANSPORTATION AND COMMUNICATIONS

1. INTERNATIONAL AIR NAVIGATION

The Convention on the Regulation of Aerial Navigation,[1] opened for signature at Paris on October 13, 1919, with its annexes, contained elaborate provisions on the subject of international air navigation, and was the first general convention dealing with the subject. It entered into force July 11, 1922 as between signatories which had ratified it. It has never been ratified by the Government of the United States. The Convention was subsequently amended, especially under the terms of a Protocol of Amendments, opened to signature at Paris, October 13, 1929.[2]

In 1929, a general air-navigation agreement was concluded between the United States and Canada.[3] Following this, a series of air-navigation agreements were entered into by the United States with European countries, the first of which was the one negotiated with the Government of Italy in 1931.[4] The Canadian agreement was superseded by a second agreement concluded in 1938.[5] On February 20, 1928, the Havana Convention on Commercial Aviation, which is a multilateral convention, was signed by representatives of the American Republics and has been ratified by the United States.[6]

United States civil aviation policy, subject to the provisions of international agreements, is set by the Civil Aeronautics Act of 1938,[7] as amended, which provided for the Civil Aeronautics Board to administer certain of its provisions.

The great technical advances made in aviation during the war have created new problems and changed and enlarged old problems of international civil aviation. The building of globe-encircling strings of air bases for military purposes with lend-lease funds has raised the special problem of the disposition of these bases and access to bases in foreign-held territory after the war is over. The reports of the five Senators (Brewster, Chandler, Lodge, Mead and Russell) on their visits to the different fighting fronts during August and September 1943,[8] laid stress on the seriousness of the problem of post-war international air transport and emphasized the need of a considered American policy and definite international understandings.

(1) Unofficial Report of Remarks of the President (Roosevelt) at His Press Conference, October 1, 1943 [9]

President Roosevelt and Prime Minister Churchill have had extensive talks about post-war aviation and have come to the informal conclusion

---

[1] *International Convention Relating to the Regulation of Aerial Navigation Dated October 13, 1919 with the Annexes to the Convention and Protocols of Proposed Amendments.* Washington, D. C., 1944, Department of State Publication 2143; also in Hudson, Manley O., *International Legislation*, I, 1919–1921. Washington, D. C., Carnegie Endowment for International Peace, 1931, p. 359.

[2] *International Convention*, p. 137, 145; Hudson, *op. cit.*, p. 384.

[3] *Executive Agreement Series 2.*   [4] *Ibid.*, 24.   [5] *Ibid.*, 129.

[6] Hudson, *op. cit.*, IV, p. 2354.

[7] 52 Stat. 973; 15 U.S.C. 21, 45; 39 U.S.C. 481–88; 46 U.S.C. 891y; 49 U.S.C. 401–681; 50 U.S.C. 151.

[8] Senate Report No. 10, Part 16, 78th Cong., 2d sess., p. 527.

[9] Article by John H. Crider, *New York Times*, October 2, 1943.

that there should be more divided [*sic*] freedom of the air, the President told his press conference today.

In this, his first statement on post-war aviation policy, the President seemed to be using the term "free air" as analogous to "freedom of the seas."

The President also came out for private ownership and operation of airlines where they could be made to pay, but said exceptions might be necessary in the case of service to remote, undeveloped places which would be unprofitable commercially. Lines of this latter class, he said, might be run by individual countries or the United Nations.

Although the question whether an airline can be profitably operated often depends largely upon what kind of competition it faces from foreign lines, especially when they are subsidized by governments, the President would not commit himself on the subsidy question, stating that plans had not been developed to the point of deciding the details of how the international lines were to make a living.

Other important points made by the President were that each country should control its internal aviation; that "free air" meant free reciprocal use of air bases, and that, presumably because all bases could be used mutually, sovereignty of the bases was unimportant.

The President discussed the post-war aviation question at length after a reporter asked about the fears of Senators just returned from a world tour of battlefronts [1] that the United States would lose its string of air bases around the world within six months after the war.

He never specifically answered this question, although it was later repeated. He said he knew no more about that than he did as to whether he and his auditors would still be alive six months after the war.

President Roosevelt said that work had been under way six or eight months on the post-war aviation problem, but there were so many "ifs" and "ands" and also the fact that nobody knew when the war would end.

However, he continued, the main objective seemed clear: We will have a free air. The Prime Minister and he had talked about it many times, he said. We all feel that internal aviation ought to be run by each country for itself, he added.

Suppose there was a Canadian line operating to Puerto Rico or the Bahamas, the President said. There was no reason why its flights should not be made over the United States with the right to stop for refueling, but it would not be allowed to pick up passengers, he said, from, say, Buffalo to the Bahamas.

Likewise, he went on, a British line might operate across the United States en route between the British Isles and Australia or New Zealand.

[1] Senate Report No. 10, Part 16, 78th Cong., 2d sess., p. 527.

It could refuel at New York and San Francisco, but would not pick up passengers here, he said.

A reporter asked if Mr. Churchill shared the President's views on free air, to which Mr. Roosevelt replied that he thought so. He said they had talked about the matter informally many times.

Also, the President asserted, further elaborating his views, commercial air transport, where it could be made to pay, should be run by private concerns. He said we did not want to put the Government in the airline business.

There would be some exceptions, the President pointed out, as when we wanted very much to operate to some undeveloped part of the world where there would not be enough business to interest private capital. In such cases, he said, a single government or the United Nations might do the job in order to open up new territory.

With regard to the ownership of air bases, the President asked why the United States should want to buy Croydon Airport in England? The President implied that ownership was unimportant so long as free access was available.

When some one remarked that there were those who thought we should claim sovereignty over airports we have built abroad, the President asked how we would like it if some other country sought to claim such jurisdiction over bases in United States territory.

The President mentioned subsidies in replying to a question on the difficulty of the airlines competing with foreign government lines. He recalled the competitive rate battles of steamship lines many years ago when rates finally got so low that one could bring immigrants across the Atlantic for $25 each. We finally came to a subsidy, he said, although it was a disguised subsidy, a mail subsidy.

One way to meet the competitive problem arising from low-priced labor abroad, he said, would be to raise the standard of living and the scale of wages in such countries, but he concluded that the discussions had not progressed to the details of how the airlines were to make their living.

(2) *Development of International Air-Transportation Services. Joint Statement of the Department of State and the Civil Aeronautics Board, Released to the Press, October 15, 1943* [1]

In order to eliminate any possible confusion in the minds of the aviation industry and the public generally, the Department of State and the Civil Aeronautics Board have felt it desirable to clarify their respective interests in the development of international air-transportation services.

[1] Department of State, *Bulletin*, IX, p. 265.

The Department of State has a primary interest in the subject from the standpoint of foreign policy and international relations, including the broad economic effects of aviation in foreign countries.

The Civil Aeronautics Board is charged with the responsibility, within the framework and guided by the policies of applicable legislation, of developing policy with respect to the organization and functioning of civil air transportation. The Board is required by law to study all of the economic and other factors which go to make up a finding of convenience and necessity for specific routes. In addition, the Board must investigate the applicant or applicants to make a determination of fitness, willingness, and ability. Findings of fact made pursuant to statutory authority in the technical fields of aviation operation, transportation economics and organization, determination of route, and the like are matters for decision by the Board, though the Department of State may bring to the attention of the Board considerations and facts relating to foreign policy which may be relevant to the subject-matter of any determination in respect of which the Department is consulted or may have an interest based on considerations of foreign relations.

The policy of both the Department of State and the Civil Aeronautics Board is that of the closest collaboration in order that the Board may be fully apprized of the Department's views on any international problems which might be involved in matters under consideration by that agency, and in order that the Department of State may be fully apprized of the views of the Board in respect of civil-aviation problems as they may affect foreign relations.

The facilities of the Department of State are freely available to the Civil Aeronautics Board for procuring from the Department or through its missions abroad such information as it may be able to secure for the use of the Board; the facilities of the Civil Aeronautics Board are freely available to the Department of State for procuring such engineering, technical, or transportation data as may be of assistance to the Department in handling its problems.

With specific reference to the development of new international air services, it is believed desirable to outline for the benefit of interested parties the procedure being followed.

Applications for certificates of public convenience and necessity, and amendments thereof, are filed with the Civil Aeronautics Board pursuant to section 401 of the Civil Aeronautics Act of 1938, as amended. Thereafter the carrier need only prepare for the hearing before the Board at which it will endeavor to prove that public convenience and necessity require the granting of its application.

The Board forwards copies of such applications to the Department of State for information and such comment as it may wish to make to the Board. Questions of landing rights and other matters affecting foreign policy will be dealt with through close consultation between the Department of State and the Civil Aeronautics Board. The Department of State, as provided in section 802 of the Civil Aeronautics Act of 1938, as amended, will conduct with foreign governments such negotiations for new or additional rights as may be determined to be desirable as a result of collaboration between the Department of State and the Civil Aeronautics Board.

Foreign air carriers who wish to apply to the Civil Aeronautics Board under section 402 of the Civil Aeronautics Act of 1938, as amended, for permits to operate into United States territory, should request their governments to forward such applications through diplomatic channels. When these applications are received in the Department of State they will be immediately transmitted to the Civil Aeronautics Board. Thereafter, pending a decision on the application, technical or other details are handled directly with the Board, and the applicant prosecutes his application directly before the Board.

(a) Letter from Assistant Secretary of State Adolf A. Berle, Jr., to Mr. John W. Cross, Representing the Alaska Star Airlines, September 25, 1943 [1]

The Department refers to your recent oral inquiry regarding the status of landing rights for American commercial aircraft which may be obtained through negotiation by the Government of the United States. Specifically you ask whether, when such landing rights may be secured, your company will have an opportunity to be heard on the question of whether it may be permitted to exercise or share in such commercial landing rights.

In reply, you are advised that it is the policy of the Department of State, when it secures commercial landing rights in foreign countries for American aircraft, to secure such rights in general terms so that they may be assigned to or allocated among American carriers in accordance with the determination of the competent authorities of this Government under the provisions of law. The competent authority for that purpose is the Civil Aeronautics Board which has authority under its certificating power to determine, with the approval of the President, what American carrier or carriers may engage in international civil aviation and what route or routes they may be permitted to fly. It is the policy of the Department of State so far as practicable when it secures commercial landing rights in foreign countries to do so in a manner which shall make them subject to the authority of the Civil Aeronautics Board. Should special circumstances exist making this impossible, it is the policy of the Department to act in consultation with the Civil Aeronautics Board.

Acting under its responsibility for developing policy with regard to the organization and functioning of international civil air transportation, the Department of State has undertaken exploratory exchanges of views with our principal allies. On March 31, the Department announced that Mr. Adolf A. Berle, Jr., Assistant Secretary of State, and Mr. Edward Warner, Vice Chairman of the Civil Aeronautics Board, were going to London for an exploratory exchange of views on

[1] *Ibid.*

civil aviation with His Majesty's Government in the United Kingdom as a first step toward preliminary international discussion during the coming summer.[1] No details have been released on the outcome of these conversations. It was reported, however, that the British Government had made concessions to the American point of view.[2]

On May 25, the Department announced that a Chinese group, consisting of Mr. Chang Kai-Ngau, Minister of Transportation; Major General P. T. Mow, Chinese Army Air Forces; and Mr. Liu Chieh, Chinese Minister and Counselor of the Embassy in Washington, had entered upon exploratory talks with an American group consisting of Ambassador Joseph C. Grew; Assistant Secretary of State Adolf A. Berle, Jr.; Mr. L. Welch Pogue, Chairman of the Civil Aeronautics Board; Mr. William A. M. Burden, Assistant Secretary of Commerce; and Mr. Stokeley W. Morgan, Chief of the Aviation Division of the Department of State. The first conference was held on Monday, May 22, 1944.

It was also announced that a Soviet group which was to hold exploratory conferences with the same American group was then in Washington and consisted of the following: Ambassador Andrei A. Gromyko; Lieutenant General L. G. Rudenko; Major General A. A. Avseevich; Major General N. I. Petrov; and Colonel P. F. Berezin. The first conference was expected to take place on Monday, May 29, 1944.[3]

It was subsequently reported that the Chinese Government was in essential agreement with the State Department's principal post-war aviation objectives.[4] At the same time it was unofficially reported on what seemed good authority that the major objectives of the State Department policy were as follows:

1. A multilateral agreement under which airlines of United Nations members could fly anywhere in the world with the right to land only for technical purposes. (The right of innocent passage.)

2. Bilateral negotiations between countries for commercial landing rights.

3. An international aviation organization with power only to recommend and without powers of enforcement as presently envisaged.

4. Elimination of uneconomic competition.

5. A surplus aircraft disposal policy that would permit friendly countries to obtain commercial planes in this country.

2. MERCHANT SHIPPING

[See *Documents, V, 1942–43*, p. 657.]

(1) *Letter from the President (Roosevelt) to the Prime Minister of the United Kingdom (Churchill), Published August 3, 1943* [5]

Because of the importance of arrangements entered into during the war to the proper appreciation of the post-war shipping problem, particularly as regards relations between the United States and Great Britain, this letter of President Roosevelt to Prime Minister Churchill is included here.

DEAR MR. PRIME MINISTER:

When you were with us during the latter part of December 1941, and the first few days of 1942, after we had become active participants in the war, plans for a division of responsibilities between your country and

---

[1] Department of State, *Bulletin*, X, p. 301.
[2] *New York Times*, April 9, 1944.
[3] Department of State, *Bulletin*, X, p. 496.
[4] *New York Times*, June 12, 1944.
[5] *Parliamentary Debates, Commons*, vol. 391, col. 2088.

mine became generally fixed in certain understandings. In matters of production, as well as in other matters, we agreed that mutual advantages were to be gained by concentrating, in so far as it was practical, our energies on doing those things which each of us was best qualified to do.

Here in this country in abundance were the natural resources of critical materials. Here there had been developed the welding technique which enables us to construct a standard merchant ship with a speed unequaled in the history of merchant shipping. Here there was waiting cargo to be moved in ships to your Island and to other theaters. If your country was to have carried out its contemplated ship construction program, it would have been necessary to move large tonnages of the raw materials that we have here across the Atlantic to your mills and yards, and then in the form of a finished ship to send them back to our ports for the cargo that was waiting to be carried.

Obviously this would have entailed a waste of materials and time. It was only natural for us then to decide that this country was to be the predominant cargo shipbuilding area for us both, while your country was to devote its facilities and resources principally to the construction of combat vessels.

You, in your country, reduced your merchant shipbuilding program and directed your resources more particularly to other fields in which you were more favorably situated, while we became the merchant shipbuilder for the two of us and have built, and are continuing to build, a vast tonnage of cargo vessels.

Our merchant fleet has become larger and will continue to grow at a rapid rate. To man its ever-increasing number of vessels will, we foresee, present difficulties of no mean proportion. On your side, the British merchant fleet has been diminished, and you have in your pool as a consequence trained seamen and licensed personnel. Clearly it would be extravagant were this body of experienced men of the sea not to be used as promptly as possible. To fail to use them would result in a wastage of manpower on your side, a wastage of manpower on our side, and what is of equal importance, a wastage of shipping facilities. We cannot afford this waste.

In order that the general understanding that we reached during the early days of our engagement together in this war may be more perfectly carried out, and in order, as a practical matter, to avoid the prodigal use of manpower and shipping that would result from pursuing any other course, I am directing the War Shipping Administration under appropriate bareboat arrangements, to transfer to your flag for temporary wartime duty during each of the suggested next ten months a minimum of 15 ships. I have, furthermore, suggested to them that this be increased to 20.

We have, as you know, been allocating to the British services on a voyage-to-voyage basis large numbers of American-controlled ships. What I am now suggesting to you, and what I am directing the War Shipping Administration to carry out, will be in the nature of a substitution, to the extent of the tonnage transferred, for the American tonnage that has been usually employed in your war program. The details of the arrangements we can properly leave to the national shipping authorities for settlement through the Combined Shipping Adjustment Board, whose function it is to concert the employment of all merchant vessels and will, in accordance with its usual practice, do so in connection with these particular ships.

(2) *Remarks of the Prime Minister of the United Kingdom (Churchill) before the House of Commons, August 3, 1943* [1]

In my discussions with the President which were furthered in great detail by the Minister of War Transport, we confined ourselves purely to the war period, leaving arrangements suitable to peacetime settlements to be discussed at a future date. The transfer to our flag of 150 to 200 ships has already begun and will be spread over ten months. It will absorb our reserves of trained seafaring population, and the resources of both countries will be economically and providently applied to the main purpose.

It gives me much pleasure to read to the House this letter from the President, which I have received his permission to make public. I think it shows a deep understanding of our problems, and of the general problems of the war, by the Head of this most powerful State, and of the intimate and sympathetic relationships prevailing between our two Allied Governments. This will I am sure be a source of keen satisfaction to the House and to the country, and certainly a powerful factor towards the abridgment of this period of war and destruction.

I should add that the Canadian Government are making a similarly generous arrangement in connection with ships built in Canada.

I could not give the classes of ships, but they are new ships which are being built in the United States. As to exactly in what proportion the different types are mingled, I have not been informed at present. There is no financial arrangement. The method we work on is that we use all things to the common advantage.

I think that whichever type they are we shall be very glad to put some of our sailors, who are accumulating surplus, and our good engineers and so forth, who are already trained for the sea, on them. These men are very eager to pursue again their dangerous avocation.

[1] *Ibid.*, col. 2089.

3. COMMUNICATIONS BY WIRE AND RADIO

(1) *Senate Resolution 187, Providing for Investigation of International Communications by Wire and Radio, Adopted October 19, 1943* [1]

Whereas efficient communication by wire and radio between the United States and foreign countries is important to the diplomatic, military and commercial interests of the United States; and

Whereas such international communications by wire and radio and the facilities and personnel employed therein are in substantial measure subject to the jurisdiction, control and influence of foreign governments and foreign nationals; and

Whereas it is necessary in the interests of the United States that a national and an international policy of the United States with respect to international communications should be determined and declared, and that the highest practical standards of operations and of service should be made effective at fair and just rates: Now, therefore, be it

Resolved, That the Interstate Commerce Committee of the Senate or a subcommittee thereof appointed by the chairman be, and it hereby is, authorized and directed to make a thorough study and investigation of international communications by wire and radio, and in particular of such communications from and to the United States; to receive and hear evidence as to (1) the ownership, control, the services rendered, the rates charged therefor, and the methods of operation, of United States carriers engaged in such communications; (2) the extent and nature of the control and influence, direct or indirect, of foreign governments over communication carriers authorized by them, the extent to which foreign governments own and operate such foreign communications services, whether such operation by government is direct or otherwise, the character and extent of the competition between foreign companies, whether owned by governments or privately, in communications to and from the United States, and in particular the nature and degree of competition of such foreign companies with American companies in such communication services; (3) the character and adequacy of services furnished by American companies now engaged in international communications to the people and the diplomatic, military and commercial interests of the United States; (4) the developments and improvements in the art of communication by wire or radio affecting, or which may be expected to affect, such international communications; (5) whether there should be competitive services between American companies in particular areas or circuits in international communications; (6) desirable forms and standards of organization of American communication companies, and in particular whether such companies

[1] *Congressional Record*, vol. 89, p. 8344, 8613 (daily editions, October 12, 19, 1943).

should be permitted or required to merge or consolidate and the general terms, conditions and obligations which should be imposed in the event of such permitted or required merger or consolidation; (7) the form and authority of the regulatory body of the United States to be charged with carrying out the policies in international communications declared by the Congress; and (8) generally to consider and to make recommendations to the Congress as to all other matters and things necessary in its judgment in meeting the purposes of the studies herein specifically set forth.

(a) Report from the Senate Committee on Interstate Commerce to Accompany Senate Resolution 187, October 18, 1943 [1]

The Committee on Interstate Commerce, to whom was referred the resolution (S. Res. 187) authorizing and directing a study of international communications by wire and radio, having considered the same, report thereon with the recommendation that it do pass.

The study and investigation proposed by Senate Resolution 187 is the direct and logical outgrowth of the consideration and enactment of the so-called Domestic Merger Act (Public Law 4, 78th Cong.).

During consideration of the latter act, which authorized the merger of domestic telegraph carriers, serious consideration was given in both the Senate Committee on Interstate Commerce and the House Committee on Interstate and Foreign Commerce to the complex problems affecting United States carriers engaged in international communications by wire and radio. In fact, in one of the early drafts of the domestic merger bill (S. 2445, 77th Cong.) a provision was included to permit merger of United States communication carriers operating in the international field; and such a provision was included in a merger bill reported in the House of Representatives in the Seventy-seventh Congress.

A number of factors made inadvisable any final congressional consideration of the international communication problem at the time of the enactment of the Domestic Merger Act.

One important objection was that the congressional committees considering the problem required far more information on the subject than was then available to them. Questions of ownership, foreign controls, control of subsidiary manufacturing entities, agreements with foreign governments, corporations, and nationals, rates, services, and many others were necessary to be answered before correct legislative action could be taken.

Of equal importance to the committee was the viewpoint on communication problems expressed at that time by military agencies in a formal report.

The Navy, in formal testimony by Rear Admiral Hooper who was authorized to express the official Navy viewpoint, opposed legislation which would have permitted merger of United States carriers engaged in international communications. Thereafter several members of the Committee on Interstate Commerce conferred with Secretary of the Navy Knox on the question. It may be noted here that the Navy has a long and continuing interest in the problem of United States international communications. The Navy was not only better informed than other Government agencies on the background and immediate problems, but presented cogent and convincing reasons against final legislative action which

[1] Senate Report No. 472, 78th Cong., 1st sess.

would have permitted merger of international communication carriers at that time and on the same terms which had been proposed for domestic carriers. The Navy Department explained that studies on the subject then under way were proceeding rapidly; that it was desirable, even vital, that any final Navy viewpoint be implemented by the wartime conditions and experiences which were even then being observed and correlated. Incidentally, these studies and findings, the committee believe, will assist greatly in the fact-finding investigation which the committee believe should now be undertaken by the Congress itself.

The Committee on Interstate Commerce, when apprised of these facts, eliminated the international merger provisions from the Domestic Merger Act. During the sessions of the conference committee of the two Houses on the Domestic Merger Act, the international question was discussed and there was informal agreement among conferees that the Congress should not long delay in conducting a comprehensive study of international communication problems.

Continuing developments and recent observations make it imperative that such a study, looking toward legislative recommendations, not be further delayed.

Deserving particular consideration are recent confidential reports on international communication matters made to the Senate by some of its members who have completed an extensive survey of the war fronts. These reports, while admittedly fragmentary, buttress certain important facts well known to cognizant military leaders concerning the restrictions under which United States communication carriers in the international field operate; their inadequacy in serving United States interests; their inability under present organization to break into powerful cartel-dominated communication empires.

A further consideration is the fact that there can be no comprehensive and clear-cut international post-war planning without the fullest consideration of the communication problem.

Still another factor of present and immediate concern to the Congress is the problem of regulation of international communication carriers. Admittedly, existing law is inadequate to cope with the communication problems that will face this country in the post-war world. The inadequacies of the law are further complicated by frequent and growing criticism of the administrative agency and its personnel — criticism which no longer can be ignored by Congress. That administrative agency is an arm of the Congress, and, as such, is responsible to it. It is the duty of the Congress to ascertain in advance whether its creature is competent and experienced enough to undertake duties which inevitably must be thrust upon it; or whether a different method of selecting administrators for technical duties must be advocated.

For these reasons, the Committee on Interstate Commerce recommend that Senate Resolution 187 be adopted.

CHAPTER X

AGRICULTURE AND USE OF NATURAL RESOURCES

1. FOOD AND AGRICULTURE

(1) *Message of the President (Roosevelt) to the Congress, November 1, 1943* [1]

[Excerpts]

In this message, the President presented an outline of his food program for the needs of our armed forces, our civilians at home, and our allies in the war. Those parts relating to purely domestic aspects of the program are omitted.

To the Congress of the United States:

Food is as important as any other weapon in the successful prosecution of the war. It will be equally important in rehabilitation and relief in the liberated areas, and in the shaping of the peace that is to come.

THE OBJECTIVES OF OUR FOOD PROGRAM

The first major objective of our food program is to raise in the most efficient manner enough food and the right kinds of foods to meet our needs. That includes: First, the needs of our armed forces; second, the needs of our civilians at home; and, third, the amount required for our shipments abroad for the essential needs of our fighting allies.

.The second major objective is to see that the food for our civilians at home is divided as fairly as possible among all of the people in all sections of the country, and that it is obtainable at reasonable prices.

I have not been content merely with a program for 1944 crops. I am thinking also about the balance of this year, and about the earlier months of 1944 before the crops are harvested. While the question of production for 1944 is an essential one, we must not lose sight of the necessity for keeping the prices of our present food supply at reasonable levels. We must see to it not only that the prices of food do not go up any further, but that the prices of those foods which have gotten out of the line are actually reduced.

One of the great difficulties is that the steps necessary to attain these two major objectives sometimes become inconsistent with each other. For example, one of the inducements for increased production of food by farmers is to see that they get an adequate price for their products.

[1] House Doc. No. 347, 78th Cong., 1st sess.

410

Such a price is necessary in order to get production. However, if these prices are too high the result will be that by the time the food reaches the grocery store or butcher shop, the housewife will have to pay too high a price for it. This in turn may force a rise in wages and an increase in the prices which farmers have to pay for what they buy. On the other hand, if the butcher shop or grocery store gets an insufficient price from the consumer for meat or groceries, then the farmer in turn will get too low a price to encourage him to raise as much food as we need. In both of these cases, our production and price objectives are not likely to be achieved unless the Government assists with equalization payments or other aid.

The efforts of this administration have consistently been directed at this double target of raising as much food as possible without placing too great a burden on the American housewife in her efforts to feed her family.

In the main our efforts have been successful. In the case of some foods, however, the objectives have not yet been attained. New measures are being taken in an effort to attain them.

＊   ・   ・   ・   ・   ・   ・   ・

Our food plans for the future are, of course, predicated on the assumption that we must not only continue our shipments overseas but actually increase them. The war is by no means won, and the global effort must be continued and accelerated. The requirements for our armed forces will be increased, not only because they will have a larger number of men and women than in 1943, but because more of them will be stationed in distant parts of the world.

The average soldier or sailor eats approximately $5\frac{1}{4}$ pounds of food per day — almost half as much again as the average civilian who eats only $3\frac{3}{4}$ pounds per day. The greater the number of men in the armed forces the larger are the demands on our food supply.

In the last war we fed 4,000,000 people in uniform — largely concentrated in the United States and in France. In this war by the end of 1943 we will have almost 11,000,000 men in uniform, and they will be scattered in all parts of the world. At the beginning of this year our armed forces totaled about 7,000,000; at the end of this year the estimated strength will be 50 percent higher. That is the reason why in 1942 approximately only $7\frac{1}{2}$ percent of our food production was allotted to our armed forces whereas in 1943 the figure will be about 14 percent. As our Army grows, as more men are sent overseas, larger food reserves will have to be accumulated, and civilian belts will have to be tightened. Furthermore our armed forces require more of the so-called protective foods such as meat, fats and oils, milk, and canned goods — foods which are, therefore, bound to run short for the increased civilian demands.

Our armed forces are now eating in each month 328,000,000 pounds of meat, 34,000,000 dozens of eggs, 28,000,000 pounds of butter, 221,000,000 pounds of potatoes — and staggering amounts of other foodstuffs. And the quality of this food is the best that we can give them.

The armed forces of our allies will also increase in 1944 and they will have to receive food assistance from us.

The amount of food going to lend-lease is gradually increasing. In 1941 it was 2 percent of our food production; in 1942, approximately 6 percent. This year because of increasing Russian shortages and other needs it will probably reach 10 percent. In 1941 and 1942 England was the largest recipient of lend-lease foods, but owing to the German invasion of the Ukraine in 1942 more food has had to be sent since then to the Soviet Union. In fact Russia, in the first 6 months of 1943, received one-third of all our lend-lease food shipments.

All these war uses will require about one-fourth of our total food supply for the year beginning October 1, 1943, leaving about three-fourths for our civilian population. This three-fourths, however, because of our increased production will amount approximately to as much, per capita, as was used during the 1935–39 period.

I am sure that the American people realize that every pound of food which we send to our fighting allies is helping our own soldiers in their battles and is speeding the day when all our fighting men and women will come home.

The food that is sent to Russia is almost all for the use of the Russian Army.

Although British farmers, by strenuous efforts, have succeeded in increasing their production from 40 percent of Britain's needs to 60 percent, she still has to rely upon imports in order to avoid starvation. American food provides only 10 percent of the entire British food supply — and yet it has been a great help in feeding Montgomery's army and the Royal Air Force and in sustaining the millions of workers in vital British factories, shipyards, and mines. I think it is safe to say that England could not have continued in the war without the help she received in American and Canadian food.

When Russia was invaded, 40 percent of her usual food production was lost. Emergency food shipments were sent from Great Britain and the Middle East, but we also had to step up our own shipments. I am sure that no one will disagree with the wisdom — to say nothing of the need and obligation — of sustaining the gallant Russian fighters with American food.

The fact is that with all our shipments, civilian diets in England and in Russia — particularly in Russia — are far below our worst shortage periods. In fact, in Russia food for civilians has been cut to the barest minimum.

Through lend-lease the United States seeks to put a share of its food resources to the most effective use against the enemy. Conversely, through reverse lend-lease, the striking power of our own armed forces abroad has been greatly augmented by substantial quantities of food provided by our allies. The United Kingdom, Australia, and New Zealand have provided the largest amount of food but we have also received food under reverse lend-lease from other parts of the British Empire and are receiving increasing quantities of foodstuffs from the French in North Africa.

Some illustrative figures may indicate the importance to our war effort and to our national economy of the food which we obtain from our allies as reverse lend-lease aid without payment.

Although we did not start receiving food under reverse lend-lease from Australia and New Zealand until a year or more after our lend-lease program started, the amounts received — in comparison to what we have lend-leased — are relatively large.

Thus, for example, through August of this year, the United States has received from Australia and New Zealand more than 90,000,000 pounds of beef and veal compared to a total of 99,000,000 pounds of beef and veal which the United States has provided under outgoing lend-lease to all lend-lease countries combined. In July and August 1943, Australia and New Zealand supplied us roughly the same amount of beef and veal under reverse lend-lease as we lend-leased to all countries.

We have received from Australia and New Zealand alone 55 percent of the amount of butter and 16 percent of the amount of lamb and mutton which we have exported under lend-lease to all countries.

During the year 1943, the United Kingdom is providing under reverse lend-lease substantial quantities of many foodstuffs — such as flour, bread, potatoes, sugar, vegetables, coffee, and cocoa — in order to supplement the food our forces receive from the United States. The foodstuffs received from the United Kingdom under reverse lend-lease save valuable shipping space, and include such commodities as fresh vegetables which cannot readily be shipped from the United States.

The United States is supplying much of the pork that England consumes. The delivery of beef to our Army from the Southern Dominions and the shipment of pork to England from the United States are good examples of sharing among the United Nations, on the basis of what each has to contribute to total war.

Most of the food for the American armed forces in the South and Southwest Pacific comes from the land and factories of that area. In order to provide for our troops, Australia and New Zealand have expanded their food production and processing facilities. Despite this, however, the large food requirements of our forces have caused shortages of many foods for the Australians and New Zealanders. Nevertheless, these two countries continue to supply our food requirements as reverse lend-lease without payment by us.

A certain small percentage of food will have to be used as the United Nations liberate presently occupied countries, until such time as the populations of these countries can have a chance to become self-supporting.

For example, a very small percentage of our food now goes to feed the liberated people of North Africa and Sicily and Italy. This includes only the bare necessities of life. Feeding people in this area is not only a military necessity, it provides strength for the hard work that has to be done by them in order to produce new supplies of food and other goods. Already the people of French Africa, with some assistance from us in expanding their agricultural production, have been able to produce a sufficiently good harvest in 1943 so that they can now even supply food to our forces there. This not only saves shipping but augments our own food supply. The people of French Africa, without payment, and under reverse lend-lease arrangements have also supplied the Allied Forces with substantial quantities of flour for use in the Italian campaign. This, too, has helped our food, as well as our shipping situation.

Agreements have just been concluded to provide the United Nations with more than 100,000 tons of fruit and vegetables. The 1944 harvests in North Africa, aided by American agricultural supplies and a year of peaceful cultivation, should ease the strain on the food supply of the United States still further. In North Africa, we and the other United Nations have truly beaten our swords into plowshares.

Food supplied to the liberated peoples also pays other dividends. It prevents epidemics. It is a potent psychological and morale weapon for those starving people whose countries are still overrun by the Axis. While starvation has been the weapon used by the Axis resulting in disease, misery, and death, the United Nations are using food as one of their most potent weapons to shorten the war and win a lasting peace.

The War Food Administration has accordingly raised its sights for 1944. A preliminary calculation calls for the planting of 380,000,000 acres of crops, as compared with 364,000,000 acres in 1943. That will be the largest farm planting in history and should result in the breaking of food-production records for the eighth successive year.

The War Food Administration, with my approval, has requested the Congress to extend the life of the Commodity Credit Corporation and to furnish additional funds. I regard this as vital to the war food program. It will also enable us to carry out our pledge to the farmers, that we will assure them against a price collapse for the 2 years following the war.   .   .   .   .

Plans are also under way to increase our food supply by the development and procurement of food abroad. I have already mentioned how our assistance in developing food production in North Africa has made and will make available food for our armed forces abroad under reverse lend-lease. Other sources of foreign food may be available to us. The functions of handling foreign food development are being centralized in the Foreign Economic Administration so that our food supply can be augmented in the most effective way.

. . . .

The objectives of our food program will, as in the past, be to grow and raise as much foodstuffs as is humanly possible.

We shall maintain our fighting men as the best fed in all the world.

We shall guarantee that every individual of our civilian population will have an ample and healthful diet. Everyone may be assured that there will be enough food to go around. No one need fear that only a comparatively few people will be able to afford an adequate and varied diet.

We shall assist in fulfilling the requirements of our fighting allies for food and shall also assist in assuring that the liberated peoples will be given sufficient food to regain their physical and economic strength.

Our farmers will receive a return over and above their costs of production that will compensate them decently and adequately for their long and arduous work. At the same time, the consumers of the Nation will be protected against rising costs which are properly chargeable to the war effort itself.

. . . .

The accomplishments of the past year have been great. We shall demonstrate to the Axis how the teamwork of a free people can make even those records fall. We shall demonstrate that freedom and teamwork make the people of a democracy the most efficient producers in the world — whether it be of battleships, tanks, planes, guns, or of the produce of the soil.

FRANKLIN D. ROOSEVELT

(2) *Food and Agriculture Organization of the United Nations. First Report to the Governments of the United Nations by the Interim Commission on Food and Agriculture, August 1, 1944* [1]

[Excerpt]

The United Nations Conference on Food and Agriculture which met at Hot Springs, Virginia, May 18–June 3, 1943 [2] adopted a resolution to the effect

[1] *First Report to the Governments of the United Nations by the Interim Commission on Food and Agriculture* (Washington, August 1, 1944), p. 11.

[2] *United Nations Conference on Food and Agriculture, Hot Springs, Virginia, May 18–June 3, 1943. Final Act and Section Reports;* also see *Documents, V, 1942–43,* p. 302.

that there should be set up an Interim Commission for carrying out the recommendations of the Conference, and that the particular function of the Commission should be "to formulate and recommend for consideration by each member government or authority:

"(a) A specific plan for a permanent organization in the field of food and agriculture;

"(b) The formal declaration or agreement referred to in the first recommendation, in which each participant shall recognize its obligation:

(i) To raise the levels of nutrition and standards of living of its own people;

(ii) To improve the efficiency of agricultural production and distribution;

(iii) To cooperate, so far as possible, with other nations for the achievement of these ends;

(iv) To undertake to submit periodically to the other participants, through the permanent organization, reports on the action taken and the progress achieved toward these ends."

Each government and authority represented at the Hot Springs Conference appointed a delegate to the Interim Commission. The United States representative was Mr. Paul H. Appleby, at that time Under Secretary of Agriculture.

The inaugural session of the Interim Commission was convened on July 15, 1943, at the Pan American Union by Assistant Secretary of State Acheson who delivered the welcoming address. In his remarks, Mr. Acheson summarized the tasks before the Commission in the following words:

"The Interim Commission has these main tasks before it: The drafting of a declaration, to be submitted to the governments represented on it with the recommendation that they issue it on their own behalf, recognizing their national responsibility to secure for each of their citizens the opportunity to acquire food and other agricultural products adequate to assure health and well-being, and the obligations of each nation to work with other nations so that all may achieve that goal. The Commission has also to survey the specific tasks that could and should be undertaken by a permanent international body and to recommend the creation of a body which can perform such functions.

"This latter task is clearly divided into two parts. There is the question of what the form of this permanent body should be and the nature of its relations to other agencies, national and international. Then there is the question, aside from its form, as to what it shall *do*. This second question seems to me the heart of the problem. If the activities of the proposed body are clearly indicated and agreed upon, it is far easier to decide upon a satisfactory organization for that body than if the organization is approached first, without references to specific functions." [1]

On July 20, 1943 the Commission met in executive session and elected the following officers: [2] Permanent Chairman: L. B. Pearson, of Canada; Vice Chairmen: Pavel I. Tchegula, of the Soviet Union, Tsou Ping-wen, of China; Secretary: Harold A. Vogel, United States Department of Agriculture. Three committees were set up as follows:

A. To draft a declaration of policy for participating governments
   Chairman: Eurico Penteado, of Brazil
   Vice Chairman: Kyriakos Varvaressos, of Greece

B. To plan the permanent organization of the Commission
   Chairman: Sir Girja Shankar Bajpai, of India
   Vice Chairman: Rafael de la Colina, of Mexico

C. To carry on interim studies and activities
   Chairman: M. P. L. Steenberghe, of the Netherlands
   Vice Chairman: Roberto MacEachen, of Uruguay

[1] Department of State, *Bulletin*, IX, p. 36.
[2] *Ibid.*, p. 52.

The deliberations of the Commission extended over a period of many months. In late February, it was reported in the press that a report would be submitted in the near future and that a proposal would be before Congress for consideration by April 1.[1] The report was finally published under date of August 1.

The text of the full report is not given. The part which is given is that dealing with the purposes and functions of the proposed Food and Agriculture Organization of the United Nations, which is important to a more complete understanding of the proposed Constitution.[2] These two documents have special significance in view of the fact that it was in the field of food and agriculture that action was first taken looking to the setting up of a permanent international organization for purposes of cooperation between governments.

In its report, the Interim Commission stressed the importance of early action. Quoting the words of the Commission's report:

"In the light of these considerations and because it is mindful of the dangers of a return to national policies of self-sufficiency, the Commission urges its constituent governments to take, with a minimum of delay, the action required to enable the Organization to be brought into effective operation, on a nucleus basis if necessary, at the earliest practicable date. The sooner it is established, the sooner will it be able to bring to bear upon post-war problems of reconstruction the disinterested, international and instructed advice and influence the provision of which is the essential purpose of the Organization." [3]

A. PURPOSES AND FUNCTIONS

18. In pursuance of paragraphs 4 (a), 5, 6, and 7 of the Resolution quoted in paragraph 1 of this Report, the Interim Commission recommends for the approval of its constituent Governments the Constitution (Appendix I) of a permanent organization for food and agriculture, hereinafter referred to as the "Organization."

19. The remainder of this section of this Report is devoted to an exposition, supplementing the Constitution, of the purposes and functions of the permanent Organization as the Commission has envisaged them, and of its structure and organization, its methods of working, its relationship with other organizations, national and international, and the need for its early establishment. References at the ends of paragraphs are to the corresponding Articles of the Constitution.

20. Throughout this Report references to the purposes, functions, duties and powers of the Organization are to be interpreted as extending to fisheries, marine products, forestry, primary forestry products and fibers and other non-food agricultural products. (Art. XVI.)

21. The purpose of the Organization as set forth in the Preamble to the Constitution is to promote the common welfare by furthering separate and collective action by the Member nations to raise levels of nutrition and standards of living, to secure improvements in the efficiency of the production and distribution of all food and agricultural products, to better the condition of rural populations and thus to contribute toward an expanding world economy.

[1] New York Times, February 28, 1944.   [2] See this volume, p. 434.
[3] First Report to the Governments of the United Nations by the Interim Commission on Food and Agriculture. Washington, August 1, 1944, p. 38.

22. The means to be employed will include the promotion of research, the dissemination of knowledge, the exchange of services and the making of recommendations for international and national action, in which the Organization might in some cases be directly involved, with regard to the improvement of nutrition; the production, distribution and consumption of foods and of fibers and other agricultural products; and the development and conservation of agricultural, forestry and marine resources. (*Art. I, IV.*)

23. These are important and far-reaching undertakings. They should be envisaged as far as possible in their entirety, so that their interrelationships may be clearly seen. But the Organization will have to develop gradually and it will probably be a considerable time before it will be able to cover the whole field described in this Report. It should be established at the earliest practicable date since there are matters falling within its scope which call urgently for action.

1. RESEARCH

24. One of the principal functions of the Organization will be to promote research in the fields relating to its work as a means of meeting the needs and helping to solve the problems of the peoples of its Member nations. Competence and persistence in the search for knowledge, and fairness and courage in promoting its application, will establish a solid basis for recommendations and action. (*Art. I.*)

25. A vast amount of knowledge in the fields to be covered by the Organization already exists. To be more widely and effectively used, it needs to be adapted to local conditions and reexamined as conditions change. In addition, new knowledge must be sought.

26. A great diversity of research in the natural and social sciences is suggested by the range of subject matter and the sources of information discussed in later paragraphs. While continually safeguarding and fostering the freedom of inquiry necessary to science, the Organization can do much to stimulate such research throughout the world; suggest and initiate projects, in many of which several institutions in more than one country might cooperate; coordinate such projects whenever possible; arrange for the use of procedures that would give comparable results; and keep research workers informed of one another's progress. The Organization should facilitate the exchange of personnel among institutions and the collection and exchange of important biological materials — breeding stocks, for example — and in some cases lend the services of members of its own technical staff to an institution or a country. Whether the Organization should supply equipment or give direct financial aid to research institutions is a matter of policy to be determined by the Conference. The question should be left for future decision whether, by arrangement with the governments primarily

concerned, the Organization should establish research stations of its own. (*Art. I, XII.*)

27. In sum, the Organization should lead in stimulating, promoting, and, where appropriate, conducting research focussed on world needs in food, agriculture, forestry and fisheries. To carry out these and other functions, it will need to assemble a great deal of information from all parts of the world. But it should not only gather data; it should find out and say what they mean.

a. *Sources of information*

28. One of the principal sources from which the Organization will gather information will be the periodic reports made by Member nations in accordance with Resolutions II, III and XV of the Hot Springs Conference. In order that these reports may serve as a basis for concerted planning and action by the Member nations it is important that they give the information needed for drawing an accurate picture of the conditions in any country and throughout the world in regard to nutrition, food consumption, production and the factors influencing them. The Organization, being charged with the responsibility of obtaining and making use of these reports, is therefore given the right to determine the lines on which they will be made and to arrange that they be furnished promptly. (*Art. XI.*)

29. The regular collection and systematic presentation of relevant statistics obtained from Member nations and international authorities will be fundamental; and continuity in the statistical series collected will be important to ensure accurate interpretation of current and future trends. The Organization should receive regularly all published statistical material, and should also have access to unpublished material relevant to its work. The basic statistical data in many countries are very imperfect. The Organization should devise effective methods for obtaining more accurate statistical information at minimum expense, and should also make the services of its technical staff available to any government needing assistance in organizing or improving national statistical services. New methods of sampling, for example, which have recently been developed, are known and used in few countries. (*Art. I, XI, XII.*)

30. All other relevant sources of information should be used, including the results of special inquiries and surveys, or the work of special committees set up by the Organization; reports and other material obtained through regional and liaison offices of the Organization; information furnished by national nutrition organizations, by any agencies that may be set up under the auspices of the Organization, and by research institutes and scientific societies; and reports and other material obtained through reciprocal arrangements with other international authorities. (*Art. XII, XIV.*)

b. *Range of subject matter*

31. The range of subject matter covered by the research, fact-finding, and interpretative work of the Organization will include all the branches of the natural and social sciences relating to food, nutrition, agriculture, forestry and fisheries. It may be useful to list some of the particularly relevant subjects as a means of sketching in broad outline the scope of the activities that would contribute to the main purpose of furthering improvements in production, distribution, consumption and nutrition. The importance of the interrelationships of the different fields and of collaboration with other institutions should be emphasized at all times.

(*i*) Natural sciences — including human nutrition in relation to health, animal nutrition, biochemistry, plant and animal genetics, plant and animal physiology and pathology, soil chemistry and physics, entomology, mycology, bacteriology and meteorology.

(*ii*) Technology — including management, selection and breeding in relation to crops and livestock; animal feeding and care; soil fertilization, drainage, irrigation and other conservation and development measures; protection of crops and livestock from natural enemies; agricultural engineering; processing, storing and transporting food and other agricultural products.

(*iii*) Economic organization of agriculture — including the production and successive stages in the distribution, marketing and consumption of food and other agricultural products; the coordinated expansion of consumption and production; the efficiency of factors of production in terms of physical output and cost per unit; methods of reducing costs of production and distribution; scale of enterprise; economical use of labor and machinery; provision and use of credit; demand and prices; gross and net income in relation to output and consumption; trends and fluctuations in production, prices, incomes and other factors bearing on the relation of agriculture to the general economy; domestic and international trade and other aspects of national and international economy, with special reference to their bearing on food and agricultural problems.

(*iv*) Other social factors — including food habits and customs, the distribution of population between agriculture and industry, population movements, land tenure, consumer and producer cooperatives, and rural roads, communications and rural electrification; rural housing, sanitation and amenities.

(*v*) Public measures of regulation and assistance: In modern states public authorities legislate so extensively in regard to standards and practices, and provide aids of so many kinds in connection with the matters included in each of the preceding subparagraphs, that investigations in these fields by the Organization are too broad to be covered by any list. They would relate, among other matters, to special planning techniques, legislation affecting the eradication of deficiency diseases, measures for improving the diets of vulnerable groups, regulations for control of plant and animal diseases and pests, grading and standards of market and nutritive quality, subsidies for production or consumption, commercial policies and measures for increasing consumption by the distribution on special terms of accumulated stocks.

2. DISSEMINATION OF KNOWLEDGE

32. The need to make useful facts about nutrition and the consumption and production of foods far more widely known is so great and so essential to progress that promoting the dissemination of knowledge is to be given equal emphasis with research. The Organization should employ various means to this end as the need arises. The development of a program of publication will be important from the beginning. Promoting education in the fields relating to the Organization's work will be another important activity. (*Art. I.*)

a. *Publications*

33. A considerable variety of publications will probably be needed, some for official or professional use, some designed to meet the needs of particular groups of producers and consumers and those of the general public. High standards should be the aim in every case. Duplication of work adequately done by others should be avoided, and the possibility of cooperative ventures should be fully explored; the Organization might do much by this means to promote world-wide coordination of efforts — for example, in the preparation and publication of scientific abstracts. (*Art. XII.*)

34. It is not possible at this time to forecast exactly what publications the Organization will find it useful to issue. Among them might be a periodic summary based on the reports by Member nations; a periodic world survey of the state of nutrition, consumption and production together with an analysis of the determining factors, with special attention to interrelated developments and the policies of different countries; a periodic digest or review of legislation and administrative rulings relating to food, agriculture, forestry and fisheries; abstracts, reviews and bibliographies of scientific literature; regular bulletins dealing with crops, production, trade, stocks, prices and other data and their interpretation; and a journal or journals containing articles for the general reader on problems and progress in the fields covered by the Organization. It will clearly be essential to publish an authoritative and comprehensive yearbook of international statistics. (*Art. I, XI.*)

b. *Education*

35. The publications of the Organization will be educational in a broad sense. It should also promote more specific educational activities in several important fields, with the central purpose of furthering improved nutrition and adequate production and consumption on a world-wide scale. (*Art. I*).

36. With a view to raising the standards of professional services and making them more widely available, the Organization should be prepared to assist governmental and other agencies in planning for expansion or improvement of the work of institutions of learning in the fields related to its work. It should be in a position to serve as consultant to institutions on courses of study and methods of training. It might well act as a clearinghouse of information on facilities for study and research in institutions throughout the world. It should encourage and facilitate the exchange between countries of students, teachers and professional workers. (*Art. I.*)

37. To what extent, and in what ways, the Organization will be of assistance to educational institutions other than those at the university or professional level cannot be foreseen at present. Nations differ widely in their educational systems, which are peculiarly a matter of national concern. But while the rural school system should be one of the most important factors in improving rural life, it is in fact in most countries at a disadvantage in comparison with urban school systems; and in both urban and rural schools there are great and often unrealized opportunities for teaching young people elementary but important facts regarding foods and nutrition. Despite the difficulties involved, the Organization should be able to perform a useful service by advising on suitable courses of study, promoting adequate teacher-training in appropriate subjects, acting in a consultative capacity, assisting in surveys and studies to determine needed improvements and in other ways. (*Art. I.*)

38. Various countries are interested in furthering adult education, particularly of the kind exemplified by agricultural extension, home demonstration and similar services. Such services depend largely on local instructors and leaders who give personal counsel and assistance and demonstrate methods to help producers and homemakers apply the principles of good farming, food preparation, nutrition, and home economics, or domestic science, in their daily work and living. The Organization should be prepared to assist governments in determining the need for these services; to promote adequate training of workers, including opportunities for study in other countries when this would be advantageous; and to assist in other ways in widening the usefulness and improving the methods and standards of such services. (*Art. I.*)

39. The Organization will be interested in improving the effectiveness with which adult education services could use such channels as newspapers, radio and motion pictures to spread practical information. In addition, it should furnish authentic information for the public regarding its own activities. To what extent it should elaborate services of its own, designed specifically to furnish material for the press, radio and other popular media, will depend upon the course of its development. Whatever may be done in this field should be safeguarded with unusual care against the risk of exploitation and misrepresentation for purposes of commercial or other propaganda. (*Art. I.*)

c. *Library and inquiry services*

40. As the work of the Organization becomes widely known, it will probably be called upon to answer a large volume of inquiries on many subjects. Furnishing adequate information in response to these inquiries will in itself be an important service in disseminating knowledge. Partly for this purpose, and also for its other work, the Organization will need an extensive library, kept fully up to date. (*Art. I.*)

3. ADVISORY FUNCTIONS

41. Much of the work of the Organization will be of an advisory character. This will include making recommendations ranging from a suggestion on some minor point to drawing up and submitting for approval an elaborate program of action on a complex problem; and from advice given to a single Member nation or even a single institution to advice given to all Member nations. (*Art. I, IV.*)

42. The Organization should have this wide scope in its advisory functions to enable it to achieve the objectives of the Hot Springs Conference. It is, however, a much more delicate matter to give advice on some subjects than on others. Special procedures are provided by which the Conference of the Organization may formulate and adopt formal recommendations to governments. In addition, a wide variety of advisory services may be developed of a less formal character. (*Art. I, IV.*)

43. The effectiveness of advice and recommendations depends on the qualifications of those who give them, the adequacy of their preparatory work, their understanding of variations in local conditions and their ability to enlist the cooperation of Member nations. The Organization should progressively establish its connections and build up a staff with a wide range of qualifications and experience. The Organization will thus be equipped to take the initiative in formulating recommendations designed to stimulate action by one or more nations or international authorities. Its initiative in making suggestions and offering advice to nations individually and collectively would be especially useful in cases

in which coordinated action is required in several fields or by a number of countries. For a variety of reasons, a nation may feel itself inhibited from initiating a discussion of problems, the solution of which appears to demand modifications of the policies of other nations as well as of its own. In such cases, particularly, the Organization would be in a favorable position to initiate discussions and make recommendations. (*Art. IV.*)

44. The advisory work of the Organization would in appropriate cases be done in cooperation with other international authorities in related fields. (*Art. XII.*)

a. *Typical cases and procedure*

45. The Organization should be ready and willing to meet requests from one or more states for advice in regard to policy or for other assistance. The extent to which the Organization's advice in regard to the problems of individual countries will be required will of course vary greatly as between countries in different stages of agricultural and economic development. But improvements resulting from sound advice given to particular countries will in the long run redound to the common benefit, and by their general as well as their particular effects will promote the basic purposes of the Organization. The following might be typical cases and procedures:

(*a*) In some cases an international convention, in the sense of a formal agreement to be ratified by a large number of nations, would be the most effective instrument to accomplish the desired objective. Or the Organization might frame a model code or form of treaty as a guide to Member nations. Either of these methods would be suitable for agreements on such matters as the standardization of terms, assaying samples, biological material of various kinds, weights and measures, containers, certain trade practices, methods of appraising the nutritive values of foods and the adequacy of diets, and measures for preventing the spread of diseases or of pests. (*Art. IV.*)

(*b*) In other cases the Conference would act by means of a resolution or by adopting reports embodying proposals for action. Such a resolution or report might call for common action by the nations affected, the acceptance of common or related policies or changes in policy, or the creation of an institution for the common use and benefit of a group of nations. (*Art. IV, XIV.*)

(*c*) Raising the nutritional level of the population will in many countries involve long-range programs including the expansion and reorientation of production, the building up of food processing and consumer-goods industries, the improvement of markets and the expansion of such services as transportation and electric power. Complementary shifts in the production and trade of other countries would often be required in such cases, and outside capital and technical assistance might be needed. The Organization could perform a useful function by helping to determine the need for such far-reaching developments, drawing up plans, coordinating action by various countries, presenting the case for loans from international credit agencies and furnishing advice and technical assistance in other ways. (*Art. I, IV, XII.*)

(*d*) Similar but even more difficult problems occur in the case of countries or regions in which such developments and improvements cannot materially relieve the poverty and malnutrition of large masses of people in a reasonable time. In some regions chronic poverty is in part the result of age-old traditions, high net rates of reproduction of populations, and the lack of education, the inadequacy of roads and communication facilities, and the absence of opportunities for industrial employment. These problems are not insoluble, but they require long-continued effort and the cooperation of many agencies. The Organization should play a leading part in such long-term efforts. Where famine is a recurrent risk the Organization should obtain information on probable requirements and sources of supply, and facilitate arrangements with the governments of Member nations or with appropriate international agencies for finding the necessary men, money and materials, free or on special terms. (*Art. I, XII.*)

(*e*) Another type of problem concerns areas where climatic or other factors have led to specialization in the production of one or a few export products. Every practicable effort should be made in these areas to diversify production, grow more food and provide alternative employment. Usually, however, the solution of the problem requires the enlargement of foreign markets for the export products of the area.

b. *Advice and recommendations on other problems*

46. In addition to dealing with the problems discussed so far, the Organization would furnish advice and make recommendations in many other cases, some of which will be of a more or less routine nature. The initiative in making proposals might be taken by one or more Member nations or by the Conference. Suggestions might be made to the Conference by general or special conferences, by the advisory committees, by the Executive Committee and by the Director-General. The Executive Committee should be especially well qualified to act as an intermediary for proposals for action to be considered by the Conference, which in turn would submit recommendations to governments. The Director-General would not make recommendations directly to a government unless it requested him to do so. (*Art. IV, V, VI, VII.*)

47. Although a distinction is drawn throughout this discussion

between the initiation of proposals by governments and by the Organization, the point should not be overemphasized. To exercise its functions effectively, the Organization would necessarily develop close working relations with governments in the course of which suggestions and advice would naturally be exchanged. (*Art. I.*)

48. The Organization will be in regular communication with governments in connection with their reports and statistical and other returns. Governments will both ask for and expect to be offered suggestions for action on their part which will amplify the information supplied and make it comparable for the various countries. In response to requests, the Organization might furnish expert advisers who, together with local officials and technical personnel, would constitute special committees or missions authorized to investigate and report in accordance with their terms of reference. In general, such inquiries would have in view the making of recommendations for action. (*Art. I, XI.*)

49. Similarly, the Organization would increasingly have occasion to map out surveys and other undertakings — for example, a world agricultural census, to be repeated at intervals — to be carried out in cooperation with the governments concerned. For these surveys, too, special committees or missions made up in part of local representatives would be effective machinery, and useful advice might be expected frequently to result. The Organization would also have regular advisory relations with national agencies such as nutrition committees and research councils. (*Art. I.*)

50. In addition, collecting and disseminating information would in themselves involve indirect advisory work which would have considerable influence. Each nation would be given the benefit of the experience of others, objectively examined as a subject of common interest. The force of example should lead governments to find out more about conditions affecting their own people, and stimulate them to introduce measures for improvement which have succeeded elsewhere, and, equally, to guard against the repetition of mistakes.

4. FISHERIES, FORESTRY AND NON-FOOD AGRICULTURAL PRODUCTS

a. *Fisheries and marine products*

51. Fisheries furnish a considerable part of the world's food supply; in some areas they are more important than agriculture as a source of food. Vitamin-rich oils extracted from the livers of cod, sharks and other fish have in recent years assumed great importance in nutrition and therapy. Fisheries also furnish important by-products, such as fertilizer materials, protein feeds for livestock, industrial oils, leather and various chemicals. The technical and economic problems of those engaged in fishing require largely similar treatment to the problems of

those engaged in farming. Improving the production, handling, storing, processing and distribution of fish is vital in any concerted effort among nations to raise the nutritional levels and the standards of living of populations.

52. Few if any types of food production yield returns as quickly as does fishing. This fact will be of special significance after the war when there will be a general scarcity of animal proteins. During 1939–44, as during 1914–18, fisheries have been substantially replenished, and at the end of the present war well-stocked fishing grounds will constitute one of the world's few reserves of foods.

53. The work of the Organization in this field would follow the same general pattern as in agriculture, including research, education, advice and recommendation. It should examine the possibilities for expansion of present fisheries, since in many parts of the world known marine resources could without harm be exploited much more intensively to supply food for human beings, feed for livestock and materials for industry. It should encourage systematic exploration for virgin marine resources and evaluate the possibilities for their development. It should encourage the setting up of additional research laboratories to study biological, economic and technical problems related to the fishery industry throughout the world. (*Art. I.*)

54. In their migrations among the waters of the world, fish have no regard for national boundaries. The conservation and wise and equitable use of fishery resources is therefore in many cases peculiarly a matter for international agreements, treaties and conventions. It would be the duty of the Organization to help to formulate and to propose such international arrangements. It should also perform functions in relation to credit, which will be needed for the development, expansion and rehabilitation of many fishery enterprises, similar to the functions suggested elsewhere in this Report in connection with agriculture. (*Art. I, IV.*)

55. As in the case of agriculture, the Organization should take the necessary steps for cooperation with other bodies — in particular, the International Labor Organization, which is concerned with the social conditions of fishermen; the Council for the Exploration of the Sea (Copenhagen); the North Atlantic Council on Fishery Investigations (Ottawa); and the several bodies administering international fisheries. (*Art. XII.*)

b. *Forestry and forestry products*

56. Forests occupy approximately 22 percent of the land surface of the earth. They play so important a part in the conservation and building up of soil and water resources that it is impossible to plan conservation measures on any extensive scale without including forest management — and frequently afforestation — in the plans. In most countries

forestry and farming or grazing constitute possible alternative uses of much of the land, and a significant part of the forest land in many countries is owned or operated by farmers. Indeed, forests are perennial crops, natural or man-made, and their products compete with or supplement other farm products for certain important uses. Farmers are among the larger users of forest products, especially for fuel, building and equipment. For these reasons many countries include forestry as a part of agriculture in their governmental organization.

57. World forest supplies have been altered by the war. New supply problems have been created and new uses developed. In some countries progress in improved methods of forest management and utilization is being made at a faster rate than ever before. Thus there are now especially urgent reasons to consider forestry in world terms and to take concerted action to bring about more efficient growing, processing and distribution of forest products, the balancing of production and distribution with needs on a world scale and the prevention of disastrous overuse of forest resources in some countries while those of other countries go to waste for lack of effective demand, to the end that the world's forest resources may make their full contribution to the needs and the well-being of the people of every nation.

58. As in the case of food and other agricultural products discussed in this Report, these objectives would be accomplished through international cooperation in bringing all branches of science to bear upon the biological, technological, economic, social and other problems involved in the production, distribution and use of primary forest products; in establishing a factual basis upon which nations, individually and in concert, could build policies and programs; in helping to work out such programs; and in promoting widespread education and public understanding of forestry problems. The Organization's work in forestry would thus closely parallel that in other fields. (*Art. I, IV.*)

59. The Commission recommends that, in accordance with the situation in each case, the Organization should establish close working relations with any existing international agencies concerned with forestry. (*Art. XII, XIV.*)

c. *Non-food agricultural products*

60. A considerable part of the world's agriculture is devoted to the production of commodities other than foods. These products are of special importance because of the contribution they make to the money income of farmers since most of them require processing and are sold as raw materials for cash. Some of them are necessities of life; others contribute in an important measure to human health, dignity and well-being. The Organization should accord these products consideration

commensurate with their importance to agriculture and to social welfare.

61. Fibers constitute one of the major groups of non-food products. Of these some, such as cotton, wool, linen and silk, are consumed mainly in clothing and household goods; others, such as jute, hemp, abacá, sisal and henequen, are used in the form of bags, ropes, cords and nets. Other categories of non-food products include the oils and fats used in paints and soaps; hides, skins and furs used in clothing and in industry; beverages and beverage materials; and tobacco. It is characteristic of most of these products that their markets are international in scope and that consumption increases and decreases with fluctuations in general prosperity. Of many, also, production over the world tends in peacetime to run ahead of effective demand, with a resulting depression of the living standards of producers. At the same time many of these products are especially subject to intercommodity competition, including the increasing competition of synthetic materials.

62. Existing information on consumption capacity and effective demand for some of these products in different countries, and on the relation of consumption levels to standards of living and levels of well-being, is meager and inadequate compared with the same information in relation to food and nutrition. In sponsoring, organizing, aiding or conducting research designed to develop more complete information, the Organization will have an opportunity for service to consumers and producers. While such fundamental facts are being sought, however, much can be done to increase and broaden the consumption of many important products — for example, clothing, household textiles, paints, soaps — through a general expansion of world economy, including agriculture, industry and trade. (*Art. I.*)

63. The functions and activities of the Organization will in the nature of the case include non-food as well as food products, with respect to such matters as agricultural organization, agricultural credit, commodity arrangements, scientific and economic research, and education. (*Art. I, IV.*)

64. The Commission recommends that, where appropriate, the Organization should establish close working relations with other public international organizations concerned with non-food agricultural products. (*Art. XII.*)

5. AGRICULTURAL CREDIT

65. The Commission has given careful thought to the functions that ought to be performed by the Organization in the domain of agricultural credit. It is manifest that the basic purposes of the Organization will not be achieved unless international credit for agricultural projects is made available and effective on a considerable scale, and it follows that

the promotion of a wise and liberal administration of international agricultural credit is among the major concerns of the Organization. Such an administration, indeed, is important not only to world agriculture but to world economy, and the doctrine of an expanding world economy, to which, at the Hot Springs Conference and elsewhere, the majority of governments have subscribed, is unlikely to be realized in the absence of sound policy and practice in regard to international agricultural credit. Investments directed toward the improvement of agricultural methods should bring quick returns in increased production, and this would not only be reflected in improved nutrition but also in increased international trade. Indeed, that portion of international investments which may be directed towards agriculture may bring about quicker effects upon world economy than larger sums needed for longer term developments.

66. The Commission conceives, however, that international credit and investment, whether related to agriculture or industrial development or to other purposes, would most suitably be administered by a single international authority charged with the appropriate functions in respect of all such purposes. It recommends that such an authority be established by agreement between the governments concerned, and that adequate arrangements be made for including the provision of agricultural credit among its functions. It further recommends that the Organization, or in the event of its not being established in time the Interim Commission itself, should be represented at any international conference that may be convened for the purpose of setting up an international credit and investment authority.

67. Credit will be needed for many agricultural developments — for example, the reequipment of agriculture, mechanization, land reclamation, irrigation, afforestation, and increased storage, processing, and marketing facilities for agricultural products. Agricultural credit should, however, be interpreted not only as covering its conventional forms but also as including credit for adjustments in other parts of the economy in the interests of agricultural reorientation and better standards of nutrition.

68. The Organization will have a direct concern with all these matters, and it is clearly appropriate, if it is to be enabled to exercise an influence in its own field commensurate with the purposes for which it is established, that it should be recognized as a complementary body to the international credit and investment authority with specific functions in regard to agricultural credit. (*Art. I.*)

69. The specific functions relating to agricultural credit which the Commission recommends should be assigned to the Organization are as follows: (*Art. I, IV, XII.*)

(*a*) The Organization should participate in the management of the international credit organization through representation on its governing body, in order to provide for due consideration of agricultural interests in the determination of general international credit and investment policies.

(b) Applications for international credit for an agricultural purpose should be considered by the international credit authority only after examination by the Food and Agriculture Organization and in the light of its recommendations.

(c) In appropriate cases, and if the Food and Agriculture Organization should so recommend, the borrowing country should be required, as a condition of the loan, to avail itself to the fullest extent, in regard to the projects for which the loan is granted, of the technical services and advice of the Organization.

6. COMMODITY ARRANGEMENTS

70. Resolution II 7 (b) of the Hot Springs Conference instructed the Commission to consider the desirability of assigning to the Organization functions in the field of agricultural commodity arrangements. The Commission has recognized the important role which such arrangements can play in (a) coordinating internationally diverse or conflicting national price and marketing policies and programs; (b) eliminating excessive fluctuations in prices; (c) mitigating some of the effects of trade cycles; (d) maintaining adequate supplies for consumers; and (e) ensuring markets for producers while promoting desirable adjustments in agricultural production. Commodity arrangements for non-agricultural products have a similar role to perform, and to secure fairness of treatment, avoid confusion and establish consistent policies, the Commission recommends to its constituent governments that international commodity arrangements for both agricultural and non-agricultural products be coordinated under the supervision and direction of a single international authority. The Commission further recommends that principles governing international commodity arrangements for all classes of products should be formulated by a special international conference and that thereafter there should be established an international authority to review in the light of experience the application of the principle so formulated and to coordinate and supervise the administration of individual commodity arrangements.

71. The Commission recommends that the Organization, or in the event of its not being established in time the Interim Commission itself, should participate in the international conference which it proposes should be held to formulate the principles to which all commodity arrangements should conform. It further recommends that the Organization should be represented on the directorate of the proposed international authority and should be associated, where appropriate, with

the working operations of that authority through mutual consultation and reference. (*Art. XII.*)

72. As in the case of international agricultural credit arrangements, the Organization will have an important, though not an exclusive, concern in international agricultural commodity arrangements. The Organization should be entitled to propose particular commodity arrangements to the proposed international authority, or in the absence of such an authority to governments, and to suggest the provisions of the arrangements so proposed. Similarly, the Organization should be entitled to propose that any existing agricultural commodity arrangement should be modified or terminated. (*Art. IV.*)

73. The Organization will have a special competence and interest in regard to such arrangements as they promote or hinder better orientation of production through agricultural adjustments and whether they may be effective in providing opportunities for supplying consumption needs from the most efficient sources of production. For example, the Organization may well study the effects of monopolistic practices, excessive price variations and similar phenomena in order to stimulate appropriate international action for maintaining a check upon the first and for diminishing, or even for preventing, the second. On its own initiative, or in response to requests either from the general administrative authority or from the individual commodity control concerned, the Organization may conduct inquiries regarding any international agricultural commodity arrangement, and should furnish to governments, to the international commodity authority or to any authority dealing with an individual commodity arrangement, information, analyses or advice. (*Art. I, IV.*)

7. ADMINISTRATIVE FUNCTIONS

74. In carrying out the duties already outlined, the Organization will necessarily undertake certain administrative work.

75. In certain circumstances the Organization might perform administrative functions in connection with a wide range of international conventions or agreements on such matters as those already mentioned. It might also, in agreement with the countries concerned, perform or organize services of an international character, such as the control of locusts and other plagues, or the search for and distribution of biological materials for the control of predatory insects and noxious weeds. (*Art. I, IV.*)

76. The Organization would be free to accept and administer endowments or gifts for the furtherance of its work, being careful to ensure that the terms are not such as might cause embarrassment to the Organization. (*Art. XV.*)

77. The Organization would be empowered to expend, if it should so decide, part of its funds, contributed by Member nations, to establish fellowships for training expert workers or carrying out research projects, to found research institutes or to make grants-in-aid for other purposes. In such cases its funds should be used, however, only for projects that have a regional or world significance and that would not be undertaken without such assistance. (*Art. I.*)

78. To the fullest possible extent the Organization should utilize the facilities and resources of other organizations, both national and international, for the achievement of its purposes and in general should be cautious about undertaking the supervision or administration of executive agencies in fields related to its work. (*Art. XII.*)

79. The Organization should be entitled to consider any proposals that might be made or itself to make proposals for the distribution on special terms, to those whose consumption is relatively very low, of abnormal stocks of food or other agricultural products; and it should be empowered to assist other international bodies in administering such schemes. The necessity of coordinating such proposals with the policies of other bodies should be borne in mind, together with the risk that such action might delay necessary basic economic adjustments by giving producers an inducement to continue production despite the lack of effective demand for their output. (*Art. IV, XII.*)

80. Much of the foregoing discussion assumes that other international authorities will be created with administrative responsibilities in related fields, and that the Organization will promote its own purposes by maintaining close and cooperative association with these other authorities. A different situation would arise if such other authorities were not set up. If governments were prepared to authorize the Organization to fill, in whole or in part, some of the gaps created by the absence of such other authorities, there would be a case for its undertaking further executive responsibilities. (*Art. XII, XIV.*)

81. In particular, the Commission has recommended that the constituent governments establish international authorities to deal with international credit as a whole, and with commodity arrangements as a whole, including agricultural credit in the one case and agricultural commodity arrangements in the other. If, however, such international authorities should not be established, or if their effective operation should be unduly delayed, the Organization would undoubtedly find itself seriously hampered in the promotion of its primary purposes. The Commission has the confident hope that this situation will not arise. If it should, the Commission conceives that it would be the duty of the Organization to represent to governments that appropriate international credit and commodity arrangements, applying to the agricultural field alone, should be made. In that event, it would no doubt be appropriate to propose

that the administrative functions involved should be performed directly by the Food and Agriculture Organization itself. (*Art. I, IV.*)

82. Collaboration with the United Nations Relief and Rehabilitation Administration also has its administrative aspects, especially in relation to agricultural rehabilitation. The Organization might well have functions to perform in connection with rehabilitation work that may need to be continued beyond the life of the Relief and Rehabilitation Administration. The Constitution of the Organization permits it to assume such responsibilities at the appropriate time. (*Art. I, IV, XII, XIV.*)

83. The Organization may initiate or concert plans with governments, in cooperation with other appropriate international bodies, for the procurement and distribution of supplies of food and producers' goods to relieve famine resulting from floods, drought, earthquakes or other calamities. (*Art. I, IV, XII.*)

(a) *Constitution of the Food and Agriculture Organization of the United Nations* [1]

PREAMBLE

The Nations accepting this Constitution, being determined to promote the common welfare by furthering separate and collective action on their part for the purposes of

raising levels of nutrition and standards of living of the peoples under their respective jurisdictions,

securing improvements in the efficiency of the production and distribution of all food and agricultural products,

bettering the condition of rural populations,

and thus contributing toward an expanding world economy,

hereby establish the Food and Agriculture Organization of the United Nations, hereinafter referred to as the "Organization," through which the Members will report to one another on the measures taken and the progress achieved in the fields of action set forth above.

ARTICLE I (FUNCTIONS OF THE ORGANIZATION)

1. The Organization shall collect, analyze, interpret and disseminate information relating to nutrition, food and agriculture.

2. The Organization shall promote and, where appropriate, shall recommend national and international action with respect to

(*a*) scientific, technological, social and economic research relating to nutrition, food and agriculture;

[1] *First Report to the Governments of the United Nations by the Interim Commission on Food and Agriculture.* Washington, August 1, 1944, p. 41.

(*b*) the improvement of education and administration relating to nutrition, food and agriculture, and the spread of public knowledge of nutritional and agricultural science and practice;

(*c*) the conservation of natural resources and the adoption of improved methods of agricultural production;

(*d*) the improvement of the processing, marketing and distribution of food and agricultural products;

(*e*) the adoption of policies for the provision of adequate agricultural credit, national and international;

(*f*) the adoption of international policies with respect to agricultural commodity arrangements.

3. It shall also be the function of the Organization

(*a*) to furnish such technical assistance as governments may request;

(*b*) to organize, in cooperation with the governments concerned, such missions as may be needed to assist them to fulfill the obligations arising from their acceptance of the recommendations of the United Nations Conference on Food and Agriculture; and

(*c*) generally to take all necessary and appropriate action to implement the purposes of the Organization as set forth in the Preamble.

ARTICLE II (MEMBERSHIP)

1. The original Members of the Organization shall be such of the nations specified in Annex I as accept this Constitution in accordance with the provisions of Article XXI.

2. Additional Members may be admitted to the Organization by a vote concurred in by a two-thirds majority of all the members of the Conference and upon acceptance of this Constitution as in force at the time of admission.

ARTICLE III (THE CONFERENCE)

1. There shall be a Conference of the Organization in which each Member nation shall be represented by one member.

2. Each Member nation may appoint an alternate, associates, and advisers to its member of the Conference. The Conference may make rules concerning the participation of alternates, associates and advisers in its proceedings, but any such participation shall be without the right to vote except in the case of an alternate or associate participating in the place of a member.

3. No member of the Conference may represent more than one Member nation.

4. Each Member nation shall have only one vote.

5. The Conference may invite any public international organization

which has responsibilities related to those of the Organization to appoint a representative who shall participate in its meetings on the conditions prescribed by the Conference. No such representative shall have the right to vote.

6. The Conference shall meet at least once in every year.

7. The Conference shall elect its own officers, regulate its own procedure, and make rules governing the convocation of sessions and the determination of agenda.

8. Except as otherwise expressly provided in this Constitution or by rules made by the Conference, all matters shall be decided by the Conference by a simple majority of the votes cast.

Article IV (Functions of the Conference)

1. The Conference shall determine the policy and approve the budget of the Organization and shall exercise the other powers conferred upon it by this Constitution.

2. The Conference may by a two-thirds majority of the votes cast make recommendations concerning questions relating to food and agriculture to be submitted to Member nations for consideration with a view to implementation by national action.

3. The Conference may by a two-thirds majority of the votes cast submit conventions concerning questions relating to food and agriculture to Member nations for consideration with a view to their acceptance by the appropriate constitutional procedure.

4. The Conference shall make rules laying down the procedure to be followed to secure:

(a) proper consultation with governments and adequate technical preparation prior to consideration by the Conference of proposed recommendations and conventions; and

(b) proper consultation with governments in regard to relations between the Organization and national institutions or private persons.

5. The Conference may make recommendations to any public international organization regarding any matter pertaining to the purpose of the Organization.

6. The Conference may by a two-thirds majority of the votes cast agree to discharge any other functions consistent with the purposes of the Organization which may be assigned to it by governments or provided for by any arrangement between the Organization and any other public international organization.

Article V (the Executive Committee)

1. The Conference shall appoint an Executive Committee consisting of not less than nine or more than fifteen members or alternate or asso-

ciate members of the Conference or their advisers who are qualified by administrative experience or other special qualifications to contribute to the attainment of the purpose of the Organization. There shall be not more than one member from any Member nation. The tenure and other conditions of office of the members of the Executive Committee shall be subject to rules to be made by the Conference.

2. Subject to the provisions of paragraph 1 of this Article, the Conference shall have regard in appointing the Executive Committee to the desirability that its membership should reflect as varied as possible an experience of different types of economy in relation to food and agriculture.

3. The Conference may delegate to the Executive Committee such powers as it may determine, with the exception of the powers set forth in paragraph 2 of Article II, Article IV, paragraph 1 of Article VII, Article XIII, and Article XX of this Constitution.

4. The members of the Executive Committee shall exercise the powers delegated to them by the Conference on behalf of the whole Conference and not as representatives of their respective governments.

5. The Executive Committee shall appoint its own officers and, subject to any decisions of the Conference, shall regulate its own procedure.

ARTICLE VI (OTHER COMMITTEES AND CONFERENCES)

1. The Conference may establish technical and regional standing committees and may appoint committees to study and report on any matter pertaining to the purpose of the Organization.

2. The Conference may convene general, technical, regional or other special conferences and may provide for the representation at such conferences, in such manner as it may determine, of national and international bodies concerned with nutrition, food and agriculture.

ARTICLE VII (THE DIRECTOR-GENERAL)

1. There shall be a Director-General of the Organization who shall be appointed by the Conference by such procedure and on such terms as it may determine.

2. Subject to the general supervision of the Conference and its Executive Committee, the Director-General shall have full power and authority to direct the work of the Organization.

3. The Director-General or a representative designated by him shall participate, without the right to vote, in all meetings of the Conference and of its Executive Committee and shall formulate for consideration by the Conference and the Executive Committee proposals for appropriate action in regard to matters coming before them.

Article VIII (Staff)

1. The staff of the Organization shall be appointed by the Director-General in accordance with such procedure as may be determined by rules made by the Conference.

2. The staff of the Organization shall be responsible to the Director-General. Their responsibilities shall be exclusively international in character and they shall not seek or receive instructions in regard to the discharge thereof from any authority external to the Organization. The Member nations undertake fully to respect the international character of the responsibilities of the staff and not to seek to influence any of their nationals in the discharge of such responsibilities.

3. In appointing the staff the Director-General shall, subject to the paramount importance of securing the highest standards of efficiency and of technical competence, pay due regard to the importance of selecting personnel recruited on as wide a geographical basis as is possible.

4. Each Member nation undertakes, insofar as it may be possible under its constitutional procedure, to accord to the Director-General and senior staff diplomatic privileges and immunities and to accord to other members of the staff all facilities and immunities accorded to non-diplomatic personnel attached to diplomatic missions, or alternatively to accord to such other members of the staff the immunities and facilities which may hereafter be accorded to equivalent members of the staffs of other public international organizations.

Article IX (Seat)

The seat of the Organization shall be determined by the Conference.

Article X (Regional and Liaison Offices)

1. There shall be such regional offices as the Director-General with the approval of the Conference may decide.

2. The Director-General may appoint officials for liaison with particular countries or areas subject to the agreement of the government concerned.

Article XI (Reports by Members)

1. Each Member nation shall communicate periodically to the Organization reports on the progress made toward achieving the purpose of the Organization set forth in the Preamble and on the action taken on the basis of recommendations made and conventions submitted by the Conference.

2. These reports shall be made at such times and in such form and shall contain such particulars as the Conference may request.

3. The Director-General shall submit these reports, together with analyses thereof, to the Conference and shall publish such reports and analyses as may be approved for publication by the Conference together with any reports relating thereto adopted by the Conference.

4. The Director-General may request any Member nation to submit information relating to the purpose of the Organization.

5. Each Member nation shall, on request, communicate to the Organization, on publication, all laws and regulations and official reports and statistics concerning nutrition, food and agriculture.

ARTICLE XII (COOPERATION WITH OTHER ORGANIZATIONS)

1. In order to provide for close cooperation between the Organization and other public international organizations with related responsibilities, the Conference may, subject to the provisions of Article XIII, enter into agreements with the competent authorities of such organizations defining the distribution of responsibilities and methods of cooperation.

2. The Director-General may, subject to any decisions of the Conference, enter into agreements with other public international organizations for the maintenance of common services, for common arrangements in regard to recruitment, training, conditions of service, and other related matters, and for interchanges of staff.

ARTICLE XIII (RELATION TO ANY GENERAL WORLD ORGANIZATION)

1. The Organization shall, in accordance with the procedure provided for in the following paragraph, constitute a part of any general international organization to which may be entrusted the coordination of the activities of international organizations with specialized responsibilities.

2. Arrangements for defining the relations between the Organization and any such general organization shall be subject to the approval of the Conference. Notwithstanding the provisions of Article XX, such arrangements may, if approved by the Conference by a two-thirds majority of the votes cast, involve modification of the provisions of this Constitution: Provided that no such arrangements shall modify the purposes and limitations of the Organization as set forth in this Constitution.

ARTICLE XIV (SUPERVISION OF OTHER ORGANIZATIONS)

The Conference may approve arrangements placing other public international organizations dealing with questions relating to food and agriculture under the general authority of the Organization on such terms as may be agreed with the competent authorities of the organization concerned.

Article XV (Legal Status)

1. The Organization shall have the capacity of a legal person to perform any legal act appropriate to its purpose which is not beyond the powers granted to it by this Constitution.

2. Each Member nation undertakes, insofar as it may be possible under its constitutional procedure, to accord to the Organization all the immunities and facilities which it accords to diplomatic missions, including inviolability of premises and archives, immunity from suit and exemptions from taxation.

3. The Conference shall make provision for the determination by an administrative tribunal of disputes relating to the conditions and terms of appointment of members of the staff.

Article XVI (Fish and Forest Products)

In this Constitution the term "agriculture" and its derivatives include fisheries, marine products, forestry and primary forestry products.

Article XVII (Interpretation of Constitution)

Any question or dispute concerning the interpretation of this Constitution or any international convention adopted thereunder shall be referred for determination to an appropriate international court or arbitral tribunal in the manner prescribed by rules to be adopted by the Conference.

Article XVIII (Expenses)

1. Subject to the provisions of Article XXV, the Director-General shall submit to the Conference an annual budget covering the anticipated expenses of the Organization. Upon approval of a budget the total amount approved shall be allocated among the Member nations in proportions determined, from time to time, by the Conference. Each Member nation undertakes, subject to the requirements of its constitutional procedure, to contribute to the Organization promptly its share of the expenses so determined.

2. Each Member nation shall, upon its acceptance of this Constitution, pay as its first contribution its proportion of the annual budget for the current financial year.

3. The financial year of the Organization shall be July 1 to June 30 unless the Conference should otherwise determine.

Article XIX (Withdrawal)

Any Member nation may give notice of withdrawal from the Organization at any time after the expiration of four years from the date of its acceptance of this Constitution. Such notice shall take effect one year after the date of its communication to the Director-General of the Organization subject to the Member nation's having at that time paid its annual contribution for each year of its membership including the financial year following the date of such notice.

ARTICLE XX (AMENDMENT OF CONSTITUTION)

1. Amendments to this Constitution involving new obligations for Member nations shall require the approval of the Conference by a vote concurred in by a two-thirds majority of all the members of the Conference and shall take effect on acceptance by two-thirds of the Member nations for each Member nation accepting the amendment and thereafter for each remaining Member nation on acceptance by it.

2. Other amendments shall take effect on adoption by the Conference by a vote concurred in by a two-thirds majority of all the members of the Conference.

ARTICLE XXI (ENTRY INTO FORCE OF CONSTITUTION)

1. This Constitution shall be open to acceptance by the nations specified in Annex I.

2. The instruments of acceptance shall be transmitted by each government to the United Nations Interim Commission on Food and Agriculture, which shall notify their receipt to the governments of the nations specified in Annex I. Acceptance may be notified to the Interim Commission through a diplomatic representative, in which case the instrument of acceptance must be transmitted to the Commission as soon as possible thereafter.

3. Upon the receipt by the Interim Commission of twenty notifications of acceptance the Interim Commission shall arrange for this Constitution to be signed in a single copy by the diplomatic representatives, duly authorized thereto, of the nations who shall have notified their acceptance, and upon being so signed on behalf of not less than twenty of the nations specified in Annex I this Constitution shall come into force immediately.

4. Acceptances the notification of which is received after the entry into force of this Constitution shall become effective upon receipt by the Interim Commission or the Organization.

ARTICLE XXII (FIRST SESSION OF THE CONFERENCE)

The United Nations Interim Commission on Food and Agriculture shall convene the first session of the Conference to meet at a suitable date after the entry into force of this Constitution.

ARTICLE XXIII (LANGUAGES)

Pending the adoption by the Conference of any rules regarding languages, the business of the Conference shall be transacted in English.

ARTICLE XXIV (TEMPORARY SEAT)

The temporary seat of the Organization shall be at Washington unless the Conference should otherwise determine.

ARTICLE XXV (FIRST FINANCIAL YEAR)

The following exceptional arrangements shall apply in respect of the financial year in which this Constitution comes into force:

(a) the budget shall be the provisional budget set forth in Annex II to this Constitution; and

(b) the amounts to be contributed by the Member nations shall be in the proportions set forth in Annex II to this Constitution: Provided that each Member nation may deduct therefrom the amount already contributed by it toward the expenses of the Interim Commission.

ARTICLE XXVI (DISSOLUTION OF THE INTERIM COMMISSION)

On the opening of the first session of the Conference, the United Nations Interim Commission on Food and Agriculture shall be deemed to be dissolved and its records and other property shall become the property of the Organization.

ANNEX I

NATIONS ELIGIBLE FOR ORIGINAL MEMBERSHIP

AUSTRALIA	INDIA
BELGIUM	IRAN
BOLIVIA	IRAQ
BRAZIL	LIBERIA
CANADA	LUXEMBURG
CHILE	MEXICO
CHINA	NETHERLANDS
COLOMBIA	NEW ZEALAND
COSTA RICA	NICARAGUA
CUBA	NORWAY
CZECHOSLOVAKIA	PANAMA
DENMARK	PARAGUAY
DOMINICAN REPUBLIC	PERU
ECUADOR	PHILIPPINE COMMONWEALTH
EGYPT	POLAND
EL SALVADOR	UNION OF SOUTH AFRICA
ETHIOPIA	UNION OF SOVIET SOCIALIST REPUBLICS
FRANCE	UNITED KINGDOM
GREECE	UNITED STATES OF AMERICA
GUATEMALA	URUGUAY
HAITI	VENEZUELA
HONDURAS	YUGOSLAVIA
ICELAND	

2. PETROLEUM

In 1939, the United States consumed petroleum products, natural gasoline, and condensates at the rate of 1,420,035,000 barrels, of which 93,060,000 barrels were from imports and stocks, indicating a depletion of United States reserves to the extent of 1,326,975,000 barrels. In 1943, calculated on a similar basis, the depletion was 1,593,000,000 barrels. The depletion for 1944 was estimated by the Petroleum Administrator for War at 1,755,000,000 barrels. During these years proven reserves have increased from 17,348,146,000 barrels to 20,082,793,000 barrels. Thus while consumption has increased 28 per cent, proven reserves have increased 15.7 per cent. On the basis of these figures it has been estimated that the domestic supply of the United States will be exhausted in 14 years.[1]

Figures such as these, combined with an awareness of the tremendous drain of the war on United States petroleum resources and the vital dependence of our future military security as well as our economic prosperity on access to adequate petroleum resources, have turned the attention of administrative officials and legislators to the question of future petroleum policy. The President in his *Thirteenth Report on Lend-Lease Operations* recognized the importance of the problem. The reports of the five Senators who made a tour of the fighting fronts in July, August, and September 1943 focused Senate and public attention on its seriousness.[2] The Arabian pipe-line proposal called attention to some of the complexities and dangers of the problem. Finally, the conversations carried on with the British conveyed some assurance that satisfactory arrangements can be worked out on an international basis.

(1) *Thirteenth Report of the President (Roosevelt) to Congress on Lend-Lease Operations, Filed January 6, 1944* [3]

[Excerpt]

After the war the nations of the world, including the United States, will require petroleum to maintain their industrialized economies. Discoveries of new oil fields will undoubtedly be made to supplement known oil reserves and, as in the past, the steady development of technological improvements in oil production will make it possible to draw on oil reserves which cannot now be tapped. Nevertheless, as in the case of other natural resources, some nations will have insufficient oil reserves to meet their petroleum requirements. Others will have a surplus. Agreed action by the nations of the world, as provided for in the master lend-lease agreements, for the expansion of production, the elimination of discriminatory treatment in commerce, and the reduction of trade barriers, will assure to the United States and other nations fair and equal access to the petroleum produced in all parts of the world.

(2) *Outline of Principles of Proposed Agreement between the Petroleum Reserves Corporation, the Arabian American Oil Co., and the Gulf Exploration Co., January 24, 1944* [4]

At the suggestion of Mr. Jesse Jones, the chairman of its Board of Directors, and with the approval of the President, the Reconstruction Finance Corporation,

[1] *Investigation of the National Defense Program. Additional Report of the Special Committee Investigating the National Defense Program*, Senate Report No. 10, Part 16, 78th Cong., 2d sess., p. 506.

[2] *Ibid.*, p. 519–71.   [3] House Doc. No. 375, 78th Cong., 2d sess., p. 45.

[4] Senate Report No. 10, Part 16, 78th Cong., 2d sess., p. 579.

on June 30, 1943, created the Petroleum Reserves Corporation with authority "to buy or otherwise acquire reserves of crude petroleum from sources outside of the United States including the purchase or acquisition of stock in corporations owning such reserves or interests therein, and to store, transport, produce, process, manufacture, sell, market, and otherwise dispose of such crude petroleum and the products derived therefrom." The Corporation was authorized to borrow from the Reconstruction Finance Corporation up to $30,000,000. The Corporation's board of directors was to consist of the Secretaries of State, War, Navy, and Interior and the Foreign Economic Administrator. The Secretary of the Interior (Ickes) was elected president of the Corporation.[1]

On February 6, 1944, Secretary Ickes announced that the Corporation had been authorized by its board of directors, with the approval of the President and the State Department, and on the recommendation of the War Department, to enter into the agreement given below. This announcement aroused widespread criticism on the part of representatives of oil companies not included in the agreement and on the part of others who doubted the wisdom of the action on broader grounds of national policy. Apparently the project was subsequently dropped, for reasons that have not been fully explained.

For brevity, Petroleum Reserves Corporation hereinafter is referred to as "Government" and the Arabian American Oil Co. and Gulf Exploration Co. are called the "Companies."

Upon the recommendation of the War Department, Navy Department, Joint Chiefs of Staff, and the Army and Navy Petroleum Board and with the approval of the Department of State, the aforementioned parties, in appreciation of the critical importance of reserves of petroleum in war and in peace and of the necessity of assuring to the military forces of the Nation and to the people of the United States adequate petroleum supplies, have agreed upon the principles of the understanding outlined below:

1. Government agrees to construct and to own and maintain a main trunk pipe-line system, including requisite facilities, for the transportation of crude petroleum from a point near the presently discovered oil fields of Saudi Arabia and Kuwait to a port at the eastern end of the Mediterranean Sea. The size, capacity, location, and terminal points of the pipe-line system shall be determined by Government. The gathering system for the delivery of oil to the intake terminus of the pipe-line shall be provided by the Companies. The Government shall determine the most feasible plan for the operation of the facilities and shall retain supervision thereof.

2. The Companies will cooperate with the various agencies of the United States Government in obtaining the necessary rights for the construction, maintenance, and operation of the pipe-line system and facilities.

3. The charges for pipe-line services shall include, in addition to current maintenance and operating costs, an amount sufficient to amortize within a period of 25 years the entire investment, together with interest

[1] *Ibid.*, p. 517.

and such net return to Government as may be agreed upon in the definitive contract. The parties shall agree upon an amount of oil to be tendered for transport by the Companies as a minimum guaranteed amount in order that the Government will be guaranteed repayment of the items above specified, within the time limited. It is the intent that the Companies will guarantee payment of the above items to the Government within the 25-year period.

4. Companies agree to perform at actual cost any work or services which the Government may request in connection with this project.

5. Government may make available to other oil producers or shippers the right to a portion of the capacity of the pipe-line system upon the agreement of such party or parties to assume pro rata the obligations undertaken by the Companies, and upon such other terms and conditions as Government may specify, and also subject to the rights of the Government of any country through which the pipe-line system passes.

6. Upon the following conditions the Companies agree to maintain a crude oil petroleum reserve available for production for the account of, and purchase by, the military forces of the United States:

(a) The reserve shall be 1,000,000,000 barrels of crude oil (gravity and specifications to be agreed upon) less amounts purchased by Government as provided for hereafter, or 20 percent of the recoverable oil content of the Companies' reserves if the total proved reserves be less than 5,000,000,000 barrels. The Companies will use their best efforts to maintain the proved reserves above this amount.

(b) Government shall have the right (transferable to other governmental agency or agencies) to purchase for a period of 50 years for the military forces the 1,000,000,000 barrels of reserved crude oil, which the Companies agree to deliver, if required by Government, at the rate of 30,000,000 barrels per year at times and quantities to be agreed upon. The aforesaid option is a continuing one and the Government is not required to purchase any crude oil during any particular period of time.

(c) Except in times of war or national emergency, if Government wishes to purchase more than 30,000,000 barrels during any calendar year, it must afford the Companies reasonable notice to provide additional facilities required to meet such increased demand.

(d) Government shall have the option to purchase said quantity of reserved oil at a discount of 25 percent below the market price in the Persian Gulf region for oil of like kind and gravity at the time and place of delivery, or at a discount of 25 percent below the average of the market prices in the United States for oil of like kind and gravity, whichever of such prices is the lower at the time of delivery. The market price of crude oil in the United States shall be determined by the selection from time to time by the parties of certain points in the United States.

(e) The Government shall have the sole right to determine when and the manner in which the aforementioned reserve is drawn upon and may, if it elects, determine that said reserve has no relation to the purchase of petroleum made by the military forces from year to year in the normal course of supplying their requirements.

7. In times of war or other national emergency, Government shall have the first right and option, in addition to that specified in paragraph 6, to purchase all of the crude petroleum produced by the Companies and all products thereof and shall pay therefor such price as the parties may agree upon at such time. Government shall specify what portion, if any, of such purchases constitutes withdrawals from the petroleum reserve provided in paragraph 6.

8. Prior notice of negotiations by Companies with Governments of any foreign countries relating in any manner to the sale of petroleum or products from their concessions in Saudi Arabia and Kuwait shall be given to the Department of State and to Government.

No sales of petroleum or products will be made by the Companies to any Government or the nationals of any Government when, in the opinion of the Department of State, such sales would militate against the interests of the United States. Companies shall be afforded appropriate notice of such opinion.

The commercial and other policies and practices of the Companies would conform to the foreign policy of the United States.

9. The agreement between the parties shall be sanctioned by the respective Governments of Saudi Arabia and Kuwait and nothing in this contract shall be construed to require action by the Companies in violation of their covenants with said Governments under existing agreements. Companies agree to lend all possible assistance to Government in carrying out its obligations hereunder.

Companies will not construct or cause to be constructed any additional main pipe-line or pipe-lines for the westward transportation of crude petroleum or products from Saudi Arabia or Kuwait unless the capacity of contemplated pipe-line system installed by Government is insufficient to meet the requirements of the Companies and, after reasonable notice from the Companies, Government declines to install additional facilities. In any event, the Companies agree at all times during the life of this agreement to utilize the pipe-line system contemplated herein to the fullest extent of its available capacity should their transportation requirements exceed the available capacity of the system.

10. This memorandum does not purport to contain a complete statement of the provisions of a contract to be entered into. It is a broad

outline of certain of the essential provisions with the details and related provisions and other matters to be incorporated therein left for future determination.

11. In the execution and performance of this agreement, it is the desire and intention of the parties not only to promote and assist in the development of petroleum in the areas affected by this agreement, but also to promote the interests of the governments of such areas, and to respect their sovereignty and protect their rights. It is the desire of the United States that American nationals that enjoy privileges with respect to petroleum in countries under foreign governments shall have an active concern for the peace and prosperity of such countries and shall exercise their rights with due regard to the rights, including that of political integrity, of the governments of such countries.

It is understood that the foregoing memorandum is subject to the approval of the board of directors of the parties and of their approval of a definitive contract containing all of the agreements of the parties. The foregoing is approved in principle and I agree to recommend its approval to my board of directors.

HAROLD L. ICKES,
Petroleum Reserves Corporation.
F. A. DAVIES,
Arabian American Oil Co.
J. F. DRAKE,
Gulf Exploration Co.

The undersigned, presidents of Standard Oil Co. of California and the Texas Co., respectively, sole stockholders of the Arabian American Oil Co., are in accord with the foregoing in principle and agree to recommend its approval by their respective boards of directors and, subject to such approval, agree to recommend its approval by the board of directors of the Arabian American Oil Co.

H. D. COLLIER.
W. S. S. RODGERS.

The undersigned, president of the Gulf Oil Corporation, is in accord with the foregoing in principle and agrees to recommend its approval by the board of directors of the Gulf Oil Corporation, and subject to such approval, agrees to recommend its approval by the board of directors of the Gulf Exploration Co. Nothing herein shall require action in violation of existing contracts with the British Government or with any corporation in which the British Government has an ownership interest.

J. F. DRAKE.

(3) *Report of Subcommittee of Special Committee Investigating the National Defense Program, Concerning Petroleum Matters, February 16, 1944* [1]

[Excerpts]

THE FUTURE OF THE UNITED STATES IN THE WORLD PETROLEUM ECONOMY

. . . .

To date, we have relied primarily on private interests and have allowed private interests to determine questions which will affect seriously our petroleum future.

The State Department has sought to keep itself informed on petroleum matters and to take action within the normal scope of its activities to protect the rights of our citizens. [A summary of its action with respect to petroleum prepared by the State Department is attached to the Report as Appendix VI.]

The acquisition of foreign oil rights has become affected with a strong national interest. To secure possession of such rights would be a determining factor in preventing future wars, for aggressive nations will hesitate to attack us if they know that we have the petroleum, as well as the other weapons, with which to defend ourselves.

It is therefore necessary for the United States to evolve a detailed policy for the exploration and development of foreign oil resources. Attention has been given to this subject by various Government agencies, especially during recent months. But it is a most difficult subject. All of the necessary information has not yet been obtained; underlying policies have not yet been decided upon.

Four approaches to our solution of the problem of petroleum readily occur. There may well be others.

The Government may continue the policy which has prevailed for at least the last two decades of leaving private American companies interested in foreign oil fields free to take whatever action they may determine upon with Government assistance limited to that available through normal diplomatic channels. With other countries conscious of the critical importance of petroleum to their national security, this course would be apt to result in difficulty for the private American oil companies concerned.

American companies since World War I have located and secured concessions for United States interests in (1) Saudi Arabia, (2) Bahrein, (3) one-half interest in Kuwait, (4) one-fourth interest in the oil fields of Iraq and Qatar, (5) Sumatra, and (6) Venezuela.

These concessions may well represent petroleum reserves equal to the

[1] Senate Report No. 10, Part 16, 78th Cong., 2d sess., p. 514.

petroleum reserves in the continental United States and may be of profound significance in considering the petroleum policy. These rights constitute a tribute to the energy and enterprise of American private industry even with limited governmental encouragement or support.

The second possible approach would be by full diplomatic backing for American enterprise in exploring and developing foreign petroleum reserves. This would mean a recognition by our Government of the vital concern of our country in foreign petroleum reserves because of their relation to our security and economic welfare.

This would mean the same sort of vigorous support that is accorded by certain other governments to their nationals abroad in cases where their national interest, as distinct from the private interests of citizens, is vitally involved.

Such a course retains the full advantage of private initiative while at the same time according protection and encouragement flowing from the recognition of the national interest involved.

The treatment of American claims in certain foreign oil reserves in the Middle East and elsewhere would present hazards to our position with respect to the oil concessions there.

The third and fourth alternatives are for the Government to participate in the ownership of the concessions or to take over sole ownership of certain foreign oil reserves. The latter possibility can immediately be ruled out. If there had been no incentive for private initiative, our concessions at Bahrein Island and in Saudi Arabia would never have been obtained. Complete Government ownership of foreign oil concessions would presuppose a radical change in our economic system.

Objections have also been advanced to partial Government ownership. It might discourage private enterprise and there are inherent difficulties in placing the Government in partnership with large private financial interests. Government control is always subject to possible political influences and has never been considered desirable except where private ownership has completely failed to do the job. On the other hand, obtaining proper oil resources is so vital to the national security and the economic complications of attempting to regulate oil production both at home and in far distant fields may present such difficulties that in the final analysis Government participation in ownership may need to be given serious consideration. Certain foreign countries containing very large reserves of petroleum forbid ownership or operation of oil properties by Government corporations. This must be taken into account in the determination of policy. American oil companies also in most instances view with some concern the entry of the Government into the oil business.

The problems of ownership and control will become even more complex in connection with any oil reserves or interests in oil reserves which we may acquire through diplomatic action as reverse lend-lease or otherwise. The Petroleum Administrator has properly stated that he believes that this Government should take some action to obtain additional petroleum concessions abroad. His expressions as a member of the administration are entitled to great weight. In addition, it is apparent that other persons in the administration are beginning to think along these lines.

It is unfortunate that we have not fully utilized the period since the First World War to obtain rights and explore and develop petroleum resources outside the borders of this country, which would be beneficial to us at this time. American companies have added greatly to the amount of our proven reserves but might have been able to accomplish more.

Now that our domestic resources are being depleted in order to provide the sinews for fighting this war, it is necessary for us to give immediate attention to the matter.

Simply because we had developed and exploited our domestic petroleum reserves to a greater extent than any other nation, the United States has been able to supply, largely out of its own domestic reserves, the bulk of the vital oil products needed to win this war directly and through lend-lease. The resulting excessive depletion of these reserves, however, affects our post-war economic position to an exceptional degree simply because our economy is built on petroleum. For that reason, it would seem fair to ask our Allies, particularly Great Britain, to recompense the United States for this excessive depletion by transfer to us of a compensating volume of proven reserves outside this country. However, even more important is an agreement with our allies on the equitable allocation of world reserves of petroleum which will be discovered and proven in the future, plus the formulation of a positive, vigorous American policy on the whole subject.

Oil resources to be obtained from the British or to be developed in the future by whatever means is determined upon will raise still another question. It will be necessary to determine whether they should be held as reserves against future use in wartime or whether they should be exploited now so that our domestic resources may be conserved. If the latter, it will be necessary to determine questions of tariff and proration of oil in the United States.

To summarize, the questions which will have to be determined before we can formulate a real policy on petroleum are very numerous. The committee does not purport to have any quick or easy answers therefor, but it does believe that immediate and continued attention should be given to these problems for the purpose of determining and putting into effect as soon as possible the best policy that can be formulated.

. . . .

Conclusion

The committee is very strongly and unanimously of the opinion that the Senate should give immediate consideration through the appropriate legislative committees to the determination of a petroleum policy for the United States that shall take properly into account both the domestic and foreign field and critical importance of petroleum in our national defense as well as our national well-being.

The security of the United States today is dependent upon adequate supplies of petroleum. The economy of the United States is also to a large extent dependent upon petroleum.

Failure to make proper provision for adequate petroleum supplies for the United States during the next few decades will vitally affect both our security and our development.

The critical importance of petroleum in the world economy is emphasized in the current emergency. There have been suggestions that international arrangements may be considered assuring the access of all nations to petroleum reserves for their peacetime economy upon an equitable basis.

Such a possibility accentuates the imperative necessity of an early determination of a national policy on petroleum by the Congress.

As preliminary discussions on petroleum policy are held between our Government and the governments of our allies, there is urgent necessity for the executive agencies of our Government to keep the appropriate congressional committees thoroughly acquainted with developments as they take place. A heavy responsibility for consideration and final approval of this Nation's petroleum policy rests upon the Congress of the United States.

In arriving at policy decisions of such magnitude that they will affect our future security for decades to come, both the legislative and executive branches of our Government should seek the practical counsel and advice of businessmen in the oil industry, particularly those with foreign experience. Their enterprise has helped to bring us this close to victory, and their judgments can be considered with profit to the national interest before final decisions are reached.

On March 23, it was announced that a special Senate Committee under the chairmanship of Senator Maloney (Connecticut) had been appointed to work out an oil policy for the United States. The other members of this Committee were Senators Connally (Texas), Johnson (Colorado), O'Mahoney (Wyoming), Lucas (Illinois), Maybank (South Carolina), LaFollette (Wisconsin), Vandenburg (Michigan), Brewster (Maine), Moore (Oklahoma) and Gurney (South Dakota).[1]

[1] *New York Times*, March 24, 1944.

(4) *Conclusion of Discussions with the United Kingdom. Department of State Release, May 3, 1944* [1]

[Excerpt]

Acting Secretary of State Stettinius made the following announcement on March 7, 1944, which was issued simultaneously in Washington and London:

"The Governments of the United States and the United Kingdom are undertaking preliminary and exploratory discussions on petroleum questions. These discussions will be, in the first instance, on an expert technical level, and will take place in Washington." [2]

The Acting Secretary of State stated that it was contemplated that these informal conversations with the British Government on problems of mutual interest relating to oil would lead at an early date to further conversations between the two Governments at a higher level. For this purpose President Roosevelt appointed a committee, under the chairmanship of the Secretary of State, consisting of Harold L. Ickes, Secretary of the Interior; Robert P. Patterson, Under Secretary of War; James V. Forrestal, Under Secretary of the Navy; Charles B. Rayner, Petroleum Adviser of the Department of State; and Charles E. Wilson, Vice Chairman of the War Production Board. Subsequently, Mr. Leo T. Crowley, Director of the Foreign Economic Administration, and Mr. Ralph K. Davies, Deputy Petroleum Administrator for War, were included in the committee.

On April 11, the Department announced the names of those who would represent the United States in the preliminary exploratory discussions on an expert technical level as follows: [3] Mr. Charles Rayner, Petroleum Adviser, Department of State, chairman; Mr. Ralph K. Davies, Deputy Petroleum Administrator for War, vice chairman; Mr. Paul Alling, Deputy Director, Officer of Near Eastern and African Affairs, Department of State; Mr. Leroy Stinebower, Adviser, Office of Economic Affairs, Department of State; Mr. George Walden, Special Assistant to the Deputy Petroleum Administrator for War; Mr. C. S. Snodgrass, Director, Foreign Refining Division, Petroleum Administration for War; Brig. Gen. Howard Peckham, War Department; Com. A. F. Carter, Navy Department.

The Department of State announced on April 13, 1944, that the Senate's Special Committee on Petroleum would be kept informed regarding the course of these preliminary exploratory discussions. Moreover, in order that the views of the American oil industry regarding problems that might arise in the discussion might be taken into account, representatives drawn from various sections of the industry were invited to meet with the group of experts representing the United States in these discussions.

This meeting took place in Washington shortly after. To facilitate the day-to-day discussions with the British representatives three of the ten oil-industry officials, Mr. John A. Brown, Mr. W. S. S. Rodgers, and Mr. A. Jacobsen, were requested to sit as advisers with the United States group of experts. It was also announced that additional advisers from among the ten oil-industry officials announced on April 13 would be asked to sit with the American expert group from time to time, should that prove desirable in the light of specific problems which might arise in the course of the discussions. Mr. James C. Sappington, 3d, Assistant Chief of the Petroleum Division, Department of State, was designated executive secretary, and Mr. John A. Loftus, also of the Petroleum Division, Department of State, was designated recording secretary of the United States group of experts. [4]

[1] Department of State, *Bulletin*, X, p. 411.
[2] *Ibid.*, p. 238.
[3] *Ibid.*, p. 346, 347.
[4] *Ibid.*, p. 372.

The preliminary exploratory discussions on petroleum began on April 18, 1944 in Washington. The discussions proceeded on the basis of the recognition that ample petroleum supplies, available in international trade, are necessary for the security and prosperity of nations; that for the foreseeable future the petroleum resources of the world are adequate to assure ample supplies for increasing post-war markets; and that expanding world demand must be met by the orderly flow of oil from the various producing countries of the world.[1]

Following the conclusion of the preliminary discussions it was announced that the report of the United States group of experts would be considered by the Cabinet committee of which Secretary Hull is chairman.[2]

The preliminary exploratory discussions on petroleum between groups of experts representing the Governments of the United States and the United Kingdom, which began in Washington on April 18, were concluded in a joint session held on May 3.[3]

In a spirit of understanding and cooperation the two groups explored the full range of both countries' interest in petroleum on the basis of broad principles looking to the orderly long-range development of abundant oil supplies. The two groups are now reporting the results of these discussions to their Governments.

After the full discussion of broad principles the two groups reviewed various specific matters of mutual interest relating to the production, distribution, and transportation of oil. These specific matters included pending problems affecting the oil operations abroad of the American and British oil industry; questions relating to oil production, particularly in the Middle East; the proposed trans-Arabian pipeline; and the Iraq Petroleum Company's project for an additional pipeline from Kirkuk, Iraq, to Haifa. The groups shared the view that the peacetime intergovernmental aspects of such matters should be resolved, as between the two Governments, within the framework of the broad principles which had been discussed. . . .

3. FISHERIES

(1) Protocol on Pelagic Whaling, Signed at London, February 7, 1944 [4]

This protocol amends in certain particulars the International Agreement for the Regulation of Whaling signed at London on June 8, 1937 and the protocol signed at London on June 24, 1938, introducing certain amendments into the agreement of 1937.

The provisions of the new protocol were agreed upon at the International Whaling Conference held in London in January 1944. The American delegates to that conference were Dr. Remington Kellogg of the United States National Museum and Mr. Loyd V. Steere, Agricultural Attaché at the American Embassy in London. These delegates were assisted by Mr. John M. Allison, Second Secretary, American Embassy, London, and Capt. Alfred C. Richmond, United States Coast Guard, as technical advisers.[5]

The Norwegian Government deposited its instrument of ratification on March 31, 1944.[6] On May 10, President Roosevelt transmitted the Protocol to the Senate with a view to receiving the advice and consent of that body to ratification,[7] which the Senate gave on June 16.[8] On June 22, the President ratified the Protocol.[9] The instrument of ratification was deposited on July 10, 1944.[10] The instrument of ratification of the United Kingdom was deposited on June 28.[11] On June 29, notification of the accession of Mexico was placed on record in accordance with the provisions of Article 6 of the Protocol.[12]

[1] Ibid.   [2] Ibid., p. 411.   [3] Ibid.   [4] Ibid., p. 592.
[5] Ibid., p. 271.   [6] Ibid., p. 400.   [7] Ibid., p. 461.   [8] Ibid., p. 568.
[9] Ibid., p. 592.   [10] Ibid., XI, p. 129.   [11] Ibid.   [12] Ibid.

The Governments of the Union of South Africa, the United States of America, the Commonwealth of Australia, the United Kingdom of Great Britain and Northern Ireland, Canada, Eire, New Zealand and Norway,

Being parties or signatories to the International Agreement for the Regulation of Whaling signed at London on the 8th June, 1937 [1] (hereinafter referred to as the Agreement of 1937), and to the Protocol signed at London on the 24th June, 1938,[2] introducing certain amendments into the Agreement of 1937 (hereinafter referred to as the Protocol of 1938); and

Desiring, in view of the fact that pelagic whaling operations in the area to which Article 7 of the 1937 Agreement applies have been interrupted for a considerable period by the existence of hostilities and in order to meet the present emergency without prejudicing the conservation of stocks of whales, to put into force by agreement such provisions as may be necessary with regard to pelagic whaling in this area when whaling operations are resumed there:

Have agreed as follows: —

ARTICLE 1. (*i*) The period fixed by Article 7 of the Agreement of 1937, during which factory ships or a whale catcher attached thereto may be used for the purpose of taking or treating baleen whales, shall be extended for the first season in which whaling operations are resumed in the area referred to in the said Article 7, so as to cover the period from the 24th November to the 24th March, both dates inclusive.

(*ii*) Each Government party to the present protocol shall give notice to the Government of the United Kingdom when whale factory ships registered under the law of any territory under its authority or otherwise under its jurisdiction engage in whaling operations in the area defined in Article 7 of the Agreement of 1937. The Government of the United Kingdom will inform the other Governments party to the present protocol of all notices received under this paragraph and shall itself similarly give notice to the other contracting Governments if whale factory ships registered under the law of any territory under its authority or otherwise under its jurisdiction engage in whaling operations in the said area.

(*iii*) For the purposes of paragraph (*i*) of this article the first season in respect of which any notice has been given under paragraph (*ii*) above, shall be deemed to be the first season in which whaling operations are resumed. This season is hereinafter referred to as "the first season."

ARTICLE 2. The provisions of Article 1 of the Protocol of 1938 relating to the taking of humpback whales in any waters south of 40 degrees south latitude shall apply during the first season.

[1] *Treaties, Conventions*, etc. 1923–1937, IV, p. 5372.
[2] United States *Treaty Series* No. 933.

ARTICLE 3. (*i*) During the first season, the number of baleen whales caught in the area referred to in Article 7 of the 1937 Agreement shall not exceed 16,000 blue whale units.

(*ii*) For the purposes of paragraph (*i*) of this article, blue whale units shall be calculated on the basis that one blue whale equals —

   (*a*) 2 fin whales, or
   (*b*) 2½ humpback whales, or
   (*c*) 6 sei whales.

(*iii*) The Government of the United Kingdom shall consult all the Governments who have given notice under Article 1 (*ii*) of this agreement in order to arrange by cooperation and agreement the measures necessary to ensure that the total number of baleen whales caught during the first season does not exceed the number specified in paragraph (*i*) of this article.

ARTICLE 4. In the absence of agreement to the contrary none of the provisions of the present protocol shall operate except in the first season.

ARTICLE 5. The present protocol shall be ratified and the instruments of ratification deposited as soon as possible with the Government of the United Kingdom.

ARTICLE 6. (*i*) The present protocol shall be open to accession on behalf of any Government which was a party to the 1937 Agreement and has not signed the present protocol.

(*ii*) Accession shall be effected by means of a notification addressed to the Government of the United Kingdom.

ARTICLE 7. (*i*) The Government of the United Kingdom shall inform the Governments of the United States of America, Canada, Eire, Mexico, New Zealand and Norway of all ratifications of this protocol or accessions thereto.

(*ii*) The present protocol shall come into force as soon as ratifications or accessions have been deposited on behalf of all Governments referred to in paragraph (*i*) of this article and of the Government of the United Kingdom.

(*iii*) The ratification of or accession to the present protocol by a Government which is a signatory but not a party to the Agreement of 1937 shall not become effective until such Government becomes a party to that agreement by ratification.

In witness whereof the undersigned plenipotentiaries, being duly authorised to this effect by their respective Governments, have signed the present protocol and affixed thereto their seals.

Done at London this 7th day of February, 1944, in a single copy which shall remain deposited in the archives of the Government of the United

Kingdom by whom certified copies will be transmitted to all the Governments referred to in Article 7 (*i*).

For the Government of the Union of South Africa:

> Deneys Reitz.
> A. P. van der Post.

For the Government of the United States of America:

> Loyd V. Steere.

For the Government of the Commonwealth of Australia:

> S. M. Bruce.

For the Government of the United Kingdom of Great Britain and Northern Ireland:

> A. T. A. Dobson.
> J. E. de Watteville.

For the Government of Canada:

> Vincent Massey

For the Government of Eire:

For the Government of New Zealand:

> W. J. Jordan.

For the Government of Norway:

> Birger Bergersen.

CHAPTER XI

LABOR AND SOCIAL RELATIONS

1. INTERNATIONAL LABOR ORGANIZATION

[See *Documents, IV, 1941–42*, p. 838.]

The twenty-sixth session of the International Labor Conference met in Philadelphia April 20–May 13, 1944. Delegations were present from 41 member countries. The Soviet Union was the only United Nation not represented. There were present 74 government delegates (each member is allowed two), 28 employers' delegates and 30 workers' delegates. Of the delegations 28 were tripartite, 11 included only government delegates and 2 included a workers' delegate but no employers' delegate. Official observers were present representing the governments of Iceland, Nicaragua and Paraguay. Danish observers also were present.

The agenda of the Conference had been prepared by the Governing Body, meeting in London in December 1943. It covered five main points: the future policy; program and status of the Organization; present and post-war social policy; organization of employment in the transition from war to peace; social security and standards of social policy in dependent territories.

The exhibits below give only the more important of the results of the Conference.[1]

(1) *Message of the President* (*Roosevelt*) *to the Opening Session of the 26th International Labor Conference, Philadelphia, April 20, 1944*[2]

To the Members of the International Labor Conference:

I send you greetings and a warm welcome. We are glad to have you in the United States. It is a privilege to welcome on our soil for the third time a general conference of your great organization. The Conference that opens today is most significant in the annals of international gatherings. The mere fact that, in the tradition of the founders of the International Labor Organization, the Conference still maintains its distinctive democratic tripartite character, is in itself of significance. As part of the regular constitutional machinery of the I.L.O., it also testifies to the vitality of one of the few international organizations which have continued to function throughout the war. The determination on the part of its member states that the I.L.O. should continue its activities during the war years is evidence of the indestructible tenacity of the democratic way of life. As representatives of the practical affairs of these nations — not only of their governments but also of their workers and employers — you have come together to make

---

[1] For report see *The Twenty-sixth Session of the International Labour Conference, Philadelphia, April to May 1944*. Montreal, 1944; *International Labour Review*, L (July 1944), p. 1.   [2] Department of State, *Bulletin*, X, p. 782.

plans and recommendations for the continuing improvement of labor standards and for raising the standard of living of the world's people.

The tasks you are undertaking, even at the moment when the tide of war is mounting, bear testimony to the fact that the welfare of the world's population and their liberty are a first and an ultimate concern of those dedicated to root out from this earth every trace of Nazi ideas and Nazi methods. We know that the conditions of a lasting peace can be secured only through soundly-organized economic institutions, fortified by humane labor standards, regular employment, and adequate income for all the people. Within the field of your activity the United Nations have no need to extemporize a new organization — the ways and means for obtaining this underwriting of a permanent peace are among the items on the agenda of your Conference. In your recommendations will lie the foundation of those agreements in the field of labor and social standards which must be part of any permanent international arrangement for a decent world. The Secretary of State, Cordell Hull, has already publicly announced that the Government of the United States is now working on plans for an international organization to maintain peace. He has also referred to the "economic and other cooperative arrangements" which must be made in order that the peoples of the world may "have the opportunity through their own efforts to improve their material condition." As part of these plans and international arrangements, I see in the I.L.O. a permanent instrument of representative character for the formulation of international policy on matters directly affecting the welfare of labor and for international collaboration in this field.

I see it as a body with the requisite authority to formulate and secure the adoption of those basic minimum standards that shall apply throughout the world to the conditions of employment. As part of these arrangements, also, I see in the I.L.O. an organization which shall serve the world for investigation and research, for discussion and debate. But more than that — it must be the agency for decision and for action on those economic and social matters related to the welfare of working people which are practical for industry and designed to enhance the opportunities for a good life for peoples the world over. It is to the I.L.O. that we shall look as the official international organization where ideas, experience, and movements in the field of labor and social development may find practical and effective expression.

(2) *Declaration of the Aims and Purposes of the International Labor Organization, Adopted by the 26th International Labor Conference, Philadelphia, May 10, 1944* [1]

The General Conference of the International Labor Organization, meeting in its Twenty-sixth Session in Philadelphia, hereby adopts, this

[1] *Ibid.*, p. 482.

day of May in the year nineteen hundred and forty-four, the present Declaration of the aims and purposes of the International Labor Organization and of the principles which should inspire the policy of its Members.

I

The Conference reaffirms the fundamental principles on which the Organization is based and, in particular, that:

(a) labor is not a commodity;

(b) freedom of expression and of association are essential to sustained progress;

(c) poverty anywhere constitutes a danger to prosperity everywhere;

(d) the war against want requires to be carried on with unrelenting vigor within each nation, and by continuous and concerted international effort in which the representatives of workers and employers, enjoying equal status with those of Governments, join with them in free discussion and democratic decision with a view to the promotion of the common welfare.

II

Believing that experience has fully demonstrated the truth of the statement in the Preamble to the Constitution of the International Labor Organization that lasting peace can be established only if it is based on social justice, the Conference affirms that:

(a) all human beings, irrespective of race, creed or sex, have the right to pursue both their material well-being and their spiritual development in conditions of freedom and dignity, of economic security and equal opportunity;

(b) the attainment of the conditions in which this shall be possible must constitute the central aim of national and international policy;

(c) all national and international policies and measures, in particular those of an economic and financial character, should be judged in this light and accepted only in so far as they may be held to promote and not to hinder the achievement of this fundamental objective;

(d) it is a responsibility of the International Labor Organization to examine and consider all international economic and financial policies and measures in the light of this fundamental objective;

(e) in discharging the tasks entrusted to it the International Labor Organization, having considered all relevant economic and financial factors, may include in its decisions and recommendations any provisions which it considers appropriate.

III

The Conference recognizes the solemn obligation of the International Labor Organization to further among the nations of the world programs which will achieve;

(a) full employment and the raising of standards of living;

(b) the employment of workers in the occupations in which they can have the satisfaction of giving the fullest measure of their skill and attainments and make their greatest contribution to the common well-being;

(c) the provision, as a means to the attainment of this end and under adequate guarantees for all concerned, of facilities for training and the transfer of labor, including migration for employment and settlement;

(d) policies in regard to wages and earnings, hours and other conditions of work calculated to ensure a just share of the fruits of progress to all, and a minimum living wage to all employed and in need of such protection;

(e) the effective recognition of the right of collective bargaining, the cooperation of management and labor in the continuous improvement of productive efficiency, and the collaboration of workers and employers in the preparation and application of social and economic measures;

(f) the extension of social security measures to provide a basic income to all in need of such protection and comprehensive medical care;

(g) adequate protection for the life and health of workers in all occupations;

(h) provision for child welfare and maternity protection;

(i) the provision of adequate nutrition, housing and facilities for recreation and culture;

(j) the assurance of equality of educational and vocational opportunity.

IV

Confident that the fuller and broader utilization of the world's productive resources necessary for the achievement of the objectives set forth in this Declaration can be secured by effective international and national action, including measures to expand production and consumption, to avoid severe economic fluctuations, to promote the economic and social advancement of the less developed regions of the world, to assure greater stability in world prices of primary products, and to promote a high and steady volume of international trade, the Conference pledges the full cooperation of the International Labor Organization with such international bodies as may be entrusted with a share of the responsibility for this great task and for the promotion of the health, education and well-being of all peoples.

V

The Conference affirms that the principles set forth in this Declaration are fully applicable to all peoples everywhere and that, while the manner of their application must be determined with due regard to the stage of social and economic development reached by each people, their progressive application to peoples who are still dependent, as well as to those who have already achieved self-government, is a matter of concern to the whole civilized world.

(3) *Resolution Concerning Social Provisions in the Peace Settlement, Adopted by the 26th International Labor Conference, Philadelphia, May 12, 1944* [1]

Whereas the Conference is called upon to make recommendations to the United Nations for present and post-war social policy, and more particularly concerning the social provisions to be inscribed in the various general or special treaties or agreements to which the United Nations will jointly or severally become parties;

Whereas the prospect of a complete victory of the United Nations makes it possible to prepare a better world order directed towards the achievement of the social objectives which these nations proclaimed in the Atlantic Charter in expressing their desire to bring about the fullest collaboration between all nations in the economic field with the object of securing for all improved labor standards, economic advancement and social security;

1.

The Conference considers that the principles stated in the following draft are appropriate for inclusion in a general or special treaty or agreement between nations desirous of giving early effect to the principles of the Atlantic Charter and Article VII of the Mutual Aid agreement:

The signatory governments

Having pledged themselves to provide conditions which will ensure an increasing measure of freedom from want to their own peoples and to all peoples; Recognizing, therefore, their common obligation to foster expanding production and employment on a sound basis, free from disruptive fluctuations, and to ensure that workers and productive resources shall not be allowed to be idle while the needs of large parts of the world remain unsatisfied;

Realizing that the economic life and conditions in each nation are increasingly dependent upon the economic life and conditions of other nations, and that hence the attainment of the above-stated objectives requires increasing collaboration among nations;

Have agreed that:

ARTICLE I. The Declaration of the Aims and Purposes of the International Labor Organization adopted by the International Labor Conference at Philadelphia, 1944, the text of which is annexed,[2] is hereby reaffirmed.

[1] *Ibid.*, p. 514.
[2] See this volume p. 458.

Article II. Each government recognizes its duty to maintain a high level of employment. Accordingly, all arrangements by and among the signatory and other like-minded governments for international economic cooperation should be framed and administered to serve the objectives set forth in Article I. They should be directed to the expansion of production, employment and the exchange and consumption of goods and to the liberation of economic activity from unreasonable restrictions. Particular consideration should be given to measures for promoting the reconstruction of economic life in countries whose economic and social life has been disrupted as the result of Axis aggression.

Article III. The following matters are of international concern and should be among the social objectives of international as well as national policy:

(1) Opportunity for useful and regular employment to all persons who want work, at fair wages or returns and under reasonable conditions, with provision for protection of health and against injury in all occupations;

(2) Raising standards of living to provide adequate nutrition, housing, medical care and education;

(3) Establishment of minimum standards of employment to prevent exploitation of workers, whether employed or self-employed, whose opportunities for high wage employment are limited;

(4) Provision for child welfare;

(5) Provision for a regular flow of income to all those whose employment is interrupted by sickness or injury, by old age or by lack of employment opportunity;

(6) The effective recognition of the right of freedom of association and of collective bargaining;

(7) Provision of facilities for training and transfer of labor.

Article IV. The International Labor Office may, under standards constitutionally determined by the International Labor Conference, as occasion requires, collect from, and interchange with, the signatory governments, uniform statistical and other economic information on the following matters which are among those of direct interest to the International Labor Organization and are of international concern:

(1) Employment, wages and conditions of work;

(2) Standards of living and the distribution of income, with particular reference to wage and salaried workers;

(3) Technical education and training for employment;

(4) Industrial health, safety and welfare;

(5) Industrial relations;

(6) Social security; and

(7) Administration of labor and social security legislation.

Article V. With respect to the matters set forth in Article III:

(1) The governments, through appropriate international agencies,

shall develop standards and statistical measures, and shall maintain uniform statistics and other information.

(2) The governments shall interchange among themselves and make available to the International Labor Organization such information and reports as may be required to assist them and the Organization to develop recommendations with respect to such matters.

(3) The governments shall take appropriate steps to assure close collaboration and full exchange of information between the International Labor Organization and any other international bodies which now exist or may be established for the promotion of economic advancement and social well-being.

(4) The governments shall take appropriate steps to have placed on the agenda of the International Labor Conference annually the subjects of the extent to which the social objectives set forth in Article I have been attained and on the measures taken during the year toward the attainment of the objectives.

ARTICLE VI. With respect to draft international conventions and recommendations adopted by the Conference in accordance with Article 19 of the Constitution of the International Labor Organization, the signatory governments undertake to report to the International Labor Office as requested by the Governing Body on the status of legislation and administration and, in so far as practicable, of practices under collective agreements between employers and workers.

2.

The Conference recommends that the Governing Body of the International Labor Organization:

(1) call a special conference of the Organization when in its opinion there is a danger of a substantial fall in general employment levels for the purpose of recommending appropriate national or international measures to prevent the development or spread of unemployment and to establish conditions under which high levels of employment may be maintained or restored;

(2) correlate the activities of the I.L.O. toward the end of maintaining full employment with those of any other international agency or agencies which may be designated by the United Nations to have primary responsibility in related economic fields.

3.

The Conference Recommends that:

(1) The United Nations should undertake —

(a) to apply to any dependent territories in respect of which they have accepted or may accept a measure of international accountability through any international or regional commission or other body the principle that all policies designed to apply to dependent territories shall be primarily directed to the well-being and development of the peoples of such territories, and to the promotion of the desire on their part for social progress;

(b) to apply to such territories the provisions of the Forced Labor Convention, 1930; the Recruiting of Indigenous Workers Convention, 1936; the Contracts of Employment (Indigenous Workers) Convention, 1939, and the Penal Sanctions (Indigenous Workers) Convention, 1939;

(c) to make a periodical report to the International Labor Office in respect of each such territory indicating the extent to which effect has been given to the provisions of the Social Policy (Dependent Territories) Recommendation, 1944;

(d) to ask the International Labor Office to appoint, in continuation of the collaboration established in the case of the Permanent Mandates Commission, a representative on any Committee which may be entrusted with the task of watching over the application of the principle of international accountability, and further to ensure that any facilities which may be afforded, in the form of inspection or otherwise, for the better implementation of this principle, shall include appropriate measures for examining the application of the above-mentioned Conventions and Recommendation.

(2) When determining the future status of dependent territories which on 1 September 1939 were controlled by Axis powers, the United Nations should specifically require the application thereto of the arrangements provided for in the preceding paragraph.

(3) In any negotiations regarding the organization, control and operation of merchant shipping and in particular in making international arrangements for the disposal of merchant shipping tonnage, the United Nations concerned should consult the competent bodies of the International Labor Organization, such as the Joint Maritime Commission, in regard to the possibility of including stipulations concerning the standard of accommodation to be provided for crews and of stipulations embodying the provisions of Conventions already adopted by the maritime sessions of the Conference, or of any further such Conventions that may be adopted before the negotiation of such agreements.

(4) In making international arrangements concerning transport by air, land, and inland waterway, the United Nations should have due regard to the repercussions of such arrangements on the working and living conditions of persons employed in transport, and should consult the International Labor Organization in regard to such repercussions and more particularly in regard to the working and living conditions of persons who, in operating such transport systems, work in or under the jurisdiction of more than one country.

(5) The International Labor Organization should make available to the United Nations any information or assistance calculated to facilitate

the implementation of the proposals contained in the resolution concerning economic policies for the attainment of social objectives and the present resolution and should be prepared to participate in any international conference which may be considering such proposals.

4.

Believing that the exceptional opportunity of the negotiations of the peace settlement should be taken to secure a concerted advance in the acceptance of binding obligations concerning conditions of labor;

The Conference reaffirming the principle of the association of management and labor in the framing of such standards,

Recommends

(a) That throughout the peace settlement the United Nations should wherever appropriate include provisions for labor standards. In a number of cases such provisions might properly be taken from conventions or recommendations that have been or may be adopted by the International Labor Conference.

(b) That the Governing Body should appoint a consultative committee on labor provisions in the peace settlement. This committee should hold itself in readiness, together with the Director of the International Labor Office, to give advice with reference to such provisions on the request of the United Nations or of particular groups of the United Nations. This committee should have the right to coopt additional members of special competence with respect to the particular sets of provisions under consideration.

(c) That the United Nations should make full use of this committee in any way in which they consider it appropriate to include labor provisions in the peace settlement.

5.

The Conference recommends to Governments that a Conference of representatives of the Governments of the United, associated, and other Nations, willing to attend, be called at any early date, in association with the Governing Body of the International Labor Office, to consider an international agreement on domestic policies of employment and unemployment; and this Conference pledges the full cooperation and the assistance of the I.L.O. in calling such a conference on employment, and in helping to carry into effect appropriate decisions it might make.

(4) *Resolution Concerning Economic Policies for the Attainment of Social Objectives, Adopted by the 26th International Labor Conference, Philadelphia, May 12, 1944* [1]

Whereas the prospect of a complete victory of the United Nations makes it possible to prepare a better world order directed towards the

[1] Department of State, *Bulletin*, X, p. 517.

achievement of the social objectives which these nations proclaimed in the Atlantic Charter in expressing their desire to bring about the fullest collaboration between all nations in the economic field with the object of securing for all improved labor standards, economic advancement and social security; and

Whereas these objectives of the United Nations coincide with the basic principles of the International Labor Organization, and the International Labor Conference, meeting in New York in 1941, pledged the full collaboration of the International Labor Organization in their implementation; and

Whereas the International Labor Conference is called upon by Item II on the Agenda of the present Session to make recommendations to the United Nations for present and post-war social policy concerning more especially the measures required to be taken internationally and nationally to ensure full employment, social security and rising standards of living; and

Whereas the initiative with regard to international policy lies with the United Nations at the present time, and it is desirable in order to attain the objectives referred to that all nations should pursue an appropriate national policy; and

Whereas the attainment of full employment and high productivity by the various nations after the war is essential to the achievement of freedom from want, the attainment of increasing living standards, the realization of genuine economic security and the continuation of peaceful economic progress; and

Whereas full employment can be achieved and maintained only through the adoption, by governments, industry and labor, of policies and measures which effectively encourage the continuing expansion of production and improvement of distribution; and

Whereas the speedy achievement of full employment requires the prompt and orderly reconversion, reconstruction and expansion of industry, trade, commerce and agriculture after the war, and the subsequent maintenance of employment and production at high levels requires the creation of an economic and social environment conducive to a progressive and expanding economy;

The Conference adopts the following resolution:

1. INTERNATIONAL POLICY

1. Believing that the relief of war-stricken peoples, repatriation of prisoners and exiles and resumption of agricultural and industrial production are matters which will be of the utmost urgency immediately on the liberation of occupied countries and that on the successful handling of these problems the possibility of achieving the long-range objectives of social and economic well-being will largely depend,

The Conference welcomes the creation of the United Nations Relief and Rehabilitation Administration, urges all States concerned to cooperate actively in the achievement of the tasks entrusted to it and assures the Administration of the readiness of the International Labor Organization to assist it in every appropriate way.

2. In view of the fact that for varying periods after the end of hostilities many essential commodities and transport facilities will be in short supply, and that international arrangements will be needed to ensure a fair allocation of available supplies and prevent excessive price movements,

The Conference considers that the Governments of the United Nations concerned should arrange to continue in operation, for such periods as any serious shortages may persist, the existing machinery of international coordination and control subject to such modification, and in particular to such enlargement of the membership of the authorities concerned, as may contribute to the equitable and efficient operation of such machinery in the transition from war to peace.

3. The Conference endorses the declaration of the United Nations Conference on Food and Agriculture held in May 1943, that while the primary responsibility lies with each nation for seeing that its own people have the food needed for life and health, each nation can fully achieve this goal only if all cooperate in appropriate international action, and urges the setting up of a permanent international organization, as recommended by the Conference on Food and Agriculture, to raise the level of nutrition and improve the efficiency of agricultural production and distribution.

4. Recognizing that a satisfactory international monetary system is essential to the full development of mutually advantageous economic relations between nations, and consequently to the raising of standards of living,

The Conference attaches great importance to the establishment at the earliest possible moment of effective international machinery for settling balances arising out of international trade and other transactions and for maintaining stability in rates of exchange, notes with satisfaction that the Governments of the United Nations are giving careful attention to this matter and urges that they include in any agreement establishing such machinery a provision requiring the authorities responsible for its application to have regard in framing and applying their policies to the effect of their decisions on employment and living standards.

5. Noting that imports of capital will be needed for reconstruction, development and the raising of living standards in many countries, and believing that the provision of such capital will contribute to the maintenance of full employment in the lending countries,

The Conference:

(a) considers that the existing machinery of the international capital market should be supplemented by the establishment of appropriate international machinery for the purpose of promoting the international movement of capital;

(b) considers that the promotion of full employment and higher living standards should be regarded as a primary objective of any such international machinery;

(c) considers that the authorities responsible for the operation of such international machinery should consult the International Labor Organization as to the appropriateness of including in the terms under which development works financed in whole or in part through such machinery are to be carried out, provisions regarding the welfare and working conditions of the labor employed; and that such provisions should be framed in consultation with the International Labor Organization;

(d) affirms the readiness of the International Labor Organization to render every assistance in its power in determining the appropriateness of the inclusion of such provisions and in their framing and application and in the promotion through the operations of such international machinery of the general objectives of full employment and higher living standards.

6. Recognizing the great contribution which the international exchange of goods and services can make to higher living standards and to high levels of employment,

The Conference:

(a) believes that the measures proposed in the foregoing paragraphs for the promotion of exchange stabilization and international lending will contribute to the expansion of international trade, but considers that the United Nations should also examine wartime changes in industrial capacity, and arrange for exchange of information on post-war industrial programs and should take vigorous action to promote the expansion of international trade by appropriate commercial policies; and considers that all countries, creditor as well as debtor, should adapt their commercial policy in such a way as to enable them to settle all obligations arising out of international transactions;

(b) considers that the United Nations should initiate measures to facilitate the coordination through appropriate international machinery of the commercial policies of all countries for the purpose of promoting a steady expansion in world trade on a multilateral basis;

(c) considers that in such coordination special consideration should be given to the need of countries which are highly dependent on returns from exports to take measures to ensure a high degree of stability in the level of their economic activity and observes that the need for these measures will decrease to the extent that international collaboration proves successful; and

(d) considers that in such coordination special account should be taken of the dislocation and the accumulated needs resulting from the devastation caused by war operations and from the prolonged diversion from peacetime production in countries which have been engaged for a long period in a sustained and total war effort.

7. In order to lay the foundation for rising levels of consumption throughout the world and at the same time to ensure more stable and adequate incomes to those primary producers whose services are needed for the production of essential raw materials and foodstuffs,

The Conference considers that the United Nations should initiate concerted action designed to ensure the constant availability to all purchasers of adequate supplies of such commodities at prices which give a reasonable return to the efficient producer and are held sufficiently stable to afford protection against major short-term fluctuations in supply or demand; and that such international arrangements (a) should provide for adequate representation of consumers as well as producers, representing both importing and exporting countries, in all authorities responsible for the determination and application of policy, and (b) should aim to assure to all workers, including the self-employed, engaged in the production of the commodities concerned, fair remuneration, satisfactory working conditions and adequate social security protection, having regard to the general standards in the countries concerned.

8. Believing that migratory movements may play an important part in the development of a dynamic economy, and that disorderly international migration may create economic and social dislocation in the countries concerned and involve serious individual hardship for the migrants themselves, while desirable migratory movements are often hampered by technical and financial difficulties which can be overcome only through international cooperation,

The Conference considers that:

(a) The United Nations should encourage by appropriate measures, with adequate safeguards for all concerned, the orderly migration of labor and settled in accordance with the economic needs and social conditions prevailing in the various countries, and in this connection should note the Conclusions adopted by the Conference of Experts on Technical and Financial Cooperation with Regard to Migration for Settlement held at the International Labor Office in 1938;

(b) Arrangements should be made for close cooperation between the International Labor Organization and any public international agency established to deal with migration;

(c) The Governing Body should take steps to bring before an early session of the Conference a report of a representative commission, with such technical assistance as it may require, on the means necessary to protect the interests of labor, on the one hand, against barriers which prevent migration from areas of limited resources, and on the other hand, against the lowering of the labor standards that might result from immigration at a rate exceeding the capacity of the receiving countries to absorb immigrants.

9. In order that reemployment may be expedited and healthy living standards established within a period of minimum duration in areas liberated from Axis occupation,

The Conference recommends that arrangements be made by those nations whose productive capacities have been maintained during the war, by all other nations which are in a position to make materials available and by the appropriate international organizations, to give the highest priority consistent with the exigencies of war to immediately supplying the territories liberated from Axis occupation with materials and equipment required for industrial installations, agriculture, transport, public works and utilities of an essential character.

10. Believing that the best possible conditions for a rise in the standard of living and the maintenance of full employment in the world can only be obtained by mutually consistent national economic, financial and social policies and by coordination of the activities of the different international institutions in this field.

The Conference considers that appropriate international measures should be taken which guarantee sufficient contact and consultation with regard to such policies between governments as well as between the different international institutions.

2. NATIONAL POLICY

11. In order that full employment at productive peacetime pursuits, freedom from want, rising standards of living and genuine economic security may be achieved with a minimum of delay after the war,

The Conference urges that governments and employers' and workers' organizations formulate comprehensive and coordinated programs, suited to the particular needs of their countries, for prompt and orderly reconversion, reconstruction and economic expansion, and that such programs be prepared and applied simultaneously with the consideration of the international measures referred to in the preceding paragraphs.

12. Recognizing that the economic situation will differ markedly among the various countries at the war's end, varying particularly with the degree and type of industrial development, the extent to which the peacetime economy has been disrupted by the war, and whether the country's territory has been occupied by the enemy; and recognizing that national post-war economic programs must vary accordingly, in

order to meet most effectively the needs of the country in which they are to be applied.

The Conference urges that, with due allowance for difference in national economic situations, programs for economic reconversion, reconstruction and expansion include the development of sound policies and procedures to provide:

(a) Effective arrangements for the orderly and expeditious demobilization and repatriation, and for the early absorption in productive peacetime employment of members of the armed forces, civilian workers, prisoners, persons who have resisted deportation, deported persons and refugees, for the prompt termination of contracts and settlement of claims, the prompt determination of policy on the peacetime use of Government-owned war production capacity and equipment and the disposition of surplus materials, with a view to the use of these items to satisfy human needs, and liberal provision for the maintenance, educational training and retraining of persons unavoidably out of employment as recommended by the 26th Session of the International Labor Conference in its Recommendation concerning employment organization in the transition from war to peace;

(b) Retention, as long as shortages exist, of such war-created economic controls — for example, price and exchange controls and rationing — as are necessary to prevent inflation, and the relaxation of such controls as rapidly thereafter as is consistent with the public welfare;

(c) Adjustment of tax systems to encourage rapid reconversion, reconstruction and economic expansion, while maintaining an equitable distribution of tax burdens and avoiding financial measures which tend to increase the dangers of inflation or deflation;

(d) Development of effective mechanisms for adequate financing of the reconversion, reconstruction and expansion of industry, trade, commerce and agriculture and particularly to assist the establishment of new and efficient enterprises.

13. The Conference urges that all practicable measures be taken to maintain a high and steady level of employment, to minimize fluctuations and business activity, and to assure a steadily expanding volume of production, more particularly by means of:

(a) Fiscal, monetary and other measures, including useful public works, to sustain the volume of demand for goods and services at a high level while avoiding the dangers of an inflationary spiral of prices and wages — in this connection attention should be paid, among other measures, to such methods as an adequate income security system, and to properly timed public works financed by borrowing in periods of depression, in accordance with the Public Works (National Planning) Recommendation, 1937;

(b) Measures to discourage monopolistic practices and to encourage technological progress, to maintain a reasonably flexible system of prices and wages, to encourage the transfer of workers and productive resources from declining to expanding industries, and to attain a high degree of mobility of resources and freedom of access to alternative employments;

(c) Measures to provide adequate incentives to engage in and expand constructive economic activity, to encourage private investment and to maintain the rate of investment — among the measures which warrant careful consideration in this connection are the adjustment of tax systems, removal of artificial barriers limiting access to resources and markets, the relaxation of unreasonable restrictions imposed by governmental agencies or by business or by labor organizations, and the maintenance of a high and stable demand for goods;

(d) Measures to provide adequate opportunity for workers to engage in productive activity and to obtain advancement — among the measures which warrant careful consideration in this connection are the provision of improved and more generally accessible educational and training facilities, provision of higher nutritional and health standards, improvement of public employment services, increased provision against economic insecurity, the maintenance of wages at a high level, and the protection, extension and improvement of collective bargaining procedures.

(5) *Remarks of the President (Roosevelt) before the Delegates to the 26th International Labor Conference, White House, May 17, 1944* [1]

MISS PERKINS, MR. GOODRICH, MR. PHELAN, DELEGATES TO THE CONFERENCE:

It is a great pleasure to have you with us here in the White House again. As I pointed out to you when we last met — two and a half years ago — taking part in a conference of the International Labor Organization is not a new experience for me. I take pride in the fact that I was permitted to play a part in the first conference of the Organization that was held here in Washington in 1919.

Those were indeed trying days when last we met in 1941. The fate of the free peoples of the entire world hung in the balance. Yet with the courage and foresight that have always characterized the International Labor Organization, you as representatives of governments, workers, and employers had the boldness to come together from all parts of the world to formulate plans for reconstruction.

You have been meeting in Philadelphia where, one hundred sixty-eight years ago, the Fathers of this Republic affirmed certain truths to be self-evident. They declared that among other things all men are endowed by their Creator with certain inalienable rights, among them

[1] *Ibid.*, p. 481.

Life, Liberty, and the Pursuit of Happiness. In these words are expressed the abiding purpose of all peoples imbued with the ideals of freedom and democracy.

The Declaration which you have formulated in Philadelphia may well acquire a similar significance. In it you have reaffirmed principles which are the essential bulwarks of any permanent peace. With the expanding use of machinery and the revolution in transportation, it is well that the world should recognize the fundamental principle of your Declaration: "Poverty anywhere constitutes a danger to prosperity everywhere." This principle is a guide to all of our international economic deliberations.

You have affirmed the right of all human beings to material well-being and spiritual development under conditions of freedom and dignity and under conditions of economic security and opportunity. The attainment of those conditions must constitute a central aim of national and international policy. Indeed, the worthiness and success of international policies will be measured in the future by the extent to which they promote the achievement of this end.

Your Declaration sums up the aspirations of an epoch which has known two world wars. I confidently believe that future generations will look back upon it as a landmark in world thinking. I am glad to have this opportunity of indorsing its specific terms on behalf of the United States. I trust, also, that within a short time its specific terms will be wholeheartedly indorsed by all of the United Nations.

As I look over the report of your work, I see that you have, for the first time in history, set out in a form which could be adopted as a treaty by the nations a particular series of social objectives. I note that among other things they include full employment, wages and working conditions calculated to insure a just share of the fruits of progress to all, the extension of social security, the recognition of the right of collective bargaining, provision for child welfare, and the assurance of adequate educational and vocational opportunities. It will be your responsibility to promote these objectives through your own organization and through such international agencies as may be created.

With great wisdom you have realized that these social objectives cannot be attained and supported without a high level of useful economic activity. You have recommended a series of economic policies and undertakings designed to bring about a material economy which will make it possible to maintain them.

You have also wisely provided for the further development and reorganization of the International Labor Organization itself so that it may be broadened and strengthened for carrying out these social objectives, and at the same time integrated on a cooperative basis with whatever new international agency or agencies are created by the United Nations. This forms an admirable pattern for formulating certain aspects of the peace. I want to assure you that this Government will do everything in its power to see that the provisions for the attainment of these social and labor objectives shall be included.

The people of the occupied countries are in deep suffering. Their representatives have agreed upon the social objectives and economic policies you have set forth. I trust that this marks the beginning of a new and better day, a period of hope for material comfort, for security, and for spiritual and personal development, for all those groups now suffering so sorely under the heel of the oppressor. The United Nations will be determined that all the oppressed of the earth shall be included in these social objectives.

I want to offer my congratulations to those of you who have participated in this Conference. You have my gratitude for the program of mutual helpfulness which you have laid out — a program which, I am sure, will inspire all of those in our generation who want to build and maintain a just peace.

(6) *Message of the President (Roosevelt) to Congress on the Results of the 26th International Labor Conference, May 29, 1944* [1]

To THE CONGRESS OF THE UNITED STATES:

The Twenty-sixth Conference of the International Labor Organization has just been held at Philadelphia. Representatives of the government, employers and workers of forty-one countries took part in its deliberations.

The Conference, by a two-thirds majority, adopted Recommendations on the following seven subjects:

1. Income Security
2. Social Security for the Armed Forces
3. Medical Care
4. Social Policy in Dependent Territories
5. Employment in the Transition from War to Peace
6. The Organization of Employment Services
7. National Planning of Public Works

Under the Constitution of the International Labor Organization, these recommendations are forwarded to the member governments for submission by them to their respective, competent national authorities. I shall accordingly submit them to the Congress in the regular way when certified copies are received.

The Conference made other important decisions of which I think the Congress should be informed.

[1] *Ibid.*, p. 514.

First, it adopted by unanimous vote a declaration of the aims and purposes of the International Labor Organization which has been referred to as the "Declaration of Philadelphia."

Secondly, it unanimously adopted resolutions concerning the social provisions of the peace settlement.

Thirdly, it unanimously adopted resolutions concerning the economic policies, international and national, required for the attainment of the social objectives of the United Nations.

Because of the interest and importance of these three documents, I am transmitting them herewith for the information of the Congress.

FRANKLIN D. ROOSEVELT

2. SUPPRESSION OF OPIUM

(1) Decision to Suppress the Use of Opium for Smoking in British and Netherlands Territories in the Far East. Statement of the Acting Secretary of State (Stettinius), November 10, 1943 [1]

I have noted with satisfaction the decision announced today by the British and the Netherlands Governments to prohibit the use of opium for smoking and to abolish opium monopolies in their territories when those territories are freed from Japanese occupation.

For many years it has been the policy of the United States Government, domestically and internationally in cooperation with other governments, to seek the eradication of the abuse of opium and its derivatives. To this end it initiated the movement resulting in the calling of the International Opium Commission at Shanghai in 1909. It participated in the conference called at The Hague which resulted in the Hague Opium Convention of 1912.[2] Article 6 of that Convention provided for the gradual suppression of the manufacture, the internal traffic in, and the use of prepared opium. Subsequently each of the governments parties to the Hague Opium Convention having possessions in the Far East enacted legislation which it deemed to be appropriate for the fulfilment of this article. The United States Government met its obligations under the Hague Convention through legislation which effectively prohibited the manufacture, importation, or sale of smoking opium both at home and in its possessions.

In view of the measures which have been taken during the last 20 years to combat the abuse of narcotic drugs, among which was the coming into force of the Narcotics Limitation Convention of 1931,[3] this Government feels that the problem of smoking opium should now be susceptible of solution.

[1] Ibid., IX, p. 331.
[2] Treaties, Conventions, etc., 1910–1923, III, p. 3025.
[3] Ibid., 1923–1937, IV, p. 5351.

With reference to the question of limitation and control of production, mentioned in the statements made by the British and Netherlands Governments, the United States Government has for many years taken every opportunity to urge that only by limiting the cultivation of the poppy for the production of opium and other narcotic drugs can clandestine manufacture be stopped and the illicit traffic be effectively combatted. This Government will therefore be glad to continue its cooperation in international efforts to bring about a solution of this problem.

On September 21, 1943 the United States Government addressed *aide-mémoire* to the British, Netherlands, and other interested governments in regard to the suppression of the non-medical use of narcotic drugs in areas in the Far East now occupied by Japanese forces when such areas are reoccupied by the armed forces of the United Nations. It is a source of deep gratification that the action taken by the British and Netherlands Governments is so closely in accord with the policy of the United States Government in this regard.

(2) *Joint Resolution (H. J. Res. 241) Requesting the President (Roosevelt) to Urge upon Governments the Limitation of Production of Opium to Amounts Required for Strictly Medicinal and Scientific Purposes, Approved July 1, 1944* [1]

Whereas for nearly forty years the United States of America has led the fight to destroy the illicit traffic in and nonmedical consumption of opium, as evidenced by its abolishing the opium monopoly system which it inherited in the Philippine Islands; its calling at Shanghai in 1909 the first International Commission to consider the opium problem; its suggesting the calling of the three International Opium Conferences at The Hague in 1912, 1913, 1914; its urging at the International Opium Conference of 1924 and 1925 sponsored by the League of Nations that the only effective way to suppress the demoralizing use of opium and its derivatives (heroin, morphine, and so forth) was to control the source of the evil by limiting the cultivation of the poppy plant to the legitimate medicinal and scientific needs of the world; and its further participation in the Geneva Conference of 1931 to restrict the manufacture and distribution of narcotic drugs; and

Whereas the laws of the Chinese Government strictly prohibit the cultivation of the opium poppy and the use of smoking opium in all territory under its control, and the people of China have valiantly resisted the attempts of the invading Japanese militarists to enslave them by encouraging and even compelling the cultivation and use of opium; and

Whereas final defeat of Japan will terminate the illicit traffic in narcotics

[1] Public Law 400, 78th Cong.

which has been carried on by the Japanese military in all territories they have occupied in the Far East; and

Whereas the British and the Netherlands Governments have recently announced their decision to prohibit the use of opium for smoking and not to reestablish their government monopolies for the sale of smoking opium in the territories formerly controlled by them in the Far East when those territories are freed from Japanese occupation, stating however that the success of their action must in the final analysis depend upon the cooperation of the opium-growing countries; and

Whereas because of our military operations in certain other areas in Asia, there are now thousands of young American citizens in countries where opium is cultivated and freely available, and other Americans are on vessels delivering war materials to those countries, which condition constitutes a real threat to the health and welfare of these Americans and affords easy opportunity for the highly profitable smuggling of opium into the United States where its use has been greatly reduced: Therefore, be it

Resolved by the Senate and House of Representatives of the United States of America in Congress assembled, That the Congress express its conviction that this World War ought to be not an occasion for permitting expansion and spreading of illicit traffic in opium, but rather an opportunity for completely eliminating it; and be it further

Resolved, That the President be, and he hereby is, requested to approach the Governments of all opium-producing countries throughout the world, urging upon them in the interest of protecting American citizens and those of our allies and of freeing the world of an age-old evil, that they take immediate steps to limit and control the growth of the opium poppy and the production of opium and its derivatives to the amount actually required for strictly medicinal and scientific purposes.

(a) Letter of the Acting Secretary of the Treasury (Gaston) to the Chairman of the House Committee on Foreign Affairs (Bloom), May 15, 1944 [1]

MY DEAR MR. CHAIRMAN: Reference is made to your letter of April 28, 1944 addressed to the Commissioner of Narcotics, relative to House Joint Resolution 241, requesting the President to urge upon the governments of those countries where the cultivation of poppy plant exists the necessity of immediately limiting the production of opium to the amount required for strictly medicinal and scientific purposes.

The Treasury Department recommends the enactment of the proposed legislation. It has long recognized the importance of preventing illicit traffic in opium

[1] Printed in report of the Committee on H. S. Res. 241, House Report No. 1515, 78th Cong., 2d sess.

and believes that such traffic can be effectively controlled only by international cooperation in limiting and controlling the growth of the opium poppy and the production of opium and its derivatives to the amount actually required for strictly medical and scientific purposes.

The Government of the United States took the initiative in bringing about the International Opium Commission at Shanghai in 1909 and the conference at The Hague, which resulted in the Opium Convention of 1912, the first international agreement on this matter. The International Opium Convention of 1912, embodying certain minimum rules concerning the production of opium, was incorporated in the Versailles Treaty. Subsequently, the governments realized that the provisions of The Hague convention were not adequate to prevent the spreading evil. The illicit traffic in opium and its derivatives rapidly grew and drug addiction became a serious menace to many countries in all parts of the world.

As a result of conditions at that time the Congress unanimously adopted and the President approved on March 2, 1923, Public Resolution No. 96, Sixty-seventh Congress, 42 Stat. 1431, declaring that the effective control of habit-forming narcotic drugs can be obtained only by limiting the production thereof to the quantity required for strictly medical and scientific purposes, thus eradicating the source or root of the conditions due to production many times greater than is necessary for such purposes. By this law, enacted in the form of a joint resolution, the President was requested to urge upon governments the immediate necessity of limiting the growth of the opium poppy or the production of opium and its derivatives exclusively to the amount actually required for strictly medical and scientific purposes. It should be noted that Public Resolution No. 96 of the Sixty-seventh Congress constitutes a precedent for the legislation now proposed.

As a result of the resolution enacted in 1923, an international conference was summoned in Geneva in 1924 to deal with the problems presented. The Geneva convention of 1925 was adopted and dealt with raw materials and manufactured drugs. Although it was a marked improvement upon The Hague Convention of 1912, this Government declined to accede to it, as the measures proposed therein were inadequate to realize the objectives, notably, in failing to provide for limitation of the production of the opium poppy. Therefore, the production of opium is governed only by the International Opium Convention of 1912 and the Geneva Convention of 1925.[1] There was, until the outbreak of the war in 1939, an enormous annual production of opium.

In connection with manufactured drugs, an international convention was summoned in Geneva in 1931, and a convention was adopted limiting the manufacture of narcotic drugs and controlling their distribution. The object of the 1931 convention has been virtually achieved. Cases in which drugs legitimately manufactured escaped into illicit traffic had, at least before the present war started, become increasingly rare.

In estimating the value of results so far achieved, it must be realized that, if they are to be conserved, constant overproduction of opium must be regarded as a permanent and latent danger. To illustrate, in 1936, the year for which the most complete statistics for raw opium production are available, the total area under cultivation (not including China with Manchuria and Afghanistan) was about 100,000 hectares. The world production of opium, excluding the above-mentioned countries, reached in that year 2,300 metric tons. In the same year 365 tons of opium were used for the manufacture of drugs and medicinal opium

---

[1] *League of Nations, Treaty Series*, LI, p. 337.

necessary for strictly medical purposes. In addition, 280 tons were used for the manufacture of smoking opium in Far Eastern countries where opium monopolies existed. For other nonmedical consumption, such as chewing, drinking, smoking, mainly in India and Iran, 475 tons were used. Thus, the total amount of opium used and accounted for was less than half of the world production in 1936. If the world production in that year, 2,300 tons, is added to the stocks on hand as reported by governments at the beginning of 1936, namely 3,690 tons, the total available world supplies of opium in 1936 reached the staggering amount of about 6,000 tons, a quantity sufficient to cover the strictly legitimate medical requirements of the world, based on the need for 1936, for $16\frac{1}{2}$ years. If the nonmedical requirements are taken into account, these 6,000 tons represent $5\frac{1}{2}$ times the total world uses in 1936.

China, the greatest producer of opium, was not included in the above figures. Although it appears that the production of opium in that country has been reduced from roughly 6,000 tons in 1934 to 360 tons in 1938, and that the Chinese Government has stated that the production has been completely prohibited since 1940, it must be assumed that large production continues in Chinese Provinces under Japanese occupation.

It has been proved that constant overproduction of opium and an increasing accumulation of huge opium stocks considerably in excess of maximum medical needs offer opportunities not only for clandestine manufacture of dangerous drugs, but also for illicit traffic in the opium. Past experience reveals that clandestine manufacture of dangerous drugs was never completely checked; and that the illicit manufacture of dangerous drugs, particularly in countries with a weak administration, was facilitated by abundant supplies of opium easily obtained. When the application of a strict system of limitation of manufacture in the United States and western European countries made it practically impossible for the illicit trafficker to obtain supplies, he moved to countries where the poppy was cultivated and opium produced and where control was inadequate.

Clandestine factories first sprang up in certain countries in the Near East. When control was tightened in these countries, the traffickers moved again to the Far East. Large quantities of dangerous drugs, often made in the crude state in remote districts with machinery of the most primitive kind, began to be produced in the Far East, and for some years created a serious problem, not only for China but also for the United States, Canada, Egypt, and other countries.

The overproduction of opium has a direct bearing on the problem of opium smoking in the Far East. As long as opium is produced in quantities far exceeding legitimate requirements, the smuggling of opium will constitute the most serious obstacle to the effective suppression of the use of opium for smoking purposes. Due mainly to American public opinion, the Netherlands Government on October 1, 1943, and the British Government on November 10, 1943, announced that opium smoking under government license (the government monopoly system) will end in all Far Eastern territories which may be returned after the war to Dutch and British control. Similar steps should be taken by the French and Portuguese Governments.

To make such a limitation completely effective, British India, the Indian States and the Shan States, which are part of British India, and Iran must cease the nonmedical use of opium. According to figures supplied by the Government of India, over 5,000 shops in the native States sell opium. While it is claimed that their system of control is so strict that it is impossible for any to leak into the illicit traffic, enforcement agents have recently seized opium sold by these Government shops which was smuggled into the United States. Therefore, if every other country should make its contribution to the common welfare by limiting the production of opium to its authorized proportion of about 300 tons for strictly medical and scientific needs, and India should continue to grow and to use between 200 and 300 tons annually for its own nonmedical purposes, the law of supply and demand from the illicit angle would inevitably render this Indian supply a most valuable reservoir for the continuance of the illicit traffic. The same argument applies to Iran where several hundred tons of opium are produced and consumed for nonmedical purposes.

Only by striking at the root of the problem, that is, by limiting the cultivation of the poppy for the production of opium to strictly medical and scientific requirements, can clandestine manufacture be stopped, illicit opium smoking completely eradicated, and the illicit traffic effectively and finally countered. It is believed that enactment of the proposed legislation would constitute an important step in achieving these objectives.

The Department has been advised by the Bureau of the Budget that there is no objection to the submission of this report to your committee.

CHAPTER XII

CULTURAL RELATIONS

1. DEVELOPMENT OF PROGRAM

A Division of Cultural Relations was first established in the Department of State in 1938 in response to special circumstances attending relations between the United States and the other American Republics. Axis expansion in Europe had created a special threat to American security in the Western Hemisphere and had given fresh urgency to the need for Inter-American unity. During the period 1938–41 the program was founded wholly upon relations with the Latin American republics. Activities which were developed and supervised directly by the Department of State included travel and study grants, exchange of professors and books, assistance to United States cultural centers such as libraries, institutes and schools, and the distribution of informational motion pictures.

During this period other government agencies have participated in cooperative projects in the neighboring republics. The Department of Agriculture, for example, has assisted in the establishment of experiment stations in several countries for the development of agricultural products complementary to United States production as part of a program of Inter-American economic cooperation. The Department of Commerce has sent equipment to aid in establishing fifteen tidal investigative stations and three radiosonde observation stations. The United States Office of Education has loaned English-teaching specialists to other Latin American governments. In all no less than a dozen government agencies have provided practical training in the United States for young technicians from other American Republics.

In November 1941 the Secretary of State informed the President that the initiation of a program of cultural relations with China was a matter of immediate concern since such a program could effectively support Chinese national resistance and would assist in building a closer understanding between China and the United States. This program was accordingly begun in January 1942 with an allocation from the Emergency Fund of the President.

The China program during 1942–43 revolved around four principal activities: sending of American technical experts requested by the Chinese Government, the exchange of professors, the awarding of study grants to Chinese students in the United States, and the sending in microfilm of technical and scholarly journals requested by the Chinese Universities.

In the spring of 1943 the Department of State concluded, after careful study of field reports, that a program in the Near East and Africa would be valuable in the development of closer relations with the countries of that area. Funds for the establishment of this program were allocated in July 1943 by the President from his Emergency Fund. Since there already existed in the Near East a number of American-founded schools and hospitals, the United States has sought to strengthen these centers in the carrying on of extension services, particularly projects in engineering, public health and agriculture. Grants of aid have been given to American institutes in Turkey, Syria and Liberia. Teachers have been sent to Afghanistan at the request of that government. Books and other cultural materials have been shipped to educational centers in these countries and to Egypt, Iran, Ethiopia and Morocco.

Toward Europe the Department has undertaken no integrated program although it has developed a number of limited activities in neutral and Allied countries.

For a more complete description of the numerous activities that have been carried out in connection with the Department's cultural relations program see *The Cultural-Cooperation Program, 1938–43,* prepared by Mr. Haldore Hanson (Department of State Publication 2137).

(1) *Message of the President (Roosevelt) to Congress, Recommending Amendment of Act of August 9, 1939, Entitled "An Act to Authorize the President to Render Closer and More Effective the Relationships between the American Republics," February 29, 1944* [1]

To the Congress of the United States of America:

I recommend to the favorable consideration of the Congress the enclosed report from the Acting Secretary of State with an accompanying memorandum, to the end that the act approved August 9, 1939, entitled "An act to authorize the President to render closer and more effective the relationships between the American Republics," may be amended to permit the development of similar programs of mutual understanding and cooperation with other nations of the world.

Franklin D. Roosevelt

(Enclosures: Report, memorandum.)

(a) *Report to the President (Roosevelt) from the Under Secretary of State (Stettinius), February 21, 1944* [2]

The President:

I have the honor to submit with a view to its transmission to the Congress, if you approve, a bill to amend the act approved August 9, 1939, entitled an Act "To authorize the President to render closer and more effective the relationship between the American Republics." The purpose of the amendment is to authorize extension to other nations of the world of programs to promote mutual understanding and cooperation in general character similar to that developed and maintained with the American republics under the authority of the existing legislation.

1. The act approved August 9, 1939 (Public No. 355, 76th Congress) authorized appropriations whereby the President was enabled to utilize the services of the Departments, agencies and independent establishments of the Government in carrying out the purposes set forth in the treaties, resolutions, declarations and recommendations signed by the twenty-one American Republics at the Inter-American Conference for the Maintenance of Peace, held at Buenos Aires in 1936, and at the Eighth International Conference of American States held at Lima, Peru in 1938. This act also authorized the creation of advisory committees composed of leaders of American thought and opinion to provide essential guidance and to enlist widespread cooperation on the part of private as well as government agencies in formulating a concrete program.

[1] House Doc. No. 474, 78th Cong., 2d sess.; *Congressional Record,* vol. 90, p. 2106 (daily edition, February 29, 1944).

[2] *Ibid.,* Department of State, *Bulletin,* X, p. 215.

Under the authority of Public No. 355, funds have been appropriated to the Department of State for "Cooperation with the American Republics," which funds are in turn allocated to the separate Departments, agencies and establishments for the purpose of carrying out specific projects relating to the other Americas.

The coordination and integration of these projects into one concrete program is carried out through the Interdepartmental Committee for Cooperation with the American Republics, which approves individual projects on the basis of their contribution to the furtherance of more effective relationships in the broad divisions of economic, social, scientific and cultural fields.

2. The last of these programs, as it relates to the other American Republics, developed and maintained pursuant to Public No. 355, is centered in the Department of State. Close cooperation has been maintained with the program carried forward by the Office of the Coordinator of Inter-American Affairs through a joint committee which has met weekly to consider and correlate all Government activities in this field. For the present year, in accordance with an exchange of letters of August 12 and 14, 1942,[1] between the Under Secretary of State and the Coordinator of Inter-American Affairs, there has been transferred to the Department of State responsibility for those activities having long-range implication which in the past have been carried on by the Office of the Coordinator. The purpose of this transfer is to place the cooperative program of the Government on a permanent basis.

3. The present scope of the program under the direct supervision of the Department of State is indicated by the following brief summary of activities.

Exchange of persons. Primary emphasis has been placed upon the increase of mutual understanding through personal relationships between leaders of thought and opinion in all fields. The exchange of persons has in the past included visits to the United States of persons of influence in the press and professions, education and the sciences from the other American republics, and a reciprocal southward movement, as well as the exchange of students, interns and professors.

The Department has cooperated with the Office of the Coordinator of Inter-American Affairs in exchanges related to the important fields of health and sanitation, of commerce, industry and agriculture.

American centers. A substantial part is played in the development of continental solidarity by the local institutions in the principal cities of the other American Republics, such as American institutes and libraries at Mexico City, Bogotá, and Rio de Janeiro. Their membership includes nationals as well as resident citizens of the United States. Among their activities are the teaching of English; maintenance of libraries of United States books and periodicals; sponsorship of radio programs, concerts, lectures and exhibits representing the United States; aid in the selection and orientation of students and other persons who plan to travel or study in the United States; and publication of articles on American life and civilization. American institutes have been formed in twenty-two important cities of the other American Republics and in addition well-equipped American libraries have been set up in Mexico City, Montevideo, and Managua.

Publications. To promote a broader knowledge and understanding of American life, books and publications are a medium of highest value. The Department has cooperated with the Office of the Coordinator and with other agencies in meeting increasingly numerous requests from libraries, universities and other institutions for materials on the United States. More than 100 outstanding titles

[1] *Documents, V, 1942–43,* p. 673.

in the fields of history, biography, technical works and social studies have already been translated or are in process of translation and publication. Thousands of volumes and copies of periodicals in English have also been distributed in answer to requests — a movement which has great significance in the light of the rapidly growing study of English.

Motion pictures and radio. Motion pictures are the world language of today and serve to reach all classes of people in foreign countries with the story of the United States. During recent months educational documentary films procured in cooperation with the Office of the Coordinator of Inter-American Affairs have reached audiences totaling more than two million persons monthly. Showings have been made through schools, universities, hospitals, army and navy officials, labor groups, government officials, political clubs, professional men and other groups of adults and children.

The radio is an indispensable instrument for creating an understanding of the United States, particularly among the "masses" of foreign countries. The Department has cooperated in this field with the Coordinator of Inter-American Affairs, the Office of War Information, and the national and other broadcasting companies in the United States.

Reciprocal aspects of the program. A program for better understanding must be a two-way process. It is as essential to inform the people of the United States concerning the other American Republics and other countries, as it is to inform those nations about the United States. Accordingly, the Department has sought, with marked success, to enlist the active cooperation of the educational, intellectual, civic and related institutions and organizations — both governmental and private — of the United States.

4. That progress has been made toward the establishment of closer and more effective relations among the American Republics is indicated by their unity of thought and action at the conferences of Foreign Ministers of the American Republics at Havana in July of 1940, and again at Rio de Janeiro in January of 1942; and by the general support of the policy of hemispheric solidarity by the peoples of the twenty-one nations.

Reports on the basis of approximately four years of operations substantiate the conclusion that the fostering of closer relations through the facilities of an educational and intellectual interchange has been an important factor in the success of the broad program both to the extent that mutual knowledge and understanding have been increased and to the extent that cooperation in the economic, scientific and social fields has thereby been facilitated.

5. As transportation and communications have progressed, economic interdependence, political interaction, social intercourse and intellectual exchange have increased among all peoples.

This circumstance, in turn, has not only added to the knowledge of peoples about one another but also emphasized the need for an ever better understanding between them.

To achieve this end, many of the nations instituted "cultural programs," involving the study and teaching of foreign languages, the exchange of scientific information, books, films and art objects, and the interchange of students, teachers and technical experts. Some of these programs have been carried on under governmental guidance, others have been spontaneous undertakings of private initiative.

As an outgrowth of this general situation, the United States undertook under the Authority of the Act of August 9, 1939 to initiate under the guidance of the Department of State, with cooperation from other Government agencies and private organizations a program to promote mutual understanding with the other American Republics.

However, from the outset an attempt was made to supply the demands for international exchanges which came from all parts of the world. Informative educational films were supplied, in addition to the other American Republics, to such countries as Belgium, South Africa, Canada and Switzerland, although in numerous other instances the Department was unable to accede to requests for films.

Since the bulk of the Department's funds for international exchanges came from appropriations authorized under Public No. 355 (and therefore restricted to use in relation to the American Republics), the program for the other areas of the world was necessarily developed on a very limited scale.

6. The changing world situation and the entrance of the United States into the war intensified the need for cooperative programs for certain areas outside the other American Republics. In January 1942, a program with China was initiated on a limited scale by means of a grant from the President's Emergency Fund. The three basic activities then inaugurated and carried forward during the 1943 fiscal year have been: (1) The provision of technical and educational leaders to China; (2) The extension of aid to Chinese students in the United States thus augmenting China's supply of skilled technicians; and (3) the furnishing of certain urgently needed informational materials such as microfilms of scholarly and scientific articles and books, and documentary and educational motion pictures.

7. Apart from the intensification of the cooperative program on an emergency basis necessitated by the conduct of the war, the widening horizon of international responsibilities opened to the United States by the war and its probable effects requires for the future a continuing and coordinated program to promote mutual understanding with other peoples. Provisions of the lend-lease agreements already negotiated commit the signatory governments to continuing collaboration and cooperation for an indefinite period after the cessation of hostilities. A program underlying and supporting these cooperative efforts, recognized as an important factor to their success in wartime, would be no less vital in the period of postwar adjustment.

If the past decades have brought close contacts among those peoples having similar interests, the post-war world, with increased facilities for transportation and communication, will undoubtedly see these contacts grow both more numerous and more continuous.

Programs of this character are an effective means of achieving international, hence national, security. Measures which spread an understanding of the democratic way of life and diffuse scientific knowledge useful in organizing it, may be made the support of political and economic peace measures. In this connection it should be emphasized that the amelioration of the lives of common men is actually achieved only as they learn new ways of doing things. Thus the cooperative program may provide means of creating necessary conditions for orderly and peaceful development. In providing the world's peoples with the means of doing better for themselves, the American people will be creating conditions favorable to the development of their own way of life; and in this prospect alone is true national security.

Since these cooperative activities provide the means of social advancement to peoples in the shape of books, trained persons, and other means of diffusing knowledge, they do not excite either political antipathy, or fear of foreign domination, or dread of interference with domestic politics. As non-political and non-patronizing activities, they are truly the means of implementing a foreign policy of a democratic people whose national interest is the maintenance and orderly development of their democracy.

8. From the foregoing it may be seen that a twofold need exists. First, it is evident that there is an urgent need for a constructive program of long-term and continuing character, not only with the republics of the Western Hemisphere but on a world-wide basis. Secondly, it is desirable that activities developed in furtherance of the program should not be inaugurated merely on an opportunistic basis as crises arise but should be part of a considered and integrated plan.

To ensure the formulation of a suitable and comprehensive program and its effective operation, funds should be provided in one appropriation administered under the direction of one responsible agency.

In developing the program applicable only to the American Republics which was authorized under Public No. 355, it is believed that suitable machinery has been set up for the centralization of appropriations, the concentration of directive responsibility and the most effective coordination of effort. Public No. 355 as now worded does not authorize the appropriation of funds for the carrying on of an active cooperative program beyond the republics of the Western Hemisphere. The limitations of Public No. 355 also preclude the use of the valuable advisory committees, already functioning in relation to the program in the Americas, for dealing with the preliminary studies of programs for other regions. Such guidance would be of inestimable benefit at this time in laying the groundwork on which the permanent post-war structure might be erected as well as in meeting the urgent current needs of the war period.

I have the honor, therefore, to recommend that the Congress be requested to enact legislation amending Public No. 355, in order to authorize extension of the program therein comprehended to any other country, countries or regions, in furtherance of the objectives of the United States in the present war and in the peace to follow.

A draft of the proposed legislation is enclosed for your convenience.

(b) Memorandum from the Under Secretary of State (Stettinius), Consisting of Draft of Proposed Bill, February 27, 1944 [1]

Be it enacted by the Senate and House of Representatives of the United States of America in Congress assembled, That the Act entitled an Act "To authorize the President to render closer and more effective the relationship between the American Republics," approved August 9, 1939 [2] (53 Stat. 1290), is hereby amended by adding at the end thereof the two following sections:

"SEC. 3. The President is also hereby authorized, subject to such appropriations as may be made available for the purpose, to develop and maintain, under the direction of the Secretary of State, such cultural and cooperative programs with other countries of the world as he may consider justified in furtherance of the purposes of the United States in the present war and in the peace to follow; and to create and utilize to such extent as may be necessary, subject to the foregoing limitations respecting salary, travel, and expenses, advisory committees for assistance in the development of such programs.

"SEC. 4. The title of this Act is hereby corrected to read, and it may be cited as 'An Act to promote, through mutual understanding with other peoples, more effective cooperation for a durable peace'."

[1] *Ibid.*, p. 218.   [2] *Documents, I, 1938–39*, p. 58.

2. EDUCATIONAL AND CULTURAL RECONSTRUCTION

(1) *American Commission for the Protection and Salvage of Artistic and Historic Monuments in Europe. Department of State Release, August 20, 1943* [1]

The President has approved the establishment of an American Commission for the Protection and Salvage of Artistic and Historic Monuments in Europe, with the Honorable Owen J. Roberts, Justice of the Supreme Court of the United States, as chairman. Mr. David E. Finley, Director of the National Gallery and a member of the Commission of Fine Arts, has been appointed vice chairman, and Mr. Huntington Cairns, secretary-treasurer of the Gallery, will serve as secretary-treasurer of the Commission. The other members of the Commission are: The Honorable Herbert Lehman, Director of Foreign Relief and Rehabilitation Operations; the Honorable Archibald MacLeish, Librarian of Congress; Dr. William Bell Dinsmoor, President of the Archeological Institute of America; Dr. Francis Henry Taylor, Director of the Metropolitan Museum in New York and President of the Association of Art Museum Directors; and Dr. Paul J. Sachs, Associate Director of the Fogg Museum of Fine Arts of Harvard University. The members will serve for three years.

The headquarters of the Commission will be in the National Gallery of Art. The Commission will cooperate with the appropriate branches of the Army and of the Department of State, including the Office of Foreign Relief and Rehabilitation Operations, as well as with appropriate civilian agencies. The Commission will also advise and work with the School of Military Government at Charlottesville, Va., and subsequent organizations of civilian character which may take over control of occupied territory when it is possible to relinquish military control.

The Commission may be called upon to furnish museum officials and art historians to the General Staff of the Army, so that, so far as is consistent with military necessity, works of cultural value may be protected in countries occupied by the armies of the United Nations. One of the principal functions of the Commission will be to act as a channel of communication between the Army and the various universities, museums, and other scholarly institutions, organizations, and individuals from whom information and services are desired. Already much valuable material has been collected and furnished to the Army by museums and universities through the efforts of individual members of the Commission and others serving in a volunteer capacity.

The Commission will function under the auspices of the United States Government and in conjunction with similar groups in other countries for the protection and conservation of works of art and of artistic and historic records in Europe, and to aid in salvaging and restoring to the lawful owners such objects as have been appropriated by the Axis powers or individuals acting under their authority or consent.

The appointment of the American Commission for the Protection and Salvage of Artistic and Historic Monuments in Europe is evidence of the concern felt by the United States Government and by artistic and learned circles in this country for the safety of artistic treasures in Europe, placed in jeopardy by the war. It is also evidence of the Government's intention that, when military operations have been concluded, there shall be restitution of public property appropriated by the Axis powers. It is expected that the Commission will use

[1] Department of State, *Bulletin*, X, p. 111.

its good offices toward this end and will advocate also that, where it is not possible to restore such property, either because it has been destroyed or cannot be found, restitution in kind should be made by the Axis powers to the countries from which property has been taken. The Commission, it is anticipated, will also urge that restitution be made of private property appropriated by the Axis nations.

(2) *Participation of the United States in Emergency Educational and Cultural Rebuilding of the War-torn United Nations, Department of State Release, March 31, 1944* [1]

War is destroying the educational and cultural organizations of the countries occupied by the enemy. Universities, schools, libraries, museums, and scientific laboratories have been wrecked or greatly damaged. Books and equipment have been stolen. Retreating Axis armies are likely to do still more injury.

Teachers, students, and scientists have been singled out for special persecution. Many have been imprisoned, deported, or killed — particularly those refusing to collaborate with the enemy. In fact, the enemy is deliberately depriving his victims of those tools of intellectual life without which their recovery is impossible.

Educational disorganization and economic and social distress are connected, one intensifying the other. Increasingly the war-torn countries are likely to suffer declines of their standards of living and health to critically low levels. The whole people will suffer, but in a special degree the children. Such conditions unavoidably tend toward internal disorder and external difficulties and may create new threats to the economic stability and political security of the world, upon which, in fact, depend the well-being and peace of the American people.

The peoples who survive this ordeal will need help — in order to help themselves. They are facing enormous problems in rebuilding educational and cultural life without essential facilities and without adequate trained personnel. Plans for these tasks must be made now and the work undertaken as soon as possible.

Because of the unprecedented crisis which must be faced in this regard, the Department of State believes that the participation of the United States Government in an international program for the rebuilding of essential educational and cultural facilities of the war-torn countries in the period immediately following hostilities is an important service in the national interest and in the interest of international security and that steps looking to this participation should be taken.

In the Department's study to date of the kind of program that would be practicable and desirable, certain conclusions have already become clear. It would be unwise for this Government to undertake to apply, much less impose, a foreign educational program or system in any liberated country or to develop a program for the placement of American teachers in the schools of these countries or for the preparation of textbooks in the United States for use in such schools.

In order to help the war-torn countries to help themselves in the rebuilding of essential educational and cultural facilities, the Department proposes to collaborate for the time being with the Conference of Allied Ministers of Education in London and to cooperate with the nations represented in this Confer-

[1] *Ibid.*, p. 299.

ence, with the other United Nations, and with the nations associated with the United Nations in the war in forming, as soon as practicable, a United Nations organization for educational and cultural reconstruction. It recognizes that a significant effort has already been made abroad and that useful work has been begun in the shaping of an emergency program to meet this need.

This program, it now appears, may consist of (1) assistance in the restocking of essential educational facilities, especially with books and scientific and other teaching aids, (2) assistance in the providing of opportunities for the training of carefully selected foreign students in American educational institutions, (3) assistance in reestablishing essential library facilities, and (4) assistance in the recovery and restoration to their rightful owners of educational, scientific, artistic, and archival materials looted by the Axis countries.

In this program, as in all other activities in educational and related fields, the Department will seek the advice and cooperation of other agencies and organizations, both governmental and private. It will attempt to operate in a manner equally advantageous to all the countries concerned. This reciprocal relationship is basic in any sound program of educational and cultural relations.

This statement concerning the participation of the United States in emergency restoration of essential educational and cultural facilities of the war-torn United Nations deals with only one of the important educational and cultural problems in the international field which are receiving active consideration. Also of very great significance is the long-range furtherance of educational and cultural relations among nations. The Department wishes increasingly to encourage democratic international cooperation in developing reciprocal and desirable educational and cultural relations among the nations and peoples of the world, especially looking toward the promotion of free and friendly intellectual intercourse among them in the interest of international peace and security.

No attempt is made here to deal with the important questions concerning the educational and cultural programs of the Axis countries.

(3) *United Nations Organization for Educational and Cultural Reconstruction. Memorandum Issued by the Secretariat of the Conference of Ministers of Education of Allied Governments, London, April 20, 1944* [1]

The Secretary of State announced on March 25, 1944, that the United States Government proposed to send a delegation in the near future to collaborate with the Conference of Allied Ministers of Education in London. It was stated that the delegation would consist of Congressman J. William Fulbright, Chairman; Mr. Archibald MacLeish, Librarian of Congress; Mr. John W. Studebaker, United States Commissioner of Education; Dean C. Mildred Thompson of Vassar College; and Messrs. Grayson N. Kefauver and Ralph E. Turner of the Department of State. [2]

The Conference was at work for most of the month of April. On May 3, Secretary Hull announced that the American delegates, other than Messrs. Kefauver and Turner, had returned.

"The discussions of the delegation with representatives of other nations," Congressman Fulbright stated, "were based on the proposition that free and unrestricted interchange between the peoples of the world of ideas and knowledge and unrestricted education are essential to the preservation of security and peace."

The delegation brought back an encouraging report of progress being made by the interested nations toward a cooperative approach to the reestablishment of essential educational and cultural facilities upon an emergency basis.

[1] *Ibid.*, p. 414.   [2] *Ibid.*, p. 293.

The discussions of the Conference, the members of the delegation reported, made clear the threat to civilization created by the cold-blooded and considered destruction by the Axis of the educational and cultural resources of great parts of the continents of Europe and Asia; the murder of teachers, artists, scientists and intellectual leaders; the burning of books; the pillaging and mutilation of works of art; the rifling of archives; and the theft of scientific apparatus.

The American delegation collaborated with the Conference on two main tasks: First, in drafting a tentative plan for a United Nations agency for educational and cultural reconstruction; and secondly, in ascertaining the essential emergency needs of the war-devastated Allied countries to reestablish educational services.

The tentative plan for a United Nations agency for educational and cultural reconstruction was formulated at open meetings presided over by Congressman Fulbright and was then accepted by the Conference for informal submission to the United Nations and Associated Nations for study and comment.

It was stated by the Department of State that the tentative plan brought back by the delegation would be studied by the interested agencies of this Government and be made the subject of discussions with members of Congress for the purpose of furnishing the Conference with the views of the United States Government concerning the proposed United Nations agency.

A tentative draft constitution for a United Nations Organization for Educational and Cultural Reconstruction was accepted by the Conference of Allied Ministers of Education yesterday, 19th April. It will be forwarded to the Allied and Associated Governments, and if adopted by them it will permit joint efforts in this field in line with parallel work already being developed by the Food Conference and UNRRA. General acceptance of the creation of an international organization to undertake cooperatively the vitally important work of restoring the educational and cultural heritages of war-torn countries would carry the United Nations past another important station on the road toward lasting peace.

The wisdom of building an international structure piece by piece on sound foundations is recognized clearly today. The projected Organization for Educational and Cultural Reconstruction would direct its activities at first to the emergency work of restoring the educational systems and the cultural institutions destroyed by the Axis powers. It is believed that the projected organization would gain experience in performing these emergency tasks which would create a basis for lasting international cooperation in educational and cultural fields.

The proposed constitution was drafted at two Open Meetings convened by the Conference of Allied Ministers of Education and the American Education Delegation, headed by Congressman Fulbright, which came to London early this month to work out plans for American collaboration with the Conference. The meetings were attended by representatives of all member and observer states currently interested in the Conference and were presided over by Congressman Fulbright. The device of holding Open Meetings enabled all representatives present to participate fully, equally, and without prejudice to their positions in the Conference. The Constitution is both broad enough and flexible enough to enable the projected organization to deal vigorously and successfully with the problems of educational and cultural reconstruction.

The need for the proposed organization is stated in the Preamble of the proposed Constitution which says in part: "To deprive any part of the interdependent modern world of the cultural resources, human and material, through which its children are trained and its people informed, is to destroy to that extent the common knowledge and the mutual understanding upon which the peace of the world and its security must rest."

The text of the tentative draft Constitution consists of seven sections. The first contains a statement of the underlying reasons why international cooperation in educational reconstruction should be attempted.

The second defines the functions of the projected organization in terms which should permit it to work effectively in the fields of educational and cultural rehabilitation and reconstruction and to develop ultimately into a permanent body with broader activities.

Section three declares that membership shall be open to all the United Nations and Associated Nations and to such other nations as shall be accepted by the Assembly, upon application thereto, after the cessation of hostilities with the Axis.

Section four, which lists the agencies of the proposed organization, provides for an Assembly with equal representation and votes for all member states, an Executive Board to be elected by the Assembly and an International Secretariat.

The fifth, or financial section, states that administrative expenses shall be shared by the member nations on a basis to be agreed by the Assembly. It also provides for the creation of an Emergency Rehabilitation Fund controlled by an Emergency Rehabilitation Fund Committee. National contributions to the Rehabilitation Fund will be fixed by the Committee subject to the approval of each contributing nation, and the Committee will also make allocations from the Fund. The Committee will consist of representatives of the three States making the largest contributions for administrative expenses and three members elected by the Executive Board.

Section six contains provisions relating to ratification, amendment, and interpretation which follow closely those in the statutes of other international bodies.

Section seven contains provisions requiring member nations to supply information about education and cultural matters, defining the legal status of the organization and its staff, providing for cooperation between the organization and existing international organizations in the educational and cultural fields, and governing the relationship of the organization to any agency for coordinating public international organizations.

CHAPTER XIII

THE WESTERN HEMISPHERE

1. RELATIONS WITH THE AMERICAN REPUBLICS

A. General

(1) *Attack by Senator Butler on the Good-Neighbor Policy. Statement by the Secretary of State (Hull), December 14, 1943* [1]

On November 26, 1943, Senator Hugh A. Butler (Nebraska) submitted to the United States Senate a report,[2] based on a "first-hand and on-the-ground" study of the activities of the United States Government in Latin America. His conclusion was that our policy toward Latin America which began as good neighborism had ceased to be that and had become "rich unclism," that the instrumentality of our policy was not goodwill but the United States Treasury, and that over $6,000,000,000 had been spent in "boondoggling." The substance of this report was earlier published in an article by Senator Butler appearing in the December 1943 number of the *Reader's Digest* under the title "Our Deep Dark Secrets in Latin America."

The propriety and truthfulness of this report were immediately challenged, particularly by Senator McKellar of Tennessee, Chairman of the Senate Appropriations Committee. In an extended reply delivered before the Senate on December 13,[3] Senator McKellar quoted at length from reports received from the Secretary of Commerce (Jones), the President of the Import-Export Bank (Pierson), the Secretary of State (Hull), the Administrator of the Foreign Economic Administration (Crowley), the Secretary of the Navy (Knox), the Secretary of War (Stimson), the Coordinator of Inter-American Affairs (Rockefeller) and the President of the Commodity Credit Corporation (Hutson) to show that the allegations contained in the report were "95 per cent wrong." [4]

The unfair attack recently made on the good-neighbor policy by Senator Butler was a matter of general astonishment throughout the Western Hemisphere. It was imperative in our national interest that these charges be analyzed and answered — answered so completely as to leave no grounds for their reiteration. Senator McKellar has provided such an answer. With painstaking analysis he has demonstrated, I believe to the satisfaction of everybody, the inaccuracies, the fallacies, and the misstatements of Senator Butler's unfortunate allegations.

[1] Department of State, *Bulletin*, IX, p. 430.
[2] *Expenditures and Commitments by the United States Government in or for Latin America*, Senate Document 132, 78th Cong., 1st sess.; *Congressional Record*, vol. 89, p. 10106 (daily edition, November 26, 1943).
[3] Senate Document 132, p. 95.
[4] *Congressional Record*, vol. 89, p. 10683 (daily edition, December 13, 1943); for texts of reports on which Senator McKellar's reply was based, see *ibid.*, p. 10692 and Senate Document 132, p. 116.

We in the Department of State are as much opposed to extravagance and waste in government expenditures as anyone can be. We have consistently practiced a policy of economy. But the question here presented is whether, especially at this serious stage of the war, we shall forget the broad essential nature of our cooperative activities in the other American Republics and turn to a controversy over a limited number of items of wartime expenditure. Senator McKellar ably and effectively presented the matter in this light. It would, of course, be too much to expect that no errors of judgment have been made in the conduct of programs conceived and carried out under the pressure of wartime emergency, but I believe that Senator McKellar has effectively demolished the figures and conclusions on which Senator Butler based all, or virtually all, his indiscriminate attacks.

Senator Butler now protests that he had no intention of misrepresenting or injuring the good-neighbor policy. Whatever his intentions may have been, the effects of what he said, its manner and its implications, were such as to constitute a most unfair and unfounded attack calculated to injure the whole policy.

Beginning 10 years ago at Montevideo we of the Americas have built a cooperative relationship to increase our trade and raise our standard of life and to serve as a bulwark in the defense of our independence and freedom.

At Buenos Aires we established the procedure of consultation before the menace of overseas aggression. At Lima we proclaimed the solidarity of the Americas and our determination jointly to face common dangers to our security. After war broke out in Europe in 1939 we had two special meetings, one at Panamá and another at Havana, where we concerted measures of mutual assistance. We agreed to consider an attack against one as an attack against all.

On December 7 attack came and with it the sternest test of inter-American solidarity. The other American Republics realized that the Axis attack against the United States was only part of a plan to conquer the entire world. Now, 13 are in a state of war with the Axis, and 6 others have broken diplomatic relations with the Axis. Argentina alone has failed to act.

We in the United States are proud of our membership in the inter-American system through which the 20 American Republics have so decisively met the challenge of our times. At the blackest moment of the war, during the meeting of Foreign Ministers at Rio de Janeiro, our sister republics raised their banners alongside ours. They opened their ports to our ships. They welcomed and quartered our troops on their soil. They devoted their mines, their forests, and their fields to the intensive production of strategic war materials. They rounded up Axis spies and saboteurs, and they shut off trade of benefit to the Axis.

They cooperated in the defense of the Panama Canal and in the suppression of the submarine menace. All this and much more they did as their contribution to victory.

The plain truth is that without this cooperation the course of the war in highly essential strategic areas might have been different. For example, consider the situation in the Near East. When Rommel was hammering at the gates of Egypt it was planes and light-tank ammunition ferried by northeastern Brazil that helped turn the tide. The value to our cause of the use of these Brazilian airports and of the cooperation of the Brazilian Army and Navy cannot be overstated.

It is distressing that at a time when the nation is engaged in a gigantic effort to defeat the assassins of civilization a wholly indefensible attack should be leveled at a policy so universally acclaimed. It is a tribute to the good sense of the people of the Americas, who have now had 10 years of experience with the good-neighbor policy, that these gross misrepresentations were not generally believed.

(2) *Pan American Day Address by the Secretary of State (Hull) before the Pan American Union, April 14, 1944* [1]

Pan American Day is an important anniversary to the nations of the Americas. We meet today to honor those whose vision and energy established and for more than 50 years have carried forward the Pan American Union and all that it signifies. It is well to ask ourselves why it is that we can meet in the midst of the greatest war of history and why it is that we have so great an achievement to commemorate. For in doing so we may more clearly see the guideposts which point the true direction in which we may go forward to new cooperation among ourselves and new cooperation with other nations of the earth.

Inter-American unity was not brought about by force and is not based upon the conception of a master race whose mission is to rule. It was not produced by nations with a homogeneous racial origin. It does not depend upon the bonds of a common language or a culture based on a common literature or common customs and habits.

Were these the only sources of international unity and common action, the future for the world would be dark indeed. But inter-American unity proves that there are other sources more subtle and even stronger — sources which offer hope to a world which can find no hope in the factors which I have mentioned. Our unity comes from a passionate devotion to human liberty and national independence which is so strong that it does not stop with the effort of each people to secure liberty for itself but goes on to respect as no less valid the desire of other peoples to achieve the same liberty in accordance with their own traditions and

[1] Department of State, *Bulletin*, X, p. 349.

historic institutions. Although the language of Bolívar and San Martín was different from that of Washington and Jefferson, they were expressing the same purposes and principles, and they led their countrymen along the same paths. These are the paths along which inter-American unity has developed, growing ever stronger as the American nations have come to understand one another and to have trust and confidence in one another's purposes and to work together for purposes so identic that they produced, not division and jealousy, but unity of thought and action.

As the years have gone on, the true principles underlying inter-American unity have been made more specific as one inter-American conference has followed another. In the years between the world wars the trust and confidence between the American nations grew ever stronger while elsewhere the growth of ambitions of conquest by force brought division and fear. It is the common pride of the American Republics and the good fortune of all mankind that the torch of international cooperation has burned at its brightest in the affairs of this hemisphere precisely at a time when it was being blacked out elsewhere. It is natural that the history of an international association which has endured longer than any other should provide encouraging guidance for the future.

At the Montevideo Conference in 1933 the American Republics affirmed their belief in certain essential principles upon which cooperation between nations and international order must be based. Among them was the principle that every nation, large and small, was equal before the law of nations. Another was the right of every nation to develop its own institutions, free from intervention by others. We already see the beginning of a wider application of these basic principles. They were stated in the Atlantic Charter, the United Nations Declaration, and the declarations made at Moscow. Specifically, it was agreed at Moscow that membership in the world security organization must be upon the basis of the sovereign equality of all nations, weak as well as strong, and the right of every nation to a government of its own choice.

The American nations spoke with a united voice at Buenos Aires as early as 1936 and Lima in 1938 of the dangers to world peace which impended, and took united action to defend the hemisphere against them. When the attack came many of the American Republics immediately sprang to the defense of the hemisphere. Shortly after the conference at Rio de Janeiro others took the same course. This chapter in our American history will ever be a gallant and glorious one. It teaches that unity of purpose, a common and passionate devotion to the maintenance of freedom, and mutual trust and confidence are the essential elements without which no amount of international organization and machinery can succeed. But it also teaches us and other nations that international organization and machinery are necessary. Successful as our common action has been, it has not been complete. And it took time, which may not always be available. Therefore, we learn that an international organization, whether in the field of inter-American cooperation or in the broader field of world peace, must have two main supports. It must gather its greatest strength from the rightness and justness of the principles upon which it is founded and the mutual trust of its members. It must also have such an essential framework and machinery and such an acceptance of their obligations on the part of its members as will enable it to act promptly and effectively in times of crisis.

Another guidepost for the future which our common experience before and during this war has raised is in the economic field. With the outbreak of the war the continent mobilized economically. The extent to which the products of the hemisphere have contributed to the growing success of the war against Germany and Japan cannot be overestimated. Millions of men and women throughout the hemisphere are devoting themselves unsparingly to the production of essential materials and to the forging of the weapons of our common victory. All this has been done under the great handicaps of the dislocations produced by the war.

At the end of the war all of our countries will be faced by problems of immense gravity. Out of the experience of our association in peace and in war we have learned that the expansion of material well-being can only come with an expansion of production and trade and hence an increase in consumption. We have learned too that no one nation can solve its problems by itself. An increase in production requires financing, a wise selection of the goods to be produced, and wise and fair commercial policies to enable goods to flow to their markets and necessary purchases to be made in return. All of this requires cooperative effort and the creation of international arrangements through which that effort may have concrete expression. But it requires something more than this. It requires the respect by each nation for each other nation, of which I have spoken, in the field of political relations. International cooperation in the economic field is the opposite of economic imperialism, by which one country seeks to exploit another. It is also the opposite of economic nationalism, by which each nation seeks to live unto itself.

We citizens of this hemisphere have great opportunities before us. The community of action among the American nations, already highly developed, will at the end of the war be indispensable in the advancement of our economic well-being and in the establishment of an international organization to prevent the recurrence of world wars. Together, as I have said, we foresaw, pointed out, and prepared against the dangers of war. Together we must foresee and prepare for the ever-greater common task of the peace. I believe that as in future years men of the Americas meet to commemorate this day they will see unfolded before their eyes ever-increasing evidence that the path along which inter-American cooperation has led is the path to human liberty and human welfare.

B. Political Solidarity and Defense

1. DECLARATIONS OF WAR, SEVERANCES OF DIPLOMATIC RELATIONS AND OTHER MANIFESTATIONS OF CONTINENTAL SOLIDARITY BY THE OTHER AMERICAN REPUBLICS

[See *Documents, IV, 1941–42*, p. 336; *V, 1942–43*, p. 358.]

The Government of Colombia announced a state of belligerency with Germany on November 27, 1943, following a series of aggressions by the German Government.[1] On December 22, the Colombian Government notified Secretary Hull of its decision to adhere to the Declaration by United Nations.[2] On December 4, the Bolivian Government promulgated a decree formally declaring that Bolivia was at war with the Axis powers, basing this action on the approval by the Bolivian Congress on November 26, 1943 of Bolivia's adherence to the Declaration by United Nations.[3] The Bolivian Ambassador informed the Department of State that the action of the Bolivian Congress sanctioned the Bolivian decree of April 7, 1943 by which a state of war was declared to exist between Bolivia and the Axis powers, and under which the Bolivian Government adhered to the United Nations Declaration.[4]

On relations with Argentina, see p. 523.

2. RECOGNITION OF NEW GOVERNMENTS INSTITUTED BY FORCE

(1) *Resolution Approved by the Emergency Advisory Committee for Political Defense, Montevideo, December 24, 1943* [5]

The forceful overthrow of recognized governments in Argentina and Bolivia under circumstances which suggested activity by pro-Axis elements led to the adoption of this resolution which was communicated to Secretary Hull in a telegram from the chairman of the Committee, Dr. Alberto Guani. Secretary Hull's reply is also given.

WHEREAS:

(*a*) That notwithstanding the lack of success in its purposes of annulling the contribution which the American peoples are making to the war effort and to the political defense of the continent, in compliance with the agreements in effect, it is evident that the Axis continues to exert itself to carry out these designs, with grave danger that totalitarian elements may through force take possession of governments of American Republics, separating them from the principles of union and solidarity adopted in the face of the common enemy and from support to the cause of the United and Associated Nations;

(*b*) That rights and duties are derived from the aforementioned agreements which consecrate the solidarity which should exist between said

---

[1] *Ibid.*, IX, p. 379.
[2] *Ibid.*, X, p. 108.
[3] *Ibid.*, IX, p. 413.
[4] See *Documents, V, 1942–43*, p. 213.
[5] Department of State, *Bulletin*, X, p. 20.

Republics for the defense of the continent against the dangers indicated in the preceding paragraph;

(c) That the third consultative meeting of the Ministers of Foreign Affairs, in creating this Committee, assigned to it the mandate of recommending measures with respect to the problems relating to all aspects of the defense of the continent against the political aggression of the Axis;

The Emergency Consultative [Advisory] Committee for Political Defense RESOLVES:

"To recommend to the American Governments which have declared war on the Axis powers or have broken relations with them, that for the duration of the present world conflict they do not proceed to the recognition of a new government instituted by force, before consulting among themselves for the purpose of determining whether this government complies with the Inter-American undertakings for the defense of the continent, nor before carrying out an exchange of information as to the circumstances which have determined the establishment of said government."

In communicating said resolution and by express provision of the Committee, I have the particular honor to express that it does not refer to any particular case, but has been adopted having in view the general interests of continental political defense.

(2) *The Secretary of State (Hull) to the Chairman of the Emergency Advisory Committee for Political Defense (Guani), December 27, 1943* [1]

I have the honor to acknowledge the receipt of Your Excellency's telegram of December 24 transmitting the text of a resolution approved by the Emergency Advisory Committee for Political Defense on December 23 in which it resolved:

"To recommend to the American Governments which have declared war on the Axis powers or have broken relations with them, that for the duration of the present world conflict they do not proceed to the recognition of a new government instituted by force, before consulting among themselves for the purpose of determining whether this government complies with the Inter-American undertakings for the defense of the continent, nor before carrying out an exchange of information as to the circumstances which have determined the establishment of said government."

I desire to inform you that this Government wholeheartedly approves of the foregoing resolution. In accordance with it, this Government stands ready to consult and exchange information with the other Ameri-

[1] *Ibid.,* p. 21.

can Republics which have declared war against or have severed diplomatic relations with the Axis, in situations to which the resolution applies.

3. MILITARY AND NAVAL COOPERATION

(1) *List of Agreements Made for Detailing of Military and Naval Missions and for Other Assistance, July 1, 1943–June 30, 1944* [1]

COUNTRY	DATE OF SIGNATURE	PURPOSE	EXECUTIVE AGREEMENT SERIES
PANAMA	Jul. 6 and Aug. 5, 1943	Renewing agreement for detail of U. S. Army officer as adviser to Minister of Foreign Affairs. In force for 1 year, effective Jul. 7, 1943	336
	Apr. 26 and May 18, 1944	Renewal of above agreement for 1 year, effective Jul. 7, 1944	414
GUATEMALA	Jul. 17, 1943	U. S. Army officer of grade of lieutenant-colonel to serve as director of the Polytechnic School. In force for 1 year, effective Jul. 17, 1943	329
	Jan. 5 and 17, 1944	Renewal of above agreement for 1 year, effective Jul. 17, 1944	397
COLOMBIA	Jul. 23 and Aug. 7, 1943	Renewing Naval Mission Agreement signed Nov. 23, 1938, as amended by supplementary agreement signed Aug. 30, 1941, and extended by agreement effected by exchange of notes, signed Sept. 22 and Nov. 5, 1942. In force for 1 year, effective Nov. 23, 1943	337
	Jun. 26 and Jul. 18, 1944	Renewal of above agreement for 1 year, effective Nov. 23, 1944	413
ECUADOR	Sept. 13, 1943	U. S. Army officer to serve as Technical Director of the Eloy Alfaro Military College. In force for 4 years, effective Sept. 13, 1943	338

[1] Compiled from information in Department of State *Bulletin*, and *Executive Agreement Series*.

Country	Date of Signature	Purpose	Executive Agreement Series
ARGENTINA	Jun. 23 and Sept. 2, 1943	U. S. Army Air Corps officers as instructors. Extension of agreement of Jun. 29, 1940 for further period of 2 years, effective Jun. 29, 1943	340
NICARAGUA	Oct. 22 and 25, 1943	Military officer to serve as Director of Military Academy of the National Guard. Continuing agreement of May 22, 1941, for further period of 2 years, effective May 22, 1943	344
PARAGUAY	Oct. 27, 1943	Military Aviation Mission. In force for 4 years, effective Oct. 27, 1943	343
PERU	Nov. 23 and Dec. 20, 1943	Renewal of agreement of Apr. 15, 1941 for military adviser to remount service of Peruvian Army, for further period of 3 years, effective Apr. 15, 1944	363
PARAGUAY	Dec. 10, 1943	Military mission. In force for 4 years, effective Dec. 10, 1943	354
VENEZUELA	Jan. 13, 1944	Military Aviation Mission. In force for 4 years, effective Jan. 13, 1944	398
PERU	Jan. 31, Feb. 9 and Mar. 21 and 31, 1944	Renewal of agreement for U. S. Naval Mission signed Jul. 31, 1940.[1] In force for 4 years, effective Jul. 31, 1944	396
PERU	Jan. 31, Feb. 18, Apr. 6 and 29, and May 2, 1944 [2]	Renewal of U. S. Naval Aviation Mission signed Jul. 31, 1940.[1] In force for 2 years, effective Jul. 31, 1944	402
ECUADOR	Jun. 29, 1944	Military Mission. In force for 4 years, effective Jun. 29, 1944	408

[1] The agreement has been amended by the addition of the following article:
"The members of the Mission are permitted and may be authorized to represent the United States of America on any mission and in any other capacity having to do with military cooperation or hemisphere defense without prejudice to this Agreement, during the present war emergency." (Department of State, *Bulletin*, X, p. 330.)

[2] The terms "Ministry of Marine and Aviation" and "Minister of Marine and Aviation" are changed to "Ministry of Aeronautics" and "Minister of Aeronautics," respectively, wherever they appear in the agreement of July 31, 1940, in conformity with a recent act approved by the Congress of Peru. (*Ibid.*, p. 490.)

C. Economic and Financial Collaboration

1. CONFERENCE OF COMMISSIONS OF INTER-AMERICAN DEVELOPMENT, NEW YORK, MAY 9–18, 1944

The Inter-American Development Commission was established on June 3, 1940 [1] as an agency of the Inter-American Financial and Economic Advisory Committee which had been organized following a resolution adopted on October 3, 1939 at the Meeting of the Foreign Ministers of the American Republics at Panama.[2] The Commission was set up to assist in mobilizing the economic forces of the American Republics (1) by stimulating the increase of non-competitive imports from Latin America to the United States; (2) by stimulating and increasing trade between the Latin American Republics themselves; and (3) by encouraging development of industry in Latin America, particularly along the lines of consumer goods.[3]

The Second Meeting of Ministers of Foreign Affairs of the American Republics, held at Havana in July 1940, endorsed the work of the Inter-American Financial and Economic Advisory Committee and enlarged its functions (Resolution XXV),[4] thus extending the scope of the Commission's work.

The Commission subsequently undertook to organize national commissions. The members of each National Commission were appointed by the Inter-American Development Commission in agreement with the government of that country.

The Third Meeting of the Ministers of Foreign Affairs, held at Rio de Janeiro in January 1942, expressed the view that "the time has come to stimulate, intensify and coordinate the work of such national commissions and of the Inter-American Development Commission in Washington in order to promote, or maintain, the economic forces of the American nations, using for this purpose to the fullest extent possible the advantages offered by the existence of such systems of inter-American commissions" and to this end recommended that the governments of the American Republics "continue to lend to the national commissions and to the Inter-American Development Commission in Washington all the assistance and support they may need to carry out the objectives for which they have been created." It instructed the Inter-American Financial and Economic Advisory Committee to create, under the auspices of the Commission, "a permanent body of technical experts to study the natural resources of each country when so requested by its government."[5] The Meeting of Ministers of Foreign Affairs also declared:

"1. That to raise the standard of living of the people, the economic policy of the American nations must be founded upon a broad and complete utilization of their natural resources and directed toward a greater industrialization of those raw materials which present favorable and permanent economic possibilities both as to production and markets; and at the same time it shall be the policy to seek to improve continental coordination through international agreements.

"2. That it is the desire of the Third Meeting of the Ministers of Foreign Affairs that the Inter-American Development Commission and the respective National Commissions endeavor to put into practice the economic policy referred to in this declaration."[6]

This Conference of Commissions of Inter-American Development, the first to be held, was called primarily for the purpose of carrying out these policy directives. Delegations were present from all the National Commissions. The

[1] *Documents, III, 1940–41*, p. 112.
[2] *Ibid., II, 1939–40*, p. 100.
[3] *Ibid., III, 1940–41*, p. 113.
[4] *Ibid.*, p. 82.
[5] *Ibid., IV, 1941–42*, p. 314.
[6] *Ibid.*, p. 316.

Chairman of the Conference was Mr. Nelson A. Rockefeller, Chairman of the Commission of Inter-American Development. The Governments of Argentina, Canada, Costa Rica, Ecuador, Nicaragua, United States and Venezuela named observers to attend the meetings. Observers were also accredited by the Pan American Union, the Inter-American Financial and Economic Advisory Committee, the International Labor Office, the Permanent Council of American Associations of Commerce and Production, and the Economic and Financial Department of the League of Nations. The United States Chamber of Commerce, the National Association of Manufacturers, the National Foreign Trade Council, the Pan American Society and the Committee for Economic Development cooperated in the proceedings.

All recommendations and resolutions were adopted unanimously. The Spanish text of each recommendation and resolution was discussed and approved by the Conference; the English text is in each case a translation. The texts of the Recommendations and Resolutions are given in the Final Act.[1]

2. COMPREHENSIVE ARRANGEMENTS FOR PROMOTION OF ECONOMIC SOLIDARITY

[For details on national arrangements previously entered into, see *Documents, IV 1941–42*, p. 356; *V, 1942–43*, p. 385]

(1) *Economic Arrangements with Haiti. Department of State Release, November 8, 1943* [2]

During the visit in Washington of His Excellency President Elie Lescot, of Haiti, in October, a number of questions relating to the joint war efforts of the two countries were discussed with President Roosevelt, Vice President Wallace, and with the leaders of the Senate and of the House of Representatives. Additional conferences were held by the President and the Cabinet Ministers of Haiti in the presidential party with officers of the Department of State and of other agencies of the United States Government.

These conferences included a consideration of the program for Cryptostegia rubber development in Haiti, an activity on which the Rubber Development Corporation of the United States Government expects to expend approximately $9,600,000 during 1944.

The occasion of the visit to Washington was also used for discussions between the Haitian Minister of Finance and the President of the Export-Import Bank of Washington, during the course of which agreements were reached regarding the schedule of repayments to the bank for a line of credit established in 1938 for a public-works program in Haiti. The Minister of Finance also indicated the intention of the Haitian Government to take steps toward the further reduction of its dollar-bond obligations.

One of the topics which the two Presidents discussed at the White House, *i.e.* the development of industries in Haiti, was explored, and decisions were taken to request the Inter-American Development Commission to conduct surveys and studies of the possible ways in which both private capital and government agencies might cooperate to develop certain small industries in Haiti, particularly after the war.

With the Office of the Coordinator of Inter-American Affairs, the Haitian Minister of Education and Agriculture laid plans for a cooperative educational

[1] *Conference of Commissions of Inter-American Development, May 9 to 18, 1944. Final Act.* Washington, Pan American Union, 1944.

[2] Department of State, *Bulletin*, IX, p. 332.

project which will involve the exchange of educators and students between Haiti and the United States. The Institute of Inter-American Affairs has also made arrangements for the continuance for an additional three years of certain projects of malaria control and public-health and sanitation improvement, which have been under way for some time in a number of Haitian communities, both urban and rural.

A number of other matters were taken up during President Lescot's visit, including the loan of the services of agricultural, educational, and taxation experts from the United States and the coordination of the two Governments in the increased production of strategic material such as rubber and sisal.

The Secretary of State on November 25 [1] announced that after consultation with His Excellency André Liautaud, the Ambassador of Haiti in Washington, it has been agreed to set up an industrial mission consisting of three representatives each of the Governments of Haiti and of the United States of America. The representatives of the United States on the mission are: Mr. Charles A. Howard, Director of the Technical Office, Inter-American Development Commission; Dr. Louis Shere, Assistant Director of the Division of Tax Research, Treasury Department; Mr. John K. Whitaker, a Director of the Cotton Textile Institute, designated upon the recommendation of the United States Commission of Inter-American Development.

(2) *Mexican-American Commission for Economic Cooperation*

For text of agreement reached by President Roosevelt and President Ávila Camacho on the occasion of their reciprocal visits in April 1943, see *Documents, V, 1942–43,* p. 404. The agreement provided for the creation of an economic committee to "study the balance of international payments and the resulting economic situation of the Republic of Mexico and formulate as the result of such study a program for economic cooperation." The committee was subsequently set up with the following membership: Honorable Wayne Chatfield Taylor, Under Secretary of Commerce, and Mr. Harry D. White, Assistant to the Secretary of the Treasury (United States members); and Mr. Valentin P. Garfias and Mr. Evaristo Araiza (Mexican members).

(a) *Report, Published July 17, 1943* [2]

As a result of the opportunity afforded by the reciprocal visits made in April by President Roosevelt and President Ávila Camacho in Mexican and United States territory, an agreement was reached between the two Presidents to create a joint commission to study the disturbances in the balance of payments and the related economic situation of Mexico and to formulate a program for economic cooperation which would provide for the indispensable assistance of the United States to the end that the economic development of Mexico be fostered and the production of strategic materials by Mexico be not jeopardized. Following the appointment of the members of the Mexican-American Commission for Economic Cooperation the Mexican members proceeded to Washington to open the discussions. Meetings of the Commission were held at intervals from May 21 to June 3, during which time the

[1] *Ibid.*, p. 283.　　　　　　　　　　[2] *Ibid.*, p. 40.

scope and objectives of the Commission's work and various technical aspects of the problems under consideration were explored.

The Commission, accompanied by its technical staffs, proceeded to Mexico City following the initial discussions in Washington and there continued its deliberations for a period of three weeks. During this period a number of subcommittees composed, on the Mexican side, of representatives of government, industry, and banking, and on the American side, of representatives of the United States Government, were formed to study disturbances in the balance of international payments of Mexico and to receive and consider programs for the production of strategic materials in Mexico and for the development of Mexican agriculture and industry. The findings of these subcommittees, all of which were reported to the Commission in Mexico City, provided the basis for its own observations and its recommendations for cooperative action.

The Commission concluded its work in Washington after a series of meetings during the period from June 28 to July 2.

In proceeding with the task entrusted to it by President Ávila Camacho and President Roosevelt, the Mexican-American Commission for Economic Cooperation has given emphasis, first, to the joint activities of the two nations in producing materials for war; second, to the maintenance of Mexican civilian economy during the war period; and, third, to analyzing ways and means by which the long-range plans for the development of Mexico's national economy may best be furthered by the closest working cooperation between governmental and private organizations of the two countries.

The Commission hopes that its recommendations will contribute materially toward the solution of some of the economic problems produced by the world-wide war in which Mexico and the United States of America are fighting side by side against the forces of totalitarian domination, but wishes to emphasize its belief that the closest economic cooperation is essential not only during the war but also in the post-war period for the maximum development of both nations, and therefore strongly recommends the preparation of plans which can be put into effect in whole or in part both now and as soon as hostilities cease.

There are many activities which are of the utmost importance in war and which are of like importance in times of peace. For example, a full supply of essential foods is a necessity in war in order to assure maximum efficiency of the armed forces and maximum production by the civilian workers who serve their needs. Likewise in peace, no nation can develop culturally or industrially if its population is undernourished. Naturally, the health of armed forces is essential to victory, and the health of the civilian population is of equal importance in both war and peace. For Mexico, increased production of food is an important goal both during and after the war.

Transportation and communications must be developed and maintained to assure victory. They are likewise essential for the development and servicing of a fully functioning national economy in times of peace.

The field of industry is more complex. Many war plants have no peacetime uses. It would appear advisable for Mexico to concentrate her industrialization program largely in those industries which will serve in peace as well as in war, thus making a permanent contribution to her economy. In many cases, tools and construction materials are not presently available, but in others a careful selection of idle machinery and a well-planned adaptation of available new equipment will permit the establishment of new industries and the expansion of existing facilities without interfering with the war effort.

Modern industry requires adequate supplies of raw materials, power, and fuel. Therefore the availability of raw materials, power, and fuel must be given primary consideration in planning any program of industrialization.

Labor must be trained for new specialized tasks, and competent technical direction and advice must be assured if the new industries are to make their full contribution.

These basic principles have guided the Commission in its discussions and in the formulation of its recommendations. In addition, consideration has been given to the trends disclosed by a study of Mexico's balance of payments and the opportunities for the sound development of Mexico's agricultural and industrial resources which these trends indicate.

STRATEGIC MATERIALS

The Commission believes that the programs for the production and sale of strategic materials by Mexico represent a major contribution to the combined war effort. In most cases these programs likewise have laid the foundations for permanent economic cooperation. In their simplest terms these programs provide that Mexico, with the indispensable cooperation of the United States, will make every effort to maintain and develop the production of raw materials directly required for the manufacture of munitions and other equipment urgently needed by the armed forces of the United Nations. Some of the end-products are used directly in equipping the armed forces of the United States. Many others are delivered under lend-lease arrangements to the other United Nations which can employ them most effectively against our common enemies.

In order to make possible the production in Mexico of these strategic materials the United States undertakes to make available the necessary supplies and equipment. While concentration on these types of production obviously affects other economic activities, like all war programs they must be vigorously pursued until final victory has been achieved. Mexico will, therefore, continue to concentrate on the production of strategic materials, and the United States will continue to deliver supplies and equipment to make the production possible. New joint programs should be developed as rapidly as circumstances and changing war requirements indicate their desirability.

Food

As indicated earlier, the Commission believes that the full development of Mexico's food supply is essential and that Mexico's climate, land resources, and people lend themselves admirably to such a development. It concurs fully in the recommendations of the United Nations Food Conference, and further recommends that the Secretaria de Agricultura of Mexico and the Department of Agriculture of the United States take all appropriate steps to insure the active and continuous cooperation which will make these splendid programs a reality. Mexico's food resources cannot be fully developed immediately, but appropriate plans can be made which will do much to assure the attainment of the final goals. These plans should cover all phases of food production, processing, storage, and distribution. Pending the development of these detailed plans, Mexico's existing food resources must be maintained, and production of basic food crops must be increased as rapidly as possible. While Mexico's agriculture has not as yet become markedly mechanized, existing equipment must be maintained at maximum efficiency. The United States undertakes to supply necessary repair and replacement parts which cannot be obtained from other sources, and new equipment must also be provided if present modest goals are to be attained.

Industry

The Commission has recognized as a guiding principle for its work that it is in the interest of both countries for the industrialization of Mexico to proceed at as rapid a pace as possible, consistent with the necessary restrictions on the use of critical materials and equipment during the war. In the light of this principle the Commission has considered programs for the orderly development in Mexico of the electrical, steel, rubber, cement, chemical, textile, sugar and alcohol, and pulp and paper industries. It has recommended the execution of both immediate and long-run projects which will contribute directly or indirectly to the war effort of the United Nations or the carrying out of which will constitute no interference with the war effort.

As a means of providing a continuing body to study programs for the development of Mexican industry in addition to those which have been considered, the Commission recommends that a small industrial commission be created by the Government of Mexico to develop and carry forward long-term programs for the industrialization of Mexico.

It is recommended that the industrial commission be composed of representatives of government, banking, and industry, and that the Government of the United States appoint a qualified person to cooperate with the industrial commission.

It is recommended that the industrial commission be assigned the task of carrying out the following functions:

(1) Continue to study and develop the plans for industrialization outlined by the Commission.

(2) Advise and consult with appropriate authorities regarding industrial projects and the financing thereof.

(3) Cooperate with, and where appropriate, utilize the facilities of the Inter-American Development Commission.

(4) Implement the immediate program outlined by the Commission by the preparation of detailed lists of machinery and equipment required, and where necessary send representatives to the United States who will be informed by the industrial commission of the type and specifications of equipment desired to carry out specific projects and who will be empowered to examine and purchase suitable idle or used equipment, lists of which will be made available to them by the appropriate agencies of the United States Government.

(5) Make recommendations to the appropriate agencies of the United States Government through existing channels in regard to the issuance of export licenses and priority assistance regarding industrial projects.

(6) Endeavor to encourage and assist in the conclusion of contracts between industrialists in Mexico and manufacturers in the United States for the carrying out of industrial projects for which needed equipment cannot presently be obtained in the United States, such contracts to be executed as soon as needed materials can be manufactured in the United States.

(7) Recommend the development of such sound industrial policies and practices as will encourage the healthy growth of industry in Mexico.

In view of the extreme difficulty of obtaining new equipment for Mexican industry, the Commission urges that every effort be made by government and private interests to procure serviceable idle or used equipment and that prompt and effective measures be taken to maintain existing equipment in use, especially through facilitating in every way possible the procurement of repair and replacement parts. The Commission recommends that used equipment be supplemented by necessary new equipment and that in urgent cases, when used equipment is not available, new equipment be furnished with the minimum possible delay.

GENERAL REQUIREMENTS

The Commission has also reviewed the general requirements (*i.e.*, requirements not related to special projects) of Mexico for commodities in short supply and has recommended revisions in estimates of supply from the United States on the basis of changed conditions in Mexico or on the basis of data heretofore not available. The Commission considers that the requirements given in the report of the subcommittee on general requirements represent the minimum requirements for the maintenance of the economy of Mexico on a wartime basis. It therefore strongly recommends that every effort be made by the appropriate agencies of the United States Government to carry out promptly the proposals contained in the report of the subcommittee.

PUBLIC WORKS AND SANITATION

The Commission has considered various public-works projects in Mexico, including drainage and flood-control projects and numerous sanitation projects. Some of these, which are clearly of immediate and vital importance, have been recommended for prompt execution. The Commission recommends that other projects, including a number which are apparently of an urgent character, be given further study by the Governments of Mexico and the United States.

TRANSPORTATION, COMMUNICATIONS, MERCHANT MARINE, AND FISHERIES

In dealing with the fundamental question of transportation in Mexico, the Commission undertook to consider Mexico's transportation requirements on the basis of the over-all program presentations furnished the Commission by the Secretaria de Comunicaciones y Obras Publicas and the Secretaria de Marina, covering railways, highways, aviation, public service and commercial automotive transport, merchant marine, and fishing. It was obvious that the importance of transportation to Mexico's economy must be fully appreciated in Mexico and in the United States.

The Commission recommends a continuing study of Mexico's transportation needs on an over-all basis and the establishment in Washington of a permanent mechanism which can cooperate effectively and continuously with the transportation authorities of Mexico.

Various specific recommendations were made calculated to maintain Mexico's transportation at its present level through adequate supply of spare parts and essential replacements. Furthermore, if Mexico is to continue her part in the production of strategic materials, while at the same time maintaining her accelerated internal economy, it is also necessary to increase transportation facilities. Recommendations were made to permit new construction by maintaining all existing equipment in constant operation, locating suitable second-hand equipment, and supplying the balance of requirements in new equipment.

The Commission recommends that further study be given to means of increasing the quantity of fish available for local consumption both by providing the necessary boats and equipment and by enlarging existing refrigeration and canning facilities ashore. A joint committee representing Mexico and the United States, it is felt, would be effective in determining present and future development.

The recommendations of the Commission should permit not only proper consideration of Mexico's immediate and wartime requirements but also the development of continuing programs that will provide Mexico with adequate transportation, in the early post-war period, for her longer-range economic requirements.

BALANCE OF PAYMENTS

During the period since the beginning of the war and especially since Pearl Harbor, the most important factors affecting the balance of payments of Mexico have been the cutting off of all important sources of supply in Europe and the Eastern Hemisphere, the conversion of the United States economy to war production, the concentration of Mexican production in strategic materials, the increase in exports to the United States, and, in the latter part of the period, a large flow of capital from other financial centers, principally the United States, to Mexico.

Mexico had in earlier years purchased much of her industrial equipment and manufactured products from the United States, but she had also established specialized sources of supply in Europe and the Far East. Thus, when these overseas sources were cut off, Mexico and other nations in this hemisphere turned to the United States as the only nation capable of filling industrial needs. Unfortunately, these demands occurred at the time when the United States was converting her vast industrial plant to war purposes. The United States might have been able to supply all the civilian needs of this hemisphere under normal conditions, but she could not act as chief arsenal of the United Nations as well. The choice was obvious — victory was far more important than trade. The United States, therefore, adopted the policy of putting war needs first and of sharing the balance available for the needs of her civilian population with other friendly nations.

The availability of transportation soon became an important factor in the allocation of existing supplies; but as Mexico and the United States could exchange goods by overland routes, their mutual trade was disturbed to a minor extent by diversion of ocean and coastwise shipping. In spite of this relative advantage, the amounts and types of goods available for export to Mexico fell far below Mexico's needs. Meanwhile, the full cooperation of Mexico in achieving the maximum production of strategic materials as her contribution to the war effort of the United Nations, regardless of the economic and transportation difficulties involved, was evidencing itself in imports into the United States from Mexico. Imports into the United States from Mexico in the calendar year 1941, according to United States statistics, amounted to $141,000,000, inclusive of silver valued at $26,000,000 and gold valued at $17,000,000. For the calendar year 1942 the total was $179,000,000, including $27,000,000 of silver and $40,000,000 of gold; and for the first 4 months of 1943 imports were approximately $73,000,000, of which $6,000,000 consisted of silver and $1,000,000 of gold.

During the same periods, exports from the United States to Mexico, according to United States statistics, were as follows: 1941 — $159,-000,000; 1942 — $147,000,000; first four months 1943 — $59,000,000 (inclusive of $9,000,000 of gold).[1] It is perhaps worth noting that in 1941 Mexico purchased United States products to a higher dollar value than in any previous year except 1920 and 1921. Thus, during 1942 and the early part of 1943 imports into the United States from Mexico, inclusive of silver and gold, exceeded exports from the United States to Mexico, whereas during 1941 the trade had resulted in a surplus of exports to Mexico. The total trade of Mexico, as revealed by Mexican statistics, showed similar trends during these periods. A typical excess of exports was converted into an excess of imports in 1941 as a result of a record volume of imports combined with a reduction in exports, while in 1942 and the early part of 1943 changes in the opposite directions produced a surplus of exports.

Although the surplus of Mexican exports over imports has been reflected in the increase in Mexico's monetary reserves, the Commission finds that an important factor contributing to the sharp increase in Mexico's holdings of dollar exchange and gold in late 1942 and in 1943 is a large capital movement. The movement represents the repatriation of Mexican balances, the transfer of refugee funds from other financial centers, and a strong transfer of the funds of United States citizens. Recent information indicates that the force of the movement was moderated by the announcement, at the end of May, of the renewal of the Mexican-United States Stabilization Agreement.

As has been indicated, the Commission believes that the inflow of capital, the increase in exports, and the restricted availability of important items which Mexico wishes to purchase abroad have all contributed to the existing balance-of-payments situation. In more normal times

[1] The figures given do not include earmarking operations. [Footnote in the report.]

a favorable trade balance accompanied by a strong inward capital movement would provide Mexico with the financial resources needed to foster a rapid development of its economy. These resources, whose full utilization is limited by the war, will be of great use to Mexico in the post-war period.

Naturally, the Commission, in tracing the effects of Mexico's trade position and capital movements, has had occasion to examine in detail some related aspects of Mexico's economic position. It has given particular attention to the increasing circulation and rapidly rising bank deposits and the movement in prices. The Commission has been informed of several remedial measures already in process or under consideration by the Government of Mexico.

At the present time the factors operative in the Mexican economy are subject to very rapid changes. The Commission notes with satisfaction that the recent renewal of the Mexican-United States Stabilization Agreement contemplates consultation between the Secretaria de Hacienda of Mexico and the Treasury Department of the United States.

CONCLUSION

The Commission believes that the specific projects which it has recommended will constitute an important contribution to Mexico's economy. The programs, while well conceived, are of necessity limited in scope. But it should be emphasized that industrial and transportation equipment available today in few cases represents the latest and most efficient designs. Wartime discoveries and wartime techniques will have a marked effect on practically every phase of industry and transportation. Mexico will have the benefit of these developments when it becomes possible fully to equip her industries and her expanded transportation system.

The recommendations covering current requirements and maintenance, especially the allocations urged for repair parts, should serve to keep Mexico's civilian economy operating on a wartime basis.

The information given to the Commission concerning Mexico's long-range development programs has been doubly useful. It has served as background for the recommendations for current action and has pointed the way to the complete economic cooperation which should follow the war and the immediate reconstruction period.

The recommendations on the development of the tourist industry in the post-war period are based on the fact that a well-developed tourist trade between the two countries will add materially to their national incomes and on the belief of the Commission that such a movement will yield a true appreciation by the residents of each country of the culture and economic possibilities of the other. The Commission is impressed particularly by the mutual advantages of a systematic exchange of students, teachers, and technicians.

The Commission strongly recommends the working out of detailed plans for the development of all phases of Mexico's economy. Agricultural production, transportation, power, production, and general industrial development all have great possibilities. As a result of the war, Mexico is acquiring reserves which will greatly facilitate their rapid development. Close cooperation between the Governments and citizens of the two countries will assure the accomplishment of the full programs. Where governmental credit may be required, as in the past, the appropriate governmental agencies of the two nations will work out ways and means of accomplishing the desired results. In the field of private investment, mutually satisfactory cooperative arrangements offer even greater possibilities. The days of exploitation or economic imperialism, whether by nations or by powerful private groups are past — no future Mexican or United States Government will condone or permit their reappearance. But now industries primarily designed to serve Mexico's own needs which combine Mexican resources, equipment, capital, and technical skills with those of the United States offer a fruitful field for the best type of economic cooperation.

Industrialization will raise the standard of living in Mexico. The industrial worker will be able to buy more of the products of agriculture, the agricultural worker will be able to buy more of the products of industry, and their combined productive and purchasing power will enable Mexico to widen its markets and increase its purchases from other nations. These obvious economic truths can become actualities more quickly in this hemisphere than in perhaps any other portion of the world, and certainly no greater possibilities exist than in the case of Mexico and the United States. Their proximity and the demonstrated interdependence of their economies offer possibilities for constructive economic cooperation which are unequalled. Their example and their continued cooperation may well set the standard for the world of tomorrow.

In closing, the members of the Commission wish to express their appreciation to President Ávila Camacho and to President Roosevelt for the unusual opportunity for service which the work of the Commission offered.

The information covering every phase of Mexican economy which has been made available so freely to the Commission constitutes a nucleus of understanding and a sound basis for cooperation which will be of great value to both nations.

Finally, the Commission wishes to emphasize the importance of promptly devising procedures which will expedite putting into operation the recommendations contained in this program of economic cooperation.

(*b*) *The President of Mexico (Ávila Camacho) to the President (Roosevelt), July 15, 1943* [1]

The Delegates designated by the Mexican Government to form part of the Joint Commission of Economic Cooperation which met in Washington on the 21st of last May, in accordance with the aims which oriented the conversations which Your Excellency and I held during our interviews at Monterrey and Corpus Christi, have informed me regarding the result of their studies and have given me an account of the frank and friendly disposition shown in every instance by their North American colleagues, as well as by the various officials of the United States with whom they had occasion to deal in the fulfillment of their work.

In expressing to Your Excellency my sincere satisfaction with the conclusions reached and confidence which I have that these results will soon be translated into acts tending to consolidate the economic cooperation between Mexico and the United States, I am pleased to express to you the conviction that everything which our Governments may do, reciprocally, to insure and strengthen our mutual assistance will make closer still the cordial relations of our peoples and will serve undoubtedly as a basis for a continental structure of conciliation, equity and human progress.

I renew to Your Excellency the assurance of my consideration and constant friendship.

(*c*) *The President (Roosevelt) to the President of Mexico (Ávila Camacho), July 15, 1943* [2]

I acknowledge with deep appreciation and satisfaction the receipt of Your Excellency's telegram regarding the completion of the work of the Mexican-United States Commission for Economic Cooperation. The recommendations made by this group of economic experts are indeed in the spirit of friendliness and mutual understanding which governed our conversations in Monterrey and Corpus Christi and fulfill the hopes which we there expressed when we determined to appoint a joint commission to study the maintenance and intensification of economic cooperation between the Government of Mexico and the Government of the United States.

I have been informed by this Government's representatives on the Commission that from the beginning the unstinted labor and cordial attitude of the Mexican representatives assured success to the deliberations of the Commission.

It is my conviction that frank discussions of the nature of those carried out by the members of the joint commission are not only the most

[1] *Ibid.*, p. 38.   [2] *Ibid.*, p. 39.

effective approach to the problems which the active prosecution of the war has brought to our economies, but are also a noteworthy example of the understanding cooperation which guides the United Nations toward the inevitable crushing victory over Axis aggression.

In renewing to Your Excellency the assurances of my highest consideration, I recall with pleasure the warm hospitality extended to me in Monterrey by Your Excellency and by the people of Mexico.

(d) Joint Statement by the Governments of Mexico and the United States, July 15, 1943 [1]

On the occasion of the visits which they made reciprocally to Mexico and the United States of America, Presidents Roosevelt and Ávila Camacho considered it opportune that experts from the two countries should study the means of coordinating their action with the object of diminishing, so far as possible, upsets occasioned by the war.

As a consequence of the foregoing, there was formed the Mexican-American Commission for Economic Cooperation, which began its labors in Washington on May 21st last and which, after continuing them in Mexico for a period of three weeks, returned to the former city in order to conclude the examination of the various problems submitted for its consideration.[2]

During the course of their conversations the delegates of Mexico and the United States took into account on one hand the desirability of giving practical application to the Resolution for Maintenance of the Internal Economies of the American Nations adopted at the Third Consultative Meeting of Foreign Ministers held at Rio de Janeiro, and, on the other hand, the necessity of stimulating, upon increasingly solid and broader bases, the collaboration which binds the two nations together.

Mexico is cooperating to the maximum of its present possibilities with the effort of its allies by sending to the United Nations — and principally to the United States of America — the strategic materials obtained from its fields, mines, and workshops.

In order that this contribution may be intensified in the present and assured in the future it is indispensable that the Mexican Republic have available in time the necessary materials and articles which the United States of America is in a position to provide, since the heavy stress which the industry and agriculture of Mexico have been supporting has resulted in considerable increase in its exports while its imports have diminished sensibly, in view of the temporary elimination of extracontinental markets and the urgent necessity felt by the North American Union to dedicate its productive capacity before everything else to the rapid winning of the victory.

[1] Ibid.   [2] See ibid., VIII, p. 376, 457, 473.

This disproportion between the imports and exports of Mexico could cause a disequilibrium which not only would affect the internal economy of the country but bring about forcedly a diminution in production and therefore of its contribution to the war supplies which the circumstances demand.

After carefully analyzing all these questions the commissioners signed the report which is published together with the present communiqué. On publishing this document the Governments of Mexico and the United States of America manifest their determination to take without delay the necessary steps to carry into effect the conclusions which are expressed therein and reaffirm the faith they hold that the cooperation of the two nations not only will redound to the equitative benefit of both but will guarantee the general economy of our hemisphere, enabling it to fulfil its high duty in the noble task of world reconstruction.

President Roosevelt on September 1, 1943 announced [1] the appointment of the Honorable Wayne C. Taylor, Under Secretary of Commerce, the Honorable Nelson A. Rockefeller, Coordinator of Inter-American Affairs and Chairman of the Inter-American Development Commission, and Mr. Thomas H. Lockett, Counselor of Embassy for Economic Affairs in Mexico City, to serve as the United States members of the Industrial Commission established by the Government of Mexico as the result of a recommendation contained in the report of the Mexican-American Commission for Economic Cooperation.[2]

The Industrial Commission was set up as a continuing body to study and develop long-term programs for the industrialization of Mexico.

The Mexican Government named as its members on the Commission Lic. Primo Villa Michel, Coordinator of Coordination and Development of Production; Ing. Evarista Araiza, Chairman of the Board of Directors of the Bank of Mexico and General Manager of the Monterrey Steel Works; and Salvador Ugarte, a well-known banker.

3. AGRICULTURAL COOPERATION

(1) *Convention on the Inter-American Institute of Agricultural Sciences. Department of State Release, January 15, 1944* [3]

A Convention on the Inter-American Institute of Agricultural Sciences was opened for signature at the Pan American Union on January 15, 1944 and was signed on that date for the United States of America, Costa Rica, Nicaragua, and Panama. The convention will remain open for signature by the other American Republics and, under the provisions of Article XV thereof, will come into force three months after the deposit of not less than five ratifications with the Pan American Union.

The convention gives permanent status to the Inter-American Institute of Agricultural Sciences, which was established as a corporation under the laws of

[1] *Ibid.*. IX, p. 155.
[2] See this volume, p. 503.
[3] Department of State, *Bulletin*, X, p. 90. For text of the convention, see *Convention on the Inter-American Institute of Agricultural Sciences*, Washington, Pan American Union, 1944.

the District of Columbia on June 18, 1942 to encourage and advance the development of agricultural sciences in the American Republics. Under the certificate of incorporation and the by-laws of the Institute, as well as under the convention, the representatives of the 21 American Republics on the Governing Board of the Pan American Union are members of the Board of Directors of the Institute.

The Institute is already functioning with funds supplied by the Government of the United States of America through the Office of the Coordinator of Inter-American Affairs. On March 19, 1943 the cornerstone of the first permanent building of the Institute at its field headquarters in Turrialba, Costa Rica, was laid by President Rafael Angel Calderón Guardia of Costa Rica and Vice President Henry A. Wallace of the United States of America. Dr. Earl N. Bressman, formerly of the Office of the Coordinator of Inter-American Affairs and of the Department of Agriculture, has been appointed Director of the Institute, and Mr. José L. Colom of the Pan American Union has been appointed as its Secretary.

Up to June 30, 1944, the Convention had been signed by the United States of America, Costa Rica, Nicaragua and Panama (January 15, 1944); Cuba and Ecuador (January 20, 1944);[1] Dominican Republic and Honduras (January 28, 1944);[2] El Salvador (February 18, 1944);[3] Guatemala (March 16, 1944);[4] Uruguay (April 17, 1944);[5] and Chile (May 13, 1944).[6]

The Convention has been ratified as follows: El Salvador — decree of ratification published and became effective April 20, 1944;[7] El Salvador — instrument of ratification dated May 16 and deposited May 31, 1944;[8] United States — Senate gave its advice and consent to ratification on June 22, 1944,[9] on June 29 the President ratified,[10] and on July 4, the instrument of ratification was deposited with the Pan American Union.[11] (U. S. *Treaty Series* 987.)

4. PRODUCTION AND PROCUREMENT OF RUBBER

[See *Documents, IV, 1941–42*, p. 378; *V, 1942–43*, p. 405.]

Costa Rica.[12] — By a note signed June 21, 1943 by the American Ambassador at San José and a note signed July 1, 1943 by the Secretary of State for Foreign Affairs of Costa Rica there was effected an agreement between the United States and Costa Rica for the extension after June 30, 1943, and until six months from the date of a notice of termination given by either Government, of the agreement for cooperative rubber investigations in Costa Rica, which was effected by an exchange of notes signed at San José on April 19 and June 16, 1941,[13] as amended by an exchange of notes signed at San José on April 3, 1943.[14]

Honduras.[15] — By a despatch dated June 30, 1943 the American Ambassador at Tegucigalpa sent to the Department of State a certified copy of a note dated June 18, 1943 addressed by the Ambassador to the Honduran Minister of Foreign

[1] *Ibid.*, X, p. 162.
[2] *Ibid.*, p. 195.
[3] *Ibid.*, p. 230.
[4] *Ibid.*, p. 294.
[5] *Ibid.*, p. 400.
[6] *Ibid.*, p. 522.
[7] *Ibid.*, p. 461.
[8] *Ibid.*, p. 567.
[9] *Ibid.*, p. 593.
[10] *Ibid.*, XI, p. 32.
[11] *Ibid.*, p. 55.
[12] *Ibid.*, IX, p. 79.
[13] *Executive Agreement Series* 222.
[14] *Ibid.*, 318.
[15] Department of State, *Bulletin*, IX, p. 21.

Affairs and the original of a note dated June 28, 1943 addressed by the Honduran Minister of Foreign Affairs to the Ambassador, effecting an agreement [1] between the United States and Honduras for the extension after June 30, 1943, and until six months from the date of a notice of termination given by either Government, of a cooperative agreement for plantation rubber investigations in Honduras which was signed on February 28, 1941, in the English and Spanish languages, by the Ministro de Fomento, Agricultura, y Trabajo of the Republic of Honduras and the Acting Secretary of Agriculture of the United States.

Nicaragua.[2] — By a despatch dated June 29, 1943 the American Ambassador at Managua sent to the Department of State a certified copy of a note dated June 23, 1943 addressed by the Ambassador to the Nicaraguan Minister of Foreign Affairs and the original of a note dated June 26, 1943 addressed by the Nicaraguan Minister of Foreign Affairs to the Ambassador, effecting an agreement[3] between the United States and Nicaragua for the extension after June 30, 1943, and until six months from the date of a notice of termination given by either Government, of an agreement for extension and continuation of plantation rubber investigations in Nicaragua which was signed on January 11, 1941, in the English and Spanish languages, by the Minister of Agriculture and Labor of the Republic of Nicaragua and the Acting Chief of the Bureau of Plant Industry of the United States Department of Agriculture.

Mexico.[4] — By a despatch dated November 9, 1943 the American Embassy at Mexico City sent to the Department of State a certified copy of a note dated July 10, 1943 addressed by the American Ambassador to the Mexican Minister of Foreign Relations and the original of a note dated September 20, 1943 addressed by the Mexican Minister of Foreign Relations to the American Ambassador, effecting an agreement [5] between the United States and Mexico for the extension after June 30, 1943, and until six months from the date of a notice of termination given by either Government, of an agreement relating to plantation-rubber investigations in Mexico, which was signed on April 11, 1941 by the Secretario de Agricultura y Fomento of the United Mexican States and the Assistant Secretary of Agriculture of the United States of America, and which was supplemented by an agreement signed on July 14, 1942 and an agreement signed on March 3, 4, and 29 and April 3, 1943.

Brazil.[6] — The American Embassy in Rio de Janeiro has transmitted to the Department of State with a despatch dated February 14, 1944 an agreement between the Government of the United States of America and the Government of Brazil regarding the rubber-development program in Brazil, effected by an exchange of notes signed at Rio de Janeiro on February 8, 1944. The original agreement was effected by an exchange of notes, signed March 3, 1942.[7] This agreement marked an important change in United States policy in that it provided for the termination of direct financial support by the United States Government of the program and the assumption by the Brazilian Government of responsibility for its financing.[8] This was announced by Dr. Valentin F. Boucas, special representative of the Brazilian Government, speaking at a meeting of the American-Brazilian Association in New York. Dr. Boucas, who is president

[1] *Executive Agreement Series* 358. [2] Department of State, *Bulletin*, IX, p. 21.
[3] *Executive Agreement Series* 357. [4] Department of State, *Bulletin*, IX, p. 404.
[5] *Executive Agreement Series* 367. [6] Department of State, *Bulletin*, X, p. 271.
[7] *Executive Agreement Series* 371. [8] *New York Times*, February 9, 1944.

of the Committee on Amazon Valley Labor and Food Supplies for Rubber Production, pointed out that under the new agreement, during the period February 9, 1944, to March 31, 1945, the price paid by the United States would be 60 cents, against the previous price of 45 cents per pound and that Brazil had made available $500,000 to finance the new production set-up.

5. FOOD PRODUCTION AND DISTRIBUTION

(1) *Extension of Inter-American Coffee Agreement. Statement of the Department of State, October 16, 1943* [1]

The Inter-American Coffee Agreement signed at Washington on November 28, 1940 [2] has been continued in effect without any change for a period of one year from October 1, 1943 as the result of a declaration made by the Inter-American Coffee Board on May 12, 1943. Pursuant to the provisions of Article XXIV of the agreement, the Inter-American Coffee Board, in its resolution adopted September 2, 1942, recommended to the participating governments the continuation without any change of the agreement for a period of one year from October 1, 1943. According to the declaration, acceptance of the aforesaid resolution was expressed by all the participating governments, namely, the Governments of Brazil, Colombia, Costa Rica, Cuba, the Dominican Republic, Ecuador, El Salvador, Guatemala, Haiti, Honduras, Mexico, Nicaragua, Peru, the United States of America, and Venezuela.

(2) *Agreements Regarding the 1944 Cuban Sugar Crop*

(a) *Department of State Release, August 21, 1943* [3]

It was announced jointly on August 21 by the Department of State, the Cuban Embassy, and the Commodity Credit Corporation that an agreement, subject to final approval by the Cuban Government, has been negotiated by a Cuban commission and officials of the United States Government, under which the Commodity Credit Corporation will purchase a minimum of 4 million short tons of 1944 crop Cuban sugar at 2.65 cents a pound, f.o.b. Cuban ports. Purchase of the 1943 crop was 3 million short tons at 2.65 cents a pound. The 1944 agreement is based on principles similar to those of the 1943 contract, with certain modifications mutually agreed upon.

The 1944 Cuban crop-purchase contract will be executed by the Commodity Credit Corporation and the Cuban Sugar Stabilization Institute, and it is expected that it will be signed at an early date.

Sugar purchased under this agreement will be utilized for supplying the requirements of this country and of other United Nations.

The agreement represents a further step in friendly reciprocal cooperation between the two Governments in the war effort.

(b) *Department of State Release, January 7, 1944* [4]

As announced by the Department of State on December 22,[5] a Cuban commission is in Washington to discuss with the Foreign Economic Administration

[1] Department of State, *Bulletin*, IX, p. 267.
[2] United States, *Treaty Series*, nos. 970 and 979.
[3] Department of State, *Bulletin*, IX, p. 116.   [4] *Ibid.*, X, p. 40.   [5] *Ibid.*, IX, p. 449.

and other Government agencies the implementation of existing contracts on
the 1944 Cuban sugar crop and the acquisition by the United States of molasses
and alcohol.

The representatives of the two Governments announced on January 7, 1944
that an agreement has been reached to produce, as part of the Cuban sugar
crop of 1944, invert molasses equivalent to 800,000 short tons, raw-sugar basis.
This invert molasses is to be purchased by the Defense Supplies Corporation
for the production of industrial alcohol, at $2\frac{1}{2}$ cents a pound total sugar content,
f.o.b. tank car at Cuban terminal or f.o.b. coastal point of delivery.

As a result of the agreement, the Cuban sugar crop can now be fixed at a
minimum of 4,827,240 short tons. Of this total, 200,000 tons will be used for
local consumption in Cuba, and 800,000 tons of sugar in the form of invert
molasses will be used for production of alcohol for the war effort. The remainder
of the 4,827,240 tons, or 3,827,240 tons, as well as any additional sugar that
can be produced in Cuba by grinding all available cane, will be acquired by the
Commodity Credit Corporation under the contract signed in September 1943.

Other phases of the negotiations are progressing, and representatives of the
two Governments expect to reach in the not distant future satisfactory conclusions in the interests of both countries and their joint efforts in the prosecution
of the war.

(3) *Agreement with the Dominican Republic. Department of State Release, February 18, 1944* [1]

On February 17 completion of an agreement whereby the entire exportable
surplus of several Dominican foodstuffs will be sold exclusively to the United
States Government through the Foreign Economic Administration in order
to help meet shortages of food in the Caribbean and other areas, was announced
jointly by the Dominican Government and the United States Department of
State. The agreement is to extend to June 30, 1945.[2]

The cooperative efforts of the Government of the Dominican Republic and of
the Dominican food producers, resulting in increases of production at this critical
time, are an important contribution to the total United Nations food-supply
program and will add to the total supplies available for distribution to deficit
areas. It will be of special value to Puerto Rico and other Caribbean islands
now largely dependent on exports of food from the United States.

Shipments of food from the Dominican Republic directly to these islands will
result in saving of shipping. The Dominican Government is contributing substantially in this respect in providing a fleet of vessels for inter-island transportation of foodstuffs.

Under an agreement signed previously,[3] the Dominican Republic is selling
exclusively to the United States for Caribbean areas its surplus of corn, rice,
and peanut cake. The new understanding adds peanuts, red kidney beans, and
live cattle to the list. In addition, the United States receives an option to buy
butter, eggs, fresh vegetables, and fruits.

[1] *Ibid.*, X, p. 195.
[2] *Executive Agreement Series* 404.
[3] *Ibid.*, 350.

D. Transportation and Communications

(1) Convention on the Regulation of Inter-American Automotive Traffic. Department of State Release, December 31, 1943 [1]

On December 31, 1943, the Honorable Cordell Hull, Secretary of State and representative of the United States of America on the Governing Board of the Pan American Union, signed in his office the Convention on the Regulation of Inter-American Automotive Traffic.

The convention was opened for signature at the Pan American Union on December 15, 1943 and was signed on that date by the representatives of nine of the American Republics, namely, Bolivia, Brazil, Cuba, Dominican Republic, Ecuador, Guatemala, Haiti, Nicaragua, and Peru.

The convention contains a preamble and 22 articles, with 2 annexes. In general, the provisions are designed to stimulate and facilitate motor travel between the countries of this hemisphere by simplifying certain formalities so far as practicable. The convention establishes certain uniform rules for international automotive traffic, in relation to such matters as registration, driving licenses, standards of size and equipment, and the keeping of records of international automotive traffic.

It is provided in Article XIX that the convention in Spanish, English, Portuguese, and French shall be opened for signature by the American Republics, and also that it shall be opened for the adherence and accession of American states which are not members of the Pan American Union. It is provided in Article XX that the convention shall be ratified in conformity with the respective constitutional procedures of the signatories, the instruments of ratification to be deposited with the Pan American Union. Article XXI provides that the convention shall come into force between the parties in the order in which they deposit their respective ratifications. Article XXII provides that the convention shall remain in effect indefinitely but may be denounced by any party, so far as such party is concerned, by means of one year's notice given to the Pan American Union.

The convention was signed for the United States subject to a reservation with respect to Article XV. Article XV provides that each government may establish requirements deemed necessary to record the passage of vehicles and operators into and out of its territory and that, if such records be maintained, they shall include a notation that the vehicle has complied with certain provisions of the convention relating to standards of size and equipment. The reservation indicates that nothing in Article XV shall be construed to require the use of personnel and facilities for the purpose of determining compliance with such provisions whenever, in the opinion of the competent authorities, there would result an impairment of essential services or an undue hindrance to the movement of automotive traffic into and from the territory of the United States. This reservation is consistent with Article IV of the convention, which provides that the contracting states shall not allow to be put into effect customs measures which will hinder international travel.

---

[1] Department of State, *Bulletin*, X, p. 22. For text of convention, see *Convention on the Regulation of Inter-American Automotive Traffic*, Washington, Pan American Union, 1944.

On January 20, 1944 the Convention was signed by a representative of Costa Rica.[1] On April 12, the President of the United States transmitted the Convention to the Senate with a view to receiving the advice and consent of that body to ratification.[2] The Convention was ratified by the National Legislative Assembly of El Salvador on June 12, 1944 and the decree of ratification was published on June 23.[3]

(2) *Problems of Newsprint Production and Transportation to Other American Republics. Department of State Release, January 12, 1944* [4]

The United States Government is vitally interested in solving the problems of newsprint production and transportation, which have adversely affected friendly publications in other American Republics. This problem continues to receive constant and careful attention with a view to arrangements equitable to all parties concerned. At the present time, an effort is being made to facilitate production for shipment to other American Republics so that newspaper services may not be interrupted.

Shipment of newsprint from the United States and Canada to the other American Republics is on a quota basis. The determination of equitable distribution is made by the appropriate local government authorities in consultation with the publications and with the advice of the American diplomatic mission in each country. Distribution lists are transmitted from the countries of the other American Republics showing the amount to be received by each consignee within the quota and the name of the supplier. Licenses are issued accordingly and manufacturing scheduled.

The quotas for the other American Republics originated in the following manner. Due to the shipping shortage that existed during August 1942 and several months thereafter through the exigencies of war, it was necessary to place a shipping quota on every exportable commodity, which also included newsprint. In order to determine a quota that could be shipped with the highest priority and that would move steadily, the newsprint requirements for each country were reduced and shipments temporarily curtailed to those countries which had large newsprint stocks on hand. Many friendly newspapers were on the point of suspending through lack of newsprint and the quota thus applied assured a regular supply.

With the cessation of the necessity to utilize certain shipping for war purposes, more tonnage became available to the other American Republics. In the meantime, however, an acute shortage developed in pulpwood, which has adversely affected the supply of pulp and paper in general and newsprint in particular. The newsprint quotas for the other American Republics, originally based on shipping considerations, are now governed by actual manufacturing potentials, the requirements of consumers heretofore not using United States and Canadian newsprint, and the general drain upon paper products as a result of substituting paper for metal in many manufactured commodities.

The quotas for newsprint to the consumers in the other American Republics represent a considerable reduction from normal requirements. With few exceptions, any failure to obtain their quotas of newsprint regularly would cause the suspension of some friendly publications in certain countries.

[1] Department of State, *Bulletin*, X, p. 162.
[2] *Ibid.*, p. 366.
[3] *Ibid.*, XI, p. 32.
[4] *Ibid.*, X, p. 88.

An attempt is being made to create a 90 days' stock position for newsprint for publications in the other American Republics, as any undue delay in delivery for any reason whatsoever would cause serious dislocations to the newspapers in the countries affected.

With very few and well-identified exceptions, the newspapers of other American Republics have editorially supported the Allied war effort and have cooperated in an equitable curtailment in the size of their editions. In view of the important foreign-relations aspects of the situation and the importance of the major portions of the publications in the other American Republics in keeping their public informed with regard to the war and relations in general with the United Nations, it is essential that no effort be spared to maintain newsprint supplies to those publications.

(3) *Statement by the Chairman of the United States Commission of the Permanent American Aeronautical Commission (Ryan), June 24, 1944* [1]

On May 27, the Department of State announced that, the terms of the original members of the United States National Commissions having expired, the President had approved the designation of new members. The names of the new members were listed as follows: [2] Mr. Oswald Ryan, Member, Civil Aeronautics Board, Department of Commerce, Chairman; The Honorable Alfred L. Bulwinkle, Member of Committee on Interstate and Foreign Commerce, House of Representatives, The Honorable William A. M. Burden, Assistant Secretary of Commerce; The Honorable Bennett Champ Clark, Chairman, Committee on Interoceanic Canals, United States Senate; Lt. Col. Louis A. Johnson, Infantry Reserve, United States Army, former Assistant Secretary of War, Clarksburg, West Virginia; Mr. Arnold W. Knauth, Attorney, Admiralty and Shipping Section, Department of Justice; Mr. Stephen Latchford, Chairman, United States Section, International Technical Committee of Aerial Legal Experts; Mr. Stokeley W. Morgan, Chief, Aviation Division, Department of State; Dr. Francis W. Reichelderfer, Chief, Weather Bureau, Department of Commerce, and Vice Chairman, National Advisory Committee for Aeronautics; Mr. Theodore P. Wright, Director of the Aircraft Resources Control Office, Aircraft Production Board, War Department.

The newly appointed United States Commission of the Permanent American Aeronautical Commission, popularly called "C.A.P.A.," held its first meeting June 21 and took steps to prepare for United States participation in the initial meeting of C.A.P.A.

The Permanent American Aeronautical Commission was established pursuant to a resolution adopted at the Inter-American Conference held at Lima, Peru, in September 1937. [3] It was contemplated that those governments which would approve the establishment of the new organization would set up national commissions to be affiliated with and to cooperate with C.A.P.A. Thirteen republics have already approved and set up their national commissions thus far.

The Lima resolution provided the following objectives for C.A.P.A.: The unification of international public and private air law and regu-

----

[1] *Ibid.*, p. 588.   [2] *Ibid.*, p. 499.   [3] Not printed.

lation; the coordination and development of mutual interests in technical subjects relating to aircraft, pilots, airways, and facilities for air navigation; and the organization and the marking of inter-American air routes and the coordination of national with international air services.

As soon as the proposals of the United States Commission are drawn up, they will be transmitted to the member Governments for the consideration of their own national commissions and with a view to the eventual drawing up of an agenda for C.A.P.A.

The Lima resolution provided that the first meeting of C.A.P.A. would take place as soon as possible after a sufficient number of the interested governments had approved the new organization. The members of the United States Commission feel that the first meeting of C.A.P.A. should be held as soon as it may be possible for the necessary arrangements to be made through diplomatic channels.

It is the intention of the United States Commission to do everything possible to make C.A.P.A. a going concern.

E. Cultural Relations

[See *Documents, IV, 1941–42*, p. 411; *V, 1942–43*, p. 409.]

The Cultural Relations program of the State Department is described in a recent publication of the Department, *The Cultural-Cooperation Program, 1938–43*, prepared by Mr. Haldore Hanson (Department of State Publication 2137).

During the period under review, the program of the Department, in so far as relations with the other American Republics have been concerned, has been developed along previously indicated lines.

F. Relations with Individual Countries

1. ARGENTINA

For background of and events surrounding the military *coup d'état* which brought General Pédro Ramírez into the office of President, see *Documents, V, 1942–43*, p. 414.

The hope was widely entertained that this change in government would result in a change of policy which would bring the conduct of the Argentine Government into line with the obligations assumed by the governments of the American Republics under the resolutions adopted at the Rio de Janeiro Meeting of Ministers of Foreign Affairs in January 1942. This hope was encouraged by a letter addressed by Foreign Minister Segundo Storni to Dr. Alberto Guani, Chairman of the Emergency Advisory Committee for the Political Defense of the Hemisphere, on July 6, 1943,[1] in which announcement was made of the formation of an Inter-Ministerial Committee to examine Argentine relations under Resolutions I (recommending rupture of relations with an aggressor against an American Republic) and XVII (dealing with subversive activities).[2] On July 31, "an authoritative source" in Buenos Aires was reported however as saying that the rapid deterioration of Germany's military position and the

[1] *New York Times*, July 9, 1943.
[2] For texts, see *Documents, IV, 1941–42*, p. 293.

anticipated early elimination of Italy from the war had virtually ended all prospects for a break with the Axis powers.[1]

On August 2, the Office of Economic Warfare announced that all outstanding licenses for export of commodities to Argentina had been revoked as of that date.[2] Foreign Minister Storni's plea for "a gesture of genuine friendship" contained in his letter of August 5 drew a stern rebuff from Secretary Hull. The British Foreign Office, on the conclusion of a trade agreement with Argentina, took the opportunity to reproach the Argentine Government for its friendly policy toward the Axis powers by expressing "disappointment" with the determination of successive Argentine Governments to maintain neutrality.[3]

On October 7, the Argentine Foreign Office announced the recall of Dr. Felipe A. Espil, Argentine Ambassador at Washington since 1931, and the designation of Dr. Adrian C. Escobar as his successor.[4] On October 12, all Buenos Aires papers appearing in Yiddish received a peremptory order from the police to cease publication.[5] On the same day occurred the simultaneous resignation of all Cabinet Ministers who had favored the immediate break of relations with the Axis powers.

A declaration demanding "effective democracy" and "loyal fulfillment of international obligations," signed by 150 prominent Argentinians, appeared on the morning of October 15 in four Argentine newspapers.[6] On the following day, President Ramírez announced the discharge of all government employees who had signed the manifesto.[7] On November 10, the establishment of a "Subsecretariat of Information and Press" with wide powers to regulate the activities of the local press and foreign correspondents was announced.[8] A decree issued on December 31 "dissolved all political parties existing in the whole territory of the nation."[9] A decree regulating the activities of the press was issued on January 5, 1944.[10]

On January 25, the Argentine Foreign Minister, General Alberto Gilbert, issued a statement to foreign diplomats saying that his Government had decided to break relations with the Axis powers.[11] A decree was issued on the 26th severing diplomatic relations with Germany and Japan.[12] On February 4, a decree was issued severing diplomatic relations with the Governments of Bulgaria, Vichy France, Hungary and Rumania.[13]

Alarmed by reports that the Government was about to declare war on the Axis powers, a group of comparatively junior army officers took possession of the Foreign Ministry on the morning of February 15.[14] On the following day, the Government announced a temporary solution of the Cabinet crisis which had been precipitated by this action.[15] Following numerous reports and rumors, General Edelmiro Farrell took the active direction of the Government as "vice-president in exercise of the Executive power." It was stated that President Ramírez, feeling the need of a rest had delegated his powers to Vice-President Farrell.[16] On March 10, General Ramírez resigned his office, and General Farrell assumed the office of President as his successor.[17]

Formal diplomatic relations with the Farrell Government were withheld by the United States and Great Britain. The Governments of Bolivia, Chile and Paraguay announced their intention to continue diplomatic relations. On June 27, the State Department announced that the United States Ambassador in Argentina, Mr. Norman Armour, had been instructed to return to Washington immediately for consultation.[18]

[1] New York Times, August 1, 1943.   [2] 8 Fed. Reg., p. 10714.
[3] New York Times, September 27, 1943.   [4] Ibid., October 8, 1943.
[5] Ibid., October 14, 1943.   [6] Ibid., October 16, 1943.
[7] Ibid., October 17, 1943.   [8] Ibid., November 11, 1943.
[9] Ibid., January 1, 1944.   [10] Ibid., January 6, 1944.
[11] Ibid., January 26, 1944.   [12] Ibid., January 27, 1944; this volume, p. 535.
[13] Ibid., February 5, 1944.   [14] Ibid., February 16, 1944.
[15] Ibid., February 17, 1944.   [16] Ibid., February 26, 1944.
[17] Ibid., March 11, 1944.   [18] Department of State, Bulletin, XI, p. 24.

(1) *The International Position of Argentina. Exchange of Notes between the Foreign Minister of Argentina (Storni) and the Secretary of State of the United States (Hull), August 5 and 30, 1943* [1]

(a) *The Foreign Minister of Argentina (Storni) to the Secretary of State of the United States (Hull), August 5, 1943*

[Translation]

MR. SECRETARY OF STATE:

Coinciding with Ambassador Armour's trip to the United States, I have thought it desirable to place myself in direct contact with you, in order to set forth confidentially to your friendly Government the situation of the new Argentine Government established as the result of the military movement of June 4, particularly with reference to the international position of this country. I do so with the full approval of the President of the Nation and in the hope that, by this means, his views may also be made known to President Roosevelt.

The military movement which has just overthrown the government of Señor Castillo assumed power as an inevitable consequence of the atmosphere of corruption that unfortunately had penetrated the political and administrative life of the country. The unanimous approval with which the renovating work of the new Government is being followed is the best justification of the movement. The Government has complete control of the situation, supported by all sound opinion in the country and fully upheld by the armed forces. But there is one factor which carries decisive weight in the work that it is doing: I refer to the international situation and to the problems of foreign policy with which the Republic is confronted.

Due to lack of adequate information or to other causes the origin of which I do not know, there has been created with respect to the situation of neutrality of the Argentine Republic an atmosphere which is prejudicial to good relations with the countries of America and especially with that great friendly nation (the United States). Thus the rumor has spread that General Ramírez, the armed forces, and the men who form this new Government profess a markedly totalitarian ideology or, at the least, that we look upon the Axis powers with great sympathy. I can affirm, and I beg that you, Mr. Secretary, accept this affirmation as the word of a man of honor, that such assumptions are absolutely false. The Argentine nation, its armed forces, and the men in its Government base their acts on the firmest democratic convictions. We are men of America: our historic tradition is very clear and it will not be modified now or in the future by the adoption of dictatorial systems of government that are repugnant to our consciences as free men — as men who,

[1] *Ibid.*, IX, p. 159.

today as in the past, feel indissolubly linked with the other inhabitants of this continent, of profoundly democratic origins.

The situation of neutrality that the Argentine Republic has had to observe up to now has not been understood. Moreover, it has given rise to suspicious comments. In judging that neutrality it has been forgotten, against all the evidence, that Argentine ships are operating exclusively in the service of the Allied nations and particularly of the American countries, extending by the decision of this new Government to the very zone of operations proclaimed by Germany. There have also been forgotten the Argentine decrees granting the status of "non-belligerency" exclusively to one of the belligerent parties. There have likewise been disregarded the protests made by Germany, Italy, and Japan after the secrecy of their official communications with their embassies here was prohibited, while the other countries continue to have the free use of their cables.

It is difficult to ignore the collaboration that the Argentine Republic is giving to the cause of the Allied nations under the conditions of a neutrality which, more than tolerant, is of an evidently benevolent character. This current of collaboration is even more effective in the field of our exports, placed at the almost exclusive service of the Allied cause and of the American countries, in so doing many times depriving our country of articles necessary for its own defense.

The effort that Argentina is making should be understood. It is not fair to forget that this new Government has sprung from a revolutionary movement which was planned and carried out in order to overthrow a government that did not understand the reality of internal and foreign policy. But the change, particularly with reference to foreign policy, could not be effected in a violent manner because our country was not ready for it. In this connection, it should not be forgotten that the Argentine Republic has been living and is still living in an atmosphere of peace, work, and comparative abundance; that our people are influenced by the ties of kinship of numerous foreign colonies; that there exists fear of the communist danger, the propagation of which in our country has corrupted even the most genuinely democratic institutions such as Acción Argentina and the Junta de la Victoria. It should be recalled that, on the other hand, the Government that was overthrown maintained its neutrality even during the most critical period of our relations with the Axis countries, as undoubtedly was the case with the repeated torpedoing of Argentine ships and the Japanese attack against Pearl Harbor.

This situation, Mr. Secretary, cannot be abruptly changed by a revolutionary government that must reconstruct the country, which is corrupted in its administration and in its educational and social institutions. The changes can be brought about only as rapidly as the internal situation may permit. The spirit in which they have been begun in the international position of the country is clear and evident and deserves to be noted in a friendly way and without bias by your Government.

Argentine sentiment, eminently American, firmly opposed to totalitarian regimes, is on the side of the United Nations in its material and spiritual action. But you, Mr. Secretary, citizen of a country that venerates freedom of conscience, will acknowledge that it is not possible, without preliminary preparation, to force the Argentine conscience with a view to leading it coldly and without any immediate motive to the breaking of relations with the Axis. The war having reached its present stage, when defeat is inexorably drawing closer to the countries of the Axis, this unexpected rupture would furthermore put Argentine chivalry to a hard test. Let it suffice to recall the judgment which Italy merited when, in a similar situation, it took its position against defeated France.

I cannot fail to point out to you, Mr. Secretary, the concern with which I view future possibilities if, because of the persistence in the present lack of comprehension, Argentina should continue to be denied the materials that it needs in order to increase its production and to arm itself in order to fulfill, should the case arise, its obligations for continental defense. It is of particular interest to recall that some time ago the Argentine Republic offered to increase shipments of fuels and heavy oils to American countries, for which purpose it sought from the United States the shipment of the machinery essential in order to increase its productive capacity. Unfortunately, thus far this request has not been heeded, no recognition being made of the sacrifice at which our country is extending its assistance to friendly countries in order to supply them so far as possible with the much-coveted fuel. Petroleum production has decreased because of the deterioration of the equipment, and our reserves have diminished considerably. Today, in order to compensate for this shortage, we find it necessary to burn in the boilers of factories and plants millions of quintals of corn, wheat, and linseed. With the aid of the United States, Argentina could burn its own petroleum, keeping that wealth of grain to supply the Allied nations and to form a reserve stock that would make it possible to feed the European peoples threatened with hunger.

The Government of General Ramírez will spare no effort to fulfill the obligations contracted. But, as I have already said, it will not be able to do so without a cause to justify it. To act otherwise would afford grounds to believe action is being taken under the pressure or threat of foreign agents, and this would not be tolerated by either the people or the armed forces of the country.

I believe that in this long letter I have explained to you, Mr. Secretary, the real situation of the Argentine Republic with respect to its sentiments of deep friendship and solidarity with the American countries. I do not doubt that in contemplating the situation from the high position that the government of President Roosevelt occupies in the world, it will be appreciated that it is not just to maintain the attitude of suspicion assumed toward a country such as ours, which has shown unmistakably its feelings of friendship and frank support for the countries that are fighting for freedom. I cannot believe that it is desired to eliminate the action of Argentina within the concert of American nations, on the basis that our neutrality — which is only theoretical — places us in an equivocal position with respect to the rest of the countries of this continent.

I can affirm to you, Mr. Secretary, that the Axis countries have nothing to hope for from our Government and that public opinion is daily more unfavorable to them. But this evolution would be more rapid and effective for the American cause if President Roosevelt should make a gesture of genuine friendship toward our people; such a gesture might be the urgent provision of airplanes, spare parts, armaments, and machinery to restore Argentina to the position of equilibrium to which it is entitled with respect to other South American countries.

This general and sincere picture of the Argentine situation will explain to you, Mr. Secretary of State, the obstacles — up to now insurmountable — encountered by this Government in fulfilling the last part of its original objectives. On the basis of the loyal understanding that we reciprocally owe to each other, I wish to rely on the spirit of good will with which we shall be heard, which would be a concrete proof of the friendship that this Government is seeking in its present difficult initial period. Moreover, Ambassador Armour, who has penetrated with intelligent and friendly understanding into all the aspects of our complicated internal situation and who was the confidential recipient of these thoughts, personally expressed by His Excellency the President of the Nation, will be able to convey to you, Mr. Secretary, a more complete personal impression obtained directly from the present reality of the life of our country.

I am very happy on this occasion to renew to you, Mr. Secretary, the assurance of my cordial and friendly consideration.

(b) *The Secretary of State of the United States (Hull) to the Foreign Minister of Argentina (Storni), August 30, 1943*

My Dear Mr. Minister:

I have received your letter of August 5, in which you were good enough to inform me regarding the situation of the new Argentine Government established as the result of the military movement of June 4, particularly with reference to the international position of Argentina. I note that your letter has the full approval of the President of Argentina and I have been pleased to make the views expressed therein known to President Roosevelt.

It is profoundly satisfactory to note your statement that the people of your country feel themselves indissolubly linked with the other inhabitants of this continent of profoundly democratic origins. This statement will be most welcome to the citizens of the United States actively engaged at the cost of tremendous sacrifices in lives and materials in a war for the survival of the principles so eloquently described by you. I feel sure that in the same spirit it will be warmly greeted by the peoples of all of the other republics of the Hemisphere which have taken measures essential to the defense of our continent against a menace now happily being overcome by the joint efforts of the friends of freedom everywhere.

However, it is with regret that my Government and the people of the United States have been forced to the conclusion that the undoubted sentiments of the Argentine people have not been implemented by action called for by the commitments freely entered into by their Government in common with the governments of the other twenty American Republics.

Your Excellency is, of course, fully familiar with those commitments. As they particularly affect the present world conflict, they are based upon Resolution XV adopted by the Foreign Ministers of the American Republics at Habana in July of 1940. That Resolution provides that any attempt on the part of a non-American state against the integrity or inviolability of the territory, the sovereignty or the political independence of an American state shall be considered as an act of aggression against the states which signed this declaration. The act of aggression contemplated in this Declaration took place on December 7, 1941. In January of 1942 the Foreign Ministers of the American Republics met at Rio de Janeiro to consider the measures which they should adopt for common defense. A Resolution recommending the break of diplomatic relations with Japan, Germany and Italy was adopted. The wording of that Resolution was the subject of prolonged discussion and the text finally agreed upon was fully responsive to the views expressed by the Argentine Government. I believe it desirable to quote the Resolution in full:

BREAKING OF DIPLOMATIC RELATIONS

I. The American Republics reaffirm their declaration to consider any act of aggression on the part of a non-American State against one of them as an act of aggression against all of them, constituting as it does an immediate threat to the liberty and independence of America.

II. The American Republics reaffirm their complete solidarity and their determination to cooperate jointly for their mutual protection until the effects of the present aggression against the Continent have disappeared.

III. The American Republics, in accordance with the procedures established by their own laws and in conformity with the position and circumstances obtaining in each country in the existing continental conflict, recommend the breaking of their diplomatic relations with Japan, Germany and Italy, since the first-mentioned State attacked and the other two declared war on an American country.

IV. Finally, the American Republics declare that, prior to the reestablishment of the relations referred to in the preceding paragraph, they will consult among themselves in order that their action may have a solidary character.

With the exception of Argentina, all of the American Republics have severed diplomatic relations with Japan, Germany and Italy and of these twenty republics thirteen are at war with the Axis powers.

Resolution V, adopted by the Consultative Meeting of Foreign Ministers at Rio de Janeiro, stipulated by unanimous agreement the immediate adoption of any additional measures necessary to cut off for the duration of the present hemispheric emergency all commercial and financial intercourse, direct or indirect, between the Western Hemisphere and the nations signatory to the Tri-Partite Pact and the territories dominated by them. The Argentine representative at the Meeting adhered to this Resolution with the following reservation:

The Argentine Delegation requests that it be recorded in the minutes, as well as at the end of this draft resolution, that the Argentine Republic agrees with the necessity of adopting economic and financial control measures with regard to all foreign and domestic activities of firms or enterprises which may, in one way or another, affect the welfare of the republics of America or the solidarity or defense of the Continent. It has adopted and is prepared to adopt further measures in this respect, in accordance with the present resolution, extending them, however, to firms or enterprises managed or controlled by aliens or from foreign belligerent countries not in the American Continent.

The Argentine Government has failed to effect the severance of financial and commercial relations called for by Resolution V. Moreover, financial transactions of direct benefit to the enemies of the United Nations have been authorized by agencies of the Argentine Government.

Resolution XVII adopted at Rio provided for a concerted effort to discover and combat subversive activities. It is notorious that Axis agents in Argentina have been and are engaging in systematic espionage which has cost the United Nations ships and lives. Vicious propaganda aimed at the United Nations appears in publications which are supported by subsidies from Axis sources. These publications have benefited by a Government decree which enables them to receive supplies of newsprint at favorable prices through the intervention of the Argentine Ministry of Agriculture.

Resolution XL adopted at the Rio de Janeiro Meeting recommended that each American Republic adopt the necessary and immediate measures to close all radiotelephone and radiotelegraph communications between the American Republics and the aggressor States and all territories subservient to them, except in so far as official communications of the American Governments are concerned. Argentina is the only one of the twenty-one American Republics now permitting radiotelephone and radiotelegraph communications with Japan, Germany and Italy.

The above summary of certain of the inter-American commitments freely entered into by Argentina, together with the twenty other American Republics, furnishes a convincing expression of the reason why the situation of neutrality which Your Excellency states the Argentine Republic has had to observe up to now has not been understood.

It is, of course, a matter solely within the competence of the Argentine Government to judge the degree to which Argentine public opinion which you state is firmly opposed to totalitarian regimes will support a foreign policy designed at the very least to reduce the assistance which Argentina's present position has rendered and is continuing to render those regimes. Nor can I pass upon the question of the nature of the motive which you believe would be necessary to enable the Argentine Government to fulfill the obligations it has contracted. I must, however, express my astonishment at your statement that for the Argentine Government to fulfill those obligations would afford grounds to believe that such action was taken under the pressure or threat of foreign agents. The obligations in question were freely entered into by all the American Republics, and have been carried out by all except Argentina.

In concluding the discussion of this subject, I believe it fitting to recall that the public and private statements made by the President of the Nation and by Your Excellency during the first few weeks of the tenure of office of the new Argentine Government gave my Government positive ground for the belief that Argentine sentiments of continental solidarity and of adherence to inter-American commitments would be translated into effective action within a specific and brief period.

It is no doubt true as indicated by Your Excellency that the products of Argentine agriculture and mining have been of the greatest value to the cause of the United Nations. Those products, however, have found markets at equitable prices in the determination of which the United Nations have consistently refused to take advantage of the fact that they are, thanks to the efficiency of their military and naval operations, the only major markets open to Argentina. A glance at Argentine economic statistics will show that Argentina's economic transactions with the United Nations have been highly beneficial to Argentina. I am, of course, not fully informed regarding the degree to which these transactions may have resulted in the sacrifice of materials essential to the defense of Argentina as mentioned in Your Excellency's letter. In this connection however, it may be noted that neither the present Argentine Government nor its predecessor has at any time evidenced a disposition to strengthen the security of Argentina by having Argentine military and naval forces take part in measures designed for the defense of the hemisphere.

With respect to Your Excellency's statement to the effect that Argentina is being denied materials which she requires to increase her production of commodities essential to the United Nations, you are, of course, aware that the conditions of the war have imposed upon the United States and the other United Nations the necessity for a very careful allocation of available materials of a critical and strategic nature in order that these materials may be used to the best advantage in furtherance of the war effort. Notwithstanding these circumstances, Argentine essential civilian requirements, particularly those related to public health and the maintenance of essential services, have received fair treatment.

With regard to the petroleum negotiations, it may be pointed out that Argentina, thanks to its natural resources, the production of which has increased during the war period, and to its ability to import, has enjoyed during the past year and a half far greater oil supplies for the consumption of its civilian population than have the neighboring republics. Those republics have received extremely limited supplies made possible through cooperative action in which the Government of the United States and of the producing republics other than Argentina have participated. Considerable hardship and sacrifice have resulted owing to the serious shortage of ocean-going tankers. Thus, while the Argentine people were enjoying gasoline supplies equivalent to about seventy percent of their normal civilian requirements, the peoples of Uruguay, Brazil, Paraguay, Chile and, in general, other republics were receiving only approximately forty percent of normal civilian requirements. Argentine assistance would have been of great value during this very difficult period.

The negotiations to which your letter refers have been concerned with the provision of materials and supplies to enable the future production of the Argentine oil fields to be maintained and even to be increased. The lack of these materials has not in any way affected the ability of Argentina to cooperate with the neighboring republics during the past eighteen months if Argentina had desired to cooperate.

With regard to the matter of arms and munitions, your letter states that the evolution of Argentine public opinion would be more rapid and effective in favor of the American countries if President Roosevelt were to make an open and friendly gesture toward the Argentine people such as would be the immediate supply of airplanes, replacement parts, armaments and machinery, in order to restore Argentina to the position of equilibrium which corresponds to her with respect to other South American countries. In reply, I must point out emphatically that questions of military and naval equilibrium as between American Republics are surely inconsistent with the inter-American doctrine of the peaceful settlement of international disputes to which so many practical contributions have been made by Argentine statesmen. In fact, one of the most specific expressions of that doctrine, known as the Treaty of Non-Aggression and Conciliation, was the work of a distinguished Argentine Minister for Foreign Affairs.[1] To furnish arms and munitions for the purpose indicated by Your Excellency would appear to this Government to be clearly inconsistent with the juridical and moral foundations upon which existing inter-American understanding and agreements are based.

I must also recall that it has been frequently indicated to representatives of your Government, including the military and naval officers who visited Washington more than a year ago, that the supply of arms and munitions by the United States to the other American Republics is exclusively for the purpose of contributing to the defense of the Hemisphere against possible aggression. In the determination of the contribution which the Government of the United States could make to the preparations for defense of the other nineteen American Republics which jointly determined upon the need for such defense, the Government of the United States has been guided exclusively by considerations of hemispheric security. Since Argentina, both by its words and its actions, has indicated clearly that the Argentine armed forces will not under present conditions be used in a manner designed to forward the cause of the security of the New World, and, thereby, the vital war interests of the United States, it would be impossible for the President of the United States to enter into an agreement to furnish arms and munitions to Argentina under the Lend-Lease Act.

I have written Your Excellency in this detail since I am sure from the frank and friendly terms in which your letter to me is couched, that you would desire an equally frank and friendly exposition of the views of this Government. I feel that I should be lacking in such frankness, however, were I to leave you under the impression that the Government and the people of the United States have not viewed with deep regret the course followed by the Argentine Government in so far as concerns hemispheric defense since the Conference of Foreign Ministers in Rio de Janeiro. I am in entire agreement with your statement that defeat is inexorably drawing closer to the countries of the Axis. In recognition of that fact the United Nations and those associated with them are devoting their attention in a wide variety of practical and constructive ways to the problems of post-war organization. Thus the failure of the Argentine Government to comply with its inter-American commitments has not only resulted in the non-participation of Argentina in the defense of the continent in a most critical period, it is also depriving Argentina of participation in the

[1] *Treaties, Conventions*, 1923–1937, IV, p. 4793.

studies, discussions, meetings and arrangements designed to solve the post-war problems mentioned above.

I am pleased to take this opportunity of extending to Your Excellency the renewed assurances of my high consideration.

(2) *Suspension by Argentina of the Publication of Jewish Newspapers. Statement of the President (Roosevelt), October 15, 1943* [1]

I have been informed that the Argentine Government has suspended the publication of Jewish newspapers, some of which have been in existence for many years. While this matter is of course one which concerns primarily the Argentine Government and people, I cannot forbear to give expression to my own feeling of apprehension at the taking in this hemisphere of action obviously anti-Semitic in nature and of a character so closely identified with the most repugnant features of Nazi doctrine. I believe that this feeling is shared by the people of the United States and by the people of the other American Republics. In this connection I recall that one of the resolutions adopted at the Eighth International Conference of American States at Lima in 1938 set forth that "any persecution on account of racial or religious motives which makes it impossible for a group of human beings to live decently, is contrary to the political and juridical systems of America."

(3) *Decree of the Argentine Government on Severance of Diplomatic Relations with the Governments of Germany and Japan, Buenos Aires, January 26, 1944* [2]

[Translation]

In view of proofs obtained by the Federal police as to the existence of a vast espionage network damaging the close and traditional ties of friendship of the republic, threatening the national sovereignty, harming the foreign policy of this Government, and plotting against the security of the continent, and considering:

That this criminal activity is directly imputable to the Governments of the Axis because such acts were similar to those perpetrated earlier by other agents who now are in the hands of justice;

That the continuance of these illicit activities makes the residence in our republic of the German and Japanese diplomatic representatives incompatible with continental security, especially in view of the exceptional privileges given diplomatists;

That the gravity and persistence of the proved facts and the evident participation of foreign diplomatic representatives in the activities of

[1] Department of State, *Bulletin*, IX, p. 264.
[2] *New York Times*, January 27, 1944.

espionage oblige the definition of Argentina's international policy in the light of new circumstances:

The President of the Argentine nation decrees:

Effective immediately, diplomatic relations are broken with the Governments of Germany and Japan. Passports are to be given the diplomatic representatives of both countries. The Ministry of Foreign Relations will take the necessary steps for the exchange of Argentine diplomatic and consular functionaries in those countries.

(a) Statement of the Argentine Government, Buenos Aires, January 26, 1944 [1]

[Translation]

The Minister of Foreign Relations and Religion, Brig. Gen. Alberto Gilbert, declared in the late hours of the night that the Argentine Government has decided to proceed immediately with the rupture of diplomatic relations with Germany and Japan.

This attitude is based on the fact that investigations ordered by the National Government, referred to in a communiqué of the Foreign Ministry of January 21, has permitted it to prove conclusively the existence in the country of a vast network of espionage. Statements made by detained persons demonstrate that the activity of espionage, which was the reason for criminal proceedings against a number of persons and for the retirement of the then German Naval Attaché, Capt. Dietrich Niebuhr, has continued to develop in prejudice to the interests of the country and in open violation of the policies of the Government and of duties imposed on the republic and its inhabitants by the Decree of Neutrality of September 4, 1939, and the decrees of December 9 and 18, 1941.

This attitude by a group of foreigners, who have forgotten their elemental obligations to the country under whose protection they were, not only involves the individuals directly responsible for this criminal activity, but also involves the personal responsibility of the diplomatic agents who gave aid and who sheltered them with the privileges and immunities conceived for the development of good and pacific relations of cordiality, but never for the protection and concealment of acts of aggression against the very country which accepts them.

The Government finds itself facing repeated acts that previously had been the object of condemnation by the Government and by public opinion.

Repetition of these activities by other persons, the organization into a band by such persons and their resources, the aid they found in the agents of the German Government, removes all possibility that this matter could be considered spontaneous acts of the spies themselves.

All of that plan evidently responds to a plan conceived by the Governments of the Axis to make the territory of the republic the center of their activities, with complete indifference to their duties to respect the Argentine Republic, and with indifference to the dangers that such activity could cause to our neutral nation.

That plan, then, consists of an unfriendly act executed in Argentina by hidden agents of the Axis countries; which obliges this nation to adopt elemental measures to secure its own defense.

[1] *Ibid.*

That systematic espionage activity within the territory of this nation has convinced the Argentine Government that it is not possible to continue maintaining diplomatic relations with the Government of Germany.

This decision made, the maintenance of diplomatic relations with Japan resulted equally incompatible.

Faced with the disregard of their rights by representatives of the Governments of the Axis, who have attempted to execute acts of aggression against other American countries from Argentine territory, the Government of the nation, in defense of its own dignity and of its sovereignty, resolved to take such measures of security that the present situation warrants, beginning with the delivery of their passports to the representatives of Germany and Japan, and recalling the Argentine diplomatic agents accredited to those countries.

We also thus give expression to the concept of American solidarity which has been the fundamental basis of Argentine foreign policy from the first days of the revolution for emancipation.

Argentina has never been remiss in affirming that sentiment of fraternal union with its neighbors. It has been and continues to be disposed to demonstrate once again that it feels — as its own — the dangers and worries of the other American countries.

(b) Telegram from the President of Argentina (Ramírez) to the President (Roosevelt), January 26, 1944 [1]

[Translation]

I have the honor to inform Your Excellency that in the exercise of constitutional powers I have proceeded to sign the decree of breach of diplomatic relations with the Governments of Germany and Japan. While advising Your Excellency of this decision which the Argentine Government adopts for the protection not only of its sovereignty but also of continental defense, I repeat to you the assurances of the firm purpose that animates us of strengthening more and more the friendly relations which so happily have always existed between our two countries.

(c) Reply of the President (Roosevelt) to the President of Argentina (Ramírez), January 28, 1944 [2]

I wish to express to Your Excellency my pleasure in learning of the decision of your Government to sever diplomatic relations with Germany and Japan. It is especially welcome to hear that Argentina has thus affirmed its intention to assist fully in the defense of the continent.

(d) Statement of the Secretary of State (Hull), January 26, 1944 [3]

It will be most gratifying to all the Allied Nations, including especially the American Republics, to learn that Argentina has broken diplomatic relations with Germany and Japan. This action was taken because the Argentine Government realizes that the Axis countries are using Argentina as a vast operating base for espionage and other activities highly dangerous to the security and internal peace of the hemisphere. It must be assumed from her action that Argentina will now proceed energetically to adopt the other measures which all the American Republics have concerted for the security of the continent.

[1] Department of State, *Bulletin*, X, p. 116.   [2] *Ibid.*   [3] *Ibid.*, p. 117.

(4) *Presentation of Letters of Credence by the Ambassador of Argentina (Escobar) to the President (Roosevelt), February 15, 1944* [1]

(a) *Remarks of the Ambassador of Argentina (Escobar)*

Mr. President:

I have the honor to deliver to you the letters of credence with which my Government accredits me as Ambassador Extraordinary and Plenipotentiary and the letters of recall of my distinguished predecessor; and in this circumstance it is a pleasure for me to transmit to you the sentiments of admiration and fraternal friendship which the Government and people of Argentina cherish toward the great Republic of the North, with which we have always been joined by spiritual, material, and moral bonds which time has consolidated to the point of their becoming indestructible.

The Argentine people has just been stirred to its innermost depths by two very grave occurrences: one of these, the tragic catastrophe of San Juan which cost many lives and enormous material destruction. That disaster furnished occasion for putting to the test once again the solidarity of feeling among the American nations, and I am pleased to repeat to Your Excellency the gratitude of my country for the part which your country had in that sincere and spontaneous gesture. The other is the categorical determination which my Government has taken, interpreting the desire of our people, to break off relations with Germany and Japan, in view of the seriousness of activities which wounded its most noble sentiments. The Argentine Government could not permit countries to which we are closely bound by traditional ties of friendship to be injured, since those activities not only infringed on the national sovereignty but compromised its foreign policy and attacked the security of the continent.

Argentina knows and feels that the destiny of America is her own destiny. This thought, Mr. President, which is a double imperative, historical and geographical, contains a high significance for the relations among the sovereign countries of America which act with rectitude — relations which cannot be altered in spite of the differences which may arise in the evaluation of some essential questions. They must be clarified and settled in a friendly and cordial atmosphere, since today, as yesterday and as tomorrow, the common objective cannot be other than the most complete reciprocal understanding. Thus ideas will be discussed, certain interests will for the moment be divergent, but over and above the occasional and ephemeral clash of ideas and interests is placed respect for the immutable principles of morality and justice.

[1] *Ibid.*, p. 191.

My country does not, in any manner, practice isolation. It has maintained and will always maintain the necessity for the closest union among the peoples of America. Its history proclaims this. It does not seek benefits, nor shares, nor advantages. It recognizes fully the rights of others and firmly maintains its own. It has an honorable and untarnished tradition: it loves peace and never soiled its name by any aggression; it submitted its fundamental questions to arbitration, it set up principles and doctrines universally recognized, and at congresses and conferences defined its policy with generous and broad concepts, which have been incorporated as juridical standards in the common patrimony of the nations of America.

We desire, Mr. President, that the legal gains achieved at the Pan American congresses be consolidated; that the solidarity sealed at Lima be a living reality. To this end we have proposed to the limitrophe countries, without the most remote political aim, the study and formation of customs unions for the better economic development of the countries, members of such unions, and the attainment of a higher standard of living for the populations concerned. And it is our keenest desire to leave the doors wide open to the whole continent to adhere to this regime, thereby converting to a harmonious reality the dreams of Washington, of Bolívar, of San Martín and so many great men of America.

The good-neighbor policy, which you initiated, Mr. President, found in my country a sympathetic echo and instantaneous welcome and, as you have said in speeches which are famous, it must be understood that this new policy of the United States has a permanent character. For our part, I need not assure you that we shall tend toward the permanence of this reciprocal good-neighborhood. We must all be good neighbors and, moreover, good and sincere friends.

From its first days as an independent nation Argentina practiced good-neighborliness and made of fraternity an article of faith: she made an offering of the blood of her sons and her well-being for other American peoples fighting on the fields of battle for most noble ideals and contributing to the freedom of half a continent.

When the peoples of America suffered misfortunes Argentina hastened to their aid with solicitude. But she did not limit her efforts to them but also offered her aid to distant and dissimilar countries when they were passing through a difficult situation. Thus, Argentina will now be present to aid the countries which are suffering the horrors of war, carrying out her mission with Christian generosity and diligent zeal.

The Government of my country will contribute, within its means, to the great work of aid, reconstruction, and rehabilitation to take care of the disasters and calamities which are scourging the world.

I hope that you, Excellency, who know my country, which had the gratification of receiving you with cordial rejoicing, will offer me the necessary opportunities to the end that I may discharge my mission which is, without reservation, that of a true rapprochement with the United States, of increasing cooperation, of sincere understanding and loyal friendship.

Mr. President, in the name of the Argentine people and Government I formulate good wishes for the prosperity of the United States, and express their warm desire for your personal happiness.

(b) *Reply of the President (Roosevelt)*

MR. AMBASSADOR:

I am indeed happy to greet you and to receive the letters accrediting you as Ambassador Extraordinary and Plenipotentiary of the Argentine Government near the Government of the United States of America. I accept at the same time the letters of recall of your distinguished predecessor, Dr. Felipe Espil, who will be remembered by his many friends in this country with deep affection and high esteem. Dr. Espil during his many years of service in the United States labored devotedly and unceasingly to bring about a deeper understanding between our two Governments and peoples.

I thank you for your expression of the sentiments of admiration and friendship cherished by the Government and people of Argentina for the United States. Similar sentiments have traditionally characterized the attitude of the Government and people of this country for the Argentine Republic. The two events referred to by you — namely, the disastrous earthquake at San Juan and the recent action of your Government in severing diplomatic relations with the Axis powers — have given rise to renewed demonstrations of that attitude.

The tragic loss of life which occurred at San Juan aroused feelings of deep sympathy here as well as a desire to be of assistance to the afflicted people of that region.

The action of the Argentine Government in severing relations with Germany and Japan and Axis satellites has been received with satisfaction by free people everywhere. The importance of this and other related matters connected with the eradication of subversive activities in the promotion of the security of the Western Hemisphere against the continuing aggressions of the enemies of our civilization is manifest.

These aggressions have taken manifold forms.

They have included espionage conducted under the auspices of the diplomatic missions of the Axis nations.

Industries producing for United Nations war purposes have been sabotaged by agents of the Axis powers.

All manner of subversive activities have been engaged in not only for the purpose of impeding the war effort of the United Nations but even in some cases with the object of overthrowing by violent means governments friendly to our common cause.

All of these activities would have involved the most serious peril to our common interests if they had not been combated by the energetic and united action of the American Republics. With the decision of your Government to cooperate fully in promoting the security of the continent, the Axis is severely handicapped in its conduct of operations in this hemisphere.

I am pleased to express my whole-hearted agreement with your observations concerning the policy of the good neighbor. That policy not only has long-term implications of incalculable importance; it has also enabled the American Republics in a time of serious peril and grave threat to their independence to concert measures and take steps in unison for their common defense. I am confident that the people of the United States have adopted this policy as a part of their permanent political philosophy.

I am very happy to extend to you, Mr. Ambassador, a most cordial welcome and to assure you of my own desire and of the desire of the officials of this Government to render you every possible assistance in the fulfilment of your mission. I am pleased also to have this opportunity of extending through you my best wishes for the happiness and welfare of the people of Argentina.

(5) Relations with the Existing Argentine Regime. Statement by the Acting Secretary of State (Stettinius), March 4, 1944 [1]

The foreign policy of the United States since the beginning of the war has been governed primarily by considerations of support to the prosecution of the war. That applies to our relations with any country. That is the single uppermost point in our policy and must remain so.

Prior to February 25, the Argentine Government had been headed by General Ramírez. On January 26, 1944 his Government broke relations with the Axis and indicated that it proposed to go further in cooperating in the defense of the Western Hemisphere and the preservation of hemispheric security.

Suddenly, on February 25, under well-known circumstances, General Ramírez abandoned the active conduct of affairs. This Government has reason to believe that groups not in sympathy with the declared Argentine policy of joining the defense of the hemisphere were active in this turn of affairs.

The Department of State thereupon instructed Ambassador Armour to refrain from entering official relations with the new regime pending

[1] *Ibid.*, p. 225.

developments. This is the present status of our relations with the existing Argentine regime.

In all matters relating to the security and defense of the hemisphere, we must look to the substance rather than the form. We are in a bitter war with a ruthless enemy whose plan has included conquest of the Western Hemisphere. To deal with such grave issues on a purely technical basis would be to close our eyes to the realities of the situation.

The support, by important elements inimical to the United Nations war effort, of movements designed to limit action already taken could only be a matter of grave anxiety.

The United States has at all times had close ties with Argentina and the Argentine people. It has consistently hoped, and continues to hope, that Argentina will take the steps necessary to bring her fully and completely into the realm of hemispheric solidarity, so that Argentina will play a part worthy of her great traditions in the world-wide struggle on which the lives of all of the American countries, including Argentina, now depend. The policies and types of action, present and future, which would effectuate this full cooperation are fully known in Argentina, as in the rest of the hemisphere.

(6) Interruption of Operations in Argentina of All America Cables, Inc. Statement of the Department of State, March 25, 1944 [1]

The Department has received information from Buenos Aires to the effect that the Argentine authorities have ordered All America Cables, Inc., to suspend all operations during the 24-hour period which expires March 25 at midnight. A fine of 1,000 pesos has been imposed upon the company. These penalties are the result of an alleged violation of censorship regulations.

It is charged that on March 8 three cables from Lima, Peru, were mistakenly forwarded by the local office of All America Cables, Inc., in Buenos Aires to the censorship official in the office of the United Press, to which the messages were addressed, instead of having received the prior approval of the censorship official in the office of All America Cables, Inc.

Thus an essential inter-American communications link serving a number of the American Republics, including the United States, has been interrupted on the ground of an apparently trivial violation of the Argentine censorship regulations. This action would appear to indicate a complete failure to appreciate the importance to the citizens of the republics concerned, including Argentina, as well as to their governments of the services performed by these communication facilities.

2. BOLIVIA

A military coup, carried out early in the morning of December 20, 1943 by a group of comparatively junior army officers, ousted the President, General Enrique Penaranda, and placed in power a mixed *junta* of officers and civilians. Major Gualberto Villarroel assumed the powers of President and José Tamayo

[1] *Ibid.*, p. 292.

542 DOCUMENTS ON AMERICAN FOREIGN RELATIONS

took the post of Foreign Minister.[1] On the following day, the new Government issued a statement formally maintaining Bolivia's alignment with the United Nations and pledging that Bolivia would continue faithfully to observe her international commitments.[2]

At his press conference on December 22 Secretary Hull indicated some doubt as to whether the revolution was inspired by elements friendly to the United States. The question of recognition was held in abeyance. On December 20, the new Government had announced the appointment of Enrique Sanchez Lozada, then in the Washington Office of the Coordinator of Inter-American Affairs, as its special confidential agent in Washington.[3] On December 23, Secretary Hull announced that information was being exchanged by the governments of the American Republics on the Bolivian situation.[4] On the 27th, it was stated that a decision concerning recognition had been postponed until the American Republics that had declared war on or severed diplomatic relations with the Axis powers had had the opportunity to consult.[5] This step was decided upon, it was announced, in consequence of a recommendation of the Inter-American Emergency Advisory Committee for Political Defense.[6]

The Argentine Government recognized the new Bolivian Government on January 3, 1944.[7] On January 24, the Department of State announced that the United States would not recognize the revolutionary government of Bolivia.[8] The British Government announced the next day its refusal to recognize the military *junta*.[9] On February 11, the revolutionary government announced that certain members who had been accused of connivance with Axis agents had resigned and been replaced by persons known to be more friendly to the United Nations.[10]

At his press conference on May 19, Under Secretary of State Stettinius made it clear that the recognition of the Bolivia and Argentine Governments were separate matters. The same day, Secretary Hull stated that results of the investigation of Bolivian affairs being made by Mr. Avra M. Warren, United States Ambassador to Panama, would be communicated to the other American Republics in line with their agreement to keep one another informed.[11] Mr. Warren arrived in Washington from Bolivia on May 23 and immediately reported to Under Secretary of State Stettinius. Later the Ambassador submitted a written report to Secretary Hull.[12] Recognition was extended on June 23. An important consideration apparently was the conviction of the American Government that the Bolivian Government had successfully eliminated or brought under control Axis agents and other persons with pro-Axis views.[13]

(1) United States Attitude Toward the New Bolivian Government. Statement of the Secretary of State (Hull), December 22, 1943 [14]

Considerations of the security of the hemisphere and of the war effort of the United Nations must have first importance in any matter of this or similar character. Included in the relevant considerations is the question whether outside influence unfriendly to the Allied cause, played any part. It must never be forgotten that the hemisphere is at present under sinister and subversive attack by the Axis, assisted by some elements from within the hemisphere itself.

[1] *New York Times*, December 21, 1943.   [2] *Ibid.*, December 22, 1943.
[3] *Ibid.*, December 23, 1943.   [4] *Ibid.*, December 24, 1943.
[5] *Ibid.*, December 28, 1943.   [6] *Ibid.;* Department of State, *Bulletin*, X, p.28.
[7] *New York Times*, January 4, 1944.   [8] Department of State, *Bulletin*, X, p. 132.
[9] *New York Times*, January 26, 1944.   [10] *Ibid.*, February 14, 1944.
[11] *Ibid.*, May 20, 1944.   [12] *Ibid.*, May 24, 1944.
[13] *Ibid.*, June 23, 1944.   [14] Department of State, *Bulletin*, IX, p. 449.

(2) *The New Government of Bolivia. Resolution of the Emergency Advisory Committee for Political Defense Regarding Recognition, Adopted at Montevideo, January 5, 1944* [1]

On December 24, 1943 the Emergency Advisory Committee for Political Defense had adopted a resolution recommending that American Governments which had declared war on the Axis powers or had broken relations with them should not, for the duration of the war, proceed to the recognition of a new government instituted by force without previous consultation and exchange of information. This resolution was approved by the United States Government.

WHEREAS:

(*a*) The Emergency Advisory Committee for Political Defense in its Resolution XXII, approved and transmitted December 24, 1943, recommended "to the American Governments which have declared war on the Axis powers or have broken relations with them, that for the duration of the present world conflict they do not proceed to the recognition of a new government instituted by force, before consulting among themselves for the purpose of determining whether this government complies with the Inter-American undertakings for the defense of the continent, nor before carrying out an exchange of information as to the circumstances which have determined the establishment of said government";

(*b*) Almost all of the governments to which the recommendation was transmitted have already advised the Committee of their acceptance, confirming the principles of Inter-American solidarity for the defense of the continent upon which the said resolution is based and recognizing that the resolution respects the free decision of each Government;

(*c*) Subsequent to the adoption of the said resolution by the Committee developments relating to the situation created through the establishment by force of a new government in Bolivia indicate, as the American Governments will appreciate, the urgent need for the application of the procedure which the Committee has recommended;

The Emergency Advisory Committee for Political Defense

RESOLVES:

To recommend to the Governments of the American Republics which have declared war on the Axis powers or have broken diplomatic relations with them, that before proceeding to recognize the new government of Bolivia they carry out as soon as possible, through regular diplomatic channels, both the consultations and the exchange of information recommended in Resolution XXII of this Committee, for the purposes therein indicated.

[1] *Ibid.*, X, p. 28.

(a) *The Secretary of State (Hull) to the President of the Emergency Advisory Committee for Political Defense (Guani), January 6, 1944*[1]

I have the honor to acknowledge the receipt of Your Excellency's telegram of January 5 transmitting to me the text of the resolution adopted by the Emergency Advisory Committee for Political Defense on that day resolving: "to recommend to the Governments of the American Republics which have declared war on the Axis powers or have broken diplomatic relations with them, that before proceeding to recognize the new Government of Bolivia they carry out as soon as possible, through regular diplomatic channels, both the consultations and the exchange of information recommended in Resolution XXII of the Committee, for the purposes therein indicated."

In reply, I desire to inform you that this Government is in hearty accord with this resolution, as with the prior resolution to which it refers, and that this Government will promptly engage in the recommended consultations and exchanges of information with the other eighteen interested Republics. In adopting these resolutions, the Committee over which you have the honor to preside has, in the judgment of this Government, rendered distinguished service to the cause of hemispheric solidarity and security.

(3) *Statement of the Secretary of State (Hull), January 7, 1944*[2]

It is my information that by the consultation now in progress there is already taking place considerable exchange of information regarding the origin of the revolution in Bolivia. This assembling of facts should soon permit each government to reach its own conclusions. The information now available here increasingly strengthens the belief that forces outside of Bolivia and unfriendly to the defense of the American Republics inspired and aided the Bolivian revolution.

(4) *Nonrecognition of the Present Revolutionary Junta in Bolivia. Department of State Release, January 24, 1944*[3]

This Government has been aware that subversive groups hostile to the Allied cause have been plotting disturbances against the American Governments operating in defense of the hemisphere against Axis aggression.

On December 20, 1943 the Bolivian Government was overthrown by force under circumstances linking this action with the subversive groups mentioned in the preceding statement.

The most important and urgent question arising from this development in Bolivia is the fact that this is but one act committed by a general subversive movement having for its purpose steadily expanding activities on the continent.

[1] *Ibid.*   [2] *Ibid.*, p. 29.   [3] *Ibid.*, p. 132.

These developments, viewed in the light of the information the American Republics have been exchanging among themselves, dispose negatively of the matter of this Government's recognizing the present revolutionary *Junta* at La Paz.

The inter-American system built up over the past 10 years has had for one of its purposes the defending of the sovereign republics of the hemisphere against aggression or intervention in their domestic affairs by influences operating outside the hemisphere and outside their individual frontiers. This Government is confident that the freedom-loving people of the American Republics, including those of Bolivia, who have the good-will of the Government and people of the United States, will understand that this decision is taken in furtherance of the aforesaid purpose.

(5) *The New Government in Bolivia. Statement of the Secretary of State (Hull), May 26, 1944* [1]

Ambassador Warren [2] has now handed me his report. I am giving the matter attention and will forward his findings to the Foreign Ministers of the other American Republics for their study and recommendations. The report should serve as the basis for an exchange of ideas and consultation among all of us.

(6) *Recognition by the United States of the New Government of Bolivia. Department of State Release, June 23, 1944* [3]

The United States Embassy in La Paz on June 23, under instructions, presented a note to the Foreign Minister of Bolivia renewing relations between the United States and Bolivia.

Between January 24 and January 28, 1944, 19 American Republics, after full exchange of information and consultation with one another, declared their intention to withhold recognition from the Bolivian *Junta*, which came into power on December 20, 1943. They concluded that recognition of the new Bolivian regime would not be in the interest of the security of the hemisphere and the success of the Allied cause. This was the criterion, and the only criterion, which they considered in passing upon the status of the Bolivian regime.

Since last January the Provisional Government of Bolivia has carried out a number of decisive and affirmative acts in support of hemisphere security and the cause of the United Nations. Accordingly, the American Governments have reviewed the situation again by exchanging information and consulting with one another. The consensus of this consultation is that there is no longer reason for withholding recognition.

The exchange of information and consultation which led to the decision by the sovereign states concerned that the Bolivian Government should be recognized took place pursuant to Resolutions XXII and XXIII [4] of the Inter-American Emergency Advisory Committee for Political Defense, located at Montevideo, which has now been apprised of the decision of this Government.

[1] *Ibid.*, p. 501.
[2] Sent on special mission to Bolivia.
[3] Department of State, *Bulletin*, X, p. 584.
[4] *Ibid.*, VII, p. 999 and X, p. 20, 28.

3. ECUADOR

After ten hours of bitter street fighting, a Provisional *Junta* was organized in Guayaquil, the capital of Ecuador, on May 29, 1944. The revolution was led by the supporters of the exiled former President, Dr. José Maria Velasco Ibarra, and was apparently aimed at forestalling the scheduled week-end presidential election.[1] The Provisional Government was first headed by Col. Pablo Borja but he was succeeded by General Larrea Alba, representing not only the Army but also the Revolutionary Vanguard, a political party. The Provisional Government, in a statement of aims, declared that its aims included "strengthening the international personality of Ecuador and intensifying its relations with the other American nations." It pledged continued strong support of the United Nations and the "repression of all Nazi-Fascist activities and other anti-democratic activities which endanger the nation and the continent."[2] The Provisional Government was also reported to have issued a proclamation against the settlement of the Ecuador-Peru boundary dispute by an exchange of notes on May 24, 1944, by which, it was claimed, the Government of Señor Arroyo del Rio gave away national territory.[3] On May 31, Dr. Ibarra assumed office as President.[4] On June 6, the Revolutionary Government received full recognition by the Government of the United States. No question apparently arose of Axis influence in the revolution.[5]

(1) Recognition by the United States of the Government of Ecuador. Department of State Release, June 6, 1944 [6]

The Acting Secretary of State, Edward R. Stettinius, Jr., announced late on the afternoon of June 6 that the Government of the United States had extended full recognition to the Government of Ecuador which is now organized under Dr. José Maria Velasco Ibarra.

At 5 o'clock P.M. on June 6 the American Ambassador in Quito informed the new Minister of Foreign Affairs of Ecuador of this action by the Government of the United States. It is understood that many other American Republics took simultaneous action in granting recognition, following consultation and exchange of information pursuant to Resolution XXII of the Committee for Political Defense at Montevideo.[7]

4. MEXICO

[On the subject of economic cooperation between the United States and Mexico, see p. 503.]

(1) Compensation for Petroleum Properties Expropriated in Mexico. Department of State Release, September 30, 1943 [8]

The manner and conditions of payment of compensation to this Government for the benefit of certain American nationals who sustained losses as a conse-

[1] *New York Times*, May 30, 1944.

[2] *Ibid.*, May 31, 1944.

[3] *Ibid.* For text of Protocol of January 29, 1942 which provided basis for ending dispute, see *Documents, IV, 1941–42*, p. 433. The exchange of notes of May 24, 1944 interpreted specific terms. For congratulatory notes from President Roosevelt and Secretary Hull, see Department of State, *Bulletin*, X, p. 487.

[4] *New York Times*, June 1, 1944.

[5] *Ibid.*, June 7, 1944.

[6] Department of State, *Bulletin*, X, p. 536.

[7] See p. 497.

[8] Department of State, *Bulletin*, IX, p. 231.

quence of the expropriation of petroleum properties in Mexico in March 1938 [1] were agreed upon through notes exchanged on September 29, 1943 by the Acting Secretary of State and the Mexican Chargé in Washington. This exchange of notes is the second and final step taken by the two Governments to implement the basic agreement of November 19, 1941,[2] in which the two Governments agreed that each Government would appoint an expert to determine the just compensation to be paid American nationals whose properties, rights, or interests were affected to their detriment by acts of the Government of Mexico subsequent to March 17, 1938. At the time of the exchange of the basic notes of November 19, 1941, the Mexican Government made a deposit of $9,000,000 on account of the compensation to be paid.

The first step in the implementation of the agreement of November 19, 1941 was the preparation and submission of the joint report of April 17, 1942 by two experts — Morris L. Cooke, representing the United States, and Manuel J. Zevada, representing the Republic of Mexico. This joint report placed an evaluation of $23,995,991 on the losses sustained by American nationals, including all elements of tangible and intangible value, and provided for interest at three percent per annum from March 18, 1938 to the date of final settlement on all balances due; in conformity with the basic agreement, the evaluation was final.

The manner and conditions of payment by the Government of Mexico to this Government are provided for in the notes as follows:

The amount due is $23,995,991 plus $5,141,709.84 interest at three percent per annum on all unpaid balances from March 18, 1938 to September 30, 1947, the date set for the final payment — a total of $29,137,700.84.

After deducting the $9,000,000 deposited in cash by the Government of Mexico at the time of the signing of the agreement of November 19, 1941, the balance due is $20,137,700.84.

The balance is to be paid in the following instalments: $3,796,391.04 on September 30, 1943, and the balance in four equal annual instalments, each of $4,085,327.45.

(2) *A Treaty between the United States of America and the United Mexican States, Relating to the Utilization of the Waters of the Colorado and Tijuana Rivers and of the Rio Grande from Fort Quitman, Texas, to the Gulf of Mexico, Signed at Washington, February 3, 1944* [3]

The treaty itself is but the latest of a long series of United States–Mexican conventions relating to the Rio Grande and the Colorado. The treaties of February 2, 1848 (9 Stat. 922) and December 3, 1853 (10 Stat. 1031) defined certain parts of these rivers with reference to the boundary and regulated the use of their waters for purposes of navigation. Aside from some conventions between 1880 and 1890 which related to the land boundary, the next treaty concerning the boundary was that of November 12, 1884 (24 Stat. 1011), which resulted from the difficulties caused by accretive and avulsive changes in the Rio Grande and the Colorado. This treaty defined the general laws of accretion and avulsion to be applied to the boundary rivers and prescribed the rules to regulate or control artificial changes in their channels, monuments on bridges across them, and property rights on cut-offs caused by avulsive changes in the river channels. The need of an international body to execute the provisions of

[1] *Executive Agreement Series* 234; *Documents, IV, 1941–42,* p. 421.

[2] *Ibid.,* p. 425; Department of State, *Bulletin,* VI, p. 351.

[3] Senate Executive A, 78th Cong., 2d sess.

the treaty of 1884 led to the signing of the treaty of March 1, 1889 (26 Stat. 1512), which provided for the organization, jurisdiction, and authority of the present International Boundary Commission, United States and Mexico.

Since 1889 three treaties of considerable importance relating to these boundary rivers have been negotiated. The treaty of March 20, 1905 (35 Stat. 1863) provided for the elimination from the effects of the treaty of November 12, 1884 of certain categories of bancos or cut-offs. The following year there was signed, on May 21 (34 Stat. 2953), a treaty by the terms of which the United States allocated to Mexico 60 thousand acre-feet of water from the Rio Grande at Ciudad Juárez.[1] After an additional quarter of a century of difficulties occasioned by the meanders and floods of the Rio Grande in the El Paso–Juárez Valley, the two countries signed, on February 1, 1933 (48 Stat. 1621), a treaty by the terms of which the river channel between El Paso–Juárez and Box Canyon was rectified and controlled by means of levees. One other treaty, the arbitral convention of June 24, 1910 (36 Stat. 2481), related to the boundary rivers only to the extent that it provided for the settlement by arbitration of the so-called "Chamizal dispute" involving a small tract of land built up by accretion on the El Paso side of the Rio Grande. This effort proved futile, and the problem of the Chamizal still remains to be settled.

With the greatly increased use of the waters of the Rio Grande and the Colorado for irrigation purposes, the natural flow of each of these streams no longer sufficed to insure enough water for irrigated areas, not to mention projects calling for a great expansion of acreage. It became necessary, therefore, not only to consider means to conserve and control the available water supply of these rivers but also to reach agreements for the equitable apportionment of the supply, both among the States of the United States and between the United States and Mexico.

During the first two decades of this century, this problem of the lower Rio Grande received the attention of the two Governments on several occasions and was the object of study by joint commissions. No material results came from these early efforts, and beginning in 1924 another serious attempt was made to reach an agreement between the two countries regarding the distribution of the waters of the Rio Grande. In that year the Congress of the United States passed an act (43 Stat. 118) approving the establishment of an International Water Commission, United States and Mexico, to make a study regarding the equitable use of the waters of this river below Fort Quitman, Texas. The refusal of the Government of Mexico to consider the Rio Grande without also considering the Colorado led to the passage by the Congress of the joint resolution of March 3, 1927 (44 Stat. 1043), amending the act of 1924 to make it cover not only the Rio Grande but also the Colorado and Tijuana Rivers. This Commission made an investigation of these rivers but was unable to reach an agreement regarding the distribution of their waters. So far as the Rio Grande was concerned, the chief difficulty lay in the fact that, whereas 70 percent of the water supply below Fort Quitman, Texas, had its origin in Mexico, most of the irrigated acreage was in Texas, and Mexico was unwilling to guarantee the perpetuation of the Texas developments, insisting instead that the water of the main stream should be divided equally, with each country retaining the right to develop its tributaries to the fullest extent.

Following the failure of the International Water Commission to reach an agreement on the Rio Grande, the situation facing the water-users grew steadily worse. In the effort to discover a rational solution for the problem, a thorough investigation was made by a panel of engineers associated with the United States Section of the International Boundary Commission, on the basis of which there was developed what is known as the Valley Gravity and Storage Project (Federal Project 5). Under this project, an initial appropriation for which was

---

[1] An acre-foot of water is the quantity required to cover one acre to the depth of one foot.

made in 1941 (55 Stat. 303), the lower valley of Texas would be protected by means of off-river storage, a gravity diversion canal to tap the Rio Grande near the town of Zapata, Texas, and a system of feeder and distribution canals, the total to cost in the neighborhood of $55,000,000. Ultimately it was planned to build storage reservoirs on the Pecos and Devils Rivers, both tributaries of the Rio Grande. The problems of the Colorado River system were approached also from both the interstate and the international angle. Mexico became involved when the Imperial Valley Project was first begun, for this development was based upon a gravity canal that headed in the Colorado River immediately above the international boundary, crossed the boundary into Mexico, and then turned west and northwest back across the boundary to the Imperial Valley of Southern California. The construction of this canal required a concession from Mexico, under the terms of which Mexico could use half the capacity of the canal.

At the same time that the two Governments were making efforts early in this century to reach an agreement on the distribution of the waters of the Rio Grande, they were seeking agreement also on the Colorado. These early diplomatic efforts failed and were not renewed until the International Water Commission, mentioned above, undertook its studies in 1928.

Meanwhile, the great increase in irrigation in the seven basin States, coupled with the gravity of the flood menace, led to efforts to reach an interstate agreement for the apportionment among these States of the water supply of the Colorado River system. In view of plans to construct a storage reservoir in the Boulder Canyon region for the better regulation of irrigation supply, for flood control, and for power production, it became important for the basin States to know in advance the extent of their rights in respect of the water supply. The result was the establishment of a Colorado River Commission composed of members from each of the seven States. This Commission finally agreed in 1922 upon the terms of a compact to govern the allocation of the waters of the Colorado River system (H. Doc. 605, 67th Cong., 4th sess., serial 8215). This compact apportions to the upper basin and lower basin respectively 7,500,000 acre-feet of water each year for beneficial consumptive use, with the lower basin having the right to increase its use by 1,000,000 acre-feet each year. The compact provides, in addition, that should the United States allocate by treaty any Colorado River water to Mexico such allocation shall be supplied first from the waters that are surplus above the 16,000,000 acre-feet apportioned to the two basins, and if this surplus is insufficient the deficiency is to be borne equally by the two basins. By still another provision the States of the upper basin guarantee to deliver during each period of 10 years not less than 75,000,000 acre-feet at Lee Ferry, which is above Boulder Dam. This compact, approved by the Congress in 1928 (45 Stat. 1057), was ratified promptly by all of the basin States except Arizona, which delayed its ratification until February 1944.

The next step was the passing of the Boulder Canyon Project Act, approved December 21, 1928 (45 Stat. 1057), by the terms of which Boulder Dam and appurtenant works were built at a total cost of approximately $150,000,000. This cost was to be repaid for the most part out of revenues from the power contracts made between the Department of the Interior and certain power interests.

In pursuance of the Colorado River Compact and Boulder Canyon Project Act, the Department of the Interior entered into certain other contracts, these being for the supply of water to California projects as follows: the Metropolitan Water District of Southern California (Los Angeles and certain nearby communities), the Imperial Irrigation District (including Coachella Valley), the Palo Verde Irrigation District, and the city of San Diego. These water contracts are for permanent service and call for the delivery of water from storage created by Boulder Dam. They recite the order of priorities set up by the State of California, but the actual delivery of water under them is made subject to the availability thereof, for use in California, under the Colorado River Compact and Boulder Canyon Project Act. Following the execution of these water contracts, the Metropolitan Water District built an aqueduct from Parker Dam to the Los Angeles area, and the Department of the Interior built Imperial Dam on the Colorado above Yuma, Arizona, and the All-American Canal running from this dam to the Imperial Valley, which thus no longer depends upon the Mexican Canal. By the terms of the All-American Canal contract the Imperial Irrigation District is obligated ultimately to repay the Government of the United States for the actual cost of the dam and the All-American Canal.

Since the California contracts were entered into, the Department of the Interior has made a contract with the State of Nevada to supply a maximum of 300,000 acre-feet each year, and the legislature of Arizona has recently approved a contract calling for the annual delivery of a maximum of 2,800,000 acre-feet, plus one half of the surplus, to that State. Both of these contracts are subject to limitations and reservations which are the same as, or similar to, those which are contained in the California contracts.

While the States of the Colorado basin and the Congress of the United States were making efforts to solve the interstate problems of this river, the International Water Commission, United States and Mexico, was endeavoring to reach an agreement on the quantity of water that the United States should guarantee to Mexico. Just as in the case of the Rio Grande, the Commission failed to reach a decision. The Mexicans demanded up to 3,600,000 acre-feet each year, but the United States representatives were willing to grant only the maximum amount that had been used in Mexico up to that time — that is, approximately 750,000 acre-feet — plus main canal losses and other waters not definitely set forth.

In the meantime, the Department of State renewed its study of the whole matter, this time in cooperation with the Committee of Fourteen and Sixteen representing the interstate water and power interests of the Colorado River Basin States. Several conferences were held during the past two or three years between this Committee and representatives of the Department. At one of these conferences held in Santa Fe, New Mexico, in April 1943, a resolution defining suggested limits for a treaty with Mexico was approved by a large majority of the members. On the basis of this resolution, the Department reopened the negotiations with the Government of Mexico that resulted in the treaty which was signed on February 3, 1944.

On February 15, President Roosevelt submitted the treaty to the Senate with a view to receiving the advice and consent of that body. Along with the treaty, he submitted a report of the Secretary of State summarizing the terms of the treaty. On February 15, the treaty was read the first time and referred to the Committee on Foreign Relations. The injunction of secrecy was removed from the treaty the same day.[1]

The above note is based largely upon, and incorporates substantial parts of, a study by Charles A. Timm, Divisional Assistant in the Division of Mexican Affairs, Department of State, entitled *Water Treaty Between the United States and Mexico*, appearing in the *Department of State Bulletin*.[2]

The Government of the United States of America and the Government of the United Mexican States: animated by the sincere spirit of cordiality and friendly cooperation which happily governs the relations between them; taking into account the fact that Articles VI and VII of the Treaty of Peace, Friendship and Limits between the United States of America and the United Mexican States signed at Guadalupe Hidalgo on February 2, 1848, and Article IV of the boundary treaty between the two coun-

[1] *Ibid.*, p. 1.

[2] Vol. X, p. 282. Maps of the Colorado River Basin and the Rio Grande Drainage basin appear at *ibid.*, p. 285, 286 and 289 respectively.

tries signed at the City of Mexico December 30, 1853 regulate the use of the waters of the Rio Grande (Rio Bravo) and the Colorado River for purposes of navigation only; considering that the utilization of these waters for other purposes is desirable in the interest of both countries, and desiring, moreover, to fix and delimit the rights of the two countries with respect to the waters of the Colorado and Tijuana Rivers, and of the Rio Grande (Rio Bravo) from Fort Quitman, Texas, United States of America, to the Gulf of Mexico, in order to obtain the most complete and satisfactory utilization thereof, have resolved to conclude a treaty and for this purpose have named as their plenipotentiaries:

The President of the United States of America:

Cordell Hull, Secretary of State of the United States of America, George S. Messersmith, Ambassador Extraordinary and Plenipotentiary of the United States of America in Mexico, and Lawrence M. Lawson, United States Commissioner, International Boundary Commission, United States and Mexico; and

The President of the United Mexican States:

Francisco Castillo Nájera, Ambassador Extraordinary and Plenipotentiary of the United Mexican States in Washington, and Rafael Fernández MacGregor, Mexican Commissioner, International Boundary Commission, United States and Mexico; who, having communicated to each other their respective Full Powers and having found them in good and due form, have agreed upon the following:

I — PRELIMINARY PROVISIONS

ARTICLE 1. For the purposes of this Treaty it shall be understood that:

(a) "The United States" means the United States of America.

(b) "Mexico" means the United Mexican States.

(c) "The Commission" means the International Boundary and Water Commission, United States and Mexico, as described in Article 2 of this Treaty.

(d) "To divert" means the deliberate act of taking water from any channel in order to convey it elsewhere for storage, or to utilize it for domestic, agricultural, stock-raising or industrial purposes whether this be done by means of dams across the channel, partition weirs, lateral intakes, pumps or any other methods.

(e) "Point of diversion" means the place where the act of diverting the water is effected.

(f) "Conservation capacity of storage reservoirs" means that part of their total capacity devoted to holding and conserving the water for disposal thereof as and when required, that is, capacity additional to that provided for silt retention and flood control.

(*g*) "Flood discharges and spills" means the voluntary or involuntary discharge of water for flood control as distinguished from releases for other purposes.

(*h*) "Return flow" means that portion of diverted water that eventually finds its way back to the source from which it was diverted.

(*i*) "Release" means the deliberate discharge of stored water for conveyance elsewhere or for direct utilization.

(*j*) "Consumptive use" means the use of water by evaporation, plant transpiration or other manner whereby the water is consumed and does not return to its source of supply. In general it is measured by the amount of water diverted less the part thereof which returns to the stream.

(*k*) "Lowest major international dam or reservoir" means the major international dam or reservoir situated farthest downstream.

(*l*) "Highest major international dam or reservoir" means the major international dam or reservoir situated farthest upstream.

ARTICLE 2. The International Boundary Commission established pursuant to the provisions of the Convention between the United States and Mexico signed in Washington March 1, 1889 to facilitate the carrying out of the principles contained in the Treaty of November 12, 1884 and to avoid difficulties occasioned by reason of the changes which take place in the beds of the Rio Grande (Rio Bravo) and the Colorado River shall hereafter be known as the International Boundary and Water Commission, United States and Mexico, which shall continue to function for the entire period during which the present Treaty shall continue in force. Accordingly, the term of the Convention of March 1, 1889 shall be considered to be indefinitely extended, and the Convention of November 21, 1900 between the United States and Mexico regarding that Convention shall be considered completely terminated.

The application of the present Treaty, the regulation and exercise of the rights and obligations which the two Governments assume thereunder, and the settlement of all disputes to which its observance and execution may give rise are hereby entrusted to the International Boundary and Water Commission, which shall function in conformity with the powers and limitations set forth in this Treaty.

The Commission shall in all respects have the status of an international body, and shall consist of a United States Section and a Mexican Section. The head of each Section shall be an Engineer Commissioner. Wherever there are provisions in this Treaty for joint action or joint agreement by the two Governments, or for the furnishing of reports, studies or plans to the two Governments, or similar provisions, it shall be understood that the particular matter in question shall be handled by or through the Department of State of the United States and the Ministry of Foreign Relations of Mexico.

The Commission or either of its two Sections may employ such assistants and engineering and legal advisers as it may deem necessary. Each Government shall accord diplomatic status to the Commissioner, designated by the other Government. The Commissioner, two principal engineers, a legal adviser, and a secretary, designated by each Government as members of its Section of the Commission, shall be entitled in the territory of the other country to the privileges and immunities appertaining to diplomatic officers. The Commission and its personnel may freely carry out their observations, studies and field work in the territory of either country.

The jurisdiction of the Commission shall extend to the limitrophe parts of the Rio Grande (Rio Bravo) and the Colorado River, to the land boundary between the two countries, and to works located upon their common boundary, each Section of the Commission retaining jurisdiction over that part of the works located within the limits of its own country. Neither Section shall assume jurisdiction or control over works located within the limits of the country of the other without the express consent of the Government of the latter. The works constructed, acquired or used in fulfillment of the provisions of this Treaty and located wholly within the territorial limits of either country, although these works may be international in character, shall remain, except as herein otherwise specifically provided, under the exclusive jurisdiction and control of the Section of the Commission in whose country the works may be situated.

The duties and powers vested in the Commission by this Treaty shall be in addition to those vested in the International Boundary Commission by the Convention of March 1, 1889 and other pertinent treaties and agreements in force between the two countries except as the provisions of any of them may be modified by the present Treaty.

Each Government shall bear the expenses incurred in the maintenance of its Section of the Commission. The joint expenses, which may be incurred as agreed upon by the Commission, shall be borne equally by the two Governments.

ARTICLE 3. In matters in which the Commission may be called upon to make provision for the joint use of international waters, the following order of preferences shall serve as a guide:

1. Domestic and municipal uses.
2. Agriculture and stock-raising.
3. Electric power.
4. Other industrial uses.
5. Navigation.
6. Fishing and hunting.
7. Any other beneficial uses which may be determined by the Commission.

All of the foregoing uses shall be subject to any sanitary measures or works which may be mutually agreed upon by the two Governments, which hereby agree to give preferential attention to the solution of all border sanitation problems.

II — Rio Grande (Rio Bravo)

Article 4. The waters of the Rio Grande (Rio Bravo) between Fort Quitman, Texas, and the Gulf of Mexico are hereby allotted to the two countries in the following manner:

A. To Mexico:

(a) All of the waters reaching the main channel of the Rio Grande (Rio Bravo) from the San Juan and Alamo Rivers, including the return flow from the lands irrigated from the latter two rivers.

(b) One-half of the flow in the main channel of the Rio Grande (Rio Bravo) below the lowest major international storage dam, so far as said flow is not specifically allotted under this Treaty to either of the two countries.

(c) Two-thirds of the flow reaching the main channel of the Rio Grande (Rio Bravo) from the Conchos, San Diego, San Rodrigo, Escondido and Salado Rivers and the Las Vacas Arroyo, subject to the provisions of subparagraph (c) of paragraph B of this Article.

(d) One-half of all other flows not otherwise allotted by this Article occurring in the main channel of the Rio Grande (Rio Bravo), including the contributions from all the unmeasured tributaries, which are those not named in this Article, between Fort Quitman and the lowest major international storage dam.

B. To the United States:

(a) All of the waters reaching the main channel of the Rio Grande (Rio Bravo) from the Pecos and Devils Rivers, Goodenough Spring, and Alamito, Terlingua, San Felipe and Pinto Creeks.

(b) One-half of the flow in the main channel of the Rio Grande (Rio Bravo) below the lowest major international storage dam, so far as said flow is not specifically allotted under this Treaty to either of the two countries.

(c) One-third of the flow reaching the main channel of the Rio Grande (Rio Bravo) from the Conchos, San Diego, San Rodrigo, Escondido and Salado Rivers and the Las Vacas Arroyo, provided that this third shall not be less, as an average amount in cycles of five consecutive years, than 350,000 acre-feet (431,721,000 cubic meters) annually. The United States shall not acquire any right by the use of the waters of the tributaries named in this subparagraph, in excess of the said 350,000 acre-feet (431,721,000 cubic meters) annually, except the right to use one-third of the flow reaching the Rio Grande (Rio Bravo) from said tributaries, although such one-third may be in excess of that amount.

(*d*) One-half of all other flows not otherwise allotted by this Article occurring in the main channel of the Rio Grande (Rio Bravo), including the contributions from all the unmeasured tributaries, which are those not named in this Article, between Fort Quitman and the lowest major international storage dam.

In the event of extraordinary drought or serious accident to the hydraulic systems on the measured Mexican tributaries, making it difficult for Mexico to make available the run-off of 350,000 acre-feet (431,721,000 cubic meters) annually, allotted in subparagraph (*c*) of paragraph B of this Article to the United States as the minimum contribution from the aforesaid Mexican tributaries, any deficiencies existing at the end of the aforesaid five-year cycle shall be made up in the following five-year cycle with water from the said measured tributaries.

Whenever the conservation capacities assigned to the United States in at least two of the major international reservoirs, including the highest major reservoir, are filled with waters belonging to the United States, a cycle of five years shall be considered as terminated and all debits fully paid, whereupon a new five-year cycle shall commence.

ARTICLE 5. The two Governments agree to construct jointly, through their respective Sections of the Commission, the following works in the main channel of the Rio Grande (Rio Bravo):

I. The dams required for the conservation, storage and regulation of the greatest quantity of the annual flow of the river in a way to ensure the continuance of existing uses and the development of the greatest number of feasible projects, within the limits imposed by the water allotments specified.

II. The dams and other joint works required for the diversion of the flow of the Rio Grande (Rio Bravo).

One of the storage dams shall be constructed in the section between Santa Helena Canyon and the mouth of the Pecos River; one in the section between Eagle Pass and Laredo, Texas (Piedras Negras and Nuevo Laredo in Mexico); and a third in the section between Laredo and Roma, Texas (Nuevo Laredo and San Pedro de Roma in Mexico). One or more of the stipulated dams may be omitted, and others than those enumerated may be built, in either case as may be determined by the Commission, subject to the approval of the two Governments.

In planning the construction of such dams the Commission shall determine:

(*a*) The most feasible sites;

(*b*) The maximum feasible reservoir capacity at each site;

(*c*) The conservation capacity required by each country at each site, taking into consideration the amount and regimen of its allotment of water and its contemplated uses;

(*d*) The capacity required for retention of silt;

(*e*) The capacity required for flood control.

The conservation and silt capacities of each reservoir shall be assigned to each country in the same proportion as the capacities required by each country in such reservoir for conservation purposes. Each country shall have an undivided interest in the flood control capacity of each reservoir.

The construction of the international storage dams shall start within two years following the approval of the respective plans by the two Governments. The works shall begin with the construction of the lowest major international storage dam, but works in the upper reaches of the river may be constructed simultaneously. The lowest major international storage dam shall be completed within a period of eight years from the date of the entry into force of this Treaty.

The construction of the dams and other joint works required for the diversion of the flows of the river shall be initiated on the dates recommended by the Commission and approved by the two Governments.

The cost of construction, operation and maintenance of each of the international storage dams shall be prorated between the two Governments in proportion to the capacity allotted to each country for conservation purposes in the reservoir at such dam.

The cost of construction, operation and maintenance of each of the dams and other joint works required for the diversion of the flows of the river shall be prorated between the two Governments in proportion to the benefits which the respective countries receive therefrom, as determined by the Commission and approved by the two Governments.

ARTICLE 6. The Commission shall study, investigate, and prepare plans for flood control works, where and when necessary, other than those referred to in Article 5 of this Treaty, on the Rio Grande (Rio Bravo) from Fort Quitman, Texas, to the Gulf of Mexico. These works may include levees along the river, floodways and grade-control structures, and works for the canalization, rectification and artificial channeling of reaches of the river. The Commission shall report to the two Governments the works which should be built, the estimated cost thereof, the part of the works to be constructed by each Government, and the part of the works to be operated and maintained by each Section of the Commission. Each Government agrees to construct, through its Section of the Commission, such works as may be recommended by the Commission and approved by the two Governments. Each Government shall pay the costs of the works constructed by it and the costs of operation and maintenance of the part of the works assigned to it for such purpose.

ARTICLE 7. The Commission shall study, investigate and prepare plans for plants for generating hydro-electric energy which it may be feasible to construct at the international storage dams on the Rio Grande (Rio Bravo). The Commission shall report to the two Governments in a Minute the works which should be built, the estimated cost thereof, and the part of the works to be constructed by each Government. Each

Government agrees to construct, through its Section of the Commission, such works as may be recommended by the Commission and approved by the two Governments. Both Governments, through their respective Sections of the Commission, shall operate and maintain jointly such hydro-electric plants. Each Government shall pay half the cost of the construction, operation and maintenance of such plants, and the energy generated shall be assigned to each country in like proportion.

ARTICLE 8. The two Governments recognize that both countries have a common interest in the conservation and storage of waters in the international reservoirs and in the maximum use of these structures for the purpose of obtaining the most beneficial, regular and constant use of the waters belonging to them. Accordingly, within the year following the placing in operation of the first of the major international storage dams which is constructed, the Commission shall submit to each Government for its approval, regulations for the storage, conveyance and delivery of the waters of the Rio Grande (Rio Bravo) from Fort Quitman, Texas, to the Gulf of Mexico. Such regulations may be modified, amended or supplemented when necessary by the Commission, subject to the approval of the two Governments. The following general rules shall severally govern until modified or amended by agreement of the Commission, with the approval of the two Governments:

(a) Storage in all major international reservoirs above the lowest shall be maintained at the maximum possible water level, consistent with flood control, irrigation use and power requirements.

(b) Inflows to each reservoir shall be credited to each country in accordance with the ownership of such inflows.

(c) In any reservoir the ownership of water belonging to the country whose conservation capacity therein is filled, and in excess of that needed to keep it filled, shall pass to the other country to the extent that such country may have unfilled conservation capacity, except that one country may at its option temporarily use the conservation capacity of the other country not currently being used in any of the upper reservoirs; provided that in the event of flood discharge or spill occurring while one country is using the conservation capacity of the other, all of such flood discharge or spill shall be charged to the country using the other's capacity, and all inflow shall be credited to the other country until the flood discharge or spill ceases or until the capacity of the other country becomes filled with its own water.

(d) Reservoir losses shall be charged in proportion to the ownership of water in storage. Releases from any reservoir shall be charged to the country requesting them, except that releases for the generation of electrical energy, or other common purpose, shall be charged in proportion to the ownership of water in storage.

(e) Flood discharges and spills from the upper reservoirs shall be divided in the same proportion as the ownership of the inflows occurring at the time of such flood discharges and spills, except as provided in subparagraph (c) of this Article. Flood discharges and spills from the lowest reservoir shall be divided equally, except that one country, with the consent of the Commission, may use such part of the share of the other country as is not used by the latter country.

(f) Either of the two countries may avail itself, whenever it so desires, of any water belonging to it and stored in the international reservoirs, provided that the water so taken is for direct beneficial use or for storage in other reservoirs. For this purpose the Commissioner of the respective country shall give appropriate notice to the Commission, which shall prescribe the proper measures for the opportune furnishing of the water.

ARTICLE 9. (a) The channel of the Rio Grande (Rio Bravo) may be used by either of the two countries to convey water belonging to it.

(b) Either of the two countries may, at any point on the main channel of the river from Fort Quitman, Texas, to the Gulf of Mexico, divert and use the water belonging to it and may for this purpose construct any necessary works. However, no such diversion or use, not existing on the date this Treaty enters into force, shall be permitted in either country, nor shall works be constructed for such purpose, until the Section of the Commission in whose country the diversion or use is proposed has made a finding that the water necessary for such diversion or use is available from the share of that country, unless the Commission has agreed to a greater diversion or use as provided by paragraph (d) of this Article. The proposed use and the plans for the diversion works to be constructed in connection therewith shall be previously made known to the Commission for its information.

(c) Consumptive uses from the main stream and from the unmeasured tributaries below Fort Quitman shall be charged against the share of the country making them.

(d) The Commission shall have the power to authorize either country to divert and use water not belonging entirely to such country, when the water belonging to the other country can be diverted and used without injury to the latter and can be replaced at some other point on the river.

(e) The Commission shall have the power to authorize temporary diversion and use by one country of water belonging to the other, when the latter does not need it or is unable to use it, provided that such authorization or the use of such water shall not establish any right to continue to divert it.

(f) In case of the occurrence of an extraordinary drought in one country with an abundant supply of water in the other country, water stored in the international storage reservoirs and belonging to the country enjoying such abundant water supply may be withdrawn, with the consent of the Commission, for the use of the country undergoing the drought.

(*g*) Each country shall have the right to divert from the main channel of the river any amount of water, including the water belonging to the other country, for the purpose of generating hydro-electric power, provided that such diversion causes no injury to the other country and does not interfere with the international generation of power and that the quantities not returning directly to the river are charged against the share of the country making the diversion. The feasibility of such diversions not existing on the date this Treaty enters into force shall be determined by the Commission, which shall also determine the amount of water consumed, such water to be charged against the country making the diversion.

(*h*) In case either of the two countries shall construct works for diverting into the main channel of the Rio Grande (Rio Bravo) or its tributaries waters that do not at the time this Treaty enters into force contribute to the flow of the Rio Grande (Rio Bravo) such water shall belong to the country making such diversion.

(*i*) Main stream channel losses shall be charged in proportion to the ownership of water being conveyed in the channel at the times and places of the losses.

(*j*) The Commission shall keep a record of the waters belonging to each country and of those that may be available at a given moment, taking into account the measurement of the allotments, the regulation of the waters in storage, the consumptive uses, the withdrawals, the diversions, and the losses. For this purpose the Commission shall construct, operate and maintain on the main channel of the Rio Grande (Rio Bravo), and each Section shall construct, operate and maintain on the measured tributaries in its own country, all the gaging stations and mechanical apparatus necessary for the purpose of making computations and of obtaining the necessary data for such record. The information with respect to the diversions and consumptive uses on the unmeasured tributaries shall be furnished to the Commission by the appropriate Section. The cost of construction of any new gaging stations located on the main channel of the Rio Grande (Rio Bravo) shall be borne equally by the two Governments. The operation and maintenance of all gaging stations or the cost of such operation and maintenance shall be apportioned between the two Sections in accordance with determinations to be made by the Commission.

III — Colorado. River

ARTICLE 10. Of the waters of the Colorado River, from any and all sources, there are allotted to Mexico:

(*a*) A guaranteed annual quantity of 1,500,000 acre-feet (1,850,234,000 cubic meters) to be delivered in accordance with the provisions of Article 15 of this Treaty.

(b) Any other quantities arriving at the Mexican points of diversion, with the understanding that in any year in which, as determined by the United States Section, there exists a surplus of waters of the Colorado River in excess of the amount necessary to supply users in the United States and the guaranteed quantity of 1,500,000 acre-feet (1,850,234,000 cubic meters) annually to Mexico, the United States undertakes to deliver to Mexico, in the manner set out in Article 15 of this Treaty, additional waters of the Colorado River system to provide a total quantity not to exceed 1,700,000 acre-feet (2,096,931,000 cubic meters) a year. Mexico shall acquire no right beyond that provided by this subparagraph by the use of the waters of the Colorado River system, for any purpose whatsoever, in excess of 1,500,000 acre-feet (1,850,234,000 cubic meters) annually.

In the event of extraordinary drought or serious accident to the irrigation system in the United States, thereby making it difficult for the United States to deliver the guaranteed quantity of 1,500,000 acre-feet (1,850,234,000 cubic meters) a year, the water allotted to Mexico under subparagraph (a) of this Article will be reduced in the same proportion as consumptive uses in the United States are reduced.

ARTICLE 11. (a) The United States shall deliver all waters allotted to Mexico wherever these waters may arrive in the bed of the limitrophe section of the Colorado River, with the exceptions hereinafter provided. Such waters shall be made up of the waters of the said river, whatever their origin, subject to the provisions of the following paragraphs of this Article.

(b) Of the waters of the Colorado River allotted to Mexico by subparagraph (a) of Article 10 of this Treaty, the United States shall deliver, wherever such waters may arrive in the limitrophe section of the river, 1,000,000 acre-feet (1,233,489,000 cubic meters) annually from the time the Davis dam and reservoir are placed in operation until January 1, 1980 and thereafter 1,125,000 acre-feet (1,387,675,000 cubic meters) annually, except that, should the main diversion structure referred to in subparagraph (a) of Article 12 of this Treaty be located entirely in Mexico and should Mexico so request, the United States shall deliver a quantity of water not exceeding 25,000 acre-feet (30,837,000 cubic meters) annually, unless a larger quantity may be mutually agreed upon, at a point, to be likewise mutually agreed upon, on the international land boundary near San Luis, Sonora, in which event the quantities of 1,000,000 acre-feet (1,233,489,000 cubic meters) and 1,125,000 acre-feet (1,387,675,000 cubic meters) provided hereinabove as deliverable in the limitrophe section of the river shall be reduced by the quantities to be delivered in the year concerned near San Luis, Sonora.

(c) During the period from the time the Davis dam and reservoir are placed in operation until January 1, 1980, the United States shall also deliver to Mexico annually, of the water allotted to it, 500,000 acre-feet (616,745,000 cubic meters), and thereafter the United States shall deliver annually 375,000 acre-feet (462,558,000 cubic meters), at the international boundary line, by means of the All-American Canal and a canal connecting the lower end of the Pilot Knob Wasteway with the Alamo Canal or with any other Mexican canal which may be substituted for the Alamo Canal. In either event the deliveries shall be made at an operating water surface elevation not higher than that of the Alamo Canal at the point where it crossed the international boundary line in the year 1943.

(d) All the deliveries of water specified above shall be made subject to the provisions of Article 15 of this Treaty.

ARTICLE 12. The two Governments agree to construct the following works:

(a) Mexico shall construct at its expense, within a period of five years from the date of the entry into force of this Treaty, a main diversion structure below the point where the northernmost part of the international land boundary line intersects the Colorado River. If such diversion structure is located in the limitrophe section of the river, its location, design and construction shall be subject to the approval of the Commission. The Commission shall thereafter maintain and operate the structure at the expense of Mexico. Regardless of where such diversion structure is located, there shall simultaneously be constructed such levees, interior drainage facilities and other works, or improvements to existing works, as in the opinion of the Commission shall be necessary to protect lands within the United States against damage from such floods and seepage as might result from the construction, operation and maintenance of this diversion structure. These protective works shall be constructed, operated and maintained at the expense of Mexico by the respective Sections of the Commission, or under their supervision, each within the territory of its own country.

(b) The United States, within a period of five years from the date of the entry into force of this Treaty, shall construct in its own territory and at its expense, and thereafter operate and maintain at its expense, the Davis storage dam and reservoir, a part of the capacity of which shall be used to make possible the regulation at the boundary of the waters to be delivered to Mexico in accordance with the provisions of Article 15 of this Treaty.

(c) The United States shall construct or acquire in its own territory the works that may be necessary to convey a part of the waters of the Colorado River allotted to Mexico to the Mexican diversion points on the international land boundary line referred to in this Treaty. Among these works shall be included: the canal and other works necessary to convey water from the lower end of the Pilot Knob Wasteway to the international boundary, and, should Mexico request it, a canal to connect the main diversion structure referred to in subparagraph (*a*) of this Article, if this diversion structure should be built in the limitrophe section of the river, with the Mexican system of canals at a point to be agreed upon by the Commission on the international land boundary near San Luis, Sonora. Such works shall be constructed or acquired and operated and maintained by the United States Section at the expense of Mexico. Mexico shall also pay the costs of any sites or rights of way required for such works.

(*d*) The Commission shall construct, operate and maintain in the limitrophe section of the Colorado River, and each Section shall construct, operate and maintain in the territory of its own country on the Colorado River below Imperial Dam and on all other carrying facilities used for the delivery of water to Mexico, all necessary gaging stations and other measuring devices for the purpose of keeping a complete record of the waters delivered to Mexico and of the flows of the river. All data obtained as to such deliveries and flows shall be periodically compiled and exchanged between the two Sections.

ARTICLE 13. The Commission shall study, investigate and prepare plans for flood control on the Lower Colorado River between Imperial Dam and the Gulf of California, in both the United States and Mexico, and shall, in a Minute, report to the two Governments the works which should be built, the estimated cost thereof, and the part of the works to be constructed by each Government. The two Governments agree to construct, through their respective Sections of the Commission, such works as may be recommended by the Commission and approved by the two Governments, each Government to pay the costs of the works constructed by it. The Commission shall likewise recommend the parts of the works to be operated and maintained jointly by the Commission and the parts to be operated and maintained by each Section. The two Governments agree to pay in equal shares the cost of joint operation and maintenance, and each Government agrees to pay the cost of operation and maintenance of the works assigned to it for such purpose.

ARTICLE 14. In consideration of the use of the All-American Canal for the delivery to Mexico, in the manner provided in Articles 11 and 15 of this Treaty, of a part of its allotment of the waters of the Colorado River, Mexico shall pay to the United States:

(*a*) A proportion of the costs actually incurred in the construction of Imperial Dam and the Imperial Dam-Pilot Knob section of the All-American Canal, this proportion and the method and terms of repayment to be determined by the two Governments, which, for this purpose, shall take into consideration the proportionate uses of these facilities by the two countries, these determinations to be made as soon as Davis dam and reservoir are placed in operation.

(b) Annually, a proportionate part of the total costs of maintenance and operation of such facilities, these costs to be prorated between the two countries in proportion to the amount of water delivered annually through such facilities for use in each of the two countries.

In the event that revenues from the sale of hydroelectric power which may be generated at Pilot Knob become available for the amortization of part or all of the costs of the facilities named in subparagraph (a) of this Article, the part that Mexico should pay of the costs of said facilities shall be reduced or repaid in the same proportion as the balance of the total costs are reduced or repaid. It is understood that any such revenue shall not become available until the cost of any works which may be constructed for the generation of hydroelectric power at said location has been fully amortized from the revenues derived therefrom.

ARTICLE 15. A. The water allotted in subparagraph (a) of Article 10 of this Treaty shall be delivered to Mexico at the points of delivery specified in Article 11, in accordance with the following two annual schedules of deliveries by months, which the Mexican Section shall formulate and present to the Commission before the beginning of each calendar year:

SCHEDULE I

Schedule I shall cover the delivery, in the limitrophe section of the Colorado River, of 1,000,000 acre-feet (1,233,489,000 cubic meters) of water each year from the date Davis dam and reservoir are placed in operation until January 1, 1980 and the delivery of 1,125,000 acre-feet (1,387,675,000 cubic meters) of water each year thereafter. This schedule shall be formulated subject to the following limitations:

With reference to the 1,000,000 acre-foot (1,233,489,000 cubic meter) quantity:

(a) During the months of January, February, October, November and December the prescribed rate of delivery shall be not less than 600 cubic feet (17.0 cubic meters) nor more than 3,500 cubic feet (99.1 cubic meters) per second.

(b) During the remaining months of the year the prescribed rate of delivery shall be not less than 1,000 cubic feet (28.3 cubic meters) nor more than 3,500 cubic feet (99.1 cubic meters) per second.

With reference to the 1,125,000 acre-foot (1,387,675,000 cubic meter) quantity:

(a) During the months of January, February, October, November and December the prescribed rate of delivery shall be not less than 675 cubic feet (19.1 cubic meters) nor more than 4,000 cubic feet (113.3 cubic meters) per second.

(b) During the remaining months of the year the prescribed rate of delivery shall be not less than 1,125 cubic feet (31.9 cubic meters) nor more than 4,000 cubic feet (113.3 cubic meters) per second.

Should deliveries of water be made at a point on the land boundary near San Luis, Sonora, as provided for in Article 11, such deliveries shall be made under a sub-schedule to be formulated and furnished by the Mexican Section. The quantities and monthly rates of deliveries under such sub-schedule shall be in proportion to those specified for Schedule I, unless otherwise agreed upon by the Commission.

Schedule II

Schedule II shall cover the delivery at the boundary line by means of the All-American Canal of 500,000 acre-feet (616,745,000 cubic meters) of water each year from the date Davis dam and reservoir are placed in operation until January 1, 1980 and the delivery of 375,000 acre-feet (462,558,000 cubic meters) of water each year thereafter. This schedule shall be formulated subject to the following limitations:

With reference to the 500,000 acre-foot (616,745,000 cubic meter) quantity:

(a) During the months of January, February, October, November and December the prescribed rate of delivery shall be not less than 300 cubic feet (8.5 cubic meters) nor more than 2,000 cubic feet (56.6 cubic meters) per second.

(b) During the remaining months of the year the prescribed rate of delivery shall be not less than 500 cubic feet (14.2 cubic meters) nor more than 2,000 cubic feet (56.6 cubic meters) per second.

With reference to the 375,000 acre-foot (462,558,000 cubic meter) quantity:

(a) During the months of January, February, October, November and December the prescribed rate of delivery shall be not less than 225 cubic feet (6.4 cubic meters) nor more than 1,500 cubic feet (42.5 cubic meters) per second.

(b) During the remaining months of the year the prescribed rate of delivery shall be not less than 375 cubic feet (10.6 cubic meters) nor more than 1,500 cubic feet (42.5 cubic meters) per second.

B. The United States shall be under no obligation to deliver, through the All-American Canal, more than 500,000 acre-feet (616,745,000 cubic meters) annually from the date Davis dam and reservoir are placed in operation until January 1, 1980 or more than 375,000 acre-feet (462,558,000 cubic meters) annually thereafter. If, by mutual agreement any part of the quantities of water specified in this paragraph are delivered to Mexico at points on the land boundary otherwise than through the All-American Canal, the above quantities of water and the rates of deliveries set out under Schedule II of this Article shall be correspondingly diminished.

C. The United States shall have the option of delivering, at the point on the land boundary mentioned in subparagraph (c) of Article 11, any part or all of the water to be delivered at that point under Schedule II of this Article during the months of January, February, October, November and December of each year, from any source whatsoever, with the understanding that the total specified annual quantities to be delivered through the All-American Canal shall not be reduced because of the exercise of this option, unless such reduction be requested by the Mexican Section, provided that the exercise of this option shall not have the effect of increasing the total amount of scheduled water to be delivered to Mexico.

D. In any year in which there shall exist in the river water in excess of that necessary to satisfy the requirements in the United States and the guaranteed quantity of 1,500,000 acre-feet (1,850,234,000 cubic meters) allotted to Mexico, the United States hereby declares its intention to cooperate with Mexico in attempting to supply additional quantities of water through the All-American Canal as such additional quantities are desired by Mexico, if such use of the Canal and facilities will not be detrimental to the United States, provided that the delivery of any additional quantities through the All-American Canal shall not have the effect of increasing the total scheduled deliveries to Mexico. Mexico hereby declares its intention to cooperate with the United States by attempting to curtail deliveries of water through the All-American Canal in years of limited supply, if such curtailment can be accomplished without detriment to Mexico and is necessary to allow full use of all available water supplies, provided that such curtailment shall not have the effect of reducing the total scheduled deliveries of water to Mexico.

E. In any year in which there shall exist in the river water in excess of that necessary to satisfy the requirements in the United States and the guaranteed quantity of 1,500,000 acre-feet (1,850,234,000 cubic meters) allotted to Mexico, the United States Section shall so inform the Mexican Section in order that the latter may schedule such surplus water to complete a quantity up to a maximum of 1,700,000 acre-feet (2,096,-931,000 cubic meters). In this circumstance the total quantities to be delivered under Schedules I and II shall be increased in proportion to their respective total quantities and the two schedules thus increased shall be subject to the same limitations as those established for each under paragraph A of this Article.

F. Subject to the limitations as to rates of deliveries and total quantities set out in Schedules I and II, Mexico shall have the right, upon thirty days' notice in advance to the United States Section, to increase or decrease each monthly quantity prescribed by those schedules by not more than 20% of the monthly quantity.

G. The total quantity of water to be delivered under Schedule I of paragraph A of this Article may be increased in any year if the amount to be delivered under Schedule II is correspondingly reduced and if the limitations as to rates of delivery under each schedule are correspondingly increased and reduced.

IV — TIJUANA RIVER

ARTICLE 16. In order to improve existing uses and to assure any feasible further development, the Commission shall study and investigate, and shall submit to the two Governments for their approval:

(1) Recommendations for the equitable distribution between the two countries of the waters of the Tijuana River system;

(2) Plans for storage and flood control to promote and develop domestic, irrigation, and other feasible uses of the waters of this system;

(3) An estimate of the cost of the proposed works and the manner in which the construction of such works or the cost thereof should be divided between the two Governments;

(4) Recommendations regarding the parts of the works to be operated and maintained by the Commission and the parts to be operated and maintained by each Section.

The two Governments through their respective Sections of the Commission shall construct such of the proposed works as are approved by both Governments, shall divide the work to be done or the cost thereof, and shall distribute between the two countries the waters of the Tijuana River system in the proportions approved by the two Governments. The two Governments agree to pay in equal shares the costs of joint operation and maintenance of the works involved, and each Government agrees to pay the cost of operation and maintenance of the works assigned to it for such purpose.

V — GENERAL PROVISIONS

ARTICLE 17. The use of the channels of the international rivers for the discharge of flood or other excess waters shall be free and not subject to limitation by either country, and neither country shall have any claim against the other in respect of any damage caused by such use. Each Government agrees to furnish the other Government, as far in advance as practicable, any information it may have in regard to such extraordinary discharges of water from reservoirs and flood flows on its own territory as may produce floods on the territory of the other.

Each Government declares its intention to operate its storage dams in such manner, consistent with the normal operations of its hydraulic systems, as to avoid, as far as feasible, material damage in the territory of the other.

ARTICLE 18. Public use of the water surface of lakes formed by international dams shall, when not harmful to the services rendered by such dams, be free and common to both countries, subject to the police regulations of each country in its territory, to such general regulations as may appropriately be prescribed and enforced by the Commission with the approval of the two Governments for the purpose of the application of the provisions of this Treaty, and to such regulations as may appropriately be prescribed and enforced for the same purpose by each Section of the Commission with respect to the areas and borders of such parts of those lakes as lie within its territory. Neither Government shall use for military purposes such water surface situated within the territory of the other country except by express agreement between the two Governments.

ARTICLE 19. The two Governments shall conclude such special agreements as may be necessary to regulate the generation, development and disposition of electric power at international plants, including the necessary provisions for the export of electric current.

ARTICLE 20. The two Governments shall, through their respective Sections of the Commission, carry out the construction of works allotted to them. For this purpose the respective Sections of the Commission may make use of any competent public or private agencies in accordance with the laws of the respective countries. With respect to such work as either Section of the Commission may have to execute on the territory of the other, it shall, in the execution of such works, observe the laws of the place where such works are located or carried out, with the exceptions hereinafter stated.

All materials, implements, equipment and repair parts intended for the construction, operation and maintenance of such works shall be exempt from import and export customs duties. The whole of the personnel employed either directly or indirectly on the construction, operation or maintenance of the works may pass freely from one country to the other for the purpose of going to and from the place of location of the works, without any immigration restrictions, passports or labor requirements. Each Government shall furnish, through its own Section of the Commission, convenient means of identification to the personnel employed by it on the aforesaid works and verification certificates covering all materials, implements, equipment and repair parts intended for the works.

Each Government shall assume responsibility for and shall adjust exclusively in accordance with its own laws all claims arising within its territory in connection with the construction, operation or maintenance of the whole or of any part of the works herein agreed upon, or of any works which may, in the execution of this Treaty, be agreed upon in the future.

ARTICLE 21. The construction of the international dams and the formation of artificial lakes shall produce no change in the fluvial international boundary, which shall continue to be governed by existing treaties and conventions in force between the two countries.

The Commission shall, with the approval of the two Governments, establish in the artificial lakes, by buoys or by other suitable markers, a practicable and convenient line to provide for the exercise of the jurisdiction and control vested by this Treaty in the Commission and its respective Sections. Such line shall also mark the boundary for the application of the customs and police regulations of each country.

ARTICLE 22. The provisions of the Convention between the United States and Mexico for the rectification of the Rio Grande (Rio Bravo) in the El Paso-Juárez Valley signed on February 1, 1933, shall govern, so far as delimitation of the boundary, distribution of jurisdiction and sovereignty, and relations with private owners are concerned, in any places where works for the artificial channeling, canalization or rectification of the Rio Grande (Rio Bravo) and the Colorado River are carried out.

ARTICLE 23. The two Governments recognize the public interest attached to the works required for the execution and performance of this Treaty and agree to acquire, in accordance with their respective domestic laws, any private property that may be required for the construction of the said works, including the main structures and their appurtenances and the construction materials therefor, and for the operation and maintenance thereof, at the cost of the country within which the property is situated, except as may be otherwise specifically provided in this Treaty.

Each Section of the Commission shall determine the extent and location of any private property to be acquired within its own country and shall make the necessary requests upon its Government for the acquisition of such property.

The Commission shall determine the cases in which it shall become necessary to locate works for the conveyance of water or electrical energy and for the servicing of any such works, for the benefit of either of the two countries, in the territory of the other country, in order that such works can be built pursuant to agreement between the two Governments. Such works shall be subject to the jurisdiction and supervision of the Section of the Commission within whose country they are located.

Construction of the works built in pursuance of the provisions of this Treaty shall not confer upon either of the two countries any rights either of property or of jurisdiction over any part whatsoever of the territory of the other. These works shall be part of the territory and be the property of the country wherein they are situated. However, in the case of any incidents occurring on works constructed across the limitrophe part of a river and with supports on both banks, the jurisdiction of each country shall be limited by the center line of such works, which shall be marked by the Commission, without thereby changing the international boundary.

Each Government shall retain, through its own Section of the Commission and within the limits and to the extent necessary to effectuate the provisions of this Treaty, direct ownership, control and jurisdiction within its own territory and in accordance with its own laws, over all real property — including that within the channel of any river — rights of way and rights *in rem*, that it may be necessary to enter upon and occupy for the construction, operation or maintenance of all the works constructed, acquired or used pursuant to this Treaty. Furthermore, each Government shall similarly acquire and retain in its own possession the titles, control and jurisdiction over such works.

ARTICLE 24. The International Boundary and Water Commission shall have, in addition to the powers and duties otherwise specifically provided in this Treaty, the following powers and duties:

(*a*) To initiate and carry on investigations and develop plans for the works which are to be constructed or established in accordance with the provisions of this and other treaties or agreements in force between the two Governments dealing with boundaries and international waters; to determine, as to such works, their location, size, kind and characteristic specifications; to estimate the cost of such works; and to recommend the division of such costs between the two Governments, the arrangements for the furnishing of the necessary funds, and the dates for the beginning of the works, to the extent that the matters mentioned in this subparagraph are not otherwise covered by specific provisions of this or any other Treaty.

(*b*) To construct the works agreed upon or to supervise their construction and to operate and maintain such works or to supervise their operation and maintenance, in accordance with the respective domestic laws of each country. Each Section shall have, to the extent necessary to give effect to the provisions of this Treaty, jurisdiction over the works constructed exclusively in the territory of its country whenever such works shall be connected with or shall directly affect the execution of the provisions of this Treaty.

(*c*) In general to exercise and discharge the specific powers and duties entrusted to the Commission by this and other treaties and agreements in force between the two countries, and to carry into execution and prevent the violation of the provisions of those treaties and agreements. The authorities of each country shall aid and support the exercise and discharge of these powers and duties, and each Commissioner shall invoke when necessary the jurisdiction of the courts or other appropriate agencies of his country to aid in the execution and enforcement of these powers and duties.

(*d*) To settle all differences that may arise between the two Governments with respect to the interpretation or application of this Treaty, subject to the approval of the two Governments. In any case in which the Commissioners do not reach an agreement, they shall so inform their respective governments reporting their respective opinions and the grounds therefor and the points upon which they differ, for discussion and adjustment of the difference through diplomatic channels and for application where proper of the general or special agreements which the two Governments have concluded for the settlement of controversies.

(*e*) To furnish the information requested of the Commissioners jointly by the two Governments on matters within their jurisdiction. In the event that the request is made by one Government alone, the Commissioner of the other Government must have the express authorization of his Government in order to comply with such request.

(*f*) The Commission shall construct, operate and maintain upon the limitrophe parts of the international streams, and each Section shall severally construct, operate and maintain upon the parts of the international streams and their tributaries within the boundaries of its own country, such stream gaging stations as may be needed to provide the hydrographic data necessary or convenient for the proper functioning of this Treaty. The data so obtained shall be compiled and periodically exchanged between the two Sections.

(*g*) The Commission shall submit annually a joint report to the two Governments on the matters in its charge. The Commission shall also submit to the two Governments joint reports on general or any particular matters at such other times as it may deem necessary or as may be requested by the two Governments.

ARTICLE 25. Except as otherwise specifically provided in this Treaty Articles III and VII of the Convention of March 1, 1889 shall govern the proceedings of the Commission in carrying out the provisions of this Treaty. Supplementary thereto the Commission shall establish a body of rules and regulations to govern its procedure, consistent with the provisions of this Treaty and of Articles III and VII of the Convention of March 1, 1889 and subject to the approval of both Governments.

Decisions of the Commission shall be recorded in the form of Minutes done in duplicate in the English and Spanish languages, signed by each Commissioner and attested by the Secretaries, and copies thereof forwarded to each Government within three days after being signed. Except where the specific approval of the two Governments is required by any provision of this Treaty, if one of the Governments fails to communicate to the Commission its approval or disapproval of a decision of the Commission within thirty days reckoned from the date of the Minute in which it shall have been pronounced, the Minute in question and the decisions which it contains shall be considered to be approved by that Government.

The Commissioners, within the limits of their respective jurisdictions, shall execute the decisions of the Commission that are approved by both Governments.

If either Government disapproves a decision of the Commission the two Governments shall take cognizance of the matter, and if an agreement regarding such matter is reached between the two Governments, the agreement shall be communicated to the Commissioners, who shall take such further proceedings as may be necessary to carry out such agreement.

VI — TRANSITORY PROVISIONS

ARTICLE 26. During a period of eight years from the date of the entry into force of this Treaty, or until the beginning of operation of the lowest major international reservoir on the Rio Grande (Rio Bravo), should it be placed in operation prior to the expiration of said period, Mexico will cooperate with the United States to relieve, in times of drought, any lack of water needed to irrigate the lands now under irrigation in the Lower Rio Grande Valley in the United States, and for this purpose Mexico will release water from El Azúcar reservoir on the San Juan River and allow that water to run through its system of canals back into the San Juan River in order that the United States may divert such water from the Rio Grande (Rio Bravo). Such releases shall be made on condition that they do not affect the Mexican irrigation system, provided that Mexico shall, in any event, except in cases of extraordinary drought or serious accident to its hydraulic works, release and make available to the United States for its use the quantities requested, under the following conditions: that during the said eight years there shall be made available a total of 160,000 acre-feet (197,358,000 cubic meters) and up to 40,000 acre-feet (49,340,000 cubic meters) in any one year; that the water shall be made available as requested at rates not exceeding 750 cubic feet (21.2 cubic meters) per second; that when the rates of flow requested and made available have been more than 500 cubic feet (14.2 cubic meters) per second the period of release shall not extend beyond fifteen consecutive days; and that at least thirty days must elapse between any two periods of release during which rates of flow in excess of 500 cubic feet (14.2 cubic meters) per second have been requested and made available. In addition to the guaranteed flow, Mexico shall release from El Azúear reservoir and conduct through its canal system and the San Juan River, for use in the United States during periods of drought and after satisfying the needs of Mexican users, any excess water that does not in the opinion of the Mexican Section have to be stored and that may be needed for the irrigation of lands which were under irrigation during the year 1943 in the Lower Rio Grande Valley in the United States.

ARTICLE 27. The provisions of Articles 10, 11, and 15 of this Treaty shall not be applied during a period of five years from the date of the entry into force of this Treaty, or until the Davis dam and the major Mexican diversion structure on the Colorado River are placed in operation, should these works be placed in operation prior to the expiration of said period. In the meantime Mexico may construct and operate at its expense a temporary diversion structure in the bed of the Colorado River in territory of the United States for the purpose of diverting water into the Alamo Canal, provided that the plans for such structure and the construction and operation thereof shall be subject to the approval of the United States Section. During this period of time the United States will make available in the river at such diversion structure river flow not currently required in the United States, and the United States will cooperate with Mexico to the end that the latter may satisfy its irrigation requirements within the limits of those requirements for lands irrigated in Mexico from the Colorado River during the year 1943.

VII — FINAL PROVISIONS

ARTICLE 28. This Treaty shall be ratified and the ratifications thereof shall be exchanged in Washington. It shall enter into force on the day of the exchange of ratifications and shall continue in force until terminated by another Treaty concluded for that purpose between the two Governments.

In witness whereof the respective Plenipotentiaries have signed this Treaty and have hereunto affixed their seals.

Done in duplicate in the English and Spanish languages, in Washington on this third day of February, 1944.

FOR THE GOVERNMENT OF THE UNITED STATES OF AMERICA:

CORDELL HULL   [SEAL]
GEORGE S. MESSERSMITH [SEAL]
LAWRENCE M. LAWSON   [SEAL]

FOR THE GOVERNMENT OF THE UNITED MEXICAN STATES:

F. CASTILLO NÁJERA   [SEAL]
RAFAEL FERNÁNDEZ MACGREGOR   [SEAL]

2. RELATIONS WITH CANADA

A. Diplomatic Representation and Privileges

The Governments of Canada and the United States announced on November 11, 1943 that arrangements had been completed whereby the Legations of the two countries at Washington and Ottawa were elevated to the rank of Embassy, the change in status to become effective with respect to each Mission upon the presentation of a letter of credence of the Ambassador-designate. The Honorable Leighton McCarthy presented his letters of credence as the first Canadian Ambassador to the United States on January 12, 1944.[1]

[1] *Ibid.*, p. 75.

B. The Alaska Highway

In the months that followed Pearl Harbor, our ability to defend Alaska, particularly the shipping lanes of the Gulf of Alaska, against Japanese attack was uncertain. Failure to defend it would have resulted in the establishment of Japanese air and naval bases for operations against the western coast of the United States and against Pacific shipping. To strengthen our defense position in Alaska, the decision was taken to build the Alaska Highway [1] and the agreement of March 17 and 18, 1942, with the Canadian Government was made.[2] For text and background of this agreement, see *Documents, IV, 1941-42*, p. 443.

With the favorable turn in the Japanese war the original need of the Highway came to be partly forgotten, and the expense and doubtful future value of the Highway became the focus of attention.

On July 1, 1943, the Senate adopted a resolution (Sen. Res. 161) authorizing the Senate Committee on Post Offices and Post Roads to make "a full and complete study and investigation with respect to the construction and maintenance of the American-Canada Highway" and to report the results of such study. The subcommittee appointed for this purpose was also instructed to report on Senate 579, to authorize the construction of a military supply highway to Alaska. The report was made on November 19, 1943, and was favorable to the Highway as then constructed as "an emergency supply route to supplement the water route," but advised against the highway proposed in Senate 579.[3]

C. The Canol Project

The Canol Project, like the Alaska Highway, was undertaken in 1942[4] as an emergency defense project. It had seemed likely that Alaska would have to be defended largely by air power. The Alaska Highway was built in part to link up a system of airfields from the United States border through Canada to Alaska, and the Canol Project was developed to furnish fuel.[5] The Project was subsequently severely criticized on the grounds that it was undertaken without adequate consideration or study and that it should have been abandoned when the difficulties became obvious. The Truman Committee made an investigation of the matter and reported to the Senate that it was "definitely of the opinion that the Canol Project should not have been undertaken, and that it should have been abandoned when the difficulties were called to the attention of the War Department." [6]

A revision of the Canol Project was effected by an Exchange of Notes signed at Ottawa on June 7, 1944.[7] The Canadian Government agreed to the withdrawal of the United States from activities in the Northwest Territories having to do with the discovery and development of oil fields.

[1] By exchange of notes, dated July 19, 1943, the official name "Alaska Highway" was accepted by the American and Canadian Governments. *Executive Agreement Series* 331.

[2] *Ibid.*, 246.

[3] Senate Report No. 548, 78th Cong., 1st sess.

[4] Agreement between United States and Canada, effected by Exchange of Notes, June 27 and 29, 1942 (*Executive Agreement Series* 386); Agreement on Pipeline, August 14 and 15, 1942 (*ibid.* 387); Agreement on Exploratory Wells, December 28, 1942 and January 13, 1943 (*ibid.* 388); and Agreement on Project Areas, January 18, February 17 and March 13, 1943 (*ibid.* 389).

[5] Testimony of Under Secretary of War Patterson before the Truman Committee. *New York Times*, November 24, 1943.

[6] *Investigation of the National Defense Program.* Senate Report No. 10, Part 14, 78th Cong., 1st sess.

[7] *Executive Agreement Series* 416.

D. Status and Future Disposition of Defense Projects

(1) *Post-War Disposition of Defense Installations and Facilities. Agreement between the Governments of the United States and Canada, Effected by Exchange of Notes, January 27, 1943* [1]

(a) *The American Chargé d'Affaires ad interim in Canada (Clark) to the Canadian Secretary of State for External Affairs (Mackenzie King)*

SIR:

Under instructions from my Government, I have the honor to refer to conversations relating to the post-war disposition of various facilities being or to be constructed in Canada by the Government of the United States.

Although in many instances the Governments of the United States of America and of Canada have reached specific agreements covering the post-war disposition of defense projects and installations which, in order more effectively to prosecute the war, the Government of the United States, with the consent and approval of the Canadian Government, has built or is building in Canada, nevertheless there seemed advantage in defining certain general principles which in the absence of special circumstances should serve as a guide to the two Governments in formulating any future agreements covering the post-war disposition of such projects or installations in Canada. The same general princ:ples would of course apply reciprocally in the event of any project or installation being built by the Canadian Government in the United States territory.

The matter was referred to the Permanent Joint Board on Defense which after careful study adopted the following Recommendation on January 13, 1943.

The Board considered the question of the post-war disposition of the defense projects and installations which the Government of the United States has built or may build in Canada. The Board noted that the two Governments have already reached specific agreements for the post-war disposition of most of the projects and installations thus far undertaken. It considers that such agreements are desirable and should be made whenever possible.

The Board recommends the approval of the following formula as a generally fair and equitable basis to be used by reference whenever appropriate in the making of agreements in the future and to cover such defense projects, if any, the post-war disposition of which has not previously been specifically provided for:

A. All immovable defense installations built or provided in Canada by the Government of the United States shall within one year after the cessation of hostilities, unless otherwise agreed by the two Governments, be relinquished to the Crown either in the right of Canada or in the right of the province in which the same or any part thereof lies, as may be appropriate under Canadian law.

[1] *Executive Agreement Series* 391.

B. All movable facilities built or provided in Canada by the Government of the United States shall within one year after the cessation of hostilities, unless otherwise agreed by the two Governments, at the option of the United States Government:

    (1) be removed from Canada;

          or

    (2) be offered for sale to the Government of Canada, or with the approval of the Government of Canada, to the Government of the appropriate Province at a price to be fixed by a Board of two appraisers, one to be chosen by each country and with power to select a third in the case of disagreement.

C. In the event that the United States Government has foregone its option as described in *B* (1), and the Canadian Government or the Provincial Government decides to forego its option as described in *B* (2), the facility under consideration shall be offered for sale in the open market, any sale to be subject to the approval of both Governments.

D. In the event of no sale being concluded the disposition of such facility shall be referred for recommendation to the Permanent Joint Board on Defense or to such other agency as the two Governments may designate.

The principles outlined above shall reciprocally apply to any defense projects and installations which may be built in the United States by the Government of Canada.

All of the foregoing provisions relate to the physical disposition and ownership of projects, installations, and facilities and are without prejudice to any agreement or agreements which may be reached between the Governments of the United States and Canada in regard to the post-war use of any of these projects, installations, and facilities.

I have today been directed to inform you that this Recommendation has been approved by the Government of the United States of America, which would welcome confirmation from you that it has likewise been approved by the Government of Canada.

(b) *The Canadian Secretary of State for External Affairs (Mackenzie King) to the American Chargé d'Affaires ad interim in Canada (Clark)*

Sir:

I have the honor to acknowledge receipt of your note of January 27, 1943, No. 827, in which you referred to recent discussions relating to the post-war disposition of various defense projects, installations and facilities being or to be constructed in Canada by the Government of the United States with the consent and approval of the Government of Canada.

It is noted with satisfaction that the Government of the United States has approved the Twenty-Eighth Recommendation of the Permanent Joint Board on Defense which dealt with this matter and which read as follows:

[Text of Recommendation is omitted.[1]]

[1] See this volume, p. 574.

It gives me pleasure to inform you that the Canadian Government has also approved this Recommendation and has so informed the Permanent Joint Board on Defense.

(2) *Provincial and Municipal Taxation of United States Defense Projects in Canada. Agreement between the Governments of the United States and Canada, Effected by Exchange of Notes, August 6 and 9, 1943* [1]

(a) *The Canadian Secretary of State for External Affairs (Mackenzie King) to the American Minister to Canada (Atherton), August 6, 1943*

SIR,

I have the honor to refer to your note No. 859 of March 23rd [2] and to your subsequent note No. 902 of May 29th,[3] concerning the possibility of exempting from Provincial and municipal taxation the United States Government and United States contractors engaged on the Alaska Highway and other United States defense projects in Canada. The Canadian Government is anxious to reach a settlement of this question which is fair to all parties concerned and which is in keeping with the spirit of mutual helpfulness which has animated both Governments with regard to the defense projects.

2. In the view of the Canadian Government the United States Government itself cannot be effectively taxed by Provincial or municipal authorities. If in any instance an attempt is made by those authorities to tax the United States Government either in respect of real property which it owns or of which it is a lessee, or in respect of license fees on motor vehicles owned by the United States Government, the Canadian Government will intervene in the legal proceedings and request the Court to accord appropriate immunities. Should the Court hold, contrary to the expectations of the Canadian Government, that the United States Government is legally liable to pay such taxes or license fees, the Canadian Government will, as a contribution to the general costs of the defense projects, reimburse the United States Government for any Provincial or municipal taxes levied in respect of such projects which the United States Government has been held liable to pay and had paid.

3. In order to keep the record clear it might be well to point out that the Canadian Government does not consider that any exemption from municipal taxation would be appropriate in the case of owners of property who have leased it to the United States Government. In cases in which improvements have been made on property so leased, assessments will normally be made against the owner who is legally bound to pay the

[1] *Executive Agreement Series* 339.   [2] Not printed.   [3] *Ibid.*

taxes exactly as he would be if the lessee were the Canadian and not the United States Government.

4. United States contractors employed by the United States Government on its military projects in Canada are, of course, legally bound to pay whatever municipal taxes may be assessed against them as owners or lease-holders of property and whatever municipal fees may be charged for building permits in connection with these lands. The Canadian Government will undertake to refund to the United States Government any amounts which that Government may pay to United States contractors in respect of this taxation. Any such payments made by the Canadian Government will form part of its contribution to the cost of the defense projects.

5. The Canadian Government will also reimburse the United States Government for any payments which it may have to make to United States contractors in respect of license fees for motor vehicles employed on the United States defense projects in Canada. Any such payments made by the Canadian Government will form part of its contribution to the cost of the defense projects.

6. The Governments of the Provinces in which United States projects are being executed will be requested by the Government of Canada not to impose license fees on non-military drivers of trucks belonging to the United States Army and not to levy head or poll taxes upon non-military personnel normally resident in the United States which is engaged on United States military projects in Canada. It appears that in the Province of Alberta the poll tax is devoted to educational purposes and the exemption of United States non-military personnel from this tax will carry with it a liability to pay school fees should any of the United States personnel wish to send their children to public schools in the Province.

7. I should be glad to receive your assurance that these proposals for dealing with the problem of the burden of Provincial and municipal taxation on United States defense projects in Canada will meet the wishes of the United States Government.

Accept, Sir, the renewed assurances of my highest consideration.

N. A. ROBERTSON
for Secretary of State for External Affairs.

(b) *The American Minister to Canada (Atherton) to the Canadian Secretary of State for External Affairs (Mackenzie King), August 9, 1943*

SIR:

I have the honor to acknowledge the receipt of your note No. 91 of August 6, 1943, concerning Provincial and municipal taxation levied upon the United States Government, the United States contractors engaged on the Alaska Highway, and other United States defense projects in Canada, and to confirm that the proposals outlined in your note for dealing with the problem meet with the wishes of the United States Government.

E. Waiver of Claims

(1) *Waiver of Claims Arising as a Result of Collisions between Vessels of War. Agreement between the Governments of the United States and Canada Concerning Application of the Agreement of May 25 and 26, 1943, Effected by Exchange of Notes, September 3 and November 11, 1943* [1]

(a) *The Secretary of State (Hull) to the Canadian Minister Counselor, Chargé d'Affaires ad interim in Washington (Pearson), September 3, 1943*

SIR:

I refer to my note dated May 25, 1943 to the Minister and to the Minister's note dated May 26, 1943,[2] effecting an agreement between the United States and Canada for the waiver of claims arising as a result of collisions between United States warships and ships of the Royal Canadian Navy.

I have received from the Secretary of War a letter in which inquiry is made whether "ships of the United States and Royal Canadian Armies, such as Army transports" are within the agreement.

I should appreciate receiving an indication of the attitude of the Canadian Government in respect of this matter.

Article I of the agreement effected by my note of May 25, 1943 and the Minister's reply note of May 26, 1943 reads as follows:

The Government of the United States of America and the Government of Canada agree that when a vessel of war of either Government shall collide with a vessel of war of the other Government, resulting in damage to either or both of such vessels, each Government shall bear all the expenses which arise directly or indirectly from the damage to its own vessel, and neither Government shall make any claim against the other Government on account of such damage or expenses.

(b) *The Canadian Minister in Washington (McCarthy) to the Secretary of State (Hull), November 11, 1943*

SIR,

I have the honor to refer to your note of September 3, 1943, regarding the agreement between Canada and the United States for the waiver of claims arising as a result of collisions between Canadian and United States vessels of war.

----

[1] *Executive Agreement Series* 366.
[2] *Ibid.*, 330, 57 Stat. 1021.

You stated in your note that the Secretary of War has enquired whether "ships of the United States and Royal Canadian Armies, such as Army transports" are within the agreement. This question has been carefully considered by the appropriate authorities of the Canadian Government, who are of the opinion that such ships are not within the agreement.

In connection with this opinion, reference is made to the opening sentence of your note of May 25, 1943, in which it was stated that the purpose of the proposed agreement was to provide for the question of damages "arising from collisions between United States warships and ships of the Royal Canadian Navy."

Accept, Sir, the renewed assurances of my highest consideration.

M. M. Mahoney
for the Minister.

F. Transport and Communications

(1) *Agreement between the Governments of the United States and Canada Regarding the Construction and Operation of Radio Broadcasting Stations in Northwestern Canada, Effected by Exchange of Notes, November 5 and 25, 1943, and January 7, 1944* [1]

(a) *The American Chargé d'Affaires ad interim in Canada (Clark) to the Canadian Under Secretary of State for External Affairs (Robertson), November 5, 1943*

Dear Mr. Robertson:

I understand that the Northwest Service Command, United States Army, feels a need for small broadcasting stations at several isolated garrisons in the Northwest Command. These stations would be similar to those established at various posts in Alaska and in the United Kingdom which are supplied with non-commercial entertainment program material by the Special Service Division, Army Service Forces.

Although there would be no aspect of competition with the Canadian Broadcasting System due to the isolated locations, a special problem has arisen in complying with Canadian laws and policies. As the stations would be operated by military personnel under the direct control of the local commanding officer, effective supervision of the operation could be exercised only through military channels. In order to ensure compliance with Canadian laws and to assure that the stations would be operated in such a manner as to serve the local populace in strict accordance with the desires of the appropriate Canadian authorities, a proposed draft of authorization which would be issued by the Secretary

[1] Department of State, *Bulletin*, X, p. 139.

of War if the Canadian Government were to approve the proposal, is enclosed herewith. I have been directed to bring this matter to your attention with the request that the Canadian Government approve the installations as outlined in the enclosure hereto. At the same time I have been directed to say that any stations placed in operation under the authority, if granted, would be closed at any time on the request of the Canadian Government and, in any event, upon the removal of the garrison or the establishment of regular broadcasting facilities. In addition, the United States War Department has said that it would be immediately responsive to the desires of the Canadian Government in any questions arising out of the operation of the proposed stations.

I understand informally that this desire of the Northwest Service Command has been made known to you through Brigadier General W. W. Foster, and that the War Committee of the Cabinet has approved it in principle. If there is any further information you desire in order to reach a final decision in this matter, I should appreciate being informed.

[Enclosure]

Subject: Military Radio Broadcasting Stations
To: Commanding General
           Northwest Service Command
           c/o Postmaster
           Seattle, Washington.

1. Reference is made to your letter of 28 September 1943, addressed to the Special Service Division, Information Branch, Radio Section, Los Angeles, California, subject: "Military Radio Broadcasting Stations." [1] With the consent and during the pleasure of the Canadian Government, you are authorized to establish armed forces radio broadcasting stations at Whitehorse, Fort Nelson, Watson Lake, Simpson, Norman Wells, and Northway.

2. The operation of these radio broadcasting stations will be subject to the following conditions:

(*a*) All applicable provisions of the Canadian Broadcasting Act of 1936, the Radio Act of 1938, and regulations made thereunder shall be observed.

(*b*) Program material will be restricted to transcriptions prepared for armed forces of the United Nations by the Special Service Division, Army Service Forces, local talent programs of a strictly entertainment character, and such Canadian programs as may be made available by Canadian Government agencies.

(*c*) Every assistance will be rendered Canadian Government authorities in the provision of wire circuits and other facilities which may be required for the delivery of news or other programs desired by them.

(*d*) A diligent and continuing survey of public reaction to programs will be maintained to the end that no criticism of any character will be permitted to develop.

(*e*) The local commanding officer will be held strictly accountable for the exercise of good taste and propriety in the selection of program material and for

---

[1] Not printed.

the complete avoidance of commercialism, sectarianism, and editorializing on political or controversial subjects.

3. Technical details such as power and the choice of frequency, etc. will be arranged through the direct channel established between the Controller of Radio, Ministry of Transport and the Office of the Chief Signal Officer in the same manner as for all other Army radio facilities in Canada.

By order of the Secretary of War.

(b) The Canadian Under Secretary of State for External Affairs (Robertson) to the American Minister to Canada (Atherton), November 25, 1943

DEAR MR. ATHERTON:

I should like to refer to Mr. Clark's letter of November 5, 1943, in which permission is requested by the United States Government to construct and operate certain radio broadcasting stations in Northwestern Canada.

I am pleased to inform you that the Canadian Government agrees to the construction and operation, by the Government of the United States, of radio broadcasting stations at Whitehorse, Watson Lake, Fort Nelson, Simpson and Norman Wells, subject to the following conditions:

(1) that the stations will be operated directly by the United States Government, and for the sole purpose of bringing entertainment and information to United States and Canadian military and civilian personnel;

(2) that the radio stations will be subject to the provisions of the Canadian Broadcasting Act, 1936, the Radio Act, 1938, the Regulations made under these Acts, and to all other applicable laws and regulations in force in Canada; provided that no fee or tax shall be paid by the United States Government to the Canadian Government in connection with the operation of these stations;

(3) that each station will be operated in accordance with the terms of an annual renewable permit to be issued by the Department of Transport;

(4) that authorization for the operation by the United States Government of the stations may be cancelled at any time by the Canadian Government, and in any case such authorization for operation shall cease with the termination of the war;

(5) that the stations may be used for the broadcasting of Canadian programs and in particular of Canadian news programs, it being understood that the amount of time to be set aside for Canadian programs will be subject to agreement between the Special Commissioner for Defense Projects in the Northwest,

and the Commanding Officer of the United States Northwest Service Command;

(6) that the United States Government will make available to the Canadian Government its wire services for the transmission of Canadian news and Canadian programs to the stations;

(7) that the sites, frequencies, power, call letters and other technical details concerning the stations shall be subject to the approval of the Department of Transport and shall be arranged directly through the channel already established between the Controller of Radio of the Department of Transport, Ottawa, and the office of the Chief Signal Officer, Washington, in the same manner as for all other radio facilities of the United States Armed Forces in Canada. Any or all necessary changes in the foregoing particulars shall be dealt with through the same channel;

(8) that the stations will be dealt with after the war in accordance with the exchange of notes of January 27, 1943, between Canada and the United States, covering post-war disposition of United States defense facilities in Canada.[1]

(9) that any land or leasehold required by the United States Government as sites for the stations shall be acquired by the Canadian Government in its name, and shall be made available to the United States Government without charge.

I trust that the foregoing arrangements will be acceptable to the United States Government.

(c) *The American Chargé d'Affaires ad interim in Canada* (Clark) *to the Canadian Under Secretary of State for External Affairs* (Robertson), *January 17, 1944*

DEAR MR. ROBERTSON:

Your letter of November 25, 1943 granting, under certain conditions, our request to construct and operate radio broadcasting stations in Northwestern Canada was forwarded immediately to Washington.

We have now been authorized to say that the stipulations made by the Canadian Government are acceptable to the United States War Department.

(2) *Operation of Pan-American Airways Over British Columbia. Department of State Release, April 1, 1944* [2]

An agreement has been effected between the Government of the United States and the Government of Canada, by an exchange of notes at Ottawa dated June 12, 1943 and January 26, 1944, whereby Canada grants permission to the

---

[1] See this volume, p. 574.
[2] Department of State, *Bulletin*, X, p. 306.

Pan-American Airways system to operate, for a period of six months from January 26, 1944, over British Columbia and to stop at Prince George for refueling while en route between Seattle, Wash., and Juneau, Alaska. The authorization granted under the present agreement and any renewal thereof in no way commits the Canadian Government with respect to post-war commercial aviation policy.

G. Water Utilization

(1) *Temporary Raising of Level of Lake St. Francis During Low Water Periods. Agreement between the Governments of the United States and Canada, Continuing in Effect the Agreement of November 10, 1941 as Continued by the Agreement of October 5 and 9, 1942, Effected by Exchange of Notes, October 5 and 9, 1943* [1]

(a) *The Canadian Minister in Washington (McCarthy) to the Secretary of State (Hull), October 5, 1943*

Sir:

I have the honor, on the instructions of my Government, to refer to the exchange of notes of November 10th, 1941,[2] whereby the Government of the United States of America agreed to a temporary raising of the levels of Lake St. Francis during low water periods for the reasons and subject to the conditions and limitations set forth in the Notes. By an exchange of notes of October 5th and 9th, 1942,[3] the arrangements made on November 10th, 1941 were continued until October 1st, 1943.

The circumstances which led the Government of the United States to agree to the temporary raising of the levels of Lake St. Francis have continued and, in view of the importance to both Canada and the United States of America of the conservation of the power supply in this area, the Canadian Government proposes that the arrangements set forth in the exchange of Notes should be continued until October 1st, 1944. The arrangements as continued would, of course, be subject to all of the conditions and limitations as contained in the exchange of Notes of November 10th, 1941.

Accept, Sir, the renewed assurance of my highest consideration.

L. B. Pearson
For the Minister.

(b) *The Secretary of State (Hull) to the Canadian Minister in Washington (McCarthy), October 9, 1943*

Sir:

I have the honor to acknowledge the receipt of your note of October 5, 1943 concerning the arrangements effected through an exchange of notes on November 10, 1941 with respect to a temporary raising of the levels of Lake St. Francis during low water periods and to inform you

---

[1] *Executive Agreement Series* 377.   [2] *Ibid.,* 291; 56 Stat. 1832.   [3] *Ibid.*

that this Government is agreeable to your Government's proposal that these arrangements should be continued until October 1, 1944 subject, of course, to all of the conditions and limitations contained in the Notes exchanged on November 10, 1941.

Accept, Sir, the renewed assurances of my highest consideration.

For the Secretary of State:

A. A. BERLE, JR.

(2) *Upper Columbia River Basin. Agreement between the Governments of the United States and Canada, Effected by Exchange of Notes, February 25 and March 3, 1944* [1]

(a) *The American Ambassador to Canada (Atherton) to the Canadian Secretary of State for External Affairs (Mackenzie King), February 25, 1944*

SIR:

I have the honor to refer to your note No. 157 of December 10, 1943,[2] concerning the desirability of having a study made by the International Joint Commission with respect to the Upper Columbia River Basin from the points of view of navigation, power development, irrigation, flood control, and other beneficial public uses and purposes.

As the result of informal exchanges of views on this subject I have been directed to bring the following suggested reference to the Commission to your attention with the request that I be informed whether it is acceptable to the Government of Canada:

1. In order to determine whether a greater use than is now being made of the waters of the Columbia River system would be feasible and advantageous, the Governments of the United States and Canada have agreed to refer the matter to the International Joint Commission for investigation and report pursuant to Article IX of the Convention concerning Boundary Waters between the United States and Canada, signed January 11th, 1909.[3]

2. It is desired that the Commission shall determine whether in its judgment further development of the water resources of the river basin would be practicable and in the public interest from the points of view of the two Governments, having in mind (A) domestic water supply and sanitation, (B) navigation, (C) efficient development of water power, (D) the control of floods, (E) the needs of irrigation, (F) reclamation of wet lands, (G) conservation of fish and wildlife, and (H) other beneficial public purposes.

3. In the event that the Commission should find that further works or projects would be feasible and desirable for one or more of the purposes indicated above, it should indicate how the interests on either side of the boundary would be benefited or adversely affected thereby, and should estimate the costs of such works or projects, including indemnification for damage to public and private property and the costs of any remedial works that may be found to be

[1] Department of State, *Bulletin*, X, p. 270, 271.
[2] Not printed.
[3] *Treaties, Conventions, etc. 1910–1923*, III, p. 2607.

necessary, and should indicate how the costs of any projects and the amounts of any resulting damage should be apportioned between the two Governments.

4. The Commission should also investigate and report on existing dams, hydroelectric plants, navigation works, and other works or projects located within the Columbia River system in so far as such investigation and report may be germane to the subject under consideration.

5. In the conduct of its investigation and otherwise in the performance of its duties under this reference, the Commission may utilize the services of engineers and other specially qualified personnel of the technical agencies of Canada and the United States and will so far as possible make use of information and technical data heretofore acquired by such technical agencies or which may become available during the course of the investigation, thus avoiding duplication of effort and unnecessary expense.

If the proposed reference is acceptable to your Government I should appreciate being informed, and this note together with your reply would be regarded as an agreement between our two Governments on the terms of reference.

(b) *The Canadian Secretary of State for External Affairs (Mackenzie King) to the American Ambassador to Canada (Atherton), March 3, 1944*

EXCELLENCY:

I have the honor to refer to your note No. 101 dated February 25, 1944, in which you brought to the attention of the Canadian Government the terms of a reference to the International Joint Commission with respect to the Upper Columbia River Basin.

The proposed reference is acceptable to the Canadian Government and your note, together with this reply, may be regarded as an agreement between our two Governments on the terms of reference.

Accept [etc.]

N. A. ROBERTSON
for Secretary of State
for External Affairs.

An arrangement between the United States and Canada providing for an additional emergency diversion for power purposes of waters of the Niagara River above the Falls was entered into, subject to approval by the Senate, by an exchange of notes dated May 3, 1944 between the Secretary of State and the Canadian Ambassador in Washington.[1]

This arrangement, which supplemented the arrangement effected by an exchange of notes of May 20, 1941 (*Executive Agreement Series* 209) and the supplementary arrangement effected by exchange of notes dated October 27 and November 27, 1941 (*Executive Agreement Series* 223), amended in its application Article V of the treaty of January 11, 1909 between the United States and His Britannic Majesty relating to the boundary between the United States and Canada (*Treaty Series* 548),[2] to permit, for the duration of the emergency unless terminated earlier by agreement, an additional diversion of the waters of the Niagara River above the Falls.

[1] Department of State, *Bulletin*, X, p. 455.
[2] *Treaties, Conventions, etc., 1910–1923*, III, p. 2607.

H. Protection of Fur Seals

The convention of 1911 between the United States and other powers providing for the preservation and protection of fur seals was signed at Washington on July 7, 1911, by plenipotentiaries representing the President of the United States, His Britannic Majesty, His Majesty the Emperor of Japan, and His Majesty the Emperor of all the Russias. Ratification was advised by the United States Senate, July 24, 1911, followed by ratification by Great Britain, Russia, and Japan. The President of the United States ratified the convention on November 24, 1911, and proclaimed it on December 14, 1911 (37 Stat. 1542).[1]

The essential provisions of the convention were as follows:

1. Pelagic sealing in the North Pacific Ocean was prohibited, and general procedures for apprehending and dealing with violators were established.

2. The use of ports of the contracting parties for operations connected with pelagic sealing was prohibited.

3. The landing of sealskins unlawfully taken was not permitted.

4. Indians, Ainos, Aleuts, and other aborigines were exempted, with certain limitations, from the prohibitions of the convention.

5. The killing of sea otters in waters more than 3 miles from the shore was prohibited.

6. The contracting parties agreed to enact and enforce legislation to make the convention effective.

7. A guard or a patrol was to be maintained in waters frequented by seal herds.

8. Mutual cooperation to prevent pelagic sealing was pledged.

9. The United States agreed to deliver to Japan 15 percent, and to the Canadian Government 15 percent, of the gross number and value of sealskins taken on the Pribilof Islands.

10. The United States was to make advance cash payments of $200,000 to Great Britain and $200,000 to Japan, in lieu of the number of fur-seal skins to which they would be entitled during the first several years after the entry into force of the convention, and a minimum share of the take of sealskins was allocated to Britain and Japan.

11. Russia agreed to deliver to Canada 15 percent and to Japan 15 percent of the sealskins taken on the Commander Islands.

12. Japan agreed to deliver to the United States 10 percent, to Canada 10 percent, and to Russia 10 percent of the sealskins taken on Robben Island.

13. Great Britain agreed that in case seals resorted to any islands or shores subject to her jurisdiction in the North Pacific Ocean she should deliver to the United States 10 percent, to Japan 10 percent, and to Russia 10 percent of the total number of skins taken.

14. The duration of the convention was specified as 15 years and was to continue thereafter until terminated by 12 months' notice given by one or more of the parties.

As a result of the notice of abrogation given by the Japanese Government on October 23, 1940, the convention terminated in October 1941. Upon receipt of the Japanese notice of abrogation steps were taken immediately by the United States with a view to the conclusion of a new agreement with the countries concerned, and efforts were being made in that direction at the time Japan declared war upon the United States.

It was then determined by representatives of the Department of State, after consultation with representatives of the Department of the Interior, as well as with appropriate officials of the Canadian Government, that a temporary arrangement should be made for the purpose of protecting the rights and interests of Canada and the United States in the fur-seal resources of the North Pacific Ocean and in the fur-seal herds on the Pribilof Islands. Accordingly, a provisional agreement was concluded between the United States and Canada by an exchange

[1] *Ibid.*, p. 2966.

of notes between the Secretary of State and the Canadian Minister in Washington, dated December 8 and 19, 1942. In general, and in so far as applicable to the circumstances that arose because of the Japanese abrogation of the 1911 convention, the provisions of that convention were incorporated in the new agreement with Canada.

This historical account has been taken from the Report of the House Committee on the Merchant Marine and Fisheries on H. R. 2924 [1] to Give Effect to the Provisional Furs Seal Agreement, with only minor changes of phraseology.

(1) *Provisional Fur-Seal Agreement Between the United States and Canada, Effected by Exchange of Notes, December 8 and 19, 1942* [2]

(a) *The Secretary of State (Hull) to the Canadian Minister in Washington (McCarthy), December 8, 1942*

SIR:

I have the honor to refer to the conversation on August 12, 1942, between Mr. Merchant M. Mahoney, counselor of the Canadian Legation, and an officer of the Department when Mr. Mahoney left an informal memorandum dated August 10, 1942, in which it is stated that the terms of the Department's note, dated May 7, 1942, and the proposed provisional fur-seal agreement between the United States and Canada contained therein are generally acceptable to the Canadian authorities, but that the Canadian Department of Fisheries desires an interpretation of certain specific points.

The first of the points on which an interpretation is desired relates to the basis for the suggestion made by this Government that the Canadian share of the fur sealskins taken annually on the Pribilof Islands be increased to 20 percent by adding to the 15 percent heretofore received by Canada under the fur-seal convention concluded on July 7, 1911, between the United States, Great Britain, Japan, and Russia, a part of the share formerly received by Japan under that convention. With regard to this I am pleased to say that, in accordance with conversations between representatives of our two Governments, this Government's proposal that the Canadian share of the fur sealskins be increased to 20 percent is in recognition of the principles underlying the fur-seal convention of July 7, 1911, and the cooperation of the Canadian Government in scientific arrangements for the conservation of the fur-seal herd. This figure is calculated with reference to the pro rata share heretofore received by Canada and to Canada's established interest in the fur-seal resources, and is intended to be provisional only for the purposes of the present agreement.

With reference to the second point mentioned in the Legation's memorandum, I have to say that no objection is perceived to the deletion

[1] House Report No. 746, 78th Cong., 1st sess.
[2] *Ibid.*, p. 14.

of the word "North" as used in the expression "North Pacific Ocean" in Article I of the text of the agreement as proposed in the Department's note of May 7, 1942.

No objection is perceived to the suggestion, made under the third point in the Legation's memorandum, that consultations between the two Governments from time to time regarding the level of population of the herd, provided for by Article VIII of the proposed agreement, shall also include other important phases of management or policy relating to the herd.

Likewise, no objection is perceived to the suggestions, made under the fourth point in the Legation's memorandum, that the agreement shall be retroactive for the 1942 season; also that it shall remain in effect for 12 months after the end of the present emergency unless either Government enacts legislation contrary to its provisions or until 12 months after either Government shall have notified the other Government of an intention of terminating the agreement.

With particular reference to the text of the proposed agreement it is understood, from conversations between representatives of our two Governments, that as far as practicable the provisions of the fur-seal convention of July 7, 1911, should be incorporated in the agreement together with the following principal changes and additions:

(1) An increase in the Canadian share of the fur sealskins taken annually on the Pribilof Islands from 15 percent to 20 percent.

(2) A provision in the agreement for pelagic sealing under emergency circumstances. It is the view of the Government of the United States that the details regarding the conditions under which pelagic sealing might be conducted and the sharing of the sealskins taken by pelagic sealing should be the subject of consultation between the two Governments in the event circumstances indicate that pelagic sealing should be resorted to in order to utilize effectively the fur-seal herd.

(3) A provision permitting the issuance of permits for the taking of fur seals for purposes of scientific research and the exchange of information obtained by such research.

(4) A provision that the two Governments consult from time to time regarding the level of population at which the seal herd is to be maintained or other important phases of management or policy.

In the light of these considerations, the Government of the United States is prepared to enter into a provisional fur-seal agreement with the Government of Canada in the following terms which embody the suggestions made by representatives of the Canadian Government:

ARTICLE I. The provisions of this Agreement shall apply to all waters of the Bering Sea and the Pacific Ocean, north of the thirtieth parallel of north latitude and east of the one hundred and eightieth meridian.

ARTICLE II. The Government of the United States of America and the Government of Canada mutually and reciprocally agree that —

(*a*) Excepting as may be authorized pursuant to paragraph (*c*) of this Article, nationals or citizens of the respective countries, and all persons and vessels subject to their laws and treaties shall be prohibited, while this Agreement remains in force, from engaging in pelagic sealing in the waters within the area defined in Article I, and that every such person and vessel offending against such prohibition may be seized, except within the territorial jurisdiction of the other Party to this Agreement, and detained by the naval or other duly commissioned officers of either of the Parties, to be delivered as soon as practicable to an authorized official of their own nation at the nearest point to the place of seizure, or elsewhere as may be mutually agreed upon; and that the authorities of the nation to which such person or vessel belongs alone shall have jurisdiction to try the offense, and impose the penalties for the same; and that the witnesses and proofs necessary to establish the offense, so far as they are under the control of either of the Parties to this Agreement, shall be furnished with all reasonable promptness to the authorities having jurisdiction to try the offense;

(*b*) No person or vessel shall be permitted to use any of the ports or harbors of either of the Parties to this Agreement or any part of the territories of such Parties for any purposes connected with the operation of pelagic sealing in the waters within the area defined in Article I; and the importation into or possession within their respective territories of skins of fur seals taken in those waters other than in accord with the provisions of this Agreement shall not be permitted; and

(*c*) Notwithstanding the foregoing provisions, pelagic sealing may be conducted, in the event of emergency circumstances, by an agency or agencies authorized by either of the two Governments under such conditions and for such a period as may be agreed upon by consultation between the two Governments, and the skins thus taken shall be shared in such a manner as may be agreed upon between them.

ARTICLE III. The United States agrees that of the total number of sealskins taken annually under the authority of the United States upon the Pribilof Islands or any other islands or shores of the waters defined in Article I subject to the jurisdiction of the United States to which any seal herds hereafter resort, there shall be delivered at the Pribilof Islands or at such other point or points as may be acceptable to both Governments, at the end of each season during the term of this Agreement 20 percent gross in number and value thereof to an authorized agent of the Canadian Government.

ARTICLE IV. It is agreed on the part of Canada that in case any fur seals hereafter resort to any islands or shores of the waters defined in Article I subject to the jurisdiction of Canada, there shall be delivered at the end of each season during the term of this Agreement 20 percent gross in number and value of the total number of sealskins taken annually from such herd to an authorized agent of the Government of the United

States of America at Vancouver, British Columbia, or at such other point or points as may be acceptable to both Governments.

ARTICLE V. The provisions of this Agreement shall not apply to Indians, Aleuts, or other aborigines dwelling on the coasts of the waters defined in Article I, who carry on pelagic sealing in canoes not transported by or used in connection with other vessels, and propelled entirely by oars, paddles, or sails, and manned by not more than five persons each, in the way hitherto practiced, and without the use of firearms; provided that such aborigines are not in the employment of other persons or under contract to deliver the skins to any person.

ARTICLE VI. The term "pelagic sealing" is hereby defined for the purposes of this Agreement as meaning the killing, capturing, or pursuing in any manner whatsoever of fur seals at sea.

ARTICLE VII. Notwithstanding anything contained in the preceding Articles of the present Agreement, either Party to this Agreement may grant to any of its nationals or agencies a special permit to take fur seals for purposes of scientific research subject to such restrictions as to number and subject to such other conditions as the Party deems appropriate. Each Party shall at the end of each calendar year inform the other Party of the number of animals taken and the data obtained under such permits.

ARTICLE VIII. Nothing contained in the present Agreement shall restrict the right of the United States at any time to suspend altogether the taking of sealskins upon the Pribilof Islands or any other islands or shores of the waters defined in Article I subject to its jurisdiction, or the right of the United States to impose such restrictions and regulations upon the total number of skins which may be taken in any season and the manner and times and places of taking skins as may seem necessary to protect and preserve the seal herd or to increase its numbers, provided, however, that the two Governments will consult from time to time regarding the level of population at which the seal herd is to be maintained or other important phases of management or policy.

ARTICLE IX. Each of the Parties agrees to enact and enforce such legislation as may be necessary to make effective the foregoing provisions with appropriate penalties for violations thereof.

The Parties further agree to cooperate with each other in taking such measures as may be appropriate for the enforcement of the foregoing provisions.

ARTICLE X. This Agreement shall enter into force on the day the President of the United States of America approves legislation enacted by the Congress of the United States for its enforcement, and the day the Government of Canada issues an Order in Council applying the provisions of the Agreement, or should the President's approval of the legislation and the issuance of the Order in Council be on different days, on the date of the later in time of such approval by the President or issuance of such Order in Council. When this Agreement shall have entered into force it shall be deemed to have been in effect as from June 1, 1942. The Agreement shall remain in effect for the duration of the present emergency and twelve months thereafter unless either the Government of the United States of America or the Government of Canada enacts legislation contrary to its provisions or until twelve months after either Government shall have notified the other Government of an intention of terminating the Agreement.

If the foregoing is acceptable to the Government of Canada, this note and your reply thereto will be regarded as placing on record the provisional agreement of the Government of the United States of America and the Government of Canada for the protection, preservation, and utilization of the fur-seal herd of the Pribilof Islands.

(b) *The Canadian Minister in Washington (McCarthy) to the Secretary of State (Hull), December 19, 1942*

SIR:

I have the honor to acknowledge the receipt of your note of December 8, 1942, setting forth the terms of the provisional fur-seal agreement which the Government of the United States is prepared to enter into with the Government of Canada.

Under instructions from my Government, I hereby advise you that the Government of Canada accepts the proposals of the Government of the United States contained in your note, and in particular the provisional agreement.

Accept, [etc.].

(2) *An Act to Give Effect to the Provisional Fur-Seal Agreement of 1942 Between the United States and Canada to Protect the Fur Seals of the Pribilof Islands, and for Other Purposes, Approved February 26, 1944* [1]

Be it enacted by the Senate and House of Representatives of the United States of America in Congress assembled, That when used in this Act —

(a) "Pelagic sealing" means the killing, capturing, or pursuing, or the attempted killing, capturing, or pursuing of fur seals at sea, whether within or without the territorial waters of the United States.

(b) "Sealing" means the killing, capturing, or pursuing, or the attempted killing, capturing, or pursuing, of fur seals in or on any lands or waters subject to the jurisdiction of the United States.

(c) "Sea otter hunting" means the killing, capturing, or pursuing, or the attempted killing, capturing, or pursuing, of sea otters at sea,

---

[1] *Public Law* 237, 78th Cong.

except in waters subject to the jurisdiction of the United States where other laws are applicable.

(*d*) "Person" includes individual, association, partnership, and corporation.

(*e*) "Secretary" means the Secretary of the Interior.

(*f*) "Fur-seal agreement" means the provisional fur-seal agreement between the United States and Canada effected by an exchange of notes signed at Washington on December 8, 1942, and on December 19, 1942, and any other treaty, convention or other agreement hereafter entered into by the United States for the protection of fur seals.

(*g*) "North Pacific Ocean" includes the Bering Sea.

(*h*) "Import" means land on or bring into, or attempt to land on or bring into, any place subject to the jurisdiction of the United States.

SEC. 2. It shall be unlawful, except as hereinafter provided, for any citizen or national of the United States, or person owing duty of obedience to the laws or treaties of the United States, or any vessel of the United States, or person belonging to or on such vessel, to engage in pelagic sealing or sea otter hunting in or on the waters of the North Pacific Ocean; or for any person or vessel to engage in sealing; or for any person or vessel to use any port or harbor or other place subject to the jurisdiction of the United States for any purpose connected in any way with the operation of pelagic sealing, sea otter hunting, or sealing; or for any person to transport, import, offer for sale, or have in possession at any port, place, or on any vessel subject to the jurisdiction of the United States, raw, dressed, or dyed skins of sea otters taken contrary to the provisions of this section or, where taken pursuant to section 3 of this Act, not officially marked and certified as having been so taken, or raw, dressed, or dyed skins of fur seals taken in or on the waters of the North Pacific Ocean or on lands subject to the jurisdiction of the United States, except sealskins which have been taken under the authority of this Act or under the authority of the respective parties to any fur-seal agreement and which have been officially marked and certified as having been so taken.

SEC. 3. Indians, Aleuts, or other aborigines dwelling on the American coasts of the waters of the North Pacific Ocean shall be permitted to carry on pelagic sealing or sea otter hunting without the use of firearms from canoes or undecked boats, propelled wholly by paddles, oars, or sails, and not transported by or used in connection with other vessels, and manned by not more than five persons each, in the way heretofore practiced by said Indians, Aleuts, or other aborigines, and shall be permitted to dispose of the skins of fur seals or sea otters so taken as they see fit, but only after such skins have been officially marked and certified as provided in section 2 of this Act. The exception made in this section shall not apply to Indians, Aleuts, or other aborigines in the employment of other persons or who shall engage in pelagic sealing or sea otter hunting under contract to deliver the skins to any person.

Sec. 4. In order to continue the proper utilization of the fur-seal herd of the North Pacific Ocean and to carry out the purposes of this Act, the Secretary is authorized to permit sealing on the Pribilof and other islands and on the shores of waters subject to the jurisdiction of the United States, by officers and employees of the Fish and Wildlife Service designated by him and by the natives of the Territory of Alaska, and to adopt suitable regulations governing the same whenever he shall determine that such sealing is necessary or desirable and not inconsistent with preservation of the fur seals of the North Pacific Ocean. The Secretary is also authorized to permit pelagic sealing in the event of emergency circumstances by officers, employees and agents of the United States and by the natives of the Territory of Alaska under such conditions and for such periods as may be agreed upon by consultation between the Government of the United States and the Government of Canada in accordance with the provisions of Article II of the Provisional Fur-Seal Agreement of 1942.

Sec. 5. Subject to the provisions of sections 3 and 15 of this Act, all seal or sea-otter skins taken under the authority conferred by this Act, or forfeited to the United States, and all sealskins delivered to the United States pursuant to the terms of any fur-seal agreement shall be sold under the direction of the Secretary in such market, at such times, and in such manner as he may deem most advantageous; and the proceeds of such sale shall be paid into the Treasury of the United States.

Sec. 6. The Pribilof Islands, including the islands of Saint Paul and Saint George, Walrus and Otter Islands, and Sea Lion Rock, in Alaska, are declared a special reservation for Government purposes. It shall be unlawful for any person other than natives of the said islands and officers and employees of the Fish and Wildlife Service to land or remain on any of those islands, except through stress of weather or like unavoidable cause or by the authority of the Secretary, and any person found on any of those islands contrary to the provisions of this section shall be summarily removed and shall be deemed guilty of a misdemeanor, punishable by a fine not exceeding $500 or by imprisonment not exceeding six months, or by both fine and imprisonment.

Sec. 7. Whenever seals are killed and sealskins taken on any of the Pribilof Islands, the native inhabitants of the islands shall be employed in such killing and in curing the skins taken, and shall receive for their labor fair compensation to be fixed from time to time by the Secretary, who shall have the authority to prescribe the manner in which such compensation shall be paid to the natives or expended or otherwise used on their behalf and for their benefit.

Sec. 8. The Secretary shall have authority to establish and maintain depots for provisions and supplies on the Pribilof Islands and to provide for the transportation of such provisions and supplies from the mainland of the United States to the islands by the charter of private vessels or by the use of public vessels of the United States which may be under his control or which may be placed at his disposal by the President; and he likewise shall have authority to furnish food, shelter, fuel, clothing, and other necessities of life to the native inhabitants of the Pribilof Islands and to provide for their comfort, maintenance, education, and protection.

Sec. 9. Under the direction of the Secretary, the Fish and Wildlife Service is authorized to investigate the conditions of seal life upon the rookeries of the Pribilof Islands, and to continue the inquiries relative to the life history and migrations of the seals frequenting the waters of the North Pacific Ocean.

Sec. 10. Any officer or employee of the Department of the Interior authorized by the Secretary, any naval or other officer designated by the President, any marshal or deputy marshal, any collector or deputy collector of customs, and any other person authorized by law to enforce the provisions of this Act shall have power, without warrant, to arrest any person committing a violation of this Act or any regulation made pursuant thereto in his presence or view, and to take such person immediately for examination or trial before an officer or court of competent jurisdiction; and shall have power, without warrant, to search any vessel within any of the territorial waters of the United States, or any vessel of the United States on the high seas, when he has reasonable cause to believe that such vessel is subject to seizure under this section. Any officer, employee, or other person authorized to enforce the provisions of this Act shall have power to execute any warrant or process issued by an officer or court of competent jurisdiction for the enforcement of the provisions of this Act; and shall have power with a search warrant to search any person, vessel, or place at any time. The judges of the courts established under the laws of the United States, and the United States commissioners, may, within their respective jurisdictions, upon proper oath or affirmation showing probable cause, issue warrants in all such cases. All fur seals and sea otters, or the skins thereof, killed, captured, transported, imported, offered for sale, or possessed contrary to the provisions of this Act or of any regulation made pursuant thereto, and any vessel used or employed contrary to the provisions of this Act or of any regulation made pursuant thereto, or which it reasonably appears has been or is about to be used or employed in or in aid of the performance of any act forbidden by the provisions of this Act or of any regulation made pursuant thereto, together with its tackle, apparel, furniture, appurtenances, and cargo, may, whenever and wherever lawfully found, be seized by any such officer, employee, or other person.

Sec. 11. Except where otherwise expressly provided in this Act, any person violating any provision of this Act or any regulation made pursuant thereto shall be punished for each such offense, upon conviction thereof, by a fine of not less than $200 nor more than $2,000, or by imprisonment for not more than six months, or by both fine and imprisonment. All fur seals or sea otters, or the skins thereof, killed, captured, transported, imported, offered for sale, or possessed contrary to any provision of this Act or any regulation made pursuant thereto shall be forfeited to the United States and shall be disposed of pursuant to section 5 of this Act. Any vessel used or employed contrary to any provision of this Act or of any regulation made pursuant thereto shall, together with its tackle, apparel, furniture, appurtenances, and cargo, be forfeited to the United States and shall be disposed of as directed by the court having jurisdiction.

Sec. 12. It shall be the duty of all collectors of customs to enforce the provisions of this Act with respect to the importation of the skins of fur seal and sea otter.

Sec. 13. Any person or vessel described in section 2 of this Act in any of the waters of the North Pacific Ocean designated in any fur-seal agreement, including in any event the waters north of the thirtieth parallel of north latitude and east of the one hundred and eightieth meridian, violating or being about to violate the prohibitions of this Act against pelagic sealing may be seized and detained by the naval or other duly commissioned officers of any of the parties to such fur-seal agreement other than the United States, except within the territorial jurisdiction of one of the other said parties, on condition, however, that when such person or vessel is so seized and detained by officers of any party other than the United States, such person or vessel shall be delivered as soon as practicable at the nearest point to the place of seizure, with witnesses and proofs necessary to establish the offense so far as they are under the control of such party, to the proper official of the United States, whose courts alone shall have jurisdiction to try the offense and impose penalties for the same. The said officers of any party to any such fur-seal agreement other than the United States shall seize and detain persons and vessels, as in this section specified, only after such party, by appropriate legislation or otherwise, shall have authorized naval or other officers of the United States duly commissioned and instructed by the President to that end to seize, detain, and deliver to the proper officers of such party vessels and persons under the jurisdiction of that government offending against any such fur-seal agreement, or any statute or regulation made by that government to enforce any such fur-seal agreement. Upon the giving of such authority by such party, such naval or other officers of the United States shall have authority to make the seizures, detentions, and deliveries described. The President of the United States shall determine by proclamation when such authority has been given by the other party to any such fur-seal agreement, and his determination shall be conclusive upon the question; such proclamation may be modified, amended, or revoked by proclamation of the President whenever in his judgment it is deemed expedient.

Sec. 14. It shall be the duty of the President to cause a guard or patrol to be maintained in the waters frequented by the seal herds and sea otter in the protection of which the United States is especially interested, composed of naval or other public vessels of the United States designated by him for such service.

Sec. 15. The Secretary shall have authority to receive on behalf of the United States any fur sealskins taken by any party to any fur-seal agreement and tendered for delivery by such party in accordance with the terms of such fur-seal agreement, and all skins which are or shall become the property of the United States from any source whatsoever shall be disposed of in accordance with the provisions of section 5 of this Act. The Secretary likewise shall have authority to deliver to the authorized agents of any government that is a party to a fur-seal agreement the skins to which such government is entitled under the provisions of such fur-seal agreement, and to do or perform, or cause to be done or performed, any act which the United States is authorized or obliged to do or perform by the provisions of such fur-seal agreement.

Sec. 16. Nothing contained in this Act shall apply to the killing, capturing, pursuing, transportation, importation, offering for sale, or possession of fur seals or sea otters, or the skins thereof, for scientific purposes under special permit issued therefor by the Secretary.

Sec. 17. The Secretary shall supervise and direct the administration of this Act through the Fish and Wildlife Service and shall make all regulations necessary for the enforcement of this Act and any fur-seal agreement. It shall be his duty to provide for the enforcement of all of the provisions of this Act and of the regulations issued thereunder, except to the extent otherwise provided for in this Act, and to cooperate with other Federal agencies and with the duly authorized officials of the government of any party to any fur-seal agreement in the enforcement of such agreement. Out of such moneys as may be appropriated for such purposes, he shall employ in Washington, District of Columbia, and elsewhere such individuals and means as he may deem necessary for the administration of this Act and of any other function imposed upon him by any fur-seal agreement.

Sec. 18. All Acts and parts of Acts inconsistent with the provisions of this Act, including but not limited to the following, are hereby repealed: Sections 1956, 1959, 1960, and 1961 of the Revised Statutes of the United States; Act of February 21, 1893 (27 Stat. 472, ch. 150); Act of April 6, 1894 (28 Stat. 52); Act of December 29, 1897 (30 Stat. 226, ch. 3); Act of April 21, 1910 (36 Stat. 326, ch. 183); Act of August 24, 1912 (37 Stat. 499, ch 373); and joint resolution of June 22, 1916 (39 Stat. 236, ch. 171), all as amended.

SEC. 19. The provisions of this Act which implement the Provisional Fur-Seal Agreement of 1942 concluded between the United States of America and Canada shall remain in effect only for the duration of the present hostilities and twelve months thereafter unless either the Government of the United States of America or the Government of Canada enacts legislation contrary thereto, or until twelve months after either Government shall have notified the other Government of its intention to terminate the agreement.

The Canadian Ambassador at Washington transmitted to the Secretary of State, with a note of June 12, 1944, copies of Order-in-Council P.C. 4112 of May 30, 1944 issued under authority of the Canadian War Measures Act applying and giving force of law, in so far as Canada is concerned, to the provisions of the Provisional Fur-Seal Agreement between the United States of America and Canada which was effected by exchange of notes signed in Washington on December 8 and 19, 1942. The Agreement entered into force on May 30, 1944, the date of issuance of the Canadian Order-in-Council, and is effective as from June 1, 1942, under the provisions of Article X of the Agreement.[1]

3. EUROPEAN POSSESSIONS IN THE WESTERN HEMISPHERE

A. Anglo-American Caribbean Commission

[For texts relating to the establishment and earlier activities of the Commission, see *Documents, IV, 1941–42*, p. 459, and *V, 1942–43*, p. 469.

(1) Joint Communiqué of the Anglo-American Caribbean Commission Meeting, Issued at Charlotte Amalie in St. Thomas, Virgin Islands, August 17, 1943 [2]

The Anglo-American Caribbean Commission is holding its fourth meeting under United States co-chairman, Mr. Charles W. Taussig, at Charlotte Amalie in St. Thomas of the Virgin Islands of the United States on August seventeenth and following days. British representation will comprise the British co-chairman, Sir Frank Stockdale, and Mr. A. J. Wakefield, Inspector General of Agriculture in the West Indies, who has been nominated as British member for the meeting. Sir John Huggins, British resident member in Washington, will not be available as he has not yet returned from discussions in London prior to assuming duty as Governor of Jamaica. Mr. Rexford G. Tugwell, Governor of

[1] Department of State, *Bulletin*, X, p. 568.
[2] *Ibid.*, IX, p. 112.

Puerto Rico and Mr. Coert duBois of the State Department, Washington, who are United States members of the commission, will also be present.

Main subject for discussion relates to agricultural research in the Caribbean. The commission has therefore taken the opportunity to invite representatives from the agricultural experimental station of the United States, Great Britain and the Netherlands in the Caribbean area to attend so that they may confer and arrange for exchange of information and coordination of such research generally. In this connection the commission will adopt as the basis of their deliberations the recommendations and report of the United Nations Food Conference at Hot Springs,[1] as these recommendations will provide the foundation for coordinated effort in the planning of agricultural and other research in the Caribbean by the participating research institutes and experimental stations now meeting at St. Thomas. These recommendations will also be of assistance to the commission in its studies of nutrition, agriculture and fisheries problems in that area. A report of this meeting will be transmitted to the governments of the participating countries and to the Interim Commission charged with carrying out the recommendations of the United Nations conference on food and agriculture.

(2) *Establishment under Anglo-American Caribbean Commission of a System of West Indian Conferences. Joint Communiqué of the United States and British Governments, January 5, 1944* [2]

In recent years the United States Government and His Majesty's Government in the United Kingdom have devoted special attention to the improvement of social and economic conditions in the territories under their jurisdiction in the Caribbean. Nearly two years ago the two Governments agreed to collaborate closely in the solution of problems of common concern in this area and to assist them in this purpose they established the Anglo-American Caribbean Commission.

With the support and cooperation of the Governments of the territories concerned and of existing United States and British agencies and organizations, much useful work has already been accomplished and long-range planning over a wide field has begun.

In the field of research there was recently established, as an advisory body to the Commission, the Caribbean Research Council for the coordination of scientific and technical work on problems of the Caribbean area.

It remained, however, to broaden the base for the approach to Caribbean problems to include consultation with local representatives — not

[1] *Documents, V, 1942–43*, p. 302; for constitution see this volume, p. 434.
[2] Department of State, *Bulletin*, X, p. 37.

necessarily officials — of the territories and colonies concerned. The value of such counsel is recognized, and provision has now been made for its expression through a regular system of West Indian conferences which, by agreement between the United States Government and His Majesty's Government in the United Kingdom, is to be inaugurated under the auspices of the Anglo-American Caribbean Commission to discuss matters of common interest and especially of social and economic significance to Caribbean countries. The Conference will convene from time to time to consider specific subjects, that is, when problems arise which are at once alive and capable of being profitably discussed by such a conference. The Conference will be a standing body: it will have a continuing existence and a central secretariat, although the representatives will change according to the nature of the subjects to be discussed.

Each United States territory and each British colony or group of colonies in the Caribbean area will be entitled to send two delegates to each session of the Conference. This representation will be achieved in the manner most appropriate to each area; in the British colonies, for example, one of each two representatives will normally be an unofficial representative. The chairman for each session of the Conference will be the United States co-chairman of the Anglo-American Caribbean Commission if the Conference meets in United States territory, or the British co-chairman if the Conference convenes in British territory. In the event of the appropriate co-chairman being absent the proceedings will be opened formally by his colleague, after which the chair will be taken by any member of the Commission of the same nationality as the absent co-chairman. Other members of the Caribbean Commission and experts invited by them will have the right to attend all meetings of the Conference. Although delegates from each territory, colony, or group of colonies will be limited to two, they may at certain sessions be accompanied by advisers.

The Conference will be purely advisory and will have no executive powers unless such powers are specifically entrusted to it by the governments of the territories and colonies which participate. If it should become advisable for the Conference to take action by voting, the question of representation and the basis of voting representation will be subject to further discussion between the United States and British Governments.

The Anglo-American Caribbean Commission will provide the secretariat for the Conference and will be responsible for sending out the necessary documents to the members of the Conference. An official report of each session of the Conference will be prepared for transmission by the Anglo-American Caribbean Commission to the Governments of the United States and the United Kingdom and to the local governments represented.

Arrangements for convening the first session of the Conference were discussed at the last meeting of the Anglo-American Caribbean Commission in August 1943, and it is hoped to convene the first session of the Conference early in 1944. The probable subjects of discussion at this meeting will be the question of obtaining supplies for the development programs which are contemplated in the various territories and colonies, the stabilization of prices of foods produced locally for local consumption, the maintenance of local food production after the war, the continuance of research on and development of fishery resources of the Caribbean, and questions pertaining to health protection and quarantine in the Caribbean area.

Although these arrangements limit the conferences to United States and British participation the Conference will be free to invite the participation of other countries on occasion.

(3) Report of the West Indian Conference, Bridgetown, Barbados, March 21–30, 1944 [1]

[Excerpt]

The first West Indian Conference, held under the auspices of the Anglo-American Caribbean Commission, for the purpose of developing a cooperative program to rebuild economic, social and health conditions in American and British possessions in the Caribbean area, was held at Bridgetown, Barbados, March 21–30, 1944.

Two delegates from each British and American area — Puerto Rico, the Virgin Islands, Jamaica, Barbados, Trinidad, British Guiana, British Honduras, the Windward Islands, the Leeward Islands, and the Bahamas — took part in the sessions, which were presided over by Sir Frank A. Stockdale, K.C.M.G., C.B.E., Comptroller for Development and Welfare in the British West Indies, British co-chairman of the Commission.

Indicative of the scope and long-range viewpoint of the Conference were the subjects on its formal agenda: means for raising the nutritional level; re-absorption in civil life of persons engaged in war employment; planning of public works for the improvement of agriculture, education, housing, and public health; health protection and quarantine procedure; industrial development; and the Caribbean Research Council — possibilities for expansion.

In addition, the Conference heard reports and recommendations from the Caribbean Research Council, an advisory body made up of British, American, and Netherlands West Indies technical experts. The Council had been making intensive studies of crop diversification; promotion of animal husbandry and fisheries; soil and forest conservation; conditions of land tenure; food-preservation and marketing possibilities; health, sanitation, and quarantine measures; and other matters vital to improvement of the economic and general welfare of the peoples of the Caribbean area.

The Commission and the West Indian Conferences, of which the Barbados meeting on March 21 was the first, have a purely advisory status. However, the British Section of the Commission is affiliated with the Colonial Office in London and with the Development and Welfare Organization in the West Indies with headquarters in Barbados. The United States Section reports directly to the President and is an integral part of the United States Department of State. It works in close cooperation with the Department of the Interior, which has jurisdiction over United States territories and island possessions, and with the President's Caribbean Advisory Committee, made up of Mr. Taussig;

---

[1] *Report of the West Indian Conference held in Barbados, 21st–30th March, 1944, under the Auspices of the Anglo-American Caribbean Commission*, p. 41.

Governor Tugwell; the Honorable Martin Travieso, Chief Justice of the Supreme Court of Puerto Rico; Judge William Hastie, Civilian Aide to the Secretary of War; and Carl Robbins, former President of the Commodity Credit Corporation.

The items of the agenda were considered by specially appointed Committees of the Conference. The reports of these Committees are included in the Report of the Conference [1] and the recommendations contained therein were adopted by the Conference. Only the resolutions bearing on general policy are here given.

1. We adopt the recommendations of the Committees set out in the preceding sections of this report.

2. We recommend that the Governments of Great Britain and of the United States and the Governments of the territories represented at the Conference should be asked to use their utmost endeavors to give immediate consideration and early effect to such of our recommendations as may be transmitted to them with the support of the Anglo-American Caribbean Commission. We feel that the situation demands prompt action.

3. This Conference has revealed to us that we have many common problems, the solution of which lies in cooperative action and we consider that everything possible should be done to maintain the continuity of the work started at this session. We recommend that the Governments of the territories concerned should take all necessary steps to maintain and develop this cooperative spirit.

4. Questions of inter-Caribbean trade have been mentioned during our discussions and we recommend that efforts should be made to expand trade within the area and that, as a first step, the various Governments should consider the abolition of import duties on foodstuffs produced within the area.

5. We recommend that the next session of the West Indian Conference should be held within twelve months.

6. We recommend that consideration be given by the Anglo-American Caribbean Commission to the establishment of a permanent secretariat to handle the work of the West Indian Conference.

The Anglo-American Caribbean Commission announced on April 18, 1944, through the State Department, that the islands of St. Thomas and St. John, of the Virgin Island group of the United States, are the first territories represented at the recent West Indian Conference in Barbados to accept and endorse the conference report.[2]

B. United States Bases in British Colonies

(1) *British Offer to Compensate for Expropriated Private Property at Bases Leased to the United States. Statement of the Department of State, August 10, 1943* [3]

In the exchange of notes dated September 2, 1940 between the Secretary of State and the late Lord Lothian, British Ambassador, providing for the leasing

[1] *Ibid.*   [2] Department of State, *Bulletin*, X, p. 384.   [3] *Ibid.*, IX, p. 96, 97.

of bases in Newfoundland and certain British colonies in the Western Hemisphere and for the transfer of destroyers to the Government of the United Kingdom,[1] the following provision was made in respect to payment by the Government of the United States for private property included in the leased areas:

"All of the bases and facilities referred to in the preceding paragraphs will be leased to the United States for a period of ninety-nine years free from all rent and charges other than such compensation to be mutually agreed on to be paid by the United States in order to compensate the owners of private property for loss by expropriation or damage arising out of the establishment of the bases and facilities in question."

To implement this provision it was agreed that the Governments of the territories concerned would acquire necessary privately owned lands to be leased to the Government of the United States for ninety-nine years, and compensate the owners. The British Government would reimburse the local governments the total expenditure involved, and the United States Government, after having the properties examined by its own appraisers, would in turn reimburse the British Government.

The British Government has now generously offered to meet, under reciprocal aid, all claims for compensation due to owners of private property in the territories concerned — namely, Newfoundland, Bermuda, Bahamas, Jamaica, Antigua, St. Lucia, Trinidad, and British Guiana. This property has been valued by United States appraisers at approximately $5,500,000 United States currency. However, the total cost to the British Government may be considerably in excess of this amount since, in addition to the actual value of the private property involved, it will also include, in many cases, the cost of moving and resettlement, awards to compensate landowners for temporary loss of business or earning power, legal fees, and, in some cases, bonuses which were paid to induce the owners to vacate immediately properties urgently needed by this Government in order to speed construction of the bases.

The exchange of notes of September 2, 1940 antedates the Lend-Lease Act of March 11, 1941, and the generous offer of the British Government to assume the obligation of this Government for the payment of compensation for the expropriated private property and other damage in the bases areas will, therefore, serve to make these bases stand out not only as effective weapons in time of war but also as tangible reminders at all times of the friendship and cooperation of the British Government.

C. French West Indies

[See Documents, IV, 1941–42, p. 460; V, 1942–43, p. 470.]

(1) New Authority in the French Antilles. Department of State Release, July 13, 1943 [2]

Mr. Henri Hoppenot, Director of Civil Services of the French Military Mission in Washington, has informed the Department of State of his designation by the French Committee of National Liberation to assume the authority over the French Antilles. Admiral Robert recently expressed a desire to relinquish his authority. The acceptance of Mr. Hoppenot's designation for the express purpose of exercising the French authority in the Antilles is not to be construed as

[1] *Executive Agreement Series* 181; *Documents, III, 1940–41,* p. 203.
[2] Department of State, *Bulletin,* IX, p. 32.

affecting either pro or con the question of this Government's relations with the French Committee of National Liberation.

Mr. Hoppenot has assured the Government of the United States that the facilities and resources of the French Antilles will be devoted to the fullest extent to the prosecution of the war against the Axis, in accord with the action already taken by all French territory not under the domination of the enemy. The military interests of the United States in the Caribbean zone are fully recognized. The use of all presently immobilized French naval and merchant ships will be made available in the prosecution of the war effort.

On the basis of the new situation created by Mr. Hoppenot's designation, the Government of the United States is despatching relief supplies to Martinique and Guadeloupe and will cooperate with the new authority in the resumption of the economic life of the islands.

Mr. Hoppenot and his assistants are expected to arrive at Martinique in the immediate future, and upon his assumption of authority relations with the French Antilles will be resumed through Consul General Marcel E. Malige, who is returning to his post.

CHAPTER XIV

EASTERN ASIA AND THE PACIFIC AREA

[For the period covered in this volume, all documents bearing upon our belligerent relations with Japan and our treatment of Japan when defeated are included in Chapter IV (The Axis Powers), p. 159.]

1. PRINCIPLES OF AMERICAN POLICY

[See also Secretary Hull's Radio Address of September 12, 1943 (p. 2) and April 9, 1944 (p. 25), the Memorandum of March 21, 1944 (p. 21), and the Cairo Declaration of December 1, 1943 (p. 232).]

(1) *United States Objectives in India and the Far East. Statement of the President (Roosevelt), February 1, 1944* [1]

The American objectives in India or elsewhere in continental Asia are to expel and defeat the Japanese, in the closest collaboration with our British, Chinese, and other Allies in that theater.

Our task in expelling the Japs from Burma, Malaya, Java, and other territory is military. We recognize that our British and Dutch brothers-in-arms are as determined to throw the Japs out of Malaya and the Dutch East Indies as we are determined to free the Philippines. We propose to help each other on the roads and waters and above them, eastward to these places and beyond to Tokyo. No matter what individual or individuals command in given areas, the purpose is the same.

There will, of course, be plenty of problems when we get there. Their solution will be easier if we all employ our utmost resources of experience, good-will, and good faith. Nobody in India or anywhere else in Asia will misunderstand the presence there of American armed forces if they will believe, as we do at home, that their job is to assure the defeat of Japan, without which there can be no opportunity for any of us to enjoy and expand the freedoms for which we fight.

2. RELATIONS WITH CHINA

A. Aid in the Prosecution of the War

An appraisal of the military situation in China during the past twelve months affords little ground for encouragement, in spite of increased efforts to bring American lend-lease supplies into China in effective quantities by way of India. The most significant event was the Cairo Conference, dealt with in greater detail elsewhere in this volume.[2] So far as the prosecution of the war is concerned,

---

[1] Department of State, *Bulletin*, X, p. 145. [2] See p. 232.

the first statement of the Declaration is of paramount importance: "The several military missions have agreed upon future military operations against Japan." The immediate effect of the Cairo Conference was to create greater confidence and closer collaboration among the Pacific Allies.

American aid to China has been marked by the increase in the number of technicians and basic supplies for building up China as a base of future operations against Japan, while American forces based in China have worked in close conjunction with the Chinese Government in the training of Chinese troops in the use of modern firearms and technical equipment, in the planning of and giving air support to local operations against the enemy, and in the building of air strips and other military facilities. Closer cooperation with the Chinese Government has moved along other lines. An agreement between the United States and China regarding military service by nationals of either country residing in the other was effected by an exchange of notes signed in Washington on November 6, 1943, May 11, 1944, and June 13, 1944.[1]

Other aid and cooperation, however, have been of a long-range nature, and can only be characterized as aimed at assisting China's over-all reconstruction. In this category is the United States Government's program of cultural relations with China, which has been much expanded and now includes the sending of American technicians and scientific data to China, and the training of Chinese technicians in the United States. In July 1943 the Department of State appointed, under this program, four American news specialists to assist the Chinese Ministry of Information at Chungking. Their duties were to correspond to those of the American city editor, feature writer, news photographer, and radio news editor, and they were required principally to demonstrate American techniques and standards of news reporting to the staff of the Chinese Ministry of Information.

In the field of industrial cooperatives, Dr. W. Mackenzie Stevens, who was sent as consultant by the Department of State in November 1942, returned in August 1943 with a report that industrial cooperatives in China were helping immensely in relieving shortages in a wide range of commodities in China. In agriculture, Dr. W. C. Lowdermilk, Assistant Chief of the Soil Conservation Service, Department of Agriculture, who was sent by the Department of State to China as an adviser in a program to increase food production, conducted a survey of a great area of loess in northwest China, to investigate "the conditions of land use, degree of erosion and loss of rainfall by immediate runoff, and to evaluate the farm practices and to discover in what way the farmers of China, who have for centuries been fighting a losing battle against soil erosion, have sought in one way or another to save their rain and save their soil." Dr. Lowdermilk expressed high respect for the experience of Chinese farmers in their long struggle with erosion.

In other fields also, such as telecommunications, where an American expert has been of great service to China's Ministry of Communications in connection with plans for the future development of China's long-distance telephone system, this Government has extended in as many ways as possible the means of helping China build a modern nation.

The year was highlighted by the visit of Vice-President Henry A. Wallace to Chungking in June 1944, as the personal representative of President Roosevelt. In Chungking, Mr. Wallace conferred with President Chiang Kai-shek, visited farmers and Chinese and American soldiers, and presented to China a gift of nearly a hundred packages of scientific instruments, books, educational films, and agricultural seeds addressed to various Chinese institutions under the auspices of the program of cultural relations of the Department of State. At the end of the conference between Mr. Wallace and Generalissimo Chiang Kai-shek the following joint statement was issued.

---

[1] *Executive Agreement Series* 426.

(1) *Joint Press Release Issued at Conclusion of Vice President Wallace's Visit to Chungking, June 24, 1944* [1]

During his visit in Chungking Vice President Wallace has had an opportunity to discuss with President Chiang and officials of the Chinese Government, in an informal, frank and friendly atmosphere, matters of common interest and concern. They have exchanged views to mutual advantage and found themselves in agreement on basic principles and objectives.

Prosecution of the war against Japan in Asia is an urgent job, and mutual assistance in every possible way to get that job done quickly and efficiently is fundamental in Chinese-American relations.

The objective of victory in the Pacific is the establishment of a democratic peace based on political and social stability deriving from government devoted to the welfare of peoples.

Enduring peace in the Pacific will depend upon: (1) effective permanent demilitarization of Japan; (2) understanding friendship and collaboration between and among the four principal powers in the Pacific area, China, the Soviet Union, the United States and the British Commonwealth of Nations, and among all United Nations willing to share in the responsibilities of post-war international order; and (3) recognition of the fundamental right of presently dependent Asiatic peoples to self-government, and the early adoption of measures in the political, economic and social fields to prepare those dependent peoples for self-government within a specified practical time limit.

Cognizance was taken of the cornerstone position of China in Asia and of the importance of China in any structure for peace in the Pacific area. It was assumed as axiomatic that essential to such a peace structure would be continuation of the ties of friendship that have characterized American-Chinese relations for over a century, and the maintenance of relations on a basis of mutual understanding between China and the Soviet Union — China's nearest great neighbor — as well as between China and her other neighbors. No balance of power arrangement would serve the ends of peace.

Seven years of resistance to Japan, during the last three of which China has been virtually cut off from physical contact with the outside world, has resulted in serious economic and financial difficulties in Free China. The Chinese people are facing these difficulties with fortitude, confident of their ability to stand the strain until greater material assistance from abroad becomes feasible.

The Chinese people and the Government are determined to implement and make real the Three People's Principles of Sun Yat-sen.

The first of these principles, national sovereignty, is now a reality.

[1] *New York Times*, June 25, 1944.

The second, democracy, is implicit in plans being formulated for the establishment of a Constitution to guarantee individual rights and freedom and to establish representative government. Concrete consideration of the third, the people's livelihood, is inherent in plans for economic reconstruction.

With regard to the people's livelihood, the fundamental importance of agricultural reconstruction in any plans for economic or industrial reconstruction was recognized. The lifelong interest of Vice President Wallace in agricultural development gave him a special understanding of China's agrarian problem and enabled him to discuss with President Chiang realistic solutions.

Vice President Wallace was confident that President Chiang would find among the American people a willingness to cooperate in every practical way with the Chinese people in solving agricultural and related problems posed in Chinese plans for economic reconstruction, implementation of which would mean trade relations between Chinese and American business men on a mutually advantageous basis.

President Chiang and Vice President Wallace were continually mindful of the fact that the fundamental purpose of their Governments is the promotion of the security and welfare of the peoples of China and the United States, respectively, and were in agreement in believing that pursuit of the broad objectives which they had discussed would be in line with accomplishment of that purpose.

B. Repeal of the Chinese Exclusion Laws

The repeal of the laws excluding the immigration of Chinese into the United States was a milestone in Sino-American relations. These laws consisted of a series of Federal statutes reaching back to 1882. From the beginning, they were mainly directed at Chinese laborers, who first came to the United States in the middle of the nineteenth century, attracted by the promise of great wealth in California, especially after the gold rush of 1848. The first immigrants were manual laborers, farmers and small merchants, at first enthusiastically welcomed by the settlers and enterprisers of the flourishing Pacific Coast states to serve their need for cheap and efficient labor. Their arrival was permitted without restriction and even encouraged by treaty. The famous Burlingame Treaty of 1868 recognized the right of the Chinese to emigrate to the United States and promised most-favored-nation treatment to such immigrants, though making a reservation with regard to the right of naturalization. But the influx of laborers increased greatly and economic competition with American labor soon produced hostility. Even before the Burlingame Treaty, California had attempted to bar Chinese immigration by legislation but these measures were subsequently invalidated by judicial decisions ruling that immigration falls exclusively in the jurisdiction of Congress. The pressure of the Pacific States, however, forced Congress to act, and in 1876 a Congressional Committee appointed to investigate conditions in California recommended legislation to restrict the influx of Asiatics.

The first attempt to pass legislation restricting Chinese immigration — a measure limiting to 15 the number of Chinese to be brought on any one vessel — was vetoed by President Hayes, who urged negotiations with China to modify the terms of the Burlingame Treaty. A commission for this purpose was accordingly appointed in 1880. It found the Chinese Government favorable to the proposals for regulation and suspension of immigration but against absolute prohibition. The treaty basis of exclusion legislation was laid by the Treaty concluded with China on November 17, 1880.[1] The first article of this treaty read, in part:

"Whenever in the opinion of the Government of the United States the coming of Chinese laborers to the United States or their residence therein, affects or threatens to affect the interests of that country, or to endanger the good order of the said country or of any locality within the territory thereof, the Government of China agrees that the Government of the United States may regulate, limit or suspend such coming into or residence, but may not absolutely prohibit it."

Provision was also made in the treaty for most-favored-nation treatment of Chinese already in the United States.

With this treaty as the basis of legislation, Congress enacted, on May 6, 1882, a measure [2] to suspend Chinese immigration for a period of ten years, on grounds that "in the opinion of the United States Government, the coming of Chinese laborers to this country endangers the good order of certain localities within the Continent of the United States." [3] "Chinese laborers" were defined as meaning "both skilled and unskilled laborers and Chinese employed in mining." [4] The act also barred Chinese from naturalization.[5]

For a quarter of a century after 1882, fully a dozen acts or parts of acts were passed by Congress on the subject of Chinese exclusion — all having the general purpose of tightening the restrictions. (The statutes concerned are included in a listing forming the objects of repeal in the text of the repeal act of December 17, 1943, hereinafter printed in full. An explanation of each such statute is appended in footnotes to the full text.)

Action of the Chinese government, after 1882, was at first directed towards protesting incidents arising from the treatment of Chinese laborers on the West coast, but with the growth of federal exclusion legislation, China undertook, during the Cleveland administration, to prohibit emigration of Chinese laborers to the United States for 20 years, and signed a treaty to this effect. The Senate added amendments forbidding Chinese laborers who had left the United States to return, no matter whether they held certificates or not. The Chinese Government did not ratify the amended treaty. Congress nevertheless enacted the law of October 1, 1888, prohibiting all readmission of Chinese and the further issuance of certificates of identity. By 1904, immigration legislation had become so stringent that it amounted to complete exclusion for an indefinite period of Chinese laborers from the continental United States, Hawaii, the Philippines and other American possessions, together with the correlative denial of the right to citizenship by naturalization of all Chinese. The severity of these laws provoked a protest boycott of American goods in China in 1904. Since 1904, no attempt has been made to conclude treaties on the matter of Chinese exclusion. Although the original occasion for the passage of the exclusion laws was now past history, their existence on the Statute-books continued to be a source of difficulty and misunderstanding with China — especially after Pearl Harbor, many groups of Americans urged Congress to repeal these laws.

· The first bill aimed at repealing outright the Chinese Exclusion Laws was introduced by Representative Kennedy of New York on February 17, 1943, as H. R. 1882. Subsequently, several bills received hearings before the House and Senate Committees on Immigration. The final bill which ultimately passed

---

[1] *Treaties, Conventions, etc., 1776–1909*, I, p. 237.
[2] 22 Stat. L. 58. See below, p. 612.
[3] 22 Stat. L. 58, Preamble.
[4] *Ibid.*, Sec. 15.
[5] *Ibid.*, Sec. 14.

the House, H. R. 3070, was introduced by Representative Magnuson of Washington. It was favorably reported to the House on October 7, 1943.[1] On October 11, the Congress received a message from the President urging passage of the bill in order to "correct a historic mistake," and "silence Japanese propaganda," and as legislation "important in the cause of winning the war and of establishing a secure peace."[2] The House began debate on H. R. 3070 on October 20, 1943.[3] Opposition was based on apprehension that the bill was the opening wedge for large Asiatic immigration; belief that it should be considered after the return of the soldiers; fear that the new Chinese influx (of 105) might aggravate a problem of post-war unemployment; and the claim that the bill still placed Chinese on an unequal plane with European immigrants while it placed China in a position superior to other Asiatic immigrants. H. R. 3070 passed the House by a voice vote on October 21, 1943, following the adoption of a committee amendment striking out the word "China" and inserting "the Chinese" in Section 2. An opposition amendment to strike out all of Sec. 2 was rejected.[4]

In the Senate, a bill to repeal Chinese exclusion was first introduced by Senator Andrews of Florida (S. 1404) on September 30, 1943. After its passage in the House, the Magnuson Bill (H. R. 3070) was substituted for S. 1404, and as amended and passed by the House was reported to the Senate on November 26, by the Senate Committee on Immigration.[5] At the same time, a letter from the Attorney-General and one from the Under Secretary of State Stettinius, both recommending strongly the passage of the bill, were placed before the Senate.[6] Opposition in the Senate was considerably less than that in the House, and the bill passed by a voice vote, without amendment, on November 26.[7] An amendment submitted by Senator Reynolds of North Carolina was rejected.

The bill received the signature of President Roosevelt on December 17, at which time he issued the following statement:[8]

"It is with particular pride and pleasure that I have today signed the bill repealing the Chinese exclusion laws. The Chinese people, I am sure, will take pleasure in knowing that this represents a manifestation on the part of the American people of their affection and regard.

"An unfortunate barrier between allies has been removed. The war effort in the Far East can now be carried on with a greater vigor and a larger understanding of our common purpose."

Acting under the power vested in him by this act, the President on February 8, 1944, issued a proclamation (No. 2603) fixing the annual quota of Chinese immigrants at 105, effective for the remainder of the fiscal year ending June 30, 1944 and for each fiscal year thereafter.[9]

The Chinese Government received the news of the repeal law with enthusiasm. Noteworthy among many statements of government leaders were those of Dr. Sun Fo, President of the Legislative Yuan, who on November 27 praised the repeal of the Chinese Exclusion Act as "reaffirming our faith in American fair play and American friendship," and Mme. Chiang Kai-shek who sent a cablegram to Vice-President Wallace and Speaker Rayburn congratulating Congress on passage of the bill.[10]

---

[1] House Report No. 732, 78th Cong., 1st sess.

[2] House Doc. No. 333, 78th Cong., 1st sess.

[3] *Congressional Record*, vol. 89, p. 8683 (daily edition, October 20, 1943).

[4] *Ibid.*, p. 8730 (daily edition, October 21, 1943).

[5] Senate Report No. 535, 78th Cong., 1st sess.; *Congressional Record*, vol. 89, p. 10093 (daily edition, November 26, 1943).

[6] *Ibid.*, p. 10095.

[7] *Ibid.*, p. 10122.

[8] Department of State, *Bulletin*, IX, p. 431.

[9] 9 *Fed. Reg.*, p. 1587.

[10] *Congressional Record*, vol. 89, p. 10397 (daily edition, December 3, 1943).

(1) *Message of the President* *(Roosevelt)* *to the Congress, October 11,* *1943* [1]

TO THE CONGRESS OF THE UNITED STATES:

There is now pending before the Congress legislation to permit the immigration of Chinese people into this country and to allow Chinese residents here to become American citizens. I regard this legislation as important in the cause of winning the war and of establishing a secure peace.

China is our ally. For many long years she stood alone in the fight against aggression. Today we fight at her side. She has continued her gallant struggle against very great odds.

China has understood that the strategy of victory in this World War first required the concentration of the greater part of our strength upon the European front. She has understood that the amount of supplies we could make available to her has been limited by difficulties of transportation. She knows that substantial aid will be forthcoming as soon as possible — aid not only in the form of weapons and supplies, but also in carrying out plans already made for offensive, effective action. We and our allies will aim our forces at the heart of Japan — in ever-increasing strength until the common enemy is driven from China's soil.

But China's resistance does not depend alone on guns and planes and on attacks on land, on the sea, and from the air. It is based as much in the spirit of her people and her faith in her allies. We owe it to the Chinese to strengthen that faith. One step in this direction is to wipe from the statute books those anachronisms in our law which forbid the immigration of Chinese people into this country and which bar Chinese residents from American citizenship.

Nations like individuals make mistakes. We must be big enough to acknowledge our mistakes of the past and to correct them.

By the repeal of the Chinese exclusion laws, we can correct a historic mistake and silence the distorted Japanese propaganda. The enactment of legislation now pending before the Congress would put Chinese immigrants on a parity with those from other countries. The Chinese quota would, therefore, be only about 100 immigrants a year. There can be no reasonable apprehension that any such number of immigrants will cause unemployment or provide competition in the search for jobs.

The extension of the privileges of citizenship to the relatively few Chinese residents in our country would operate as another meaningful display of friendship. It would be additional proof that we regard China not only as a partner in waging war but that we shall regard her as a partner in days of peace. While it would give the Chinese a preferred

---

[1] House Doc. No. 333, 78th Cong., 1st sess.

status over certain other oriental people, their great contribution to the cause of decency and freedom entitles them to such preference.

I feel confident that the Congress is in full agreement that these measures — long overdue — should be taken to correct an injustice to our friends. Action by the Congress now will be an earnest of our purpose to apply the policy of the good neighbor to our relations with other peoples.

FRANKLIN D. ROOSEVELT.

(2) *An Act to Repeal the Chinese Exclusion Acts, to Establish Quotas, and for Other Purposes, Approved December 17, 1943* [1]

Be it enacted by the Senate and House of Representatives of the United States of America in Congress assembled, That the following Acts or parts of Acts relating to the exclusion or deportation of persons of the Chinese race are hereby repealed: May 6, 1882 (22 Stat. L. 58); July 5, 1884 (23 Stat. L. 115); September 13, 1888 (25 Stat. L. 476); October 1, 1888 (25 Stat. L. 504); May 5, 1892 (27 Stat. L. 25); November 3, 1893 (28 Stat. L. 7); that portion of section 1 of the Act of July 7, 1898 (30 Stat. L. 750, 751), which reads as follows: "There shall be no further immigration of Chinese into the Hawaiian Islands except upon such conditions as are now or may hereafter be allowed by the laws of the United States; and no Chinese, by reason of anything herein contained, shall be allowed to enter the United States from the Hawaiian Islands"; section 101 of the Act of April 30, 1900 (31 Stat. L. 141, 161); those portions of section 1 of the Act of June 6, 1900 (31 Stat. L. 588, 611), which read as follows: "And nothing in section four of the Act of August fifth, eighteen hundred and eighty-two (Twenty-second Statutes at Large, page two hundred and twenty-five), shall be construed to prevent the Secretary of the Treasury from hereafter detailing one officer employed in the enforcement of the Chinese Exclusion Acts for duty at the Treasury Department at Washington. . . . and hereafter the Commissioner-General of Immigration, in addition to his other duties, shall have charge of the administration of the Chinese exclusion law . . ., under the supervision and direction of the Secretary of the Treasury"; March 3, 1901 (31 Stat. L. 1093); April 29, 1902 (32 Stat. L. 176); April 27, 1904 (33 Stat. L. 428); section 25 of the Act of March 3, 1911 (36 Stat. L. 1087, 1094); that portion of the Act of August 24, 1912 (37 Stat. L. 417, 476), which reads as follows: "*Provided,* That all charges for maintenance or return of Chinese persons applying for admission to the United States shall hereafter be paid or reimbursed to the United States by the person, company, partnership, or corporation, bringing such Chinese to a port of the United States as applicants for admission"; that portion of the Act of June 23, 1913 (38 Stat. L. 4, 65), which reads

[1] Public Law 199, 78th Cong.

as follows: "*Provided,* That from and after July first, nineteen hundred and thirteen, all Chinese persons ordered deported under judicial writs shall be delivered by the marshal of the district or his deputy into the custody of any officer designated for that purpose by the Secretary of Commerce and Labor, for conveyance to the frontier or seaboard for deportation in the same manner as aliens deported under the immigration laws."

Sec. 2. With the exception of those coming under subsections (*b*), (*d*), (*e*), and (*f*) of section 4, Immigration Act of 1924 (43 Stat. 155; 44 Stat. 812; 45 Stat. 1009; 46 Stat. 854; 47 Stat. 656; 8 U. S. C. 204), all Chinese persons entering the United States annually as immigrants shall be allocated to the quota for the Chinese computed under the provisions of section 11 of the said Act. A preference up to 75 per centum of the quota shall be given to Chinese born and resident in China.

Sec. 3. Section 303 of the Nationality Act of 1940, as amended (54 Stat. 1140; 8 U. S. C. 703), is hereby amended by striking out the word "and" before the word "descendants," changing the colon after the word "Hemisphere" to a comma, and adding the following: "and Chinese persons or persons of Chinese descent":

(a) Memorandum Summarizing Laws Relating to Exclusion of Chinese from the United States, Contained in Report of the Senate Committee on Immigration (to Accompany H. R. 3070), November 16, 1943 [1]

EXPLANATORY COMMENT

This memorandum sets forth the salient features of the laws relating to the exclusion of Chinese from the United States. It does not purport to be exhaustive, but is devised to present, as briefly and as clearly as possible, a comprehensive statement of the important statutory provisions.

Act of May 6, 1882 (22 Stat. 58) (the basic Chinese Exclusion Act).

1. Suspended immigration of Chinese laborers for 10 years (sec. 1).
2. Permitted Chinese laborers resident in the United States November 17, 1880, to obtain certificate from collector of customs entitling them to return to United States after temporary absence (sec. 3).
3. Chinese persons other than laborers could be admitted to United States only upon production of a certificate from the Chinese Government in the English language describing the immigrant and certifying to his right to come to the United States under the terms of the treaty with China. This document, which came to be known as the Section Six Certificate, was to be prima facie evidence of the facts therein stated (sec. 6).
4. Chinese persons who entered the United States improperly after passage of the act were to be deported upon order of a judge or commissioner of a court of the United States (sec. 12).
5. "That hereafter no State court or court of the United States shall admit Chinese to citizenship" (sec. 14).

[1] Senate Report No. 535, 78th Cong., 1st sess., p. 7.

Act of July 5, 1884 (23 Stat. 115) (amended the act of May 6, 1882).

1. Section Six Certificate could be issued by any foreign government of which Chinese person was then subject (sec. 6).

Section Six Certificate required an antecedent visa at the place of departure by the American consul, who was instructed to inquire into the veracity of the statements in the certificate and to refuse his visa where he found the statements untrue. It was also provided that the Section Six Certificate should be "the sole evidence permissible on the part of the person so producing the same to establish a right of entry into the United States; but said certificate may be controverted and the facts therein stated disproved by the United States authorities" (*ibid.*).

Act of September 13, 1888 (25 Stat. 476).

A Chinese laborer who departed from the United States was not permitted to return unless he had a lawful wife, child, or parent in the United States, or property therein valued at $1,000. A Chinese laborer within these exemptions who desired to depart temporarily was required to obtain from the local collector of customs a return certificate which was valid for 1 year and could be extended for a further 1-year period only in certain contingencies (sec. 7).

NOTE. — Sections 1 to 4 of this statute were predicated on a treaty with China concluded earlier in 1888, which was never ratified. Those sections consequently never became effective, and their provisions are not recited herein.

Act of October 1, 1888 (25 Stat. 504) (known as Scott Act).

1. Prohibited return of any Chinese laborers who departed from United States (sec. 1).

2. Forbade the issuance of return certificates to Chinese laborers resident in the United States and canceled outstanding return certificates which had been issued under sections 4 and 5 of the act of May 5, 1882, to Chinese laborers in the United States who had left this country on temporary visits abroad (sec. 2).

NOTE. — This statute has apparently never been specifically repealed, but it appears to have been abrogated under the terms of the treaty subsequently concluded with China in 1894 (28 Stat. 1210).

Act of May 5, 1892 (27 Stat. 25) (known as the Geary Act).

1. Extended all Chinese exclusion laws for a period of 10 years (sec. 1).

2. Placed on Chinese persons apprehended in deportation proceedings the burden of establishing their lawful right to remain in the United States (sec. 3).

3. Prohibited allowance of bail to Chinese persons who had been denied privilege of landing in United States and who thereafter brought habeas corpus proceedings (sec. 5).

4. Required registration within 1 year of all Chinese laborers then in the United States and provided for the issuance of certificates of residence to those who could establish the legality of their presence in the United States. Those thereafter found in the United States without such certificate of residence were deemed unlawfully in the United States, and were to be deported upon order of a United States judge, unless they satisfied such judge (1) that the failure to obtain the certificate of residence was caused by accident, sickness, or other unavoidable cause, and (2) that they were resident in the United States on May 5, 1892, which fact had to be proved by the testimony of at least one credible white witness (sec. 6).

Act of November 3, 1893 (28 Stat. 7) (amended act of May 5, 1892).

1. Extended time for registration of Chinese laborers for 6 months (sec. 1).

2. Defined "laborer" and "merchant," as those terms are used in the Chinese exclusion laws (sec. 2). Prohibited release on bail of Chinese persons under order of deportation (*ibid.*).

Act of July 7, 1898 (30 Stat. 750).

Prohibited further immigration of Chinese into Hawaiian Islands except upon such conditions as they were admissible to the United States (sec. 1).

Act of April 30, 1900 (31 Stat. 141).

Required Chinese then in Hawaii to register and obtain certificates of residence within 1 year in same manner as required in United States under act of May 5, 1892 (sec. 101).

Act of June 6, 1900 (31 Stat. 588).

Authorized detailing of one officer to specialize in enforcement of Chinese Exclusion Acts in Treasury (now Justice) Department, and directing that Commissioner General of Immigration (now Commissioner of Immigration and Naturalization) shall have charge of enforcement of Chinese exclusion laws (31 Stat. 611).

Act of March 3, 1901 (31 Stat. 1093).

No warrant of arrest for violation of Chinese exclusion laws to be issued except upon sworn complaint of designated Government officials, unless the issuing of such warrant of arrest shall first be approved or requested in writing by the United States attorney of the district in which the warrant is issued (sec. 3).

Act of April 29, 1902 (32 Stat. 176).

1. Extended all Chinese exclusion laws then in force, so far as same were not inconsistent with treaty obligations (sec. 1).

2. Required registration and obtaining of certificates of residence by Chinese persons in insular possession of United States (sec. 4).

Act of April 27, 1904 (33 Stat. 428).

Extended all Chinese exclusion laws without any further limitation in time, made such laws applicable to the island territory under the jurisdiction of the United States, and prohibited immigration of Chinese laborers from such island territory of the United States to the mainland territory of the United States (sec. 5).

Act of March 3, 1911, section 25 (36 Stat. 1094).

Conferred appellate jurisdiction on United States district courts of the judgments and orders of United States Commissioners in cases arising under the Chinese exclusion laws.

Act of August 24, 1912 (37 Stat. 417).

Reimbursement for all charges for maintenance or return of Chinese persons applying for admission to the United States to be made to the United States by the person, company, partnership, or corporation bringing such persons to a port of the United States as applicants for admission (37 Stat. 476).

Act of June 23, 1913 (38 Stat. 4).

All Chinese persons ordered deported under judicial writs to be delivered by United States marshal to custody of officers of the Immigration and Naturalization Service, for deportation in the same manner as aliens deported under the immigration laws (38 Stat. 65).

(b) Relevant Provisions of the Immigration Act of 1924 [1]

SEC. 4. When used in this Act the term "non-quota immigrant" means —

. . .

(b) An immigrant previously lawfully admitted to the United States who is returning from a temporary visit abroad;

. . .

(d) An immigrant who continuously for at least two years immediately preceding the time of his application for admission to the United States has been, and who seeks to enter the United States solely for the purpose of, carrying on the vocation of minister of any religious denomination, or professor of a college, academy, seminary, or university; and his wife, and his unmarried children under eighteen years of age, if accompanying or following to join him;

(e) An immigrant who is a bona fide student at least fifteen years of age and who seeks to enter the United States solely for the purpose of study at an accredited school, college, academy, seminary, or university, particularly designated by him and approved by the Attorney General, which shall have agreed to report to the Attorney General the termination of attendance of each immigrant student, and if any such institution of learning fails to make such reports promptly the approval shall be withdrawn; or

(f) A woman who was a citizen of the United States and lost her citizenship by reason of her marriage to an alien, or the loss of United States citizenship by her husband, or by marriage to an alien and residence in a foreign country.

SEC. 11:

(a) The annual quota of any nationality shall be 2% of the number of foreign-born individuals of such nationality resident in continental United States as determined by the United States census of 1890, but the minimum quota of any nationality shall be 100.

(b) The annual quota of any nationality for the fiscal year beginning July 1, 1927 and for each fiscal year thereafter shall be a number which bears the same ratio to 150,000 as the inhabitants in continental United States in 1920 having their national origin (ascertained as hereinafter provided in this section) bears to the number of inhabitants in continental United States in 1920, but the minimum quota of any nationality shall be 100.

Before the passage of the present Act, a quota of 100 per annum had already been allotted to China under SEC. 11 above, but this quota has been available only to persons born in China but of races eligible to American citizenship, provisions of law previously prohibiting the coming of Chinese to the United States.

Under the present Act, the quota for persons of Chinese race is computed under SEC. 11 (b) of the Act of 1924, above, and amounts to 105 per annum. This provision, however, does not place Chinese on a full quota parity basis

[1] 43 Stat. 155; 44 Stat. 812; 45 Stat. 1009; 46 Stat. 854; 47 Stat. 656; 8 U.S.C. 204.

with other immigrants because while other aliens are charged to the quota of the country in which they were born, all Chinese persons entering the United States as immigrants must be charged to the one separate quota for Chinese, no matter where their place of birth.

(c) Relevant Provisions of the Nationality Act of 1940 [1]

SEC. 303:

The right to become a naturalized citizen under the provisions of this Act shall extend only to white persons, persons of African nativity or descent, and descendants of races indigenous to the Western Hemisphere: Provided, That nothing in this section shall prevent the naturalization of native-born Filipinos having the honorable service in the United States Army, Navy, Marine Corps, or Coast Guard as specified in SEC. 324, nor of former citizens of the United States who are otherwise eligible to naturalization under the provisions of SEC. 317.

The amendment made by the Act of December 17, 1943 makes eligible for citizenship some 45,000 Chinese aliens in the United States. But the actual number eligible is much reduced, since a large number of these Chinese have never been admitted for lawful permanent residence and hence cannot meet statutory requirements for naturalization. A further consideration is that the great majority of them are also advanced in years.

(d) Report of the House Committee on Immigration and Naturalization (to Accompany H. R. 3070), October 7, 1943 [2]

[Excerpt]

The following general statement relating to all sections of the Act was submitted by the House Committee on Immigration and Naturalization, in reporting favorably H. R. 3070: (House Report No. 732). A general statement similar in substance was submitted in the Senate Committee Report. (Senate Report No. 535, 78th Cong.)

From a reading of the bill and a study of this report it will be seen that it is proposed to remove discriminations against the Chinese which have been a source of misunderstanding in the relations between our two peoples for over 60 years and have aroused widespread resentment among the Chinese people.

The original act of exclusion was not born of ill will toward the Chinese people. The motivation was exclusively economic. But profound changes have taken place in 60 years.

We have had time and abundant occasion to reflect on the extraordinary qualities of the Chinese people. Above all, the tenacity and courage of the Chinese in their terrible ordeal of the last 7 years has impelled a respect that we are proud to acknowledge.

It is clear today that only a few short years stand between the Chinese people and the full use of their vast resources, both human and material, for their own betterment and well-being, free from any outside control. It has always been the policy of the United States to help China in her struggle against encroachment upon her independence and sovereignty and we are now brothers in arms in that cause. It is fitting, therefore, that the incongruity of discriminatory legislation, inconsistent with the dignity of both our peoples, should be eliminated.

In reporting favorably a bill for the repeal of the Chinese Exclusion Acts, this committee is expressing what it believes to be the will of the American people.

[1] 54 Stat. 1140; 8 U.S.C. 703.   [2] House Report No. 732, 78th Cong., 1st sess.

It is expressing, also, the realization of the American people that freedom depends upon respect for the integrity of others and that their own freedom and security demand that they accord to others the respect that they ask for themselves.

The committee held public hearings on a number of bills relating to the principle in H. R. 3070 over a period of several weeks. A great majority of the witnesses spoke in favor of the principle of this bill. Likewise, the comment of the press throughout the country appears to be overwhelmingly in its favor. The Attorney General, in a letter to the chairman of the committee under date of September 6, strongly endorsed H. R. 3070.

The committee were of the opinion that such legislation was necessary and reported the same and urge early and favorable consideration.

3. INDIA

[See statement by President Roosevelt on United States objectives in India and the Far East, given to the press on February 1, 1944 and printed in this volume, p. 604.]

4. THE PHILIPPINES

The question of the future policy of the United States with regard to the Philippines became urgent with the disclosure of a Japanese propaganda campaign intended to convince the people of those islands that their best chance of eventual independence lay in collaboration with the Japanese.

On October 14, 1943, the Japanese set up a puppet government in the Philippine Islands with José P. Laurel, previously a justice of the Philippine Supreme Court, as president. One of the first acts of this "government" was to sign a military alliance with Japan.

By the provisions of the Tydings-McDuffie Act of March 24, 1934, the Philippine Islands were to acquire their full independence on July 4, 1946.

Under the Constitution which was subsequently adopted, Manuel Quezon was elected President and Sergio Osmena, Vice President, for terms of 8 years, beginning November 15, 1936. When the Japanese occupied the Philippines, President Quezon and Vice President Osmena took refuge in the United States and continued to practice as heads of the Government in Washington. With the approach of the ends of their elected terms, the question arose as to how legal provision might be made for the continued exercise of the executive powers pending the possibility of new elections. S. J. Res. 95, passed by both Houses of Congress and approved by the President on November 12, 1943,[1] extended the terms of President Quezon and Vice President Osmena until the expulsion of the Japanese from the Philippines.

For a review of our relations with the Philippines since the outbreak of war, see Richardson Dougall, *Philippine-American Relations Since 1939* (Department of State, *Bulletin*, XI, p. 182).

(1) *Address by the President* (*Roosevelt*) *to the People of the Philippines, August 13, 1943* [2]

TO THE PEOPLE OF THE PHILIPPINES:

On December 28, 1941, three weeks after the armies of the Japanese launched their attack on Philippine soil, I sent a proclamation to you, the gallant people of the Philippines.[3] I said then:

I give to the people of the Philippines my solemn pledge that their freedom will be redeemed and their independence established and protected. The entire resources, in men and in material, of the United States stand behind that pledge.

---

[1] *Congressional Record*, vol. 89, p. 9593 (daily edition, November 15, 1943).

[2] Department of State, *Bulletin*, IX, p. 91.   [3] *Documents, IV, 1941-42*, p. 575.

We shall keep this promise, just as we have kept every promise which America has made to the Filipino people.

The story of the fighting on Bataan and Corregidor — and, indeed, everywhere in the Philippines — will be remembered so long as men continue to respect bravery and devotion and determination. When the Filipino people resisted the Japanese invaders with their very lives, they gave final proof that here was a nation fit to be respected as the equal to any on earth, not in size or wealth, but in the stout heart and national dignity which are the true measures of a people.

That is why the United States, in practice, regards your lawful Government as having the same status as the governments of other independent nations. That is why I have looked upon President Quezon and Vice President Osmena not only as old friends but also as trusted collaborators in our united task of destroying our common enemies in the east as well as in the west.

The Philippine Government is a signatory of the Declaration by the United Nations, along with 31 other nations. President Quezon and Vice President Osmena attend the meetings of the Pacific War Council, where the war in the Pacific is charted and planned. Your Government has participated fully and equally in the United Nations Conference on Food and Agriculture, and a Philippine representative is a member of the Interim Commission created by that conference. And, of course, the Philippine Government will have its rightful place in the conferences which will follow the defeat of Japan.

These are the attributes of complete and respected nationhood for the Philippines — not a promise but a fact.

As President Quezon himself has told you, "The only thing lacking is the formal establishment of the Philippine Republic." These words of your President were uttered to you with my prior knowledge and approval. I now repeat them to you myself. I give the Filipino people my word that the Republic of the Philippines will be established the moment the power of our Japanese enemies is destroyed. The Congress of the United States has acted to set up the independence of the Philippines. The time will come quickly when that goes into full effect. You will soon be redeemed from the Japanese yoke and you will be assisted in the full repair of the ravages caused by the war.

We shall fight with ever-increasing strength and vigor until that end is achieved. Already Japan is tasting defeat in the islands of the Southwest Pacific. But that is only the beginning. I call upon you, the heroic people of the Philippines, to stand firm in your faith — to stand firm against the false promises of the Japanese, just as your fighting men and our fighting men stood firm together against their barbaric attacks.

The great day of your liberation will come, as surely as there is a God in Heaven.

The United States and the Philippines have learned the principles of honest cooperation, of mutual respect, in peace and in war.

For those principles we have fought — and by those principles we shall live.

(2) *Independence for the Philippine Islands. Message of the President (Roosevelt) to the Congress, October 6, 1943* [1]

To the Congress of the United States:

Since the Japanese launched their attack on the Philippine Islands, I have on several occasions addressed messages on behalf of the American people to the courageous people of the Philippines — expressing our admiration of their heroism and loyalty. I have assured them that the Government of the United States of America will see to it that their independence will be promptly established and — still more important — that it will be protected. The resources of the United States, in men and material, stand behind that pledge to the people of the Philippines. We shall keep that promise just as we have kept every promise which the United States has made to the Filipino people.

The Philippine Government, now in the United States, has been collaborating with the rest of the United Nations in the united task of destroying our common enemies in the East and in the West. As I stated on August 12, 1943, the United States, in practice, regards the Philippines as having now the same status as the governments of other independent nations — in fact all the attributes of complete and respected nationhood.

I am sure that the American people believe that the Filipino people have earned the right juridically to be free and independent.

The date now set by statute and by the vote of the people and the Legislature of the Philippine Islands for independence is July 4, 1946. It is possible, however, that the fortunes of war will permit an earlier consummation of this joint will of the American and Filipino peoples.

I, therefore, recommend legislation by the Congress giving the President the authority, after consultation with the President of the Commonwealth of the Philippine Islands, to advance the date provided in existing law and to proclaim the legal independence of the Philippines, as a separate and self-governing nation, as soon as feasible.

If the Congress takes this action, there are several steps which, in my opinion, are necessary to make good our pledge that the independence of the Philippines will be protected in the future and to give them the opportunity of economic rehabilitation which is their due.

[1] Senate Doc. No. 101, 78th Cong., 1st sess.

I, therefore, also recommend:

1. That the Congress make provision authorizing the President of the United States and the President of the Commonwealth of the Philippine Islands to enter into immediate negotiations and take the necessary steps to provide for full security for the Philippines, for the mutual protection of the islands and of the United States, and for the future maintenance of peace in the Pacific.

2. That the Congress make provision for determining the adjustments necessary in the existing provisions of law which govern the economic relations between the United States and the Philippines, so as to assist in making the Philippines, as an independent nation, economically secure wherever possible.

3. That the Congress make provision for the physical and economic rehabilitation of the Philippines made necessary by the ravages of war which the invaders have inflicted upon them.

All of this is due to the Filipino people in recognition of their heroic role in this war, the political ties which have bound us together, and the bonds of friendship which will join us together in the future.

Such action on the part of the Congress would assure the Philippine people again of our sincerity of purpose, and of our resolution to accord them as soon as feasible the legal status of complete freedom, independence and nationhood to which, as a member of the United Nations, they are entitled.

(3) *Statement of the President (Roosevelt) Regarding the [Puppet Government in the Philippines, October 22, 1943* [1]

On the fourteenth of this month a puppet government was set up in the Philippine Islands with José P. Laurel, formerly a justice of the Philippine Supreme Court, as "president." Jorge Vargas, formerly a member of the Philippine Commonwealth Cabinet, and Benigno Aquino, also formerly a member of that Cabinet, were closely associated with Laurel in this movement. The first act of the new puppet regime was to sign a military alliance with Japan. The second act was a hypocritical appeal for American sympathy which was made in fraud and deceit and was designed to confuse and mislead the Filipino people.

I wish to make it clear that neither the former collaborationist "Philippine Executive Commission" nor the present "Philippine Republic" has the recognition or sympathy of the Government of the United States. No act of either body is now or ever will be considered lawful or binding by this Government.

[1] Department of State, *Bulletin*, IX, p. 274.

The only Philippine government is that established by the people of the Philippines under the authorization of the Congress of the United States — the Government of the Commonwealth of the Philippine Islands. At my request, the principal executive officers of the Commonwealth were transferred in 1942 from Corregidor to Washington.

Further, it is our expressed policy that all the resources of the United States, both of men and materials, shall be employed to drive the treacherous, invading Japanese from the Philippine Islands, to restore as quickly as possible orderly and free democratic processes of government in the islands, and to establish there a truly independent Philippine nation.

Our sympathy goes out to those who remain loyal to the United States and the Commonwealth — to that great majority of the Filipino people who have not been deceived by the promises of the enemy and who look forward to the day when the scheming, perfidious Japanese shall have been driven from the Philippines. That day will come.

(4) *Statement of the Secretary of State (Hull) on the Eighth Anniversary of the Establishment of the Philippine Commonwealth, November 13, 1943* [1]

The President's pledge to redeem the Philippines is certain of fulfilment.[2] His message to the Congress on October 6, 1943, recommending that authority be granted to him to proclaim the legal independence of the Islands as soon as feasible and to provide measures for their protection and rehabilitation, is but a step in that direction.

It is worthwhile to recall briefly how the Filipinos fared before the Japanese invaded their homeland. Freedom, independence, and sovereignty of the Filipino people were a foregone conclusion from the time the flag of the United States was raised over the Islands. After November 15, 1935, the Filipino people enjoyed the true substance of freedom, for Filipino officials elected by the Filipino people carried on the internal affairs of the Philippines. American authorities remained in the Islands on a temporary basis and enjoyed happy and harmonious relations with the Filipino authorities and people. The armed forces of the United States labored shoulder to shoulder with their Filipino comrades, solely for the protection of the Filipino people themselves.

In contrast to the freedom which the Filipinos knew before the Japanese invasion, the Filipino people became enslaved — forced by guns to do the bidding of the enemy. Japan not only coerced the Filipinos but also deluged them with propaganda, blandishment, and cajolery. No one knows better than the Filipinos themselves that so-called independence at the hands of the Japanese — whose one thought is to stifle Filipino initiative, to stunt Filipino culture, and to mold the Filipino people

---

[1] *Ibid.*, p. 321.   [2] *Documents, IV, 1941–42*, p. 575.

to Japan's purposes of empire and self-aggrandizement — denotes independence only in name. The Filipinos know, and we all know, that the Japanese, until they are driven from the Islands, will continue their attempts to control all principal aspects of Filipino life: spiritual, educational, financial, economic, and personal. They will continue their efforts through debased ideologies and false values to reach into the very minds of the Filipinos and to change the Filipino way of thinking and of living.

Remembering their life before Japan came, the Filipinos will not forget their rightful heritage and will wonder how Japan, itself the slave of its own military, could hope to grant real independence to another people.

As the Filipino people recall what the Japanese enemy has done and is doing to the natives of Formosa, of Korea, of China, of Thailand, and of Burma, and of all the areas overrun and invaded by Japanese, it will be apparent to them, and to all of us, that Japan will never voluntarily withdraw from the Philippines but rather will put forth its utmost effort to remain there for the purpose of exploiting those areas and those peoples in the sole interest of the Japanese Government.

They will not remain. They will be driven out.

(5) *Joint Resolution (S. J. Res. 93) Declaring the Policy of the Congress with Respect to the Independence of the Philippine Islands, and for Other Purposes, Approved June 29, 1944* [1]

Whereas, on December 7, 1941, while the people of the Philippine Islands were peacefully engaged in achieving for themselves their complete political independence in the manner mutually agreed upon by the Government of the United States and the people of the Philippine Islands, which independence was to become fully effective July 4, 1946, the Japanese in a wholly unprovoked, wantonly treacherous, and surprise attack on the people of the Philippines and of the United States, did by military invasion interrupt these orderly and mutually agreeable processes for complete independence of the Philippines; and

Whereas the American and Filipino troops made a valiant and courageous defense to the aggression of the Japanese invader and were overwhelmed only by the surprise and superior numbers and equipment of the enemy; and

Whereas the Japanese are now in possession and control of the land, peoples, business, communication, and institutions of the Commonwealth of the Philippines, and because of these circumstances the Filipino people are denied the free use and employment of the processes

[1] Public Law 380, 78th Cong.

and political institutions jointly established by the Government of the United States and the Commonwealth of the Philippines for the transaction of private and public business and for the maintenance of liberty, law and order, and justice in the Philippine Islands; and

Whereas by this possession and invasion the Japanese have attempted to frustrate the free processes to independence in the Philippines by substituting therefor their own puppet government which was conceived in intrigue, born in coercion, and reared primarily for the purpose of Japanese selfishness and aggrandizement and not to achieve the independence and freedom of the Filipino people; and

Whereas the Government of the United States has solemnly guaranteed to the people of the Philippine Islands the right to be completely free and independent and to select by a free ballot, without any kind of inducement or coercion whatsoever, those who shall hold the elective offices in such government and exercise the power and authority thereof, which solemn guaranties have been temporarily made impossible of fulfillment due to the wantonly treacherous and surprise attack on the free people of the Philippine Islands; and

Whereas, because of the valiant resistance by the Philippine people, which is even now continuing while the invader occupies parts of the Philippines, and because of the long and unbroken record of loyalty of the Filipino people, both to the cause of complete independence for themselves and to the sovereignty of the United States while they have been under our flag, and because they have abundantly demonstrated their will to independence through the processes mutually agreed upon by the people of the Philippines and the Government of the United States, and their will to resist all outside invasion and encroachment, which seek to destroy or set aside their march to independence, and because they have abundantly proved their capacity to govern themselves in an enlightened, progressive, and democratic manner: Now, therefore, be it

Resolved by the Senate and House of Representatives of the United States of America in Congress assembled, That it is hereby declared to be the policy of the Congress that the United States shall drive the treacherous, invading Japanese from the Philippine Islands, restore as quickly as possible the orderly and free democratic processes of government to the Filipino people, and thereupon establish the complete independence of the Philippine Islands as a separate and self-governing nation.

SEC. 2. After negotiation with the President of the Commonwealth of the Philippines, or the President of the Filipino Republic, the President of the United States is hereby authorized by such means as he finds appropriate to withhold or to acquire and to retain such bases, necessary appurtenances to such bases, and the rights incident thereto, in addition to any provided for by the Act of March 24, 1934, as he may deem necessary for the mutual protection of the Philippine Islands and of the United States.

SEC. 3. In order speedily to effectuate the policy declared in section 1, the President of the United States is hereby authorized, after proclaiming that constitutional processes and normal functions of government have been restored in the Philippine Islands and after consultation with the President of the Commonwealth of the Philippines, to advance the date of the independence of the Philippine Islands by proclaiming their independence as a separate and self-governing nation prior to July 4, 1946.

SEC. 4. Meanwhile the resources of the United States, both of men and materials, are pledged for continued use to redeem the Philippines from the invader and to speed the day of ultimate and complete independence for the people of the Philippine Islands.

(6) *Joint Resolution (S. J. Res. 94) to Amend Section 13 of Philippine Independence Act, as Amended, Establishing the Filipino Rehabilitation Commission, Defining Its Powers and Duties, and for Other Purposes, Approved June 29, 1944* [1]

Resolved by the Senate and House of Representatives of the United States of America in Congress assembled, That section 13 of the Act of March 24, 1934, as amended, is hereby further amended by striking out the proviso and inserting in lieu thereof the following:

There shall promptly be held a conference of representatives of the Government of the United States and the Government of the Commonwealth of the Philippines, such representatives on the part of the Government of the United States to consist of three United States Senators appointed by the President of the Senate, three Members of the House of Representatives appointed by the Speaker of the House, and three persons appointed by the President of the United States, and on the part of the Philippines to consist of nine representatives to be appointed by the President of the Commonwealth of the Philippines; each appointee shall serve at the pleasure of his appropriate appointing authority; the said Commission to be known as the Filipino Rehabilitation Commission, subject to the following conditions and with the following powers and duties:

(a) The members of the Commission shall be appointed not later than fifteen days after the passage of this Act. Within ten days there-

_____
[1] Public Law 381, 78th Cong.

after the ranking member of the Senate appointees and the ranking member of the Filipino appointees shall jointly call a meeting of the Commission to be held in the Capitol of the United States for the purpose of organization. In case of death or resignation of a member, such vacancy shall be filled by the original appointing power.

(*b*) The Commission shall investigate all matters affecting post-war economy, trade, finance, economic stability, and rehabilitation of the Philippine Islands, including the matter of damages to public and private property and to persons occasioned by enemy attack and occupation.

(*c*) To formulate recommendations based upon such investigations and for future trade relations between the United States and the independent Philippine Republic when established and to consider the extension of the present or heretofore agreed upon trade relations or otherwise for a period of years to make adjustments for the period of occupancy by the Japanese in order to reestablish trade relations as provided for in the original Independence Act.

(*d*) The Commission is authorized to employ expert legal and clerical assistance, to establish offices in the Philippine Islands and in the United States, and to make rules and regulations for the transaction of its business pertinent to the provisions of this Act.

(*e*) The Commission shall make annual reports to the President of the United States and to the Congress, and to the President and the Congress of the Philippines, and more frequently if so desired, and make such recommendations from time to time as it deems necessary to carry out the purposes and intents of this Act.

(*f*) The Commission is authorized to fix the salary of all necessary expert and clerical assistance, to provide for travel and other expenses incident to its labor, and to do all other things pertinent to this Act. The annual compensation of the United States members of this Commission, other than those holding official positions under the United States Government, shall be on a per diem basis at the rate of $10,000 per annum. The compensation of the Philippine members of the Commission shall be determined by the Government of the Philippine Commonwealth. The United States, as herein provided, shall compensate the members of the Commission who represent it, and the Commonwealth of the Philippines, or the Filipino Republic, as the case may be, shall compensate the members of the Commission appointed by it or them. Otherwise, the expenses of the Commission shall be equally borne by the United States and the Commonwealth of the Philippines, or the Filipino Republic, as the case may be.

SEC. 2. For the purpose of carrying on its duties, there is hereby authorized to be appropriated, out of any money in the Treasury not otherwise appropriated, such sums as may be necessary.

(7) *Joint Resolutions Concerning the Philippines. Statement of the President (Roosevelt), June 29, 1944* [1]

I have signed today two joint resolutions of Congress respecting the Philippines. The first of these resolutions lays down a policy for the granting of independence, and for the acquisition of bases adequate to provide for the mutual protection of the United States and the Philippine Islands.

In that resolution it is declared to be the policy of "the Congress that the United States shall drive the treacherous, invading Japanese from the Philippine Islands, restore as quickly as possible the orderly, free democratic processes of government to the Filipino people, and thereupon establish the complete independence of the Philippine Islands as a separate self-governing nation." The measure makes it possible to proclaim independence as soon as practicable after constitutional processes and normal functions of government have been restored in the Philippines.

It is contemplated that as soon as conditions warrant, civil government will be set up under constitutional officers. It will be their duty forthwith to take emergency measures to alleviate the physical and economic hardships of the Philippine people and to prepare the Commonwealth to receive and exercise the independence which we have promised them. The latter includes two tasks of great importance: Those who have collaborated with the enemy must be removed from authority and influence over the political and economic life of the country; and the democratic form of government guaranteed in the Constitution of the Philippines must be restored for the benefit of the people of the islands.

On the problem of bases, the present organic act permitted acquisition only of naval bases and fueling stations, a situation wholly inadequate to meet the conditions of modern warfare. The measure approved today will permit the acquisition of air and land bases in addition to naval bases and fueling stations. I have been informed that this action is most welcome to Commonwealth authorities and that they will gladly cooperate in the establishment and maintenance of bases both as a restored Commonwealth and as an independent nation. By this we shall have an outstanding example of cooperation designed to prevent a recurrence of armed aggression and to assure the peaceful use of a great ocean by those in pursuit of peaceful ends.

The second joint resolution signed today brings into effect the joint economic commission first ordained in the present organic act, and

[1] Made in connection with the signing of S. J. Res. 93 and S. J. Res. 94; Department of State, *Bulletin*, XI, p. 17.

enlarges its scope to include consideration of proposals for the economic and financial rehabilitation of the Philippines.

We are ever mindful of the heroic role of the Philippines and their people in the present conflict. Theirs is the only substantial area and theirs the only substantial population under the American flag to suffer lengthy invasion by the enemy. History will attest the heroic resistance of the combined armies of the United States and the Philippines in Luzon, Cebu, Iloilo, and other islands of the archipelago. Our character as a nation will be judged for years to come by the human understanding and the physical efficiency with which we help in the immense task of rehabilitating the Philippines. The resolution creates the Philippine Rehabilitation Commission whose functions shall be to study all aspects of the problem and, after due investigation, report its recommendations to the President of the United States and the Congress, and to the President and the Congress of the Philippines.

5. AUSTRALIA AND NEW ZEALAND

(1) *Agreement Between the Commonwealth of Australia and the Dominion of New Zealand, Signed at Canberra, January 21, 1944* [1]

His Majesty's Government in the Commonwealth of Australia and His Majesty's Government in the Dominion of New Zealand (hereinafter referred to as the two Governments) represented as follows:

The Governor of the Commonwealth of Australia by the Right Honorable John Curtin, Prime Minister of Australia and Minister for Defense; the Honorable Francis Michael Forde, Minister for the Army; the Honorable Joseph Benedict Chifley, Treasurer and Minister for Postwar Reconstruction; the Right Honorable Herbert Vere Evatt, LL.D., K.C., Attorney-General and Minister for External Affairs; the Honorable John Albert Beasley, Minister for Supply and Shipping; the Honorable Norman John Oswald Makin, Minister for the Navy and Minister for Munitions; the Honorable Arthur Samuel Drakeford, Minister for Air and Minister for Civil Aviation; the Honorable John Johnstone Dedman, Minister for War Organization of Industry; the Honorable Edward John Ward, Minister for Transport and Minister for External Territories; and the Honorable Thomas George de Largie D'Alton, High Commissioner for Australia in New Zealand, and

The Government of the Dominion of New Zealand by the Right Honorable Peter Fraser, Prime Minister of New Zealand, Minister for External Affairs and Minister of Island Territories; the Honorable Frederick Jones, Minister of Defense and Minister in Charge of Civil Aviation; the Honorable Patrick Charles Webb, Postmaster-General

---

[1] From the Information Office of the Australian and New Zealand Governments.

and Minister of Labor; and Carl August Berendsen, Esquire, C.M.G., High Commissioner for New Zealand in Australia:

having met in conference at Canberra from the 17th to the 21st January, 1944, and desiring to maintain and strengthen the close and cordial relations between the two Governments, do hereby enter into this agreement:

DEFINITION OF OBJECTIVES OF AUSTRALIAN-NEW ZEALAND COOPERATION

1. The two Governments agree that as a preliminary, provision shall be made for fuller exchange of information regarding both the view of each Government and the facts in the possession of either bearing on matters of common interest.

2. The two Governments give mutual assurances that on matters which appear to be of common concern each Government will so far as possible be made acquainted with the mind of the other before views are expressed elsewhere by either.

3. In furtherance of the above provisions with respect to exchange of views and information, the two Governments agree that there shall be the maximum degree of unity in the presentation elsewhere of the views of the two countries.

4. The two Governments agree to adopt an expeditious and continuous means of consultation by which each party will obtain directly the opinions of the other.

5. The two Governments agree to act together in matters of common concern in the Southwest and South Pacific areas.

6. So far as compatible with the existence of separate military commands the two Governments agree to coordinate their efforts for the purpose of prosecution of the war to a successful conclusion.

ARMISTICE AND SUBSEQUENT ARRANGEMENTS

7. The two Governments declare that they have vital interests in all preparations for any armistice ending the present hostilities or any part thereof, and also in arrangements subsequent to any such armistice and agree that their interests should be protected by representation at the highest level on all armistice planning and executive bodies.

8. The two Governments are in agreement that the final peace settlement should be made in respect of all our enemies after hostilities with all of them are concluded.

9. Subject to the last two preceding clauses, the two Governments will seek agreement with each other on the terms of any armistice to be concluded.

10. The two Governments declare that they should actively participate in any armistice commission to be set up.

11. His Majesty's Government in the Commonwealth of Australia
shall set up in Australia, and His Majesty's Government in the Dominion
of New Zealand shall set up in New Zealand armistice and post-hostilities
planning committees and shall arrange for the work of these committees
to be coordinated in order to give effect to the views of the respective
Governments.

12. The two Governments will collaborate generally with regard to the
location of machinery set up under international organization such as the
United Nations Relief and Rehabilitation Administration, and in particular with regard to the location of the Far Eastern Committee of that
Administration.

Security and Defense

13. The two Governments agree that within the framework of a
general system of world security a regional zone of defense comprising
the Southwest and South Pacific areas shall be established and that this
zone should be based on Australia and New Zealand, stretching through
the arc of islands north and northeast of Australia to Western Samoa
and the Cook Islands.

14. The two Governments regard it as a matter of cardinal importance
that they should both be associated not only in the membership but also
on the planning and establishment of the general international organization referred to in the Moscow Declaration of October 1943, which organization is based on the principle of the sovereign equality of all peace-
loving States and open to membership by all such States large or small for
the maintenance of international peace and security.

15. Pending the reestablishment of law and order and the inauguration of a system of general security the two Governments hereby declare
their vital interest in the action on behalf of the community of nations
contemplated in Article V of the Moscow Declaration of October 1943.
For that purpose it is agreed that it would be proper for Australia and
New Zealand to assume full responsibility for policing or sharing in
policing such areas in the Southwest and South Pacific as may from time
to time be agreed upon.

16. The two Governments accept as a recognized principle of international practice that the construction and use in time of war by any
power of naval, military or air installation in any territory under the
sovereignty or control of another power does not in itself afford any
basis for territorial claims or rights of sovereignty or control after the
conclusion of hostilities.

CIVIL AVIATION

17. The two Governments agree that the regulation of all air transport services should be subject to the terms of a convention which will supersede the convention relating to the regulation of aerial navigation.

18. The two Governments declare that the air services using the international air trunk routes should be operated by an international air transport authority.

19. The two Governments support the principles that

(a) Full control of the international air trunk routes and the ownership of all aircraft and ancillary equipment should be vested in the international air transport authority, and

(b) the international air trunk routes should themselves be specified in the international agreement referred to in the next succeeding clause.

20. The two Governments agree that the creation of the international air transport authority should be effected by an international agreement.

21. Within the framework of the system set up under any such international agreement, the two Governments support

(a) the right of each country to conduct all air transport services within its own national jurisdiction including its own contiguous territories, subject only to agreed international requirements regarding safety facilities, landing and transit rights for international services and exchange of mails.

(b) the right of Australia and New Zealand to utilize to the fullest extent their productive capacity in respect of aircraft and raw materials for the production of aircraft.

(c) the right of Australia and New Zealand to use a fair proportion of their own personnel, agencies and materials in operating and maintaining international air trunk routes.

22. In the event of failure to obtain a satisfactory international agreement to establish and govern the use of international air trunk routes, the two Governments will support a system of air trunk routes controlled and operated by Governments of the British Commonwealth of Nations under Government ownership.

23. The two Governments will act jointly in support of the above-mentioned principles with respect to civil aviation, and each will inform the other of its existing interests and commitments as a basis of advancing the policy herein agreed upon.

DEPENDENCIES AND TERRITORIES

24. Following the procedure adopted at the conference which has just concluded the two Governments will regularly exchange information and views in regard to all developments in or affecting the islands of the Pacific.

25. The two Governments take note of the intention of the Australian Government to resume administration at the earliest possible moment of those parts of its territories which have not yet been reoccupied.

26. The two Governments declare that the interim administration and ultimate disposal of enemy territories in the Pacific is of vital importance to Australia and New Zealand, and that any such disposal should be effected only with their agreement and as part of a general Pacific settlement.

27. The two Governments declare that no change in the sovereignty or system of control of any of the islands of the Pacific should be effected except as a result of an agreement to which they are parties or in the terms of which they have both concurred.

WELFARE AND ADVANCEMENT OF NATIVE PEOPLES OF THE PACIFIC

28. The two Governments declare that in applying the principles of the Atlantic Charter to the Pacific, the doctrine of trusteeship (already applicable in the case of the mandated territories of which the two Governments are mandatory powers) is applicable in broad principle to all colonial territories in the Pacific and elsewhere, and that the main purpose of the trust is the welfare of the native peoples and their social, economic and political development.

29. The two Governments agree that the future of the various territories of the Pacific and the welfare of their inhabitants cannot be successfully promoted without a greater measure of collaboration between the numerous authorities concerned in their control, and that such collaboration is particularly desirable in regard to health services and communications, matters of native education, anthropological investigation, assistance in native production and material developments generally.

30. The two Governments agree to promote the establishment at the earliest possible date of a regional organization with advisory powers which could be called the South Seas Regional Commission, and to which in addition to representatives of Australia and New Zealand, there might be accredited representatives of the Governments of the United Kingdom and the United States of America, and of the French Committee of National Liberation.

31. The two Governments agree that it shall be the function of such South Seas Regional Commission as may be established to secure a common policy on social, economic and political development, directed towards the advancement and well-being of the native peoples themselves, and in particular, the Commission shall:

(a) recommend arrangements for the participation of natives in administration in increasing measure with a view to promoting the ultimate attainment of self-government in the form most suited to the circumstances of the native peoples concerned;

(b) recommend arrangements for material development, including production, finance, communications and marketing;

(c) recommend arrangements for coordination of health and medical services and education;

(d) recommend arrangements for maintenance and improvement of standards of native welfare in regard to labor conditions;

(e) recommend arrangements for collaboration in economic, social, medical and anthropological research;

(f) make and publish periodical reviews of progress towards development of self-governing institutions in the islands of the Pacific and in the improvement of standards of living conditions, of work, education, health and general welfare.

MIGRATION

32. In the peace settlement or other negotiations the two Governments will accord one another full support in maintaining the accepted principle that every Government has the right to control immigration and emigration in regard to all territories within its jurisdiction.

33. The two Governments will collaborate, exchange full information, and render full assistance to one another in all matters concerning migration to their respective territories.

INTERNATIONAL CONFERENCES RELATING TO THE SOUTHWEST AND SOUTH PACIFIC

34. The two Governments agree that as soon as practicable, there should be a frank exchange of views on the problems of security, postwar development and native welfare between properly accredited representatives of the Governments with existing territorial interests in the Southwest Pacific area or in the South Pacific area or in both, namely, in addition to the two Governments, His Majesty's Government in the United Kingdom, the Government of the United States of America, the Government of the Netherlands, the French Committee of National Liberation and the Government of Portugal, and His Majesty's Government in the Commonwealth of Australia should take the necessary steps to call a conference of the Governments concerned.

PERMANENT MACHINERY FOR COLLABORATION AND COOPERATION BETWEEN AUSTRALIA AND NEW ZEALAND

35. The two Governments agree that

(a) Their cooperation for defense should be developed by

   (I) Continuous consultation in all defense matters of mutual interest;

  (II) The organization, equipment, training and exercising of the armed forces under a common doctrine;

 (III) Joint planning;

 (IV) Interchange of staff; and,

  (V) The coordination of policy for the production of munitions, aircraft and supply items and for shipping to ensure the greatest possible degree of mutual aid consistent with the maintenance of the policy of self-sufficiency on local production;

(b) Collaboration in external policy on all matters affecting the peace, welfare and good government of the Pacific should be secured through the exchange of information and frequent Ministerial consultation;

(c) The development of commerce between Australia and New Zealand and their industrial development should be pursued by consultation and in agreed cases by joint planning;

(d) There should be cooperation in achieving full employment in Australia and New Zealand and the highest standards of social security both within their borders and throughout the islands of the Pacific and other territories for which they are responsible;

(e) There should be cooperation in encouraging missionary work and all other activities directed towards the improvement of the welfare of the native peoples in the islands and territories of the Pacific.

36. The two Governments declare their desire to have the adherence to the objectives set out in the last preceding clause of any other Government having or controlling territories in the Pacific.

37. The two Governments agree that the methods to be used for carrying out the provisions of Clause 35 of this agreement and of other provisions of this agreement shall be consultation, exchange of information and where applicable joint planning. They further agree that such methods shall include

(a) Conferences of Ministers of State to be held alternately in Canberra and Wellington, it being the aim of the two Governments that these conferences be held at least twice a year;

(b) conferences of departmental officers and technical experts;

(c) meeting of standing intergovernmental committees on such subjects as are agreed to by the two Governments;

(d) the fullest use of the status and functions of the High Commissioner of the Commonwealth of Australia in New Zealand and the High Commissioner of the Dominion of New Zealand in Australia;

(e) regular exchange of information;

(f) exchange of officers; and

(g) the development of institutions in either country to serve the common purposes of both.

Permanent Secretariat

38. In order to ensure continuous collaboration on the lines set out in this agreement, and to facilitate the carrying out of the duties and functions involved, the two Governments agree that a permanent secretariat shall be established in Australia and New Zealand.

39. The Secretariat shall be known as the Australian-New Zealand Affairs Secretariat, and shall consist of a Secretariat of the like name to be set up in Australia and a Secretariat of the like name to be set up in New Zealand, each under the controller of the Ministry of External Affairs in the country concerned.

40. The functions of the secretariat shall be:

(a) To take the initiative in ensuring that effect is given to the provisions of this agreement;

(b) To make arrangements as the occasion arises for the holding of conferences or meetings;

(c) To carry out the directions of those conferences in regard to further consultation, exchange of information or the examination of particular questions;

(d) To coordinate all forms of collaboration between the two Governments;

(e) To raise for joint discussion and action such other matters as may seem from day to day to require attention by the two Governments, and

(f) generally to provide for more frequent and regular exchanges of information and views, these exchanges between the two Governments to take place normally through the respective High Commissioners.

41. His Majesty's Government in the Commonwealth of Australia and His Majesty's Government in the Dominion of New Zealand each shall nominate an officer or officers from the staff of their respective High Commissioners to act in closer collaboration with the Secretariat in which they shall be accorded full access to all relevant sources of information.

42. In each country the Minister of State for External Affairs and the resident High Commissioner shall have joint responsibility for the effective functioning of the Secretariat.

Ratification and Title of Agreement

43. This agreement is subject to ratification by the respective Governments, and shall come into force as soon as both Governments have ratified the agreement and have notified each other accordingly. It is intended that such notification will take place as soon as possible after the signing of this agreement.

44. This agreement shall be known as the Australian-New Zealand Agreement 1944.

Dated this 21st day of January One Thousand Nine Hundred and Forty Four.

Signed on behalf of His Majesty's Government in the Dominion of New Zealand.

Signed on behalf of His Majesty's Government in the Commonwealth of Australia.

CHAPTER XV

EUROPE, AFRICA AND WESTERN ASIA

1. RELATIONS WITH PARTICULAR EUROPEAN COUNTRIES

A. The United Kingdom

During the period under review, the relations between the United States and the United Kingdom have been largely carried on within the framework of the United Nations concept and for the purpose of achieving common United Nations purposes. For that reason, even though these relations have often been conducted on a two-party basis, they have been described and documented in Chapter IV (The United Nations). The texts of the communiqués signed by Prime Minister Churchill at the various international conferences have been printed as follows: Quebec, p. 224; Moscow, p. 226–32; Cairo, p. 232; Tehran, p. 234, and Second Cairo, p. 237.

For a description of the international agencies dealing with the prosecution of the war, see p. 238–47.

The amount of lend-lease operations with the United Kingdom appears at p. 124 and the reverse lend-lease furnished to the United States by the United Kingdom is given at p. 136.

1. POST-WAR RELATIONS

(1) *Address by the Prime Minister (Churchill) at Harvard University, September 6, 1943* [1]

President Conant, Mr. Governor of the Commonwealth of Massachusetts, gentlemen of the University, ladies and gentlemen here assembled, the last time I attended a ceremony of this character was in the spring of 1941 when, as Chancellor of Bristol University, I conferred a degree upon United States Ambassador Winant and, *in absentia*, our President who is here today and presiding over this ceremony.

. . . .

Twice in my lifetime the long arm of destiny has reached across the ocean and involved the entire life and manhood of the United States in a deadly struggle. There was no use saying: "We don't want it. We won't have it. Our forebears left Europe to avoid these quarrels. We have founded a new world which has no contact with the old." There was no use in that. The long arm reaches out remorselessly and everyone's existence, environment and outlook undergo a swift and irresistible change.

[1] British Information Services, *British Speeches of the Day*, No. 7, September 1943, p. 1.

What is the explanation, Mr. President, of these strange facts and what are the deep laws to which they respond? I will offer you one explanation. There are others, but one will suffice.

The price of greatness is responsibility. If the people of the United States had remained in a mediocre station, struggling with the wilderness, absorbed in their own affairs, and a factor of no consequence in the movement of the world, they might have remained forgotten and undisturbed beyond their protecting ocean. But one cannot rise to be in many ways the leading community in the civilized world without being involved in its problems, without being convulsed by its agony and inspired by its causes. If this has been true in the past, as it has been, it will become indisputable in the future. The people of the United States cannot escape world responsibility.

Although we live in a period so tumultuous that little can be predicted, we may be quite sure that this process will be intensified with every forward step the United States makes in wealth and in power. Not only are the responsibilities of this great republic growing, but the world over which they range is itself contracting in relation to our powers of locomotion at a positively alarming rate.

We have learned to fly. What prodigious changes are involved in that new accomplishment! Man has parted company with his trusty friend the horse and has sailed into the azure with the eagle — eagles being represented by the internal combustion engine. Where, then, are those broad oceans or vast glaring deserts? They are shrinking beneath our very eyes. Even elderly parliamentarians like myself are forced to acquire a high degree of mobility. But to the youth of America as to the youth of all the Britains I say:

We cannot stop. There is no halting place at this point. We have now reached the point in the journey where there can be no pause. We must go on. It must be world anarchy or world order.

Throughout all this ordeal and struggle which is characteristic of our age, you will find in the British Commonwealth and the Empire good comrades to whom you are united by other ties besides those of state policy and public needs. To a large extent there are the ties of blood and history. Naturally, I am a child of both worlds and conscious of these. Law, language, literature — these are considerable factors. Common conceptions of what is right and decent, a marked desire for fair play, especially to the weak and poor, a stern sentiment of impartial justice and above all, the love of personal freedom or, as Kipling put it, "leave to live by no man's leave underneath the law," these are common conceptions on both sides of the ocean among the English-speaking peoples. We hold to these conceptions as strongly as you do.

We do not war primarily with races as such. As you have said, Mr. Governor, tyranny is our foe. Tyranny is our foe whatever trappings or disguise it wears, whatever language it speaks. Be it external or internal, we must forever be on our guard, ever mobilized, ever vigilant, always ready to spring at its throat. In all this we march together. Not only do we march and strive shoulder to shoulder at this moment under the fire of the enemy on the fields of war, or in the air, but also in those realms of thought which are consecrated to the rights and dignity of man.

At the present time, Mr. President, we have in continual vigorous action the British and United States Combined Chiefs of Staff Committee which works immediately under the President and myself as representative of the British War Cabinet.

This Committee, with its elaborate organization of Staff officers of every grade, disposes of all our resources; and, in practice, uses British and American troopships, aircraft and munitions just as if they were the resources of a single state or nation.

I would not say there are never divergencies of view among these high professional authorities. It would be unnatural if there were not. That is why it is necessary to have plenary meetings of principals every two or three months. All these men now know each other, they trust each other, they like each other and most of them have been at work together for a long time. When they meet they thrash things out with great candor and plain blunt speech. But after a few days the President and I find ourselves furnished with sincere and united advice.

This is a wonderful system. There was nothing like it in the last war. There never has been anything like it between two allies. It is reproduced in an even more tightly-knit form at General Eisenhower's headquarters in the Mediterranean where everything is completely intermingled and soldiers are ordered into battle by the Supreme Commander or his deputy, General Alexander, without the slightest regard as to whether they are British, American or Canadian, but simply in accordance with the fighting needs.

Now, in my opinion, it would be a most foolish and improvident act on the part of our two governments, or either of them, to break up this smooth running and immensely powerful machinery the moment the war is over; but for our own safety, as well as for the security of the rest of the world, we are bound to keep it working and in running order after the war, probably for a good many years not only till we have set up some world arrangement to keep the peace but until we know that it is an arrangement which will really give us that protection we must have from danger and aggression — a protection we have already had to seek across two vast world wars.

.   .   .   .

Various schemes for achieving world security, while yet preserving national rights, traditions and customs, are being studied and probed.

We have all the fine work that was done a quarter of a century ago by those who devised and tried to make effective the League of Nations after the last war. It is said that the League of Nations failed. If so, that is largely because it was abandoned and, later on, betrayed; because those who were its best friends were still at very late periods infected with a futile pacificism; because the United States, the originating impulse, fell out of the line; because, while France had been bled white and England was supine and bewildered, a monstrous growth of aggression sprang up in Germany, in Italy and Japan.

We have learned from hard experience that stronger, more efficient, more rigorous world institutions must be created to prevent wars and to forestall the causes of future wars. In this task, the strongest, victorious nations must be combined, and also those who have borne the burden and heat of the day and suffered under the flail of adversity.

And in this task, creative task, there are some who say: "Let us have a world council and under it regional or continental councils." And there are others who prefer a somewhat different organization. All these matters weigh with us now in spite of the war, which none can say has reached its climax, which is perhaps entering for us, British and Americans, upon its most severe and costly stage.

But I am here to tell you that, whatever form your system of world security may take, however the nations are grouped and ranged, whatever derogations are made from national sovereignty for the sake of the larger synthesis, nothing will work soundly or for long without the united efforts of the British and American people. If we are together, nothing is impossible. If we are divided, all will fail.

I, therefore, preach continually the doctrine of the fraternal association of our two peoples, not for any purpose of gaining invidious material advantages for either of them, not for territorial aggrandizement or the vain pomp of earthly domination, but for the sake of service for mankind and for the honor that comes to those who faithfully serve great causes.

And here let me say how proud we ought to be, young and old, to live in this tremendous, thrilling, formative epoch in the human story; and how fortunate it was for the world that when these great trials came upon it there was a generation that terror could not conquer and brutal violence could not enslave.

Let all who are here remember, as the words of the hymn we have just sung suggest — let all of us that are here remember that we are on the stage of history and that whatever our station may be, whatever part we have to play, great or small, our conduct is liable to be scrutinized not only by history but by our own descendants. Let us rise to the full level of our duty and of our opportunity, and let us thank God for the spiritual reward He has granted for all forms of valiant and faithful service.

2. COMMONWEALTH POLICY

(1) Declaration of the King's Prime Ministers of the United Kingdom, Canada, Australia, New Zealand and South Africa, London, May 17, 1944 [1]

We, the King's Prime Ministers of the United Kingdom, Canada, Australia, New Zealand and South Africa, have now, for the first time since the outbreak of the war, been able to meet together to discuss common problems and future plans. The representative of India at the War Cabinet and the Prime Minister of Southern Rhodesia have joined in our deliberations and are united with us.

At this memorable meeting in the fifth year of the war we give thanks for deliverance from the worst perils which have menaced us in the course of this long and terrible struggle against tyranny.

Though hard and bitter battles lie ahead, we now see before us, in the ever-growing might of the forces of the United Nations and in the defeats already inflicted upon the foe by land, by sea and in the air, the sure presage of our future victory.

To all our armed forces, who in many lands are preserving our liberty with their lives, and to peoples of all our countries whose efforts, fortitude and conviction have sustained the struggle, we express our admiration and gratitude.

We honor the famous deeds of the forces of the United States and of Soviet Russia and pay our tribute to the fighting tenacity of the many states and nations joined with us.

We remember, indeed, the prolonged stubborn resistance of China, the first to be attacked by the author of world-aggression, and we rejoice in the unquenchable spirit of our comrades in every country still in the grip of the enemy. We shall not turn from the conflict till they are restored to freedom. Not one who marches with us shall be abandoned.

We have examined the part which the British Empire and Commonwealth of Nations should bear against Germany and Japan, in harmony with our Allies. We are in cordial agreement with the general plans which have been laid before us. As in the days when we stood all alone against Germany, we affirm our inflexible and unwavering resolve to continue in the general war with the utmost of our strength until the defeat and downfall of our cruel and barbarous foe has been accomplished. We shall hold back nothing to reach the goal and bring to the speediest end the agony of mankind.

We have also examined together the principles which determine our foreign policies, and their application to current problems. Here, too, we are in complete agreement. We are unitedly resolved to continue, shoulder to shoulder with our Allies, all needful exertion which will aid our

[1] *Ibid.*, Vol. II, No. 6 — Supplement, June 1944, p. 54.

fleets, armies and air forces during the war, and therefore to make sure of an enduring peace. We trust and pray that victory, which will certainly be won, will carry with it a sense of hope and freedom for all the world.

It is our aim that, when the storm and passion of war have passed away, all countries now overrun by the enemy shall be free to decide for themselves their future form of democratic government.

Mutual respect and honest conduct between nations is our chief desire. We are determined to work with all peace-loving peoples in order that tyranny and aggression shall be removed or, if need be, struck down wherever it raises its head. The people of the British Empire and Commonwealth of Nations willingly make their sacrifices to the common cause. We seek no advantages for ourselves at the cost of others. We desire the welfare and social advancement of all nations and that they may help each other to better and broader days.

We affirm that after the war a world organization to maintain peace and security should be set up and endowed with the necessary power and authority to prevent aggression and violence.

In a world torn by strife we have met here in unity. That unity finds its strength not in any formal bond but in the hidden spring from which human action flows. We rejoice in our inheritance, loyalties and ideals, and proclaim our sense of kinship to one another. Our system of free association has enabled us, each and all, to claim a full share of the common burden.

Although spread across the globe, we have stood together through the stress of two world wars, and have been welded the stronger thereby. We believe that when the war is won and peace returns, this same free association, this inherent unity of purpose, will make us able to do further service to mankind.

WINSTON S. CHURCHILL, Prime Minister of the United Kingdom of Great Britain and Northern Ireland.

W. L. MACKENZIE KING, Prime Minister of Canada.

JOHN CURTIN, Prime Minister of the Commonwealth of Australia.

PETER FRASER, Prime Minister of New Zealand.

J. C. SMUTS, Prime Minister of the Union of South Africa.

B. The Union of Soviet Socialist Republics

1. PROSECUTION OF THE WAR

During the period under review, two events occurred which had an important bearing on the relations of the Soviet Union with her principal allies: (1) the Moscow Conference of Foreign Ministers (see p. 226), followed by the Tehran Conference of heads of Governments (see p. 234); and (2) the invasion of Normandy on June 6. The Moscow and Tehran Conferences consummated a series of efforts by the American and British Governments to bring the Government of the Soviet Union into more effective cooperation in the over-all planning of the war and in dealing with war and post-war political problems. The invasion of Normandy was the first step in the realization of a second land front in the West which Premier Stalin had long been demanding and regarding which he had apparently received assurances at the Tehran Conference in December.

The United States continued during the period under review to give important lend-lease aid to the Soviet Union. For details, see p. 222. An interesting detail of lend-lease assistance, first brought up by Senator Bridges of New Hampshire in the course of Senate debate as a report which had come to him, and later confirmed by Senator Walsh of Massachusetts, Chairman of the Senate Committee on Naval Affairs, was the transfer to the Soviet Union of a light cruiser by the Navy Department.[1]

(1) Consultation with the Soviet Government. Department of State Release, September 1, 1943 [2]

The Soviet Government has been consulted and has been kept fully informed by the United States and British Governments in regard to all aspects of the military situation as it has developed in connection with operations against Italy and other operations in the European theater, and with respect to political situations arising directly out of military operations.

2. SOVIET RELATIONS WITH CZECHOSLOVAKIA

While relations between the Soviet Union and Czechoslovakia had been more friendly than Soviet relations with her other European neighbors, the agreements that were signed by representatives of these two governments providing for mutual assistance and defining the relations between Soviet and Czechoslovak authorities following liberation were regarded as giving some indication of what Soviet policy might be toward its eastern European neighbors. The terms of the Mutual Aid Treaty are to be compared with those of the Anglo-Soviet Treaty of May 26, 1942 (See *Documents, IV, 1941–42,* p. 254).

(1) Agreement of Friendship, Mutual Assistance and Post-War Collaboration between the Union of Soviet Socialist Republics and the Czechoslovak Republic, Signed at Moscow, December 12, 1943 [3]

The Presidium of the Supreme Soviet of the Union of Soviet Socialist Republics and the President of the Czechoslovak Republic, desiring to modify and supplement the Treaty on Mutual Assistance existing between the Union of Soviet Socialist Republics and the Czechoslovak Republic and signed in Prague on May 16, 1935,[4] confirm the provisions

[1] *New York Times*, June 8, 1944.
[2] Department of State, *Bulletin*, IX, p. 154.
[3] Embassy of the Union of Soviet Socialist Republics, *Information Bulletin*, No. 139, December 16, 1943, p. 1.
[4] League of Nations, *Treaty Series*, CLIX (1935–36), p. 347.

of the Agreement between the Government of the Union of Soviet Socialist Republics and the Government of the Czechoslovak Republic on
Joint Actions in War Against Germany signed in London on July 18,
1941,[1] desiring to assist after the war in the maintenance of peace and in
averting further aggression on the part of Germany and to insure continuous friendship and peaceful collaboration between themselves after
the war, have decided to conclude a treaty with this purpose and appointed as their Plenipotentiaries:

For the Presidium of the Supreme Soviet of the Union of Soviet
Socialist Republics — Vyacheslav Mikhailovich Molotov, People's
Commissar of Foreign Affairs; for the President of the Czechoslovak
Republic — Zdenek Firlinger, the Ambassador of the Czechoslovak
Republic in the Soviet Union, who upon the exchange of their credentials
found in due form and good order have agreed upon the following:

ARTICLE I. The high contracting parties, having mutually agreed to
unite in the policy of continuous friendship and friendly collaboration
after the war as well as of mutual assistance, undertake to render each
other military and other assistance and support of all kind in the present
war against Germany and all those states which are associated with her
in acts of aggression in Europe.

ARTICLE II. The high contracting parties undertake not to enter in
the course of the present war into any negotiations with the Hitler government or with any other government in Germany which does not
clearly renounce all aggressive intentions, and not to negotiate or conclude without mutual consent any armistice or peace treaty with Germany
or with any other state associated with her in acts of aggression in Europe.

ARTICLE III. Confirming their prewar policy of peace and mutual
assistance expressed in their treaty signed in Prague on May 16, 1935, the
high contracting parties undertake that, in the event one of them finds
itself in the postwar period involved in hostilities with Germany which
would resume her "Drang nach Osten" policy, or with any other state
which would unite with Germany directly or in any other form in such a
war, the other high contracting party will immediately render the contracting party thus involved in hostilities every military and other
support and assistance within its disposal.

ARTICLE IV. The high contracting parties, considering the interests of
security of each of them, agree to maintain close and friendly collaboration in the period after the reestablishment of peace and to act in conformity with the principles of mutual respect for their independence and
sovereignty, as well as for non-intervention in internal affairs of the
other State. They agree to develop their economic relations on the widest
possible scale and to render each other every possible economic assistance
after the war.

[1] *Inter-Allied Review,* I (1941), p. 5.

ARTICLE V. Each of the high contracting parties undertakes not to conclude any alliance and not to take part in any coalition directed against the other high contracting party.

ARTICLE VI. The present treaty comes into force immediately upon being signed and is subject to ratification within the shortest possible time; the exchange of the instruments of ratification shall be effected in Moscow as soon as possible. The present treaty shall remain in force for twenty years from its signature and, if at the end of the said period of twenty years one of the high contracting parties does not declare, twelve months prior to the expiration of the term, its desire to renounce the treaty, it shall remain in force for the next five years, and thus each time until one of the high contracting parties, twelve months prior to the expiration of the current five-year term, presents notice in writing of its intention to discontinue its operation. In testimony whereof the Plenipotentiaries have signed this treaty and have affixed their seals thereto. Made in two copies, each in the Russian and the Czechoslovak languages. Both texts have equal force.

Moscow, December 12, 1943
(*Signed*)

On authorization of the Presidium of the Supreme Soviet of the U.S.S.R.
MOLOTOV

On authorization of the President of the Czechoslovak Republic
FIRLINGER

(2) *Agreement between the Soviet and Czechoslovak Governments Regarding the Administration of Liberated Czechoslovak Territory, Signed at London, May 8, 1944* [1]

Details of the accord were announced simultaneously in Moscow and in London. In a statement broadcast to Czechoslovakia from London, Foreign Minister Ripka announced that his Government had drafted the text of the accord, that the Soviet Union had accepted the text without alteration, and that the British and United States Governments had expressed their approval.

The Government of the Czechoslovak Republic and the Government of the Union of Soviet Socialist Republics, desiring that the relationship between the Czechoslovak administration on territory of the Czechoslovak Republic and the Soviet (Allied) Commander-in-Chief on the entry of Soviet (Allied) troops into Czechoslovak territory should be adjusted in the spirit of friendship and of alliance existing between the two countries, have agreed upon the following:

ARTICLE I. After the entry, as a result of military operations, of Soviet and Allied troops on Czechoslovak territory, the sovereign power and responsibility in all matters concerning the prosecution of war will

[1] *Czechoslovak Government Press Bureau*, May 19, 1944, Vol. 4, No. 40; *New York Times*, May 9, 1944. See also *United Nations Review*, July 15, 1944, p. 185.

lie, as far as military operations and all measures necessary for their execution are concerned, in the hands of the Supreme commander of the Soviet and Allied troops.

ARTICLE II. A Czechoslovak Government Commissioner is to be appointed for the liberated territories whose duties will be as follows:

(a) To establish and conduct, according to Czechoslovak laws, the administration of the territory liberated from the enemy;

(b) To rebuild the Czechoslovak military forces.

(c) To secure active support by the Czechoslovak Administration for the Soviet and Allied Commanders in Chief; namely to give appropriate directives to the local authorities regarding the needs and desire of the Soviet and Allied Commander.

ARTICLE III. Czechoslovak military units which will be part of the Soviet and Allied Armies at the time of their entry into Czechoslovak territory are to be immediately used on Czechoslovak territory.

ARTICLE IV. To insure liaison between the Soviet and Allied Command and the Czechoslovak Government, a representative Czechoslovak Military Mission is to be appointed with the Soviet and Allied Command.

ARTICLE V. In the zones under the supreme authority of the Soviet and Allied Commander, Czechoslovak Government organs on liberated territory will keep contact with the Soviet and Allied Command through a Czechoslovak representative.

ARTICLE VI. As soon as any part of the liberated territory ceases to be a zone of direct military operations, the Czechoslovak Government takes over completely the power of administration of public affairs and will give the Soviet and Allied Commander, through its civil and military organs, every assistance and help.

ARTICLE VII. All persons belonging to the Soviet and Allied troops on the territory of Czechoslovakia are to be subject to the jurisdiction of the Soviet and Allied Commander. All persons belonging to the Czechoslovak military forces are to be subject to Czechoslovak jurisdiction. To this jurisdiction are also to be subject the civil population on Czechoslovak territory even in cases of crimes committed against Soviet and Allied troops, except crimes committed in a zone of military operations where they will be subject to the jurisdiction of the Soviet and Allied Command. In doubtful cases the question is to be decided by a mutual agreement between the Soviet and Allied Commander and the Czechoslovak Government representative.

ARTICLE VIII. Concerning financial problems having a bearing on the entry into Czechoslovak territory of Soviet and Allied troops, a special agreement will be reached.

ARTICLE IX. The present agreement comes into force immediately after it is signed. The agreement is made out in two copies, each in the Russian and Czechoslovak languages. Both texts are equally valid.

3. SOVIET RELATIONS WITH POLAND

[See *Documents, V, 1942–43*, p. 531.]

The death of General Wladyslaw Sikorski, in an airplane accident on July 4, 1943, created a serious crisis in Polish affairs, especially in relations with the Soviet Union, although the optimism which he expressed shortly before his death was perhaps not fully justified.[1] In the reorganization of the Government-in-Exile General Kazimierz Sosnowski became Commander-in-Chief of Poland's armed forces after promising to renounce the right which he would have as Commander-in-Chief to succeed to the Presidency.[2] Tadeusz Romer, Polish Ambassador to Moscow until the Soviet severance of diplomatic relations, became Minister of Foreign Affairs.[3]

In a speech delivered in Mexico City, November 12, 1943, Constantine Oumansky, the Soviet Ambassador to Mexico, indicated that the Soviet Union was determined to retain that part of the territory of pre-war Poland which she received on the basis of the German-Soviet Agreement of September 29, 1939.[4] This, coming after the discussion between the foreign ministers at Moscow, seemed to indicate that the Soviet Government had not changed its position on this issue, which had been one of the difficulties in the way of establishing good relations between the Soviet Government and the Polish Government-in-Exile.[5]

On January 1, President Wladyslaw Raczkiewicz declared that Poland wanted "respect for our undoubted right to that which belonged to us as a state before the war." On January 5 following a report that Soviet forces had crossed into pre-war Poland, the Polish Government issued a statement reaffirming its position and stating that it had instructed underground forces in Poland to continue resistance to the Germans, to avoid conflicts with Soviet troops in Poland and to cooperate with them if Soviet-Polish diplomatic relations were resumed.[6] On the following day, the Union of Polish Patriots in Moscow countered the statement of the Government-in-Exile with the following five-point program.[7]

1. Extension of Poland's strategic frontier westward.
2. Cession of the western Ukraine and western White Russia to the Soviet Union and settlement of all difficulties with Russia.
3. Establishment of a parliamentary democratic regime.
4. Wiping out of all "reactionary" elements and distribution of land to peasants.
5. Unification of all Poles, regardless of political creed, with the exclusion of "reactionary emigré elements abroad."

On January 11, a Soviet Government statement was issued stating the Soviet position.[8] The statement of the Soviet Government appeared to offer some hope of a compromise agreement which would permit the restoration of diplomatic relations between the Soviet Government and the Polish Government-in-Exile, recognized by the British and United States Governments, and the eventual establishment of friendly and cooperative relations between the two governments and their respective peoples. Clearly the British and United States Governments were exercising their influence to that end. On January 14 the Polish Government-in-Exile announced its willingness to discuss all outstanding questions with

[1] Article by Pertinax, *New York Times*, July 9, 1943.

[2] *New York Times*, July 11, 1943.

[3] *Ibid.*, July 15, 1943.

[4] An agreement was signed between Poland and the Soviet Union in London on July 30, 1941 abrogating the German-Soviet accord partitioning Poland.

[5] *New York Times*, November 15, 1943.

[6] *Ibid.*, January 6, 1944; this volume, p. 647.

[7] *New York Times*, January 7, 1944.

[8] Embassy of the Union of Soviet Socialist Republics, *Information Bulletin*, No. 5, January 13, 1944, p. 1; this volume, p. 649.

the Soviet Union and indicated that it was approaching the United States and British Governments with a view to having them act as intermediaries.[1] The Moscow radio broadcast a statement on January 17, in which it was announced that the evasion in the Polish declaration of the question of the recognition of the Curzon Line [2] could only be interpreted as a rejection of the offer. The Soviet Government could not, it was stated, enter into official relations with the Polish Government-in-Exile since diplomatic relations were broken off between them. These circumstances, in the opinion of the Soviet Government, demonstrated that the existing Polish Government did not desire to establish good neighborly relations with the Soviet Union.[3] On January 26, Secretary Hull announced that the Soviet Government had rejected a tender of good offices by the United States.

It became increasingly clear that the Soviet Government was averse to dealing with the Polish Government-in-Exile. *Wolna Polska*, the organ of the Union of Polish Patriots in Russia, announced on February 21 that a National Council had been created inside Poland, elected "by the most democratic methods" and uniting all groups actively engaged in the fight against the Germans. It stated that the Free Polish radio had announced on January 30 the creation of this Council, which had issued a manifesto urging the merging of all parties fighting against the Nazis, collaboration with the Allied troops, and the setting up of cordial relations with Russia, Britain, and the United States. This policy was described as the path to "a free, independent, strong, democratic Poland," and the Polish Government in London was described as "an émigré, Fascist clique." [4]

The position of the British and United States Governments continued to be that of recognizing the Government-in-Exile as the *de jure* Government of Poland. On the boundary question, Secretary Hull made it clear in his address to Congress following the Moscow Conference that American policy was to leave such problems "in abeyance until the termination of hostilities." [5] Anthony Eden, Secretary of State for Foreign Affairs in the United Kingdom Government, stated to the House of Commons on January 26 that "we do not propose to recognize any territorial changes which take place during the war unless they take place with the free consent and good-will of the parties concerned." [6]

(1) *Statement of the Polish Government, London, January 5, 1944* [7]

In their victorious struggle against the German invader, Soviet forces are reported to have crossed the frontier of Poland.

This fact is another proof of the breaking down of German resistance and it foreshadows the inevitable military defeat of Germany. It fills the Polish nation with hope that the hour of liberation is drawing near. Poland was the first nation to take up the German challenge and it has been fighting against the invaders for more than four years, at a cost of

[1] See below, p. 651.

[2] The Supreme Council of the Allied Powers on December 8, 1919 fixed the so-called Curzon Line as the provisional frontier of Poland by virtue of Article 87, par. 3, of the Treaty of Versailles.

[3] Royal Institute of International Affairs, *Bulletin of International News*, XXI (1944), p. 66.

[4] *Ibid.*, p. 207.

[5] Department of State, *Bulletin*, IX, p. 344; this volume, p. 11.

[6] *New York Times*, January 27, 1944.

[7] *Ibid.*, January 6, 1944; *United Nations Review*, February 15, 1944, p. 79.

tremendous sacrifices and sufferings, without producing a single Quisling and rejecting every form of compromise or collaboration with the aggressor.

The underground movement, among its many activities, concentrated upon attacking the Germans in their most sensitive spots, upon sabotage in every possible form and upon the carrying out of many death sentences on German officials whose conduct had been particularly outrageous.

Polish forces, twice reorganized outside their country, have been fighting ceaselessly in the air, at sea and on land, side by side with our Allies, and there is no front on which Polish blood has not been mingled with the blood of other defenders of freedom.

There is no country in the world where Poles have not contributed to furthering the common cause. The Polish nation, therefore, is entitled to expect full justice and redress as soon as it is set free from enemy occupation.

The first condition of such justice is the earliest reestablishment of Polish sovereign administration in the liberated territories of the Polish Republic, and the protection of the lives and property of Polish citizens.

The Polish Government, as the only legal steward and spokesman of the Polish nation, recognized by Poles at home and abroad as well as by the Allied and free governments, is conscious of the contribution of Poland to the war and is responsible for the fate of the nation. It affirms its indestructible right to independence, confirmed by the principles of the Atlantic Charter common to all the United Nations and by binding international treaties.

The provisions of those treaties, based on the free agreement of the parties, not on the enforcement of the will of one side to the detriment of the other, cannot be revised by accomplished facts. The conduct of the Polish nation in the course of the present war has proved that it has never recognized and will not recognize solutions imposed by force.

The Polish Government expects that the Soviet Union, sharing its view as to the importance of future friendly relations between the two countries, in the interests of peace and with the view of preventing German revenge, will not fail to respect the rights and interests of the Polish Republic and its citizens.

Acting in that belief, the Polish Government instructed the underground authorities in Poland on October 27, 1943, to continue and to intensify their resistance to the German invaders, to avoid all conflicts with Soviet armies entering Poland in their battle against the Germans and to enter into cooperation with Soviet commanders in the event of resumption of Polish-Soviet relations.

If a Polish-Soviet agreement, such as the Polish Government has declared itself willing to conclude, had preceded the crossing of the frontier of Poland by Soviet forces, such an agreement would have enabled the

Polish underground army to coordinate its action against the Germans with Soviet military authorities.

The Polish Government still considers such an arrangement highly desirable. At this crucial moment, the importance of which in relation to the outcome of the war in Europe is evident to everyone, the Polish Government issues the above declaration, confident in final victory and in the triumph of the just principles for which the United Nations stand.

This declaration has been handed to all the United Nations with which the Polish Government has diplomatic relations.

(2) *Declaration of the Soviet Government on Soviet-Polish Relations, Moscow, January 11, 1944* [1]

On January 5 in London was published a declaration of the emigré Polish Government on Soviet-Polish relations which contains a number of incorrect assertions, including an incorrect assertion about the Soviet-Polish frontier.

As is well known, the Soviet Constitution established the Soviet-Polish frontier in conformity with the will of the population of Western Ukraine and Western Byelorussia, as expressed through a plebiscite conducted on a broad democratic basis in 1939. Then the territories of the Western Ukraine in which Ukrainians form the overwhelming majority of the population were incorporated with the Soviet Ukraine, and the territories of Western Byelorussia in which Byelorussians form an overwhelming majority of the population were incorporated with Soviet Byelorussia. The injustice committed by the Riga Treaty of 1921, which was imposed upon the Soviet Union, in regard to the Ukrainians inhabiting the Western Ukraine and the Byelorussians inhabiting Western Byelorussia, was thus rectified.

The incorporation of Western Ukraine and Western Byelorussia with the Soviet Union not only did not violate the interests of Poland, but on the contrary created a reliable foundation for stable and permanent friendship between the Polish people and its neighbors, the Ukrainian and Byelorussian and Russian peoples.

The Soviet Government has repeatedly stated that it stands for the reestablishment of a strong and independent Poland and for friendship between the Soviet Union and Poland. The Soviet Government declares again that it seeks to establish friendship between the U.S.S.R. and Poland on the basis of stable, good-neighborly relations and mutual respect and, if the Polish people will so desire, on the basis of an alliance for mutual assistance against the Germans as the chief enemies of the Soviet Union and Poland.

Poland's joining of the Soviet-Czechoslovak treaty of friendship,

[1] Embassy of the Union of Soviet Socialist Republics, *Information Bulletin*, No. 5, January 13, 1944, p. 1.

mutual assistance and post-war collaboration could contribute to the accomplishment of this task.

The successes scored by Soviet troops on the Soviet-German front daily accelerate the liberation of the occupied territories of the Soviet Union from the German invaders. The self-sacrificing struggle of the Red Army and the developing war operations of our Allies bring nearer the utter defeat of the Hitlerite war-machine and are bringing to Poland and other nations liberation from the yoke to the German occupationists.

The Union of Polish Patriots in the U.S.S.R. and the Polish Army Corps formed by it, which acts on the front against the Germans hand-in-hand with the Red Army, are already fulfilling their glorious tasks in this struggle for liberation.

At present the possibility is opening for the rebirth of Poland as a strong and independent state. However, Poland must be reborn not through the seizure of Ukrainian and Byelorussian lands, but through the restoration to Poland of lands which belonged to Poland from time immemorial and were wrested by the Germans from her. Only in this way trust and friendship could be established between the Polish, Ukrainian, Byelorussian and Russian peoples.

The eastern frontiers of Poland can be established by agreement with the Soviet Union. The Soviet Government does not regard the frontiers of 1939 as unalterable. These frontiers can be modified in Poland's favor so that the areas in which the Polish population forms a majority be turned over to Poland. In this case the Soviet-Polish frontier could pass approximately along the so-called Curzon line, which was adopted in 1919 by the Supreme Council of the Allied Powers, and which provides for inclusion of the Western Ukraine and Western Byelorussia into the Soviet Union.

The western frontiers of Poland must be extended through incorporation with Poland of ancient Polish lands previously wrested by Germany, without which it is impossible to unite the whole Polish people in its state, which thereby will receive a needed outlet to the Baltic Sea.

The just aspiration of the Polish people for its full reunion in a strong and independent state must receive recognition and support.

The emigré Polish Government, isolated from its people, proved incapable of establishment of friendly relations with the Soviet Union. It also proved incapable of organizing active struggle against the German invaders within Poland herself. Furthermore, by its incorrect policy it not infrequently plays into the hands of the German occupationists.

However, the interests of Poland and the Soviet Union consist in that stable, friendly relations be established between our countries and that the people of Poland and the Soviet Union unite in struggle against the common external enemy, as demanded by the common cause of all the Allies.

(3) *Declaration of the Polish Government, London, January 14, 1944* [1]

The Polish Government have taken cognizance of the Declaration of the Soviet Government contained in the *Tass* communiqué of January 11, 1944, which was issued as a reply to the Declaration of the Polish Government of January 5.

The Soviet communiqué contains a number of statements to which a complete answer is afforded by the ceaseless struggle against the Germans waged at the heaviest cost by the Polish Nation under the direction of the Polish Government.

In their earnest anxiety to safeguard the complete solidarity of the United Nations especially at a decisive stage of their struggle against the common enemy, the Polish Government consider it to be preferable now to refrain from further public discussions. While the Polish Government cannot recognize unilateral decisions or accomplished facts which have taken place or might take place on the territory of the Polish Republic, they have repeatedly expressed their sincere desire for a Polish-Soviet agreement on terms which would be just and acceptable to both sides. To this end the Polish Government are approaching the British and United States Governments with a view to securing through their intermediary the discussion by the Polish and Soviet Governments with the participation of the British and American Governments of all outstanding questions, the settlement of which should lead to a friendly and permanent cooperation between Poland and the Soviet Union. The Polish Government believe this to be desirable in the interest of the victory of the United Nations and harmonious relations in post-war Europe.

(4) *Statement by the Secretary of State (Hull). Department of State Release, January 17, 1944* [2]

At his press and radio news conference on January 17 the Secretary of State said that having received officially the request of the Polish Government contained in its public statement of January 14, this Government through its Ambassador in Moscow, informed the Soviet Government of its willingness, if agreeable to the Soviet Government, to extend its good offices with a view to arranging for the initiation of discussions between the two Governments looking to a resumption of official relations between them. The Secretary said that without going into the merits of the case it is our hope that some satisfactory means may be found for the resumption of friendly relations between these two fellow members of the United Nations.

The Secretary added that no reply has been received from the Soviet Government.

(5) *Reply of the Soviet Government to the United States Inquiry Regarding the Polish Declaration of January 14, 1944. Statement of the Department of State, January 26, 1944* [3]

At his press and radio news conference on January 26 the Secretary of State declared that the Soviet Government had replied to the inquiry whether the

[1] Department of State, *Bulletin,* X, p. 97.　　[2] *Ibid.*, p. 96.　　[3] *Ibid.*, p. 116.

good offices of the United States with a view to arranging for the initiation of discussions between the Polish and Soviet Governments looking to a resumption of official relations between them would be agreeable to the Soviet Government. He added that the Soviet Government, after expressing appreciation of the offer made by the United States, had stated that it felt that conditions had not yet reached the stage where such good offices could be utilized to advantage.

4. SOVIET RELATIONS WITH RUMANIA

(1) Statement of the People's Commissar of Foreign Affairs of the Union of Soviet Socialist Republics (Molotov) to Representatives of the Soviet and Foreign Press, April 2, 1944 [1]

This statement was made at the time of the arrival of the Red Army on the Prut River, the frontier between Rumania and the Soviet Union when the German invasion of the Soviet Union took place on June 22, 1941.

As a result of a successful advance, the Red Army emerged on the Prut River, which forms the State frontier between the Union of Soviet Socialist Republics and Rumania. This laid the beginning of the full reestablishment of the Soviet State frontier established in 1940 by a treaty between the Soviet Union and Rumania, which was treacherously violated in 1941 by the Rumanian Government in alliance with Hitlerite Germany.

At present the Red Army is clearing Soviet territory of all enemy troops present on it, and the time is not far off when the entire Soviet frontier with Rumania will be fully reestablished.

The Soviet Government announces that advancing Red Army troops, pursuing the German armies and their allies, the Rumanian troops, crossed the Prut River in several sectors and entered Rumanian territory.

The Supreme Command of the Red Army has ordered the advancing Soviet troops to pursue the enemy until he is routed and surrenders.

At the same time the Soviet Government declares that it does not pursue the purpose of acquiring any part of Rumanian territory or of changing the social system existing in Rumania, and that the entry of Soviet troops into Rumania is dictated exclusively by military necessity and by the continued resistance of enemy troops.

(a) Statement of the Secretary of State (Hull), April 3, 1944 [2]

I have noted with considerable interest the statement made by Mr. Molotov in connection with the military operations now being conducted in Rumania. This statement makes clear to the Rumanian people that the main business of the armies of Soviet Russia is to defeat the enemy in the field. The political assurances which the statement contains should help the Rumanians to see that their own ultimate interests require that German forces be driven from their country.

[1] Embassy of the Union of Soviet Socialist Republics, *Information Bulletin*, No. 41, April 6, 1944, p. 1.
[2] Department of State, *Bulletin*, X, p. 315.

5. AUTONOMY OF SOVIET REPUBLICS IN FOREIGN RELATIONS

(1) *Report of the People's Commissar of Foreign Affairs of the Union of Soviet Socialist Republics (Molotov) to the Supreme Soviet, February 1, 1944* [1]

COMRADES DEPUTIES:

The question of the transformation of two People's Commissariats — the People's Commissariat of Defense and the People's Commissariat of Foreign Affairs — from Union into Union-Republican People's Commissariats has been posed before the Supreme Soviet.

The Council of People's Commissars believes that this question is quite ripe. This is not a matter of the ordinary reorganization of two People's Commissariats. This is primarily a matter of placing new and most responsible tasks before the Union Republics. The question has been posed of new tasks and rights of Union Republics, firstly in the matter of the defense of our country, and secondly in the sphere of external relations with foreign states, and in this connection, of important transformations in our Union State.

Heretofore the Union Republics took part in the common work of creation of the organization and equipment of the Red Army. Our Army was created as an All-Union Army, and there existed no separate army formations of the Republics. Now it is proposed to institute army formations of Republics, which should form component parts of the Red Army. In this connection there arises the need for the creation of People's Commissariats of Defense in the Union Republics, as well as the necessity of the transformation of the Union People's Commissariat of Defense into a Union-Republican People's Commissariat.

After the foundation of the Union of Soviet Republics in 1922, foreign political relations were wholly concentrated in the Union People's Commissariat of Foreign Affairs, to which individual Republics delegated their powers in foreign relations. Now the Government of the Union proposes that Union Republics be granted powers to enter into direct relations with foreign states and conclude agreements with them. Naturally, the granting of powers to the Republics in the sphere of foreign relations renders it necessary to create People's Commissariats of Foreign Affairs in the Union Republics and to transform the Union People's Commissariat of Foreign Affairs into a Union-Republican People's Commissariat.

The meaning of the proposed transformation is perfectly clear. This transformation signifies the great expansion of activities of the Union Republics which has become possible as a result of their political, economic and cultural growth, or, in other words, as a result of their national

[1] Embassy of the Union of Soviet Socialist Republics, *Information Bulletin*, No. 15, February 5, 1944, p. 1.

development. One cannot fail to see in this a new, important step in the practical solution of the national problem in the multi-national Soviet State, one cannot fail to see in this a new victory for our Lenin-Stalin national policy.

This transformation, however, has become possible not merely as a result of the strengthening of our Republics. It has become possible as a result of the achieved strengthening of our Union State as a whole. The strengthening of the Soviet Union that has taken place is most convincingly proved by the manner in which our Red Army, which bears the whole brunt of the struggle with the main forces of the most dangerous enemy, is beating the German-fascist army and successfully brings nearer the time of the complete expulsion of the enemy from Soviet territory and his utter defeat.

Now it is more than obvious how scandalously the enemy's calculations on the Red Army's defeat fell through and how nearsighted were the Hitlerites' calculations on causing disunity among the peoples of the Soviet Union. Our Army, which was joined by millions of people from all the nations in the Soviet Union and which receives such invaluable help from our guerrillas in the enemy's rear, proves more and more successfully with every day how strong our country has become, how powerful the Soviet system is, how great the friendship of the Soviet peoples is.

The present proposal on the transformations in the organization of defense and in foreign relations, providing for a great expansion of the functions of the Union Republics, should serve as a new confirmation of our confidence in the strength and growth of the forces of the Soviet Union. This confidence is demonstrated all the more forcefully that we propose to effect these transformations at the height of a Patriotic War, when the forces of our peoples are strained so greatly and when not every state would venture to undertake such important transformations.

I

Transformation of the People's Commissariat of Defense

I proceed to the question of the transformation of the People's Commissariat of Defense. It is proposed by the draft of the law to establish that the Union Republics organize army formations of the Republics, and that the People's Commissariat of Defense is transformed from a Union into a Union-Republican People's Commissariat. It is proposed accordingly to make the necessary addenda to the All-Union Constitution.

Now, too, we have national army formations in the Red Army. Our Army has Lithuanian, Latvian, Estonian, Georgian, Azerbaijanian, Armenian, Kazakh and certain other army formations. Some of these army units were created during the Patriotic War. Now that all the peoples of the Soviet Union strive to take their place in the ranks of the Red Army, creation of army formations of the Republics is of great importance to us. As is well known, in Tsarist Russia certain national-ities and peoples were not conscripted for military service. For instance, the Uzbeks, Kazakhs, Tajiks, Turkmenians, Kirghizians, and most of the peoples of the Northern Caucasus, also peoples of the North, were not subject to conscription. Tsarism, naturally, did not trust peoples which it kept in a colonial or semi-colonial status. The Tsarist power even did not do anything to prepare these peoples for gradual induction into the army.

In the Soviet time, the situation has changed radically. The legis-lation naturally contains no legal restrictions for some or other nation-alities as regards conscription. But a certain time had to pass in order to render possible actual realization of conscriptions to the Red Army in all parts of the Soviet Union. Partial conscriptions to the Red Army were carried out in past years even in those districts of the U.S.S.R. where no conscriptions took place in old times. National army units were formed in the Red Army as well, but up to recent time these formations could not really develop. Now the situation has changed for the better. Adequate possibilities have been created for army formations in the Union Republics. All the Republics have not only cadres of rank and file fighters, but also certain cadres of commanding personnel capable of directing respective army units. Thus at present the creation of army formations in the Union Republics can be placed on a firm foundation.

But to realize this task it is necessary to have Republican People's Commissariats of Defense, and consequently there arises the necessity of the transformation of the Union People's Commissariat of Defense into a Union-Republic People's Commissariat. It is to be expected that this will also increase the attention paid by the Republics to the organization of military training in schools and institutions of higher education, of which we stand in need. Under such conditions, the creation of army formations in the Republics as component parts of the Red Army will play a noninsignificant, positive part.

How will this affect our Red Army? Will this contribute to its strength-ening, to the growth of its might? Yes, this is beyond any doubt. Our Army has always been close to and cherished by the peoples of the Soviet Union. In the course of the Patriotic War, still stronger became the love of the peoples of the U.S.S.R. for their Army, still stronger and more universal became the pride of the Soviet people in the successes and heroism of the Red Army. Indeed, who fails to see what a glorious struggle is waged by our Army for the liberation of the Ukraine, for the liberation of Byelorussia? Who fails to appreciate whole-heartedly what the Red Army does to prepare the imminent liberation of Lithuania,

Latvia, Estonia, Moldavia and the Karelo-Finnish Republic? Who fails to remember that Soviet troops saved Azerbaijan, Georgia and Armenia from the invasion of German fascism? Who of our Soviet people does not glorify our Army for having defended our Capital — Moscow, for having routed the Germans at Stalingrad and launched an offensive along the whole front, for having defended Leningrad and fully lifted the blockade from it, and for now chasing the enemy hordes from the native soil without giving him any respite? Who, save those plagued by fascism, fails to understand now that the Red Army fulfills a mission of liberation not only with regard to its own motherland, but also with regard to all democratic countries which fight for their honor, freedom and independence against the mortal danger presented by fascism?

Who further does not know that the men and women workers of our mills and factories, that the men and women peasants on the collective farms, that our intelligentsia, that all the Soviet people, are ready to give all their strength to enhance the might of the Red Army, that by their self-sacrificing labor they discharge by actual deeds their duty to the motherland, to the heroic Red Army?

The formation of army units of the Republics should serve to strengthen further our Army as the defender of our country, as the reliable bulwark of the Soviet Union. The enemies of the Soviet Union need not doubt that as a result of these new army formations the forces of our State will grow still stronger. This will make them more cautious in the future.

This new embodiment of the growing friendship of the peoples of the Soviet Union will contribute to the further growth of the prestige of our country with the nations of the East and West.

II

TRANSFORMATION OF PEOPLE'S COMMISSARIAT OF FOREIGN AFFAIRS

Of no lesser significance is the transformation of the All-Union People's Commissariat of Foreign Affairs into a Union-Republican People's Commissariat. Before the foundation of the Soviet Union, along with the People's Commissariat of Foreign Affairs of the Russian Soviet Federative Socialist Republic, there existed People's Commissariats of Foreign Affairs in the Ukraine, Byelorussia, Georgia, Armenia and Azerbaijan, which on certain occasions maintained foreign relations with other states. During the early period when our State was not yet gathered into one Union State, but consisted of separate parts, a number of treaties and agreements were concluded between individual Soviet Republics and foreign states. On some occasions representatives of the Russian S.F.S.R. were specially authorized by other Soviet Republics to participate in international conferences and to conclude treaties with other states on behalf of all or several Soviet Republics.

Comrade Stalin said at the first All-Union Congress of Soviets that "at the time the Soviet Republics, although they acted together, marched separately, occupied primarily by the problem of their existence." That was inevitable at the initial stage. When the U.S.S.R. was founded in accordance with the common will of the Union Republics, it was decided to unify relations with foreign states in one center. Then was created the All-Union People's Commissariat of Foreign Affairs, in which were vested the powers of the People's Commissariats of Foreign Affairs of the separate Soviet Republics. Since then, up to our days, the Soviet State was represented abroad through All-Union diplomatic representatives. Treaties and agreements with foreign states were also concluded only on behalf of the Union. This was necessary at a certain stage of the development of our State and yielded its positive results by having strengthened the State and highly enhanced its part in international affairs. But even then, as far back as at the Party Congress in 1923, Comrade Stalin said: "We shall still take up the national question more than once, since national and international conditions are subject to changes and may still change. I do not preclude the possibility that subsequently we may have to separate certain commissariats which we are now merging in the Union of Republics . . ."

Being the best authority on the national question, not only in our Party and not only in our country, Comrade Stalin, who together with the great Lenin laid the foundation of the Soviet Union, pointed out even then that changes in the international situation and the national development would more than once call forth organizational changes in the machine of the Soviet State. No other state of affairs can be imagined, especially in such a young and rapidly gaining strength organism as the Soviet Union is.

Now the question of the foreign relations of the Union Republics stands differently from the way it stood two decades ago when the Soviet Union was being founded. It grew out of the vital needs of the Republics and its solution is dictated by the interests of the Union as a whole. The time is long past when certain foreign states tried not to notice the existence of the Soviet Republic born in the October Revolution. Now, on the contrary, among foreign states there is a growing desire to establish and develop diplomatic relations with our State.

Certainly under conditions of World War this meets with peculiar, not insignificant difficulties, but still even in the years of war the international connections of the U.S.S.R. have been steadily extending. One may even say that it was just in the years of the war that the international connections of the Soviet Union have risen to a new and higher level. The facts are universally known. For the first time during the existence of Soviet power, we have established not only friendly but even allied relations with Great Britain. Similar good relations have been formed between us and the United States of America. A powerful anti-Hitler coalition has been formed, headed by the Soviet Union, Great Britain and the United States of America, a coalition whose military and political importance for the whole range of democratic states can hardly be overestimated. The recently concluded Soviet-Czechoslovak Treaty may serve as an example of the strengthening of friendly relations of the Soviet Union with European states. The foundations have been laid for the cooperation of large and small democratic countries, not only in time of war against a common enemy, but also in the post-war period for the sake of safeguarding peace against new encroachments on the part of aggressive powers.

As is well known, the Moscow and Tehran Conferences played a most eminent part in the development and strengthening of the anti-Hitler coalition. Now as never before, great is the confidence of the peoples of the anti-Hitler camp in near and complete victory, in joint crushing blows of the Allies at the common enemy, which are already not distant, as well as confidence that the alliance and friendship of the anti-fascist countries will be steeled in this common struggle.

And still it cannot be said that this general positive course of development of the international connections of the Soviet Union could fully cover not only the requirements of the whole Union but also the multifarious and growing requirements of the Union Republics in foreign affairs. Thus the Union Republics have quite a few specific economic and cultural requirements which cannot be covered in full measure by All-Union representation abroad and also by treaties and agreements of the Union with other states. These national requirements of the Republics can be met better by means of direct relations of the Republics with the corresponding states. Naturally, questions of this kind require special concrete elaboration in Union and Republican organs. It cannot be denied either that a certain time will be required to organize these external activities of the Republics. Such questions are not solved after a cut and dried pattern. It is indisputable, however, that the problem of emerging into the arena of external activities has already acquired vital importance for a number of Republics.

Lastly, it should be acknowledged that this is in the interests not only of this or that individual Union Republic, but also in the interests of the entire cause of the expansion of international connections and the strengthening of the cooperation of the U.S.S.R. with other states, which is of such importance in time of war and which will yield fruit also in the post-war period.

Such are the grounds on which the necessity of the transformation of the People's Commissariat of Foreign Affairs from a Union into a Union-Republican People's Commissariat should be recognized. Whereas in the initial period there existed only Republican People's C

Foreign Affairs, and in the second period only a Union Commissariat of Foreign Affairs, now the People's Commissariat of Foreign Affairs should be transformed into a more complex and ramified organization — into a Union-Republican People's Commissariat.

It remains for me to add a few words on our diplomatic practice. It is necessary to note that the absence of special provisions in the Soviet Constitution as regards the rights of Union Republics to exchange of representations with other states and to the maintenance of foreign relations, is sometimes interpreted to the direct detriment of the interests of the Soviet Republics and of the Soviet Union as a whole. The proposed addition will serve to eliminate facts of this kind.

III

New Forward Stride in Solution of National Problem

The proposed transformation of the People's Commissariat of Foreign Affairs and the People's Commissariat of Defense is a new forward stride in the solution of the national problem in the Soviet Union. This transformation is in direct accord with the principles of our Lenin-Stalin national policy. The realization of measures of this kind at the present time means that the Soviet State has reached a new level in its development, turning into a more complex and virile organism. In this one cannot fail to see fresh evidence of the great significance of the socialist principles of the organization of the Soviet Union.

In his report to the Congress of Soviets which adopted the Constitution of the U.S.S.R. in 1936, Comrade Stalin thus characterized the victory of the national policy of the Soviet power which insured the success of the formation of a multi-national state on the basis of socialism:

The absence of exploiting classes which are the principal organizers of strife between nations; the absence of exploitation which cultivates mutual distrust and kindles nationalist passions; the fact that power is in the hands of the working class which is the foe of all enslavement and the true vehicle of the ideas of internationalism; the actual practice of mutual aid among the peoples in all spheres of economic and social life; and finally, the flourishing national culture of the peoples of the U.S.S.R., a culture which is national in form and socialist in content — all these amd similar factors have brought about a radical change in the aspect of the peoples of the U.S.S.R.; their feeling of mutual distrust has disappeared, a feeling of mutual friendship has developed among them, and thus real fraternal cooperation among the peoples has been established within a system of a single Union State. As a result, we now have a fully-formed multi-national socialist State which has stood all tests and whose stability might well be envied by any national state in any part of the world.

Seven years — and what years! — have passed since then. Soon it will be three years that we have been waging the great Patriotic War against German fascism and its allies, which use the material and man-power resources of nearly the whole of Europe in their struggle against the Soviet Union. This has been a new — and the most serious at that — test for our multi-national State. But the Soviet Union has passed this test, too, with flying colors.

On the 26th anniversary of the October Revolution, Comrade Stalin thus summed up the latest period:

All the peoples of the Soviet Union have risen as one to defend their mother-land, rightly considering the present Patriotic War the common cause of all working people, irrespective of nationality or religion. By now the Hitlerite politicians have themselves seen how hopelessly stupid were their hopes of dis-cord and strife among the peoples of the Soviet Union. Their friendship of the peoples of our country has withstood all hardships and trials of war and has become tempered still further in the common struggle of all Soviet people against the fascist invaders.

This — in Comrade Stalin's words — is one of the decisive sources of the strength of the Soviet Union.

Let us sum up. Carrying out under the present conditions important State transformations, we must of course pose the question of how this will affect the Red Army and its deep rear in the country. In other words, are we making a step toward the strengthening or toward the weakening of the U.S.S.R.?

Everything said above permits to give a definite answer to this question. The transformation of the People's Commissariat of Foreign Affairs and the People's Commissariat of Defense which follows from the expansion of the tasks and functions of the Union Republics within the country and beyond its confines, far from running counter to the interests of the strengthening of our Union, on the contrary is being effected in the name of and for the purpose of the further strengthening of our great State.

Since the time when the Soviet Union was founded, the Constitution has insured to the Union Republics such a supreme expression of their sovereign rights as the right of free secession from the U.S.S.R. But as time passes the stronger becomes the desire of the peoples of the Soviet Union to live in close friendship among themselves, to help one another and to march together through all trials under the guidance of Soviet power.

The recognition by the Union of the increased requirements of the Republics in their state activities, including foreign activities, and legis-lative provision for these needs of the Republics, only serve to strengthen the fraternal relations among the peoples of our country and reveal still more fully the historic meaning of the existence of the Soviet Union to the peoples of the East and West.

It should be recognized further that the new forward stride in the solution of the national problem in the U.S.S.R. is of great importance from the viewpoint of all progressive humanity. At a time when German fascism — this worst product of imperialism! — has reared its head and unleashed a World War to strangle its neighbors, to destroy free states and impose its bandit imperialist policy upon other peoples of Europe, and after that upon the peoples of the whole world — the new success in the realization of the Lenin-Stalin national policy in the Soviet State will have especially great international significance. This step of the Soviet power will constitute a new moral-political blow at fascism and its man-hating policy, hostile to its core to the interest of the free national development of peoples.

The Soviet Union and its Allies are already successfully beating fascism, which imposed this war, hastening the time of its utter military defeat. But we know the matters should not be restricted to the military defeat of the fascist forces. It is necessary to bring to completion the moral-political defeat of fascism as well. To this, we are certain, will successfully contribute those State transformations in the Soviet Union which are now submitted for your approval.

I express assurance that the Supreme Soviet will demonstrate the unanimity of the Soviet people in the solution of the question of the proposed State transformations.

(2) *Law for the Granting to the Union Republics of Plenipotentiary Powers in the Field of Foreign Relations, Kremlin, Moscow, February 1, 1944* [1]

[Translation]

[For text of the law granting autonomy to the Republics in defense matters, see *New York Times*, February 3, 1944.]

With a view to extending international relations and to strengthening the collaboration of the Union of Soviet Socialist Republics with other states and in view of the growing need of the Union Republics to establish direct relations with foreign states, the Supreme Soviet of the Union of Soviet Socialist Republics resolves:

1. To provide that the Union Republics may enter into direct relations with foreign states and conclude agreements with them.

2. To include in the Constitution of the U.S.S.R. the following amendments:

(*a*) Add to Article 14 point "*a*" of the Constitution of the U.S.S.R. after the words "representation of the Union in international relations, conclusion and ratification of treaties" the words "the establishment of

[1] Department of State, *Bulletin*, X, p. 421.

the general form of mutual relations of the Union Republics with foreign states" whereby this point will read as follows:

"(*a*) Representation of the Union in international relations, conclusion and ratification of treaties with other states, and the establishment of the general form of mutual relations of the Union Republics with foreign states."

(*b*) Add to the Constitution of the U.S.S.R. Article 18–*a* with the following content:
"Article 18–*a*. Each Union Republic has the right to enter into direct relations with foreign states, to conclude agreements with them and to exchange diplomatic and consular representatives."

(*c*) Add to Article 60 of the Constitution of the U.S.S.R. point "*e*" with the following content:

"(*e*) Establishes representation of the Union Republic in international relations."

3. To reorganize the People's Commissariat for Foreign Affairs from an All-Union to a Union-Republican People's Commissariat.

President of the Presidium of the Supreme Soviet of the U.S.S.R.,
M. KALININ.
Secretary of the Presidium of the Supreme Soviet of the U.S.S.R.,
A. GORKIN.

(a) Circular Note from the Commissariat of Foreign Affairs of the Union of Soviet Socialist Republics, February 11, 1944 [1]

[Excerpt]

With a view to expanding international relations and to strengthening the collaboration of the Union of Soviet Socialist Republics with other states, and in view of the growing need of the Soviet Republics for establishing direct relations with foreign states, the new Law provides that each Soviet Republic has the right to enter into direct relations with foreign states, to conclude agreements with them and to exchange diplomatic and consular representatives. The Law of February 1, 1944, introduces appropriate amendments into the present Constitution of the Union of Soviet Socialist Republics of December 5, 1936.

C. France

[See *Documents, IV, 1941–42*, p. 623; *V, 1942–43*, p. 535.]

The formation of the French Committee of National Liberation under the joint chairmanship of Generals de Gaulle and Giraud on June 3, 1943,[2] raised the general question of the attitude to be adopted by the United States and Allied governments and, more particularly, the degree of recognition to be accorded.

[1] *Ibid.*
[2] *Documents, V, 1942–43*, p. 589.

The policy of the United States Government, apparently supported by that of Great Britain, had been to unify French resistance forces in effective opposition to Germany, and once victory was won, provide the French people with the freest opportunity to select their own leaders and form of government.[1] In line with this general policy, the United States Government, with the support of the British Government, used its influence to keep General Giraud in command of the French forces. On July 7, General Giraud arrived in Washington for a visit, the guest of the United States.[2] The General's visit was officially described as mainly military. On July 9 he announced that he had "made an agreement with the President for the rearming of 300,000 men with American equipment." [3]

Meantime, in Algiers on Bastille Day, July 14, General de Gaulle in a speech called for a Fourth Republic free of privilege and exploitation. He declared that it was impossible "to consider the action of the French armies independently of the sentiment and wishes of the great mass of people." [4] In an exclusive interview with Drew Middleton of the *New York Times* on July 21, General de Gaulle outlined three main objectives of the French after victory: first, the return of democracy, second, treatment as a sovereign nation, and third, economic, social and political resurrection.[5]

On July 31, the French Committee of National Liberation announced the unification of all French fighting forces by the appointment of General Giraud as the Commander-in-Chief of all French forces, and the appointment of General de Gaulle as the permanent president of a Committee of National Defense.[6] It was announced that General Giraud would preside over the Committee of National Liberation when military affairs were being discussed, and General de Gaulle when other matters were being considered.

One of the first major political results of the Quebec Conference was the recognition of the French Committee of National Liberation by the American and British Governments on August 26.[7] The recognition was limited in nature and did not go as far as the French themselves probably would have liked. In general the attitude at Algiers was that of hopefulness.[8] The recognition by the Soviet Government reported on August 27 was interpreted as going somewhat beyond that of the British and United States Governments.[9]

The Committee of National Liberation announced its first important change in composition on September 6 with the appointment of François de Menthon, a coordinator of "Combat," one of the large underground resistance organizations in France, as Commissioner for Justice.[10] On September 7, it was announced that the Provisional Consultative Assembly, due to open on November 3, would be enlarged to eighty members, of whom half were to represent the resistance movements in France.[11]

On September 27, the question of the control of the armed forces was given a new solution with the decision of the Committee of National Liberation to establish a new Commissariat for National Defense.[12] General Paul Le Gentilhomme was appointed to the new post. When the Provisional Consultative

[1] See Statement of Secretary Hull, December 17, 1942, *ibid.*, p. 553.

[2] *New York Times*, July 7, 1943.

[3] *Ibid.*, July 10, 1943.

[4] *Ibid.*, July 15, 1943.

[5] *Ibid.*, July 22, 1943.

[6] *Ibid.*, August 1, 1943; *Free France*, November–December, 1943, p. 182.

[7] *New York Times*, August 27, 1943.

[8] *Ibid.*

[9] *Ibid.*, August 28, 1943.

[10] *Ibid.*, September 7, 1943.

[11] *Ibid.*, September 8, 1943. For texts of Ordinance Concerning the Establishment of the Provisional Consultative Assembly of September 17, 1943 and the Modifying Ordinance of December 6, 1943, see *Free France*, Special Issue No. 1 (April, 1944), p. 15, 18.

[12] *New York Times*, September 28, 1943.

Assembly met at Algiers on November 3, General de Gaulle opened the meeting with a "restrained but unqualified reminder" to the three major Allies that any world settlement without France would be a mistake.[1]

On November 9, General Giraud resigned as co-chairman of the French Committee of National Liberation, leaving General de Gaulle with full powers in a reshuffling of positions which eliminated all but two "Giraudists."[2] General de Gaulle subsequently emphasized that the Committee was the only authority that had any value within France or which would be accepted by the French.[3]

On December 21, details of the plan of the Committee for the restoration of republican government in France were released. The plan received final approval from the Committee on December 18.[4] When the plan was presented to the Provisional Consultative Assembly, strong objections were raised to certain features. The Committee on Legislation and State Reforms drew up another draft.[5] Following the debates in the Assembly, the French Committee of National Liberation adopted on April 21, 1944, the Ordinance on Organized Public Powers in Liberated France.[6]

The demand of the Committee for fuller recognition by the United States and British Governments and greater participation in military and political discussions and decisions met a considerable measure of recognition when the British Government on February 8 signed a financial agreement fixing the exchange rate and a mutual-aid agreement with the Committee.[7]

Belief that invasion of continental France was imminent increased demands from many quarters that the status of the Committee of National Liberation should be further clarified. On March 17, President Roosevelt confirmed a report that he had drafted a new formula for partial recognition of the Committee.[8] This aroused considerable speculation as to what the intentions of the United States Government were. On March 26, in an address to the Provisional Consultative Assembly, General de Gaulle referred to the Committee as "the Provisional Government of the French Republic" and stated that the Government need listen only to the French nation.[9]

Presumably with a view to making the Committee more representative of the French Nation, announcement was made on April 4 of the inclusion of two Communists in the Committee.[10] At the same time, General de Gaulle became supreme commander of the armed forces. General Giraud was offered the post of Inspector General, a position which he refused. As a consequence, he was placed "en reserve de commandement."[11]

The failure of the United States and British Governments to accord the Committee fuller recognition and to reach agreement with the Committee on French participation in military operations incident to the invasion of continental France and in the administration of freed territory, combined with the action of the British Government on April 7 in restricting on security grounds communications between foreign embassies and consulates in Great Britain and their governments, other than those of the United States, the Soviet Union and the Dominions, aroused considerable feeling in the French Committee and among its supporters. General de Gaulle's reference to the Committee as the "Provisional

[1] *Ibid.*, November 3, 1943.
[2] *Ibid.*, November 10, 1943.
[3] *Ibid.*, November 11, 1943.
[4] Article by Harold Callender, *New York Times*, December 22, 1943; *Free France*, May 1, 1944, p. 334.
[5] *Free France*, May 1, 1944, p. 334.
[6] *Ibid.*, p. 337.
[7] *New York Times*, February 9, 1944.
[8] *Ibid.*, March 17, 1944.
[9] *Ibid.*, March 28, 1944.
[10] *Ibid.*, April 5, 1944.
[11] *Ibid.*, April 15, 1944.

Government of the French Republic" was one manifestation of independence born of resentment. On April 1, the Committee published the text of an ordinance communicated to the United States, British and Soviet Governments, setting forth proposals for the establishment of civilian and military authorities to operate in France following Allied landings.[1] On May 7, General de Gaulle, in a speech in Tunis referred to future French relations with the Soviet Union in particularly friendly terms.[2] On May 15, General de Gaulle announced to the Provisional Consultative Assembly that the Darlan-Clark agreements, on which Allied military authority rested in North Africa, were not binding in the eyes of France.[3] On the same day the Assembly voted unanimously to change the name of the Committee to "Provisional Government of the French Republic." On June 2, the Committee adopted an ordinance to that effect.[4]

On June 5, the day before the invasion of Normandy commenced, General Eisenhower told correspondents that there was complete agreement between the French Committee and him on the military level. This statement was made after a conference in which General de Gaulle, Prime Minister Churchill and others participated.[5] On June 6, D-day, General de Gaulle made an appeal to the people of France. In this appeal, he stated that "the good conduct of the battle" required "that the directives given by the French Government and the French chiefs it has qualified, locally and nationally, be carefully followed, in letter and in spirit."[6] On the 10th, he stated to the Agence Française Independente that "at present there is unfortunately no agreement between the French Government and the Allied Governments concerning the cooperation of the French administration with the Allies' armies in liberated French metropolitan territory."[7] "Furthermore," he said, "the proclamation addressed to the French people on June 6 and the one published today seem to foreshadow a sort of taking over of power in France by the Allies' military command. This situation is obviously not acceptable to us. . . ."[8] It was announced in Algiers on June 13 that the French Committee of National Liberation, acting as the "Provisional Government of the French Republic" had appointed military and civilian leaders for freed areas of Normandy.[9]

On June 15 General de Gaulle installed M. François Coulet as Commissioner for Civil Affairs in Normandy.[10] It was reported "on high authority" from Algiers on June 22 that an agreement had been reached between General Eisenhower and General de Gaulle for the use of some 230 French liaison officers, these officers to go to France on the staff of Brigadier General Joseph Pierre Koenig, Algiers liaison officer in London.[11] On June 28, it was announced that the French Committee had appointed four more regional commissioners for liberated areas.[12]

On June 27, it was announced in Washington that General de Gaulle was expected to visit Washington between July 5 and 9.

(1) Statement of the President (Roosevelt) on Bastille Day, July 14, 1943 [13]

The 14th of July is, for all the peoples of the world devoted to the ideals of liberty, a day of celebration. We observe it this year, here in the United States, with special fervor. Immortal France has reaffirmed once again, in the most heroic circumstances, her greatness and her glory.

[1] Free France, May 1, 1944, p. 328.   [2] New York Times, May 8, 1944.
[3] Ibid., May 16, 1944.   [4] Ibid., June 3, 1944; Free France, July 1, 1944, p. 15.
[5] New York Times, June 8, 1944.   [6] Free France, July 1, 1944, p. 2.
[7] New York Times, June 11, 1944.   [8] Ibid.   [9] Ibid., June 14, 1944.
[10] Ibid., June 16, 1944.   [11] Ibid., June 23, 1944.
[12] Ibid., June 29, 1944.   [13] Department of State, Bulletin, IX, p. 28.

On this anniversary of the winning by the French people of their liberties I wish to recall again that the fundamental principles which guide our democracies were evolved from the American and the French Revolutions. The keystone of our democratic structure is the principle which places governmental authority in the people, and in the people only. There can be one symbol only for Frenchmen — France herself. She transcends all parties, personalities, and groups: they live indeed only in the glory of French nationhood.

One of our war aims, as set forth in the Atlantic Charter, is to restore the mastery of their destinies to the peoples now under the invaders' yoke. There must be no doubt anywhere of the unalterable determination of the United Nations to restore to the oppressed peoples their full and sacred rights.

French sovereignty resides in the people of France.

Today this people is shackled by barbaric oppression. In the freedom of tomorrow, when Frenchmen and their brothers in arms of the United Nations have cleansed French soil of the enemy, the French people will again give expression to their freedom in the erecting of a government of their own free choice.

Long live Liberty, Equality, Fraternity. May France live forever!

(2) *Report of Remarks of the President (Roosevelt) at His Press Conference, July 16, 1943* [1]

President Roosevelt suddenly started talking about the Martinique situation, speaking of a development [2] that he said had worked out rather well since his press conference on Tuesday.

We have had a problem in Martinique and Guadeloupe and several other French islands down there, the President said, and we had a somewhat difficult problem in Admiral Robert. This, he said, was a very polite way of saying it.

There were a great many people, even a lot of isolationists, who wanted us immediately to go down there with a great fleet and a landing force and take Martinique and Guadeloupe, with a lot of bloodshed and so forth, at the same time buying a large-sized headache in the actual running of those French islands, he continued. For about two years now, we have been just taking it on the chin — keeping quiet, the President asserted. We wanted to avoid bloodshed and we hoped that the matter would be peacefully resolved without bloodshed and without landing an expeditionary force.

So we waited it out, the President continued, and we got the base on balls, which we hoped we would get from the beginning.

[1] *New York Times*, July 17, 1943.
[2] See this volume, p. 602.

Now it seems quite clear that virtually every part of the French Empire has joined in working in the common cause for the defeat of Germany and the liberation of France itself, he declared. He added that we had kept aloof and away from the internal political side of affairs, especially in the Axis-occupied countries, and have consistently refused to become involved in political rivalries and political ambitions of individuals or groups.

Out of this, the President added, have come all kinds of vicious propaganda attacking the State Department and the Government as a whole. There were many unfair and incorrect rumors, reports and statements that were derogatory to a perfectly well-ordered plan that went back several years, he added.

We have had a consistent policy since the fall of France, he continued, our policy being the preservation of the French fleet and the naval and air bases from falling into Axis hands until last November, when the Axis occupied the balance of France. The President said that, while France had lost her fleet, we had got the North African landing operation successfully concluded and have been working in close cooperation with all Frenchmen everywhere who were patriotically resisting the Axis powers and who had been working to encourage the people of France to keep thoroughly alive the principles of liberty and freedom. So far, he concluded, it has worked pretty well.

(3) *Letter of Assistant Secretary of State Berle to Mr. Mortimer Hayes, Published July 25, 1943* [1]

[Excerpt]

This letter was sent in reply to one addressed by Mr. Hayes to Secretary Hull, in which Mr. Hayes suggested that the United States recognize the French Committee of National Liberation.

Unfortunately, this is not the case with France and no French group today can authoritatively claim to represent the will of the French people under Axis domination. The French Government of early 1940 disappeared and since that time the French people have had no opportunity to express themselves politically.

In the circumstances it seems to me that the only truly democratic course for the friends of France to take is along the lines of the policy which this Government has consistently followed, namely, to refrain from recognizing any group of Frenchmen as the Government of France until the French people are liberated and are again in a position to exercise their free will in the choice of their leaders.

Naturally, the withholding of such recognition does not mean that we have no relations with those Frenchmen who have succeeded in escaping

[1] *New York Times*, July 25, 1943.

from their conquered country. On the contrary we have from the beginning eagerly sought the cooperation of all Frenchmen sincerely desirous of taking an active part in the war against the Axis and will continue to cooperate with them in all matters dealing with the prosecution of the war.

It is for this reason that General Giraud was invited to visit the United States. You may be sure that, if the extension of an invitation to General de Gaulle would further our present military objectives, that invitation would be extended without delay.

(4) *Statement of the President (Roosevelt) on the Recognition of the French Committee of National Liberation, August 26, 1943* [1]

The Government of the United States desires again to make clear its purpose of cooperating with all patriotic Frenchmen, looking to the liberation of the French people and French territories from the oppressions of the enemy.

The Government of the United States, accordingly, welcomes the establishment of the French Committee of National Liberation. It is our expectation that the Committee will function on the principle of collective responsibility of all its members for the active prosecution of the war.

In view of the paramount importance of the common war effort, the relationship with the French Committee of National Liberation must continue to be subject to the military requirements of the Allied commanders.

The Government of the United States takes note, with sympathy, of the desire of the Committee to be regarded as the body qualified to insure the administration and defense of French interests. The extent to which it may be possible to give effect to this desire must however be reserved for consideration in each case as it arises.

On these understandings the Government of the United States recognizes the French Committee of National Liberation as administering those French overseas territories which acknowledge its authority.

This statement does not constitute recognition of a government of France or of the French Empire by the Government of the United States.

It does constitute recognition of the French Committee of National Liberation as functioning within specific limitations during the war. Later on the people of France, in a free and untrammeled manner, will proceed in due course to select their own government and their own officials to administer it.

The Government of the United States welcomes the Committee's expressed determination to continue the common struggle in close co-

[1] Department of State, *Bulletin*, IX, p. 125.

operation with all the Allies until French soil is freed from its invaders and until victory is complete over all enemy powers.

May the restoration of France come with the utmost speed.

(a) Statement of the United Kingdom Government Announcing Recognition of the French Committee of National Liberation, August 27, 1943 [1]

His Majesty's Government in the United Kingdom desire again to make clear their purpose of cooperating with all patriotic Frenchmen looking to the liberation of the French people and French territories from oppressions of the enemy.

His Majesty's Government in the United Kingdom accordingly welcome the establishment of the French Committee of National Liberation. It is their understanding that the committee has been conceived and will function on the principle of collective responsibility of all its members for prosecution of the war.

It is also, they are assured, a common ground between themselves and the committee that it will be for the French people themselves to settle their own constitution and to establish their own government after they have had an opportunity to express themselves freely. On this understanding His Majesty's Government in the United Kingdom wish to make the following statement:

His Majesty's Government in the United Kingdom recognize forthwith the French Committee of National Liberation as administering those French overseas territories which acknowledge its authority and as having assumed functions of the former French National Committee in respect of the territories in the Levant. His Majesty's Government in the United Kingdom also recognize the committee as a body qualified to ensure the conduct of the French effort in the war within the framework of inter-Allied cooperation.

They take note with sympathy of the desire of the committee to be regarded as a body qualified to ensure the administration and defense of all French interests. It is the intention of His Majesty's Government to give effect to this request as far as possible while reserving the right to consider, in consultation with the committee, the practical application of this principle in particular cases as they arise.

His Majesty's Government in the United Kingdom welcome the committee's determination to continue the common struggle in close cooperation with all the Allies until French and Allied territories are completely liberated and until victory is complete over all enemy powers.

During the war military needs are paramount and all controls necessary for operational purposes are in consequence reserved to the supreme commander of Allied armies in any theatre of operations. In respect of certain of the territories under administration of the committee, agreements already exist between French authorities and United Kingdom authorities.

The creation of the French Committee of National Liberation may make it necessary to revise these agreements, and His Majesty's Government in the United Kingdom assume that pending their revision all such agreements concluded since June 1940, except in so far as these have been automatically made inapplicable by formation of the French Committee of National Liberation, will remain in force as between His Majesty's Government in the United Kingdom and the French Committee of National Liberation.

[1] *New York Times*, August 27, 1943.

(b) Statement of the Canadian Government Announcing Recognition of the French Committee of National Liberation, August 25, 1943 [1]

The Government of Canada has welcomed the establishment of the French Committee of National Liberation.

It has been and remains the intention of the Government of Canada to co-operate with all patriotic Frenchmen in freeing France and the French people from the oppression of the enemy. This Government is deeply interested in the early return of France to her high place among the nations and regards the institution of the committee as an important contribution to that end.

Early in July the committee was informed that Canada was prepared to consider promptly and sympathetically any requests which the committee might care to present for assistance in the equipment and training of the French forces under its control.

It is understood that the committee will operate on the principle of the collective responsibility of all its members for the prosecution of the war. It is also understood that the committee is in accord with the view of the Canadian Government that the French people themselves, as soon as they have an opportunity of freely expressing their wishes, should establish in France the Government of their choice.

On this basis the Government of Canada recognizes the French Committee of National Liberation as administering the French overseas territories which acknowledge its authority, and as the body qualified to ensure the conduct of the French effort in the war within the framework of inter-Allied cooperation.

It is the intention of the Canadian Government to give effect to this request as far as possible while reserving the right to consider in consultation with the committee the practical application of this principle in particular cases as they arise.

The Government of Canada warmly welcomes the committee's determination to carry on the common struggle in close cooperation with all the Allies until French and Allied territories are entirely liberated and complete victory over all enemy powers has been achieved.

It is understood that the committee will afford in territories under its administration whatever military and economic facilities are required by the Governments of the United Nations for the prosecution of the war.

(c) Note of the Soviet Government to the French Committee of National Liberation, August 26, 1943 [2]

The Government of the Union of Soviet Socialist Republics, having acquainted itself with the declaration of the French Committee of National Liberation, has decided to recognize the French Committee of National Liberation as the representatives of the State interests of the French Republic, and leader of all French patriots fighting against Hitlerite tyranny, and to exchange with it plenipotentiary representatives.

[1] *Ibid.*
[2] *Free France*, November–December, 1943, p. 187.

(5) *False Rumors of Possible Future Collaboration between the United States and the Vichy Regime. Statement of the Department of State, March 21, 1944* [1]

The statement below was issued in response to a request for comment on reports emanating from Algiers to the effect that concern had been expressed there that the United States Government might in the future collaborate with officials of the Vichy regime.

The absurd reports and rumors periodically occurring, which are evidently inspired, endeavoring to create the impression that this Government upon the liberation of France intends to deal with the Vichy regime or with certain individuals directly or indirectly supporting the policy of collaboration with Germany, are false on their face. The fact that this Government kept representatives at Vichy for some time for such vital purposes as combating Nazi designs, the preservation of the French fleet from German hands, and the prevention of Nazi occupation of French Africa or the establishment of military bases there, has been most amazingly and falsely represented as founded upon a sympathetic relationship between the American Government and pro-Axis supporters at Vichy. Every person at all informed knew that throughout the entire period just the opposite was the truth.

No loyal supporter of the Allied cause would make the ridiculous charge that the United States Government, while sending its military forces and vast military supplies to the most distant battlefields to prosecute the war against the Axis powers, would at the same time have any dealings or relations with the Vichy regime except for the purpose of abolishing it.

(6) *Proclamation by the Commander-in-Chief of the Allied Expeditionary Force (Eisenhower), Addressed to the People of France, Dropped in Enemy-Held Areas and Posted in Liberated Areas in France* [2]

[Translation]

On June 9, Supreme Headquarters made public the English translation of the proclamation of General Dwight D. Eisenhower to the people of France. This proclamation to the French people, which was dropped over enemy-held territory and posted where liberation already had taken place, was couched in terms similar to the words he had addressed to the peoples of occupied Europe a few

[1] Department of State, *Bulletin*, X, p. 278.
[2] *New York Times*, June 10, 1944.

hours after the invasion had begun except that it mentioned the French mission that is assisting him.

Citizens of France:

The day of liberation has dawned. Your comrades in arms are on French soil.

I am proud to have under my command the gallant forces of France who have so long trained and waited for this day when they can take part in the liberation of their home country.

United we come to settle on the battlefield the war you have continued heroically through years of stubborn resistance. We shall destroy the Nazi tyranny root and branch so that the peoples of Europe may have a new birth of freedom.

As Supreme Commander of the Allied Expeditionary Force, there is imposed on me the duty and responsibility of taking all measures essential to the prosecution of the war. Prompt obedience to such orders as I may issue is necessary.

All persons must continue in the performance of their present duties unless otherwise instructed. Those who have made common cause with the enemy and so betrayed their country will be removed. It will be for the French people to provide their own civil administration and to safeguard my troops by the effective maintenance of law and order. Members of the French Military Mission attached to me will furnish assistance to this end.

The valor and extreme sacrifice of the millions who have fought under the banner of resistance have helped and will continue to help the success of our arms. The presence of the enemy among you has made tragically necessary the aerial bombardment and military and naval operations which have caused you loss and suffering. This you have accepted courageously, in the heroic tradition of France, as part of the inevitable price we all must pay to attain our goal — which is our freedom.

Every resource will be required for the expulsion of the enemy from your country. Battle may inflict on you further deprivation. You will realize that munitions of war must come first, but every endeavor will be made to bring to you assistance that you need so sorely.

I rely on your assistance in the final crushing of Hitlerite Germany and the reestablishment of the historic French liberties. When victory is won and France is liberated from her oppressors the French people will be free to choose at the earliest possible moment, under democratic methods and conditions, the government under which they wish to live.

The enemy will fight with the courage of despair. He will neglect no measure, however ruthless, which he thinks may delay our progress. But our cause is just, our armies are strong. With our valiant Russian allies from the East we shall march to certain victory.

D. Eire

1. SALE OF MERCHANT SHIPS

(1) *The American Minister to Eire* (Gray) *to the Irish Prime Minister* (*de Valera*), *January 6, 1944* [1]

I have the honor to refer to recent efforts of the Irish Government, through its officials in Washington, to obtain additional merchant ships in the United States. Several weeks ago the Irish Shipping Limited, an agency of the Irish Government, entered into negotiations with the States Marine Corporation in New York for the purchase of the SS *Wolverine*, a vessel of approximately eight thousand tons under charter to the United States War Shipping Administration. Application was made to the Maritime Commission for approval of the proposed sale and the Irish Legation in Washington, in a note of December 4, requested the State Department to recommend to the War Shipping Administration that the application be approved.

I am instructed to inform you that the State Department in consultation with the President has given this matter careful consideration and for the reasons set forth below has been unable to make the recommendation requested by the Irish Government. The United States Maritime Commission on December 7 denied the application for the proposed sale as not being in the interests of the United States.

You will recall that in September 1941, in the face of a growing world shortage of shipping, the American Government made available to the Irish Government by charter two American merchant ships. These two ships have now both been destroyed and, in view of all the circumstances, we must assume they were destroyed by Axis submarines. The American Government understands that the *Irish Pine* (formerly the *West Hematite*) sailed from Ireland October 28, 1942 and failed to arrive at its destination and that the *Irish Oak* (formerly *West Neris*) was torpedoed on the morning of May 15, 1943 in open daylight and under conditions of good visibility. Although no definite information seems to be available regarding the precise manner of the sinking of the *Irish Pine*, the torpedoing of the *Irish Oak* appears to have been definitely established, as well as the fact that a German submarine was observed by the crew of the *Irish Oak* some hours prior to the sinking. The sinking of the *Irish Oak*, which you have rightly described as a " wanton and inexcusable act," and of other Irish ships must be presumed in the absence of evidence to the contrary to be the work of Axis submarines in their campaign of indiscriminate warfare against all ships whether belligerent or neutral.

[1] Department of State, *Bulletin*, X, p. 236.

In chartering the *West Hematite* (*Irish Pine*) and the *West Neris* (*Irish Oak*) to the Irish Government the American Government was motivated by the most friendly considerations and by the sole purpose of helping the Irish Government and the Irish people to carry to their shores foodstuffs and other supplies of critical necessity. This, of course, constitutes only a part of the efforts of the American Government since the outbreak of the war to assist the Irish people in obtaining needed supplies. The chartering of these ships to the Irish Government represented a real sacrifice on the part of the United States at a time when shipping space was most badly needed. The Irish Government sailed these ships with distinct neutral markings and they carried supplies in no way connected with the war. The action of the Axis submarines in sinking these ships without warning is, therefore, to repeat your own language, a " wanton and inexcusable act."

So far as the American Government is informed, the Irish Government has taken no steps against the Axis Governments, and, thus far, has offered no word of protest to the Axis Governments against these wanton acts. These repeated attacks on Irish ships appear to be conclusive proof, if further proof were needed, that the Axis powers are in fact making war upon Ireland while at the same time using Ireland's friendship to the detriment of the United Nations war effort. The loss of the *West Hematite* (*Irish Pine*) and the *West Neris* (*Irish Oak*) has harmed not only Ireland but the United States, to whom those vessels belonged, and the whole United Nations war effort.

The fact that ships sailing under the Irish flag bear distinct neutral markings and travel fully lighted at night should make them immune from belligerent attack but in reality serves only to make them easy targets for Nazi submarines. Any further ships transferred to the Irish flag would be subjected to these same hazards.

In view of the foregoing circumstances, it is regretted that the State Department cannot comply with your request that it recommend to the Maritime Commission the approval of the sale now in question.

2. RELATIONS WITH AXIS POWERS

The neutrality of Eire, carrying with it the maintenance of diplomatic and consular relations with Germany, raised certain serious problems for the British and United States Governments in the period preceding the invasion of the continent of Europe. Through channels of communication thus available to the German Government there was always the possibility that important information could be obtained regarding plans for the Allied invasion of Europe which would be of great value to the German High Command. It thus became desirable in the view of the British and United States Governments that diplomatic and consular relations between Ireland and the Axis powers be terminated.

At the time the text of the note of February 21 was released, the Department of State also released the text of a message which President Roosevelt had sent to Prime Minister de Valera on February 26, 1942, following a public statement by the Prime Minister of concern over the landing of American troops in North-ern Ireland. In his message, President Roosevelt said:

"At some future date when Axis aggression has been crushed by the military might of free peoples, the nations of the earth must gather about a peace table to plan the future world on foundations of liberty and justice everywhere. I think it only right that I make plain at this time that when that time comes the Irish Government in its own best interest should not stand alone but should be associated with its traditional friends, and, among them, the United States of America."

(1) *Request for the Removal of Axis Diplomatic and Consular Repre-sentatives. The United States Government to the Irish Prime Minister (de Valera), February 21, 1944* [1]

Your Excellency will recall that in your speech at Cork delivered on the fourteenth of December, 1941 you expressed sentiments of special friendship for the American people on the occasion of their entry into the present war and closed by saying, "The policy of the state remains unchanged. We can only be a friendly neutral." As you will also recall, extracts of this speech were transmitted to the President by your Min-ister in Washington. The President, while conveying his appreciation for this expression of friendship, stated his confidence that the Irish Gov-ernment and the Irish people, whose freedom is at stake no less than ours, would know how to meet their responsibilities in this situation.

It has become increasingly apparent that despite the declared desire of the Irish Government that its neutrality should not operate in favor of either of the belligerents, it has in fact operated and continues to operate in favor of the Axis powers and against the United Nations on whom your security and the maintenance of your national economy depend. One of the gravest and most inequitable results of this situation is the oppor-tunity for highly organized espionage which the geographical position of Ireland affords the Axis and denies the United Nations. Situated as you are in close proximity to Britain, divided only by an intangible boundary from Northern Ireland, where are situated important Amer-ican bases, with continuous traffic to and from both countries, Axis agents enjoy almost unrestricted opportunity for bringing military in-formation of vital importance from Great Britain and Northern Ireland into Ireland and from there transmitting it by various routes and methods to Germany. No opportunity corresponding to this is open to the United Nations, for the Axis has no military dispositions which may be observed from Ireland.

We do not question the good faith of the Irish Government in its efforts to suppress Axis espionage. Whether or to what extent it has suc-ceeded in preventing acts of espionage against American shipping and American forces in Great Britain and Northern Ireland is, of course, im-

[1] *Ibid.*, p. 235.

possible to determine with certainty. Nevertheless it is a fact that German and Japanese diplomatic and consular representatives still continue to reside in Dublin and enjoy the special privileges and immunities customarily accorded to such officials. That Axis representatives in neutral countries use these special privileges and immunities as a cloak for espionage activities against the United Nations has been demonstrated over and over again. It would be naïve to assume that Axis agencies have not exploited conditions to the full in Ireland as they have in other countries. It is our understanding that the German Legation in Dublin, until recently at least, has had in its possession a radio sending set. This is evidence of the intention of the German Government to use this means of communication. Supporting evidence is furnished by the two parachutists equipped with radio sending sets recently dropped on your territory by German planes.

As you know from common report, United Nations military operations are in preparation in both Britain and Northern Ireland. It is vital that information from which may be deduced their nature and direction should not reach the enemy. Not only the success of the operations but the lives of thousands of United Nations' soldiers are at stake.

We request therefore, that the Irish Government take appropriate steps for the recall of German and Japanese representatives in Ireland. We should be lacking in candor if we did not state our hope that this action will take the form of severance of all diplomatic relations between Ireland and these two countries. You will, of course, readily understand the compelling reasons why we ask as an absolute minimum the removal of these Axis representatives whose presence in Ireland must inevitably be regarded as constituting a danger to the lives of American soldiers and to the success of Allied military operations.

It is hardly necessary to point out that time is of extreme importance and that we trust Your Excellency will favor us with your reply at your early convenience.

(2) *The Irish Prime Minister (de Valera) to the United States Government. Released by the Irish Legation in Washington, March 10, 1944* [1]

The note of the American Government was handed to me by the American Minister on February 21. I informed him at once that the request it contained was one with which it was impossible for the Irish Government to comply. The Irish Government have since given the matter careful consideration and I now confirm the reply which I then gave verbally.

The Irish Government have also received the assurance of the American Government, conveyed to the Irish Minister at Washington and

[1] *New York Times,* March 11, 1944.

later confirmed by the American Minister here in an interview with me on February 29, to the effect that the American Government did not contemplate proceeding to military or other measures because of the reply which had been given.

The American Minister quoted in particular the President's personal message to me of February 26, 1942, that "there is not now nor was there then the slightest thought or intention of invading the territory of Ireland or of threatening the security of the Irish" and added that this attitude was unchanged.

The Irish Government wish to express their appreciation of this assurance. They were indeed surprised that so grave a note as that of February 21 should have been addressed to them. The terms of the note seemed to them altogether out of harmony with the facts and with the traditional relations of friendship between the Irish and American peoples.

They doubted that such a note could have been presented had the American Government been fully aware of the uniform friendly character of Irish neutrality in relation to the United States and of the measures which had been taken by the Irish Government, within the limits of their power, to safeguard American interests.

They felt, moreover, that the American Government should have realized that the removal of representatives of a foreign State on the demand of the Government to which they are accredited is universally recognized as the first step toward war, and that the Irish Government could not entertain the American proposal without a complete betrayal of their democratic trust. Irish neutrality represents the united will of the people and Parliament. It is the logical consequence of Irish history and of the forced partition of national territory.

Already before American entry into the war, the policy of the Irish Government toward Britain, America's ally, had been directed toward carrying out the intentions indicated in a statement of policy made by me in the Dail Eireann on May 29, 1935, namely that "our territory would never be permitted to be used as a base for attack upon Britain."

That policy has during the war been faithfully pursued. From the beginning, by the establishment of strong observation and defense forces, by a wide and rigorous censorship of press and communications, by an extensive anti-espionage organization and by every other means within our power, we have endeavored to prevent the leakage through Ireland of any information which might in any way endanger British lives or the safety of Great Britain.

Since the United States entered the war the same spirit of scrupulous regard for American interests has been shown. American officials have had an opportunity of seeing the measures which have been taken — they have indeed made favorable comments on their effectiveness — and it is satisfactory to observe that in the note itself not a single instance of neglect is alleged and no proof of injury to American interests is adduced. Should American lives be lost it will not be through any indifference or neglect of its duty on the part of this State.

As was known to the American officials, it is true that the German Minister had a wireless transmitter, but he had been for a long time debarred from using it and it has been in the custody of the Irish Government for some months. As regards the two parachutists dropped in Ireland last December, they were apprehended within a few hours. Two other agents dropped here since the war began met with a similar fate. The fifth, who arrived during the first year of the war, remained at large until December 3, 1941, but the police were aware of his presence here almost from the first moment of landing, and successful activities on his part were rendered impossible.

The total number of persons, inclusive of these parachutists, suspected of intentions to engage in espionage, and now held in Irish prisons, is ten foreign and two Irish nationals. These are the facts, and it is doubtful if any other country can show such a record of care and successful vigilance.

The British Government have informed the Irish Government that they welcome the initiative of the American Government in sending the note and that they attached the utmost importance to it. The Irish Government do not wish to comment on this, except to remark that it is perhaps not known to the American Government that the feelings of the Irish people toward Britain have, during the war, undergone a considerable change, precisely because Britain has not attempted to violate our neutrality.

The Irish Government feels sure that the American Government would agree that it would be regrettable if any incident now should alter that happy result.

The Irish Government are therefore safeguarding, and will continue to safeguard, the interests of the United States, but they must in all circumstances protect the neutrality of the Irish State and the democratic way of life of the Irish people. Their attitude will continue to be determined not by fear of any measures which could be employed against them, but by goodwill and the fundamental friendship existing between the two peoples.

(3) *The United Kingdom Representative (Maffey) to the Irish Prime Minister (de Valera), February 22, 1944* [1]

The Government of the United States of America recently consulted His Majesty's Government in the United Kingdom on their proposal to

[1] *Ibid.*, March 12, 1944.

address to the Government of Eire a request for the removal of Axis diplomatic and consular representatives in Eire.

It was with the full concurrence of His Majesty's Government that the United States Government made this approach to the Government of Eire in their note of February 21, 1944.

The United Kingdom Government desire to make it clear to the Government of Eire that, for their part, they warmly welcome the initiative which has been taken by the United States Government and they fully support the request for the removal from Eire of German and Japanese diplomatic and consular representatives.

The United Kingdom Government wish to emphasize the importance which they attach to this request.

(a) *The Irish Prime Minister (de Valera) to the United Kingdom Representative (Maffey), Released March 11, 1944* [1]

EXCELLENCY:

I have the honor to acknowledge receipt of the note of the British Government handed to me by you on February 22, welcoming the initiative taken by the American Government in their note of February 21.

I enclose for transmission to your Government a copy of the reply which was handed to the Department of State by the Irish Minister at Washington on March 7.

Accept, Excellency, the renewed assurance of my highest consideration.

A revised blacklist of pro-Axis firms with which trading would not be permitted was issued May 6 by the State Department and contained for the first time the names of companies and individuals in Eire. Thirty-eight such firms and individuals were listed. Nineteen of them bore such obviously German titles as AEG Electric Company, Ackermans & Van Haaren, Siemens-Schuckert, German Academy and German News Agency. Three had Italian names such as Berni's Café and Restaurant. Nearly all were in Dublin.[2]

E. Finland

[See *Documents, IV, 1941–42,* p. 637; *V, 1942–43,* p. 589.]

1. RELATIONS WITH THE SOVIET UNION

(1) *Soviet Terms to Finland. Statement of the Information Bureau of the Soviet Commissariat of Foreign Affairs, Broadcast of March 1, 1944* [3]

Various rumors have been disseminated in the foreign press recently with regard to negotiations which have been conducted between the

[1] *Ibid.*

[2] *The Proclaimed List of Certain Blocked Nationals.* Cumulative Supp. No. 2, May 5, 1944 of Revision VII of March 23, 1944, p. 17.

[3] *New York Times,* March 1, 1944.

Soviet Union and Finland and which allegedly concerned the termination of hostilities by Finland against the Soviet Union, and withdrawal of Finland from the war.

In actual fact official negotiations between the Soviet Union and Finland have not yet begun, but preparations for such negotiations have been initiated.

In mid-February this year a well-known Swedish industrialist approached the Soviet Ambassador at Stockholm, A. M. Kollontay, informing the Ambassador that a representative of the Finnish Government, Dr. Paasikivi, had arrived at Stockholm and had been authorized to find out conditions for Finland's getting out of the war.

During the meeting Mme. Kollontay was asked whether the Soviet Government would agree to negotiate with the present Finnish Government and whether she would meet a representative of that Government, Dr. Paasikivi.

In the name of the Soviet Government Mme. Kollontay declared that the Soviet Government had no reason to have particular confidence in the present Finnish Government, but that should the Finns see no other possibility the Soviet Government, in the interests of peace, would agree to conduct negotiations on the cessation of military operations with the present Finnish Government.

During an unofficial meeting which took place February 16 at the request of Dr. Paasikivi, Dr. Paasikivi declared to Mme. Kollontay that he was authorized by the Finnish Government to find out the Soviet Government's conditions with regard to the cessation of military operations on the part of Finland and with regard to Finland's withdrawal from the war.

During the meeting that followed Mme. Kollontay conveyed to Dr. Paasikivi the reply of the Soviet Government containing the following armistice terms:

1. The rupture of relations with Germany and the internment of German troops and ships in Finland. And furthermore, should Finland consider this latter task beyond her powers, the Soviet Union is prepared to render her the necessary assistance with her troops and air force.

2. Reestablishment of the Soviet-Finnish agreement of 1940 [1] and withdrawal of Finnish troops to the 1940 boundaries.

3. Immediate return of Soviet and Allied war prisoners as well as Soviet and Allied persons of the civilian population now being held in concentration camps or being used for labor.

4. The question concerning part or complete demobilization of the Finnish Army to be left for negotiations in Moscow.

5. The question concerning reparations of damage caused to the Soviet

---

[1] *Documents, II, 1939–40*, p. 392.

Union through military operations and occupation of Soviet territories to be left for negotiations in Moscow.

6. The question concerning the Petsamo region to be left for negotiations in Moscow.

It was declared to Dr. Paasikivi that if the Finnish Government agreed to accept these conditions immediately the Soviet Government would be prepared to receive in Moscow Finland's representatives for negotiations for conclusion of a concrete agreement.

Rumors which have been disseminated in certain organs of the foreign press purporting that the Soviet Government had presented demands to Finland for unconditional surrender and that the Soviet Government had demanded Finland's agreement for occupation by Soviet troops of the town of Helsinki and other large Finnish towns are unfounded.

(2) *Statement of the Finnish Government on Rejection of the Soviet Armistice Terms, Broadcast of March 21, 1944* [1]

It is the duty of the Finnish Government to study all possibilities of safeguarding the freedom and independence of Finland. The Government therefore considered it their duty to find out on what terms it would be possible to return to peaceful relationships with the Soviet Government and on what terms an honorable and lasting peace could be attained.

As a result of these activities the Government on February 29 presented to the Diet the armistice terms that J. K. Paasikivi had received from the Soviet envoy in Stockholm. These terms have already been published. Although the terms were harsh and although their acceptance in the form presented by the Soviet Government was out of the question, the Government did not reject the possibility of continuing discussions to clear the situation.

Therefore, the Government proposed to the Diet that the discussions should be continued. The majority of the Diet approved the manner in which the Government had conducted the matter and voted adjournment to the agenda of the day. The minority of the Diet stressed that the terms on some points could not be accepted and opposed adjournment to the agenda of the day. The Diet agreed by 105 votes against 80 to adjourn to the ordinary agenda of the day.

After the Diet had accepted the Government's attitude and even the minority in their statement had agreed that the Government was studying the possibilities of retaining our independence, freedom and security, the Government, in reply to the Soviet Government, expressed sincere hopes of resuming friendly relations with the Soviet Government and

[1] *New York Times*, March 22, 1944.

therefore, having carefully weighed the armistice terms, expressed the desire to be given the opportunity to state their own view of all these questions.

On March 10 a reply was received in which the Soviet Government expressed dissatisfaction in the Finnish Government's reply and stated that the terms presented on February 19 could be considered as preliminary terms and that only after these had been accepted could cessation of hostilities be discussed. A reply in the affirmative was demanded within a specified time.

In a secret session of the Diet on March 14, Prime Minister Linkomies presented to the Diet the Finnish Government's proposal to the Soviet Government and the reply. As the Soviet Government had not found it possible to agree to the reasonable request of giving an opinion before acceptance of the terms, the Prime Minister regretted that in this situation there was no other possibility than to reply in the negative to the demands of the Soviet Government.

The Prime Minister expected the Diet, after having heard his statement, to approve a motion to return to the agenda of the day, which the Diet did on the following day after an hour's discussion. Thereupon the Finnish Government again emphasized in its reply to the Soviet Government how indispensable it would have been for the Finnish Diet to have obtained more detailed information, both on the formal interpretation of different paragraphs of the terms as well as on their factual content.

In its reply the Finnish Government regrets that the Soviet Government has not seen its way to provide Finland with an opportunity of submitting its views on the different questions and that negotiations were declared to be possible only after an acceptance by the Finnish Government of the conditions presented by the Soviet Government.

Although the Finnish Government's persistent and earnest aim is the reestablishment of peaceful relations, it has not been able to see its way to accept in advance terms that deeply affect the very existence of the nation without even having obtained certainty as to their interpretation and contents.

(3) *Statement of the Information Bureau of the Soviet Commissariat of Foreign Affairs, Broadcast of March 21, 1944* [1]

On March 1 the Information Bureau of the People's Commissariat of Foreign Affairs of the U.S.S.R. published the Soviet armistice terms offered by the Soviet Government to Finland.

On March 8 the Soviet mission in Stockholm received the reply of the Finnish Government. From this reply it appeared that the Finnish Government found it difficult to accept Soviet armistice terms without preliminary discussions.

[1] *Ibid.*

The Soviet Government informed the Finnish Government that it considered the Finnish reply unsatisfactory.

The Soviet Government therefore brought to the attention of the Finnish Government the fact that the Soviet armistice terms in the six points given to J. K. Paasikivi were the minimum and the elementary ones and that only acceptance of these terms by the Finnish Government would make possible Soviet-Finnish discussions for cessation of hostilities.

The Soviet Government also stated that it would await a reply from the Finnish Government until March 18. On March 17 the Finnish Government gave a negative reply to the Soviet statement. By this action it has taken upon itself full responsibility for what will follow.

2. WITHDRAWAL OF DIPLOMATIC REPRESENTATION

Until the request for withdrawal of Finnish diplomatic representatives the United States pursued the policy of attempting to disassociate Finland from her collaboration with Germany and the other Axis powers. On February 8, 1944, Secretary Hull stated that the United States Government had recently taken the occasion to say to the Finnish Government that the responsibility for continued collaboration must be borne "solely by the Finnish Government." [1] Following the publication of Soviet armistice terms, President Roosevelt made a statement in which he reminded the Finnish people that "the longer they stay at Germany's side, the more sorrow and suffering is bound to come to them." [2]

(1) *Department of State Release, June 16, 1944* [3]

The Minister of Finland, Mr. Hjalmar J. Procopé, and three counselors of the Finnish Legation, Mr. T. O. Vahervuori, Mr. Urho Toivola, and Mr. Risto Solanko, were handed their passports on June 16 and requested to leave the country at the earliest moment because of activities on their part inimical to the interests of the United States.

This action does not constitute a rupture of diplomatic relations between the United States and Finland.

———

The Department of State announced on June 21 that it had completed arrangements for the departure from the United States of Mr. Hjalmar J. Procopé, lately Minister of Finland, and of Messrs. Vahervuori and Solanko, lately Counselors of the Finnish Legation, with the families of the latter two officers.

The Department had been informed by Mr. Procopé that it was his desire to proceed unaccompanied by his family. He did not act on the suggestion made by the Department that, if he so desired, he could remain in the United States with Madame Procopé and their children pending the restoration of her health.

The Department received a request from Mr. Urho Toivola, lately a Counselor of the Finnish Legation, who had been expected to depart from the United States with Mr. Procopé and Messrs. Vahervuori and Solanko, that he be permitted to remain in this country owing to the serious illness of Madame Toivola. This request was granted.

[1] Department of State, *Bulletin*, X, p. 179.   [2] *Ibid.*, p. 253.   [3] *Ibid.*, p. 565.

(2) *The Secretary of State (Hull) to the Finnish Chargé d'Affaires (Thesleff), June 30, 1944* [1]

Sir:

On June 27, 1944, the Finnish Government made the following announcement:

The German Foreign Minister von Ribbentrop has concluded his visit to the Finnish Government.

During this visit questions of interest to Finland and Germany were discussed, especially Finland's expressed desire with respect to military aid. The German Government has declared itself prepared to comply with this wish of the Finnish Government.

The discussions which were conducted between the President of the Finnish Republic Ryti and Foreign Minister Ramsay on one side and the German Foreign Minister on the other, are sustained by the spirit which has its roots in the comradeship in arms between the armies and the existing friendship between the two peoples.

Complete agreement and understanding were reached on all points between the Finnish Government and the German Government.

The Finnish Government has thus formally admitted to the world that it has now entered a hard-and-fast military partnership with Nazi Germany irrevocable throughout the war, for the purpose of fighting the Allies of the United States, in alliance with the enemies of the United States. This action was taken without recourse to the established democratic procedure of Finland, and responsibility for the consequences must rest solely on the Finnish Government.

The American Government is not unaware of the fact that the infiltration of German troops into Finland, with the consent of the Finnish Government and German infiltration into the councils of the Finnish Government have deprived Finland of liberty of action and reduced the Government of the Republic of Finland to the condition of a puppet of Nazi Germany.

This necessarily changes the status of the Finnish Government. The United States, up to the present, has taken every opportunity, publicly and through diplomatic representations, to warn the Finnish Government of the inevitable consequences of continuing its association with Nazi Germany. These warnings have been ignored, and the partnership is now complete.

The Government of the United States must take into account the fact that at this decisive stage in the combined operations of the military, naval and air forces of the United States and the other United Nations, the Finnish operations have a direct bearing on the success of the Allied effort. Notwithstanding the esteem in which the American people have held the people of Finland, further relations between the Government

[1] *Ibid.*, XI, p. 3.

of the United States and the Government of Finland are now impossible.

The American Chargé d'Affaires in Helsinki has therefore been instructed to request passports for himself and for the members of his staff and their families.

The American Government is requesting the Swiss Government to assume immediately the representation of American interests in Finland.

F. Portugal

(1) *Use of Facilities in the Azores. Statement of the British Prime Minister (Churchill) in the House of Commons, October 12, 1943* [1]

I have an announcement to make to the House arising out of the Treaty signed between this country and Portugal in the year 1373 between His Majesty King Edward III and King Ferdinand and Queen Eleanor of Portugal. This Treaty was reinforced in various forms by Treaties of 1386, 1643, 1654, 1660, 1661, 1703 and 1815 and in a secret declaration of 1899.

In more modern times, the validity of the old Treaties was recognized in the Treaties of Arbitration concluded with Portugal in 1904 and 1914. Article I of the Treaty of 1373 runs as follows:

In the first place we settle the covenant that there shall be from this day forward true, faithful, constant, mutual and perpetual friendships, unions, alliances and needs of sincere affection and that as true and faithful friends we shall henceforth, reciprocally, be friends to friends and enemies to enemies, and shall assist, maintain and uphold each other mutually, by sea and by land, against all men that may live or die.

This engagement has lasted now for over 600 years and is without parallel in world history. I have now to announce its latest application. At the outset of the war the Portuguese Government, in full agreement with His Majesty's Government in the United Kingdom, adopted a policy of neutrality with a view to preventing the war spreading into the Iberian Peninsula. The Portuguese Government have stated repeatedly, most recently in Dr. Salazar's speech of April 27th, that the above policy is in no way inconsistent with the Anglo-Portuguese Alliance which was reaffirmed by the Portuguese Government in the early days of the war.

His Majesty's Government in the United Kingdom, basing themselves upon this ancient Alliance, have now requested the Portuguese Government to accord them certain facilities in the Azores which will enable better protection to be provided for merchant shipping in the Atlantic. The Portuguese Government have agreed to grant this request, and arrangements, which enter into force immediately, have been concluded

---

[1] *The United Nations Review*, November 15, 1943, p. 433; *New York Times*, October 13, 1944.

between the two governments regarding (1) the conditions governing the use of the above facilities by His Majesty's Government in the United Kingdom and (2) British assistance in furnishing essential material and supplies to the Portuguese armed forces and the maintenance of the Portuguese national economy. The Agreement concerning the use of facilities in the Azores is of a temporary nature only, and in no way prejudices the maintenance of Portuguese sovereignty over Portuguese territory. All British Forces will be withdrawn from the Azores at the end of hostilities. Nothing in this Agreement affects the continued desire of the Portuguese Government, with which His Majesty's Government have declared themselves in full sympathy, to continue their policy of neutrality on the European mainland and thus maintain a zone of peace in the Iberian Peninsula.

In the view of His Majesty's Government, this Agreement should give new life and vigor to the Alliance which has so long existed between the United Kingdom and Portugal to their mutual advantage. It not only confirms and strengthens the political guarantees resulting from the Treaties of Alliance, but also affords a new proof of Anglo-Portuguese friendship and provides an additional guarantee for the development of this friendship in the future. On the conclusion of these negotiations my right hon. Friend the Foreign Secretary, who has, I think, conducted them with the very greatest skill and patience, has exchanged most cordial messages with the Portuguese President of the Council. In his message, my right hon. Friend affirmed his conviction that the facilities now granted by the Portuguese Government will greatly contribute to the effective defense of our shipping and thus prove an important factor in shortening the war. He added that the Agreement would give fresh vitality to the ancient Alliance and enhance the close and friendly relations which have so long subsisted between Portugal and Great Britain. In replying to this message, Dr. Salazar stated that he shared the hope that the facilities granted by Portugal to her Ally would help to bring about greater safety for shipping in the Atlantic and that he trusted that this new proof of Portugal's loyalty to her traditions would fortify the secular Alliance and serve to draw still closer the bonds of friendship between the two peoples.

I take this opportunity of placing on record the appreciation by His Majesty's Government, which I have no doubt is shared by Parliament and the British nation, of the attitude of the Portuguese Government, whose loyalty to their British Ally never wavered in the darkest hours of the war.

The Department of State announced on October 12 that the United States Government had been informed of and had approved the arrangements made.[1]

[1] Department of State, *Bulletin*, IX, p. 263.

At his press conference, President Roosevelt indicated that the United States would use these facilities as well as Great Britain. The British had made the arrangements, the President said, because their treaty relations with Portugal made that course feasible.[1]

(2) *Embassy Rank for Representation. Department of State Release, April 21, 1944* [2]

The Government of the United States of America, having in mind the character and the growing importance of relations between the two countries, has expressed the intention of raising its legation in Lisbon to the rank of embassy and has expressed at the same time the hope that the Portuguese Government would accredit a representative from Portugal at Washington with equal rank.

The Portuguese Government, having taken note of this contemplated action with the greatest pleasure, has expressed its appreciation to the American Government for its initiative and has declared itself readily willing to reciprocate.

Accordingly, the two Governments have agreed to raise the r respective legations at Washington and Lisbon to embassies.

(3) *Portuguese Action Concerning the Exportation and Production of Wolfram. Announcement by the Acting Secretary of State (Stettinius), June 6, 1944* [3]

Portuguese agreement to send Germany no more wolfram, which is invaluable for the hardening of steels in armaments, was announced in the House of Commons on June 7, 1944 by Foreign Secretary Anthony Eden. His statement stressed the historic friendship of England and Portugal embodied in the series of treaties of alliance dating back to the fourteenth century. Britain had asked Premier Antonio de Oliveira Salazar to impose a total ban on wolfram for the Germans, and on June 5 the request was granted.

A factor relating to British-Portuguese commerce in general is seen in the development. Britain owes Portugal for war purchases about £60,000,000, which is held in London and which Premier Salazar is eager to have released for trade or credit purposes. A new agreement for payment is being studied by the British Treasury to replace terms that have given Portugal the right to call for British gold.

The Portuguese Government undertook on June 5 to impose a total prohibition upon the export of wolfram and to bring about an immediate cessation of wolfram production in Portugal.

The action of the Portuguese Government should prove a factor in shortening the war, in as much as it will deprive the enemy in Europe of important quantities of a vital war material.

The United States Government has been active in the negotiations which have led up to this satisfactory conclusion in close consultation with the British and Brazilian Governments.

[1] *New York Times*, October 13, 1943.
[2] Department of State, *Bulletin*, X, p. 388.
[3] *Ibid.*, p. 535.

G. Spain

(1) *Note from the Spanish Government Regarding Message of Spanish Foreign Minister to the Philippine Puppet Government, November 9, 1943* [1]

[Translation]

At the press conference of the Acting Secretary of State, Mr. Stettinius, on the afternoon of November 9, a news correspondent inquired regarding a recent message of the Minister of Foreign Affairs of Spain addressed to José P. Laurel, "President" of the puppet government which has been set up by Japan in the Philippines. The Acting Secretary replied that the Spanish Ambassador in Washington, Señor Don Juan Francisco de Cárdenas, had called on him that afternoon and had left a note in the Spanish language, a literal translation of which is given below.

In view of the erroneous interpretation ascribed to the cablegram of courtesy which the Minister of Foreign Affairs sent on October 18th in reply to one addressed to him by Mr. J. P. Laurel from Manila, on the 13th of the same month, the Spanish Government is interested in letting the United States Government know what follows:

1. The cable in question is an act of courtesy towards the Philippine people, taking advantage of the opportunity offered by this same people in addressing our own. It was dictated exclusively by the sentiments which every phase of the Philippine life inspires to Spain, because of the affinity of blood, religion and language which link the Spanish people to the Philippines, with which they shared life until fifty years ago, creating between both countries a confraternity which embraces all moral and material phases, and which makes of the Philippines, independently from whatever its political situation and its international position may be, a country spiritually bound to Spanish tradition. It is precisely because of that, that Spain, appreciating as it does appreciate the Philippine people without distinctions of any kind, refrains from any act of a political character which might be interpreted as partiality towards a country for which it only wishes all kinds of prosperity and well-being.

2. In thus establishing the true significance of the cable, completely devoid of all political aspects, and, consequently, of all act implying, even indirectly, recognition, the Minister of Foreign Affairs wishes to emphasize the point, so as to avoid at any time a disfigured interpretation which might serve as a foundation for a campaign tending to disturb the good relations existing between the Governments of Spain and the United States, and which, for our own part, have been proved time and again by evident and ostensible acts of a manifest good will.

[1] *Ibid.*, IX, p. 325.

(2) Suspension of Oil Shipments to Spain. Department of State Release, January 28, 1944 [1]

The loadings of Spanish tankers with petroleum products for Spain have been suspended through action of the State Department, pending a reconsideration of trade and general relations between Spain and the United States in the light of trends in Spanish policy. The Spanish Government has shown a certain reluctance to satisfy requests deemed both reasonable and important by the State Department and concerning which representations have continuously been addressed to the Spanish Government for some time past. Certain Italian warships and merchant vessels continue interned in Spanish ports; Spain continues to permit the export to Germany of certain vital war materials such as wolfram; Axis agents are active both in continental Spain and in Spanish African territory as well as in Tangier; some portion of the Blue Division appears still involved in the war against one of our allies; and reports have been received indicating the conclusion of a financial arrangement between the Spanish Government and Germany designed to make available to Germany substantial peseta credits which Germany unquestionably expects to apply to augmenting espionage and sabotage in Spanish territory and to intensifying opposition to us in the peninsula.

This action has been taken after consultation and agreement with the British Government.

(3) Suspension of Oil Shipments to Spain. Department of State Release, March 4, 1944 [2]

On January 28, 1944 the Department of State issued a press release of which the opening sentence reads as follows: "The loadings of Spanish tankers with petroleum products for Spain have been suspended through action of the State Department, pending a reconsideration of trade and general relations between Spain and the United States in the light of trends in Spanish policy."

The foregoing statement related only to Spanish tanker loadings in the Caribbean area. In addition to the suspension of tanker loadings, the Department decided to suspend the granting of export licenses for the shipment of packaged petroleum products, including lubricants, from the United States, so long as the tanker loadings were suspended. In taking this decision, however, the Department did not cancel outstanding licenses for packaged petroleum goods. The packaged goods in question are being shipped under licenses granted before the suspension took effect.

Incidentally, under the petroleum program in effect prior to the suspension or loadings, Spain would ship from United States ports less than 3 percent of her total limited liftings in the Western Hemisphere. The amount of lubricants being shipped on the vessel referred to in the morning press of March 4 [3] represents a very small portion of the petroleum products which Spain could otherwise import were it not for the suspension of loadings.

[1] *Ibid.*, X, p. 116.
[2] *Ibid.*, p. 225.
[3] This referred to a shipment of barreled petroleum from Philadelphia.

(4) Agreement with Spain on Certain Outstanding Issues. Department of State Release, May 2, 1944 [1]

After a protracted period of negotiation with the Spanish Government, the American and British Governments have received assurances from the Spanish Government which permit a settlement of certain outstanding issues.

The Spanish Government has agreed to expel designated Axis agents from Tangier, the Spanish Zone in North Africa, and from the Spanish mainland. It has agreed to the closing of the German Consulate and other Axis agencies in Tangier. It has agreed to the release of certain Italian commercial ships now interned in Spanish waters and to the submission to arbitration of the question of releasing Italian warships likewise interned in Spanish waters. It has withdrawn all Spanish military forces from the eastern front. It has maintained a complete embargo on exports of wolfram since February 1, 1944, at which time bulk petroleum shipments were suspended, and has now agreed for the remainder of the year to impose a drastic curtailment of wolfram exports to Germany.

One of our objectives in these negotiations was to continue to deprive Germany of Spanish wolfram. Although agreement was reached on a basis less than a total embargo of wolfram shipments, this action was taken to obtain immediate settlement on the urgent request of the British Government. Under the curtailed program not more than 20 tons of wolfram may be exported to Germany from Spain in each of the months May and June. Thereafter for the remainder of the year, if as a practical matter they can be made, exports may not exceed 40 tons per month. It is improbable that any of this can be utilized in military products during this year.

In view of the foregoing negotiations, permission will now be given for the renewal of bulk petroleum loadings by Spanish tankers in the Caribbean and the lifting from the United States ports of minor quantities of packaged petroleum products in accordance with the controlled program in operation prior to the suspension of such loadings.

(a) Communiqué of the Spanish Foreign Office, Madrid, May 2, 1944 [2]

After negotiations, which were necessarily lengthy on account of the breadth and complexity of the problems involved, an agreement has been reached which in general embraces all points awaiting settlement especially in reference to our commercial relations with Great Britain and the United States. The agreement, which has been reached within the limits and understanding of our position of strict neutrality and in view of present realities, will assure the immediate normalization of relations between Spain and those nations. These relations, as every one knows, have gone through a period of crisis in the past weeks, and it has been possible to reach a settlement without impairment of the advantage and the honor of the interested countries, thus ending the difficulties which have arisen.

———

At his press conference on May 30, President Roosevelt indicated that in his opinion, while the amount of exports from Spain to Germany had been materially

[1] *Ibid.*, p. 412.
[2] *New York Times*, May 3, 1944.

cut, the cut was not great enough.[1] This comment was prompted by a reference to Prime Minister Churchill's address to the House of Commons on May 24 in which he spoke appreciatively of the service rendered by Spain to the cause of the United Nations.[2]

2. THE OCCUPIED TERRITORIES

(1) *Letter from Assistant Secretary of State Berle to Mr. M. B. Schnapper, Published August 30, 1943* [3]

The text of the letter from Mr. M. B. Schnapper, Executive Secretary, American Council on Public Affairs, to Assistant Secretary of State Berle, dated July 23, 1943, to which this letter was written in reply, is given in the first paragraph of the letter below.

MY DEAR MR. SCHNAPPER:

In your letter of July 23, 1943 you state that:

"The assertion is frequently made — sometimes by men and journals of good will — that the Department of State has pursued a policy of rebuffing and ignoring exiled leaders who look to a democratic revitalization of Europe and that, on the other hand, it has been favorably disposed toward highly conservative and reactionary persons who are desirous of retaining the evils of pre-war Europe. Assertions of this sort have been particularly emphatic of late in connection with the Department's policy with regard to Italy."

You suggest a clarifying statement if the present time is appropriate.

The Government of the United States has consistently maintained a policy directed towards a democratic solution in the occupied countries and in the enemy countries, as and when the people of these countries shall be free to speak. The Atlantic Charter declares the right of the people of each country to live under a government of their own choosing.

The assertion that the Department of State has favored persons desirous of retaining the evils of pre-war Europe is really amazing in view of the long and tenaciously held policies of this country. Under them, refugees from Europe seeking safety from oppression have been admitted to the United States. They have been permitted to come to the United States and to state their views and political platforms to an extent not permitted by any other country on earth. They can and do offer their views through the American institution of free speech and free press for acceptance or rejection by our public opinion. Under the American tradition the Department of State can scarcely do more. By doing it, the Department has given greater privilege to those who wish a revitalization of Europe than has been granted anywhere else in the world. This is the American — the democratic — way.

---

[1] *Ibid.*, May 31, 1944.

[2] *Ibid.*, May 25, 1944; British Information Services, *British Speeches of the Day*, II (1944), No. 6, p. 41.

[3] Department of State, *Bulletin*, IX, p. 151.

Europeans reaching this country cannot be judged merely on the basis of political "name-calling." Conservatives who have consistently and vigorously fought Fascism are often attacked by groups who also are fighting Fascism but who are pleading for particular reforms, and these in turn are commonly accused of being reactionary or even Fascist by more radical groups. Frequently foreign racial or political issues are brought into the discussion. In general, the United States public with great good sense has declined to become excited about this name-calling; and is properly suspicious when these controversies reach the point, as they often do, of becoming campaigns of defamation.

At no time has the Department pursued a policy of rebuffing leaders who look toward a democratic revitalization of Europe, nor has it engaged in any policy of encouraging conservative and reactionary persons desirous of retaining the evils of pre-war Europe.

Leaders and groups of all shades of thought have sought here the refuge which we have gladly offered. Many of them have asked to be recognized or accepted or dealt with as representing the country from which they came. Their claims thus to speak for an invaded or silenced country are often disputed by other groups and leaders of the same nationality, and attacked by leaders and groups of other nationalities. These claims properly ought to be settled by the people of their own country, not by the State Department.

The degree of support which free movements or leaders in exile may have in their own countries in most cases can be only a matter of conjecture until there are means of access to their own people. It is probable that no political group in exile would have much chance of permanent success in rallying the people of the country to its cause if its strength lay chiefly in the support of foreign states. For these reasons the United States has not felt it possible to extend recognition to these individuals or groups, even though in many cases their views and sentiments may be highly praiseworthy.

As early as December 1941, the Department adopted a policy which has proved both wise and necessary. The policy then enunciated included the following declarations:

In harmony with the basic principles of liberty, the people of the United States do have a sympathetic interest in movements by aliens in this country who desire to liberate their countries from Axis domination.

The Department of State is glad to be informed of the plans and proposed activities of such "free movements" and of organizations representing such movements. . . .

The Department has taken cognizance of the existence of a number of committees representing free movements but has not extended any form of recognition to them, formal or informal. . . .[1]

[1] *Documents, IV, 1941–42*, p. 806; Department of State, *Bulletin*, V, p. 519.

The Government of the United States has been glad to receive the suggestions, the ideas, the plans, of all of these "free" movements and their leaders. But decision upon their claims rests not in the hands of this Government, but in the hands of their own people.

All of us appreciate to the full the devotion to ideals of freedom and democracy which those who have struggled against Nazism and Fascism share with us. At the same time we must be careful not to take any steps whose effect might be to prejudice the freedom of choice of any people whose voice is now silent.

The United States ran up the flag of democracy in 1776 by asserting that government rested on the just consent of the governed. Upon its shores from that day to this, Frenchmen, Germans, Hungarians, Poles, Italians, Spaniards, Russians, and representatives of every race in the world have maintained the doctrine of freedom upon the soil of the United States. This is as true today as it has been from the beginning of our history. I am confident that no baseless rumors nor even statements, frequently circulated for ulterior propaganda purposes, will long mislead men of good-will or the American public generally. You will have noticed, in respect to the assertions you cite, that they are never even remotely backed up by evidence.

Your letter was occasioned in part by certain wild yarns which are hardly worth the trouble of denying. Some of these seem, indeed, to have been circulated by foreign political personages enjoying American hospitality. One such was the rumor circulated a few weeks ago that Count Ciano was in the United States; another, that some plan for a "Catholic Axis" was being elaborated in Washington; a third, that some scheme of Fascist federation of Eastern Europe aimed against the Soviet Union was being worked up, and so forth and so on. A very recent illustration was the story industriously circulated in some quarters that this Government was seeking to establish contact with Laval or other representatives of the defunct Pétain Administration in Occupied France. These are truthless trifles which circulate in wartime, all too often borne on currents of factional dispute or European propaganda. They merit no attention.

(2) *Address by Assistant Secretary of State Berle Before the Knoxville Rotary Club, November 23, 1943* [1]

[Excerpt]

The independence and safety of the United States depend immediately on winning a huge war. It has been fashionable in some circles to assume that this war is a revolution; that all conservatives, moderates, or other non-revolutionaries must be Nazis or Fascists, and that the

[1] *Ibid.*, IX, p. 384.

only true defenders of liberty were found in extreme left-wing groups. Some say, therefore, the war is chiefly to be won by encouraging social upheaval the world over. This is an easy generalization which goes along nicely until it bumps up against the hard facts.

Undoubtedly great social changes are abroad in the world. Undoubtedly the forces set in motion by this war will liberate vast popular forces both here and abroad. But the fact was, Hitler — not the democracies — wanted to create a class war. He hoped, by bribery and threat and propaganda, to make allies for himself in every country in the world and thereby to create fifth columns and open the way for his panzer divisions. In the main he lost that fight, though in a few places he had a degree of success. His victims did not split along class lines. They refused to engage in civil wars. He did not succeed in bringing to his support great classes in the victim countries. Instead, in nation after nation, all groups arrayed themselves solidly against him, irrespective of their social doctrines. Poland, with a conservative government, fought him to the death, just as did Soviet Russia with a Communist government. Norway and the Netherlands have resisted him both before and after their invasion as bitterly as Czechoslovakia. The British resistance, turning-point of the war, was first carried on by a Tory government, just as the American war effort was organized by the liberal government of President Roosevelt. The men who come out of the undergrounds in Europe — we have the privilege of seeing them in the State Department from time to time — are of every political and religious belief: Conservative and Communist; Capitalist and Socialist; Catholic, Protestant, and Jewish. Nor is the situation different in the Western Hemisphere: Liberal governments like that of Mexico find common cause with conservative governments like that of Brazil.

It would be merely playing Hitler's game to pretend that the spirit of resistance is possessed only by those holding a particular social faith. The war is essentially the defense of freedom and national life for this nation and for all nations. Without exception, every one of the United Nations has placed its national existence above every other objective; though all realize that their safety must lie in common action.

We in the State Department, accordingly, have been unable to accept the idea that social upheaval was the primary means of defeating Hitler. Rather, the principle has been and must continue to be that of unity in the face of enemies of civilization.

The liberated countries undoubtedly will wish to rebuild their social structures when the enemy is expelled. They may wish to modify and change those structures. But this is a choice for them to make, and not for us. Our obligation was set forth in the Atlantic Charter which contains a declaration that nations have the right to live under governments of their own choosing.

At the close of the Moscow Conference, Premier Stalin made a speech in which he set forth the same view. He said: "The liberated countries of Europe must receive full right and freedom to decide for themselves their form of state."

It may be added that, from a military point of view, the proposition that the United States should engage in a series of adventures for the purpose of intervening in the affairs of other states seems merely absurd. Our divisions are thoroughly engaged in the task of smashing the Japanese and the Germans. Nor have we any intention to scrap the well-settled policy of non-intervention in the affairs of other states. The policy of non-intervention in other peoples' affairs is and must be the first principle of sound doctrine. Unless this is the settled practice of nations, there can be no principle of sovereign equality among peace-loving states and probably no permanent peace at all. The Nazis practiced the principle of forcing their neighbor nations to instal governments satisfactory to their ideas. We are content to leave to them the patent on that idea.

In following this line the Government of the United States follows the oldest, strongest, and most successful liberal tradition in the world. The doctrine of democracy established itself spontaneously in the United States in 1776. In the century which followed, representative democracy became the rule throughout the Western World. But this was done by force of example and by the free process of men's minds. We need not apologize for that record; and nothing in the history of European controversy during the past two generations justifies us in departing from this American principle.

The application of this principle is translated into the day-by-day work, dealing with the territories which we are progressively liberating, in company with our Allies. We have not used the force of American armies, destined to fight the Nazis, to compel erection of improvised political governments against the will of their peoples, in spite of the fact that certain factions have earnestly and sometimes bitterly urged this course upon us. Rather, the attempt has been made to open the way for healthy political evolution in these countries. It has been necessary to provide a reasonably stable economic life and to open the streams of information and public thought. Once this is done, and subject to military necessity, we can rely on the peoples of these countries to re-create their own political life. This does not please some who are anxious for partisans of particular political factions; nor does it satisfy some European political personalities who have found refuge on our shores. Yet it is, I think, the only wise and sound course.

There are some who say that the United Nations should boldly announce that there will be no return to the system previously existing in Europe; that every effort should be made, now, to assist in destroying the political life which existed before 1939. Since the continent of Europe is at present silenced, the first effect of any such policy would be to leave every European country voiceless, without even the external symbols of their continued life. Until these countries are liberated, no one outside them can secure a new mandate. Every government in refuge has recognized and declared that its first act, on liberation, must be to submit itself to the judgment of its people, who can then make such changes as they choose. Quite likely there will be changes; for those who have fought out, underground, in their own countries, the terrible and bloody battle against the Nazi invaders, will unquestionably emerge from the struggle, covered with wounds and sweat, claiming their right to be heard as representatives of the silenced and struggling masses. Having faith, as we do, in the common and kindly people who are the mass of Europe, we can safely leave it to them to decide the forms of their government. The contribution we can make is to give them, by force of arms and continuing victory, their freedom to speak once more without fear of Gestapo or danger from German bayonets. To take any other course would be to deny the essential democracy of our being.

Many of the arguments addressed to the Department of State — and I have no doubt the same arguments are directed likewise to the British Foreign Office and to the Soviet Commissar of Foreign Affairs — should more properly be directed to the people of the countries whose affairs are discussed.

In terms of day-to-day work, these problems present themselves in a light somewhat more difficult than that of mere generalization. An army moves into a country and frees it from German domination. At that moment the only organized force in the country is that of a group which had maintained itself through the previous phase. Every other element of political life is either dead, in concentration camps, in hiding, or in exile. Even information as to the outside world has been cut off. Slowly the elements of political choice have to be reassembled; the news of the world has to be readmitted. Relationships of neighborhoods, trades-unions, town and city governments, provincial life, and eventually national life, have to be reestablished. The evolution goes on; representative men appear; they take their places in the public life of the country, set out the doctrines they represent, and enter into the structure of the government as public opinion accepts their ideas.

It is natural to expect controversy in the difficult work of European reconstruction. These controversies largely arise from, or continue, the bitter political divisions in the Europe of before the war. Representatives of practically every European party and from practically every European country are present in the United States. Between themselves they carry on much the same sort of warfare that went on in the European capitals. Being exiled, each of these representatives claims to speak not for his party but for his country; for a purely party-claim would have little appeal to the public opinion of the United States.

When opportunity arises, these claims to represent other countries can be referred to the people of that country, who are and must be the final judges. This does not satisfy some claimants, who wish to be recognized now as spokesmen for their still captive countries and to be assisted with American money and men to take power in those countries. The United States Government has consistently taken the view that it had no right to make such decisions, least of all in respect to friendly countries. In some quarters the disappointed candidates have turned their criticism on the State Department; and some of that criticism has been both ill-founded and unscrupulous.

To all non-enemy groups the Department has zealously guarded their freedom of speech, their freedom to organize, and their right to state their own case and to present themselves to such public opinion as may be available. Each group has been very glad to avail itself of this right. Some groups, unhappily, are very anxious to see this right denied to other groups with whose views or aspirations they disagree, and seem to feel that the Government of the United States in some dictatorial fashion should suppress their rival groups. I need hardly say that there is no likelihood that this Government will depart from its traditional position — which is in fact the strongest liberal tradition in the world.

The true aim of enlightened foreign policy now must be to place world affairs on a new footing — a basis in which, as Secretary Hull observed the other day, spheres of influence, special alliances, and all the shoddy tricks of balance-of-power politics and imperialist operations can be discarded. This has to be done in the name of common humanity, but it equally has to be done in the interest of the United States. It is a titanic job.

It will not be achieved by cultivating hatreds or taking sides in stale European controversies. It cannot be based on civil wars, disingenuous propaganda, or political trickery. The vast problem of securing a recon-stituted world system which can maintain peace and recognize human rights can only be carried forward by finding and increasing a common denominator of public opinion. This must be such as will enable countries to establish peace within their own borders and to join in establishing a peaceful framework for the whole world. Increasing bitterness and factional fights within nations, or the differences between nations, can only impede the largest and most important work we have to do. And it can only hinder and impede the pressing and immediate necessity for winning the war.

The time is long since past when any group seeking to lead public opinion in international affairs can be merely negative. Progress today depends, not on the number of things you can find to oppose, but on the number of things you can find to support. Tangible and permanent advances, embodied in well-founded institutions, have to be based on programs studied, thought out, and commanding such widespread approval that they can be put into effect. None of these plans will satisfy everyone's hopes.

But we have arrived at the stage where a modest achievement which has in it the power of growth is better than a lost cause and another generation of want and fear and agony.

I think that the true forward movements when they come will not talk the language of hatred. They will not endeavor to set neighbor against neighbor. Their political weapons will not be slander and falsehood. They will be based on the age-old constructive principles of justice, kindliness, and a search for truth. Not otherwise has any society been permanently founded; and no international society will well serve either the United States or any other nation unless it rests on these timeless qualities in human life.

(3) Civil-Affairs Agreements with Belgium, the Netherlands and Norway. Department of State Release, May 16, 1944 [1]

Agreements in identical terms were concluded on May 16 by the United States of America and the United Kingdom with the Governments of Belgium and the Netherlands and by the United States of America, the United Kingdom, and the U.S.S.R. with the Government of Norway. These agreements concern arrangements to be made for civil administration and jurisdiction in the Belgian, Netherlands, and Norwegian territories when they are liberated by the Allied forces.[2] The Soviet Government has been consulted concerning the arrangements with Belgium and the Netherlands and has expressed its agreement.

These agreements are intended to be essentially temporary and practical in character. They are designed to facilitate the task of Allied commanders and to further the common purpose of the Governments concerned, namely, the speedy expulsion of the Germans from Allied territory and final victory of the Allies over Germany.

The agreements recognize that the Allied Supreme Commander must enjoy *de facto* during the first or military phase of the liberation of the Netherlands such measure of supreme responsibility and authority over civil administration as may be required by the military situation. It is laid down that, as soon as the military situation permits, the Netherlands Government shall resume their full constitutional responsibility for civil administration on the understanding that such special facilities as the Allied forces may continue to require on Netherlands territory will be made available for the prosecution of the war to its final conclusion.

[1] *Ibid.*, p. 479.

[2] In the case of the agreements with Belgium and the Netherlands, the press releases contain the following variation: "liberated by the Allied Expeditionary Force under the Supreme Allied Commander."

3. AFRICA AND WESTERN ASIA

A. Iran

See p. 236 for text of Declaration of the Governments of the United States, Great Britain and the Soviet Union on Iran.

On February 10, it was announced that the status of the United States diplomatic mission to Tehran had been raised from that of legation to an embassy.[1] On March 31, 1944, President Roosevelt proclaimed a trade agreement with Iran which had been effected by an exchange of notes dated April 8, 1943.[2]

On general topic of American advisers in Iran, see article by George V. Allen, Chief of the Division of Middle Eastern Affairs in the Department of State, *Bulletin*, XI, p. 88.

(1) *Military Mission to Iran. Announcement of the Department of State, January 1, 1944* [3]

The American Legation at Tehran has transmitted to the Department of State with its despatch 748 of December 1, 1943 the signed originals in English and Persian of a military-mission agreement between the United States and Iran, signed at Tehran November 27, 1943 by Louis G. Dreyfus, Jr., American Minister at Tehran, and Mohammed Saed, Minister of Foreign Affairs of Iran.[4]

This agreement, which was concluded in conformity with the request of the Government of Iran, is made effective as of October 2, 1942 and will continue in force for two years, but may be extended beyond the two-year period by mutual agreement of the two Governments.

The purpose of the military mission to which the agreement relates is to advise and assist the Ministry of Interior of Iran in the reorganization of the Imperial Iranian Gendarmerie. The agreement contains provisions similar in general to provisions contained in agreements between the United States and a number of the other American Republics providing for the detail of officers of the United States Army or Navy to advise the armed forces of those countries.

B. Syria and Lebanon

[See *Documents, IV, 1941–42*, p. 667; *V, 1942–43*, p. 607.]

(1) *Restoration of the Government in the Lebanese Republic. Department of State Release, November 26, 1943* [5]

The Government of the United States has noted with approval the action of the French Committee of National Liberation in releasing and restoring to office the President and Ministers of the Lebanese Republic and in abrogating the decrees issued on November 11, 1943, suspending the Lebanese Constitution, dissolving the Lebanese Parliament, and naming a "Chief of State, Chief of Government."

[1] Department of State, *Bulletin*, X, p. 181.
[2] *Executive Agreement Series* 410.
[3] Department of State, *Bulletin*, X, p. 22.
[4] *Executive Agreement Series* 361.
[5] Department of State, *Bulletin*, IX, p. 381, 382.

The situation in Lebanon is thus restored to a normal basis, and it is the earnest hope of this Government that friendly negotiations can now proceed in an atmosphere of good-will on both sides for the solution of the underlying issue of the independence of the Levant States.

By way of background it may be recalled that the independence of Syria and Lebanon was contemplated in the terms of the Class A Mandate over these States entrusted to France by the League of Nations. American rights in these States were defined in the treaty of [April 4] 1924 between the United States and France.[1] The Government of the United States has subsequently expressed its sympathy and that of the American people with the aspirations of the Syrian and Lebanese peoples for the full enjoyment of sovereign independence. The proclamations of independence issued in the name of the French National Committee in 1941 were welcomed as steps toward the realization of these aspirations,[2] and this Government extended limited recognition to the local governments established thereunder by accrediting to them a diplomatic agent.[3] More recently, this Government observed with satisfaction the successful establishment of elected governments in these States. Moreover, the eastern Mediterranean is a theater of war. While it is an area of primary British strategic responsibility, any activities therein which hamper the general war effort are of concern to all the United Nations.

[1] *Treaties, Conventions, etc. 1923–1937*, IV, p. 4169.
[2] Department of State, *Bulletin*, V, p. 440.
[3] *Ibid.*, VII, p. 828.

INDEX